ASCRIPTION
AND
ACHIEVEMENT

D1712758

THE CARLETON LIBRARY SERIES

A series of original works, reprints, and new collections of source material relating to Canada, issued under the supervision of the Editorial Board, Carleton Library Series, Carleton University Press Inc., Ottawa, Canada.

GENERAL EDITOR

Michael Gnarowski

ASCRIPTION AND ACHIEVEMENT:

Studies in Mobility
and
Status Attainment
in Canada

BY

Monica Boyd, John Goyder, Frank E. Jones,
Hugh A. McRoberts, Peter C. Pineo and
John Porter

CARLETON UNIVERSITY PRESS
OTTAWA, CANADA

© Carleton University Press Inc., 1985
ISBN 0-88629-023-6 (paperback)

Printed and bound in Canada

Canadian Cataloguing in Publication Data

Main entry under title:
  Ascription and achievement : studies in
mobility and status attainment in Canada

(The Carleton library ; no. 133)
ISBN 0-88629-023-6

1. Social mobility—Canada. I. Boyd, Monica
II. Series.

HN110.Z9S65 1985   305.5′13′0971   C85-090090-5

Distributed by:
  Oxford University Press Canada
  70 Wynford Drive
  DON MILLS, Ontario, Canada, M3C 1J9
  (416) 441-2941

ACKNOWLEDGEMENT

Carleton University Press gratefully acknowledges the support extended to its
publishing programme by the Canada Council and the Ontario Arts Council.

Preface

The research reported in this volume was the product of collaboration which took a variety of forms. Even so, collaboration did not eliminate differences in analytical styles adopted by members of the research team. Thus, for reporting our research, we decided, after extensive discussion, to write our chapters independently rather than to struggle for the compromises which joint authorship would require. We hope our decision is to the advantage of the reader.

Although Chapter 1 was written after John Porter's death, he had drafted a section for it and we have incorporated this section, largely as he wrote it, in the section titled, "Mobility and Attainment in Canada: Conceptual and Analytical Frameworks." As well, John had set the stage for the monograph by writing Chapter 2 which was also in draft form at the time of his death. We were very fortunate that Marian Porter agreed to carry out the final revisions of this chapter.

It has, of course, been some time between the gathering of the data in 1973 and the publication of this basic volume. The reasons for this time gap are partly told elsewhere in this volume. We would note that in contrast to similar research projects undertaken elsewhere, we did our work with limited resources. Except for occasions when some of us were on sabbatical or leaves of absence, we all had full-time university responsibilities to meet. Our funding did, however, allow us to employ a full-time research assistant at each university, Carleton and McMaster. Christine Kluck Davis served with full commitment and complete loyalty in this capacity at McMaster. Despite the problems of meeting the different computational requirements of three researchers, of responding to requests for bibliographic information, of looking after the accounts and a variety of other details related to the research, her enthusiasm for the project never waned and her skills increased. There are others at McMaster who helped us, too. Drs. Frank Henry and Charles Jones provided advice on statistical and programming problems. Lillian Giavedoni, the Department of Sociology's research assistant, provided valuable back-up support for Chris Davis and, when Chris's work terminated, took over the responsibility for computer runs.

Those of us at Carleton were fortunate to have had the aid in turn of three excellent research assistants: Martha Bird Van Dine, who did much of the early work in setting up the data processing and documentation systems for the analysis; Gillian Stevens, who handled data processing chores and carried out methodological investigations for us; and finally Bonnie Shiell who did much of the final data processing for us for this volume and who organized and documented the enormous amount of information which the study had accumulated so that we could archive the data. We must also thank Bill Bradley and Randall Levitt at the Carleton University Computing Centre whose assistance in computing matters (including rewriting parts of Xerox SPSS) was invaluable. Finally, we wish to thank Greg Morrison and Jane Wilson of the Social Sciences Data Archives at Carleton University for their programming assistance with programs such as PATH and ECTA.

At Waterloo, Goyder benefitted from consultation with several colleagues: Alf Hunter and James Curtis in the Department of Sociology, and George Barnard and Greg Bennett in the Statistics Department. Hubert M. Blalock, Jr., at the University of Washington, generously responded to some written queries about statistical matters.

We thank Carleton University and McMaster University for assistance in the administration of our grant and for providing various necessary services. Thanks also are given to the Centre for Demography and Ecology, University of Wisconsin — Madison, which under support from the National Institutes of Health Centre grant #HDO5876 provided free computer time, office space and assistance to Monica Boyd, who was there in 1975-76 as a Canada Council Post-doctoral Fellow. Finally, not only do we express our appreciation to the Canada Council for Research Grants S72-1419 and S73-1894, but for the readiness of Council staff, especially Mireille Badour and Patrick Mates, to help at those times when the realities of research had to be fitted to the image of research described in our original application. We also remember, with gratitude, the sympathetic assistance given to us by the late Jean Morrison when the project was launched.

We would also like to thank a number of people at Statistics Canada without whose support and expertise this study could not have been done. First, we would thank Sylvia Ostry, Chief Statistician; Jenny Podoluk, Director General, Household Surveys Branch; and Peter Hicks, Director, Labour Force Survey Division, for their support, cooperation, and various acts of executive will which enabled the survey to be carried out. Secondly, we would thank the members of the Supplementary Survey Unit at Statistics Canada who carried out our study. In particular we owe a debt to: Ron C. Corbeil, Chief of the Unit who worked with us as a collaborator in the design and layout of the questionnaire, and who piloted the project through the shoals of bureaucracy and Treasury Board regulations; Ray Ryan, Ron's successor who picked up the project after the field work stage and saw it through coding, editing, and release; and Frank Gallager, who was the staff member most involved in the project who handled much of the detailed planning and was responsible for the data processing work at Statistics Canada.

At different times and in different ways, the academic community has expressed its sorrow over John Porter's untimely death. For us, his colleagues on this project, his death was especially sad. Not only do we wish that he had lived to see this monograph in print, but we wish he had lived to join us in discussing how to ensure that research on this important problem is repeated periodically in the future. Even though our wishes must go unfulfilled, we can say, in all truth, that his presence has been with us as we readied this manuscript for publication. As we worked, we could readily imagine what his views on various topics were and what his reactions would be to what we wrote. This manuscript has benefited through our awareness of his scholarly concerns and standards.

MONICA BOYD
HUGH McROBERTS
Ottawa

JOHN GOYDER
Waterloo

FRANK JONES
PETER PINEO
Hamilton

Contents

CHAPTER 1

Introduction: The Canadian Mobility Study; Approaches and Procedures

MONICA BOYD, JOHN GOYDER, FRANK E. JONES, HUGH A. McROBERTS, PETER C. PINEO, and JOHN PORTER

The association between the social location of parents and offspring and the processes of status transmission from one generation to another are the central issues explored in this book. These are not new issues. In one form or another and in varying degrees of centrality, they have long intrigued social analysts of often sharply divergent ideological positions (see Goldthorpe, 1980). As a consequence, considerable diversity exists in studies of social inheritance, and its analogue social mobility, with respect to questions asked, theoretical frameworks employed, and methods of analysis.

From its inception, the Canadian Mobility Study was designed to parallel the benchmark 1962 Occupational Change in a Generation Study in the United States (Blau and Duncan, 1967) and its 1973 replication (Hauser and Featherman, 1977). As a result, our analyses are shaped by the conceptual and analytical paradigms which stress mobility as a measure of social opportunity and which investigate the effect of social origins and education on social mobility and opportunity. Chapter 2 provides the rationale for the areas of inquiry investigated in the remainder of the book. In this chapter, we present an overview of the analytical and conceptual models as they shaped the design of the Canadian Mobility study. We also discuss the history of the Canadian Mobility Study, and we conclude with a look at the topics of investigation which are examined more extensively in the remainder of the book.

1

Mobility and Attainment in Canada: Analytical and Conceptual Frameworks

Studies of social mobility have as their principal concerns the measurement of the rate of transmission of inequality from one generation to another and the identification of those factors which determine the level people attain within the structure of inequality. Such similarity of concern does not imply homogeneity of interpretation. Within the tradition of mobility research, different questions are raised and answered within different theoretical perspectives (Goldthorpe, 1980: 1-37; Matras, 1980).

The research presented in this book addresses several of the many questions found in mobility research (see Matras, 1980), and it interprets the answers in light of one of several perspectives. In keeping with much of the postwar North American and European research, attention is focused on the amount of social mobility which exists in Canada, defined as mobility between generations (inter-generational mobility) and during a generation (intra-generational or career mobility). With respect to inter-generational mobility we ask to what extent various strata tend to be self-recruiting or open to persons of other social origins. What explains the transformation from origins to destination is also a focus of inquiry, and underlies our analyses of education and first-job variables which affect the transmission of occupational status across generations. By design and conceptualization, our study will not shed much light on other variables known to affect the mobility process, such as the class location of the individual, the relations between classes, the role of the state, the structure of the educational system, and the structure of the economy to name a few. Nor will the study deal directly with other issues related to mobility such as the de-skilling of labour or the existence of a credential society in which the labour force is over-educated for its needs.

Our decision to narrow our focus to Canada and to occupational mobility in our initial research has meant that certain legitimate research concerns are not addressed in this volume. However, subsequent research has compared mobility in Canada and the United States (McRoberts and Selbee, 1981) and has investigated the income attainment of Canadians (Adsett, 1981; Boyd and Humphreys, 1980; Callan, 1979; Goyder, 1981). Our study was designed within a tradition which stresses the centrality of occupations as a measure of status location, and which emphasizes the allocating role of individual statuses such as family or origin characteristics and education and occupational achievements. Such a study provides important insights into the degree of status inheritance and into one set of factors which do or do not affect the destination statuses of offspring.

Two approaches dominate the analysis in this book. One approach asks about the degree and nature of the association between the location of fathers and respondents in a hierarchy of occupational categories. This analysis of mobility matrices extends backwards through virtually all empirical studies of occupational mobility. The second approach, proposed initially by Blau and Duncan (1967), derives from the earlier study of father-son occupational association but conceptualizes the process of status inheritance as occurring over the life cycle. The status attainment model, as it is called, envisions family of origin characteristics as affecting current occupational achievement via education and prior occupational experience acquired by offspring as they mature, complete their education, and enter the work world.

Each approach addresses a slightly different issue in stratification research. In the early studies of occupational or social mobility, the basic question posed was: "To what extent is a son's occupation or social status related to that of his father?" This question was answered by obtaining a sample and arranging information on father's and son's occupations, or social status, into a bivariate cross-classification called a mobility matrix. From this matrix, percentages and/or measures of association were calculated, to measure the relation between origins and occupational outcomes. The matrix itself is theoretically neutral. The meaning is imposed upon the data by the researcher through the decisions about the attributes to be measured (occupations, status groups, or classes) and the meanings imposed upon the findings (see Horan, 1978). Clearly the data have greater import for those analyses which view equality of opportunity as relatively central to their understanding of what is implied by social justice, and they have lesser import for those whose analysis derives from a simple insistence upon equality of condition as the *sine qua non* of justice.

Compared to mobility matrix analysis, the status attainment model is more complex. This difference in part derives from the different purposes underlying the matrix and status attainment procedures. In the former, as typically used, the concern is largely descriptive: Is there an association between fathers and sons occupational statuses? How strong is it? As bivariate analysis provides limited scope for theory, it is not surprising that mobility matrix analysis has been regarded as being largely descriptive. However, given contemporary developments in the analysis of categorical data, such as log-linear analysis, and the extension of mobility analysis from bivariate to multivariate, matrix analysis may attempt explanation.

In the case of the status attainment model, the purpose is to offer an explanation of the phenomena which were observed in the matrix: how is it that parents are able to affect for good or ill the socioeconomic destinies of their children? One answer to this question is provided by a model of the attainment process in which current occupational status is conceptualized as an outcome of family of origin characteristics, educational attainments, and first-job status (Blau and Duncan, 1967; Boyd *et al.*, 1981; Cuneo and Curtis, 1975). Because this model decomposes the association between family of origin characteristics and the respondent's occupational status into the intervening attainments of education and first-job status, it is especially useful in showing the mechanisms by which social origins affect the socioeconomic statuses of the offspring. Social origin variables are considered to influence the subsequent educational and occupational attainments both because they are indicators of the levels of economic resources in a family and because they also capture role modelling and other socialization effects (Blau and Duncan, 1967; Duncan, Featherman and Duncan, 1972). Education is included because it represents a resource which is utilized in the labour market. In particular, formal schooling has certification properties which qualify or disqualify people for certain kinds of occupations. In turn, the status of the first job is related to the status of the current occupations, in part because certain occupations have career trajectories associated with them (e.g., factory worker to foreman) and in part because the requirements of certain occupations (e.g. physician) make recruitment from other occupations (e.g. garment worker) unlikely.

Analytically, these variables are considered to be sequentially ordered. Educational attainment represents the first stage of socioeconomic achievements over the life cycle, first job the next stage occurring after school completion, and so on. This temporal ordering of successive achievements has been depicted graphically by means of path models (see Blau and Duncan, 1967; Cuneo and Curtis, 1975). As revealed in these path diagrams, social origin variables and education and first-job attainment influence current occupational attainment in two possible ways. Past ascribed or achieved statuses can influence current occupational status directly, as is the case when the offspring of a farmer becomes a farmer. And the past status can affect indirectly the current status of a respondent by virtue of its influence on a temporally prior attainment as when a graduate of a teachers' college becomes a high school principal, in later years, largely through the mechanism of becoming a teacher first.

Although the data-gathering and analytical strategies may be neutral, interpretation of the findings of such research requires a theoretical framework. As all the contributions in this volume refer to specific aspects of the theories of occupational mobility and status attainment, an elaborate review of these theories is not presented here. However, since we are, in the main, following conventional analytical procedures, it may be useful to outline the sociologist's conventional wisdom about mobility research and the criticisms which we acknowledge it invokes.

Most studies of occupational mobility assume an association between the growth of industrialization and an improvement in the quality of a national labour force because technological exigencies require or create more highly qualified workers. The great expansion of education which has come with advanced industrialism has been viewed as investment in human capital, and increasingly high levels of educational attainment of the labour force have accompanied economic growth. Changes in the occupational structure reflecting this "upgraded" quality of labour have been traced from census to census in all industrial societies as the tertiary level of white-collar, skilled technological, and professional classes of workers has constantly expanded. It has been argued that at a later stage of modernity, namely post-industrialism, the labour force becomes further enriched in highly qualified manpower. Since these emerging higher positions cannot all be filled from families already well placed in the social hierarchy, they are filled from lower in the social structure, where in the past families have been larger, and as improved access to public education has provided the necessary schooling. Thus, industrialization brings with it an "opportunity structure" of an ever greater number of higher-level, "better" jobs.

Another assumption of the conventional model for mobility studies is that the allocation of individuals to occupational roles is more rational than in pre-industrial periods in the sense that ability, trained capacity and experience are the most important criteria in job recruitment. This rational selection process is summed up in the term universalism and contrasts sharply with the particularism of earlier periods when non-rational attributes such as the social status of the family of origin, religion, ethnicity, race, and sex were all used as recruiting and excluding devices for the higher-level jobs. Because an industrial occupational structure demands talent, the universalistic criteria become paramount and, although vestiges of particularism remain, they are viewed as "irrationalities." In this model, education plays an important role in the allocative process by training and developing intrinsic talents so that the most able get the most and best education. Thus, educational achievement reflects ability and assures a maximal fit between the talent demands of the occupational structure and the talent outputs of the educational system.

As the conventional model portrays an ideal smoothly running allocative system, it has been a task of mobility and status attainment studies to determine how closely any actual system conforms to the ideal. The model is ideal in another sense: it supports the ethical notion of equality of opportunity and therefore is important in the legitimation of the allocative system and of the distribution of rewards — that is, the inequality of income — that follows from it. As with any ideal model, the assumptions underlying it can be, and have been, questioned. For example, much sociological research has demonstrated that education systems in industrialized societies are neither fair nor rational because children from better-off families, regardless of their intrinsic ability, bring superior cultural and material resources from their homes to the school, and this gives them an advantage over children from less favoured backgrounds. A more severe criticism, from contemporary Marxist analysis, is that schools in capitalist societies reproduce the existing structure of inequality by giving the children from less privileged classes a different kind of training in different types of programs and streams than is given children of the more privileged. The education both receive is appropriate to the stations in life from which they have come and to which they are most likely to go. Thus, rather than serving mobility, public education is said to have thwarted mobility.

An even more severe criticism by Marxist writers (e.g., Braverman, 1974) is that the changes in the occupational structure produced by industrialization do not provide upward mobility at all. Industrial technique and the division of labour "degrades" the labour force rather than upgrades it, as many former skills, it is argued, have been simplified through increases in the division of labour. White-collar workers have lost much of the status and independence they once had as they are absorbed into white-collar production lines and increasingly take on characteristics, including unionization, of blue-collar workers. Thus, the hierarchical occupational scaling used to measure the transmission of status is not a proper measure of a job's standing. Marxists, of course, do not accept the ranking dimension for which occupational scales were devised, since they view most work in capitalist regimes as "exploitative" and hold that greater proportions of the labour force become degraded into exploited forms of labour as capitalist industrialization proceeds. Thus upward mobility is an illusory process and attempts to measure it a hopeless undertaking (see for example, Poulantzas, 1974).

A further criticism of the supposed functional relationship between education and work is that the educational requirements of jobs have become greatly inflated leading to "credentialism" by which is meant too great an emphasis on formal certification for entry to occupations. This description of a labour force over-educated for its needs could be consistent with the degrading thesis. However, as long as educational requirements are essential to entry and advancement within sectors of the occupational structure, the "functional" relationship remains regardless of whether the jobs have the intrinsic educational require- ments that job describers and recruiters maintain they do. As long as this condition of "education before work" remains, it seems correct to consider how important education is for occupational mobility.

Thus, despite the criticisms that have been made of the conventional linking of occupational change, the growth of education, and mobility opportunity, we adopt the conventional framework in most of the analysis in this study. Throughout, the analysis provides a test of deviation from the rationality of the conventional model so that we might find out, for example, if and how particularistic elements of social background affect occupational attainment, or how much education — even if its only purpose is to acquire certificates — helps to overcome disadvantaged social origins. Moreover, while the degrading thesis may have some validity, there is little doubt that some proportion of the labour force now requires more skill than formerly. Occupations based on science and technology which require a greater level of education to perform have undoubtedly increased in number, although it appears that we may have assumed too readily that lower-level jobs now require greater educational content. Perhaps when credentialism has been removed we are left, in real terms of occupational needs, with a bimodal distribution of good and bad jobs rather than a graded hierarchy of jobs.

Education, rightly or wrongly, is widely perceived as an important element in the value of a job and the rewards which it can command. Employers seem convinced that the more education an employee has, the more productive a worker he is likely to be, and the more he will be able to improve through experience. Workers themselves believe that some jobs, often their own, require more skill than others and bargain collectively with great force to maintain historical differentials in pay. High incomes of professionals are justified in terms of returns to their investment in education, and indeed, personal investment in education is not considered worthwhile unless there is a substantial return on it in higher income. It is not our task here to render a verdict on the so-called "great training robbery" (Berg, 1970) but we do assert that education has been and continues to be important in occupational recruitment.

Controversies about the upgrading or degrading of the labour force we also set aside, interesting as they are in attempting to assess the true consequences of industrialization. Whatever the outcome of such controversies, the fact that the entire labour force and work world is endowed with prestige is unlikely to change. Very many and surprisingly consistent studies of the public evaluation of occupations have been undertaken in many countries. The public has no difficulty in ranking occupations in terms of their standing in the community, although it must be accepted that for many occupations the variance in the rankings is considerable. These prestige rankings have been variously interpreted as reflecting the subjectively perceived properties of preferability, desirability, and social standing that jobs have and that make up their generalized status. There are many theories which seek to explain why occupational roles are ranked in this way. Some jobs, it is said, are more important for the survival of the society, some require more of the scarce talent that is available, and some are so onerous that they must have both material and prestige rewards to induce people to take them on. Some jobs of high prestige, such as supreme court justices, prime ministers, archbishops, nuclear scientists, and the like, are highly ranked because they deal with cosmic forces beyond the ken of ordinary people and being so remote are endowed with "presumptive charisma." These practitioners engender awe and respect. As we descend the job hierarchy, profane and ordinary qualities are sufficient for the performance of less valued work.

Once again we do not need to choose between these theories; but we can take as given that the world of occupations does have a status hierarchy which is in good measure captured by the scales and classifications we employ, and that the movement up or down this occupational hierarchy between generations or during the career of an individual represents occupational and social mobility. The legitimate questions of whether there ought to be differential ranking and unequal rewards or how extensive the differentials ought to be in the modern world are set aside. We live in an unequal, stratified society which may, for some, be ethically indefensible. To study occupational mobility with the conventional analytical tools is not to accept that inequality; rather it is to throw more light on the nature and consequences of social stratification.

The Origins of the 1973 Canadian Mobility Study

The genre of empirical studies, of which our study is a part, had its beginnings in the early 1950s with the investigation of social mobility in Great Britain, carried out under the direction of David V. Glass (1954). This study provided a detailed description of class and stratification in Great Britain, and it also involved the development of indices of association and related statistics which methodologically advanced the study of social mobility. Natalie Rogoff's research (Rogoff, 1953) must also be regarded as a major early contribution to mobility research. Although it was undertaken about the same time as the Glass research, her development of the Rogoff ratios was carried out independently of Glass and his co-workers. She and the Glass group deserve joint credit.

While Rogoff's research was limited to one city in the United States, the Glass study was the first of several large national investigations which were subsequently conducted in the United States (Blau and Duncan, 1967), Australia (Broom, Jones and Zubrzycki, 1968), and Italy (Lopreato, 1966). Aside from the study of elites (Clement, 1975; Olsen, 1980; Porter, 1965), the area of social mobility has received only limited attention from Canadian sociologists. Findings on social mobility have been reported by Goyder and Curtis (1977), McRoberts (1971, 1975) and Pineo (1976). The remainder of the Canadian studies are not national in scope (i.e., Cuneo and Curtis, 1975; deJocas and Rocher, 1957; Richmond, 1967) and hence their findings have limited generalizability.

Canadian sociologists have long been aware that Canada is one of the few western nations which does not possess any reliable national data on the important issues of occupational mobility and the process of occupational attainment. In response to the void, three of the members of the present team of investigators — Frank Jones and Peter Pineo (McMaster University), and John Porter (Carleton University) — in 1967 investigated the possibility of undertaking such a national study. Although the efforts of Jones and Pineo resulted in several pilot studies known as the Four Cities Study, a national investigation into occupational mobility became a reality only in 1972. During the summer of 1972, John Porter, with the assistance of Hugh McRoberts, hosted a conference at Carleton University which provided a forum for the discussion of a national mobility study among the invited representatives, of the Canada Council, Statistics Canada and other federal government departments. Robert Hauser and David Featherman (University of Wisconsin) and Donald Treiman (Columbia University) were present as consultants on the basis of their expertise in similar American endeavours. Following the assurances of Statistics Canada that it would serve as the data collection agency, a grant proposal was submitted to Canada Council and subsequently approved.

We initially considered data collection by a private research agency but a consideration of costs versus benefits resulted in the decision to have Statistics Canada gather the data. In making this choice, we were aware that there would be certain constraints and that some compromises would have to be made between what would be ideal and what Statistics

Canada would be prepared to do. However, our study benefited enormously from the collaboration. Initially and throughout the fielding and processing stages, meetings were held with Statistics Canada representatives, of whom Ron Corbett, Ray Ryan, and Frank Gallager were the most central figures. Under this collaboration arrangement, Statistics Canada administered the instrument as a supplement to their Monthly Labour Force Survey, and collected, coded, and edited the data prior to their release as a set of individual records.

The study was fielded in July 1973 with the final release of the data coming in June 1975. We obtained usable information on approximately 23,000 females and 22,000 males who were age 18 and over and not full-time students. Because of the sampling design employed in the Labour Force Survey, these data when appropriately weighted are representative of the target population.

The Labour Force Study: Implications for the Canadian Mobility Study

Although the Canadian Mobility Study was designed to be distinct from the Labour Force Survey, it was fielded as an adjunct to the Statistics Canada Labour Force Survey. As a result of this arrangement, the data-gathering stages of the Canadian Mobility Study were shaped somewhat by the policies and procedures of Statistics Canada on data collection and micro data release. Two factors were particularly important in shaping our research design: the nature of the Labour Force Survey and the nature of the Statistics Act (1970-71-72) of Canada, under which the data were gathered.

In Canada, the primary purpose of the Labour Force Survey is to establish monthly, quarterly, and annual estimates of employment and unemployment. These estimates have both a policy value and a political value. Because of the political debate surrounding unemployment, considerable care must be taken to ensure that nothing interferes with the continuing accuracy of the rates. In particular, Statistics Canada is very concerned with respondent dropout. Respondents are in the survey for six months with one-sixth of the sample rotating out and a new panel selected each month. If respondents refuse to participate at any point in that period, they are lost for the remainder of the time their panel is in the survey.

This concern about respondent dropout produced constraints concerning when the data were to be collected and the length of the Canadian Mobility Study questionnaire. To reduce respondent fatigue, Statistics Canada has made a policy decision to run only four major supplements per year, one every three months. With the exception of July 1973, all the other major supplement dates were booked until 1975. Because the comparative value of the survey would be significantly reduced by waiting for two years, the 1973 date was selected. However, there were problems associated with the July 1973 date.

First, there was less than one year to fund the project, design the instrument, and to get into the field. This very tight time schedule prohibited a pre-test on the instrument. While a pre-test would have been desirable, much of the background information which we wished to gather had been previously gathered by Statistics Canada in various surveys. As a result, we were able to "lift" many standard items from their work. The McMaster team had also done some development work prior to the launching of the national study. Further, the questionnaire design benefited from the work conducted by Blau and Duncan (1967) and Featherman and Hauser (1975) on occupational mobility and attainment in the United States.

The second problem with the choice of the 1973 date was that the survey was conducted in the last week of July, which is the prime vacation period. Due to a considerable portion of the sample not being at home, there was a lower response rate to the July Labour Force Survey and to the supplementary Canadian Mobility Study questionnaire than would have been the case in other months (Table 1:1). For the regular Labour Force Survey, a large number of these non-responses due to vacations can be eliminated by matching with the corresponding June survey responses. Such a procedure is not applicable to the Canadian Mobility Study questionnaire which was fielded at only one point in time, and hence it suffers the full non-response load.

We did consider administering the instrument to each panel in its last month in the survey as an alternative to doing the survey at one point in time. However, we rejected this option in view of the cost, the problems of establishing a common reference period, and the problems of loss of respondents who either had moved or had refused to participate in earlier Labour Force Surveys.

In addition to the July 1973 date, the relationship between the length of the instrument and respondent fatigue placed a further constraint on the design of the Canadian Mobility Study. After considerable discussion with Statistics Canada's field and methods staff, it was decided that the questionnaire must not exceed seventy-five questions and must not cover more than eight legal size pages. Such a constraint meant that some areas considered important received less attention than we would have liked.

A final constraint arose out of the Statistics Act itself. The act prohibits the release of any information in such a way that individuals

TABLE 1:1 — **Comparison of July 1973 Non-response with Averages for 1973 and 1974 by Reasons for Non-response, Labour Force Surveys**

		Reasons for Non-response			
	Total	*Temporarily[1] absent*	*No one[2] home*	*Refusal[3]*	*Other[4]*
July 1973	15.1	9.1	3.2	1.9	.9
Average: Jan.-June 1973	7.4	2.2	2.4	1.9	.9
Average: 1972 (excluding July)	8.1	2.2	2.7	1.9	1.3

SOURCE: Derived from information provided by Statistics Canada, Labour Force Survey Division, Unpublished Mimeo, 1973.

[1] *Temporarily absent.* When all household members are away for the entire interview week.

[2] *No one home.* When after a reasonable number of callbacks, there is no responsible member to interview.

[3] *Refusal.* When a responsible member of the household definitely refuses to provide the survey information requested.

[4] *Other.* When one of the foregoing reasons are applicable, e.g., roads impassable, enumerator not available, death, illness, language problems, etc.

can be identified. (For additional discussion of the confidentiality issue, see Fellegi, 1972.) Loss of detail in the information on occupation was the most serious consequence of this constraint. Although the occupational data were coded to the four-digit 1971 Census Occupational Classification, the occupational data made available to us were coded by Blishen values and to the sixteen-category occupational classification devised for the project. Categories were collapsed for several other variables, notably place of residence, which was identified for us only at the level of province and in terms of five categories of an urban-rural scale.

THE SAMPLE DESIGN OF THE CANADIAN MOBILITY STUDY

The sample used for the study is the sample ordinarily used by the Labour Force Survey, and complete descriptions of its design are available in Statistics Canada publications (1966). The basic unit which is sampled is the household and for Labour Force Survey purposes information is collected on all individuals who are 14 years of age or older in the households falling into the sample. The total sample has around 35,000 households in it. As households are kept in the sample, operating as panels, for six months, some 6,000 new households are added to it each month and an equivalent number retired from it. The sampling procedures would be familiar to any survey researcher: basically, it is a multi-stage areal probability sample. For the larger urban areas, called "self-representing units," a two-stage sampling procedure is used. For the rural areas and smaller cities, called "non-self-representing units," a four-stage design is used. The special design for the rural and mixed areas achieves a form of clustering of cases that minimizes interviewer travel time. In all, the sampling procedures appear to us to be thoroughly professional. In fact, at certain stages they reflected greater care in design than would be expected of a university-based survey research centre. The design included, for example, a double selection of units so that two parallel samples could be used to generate estimates of standard errors where ordinary mathematical procedures are not yet developed. We did note a departure from ideal design, however. Interviewers do form lists of the households within selected clusters but the actual selection of households is not wholly random: there is a random start and then an interval is used.

The Labour Force Survey is designed to generate estimates of unemployment not just for the whole country but also for each of the provinces. To achieve this, the smaller provinces must be sampled at higher rates than the larger ones. It is, then, a stratified sample, and weighting procedures must be used to counteract the varying sampling rates. Without weighting procedures our estimates would be biased — over-representing Prince Edward Island and under-representing Ontario and Quebec. The weights which we use are provided by Statistics Canada. They include a term which corrects for the varying sampling rates and also three other terms. The extra terms are developed to compensate for changes in the population which have occurred since the sample was designed (1961) and ensure that the sample is representative on age, sex, and proportion rural or urban. Also included in the weight, for the purposes of our study was a term developed to correct for the less-than-perfect completion rate. All these terms are summed to a single number in the data presented to us, and so cannot be disaggregated. When the weight is used the frequencies produced from the sample are of the magnitude that would appear in the census, often in the millions. This turns out to have a disadvantage, as normal significance tests can no longer be applied. Particularly in the use of regression techniques and in Chi-square measures, where the power of the statistical test rises with the size of population, the inflated sample exaggerates the significance of the results. (For regression the error varies as $1 / \sqrt{N}$ and for

Chi-square, the ß error varies as 1/n). To give a more realistic sense of the relative importance of results, we employ a procedure used by other analysts who have faced the same problem (see Featherman and Hauser, 1978:511, for example). This procedure consists of dividing the weight term by some constant, in our case 300.55, which reduces the frequencies back to a size roughly equivalent to the original sample. This "downweight" does not simply cancel out the effects of the weight, of course, because while the weight varies in value from case to case, the downweight is the same for all cases. This procedure does not wholly solve the problem. The significance tests in general become more realistic but for subgroups which include many cases with particularly small or large weights, the significance tests will be biased, either being too conservative or too rigorous. As the foreign-born were inadvertently undersampled by virtue of their concentration in large urban areas, more appropriate average weights were calculated for downweighting purposes for use in the analysis reported in Chapter 11.

As indicated above, the Labour Force Survey sampling procedures determined the target population and the sample for the Canadian Mobility Study. However, because the instrument was not relevant to persons under 18 years of age and to full-time students, they were dropped from our sample. Consultation with Statistics Canada assured us that deletion could be made without biasing the sample or the weights.

FIELD PROCEDURES

Given the decision to conduct the survey at a single point in time, the instrument was dropped off at the time of the July 1973 Labour Force Survey interview and picked up later in the week by the enumerator. This procedure was particularly useful in determining the eligibility of persons in the Labour Force Survey for the Canadian Mobility Study. A covering letter by the then Chief Statistician of Canada, Dr. Sylvia Ostry, both requested the cooperation of respondents and gave them strong assurances of confidentiality for their responses. The enumerator was instructed to note on a control form whether or not each member of the household was eligible for the Canadian Mobility Study (over 18 and not a full-time student). Eligible respondents were then given a question-naire called the Job Mobility Survey (See Appendix 1:1), and asked the time at which the enumerator could call back to collect the completed instrument. Up to three call-backs were made in some cases. There were two exceptions to these procedures of sample selection and call-backs. First, in remote areas where consideration of time and distance made call-backs impossible, a stamped return envelope was left with the respondent. Secondly, where a family was not at home, copies of the instrument and stamped return envelopes were left for every member of the household. It should be noted that the Canadian Mobility Study and Labour Force Survey samples differ in that in the latter one member of the household acts as a proxy for all members. In the Canadian Mobility Study, each eligible individual in the household was asked to complete his/her own questionnaire. The result of these field procedures was the completion of some 49,324 questionnaires, which after the exclusion of mismatching, blank, and otherwise unusable cases gave us a set of 44,869 cases representing a response rate of 78 per cent.

The Canadian Mobility Questionnaire Design

In approach and in the type of data collected, the Canadian Mobility Study questionnaire is similar to that of the Occupational Changes in a Generation Surveys I and II in the United States (Blau and Duncan, 1967; Featherman, Hauser, 1978: Appendix A; Featherman and Hauser, 1975), and to a variety of investigations fielded in Great Britain, Ireland, West Germany, Hungary, Finland, Japan, and Australia (Featherman, Hauser and Sewell, 1974). With respect to family of origin characteristics, our questionnaire asked respondents for information on parental education and occupation and on family structure, including number of siblings, ordinal position, and family type, defined by who was head of the household. In keeping with the objective of measuring the transmission of status from generation to generation the question-naire also asked about respondents' education, their first full-time job, their current job and a variety of additional labour force questions concerning employee-employer status, hours worked, and 1972 income. The exact wording of these questions appear in Appendix 1:1, pp. 529-35. Additional labour force information was provided by the record linkage of our Job Mobility Survey with the July Labour Force Survey. This linkage provided us with data on province of current residence, size of place, age, sex, labour force status, hours worked in the reference week, job search experience in the reference week, 1961 and 1971 census occupational classifications, industry codes, and class of worker.

Mindful of the Canadian experience of continued immigration and its traditions of bi- and multi-culturalism, we also asked respondents about their or their parents' immigration background, their internal migration experiences, their religion, their linguistic abilities, and their ethnic origins. Many of these questions reflect the collaboration with Statistics Canada and they are similar in wording to those appearing in the 1971

Census of Canada. But some of our questions provide information not found in the census. For example, because the census question on ethnicity, which probes paternal ethnic origins, is not without criticism (Ryder, 1955; DeVries, 1977), we also asked respondents to indicate the ethnic or cultural group to which they felt they now belonged. Also, a variety of questions were asked on the language first spoken, the language now most comfortable speaking, conversational knowledge of French and/or English, and language spoken on the first job and on currently held job.

The fact that the Statistics Canada Labour Force Survey included both sexes provided us with the opportunity to study the mobility and attainment experiences of women. Since most mobility studies in industrial nations had previously examined only the mobility experiences of males, we found ourselves designing questions which we hoped would measure the female experience of labour force involvement and occupational mobility more accurately than a male-specific questionnaire. Initially, we had hoped to design a separate questionnaire for women but we were prevented from doing so by budget constraints on the coding and processing of such data. As a result, women were asked the same questions as men but questions which were particularly germane to women were incorporated into the questionnaire, and a series of flow instructions were used to route both male and female respondents either through or around them. While budget constraints, potential respondent fatigue, and question sensitivity prevented us from asking many of the questions appropriate to a study of female status attainment, a number of questions were asked concerning the discontinuity of work experience for all women. Some of these questions were a telescoping of the Parnes Longitudinal Survey design (Parnes, 1970). Although our attempt at capturing life history data at one point in time was not altogether successful, we were able to obtain useful information on length of time in the labour force. In addition, questions were asked concerning maternal employment, respondents' marital status, age at first marriage, number of children and the labour force anticipation of married women while children were pre-schoolers or later in school (see Appendix 1:1).

Overall, the research design strongly reflects the status attainment perspective which guided much of North American stratification during the 1960s and early 1970s. As discussed earlier, this perspective directs attention to the processes by which individuals acquire education and attain occupational status. Of central interest is the way in which such processes are shaped by major axes of differentiation and stratification in Canadian society. Many of the questions in the Canadian Mobility

Study were designed to provide information on such axes of stratification (sex, nativity, language, ethnicity) and the rationale for their
centrality in our study is developed in Chapter 2.

In any status attainment study, education and occupation are
important variables, both conceptually and analytically. The Canadian
Mobility Study questionnaire asked respondents two questions about
their formal schooling. The first question asked what was the highest
level of education completed. Because of interprovincial differences
both in the age of starting school (ranging from age 4 to age 7) and in the
length of secondary schooling (ranging from three to five years), the
second question asked respondents to indicate the number of years
spent in school altogether. These two questions gave us rather different
measures of education. The analyses reported in this book use a scale
which orders the categories according to our sociological judgment into
the arrangement shown in Table 1:2.

Two different measures are used to represent the occupational
hierarchy in Canada: the Blishen-McRoberts socioeconomic scale and
the Pineo-Porter-McRoberts occupational classification. The Blishen-
McRoberts scores are based on the regression of occupational prestige
rankings on education and income measures, using data from the 1971
census (Blishen and McRoberts, 1976). Blishen (1958, 1967) pioneered
the development of this type of scale in Canada with his work on the
1951 census and his approach is similar to that employed by Duncan
(1961) in the development of socioeconomic status scores for the United
States. Both the Blishen-McRoberts and the Duncan scores denote the
status accorded to a particular occupational position. Derived as they are
from education and income characteristics of occupations, the usefulness of these scores for the examination of occupational attainment has
been hotly debated along two lines. First, critics of the scores have
argued that the inclusion of education in deriving the scale underlies the
centrality of education as a variable mediating between the occupational
statuses of father/parent and offspring. This criticism appears based on
a confusion of group attributes versus individual characteristics. Blau
and Duncan (1967: 124-128) have shown that the scores assigned do not
change appreciably if education is removed as a component of the score.
In their regression analysis, Duncan, Featherman and Duncan (1972:
49) also found no support for the existence of an education bias in the
socioeconomic scores of occupation.

Such research indicates that the inclusion of an educational component in deriving the overall occupational status scores does not
contaminate analyses based on this measure. A more relevant concern
would appear to be what the scores actually represent. Recent research

TABLE 1:2 — Response Categories and Codes for Education Variables

Level of Education Attainment	Code Assigned
No formal schooling	1
Elementary school	
Some	4
Completed	8
High school	
Academic	
Some	10
Completed	12
Vocational or technical	
Some	10
Completed	12
After high school but not university	
Business or trades training: (e.g., secretarial schooling, hairdressing school, barbering school, trade school, etc.)	
Some	12
Completed	13
Nursing school or Teacher's College	
Some	12
Completed	13
Community College, Junior College, CEGEP, Technical Institute	
Some	13
Completed	14
University	
Some	14
Completed:	
Certificate or diploma	14
Bachelor's degree	16
Master's degree	19
Doctorate	19
Professional degree (e.g., MD, LLB, CA, etc.)	18

clearly indicates that the resultant hierarchy of occupations based on socioeconomic scores closely corresponds to the perceived "goodness" of an occupation — a goodness which is evaluated in terms of the socioeconomic attributes and desirability of the occupation in question (see Featherman and Hauser, 1976; Featherman, Jones and Hauser, 1975; Goldthorpe and Hope, 1972).

Because it is possible for two or more occupations to have identical socioeconomic scores, the Blishen-McRoberts scores represent an abstraction of popularly known and understood occupational categories. The Pineo-Porter-McRoberts classification, however, preserves the distinction between different categories of occupations. As developed by three members of the Canadian Mobility Study (Pineo, Porter, McRoberts, 1977), this classification scheme reorganizes occupational data into a set of sixteen categories defined by type of occupation and skill criteria (see also Jones, 1980). The result is an occupational classification that is more appropriate than the broad occupational categories devised for the 1971 census (Major Groups) for detailed analysis of inter-generational occupational mobility.

PROCESSING THE DATA

Once returned to Statistics Canada, the questionnaires were coded, keypunched, and edited by Statistics Canada prior to the data release to us. The first stage of the data preparation was a manual edit in which each questionnaire was examined for unanswered questions, multiple responses, or written responses. Contrary to the standard Statistics Canada procedure, item non-responses were not subjected to substitution but were coded as missing data. The questionnaire was designed to be "self coding" with the exception of questions on occupations, and after the initial manual edit, the questionnaires were then sent for occupational coding into the four-digit 1971 Census Occupational Classification which is based on the Canadian Classification and Dictionary of Occupations (CCDO). The data were converted to machine-readable form by a key edit process which involved a direct verification procedure, producing a wild keypunching error of approximately 1 per cent. The final stage in the data preparation was a series of computer-based edits, which checked for three types of errors: "wild punches," or punches which lie outside of the valid range of a variable; dates which are out of sequence, such as when a person reports being in the armed forces beginning in 1943 and ending in 1927; and answers which in combination are logically inconsistent, such as a female respondent who reports two brothers, four of whom are older than she. Several meetings were held with Statistics Canada on the results of these edits and several more were held involving only the members of the Canadian Mobility Study. In some instances, inconsistencies were recorded as blanks but for the most part no action was taken on resolving the errors identified by the validation checks. The checks did alert us, however, to the confusion and misreporting which occurred in the job discontinuity section of the questionnaire, and to other inaccuracies in the data, such as when some respondents indicated a very early age at first job, which suggested a failure to give first full-time job, and a tendency of retirees not to give last occupation.

In addition to validation procedures, reliability of the data was another concern. Early in the history of the project we had hoped to reinterview a subsample of our respondents in order to provide reliability estimates for the occupational, educational, and background data. However, time constraints prevented us from doing so. As noted earlier, we had less than a year to fund the project, design the questionnaire, and get into the field. Reinterviewing a panel of respondents meant an even tighter time-frame since respondents stayed in the Labour Force Survey sample for a maximum of six months. The time problems also were compounded by the fact that such reinterviewing was not part of our original agreement with Statistics Canada, and to fund it would have required an additional application to, and review period by, the Canada Council. While it is regrettable that we were not able to obtain estimates of reliability from a reinterview procedure, such estimates were available from the extensive investigations in measurement error in stratification research in the United States (Alwin, 1980; Bielby, 1976; Bielby, Hauser and Featherman, 1977a, 1977b). Such investigations suggest that retrospective reports of status variables are as reliable as contemporaneous ones for white males so that when measurement error is ignored, the socioeconomic inequality which is attributed to variation in socioeconomic background and educational attainment is slightly underestimated.

In addition to coding, keypunching, and editing the data in the Canadian Mobility Study questionnaires, Statistics Canada also converted the Census Occupational Classification codes into two occupational measures: the Blishen-McRoberts (1976) socioeconomic status scores and the Pineo-Porter-McRoberts (1977) occupational classification. These transformations were made both because of the theoretical perspectives and the analytical requirements of the Canadian Mobility Study and, as noted earlier, because Statistics Canada could not release the very detailed four-digit census codes to us under their guidelines for maintaining the confidentiality of respondents.

With the final release of the data from Statistics Canada to us in June 1975, individual members of the research team made checks on the data and created certain composite measures, such as numbers of siblings and educational achievement.

In addition to devising a measure of educational achievement, a number of internal checks were performed on the data. In the course of her analysis on immigrants, Professor Boyd discovered an apparent misreporting of first job by the foreign-born (see Chapter 7). Non-response to the current occupation question was higher than we would have liked (Table 1:3). In the case of males, where the overall rate was 15 per cent, some non-response was associated with low education, employment in lower-level occupations and, of course, being out of the

TABLE 1:3 — Non-response Rates to Current Occupation by Education and Labour Force Characteristics for Men and Women, Age 25-64.

Characteristics	*Percent Not Giving Current Occupation*	
	Male	*Female*
Total	15.2	51.1
Education		
Zero or Some Elementary	20.2	63.5
Completed Elementary	12.2	51.6
High School or More	8.5	33.6
Labour Force Participation		
Employed	12.8	24.4
Unemployed	29.8	41.6
Not in Labour Force	48.2	68.4
Worker Status (Labour Force Only)		
Full Time	12.7	19.5
Part Time	20.4	41.8
Occupation (Labour Force Only)		
Manager and Administration	6.5	11.2
Professional and Semi-professional	8.3	16.2
Clerical	11.1	18.4
Sales	10.6	29.8
Services	16.9	38.2
Farm, Fishing, Logging	21.7	70.8
Mining and Quarrying	15.5	24.6
Production, Fabrication		
Assembling and Repairing	13.2	28.8
Construction and Trades	15.4	—
Transportation and Crafts	14.2	25.2

labour force. The apparently high non-response rate among women (51 per cent) is less problematical than would appear, as the rate falls to slightly under 20 per cent among women employed full-time compared to 42 per cent for those employed part-time. Among the latter, some respondents were not required, because of flow design, to complete the current occupation question. Another group of women who by-passed the current occupation question were those who did not report a first full-time occupation. Thus, 78 per cent and 86 per cent of these women, employed respectively full-time and part-time, did not report a current occupation. However, among those reporting a first occupation, 30 per cent of those employed part-time, compared to 10 per cent of those employed full-time, did not report a current occupation.

Analysing the Canadian Mobility Data

The analysis of the data was accomplished over a period of two and a half years during which, under the conditions of the Canada Council grant, the principal investigators maintained their full teaching and advising responsibilities and were assisted in the research endeavours by two research assistants, one located at Carleton University and one at McMaster University. This volume reports initial analysis of our data which focused on the educational and occupational attainment processes of Canadians. Other measures of attainment, such as income, other topics, and more in-depth analyses were reserved for subsequent analysis and Appendix 1:2 provides a bibliography on work prepared to date. Among the topics examined in this volume are the basic models of attainment, which assess the impact of the number of siblings, and paternal education and occupation on respondents' own educational and occupational achievements (chapters 3, 4, and 6). In addition, temporal variation in the transmission of status across generations is examined (Chapter 5). Central to these analyses is a general concern with the degree and way in which achievements of individuals are influenced by ascriptive variables, or those attributes with which people are born and which generally are unalterable. These analyses examine the achievements of males in the labour force. However, two subsequent analyses extended the basic findings to females. Chapter 7 in this volume compares native-born men and women, using occupational status (the Blishen-McRoberts scores) as a dimension of occupational achievement. Chapter 8 augments this analysis by examining the experiences of men and women in terms of location on a distribution of occupational categories (the Pineo-Porter-McRoberts classification), and it enlarges the analysis to include all men and women in Canada (see Table 1:4 for a

TABLE 1:4 — Canadian Mobility Study: Sample Characteristics

Chapter	Sex	Age	Birth place	Labour force status	Farm owners/ Farm labourers	Unweighted N
3	Male	25-64	Native born	In	Both	8,204
4	Male	25-64	Native born & Foreign born	In & out	Both	15,710
5	Male	25 & over	Native born	In & out	Both	17,594
6	Male & female	25 & over	Native born & Foreign born	In & out	Both	20,265
7	Male & female	25-64	Native born	In	Both	13,943 (M)* 4,325 (F)
8	Male & female	25-64†	Native born & Foreign born	In & out	Both	16,416‡
9	Male	25-64	Native born	In	Both	8,204
10	Male	18 & over	Native born & Foreign born	In & out	Both	21,753
11	Male	25-64	Native born & Foreign born	In	Both	11,950 (NB) 2,571 (FB)
12	Male	25-64	Native Born & Foreign born	In & out	Both	15,710
13	Male & female	18/25 & over	Native born & Foreign born	In & out	Both	21,753

* For analyses involving Current Occupation; where the dependent variable was First Occupation or Educational Attainment, male and female unweighted samples were, respectively, 13,561 and 11,765, 13,317 and 15,317 and 16,043.
† 18 years and over for Table 8:1.
‡ N for females; male N as in Chapter 3.

description of the subsamples used for analysis). In addition to sex, language and ethnicity also are known to differentiate and stratify the Canadian population, and the occupational achievements of the male French- and English-language groups and various ethnic groups are studied in chapters 9 and 10. The occupational attainments of the native- and foreign-born groups are examined in chapters 11 and 12. The book concludes with an analysis of the impact of place of residence and migration in Canada on the attainment process.

References

ADSETT, MARGARET A.
   1981 "Sex Differences in Rates of Return from Human Capital to Earnings for Married Full Time Workers in the Canadian Labour Force: A Case of Women's Work History?" M.A. thesis. Department of Sociology and Anthropology, Carleton University, Ottawa.

ALWIN, DUANE F.
   1980 "Measurement Models for Response Errors in Surveys: Issues and Applications." In K.F. Schuessler, ed., *Sociological Methodology*. San Francisco: Jossey Bass.

BERG, IVAR
   1970 *Education and Jobs: The Great Training Robbery*. New York: Praeger.

BIELBY, WILLIAM T.
   1976 "Response Errors in Models of Intergenerational Transmission of Socioeconomic Status." Ph.D. dissertation. Department of Sociology, University of Wisconsin, Madison. Also published as *Working Paper 76-26*. Center of Demography and Ecology, University of Wisconsin, Madison.

BIELBY, WILLIAM T., ROBERT M. HAUSER, DAVID L. FEATHERMAN
   1977a "Response Errors of Black and Non-black Males in Models of the Intergenerational Transmission of Socioeconomic Status." *American Journal of Sociology*, 82: 1,242-88.
   1977b "Response Errors of Non-black Males in Models of the Stratification Process." *Journal of the American Statistical Association*, 72: 723-35.

BLAU, PETER and OTIS DUDLEY DUNCAN
   1967 *The American Occupational Structure*. New York: John Wiley.

BLISHEN, BERNARD and HUGH A. MCROBERTS
   1976 "A Revised Socioeconomic Index for Occupations in Canada." *Canadian Review of Sociology and Anthropology*, 13(1): 71-79.

BLISHEN, BERNARD R.
   1967 "A Socioeconomic Index for Occupation in Canada." *Canadian Review of Sociology and Anthropology*, 4: 41-53.

1958 "The Construction and Use of an Occupational Class Scale." *Canadian Journal of Economics and Political Science,* 24: 519-31.

BOYD, MONICA, HUGH A. MCROBERTS, JOHN PORTER, JOHN GOYDER, FRANK E. JONES and PETER PINEO
1977 "The Canadian National Mobility Study." *Canadian Studies in Population,* 4: 94-96.

BOYD, MONICA, JOHN GOYDER, HUGH A. MCROBERTS, FRANK E. JONES, PETER C. PINEO and JOHN PORTER
1981 "Status Attainment in Canada: Findings of the Canadian Mobility Study." *Canadian Review of Sociology and Anthropology,* 18: 657-73.

BOYD, MONICA and ELIZABETH HUMPHREYS
1980 "Sex Differences in Canada: Incomes and Labour Markets," pp. 401-20 in Economic Council of Canada, *Reflections on Canadian Incomes.* Ottawa: Minister of Supply and Services, Catalogue No: EC 22-78/1980E.

BRAVERMAN, H.
1974 *Labor and Monopoly Capital,* New York: Monthly Review Press.

BROOM, LEONARD, F. LANCASTER JONES and JERGE ZUBRZYCKI
1968 "Social Stratification in Australia." In John A. Jackson, ed., *Sociological Studies,* Vol. 1. Cambridge University Press, 212-33.

CALLAN, FERN E.
1979 "The Role of Language in the Income Attainments of Quebec Women." M.A. thesis. Department of Sociology and Anthropology, Carleton University, Ottawa.

CLEMENT, WALLACE
1975 *The Canadian Corporate Elite: An Analysis of Economic Power.* Toronto: Carleton Library, No. 89.

CUNEO, CARL J. and JAMES E. CURTIS
1975 "Social Ascription in the Education and Occupational Status Attainment of Urban Canadians". *Canadian Review of Sociology and Anthropology,* 12: 6-24.

deJOCAS, YVES and GUY ROCHER
1957 "Inter-generation Occupational Mobility in the Province of Quebec." *Canadian Journal of Economics and Political Science,* 23: 57-68.

deVRIES, JOHN
1977 "Explorations in the Demography of Language: The Case of the Ukrainians in Canada." Unpublished paper. Department of Sociology and Anthropology, Carleton University, Ottawa.

DUNCAN, OTIS DUDLEY
1961 "A Socioeconomic Index for All Occupations." Pp. 109-38 in Albert Reiss, *et al., Occupations and Social Status.* New York: Free Press.

DUNCAN, OTIS DUDLEY, DAVID L. FEATHERMAN and BEVERLY DUNCAN
1972 *Socioeconomic Background and Achievement.* New York: Seminar Press.

FEATHERMAN, DAVID L. and ROBERT M. HAUSER
  1975   "Design for a Replicate Study of Social Mobility in the United States."
         Pp. 219-51 in Kenneth C. Land and Seymour Spilerman, eds., *Social
         Indicator Models*. New York: Russell Sage.
FEATHERMAN, DAVID L. and ROBERT M. HAUSER
  1976   "Prestige or Socioeconomic Scales in the Study of Occupational
         Achievement." *Sociological Methods of Research*, 4: 403-22.
  1978   *Opportunity and Change*. New York: Academic Press.
FEATHERMAN, DAVID L., ROBERT M. HAUSER and WILLIAM SEWELL
  1974   "Toward Comparable Data on Inequality and Stratification." *American
         Sociologist*, 9: 19-25.
FEATHERMAN, DAVID L., F. LANCASTER JONES and ROBERT M. HAUSER
  1975   "Assumptions of Social Mobility Research in the United States: The
         Case of Occupational Status." *Social Science Research*, 4: 329-60.
FELLEGI, IVAN P.
  1972   "On the Question of Statistical Confidentiality." *Journal of American
         Statistical Association*, 67: 7-18.
GLASS, DAVID V., ed.
  1954   *Social Mobility in Britain*. London: Routledge, Kegan Paul.
GOLDTHORPE, JOHN H.
  1980   *Social Mobility and Class Structure in Modern Britain*. Oxford: Clarendon
         Press.
GOLDTHORPE, JOHN H. and KEITH HOPE
  1972   "Occupational Grading and Occupational Prestige." Pp. 19-80 in Keith
         Hope, ed., *The Analysis of Social Mobility Methods and Approaches*. Oxford:
         Clarendon Press.
GOYDER, JOHN C.
  1981   "Income Differences between the Sexes: Findings from a National
         Canadian Survey." *Canadian Review of Sociology and Anthropology*, 18:
         321-42.
GOYDER, JOHN and JAMES CURTIS
  1977   "Occupational Mobility in Canada Over Four Generations." *Canadian
         Review of Sociology and Anthropology*, 14: 303-19.
HAUSER, ROBERT M. and DAVID L. FEATHERMAN
  1977   *The Process of Stratification: Trends and Analysis*. New York: Academic
         Press.
HORAN PATRICK
  1978   "Is Status Attainment Research Atheoretical?" *American Sociological
         Review*, 43: 534-40.
JONES, FRANK E.
  1980   "Skill as a Dimension of Occupational Classification.. *Canadian Reivew
         of Sociology and Anthropology*, 17: 176-83.

LOPREATO, J.
1966 "Social Mobility in Italy." *American Journal of Sociology*, 71: 311-14.

MATRAS, JUDAH
1980 "Comparative Social Mobility," pp. 401-431 in Alex Inkeles, ed. *Annual Review of Sociology*, Vol. 6. Palo Alto, California: Annual Reviews Inc.

McROBERTS, HUGH A.
1971 "Explorations in Canadian Occupational Mobility." M.A. Thesis. Carleton University, Ottawa.

1975 "Social Stratification in Canada: A Preliminary Analysis." Ph.D. Dissertation. Department of Sociology, Carleton University, Ottawa.

McROBERTS, HUGH A. and KEVIN SELBEE
1981 "Trends in Occupational Mobility: Canada and the U.S." *American Sociological Review*, 46: 406-21.

OLSEN, DENNIS
1980 *The State Elite.* Toronto: McClelland and Stewart.

PARNES, HERBERT S. *et al.*
1970 *Dual Careers.* Washington: U.S. Department of Labor, Manpower Research Monograph, No. 21.

PINEO, PETER C.
1976 "Social Mobility in Canada: The Current Picture." *Sociological Focus*, 9: 109-23.

PINEO, PETER C., JOHN PORTER and HUGH A. McROBERTS
1977 "The 1971 Census and the Socioeconomic Classification of Occupations." *Canadian Review of Sociology and Anthropology*, 14(1): 91-102.

PORTER, JOHN
1965 *The Vertical Mosaic: An Analysis of Social Class and Power in Canada.* Toronto: University of Toronto Press.

POULANTZAS, N.
1974 *Les Classes Sociales dans le Capitalism Aujourd'hui.* Paris, Seuil.

RICHMOND, ANTHONY, H.
1967 *Postwar Immigrants in Canada.* Toronto: University of Toronto Press.

ROGOFF, NATALIE
1953 *Recent Trends in Occupational Mobility.* Glencoe: Free Press.

RYDER, NORMAN
1955 "The Interpretation of Origin Statistics." *Canadian Journal of Economics and Political Science*, 21: 466-79.

CHAPTER 2

Canada: The Societal Context of Occupational Allocation

JOHN PORTER

Occupational mobility, or occupational attainment, the process which we are seeking to analyse in this study, takes place within an established social order. Social order implies a relatively stable and persistent set of arrangements through which the major tasks and essential needs of the society are met. The configuration of a social order, or a social structure, is made up of the major institutional sub-orders, such as: the economy, which organizes the production and distribution of a society's material goods, that is, its wealth; the polity, which provides the mechanisms for controlling, coordinating, and directing people and the groups they form in their need to attain common objectives, that is, the institutions of government; the family, the institution through which human reproduction takes place and the young are nurtured and socialized to become adults; and the educational system, which shares the socializing function with the family, but which also, at its higher levels, creates and maintains a society's culture, trains highly qualified manpower, and conducts scientific inquiry.

All human societies fulfill their needs through established institutional patterns with which all members are familiar and to which in a large measure they conform. For example, in all industrialized societies — and we will confine our observations to the advanced type of society — children are brought up in families in which the parents, mainly the father but increasingly the mother also, work outside the home for income to pay for the family members' individual and joint needs.

Although industrial societies have many features in common, there are also respects in which they differ. In some industrial societies

29

political institutions are authoritarian, where there is a high degree of direction from above and little if any control of the decision-making elites by the masses. There are other types of industrialized societies where the governing elites must contest elections and therefore seek some degree of mass approval for continuation in office. Some industrialized societies have tightly planned economies where all the pieces of a complex productive machinery, including manpower needs, are designed beforehand, cut out, and put together in a way which it is hoped will work. Other industrial societies depend for their economic activities on a relatively free market in which many groups, corporations, unions, and individuals do their own planning in the light of their interests, a process which, it is hoped also will work.

Some industrialized societies have relatively homogeneous populations facilitating centralized political systems; others are more pluralistic in the sense that they are made up of different ethnic or descent groups leading to some form of federated political structures. In some industrialized societies all speak, with varying degrees of conformity, to the "correct" version, the same language; in other industrial societies more than one language is spoken. Industrialized societies differ also in their histories and traditions. Some have taken on their present territorial outlines and commenced their histories before the onset of industrialization, or, in the western nations, the emergence of capitalistic forms of production. Others are "new nations" whose territorial outlines and nation-building have taken shape along with the development of capitalism and industrialization. These latter have depended on large numbers of immigrants to achieve industrial growth.

There are then both similarities and differences in the established social orders of modern industrial societies. In some, particular features of social structure will be of particular importance; in others some other components will be emphasized. For example, in an ethnically plural society differences of colour or language may be salient to a point that people's colour or language group become of great consequence for them, as has been the case, for example, with colour in the United States, language in Canada, and religion in Northern Ireland.

Whatever they might be, the established features of social structure in their varying degrees of saliency provide a set of conditions against which occupational mobility takes place. In the more strict sense of conditional probabilities, they affect the chances that individuals have for particular occupational attainments. Social structure interferes with the rational allocation of individuals to occupations on the basis of the competence they have acquired through education and experience. Ideally in an industrialized society the allocation should be independent of factors which have no bearing on the capacity to work at particular occupations. Thus, in a free system of allocation, providing he has met the professional standards required, a person should not be prevented from working as a physician or lawyer, for example, by the colour of his skin, his ethnic origin, or his religion since these could not affect his technical competence. The point could equally have been made if we had used "she" rather than "he" in the preceding sentence and the point might have been made more forcibly for it is well known that there are for women additional barriers to those for men in the occupational world — barriers which are determined by social arrangements rather than by differences in intrinsic abilities between the sexes.

A system of recruitment to occupations which showed no interferences from factors of social structure would be ideal. Under such free and open circumstances an individual would find himself at an occupational level which was consistent with his education, his work experience, his ability, and his motivation relative to other individuals. Differences in natural endowment, the degree of willingness to put up with the irksomeness of learning, the amount of ambition and energy all ensure that everyone will not be striving for the same occupational levels. In the ideal system differences in these factors alone would go a long way towards explaining how people get the kinds of jobs they do. We know, however, from many sociological studies that qualities such as ambition and energy, which depend on good health, are themselves affected by conditions of social structure. In school, for example, it has frequently been shown that children at the lower end of the social class structure do not aspire to as much education or such high-level jobs as children from upper parts of the social class structure. Thus even before facing the hazards of access to the occupational world individuals will have experienced effects imposed by the social structure, which in the case of the preceding illustration is the existence of social classes.

In our ideal model of occupational recruitment it is conceivable that large numbers of well-educated people, all equally ambitious and talented, could be chasing a limited number of higher-level occupations — a condition which some critics of the so-called over-production of "human capital" claim has already been reached. Such a situation might arise, of course, where an economy has become stationary or contracting. However, if these circumstances should arise, allocation on the basis of competence could still work with the more competent receiving the better opportunities so that trained competence and experience would still explain in large measure how people got where they did.

However, societies are not ideal in that allocation is independent of social factors. Conditions of social structure intervene to become barriers for some and bridges for others in the process of occupational attainment so that these conditions, more than competence, explain how people get to where they do. As we have said, some features of social structure which are salient and which might interfere with the free and rational allocation of competences to occupations can be the same for all societies; others are specific to particular societies. Sex, for example, is an almost universal basis of discrimination, and lower social class origins have in every society a depressing effect on achievement. On the other hand, language can only be of importance where there is more than one language widely used, and the status of being an immigrant is likely to affect the conditions of work where there are large numbers of immigrants in the work force. Here we seek to review those features of Canadian social structure which we would assume to have some effects on mobility chances of Canadians.

SOCIAL STRUCTURE AND VALUES

All social structures are supported by appropriate values and beliefs. For example, modern industrialized societies could not exist without beliefs which support the rational allocation of resources within the economy, the calculation of costs, the planning of a complex division of labour, bureaucratic control and responsibility for productive processes, and the accountability of units within large-scale organizations for their be-haviour. Nor could they exist without beliefs supporting the notion that the "free" adult should be able to pursue his career independently of the social group or family in which he was reared or of the restrictive obligations of traditional ways of living. Most industrial societies also support the value of equality of opportunity and the career open to the talents. An industrialized society requires trained ability, that is, a constant supply of highly qualified manpower. If there were substantial barriers to opportunity, if there was recruitment to the more important occupations on the basis of favoured groups, some proportion of a society's talent would be wasted and hence an "irrationality" would be introduced into the allocative process. Public education, in which all societies embarked in the early stages of their transition to industrializa-tion, was implemented to train the potential talent which lay within all sectors of their populations.

All societies fall short of a total commitment to the values which support them. For example, no society has yet provided full equality of opportunity in which all social barriers to achievement are removed. Some have done more than others in providing the resources to maintain high levels of educational attainment of their young people and, to the extent that they have, they provide greater opportunities in turn for occupational attainment.

Values and beliefs are slow to change or to catch up with the material changes which have come about or have been forced upon a society. Thus in the transition from rural-farming to urban-industrial modes of living, some groups may cling to the old ways and so create for themselves a lag or disjunction between the exigencies of industrialism and their preparedness for it. We might expect, then, that along with the interferences with the rational allocation of individuals to occupations presented by social structure, there would also be interferences caused by differing values among different groups in the society, or by the varying intensities with which the prevailing values are held within the different segments. For example, some groups might not consider education to be as worthwhile as other groups do. Some might feel that attachment to family and region or cultural group should be stronger than the call of personal ambition and that the latter should be sacrificed for the former. If groups are different in their commitment to values, and some sociologists say they are, then obviously we would expect such values also to condition the probabilities associated with occupational attainment.

Unfortunately values are difficult to measure. Often social commentators resort to their imaginations and invoke value differences to explain differences in social experiences of groups. For example, in what is perhaps the largest social investigation undertaken in Canada, that of the Royal Commission on Bilingualism and Biculturalism, many of the differences between the English and the French were attributed to differences in values. There is generally in Canada an absence of information, which might be obtained through surveys of opinions and attitudes, about the values of Canadians. As a consequence in this review of the dominant features of Canadian social structure which provide the context for occupational attainment, we can say very little of an empirical nature about values or the cultural components of social structure.

SOCIAL STRUCTURE AND TIME

In mapping out the dominant features of Canadian social structure which are of some relevance to the analysis of occupational attainment several problems arise. One is that we are dealing in this study with a sample of men and women over 18 years of age who have been educated and who have begun their careers over a time span of forty to fifty years. Their parents, whose conditions of living have been important for the life chances of those in our sample, have lived in Canada, or elsewhere, at any time from the 1960s back at least to the 1920s if not earlier. However persistent, social structures will change, if not basically at least in outline, and it therefore becomes a question of the period which should be used to best illustrate those features which we consider important in shaping the context within which mobility takes place. Moreover, there is some reason to be up-to-date, to give a sketch of what things were like in 1973 at the time of the survey, because that was the time when people held the jobs they did.

Problems arise because of the availability of statistical data for different periods. The more recent the period the more complete can our picture be. If all the data were comparable say between 1930 and 1970, we would be able to establish clear trends. Unfortunately data are not always comparable because of the way in which they were collected and presented at different times. To strike a middle course would be to present data for the decade from 1950 to 1960. People who were 35 to 40 years old and approaching midcareer in 1973 would have been 16 years old — when family influences would have been most important — between 1949 and 1954. For older groups the war years and the depression created quite different conditions for maturing.

Our way out of these difficulties is to try to provide, from whatever data are available, a broad picture of social structure in Canada during the present century, but highlighting particularly the post-Second World War period. Our narrative may at times seem kaleidoscopic as we attempt to incorporate various fragments of time into this perspective, but we hope it will provide both a source of speculation about avenues of analysis we might pursue and a background against which to interpret findings about occupational mobility.

THE RURAL-URBAN TRANSITION

Perhaps the most striking feature of Canadian social structure during the lifetime of our sample of adults and that of their parents has been the transition from a rural way of life based on farming to an urban way of life based on industrial and commercial occupations. If we trace these changes from the 1901 census, we see that at the beginning almost two-thirds (65 per cent) of the population of Canada were classified as rural, but in 1971 less than one-quarter (23 per cent) were (Canada, Statistics Canada, 1974: Table 1.1). In 1901 46 per cent of male workers were engaged in agriculture. If all others in fishing, logging and mining are added, the proportion in primary occupations was 51 per cent. In 1971 the proportions were 8 per cent in agriculture and 11 per cent if the workers in other primary industries are added (Ostry, 1968; Statistics Canada, 1978).

This rural-urban transition was accompanied by an extensive growth of the population from 5.3 million in 1901 to 21.6 million in 1971 (Statistics Canada, 1974: Table 1.1). Growth in population has not been even throughout this time but has proceeded in bursts particularly during the decade before the First World War and after the Second when, in both, population increased by one-third. The period of the depression in the 1930s was the low point of expansion with an increase of only 11 per cent. There was some slowing down also in the period between 1961 and 1971 when the increase was 18 per cent (Statistics Canada, 1974: Table 1.3).

The movement off farms after the Second World War was accompanied by qualitative as well as quantitative changes in the structure of agriculture. From 1951 to 1971 the number of farms in Canada was reduced by four-tenths from 623,000 to 366,000. During this twenty-year period half the small farms (those under 240 acres) disappeared while the number of large farms (those over 1,600 acres) more than doubled, increasing by 113 per cent (Canada, Federal Task Force on Agriculture, 1969). It is clear, then, that one of the significant inter-generational changes we can anticipate among our respondents who were born in Canada is that many of them will have come from farm origins, but that themselves will be neither farmers nor farm workers.

To come from farm origins usually implies having less education than those who come from cities and thus poorer initial advantages in opportunities for higher-level jobs. Not only are those raised on farms less likely than those raised in cities to have the range of competences for the industrialized occupational world; but it is very likely that they will not have as strong value commitments to occupational attainment as their urban counterparts. For those who remain in farming, its transformation into large-scale operations, as indicated by the increased size of farms and the emergence of what is called "agribusiness," required special skills in the management of large amounts of capital equipment and personnel, and in the application of scientific methods to farming, so that in the 1970s even in farming there would be a premium on education and occupational competence which did not exist in an earlier period (Federal Task Force on Agriculture, 1969).

The other side of the coin to the movement off farms is the growth of cities and the major metropolitan centres where industry has become concentrated. In 1901 only about one-third lived in areas the census defined as urban: by 1971 three-quarters did (Statistics Canada, 1974: Table 1.8). At the turn of the century there were only two cities with more than 100,000 population and they contained less than one-tenth (8.9 per cent) of the population of the country. In 1971 there were nineteen such cities containing 27 per cent of the population (Statistics Canada, 1974: Table 1.1). To look only at cities is to understate the degree of urban growth because many cities spill into each other and some merge with suburbs that have grown up around the city boundaries. Thus the real measure of urbanization is the metropolitan conurbation, or the census metropolitan area, of which there were twenty-two in 1971 containing over half (55 per cent) of the Canadian population compared to the 45 per cent who lived in them in 1951 (Statistics Canada, 1974: Table 1.10). Any image of Canada as an outdoor rural society created by its history or its vast land area is inappropriate. In 1971, the large majority lived in cities of considerable size.

Since large cities are the locus of industrialization and the corresponding complex hierarchical occupational structure, being raised in a city, or moving to one, particularly to the large metropolises, can no doubt affect the chances that people have of exploiting the opportunities that exist. Not only is the occupational structure more visible and familiar for the city dweller than the countryman, but also the range and accessibility of educational facilities to fit a person for industrial occupations are likely to be greater in the city. In general it might be speculated that the prospect for opportunity increases with the size of city of residence, particularly in the early stages of a person's career.

THE CHANGING STRUCTURE OF OCCUPATIONS

The rural-urban transition and the growth of industrialization was a process of social and economic change which culminated at the post-industrial level of development where the economy was producing more services than goods. For Canada this threshold had been reached by 1960 when 54 per cent of those at work were producing services which amounted to 55 per cent of employment and 61 per cent of the value of output. These were substantial changes from 1946 when four out of ten workers only were producing services and six out of ten producing goods (Canada, Economic Council of Canada, 1978:70). This movement from a goods-producing industrial society to a service-producing post-industrial society (Bell, 1974) was accompanied by another important structural change in the national economy — the increase in government participation in the disposal of goods and services. By 1970 government expenditures were amounting to over one-third (35 per cent) of the gross national product whereas in 1950 the proportion had been less than one-quarter (23 per cent) (Economic Council of Canada, 1971:8).

The increase of government bureaucracy in the public sector and of service-producing activity such as wholesale and retail trade, finance, insurance and real estate, community services, and business services in the private sector brought about a great expansion of white-collar or non-manual occupations. Because these occupations, generally speaking, require higher levels of education than most forms of manual work and because they are usually ranked higher by members of the community in terms of prestige or social standing (Pineo and Porter, 1967:24-40), the shift to service-producing economies results in an expansion at the higher levels of the occupational structure and a contraction at the lower levels of unskilled and labouring occupations. We can speak of an upgrading of the labour force. It is this upgrading of the labour force from less skill to more skill inherent in the growth of industrialization and post-industrialism that constitutes the demand side of occupational mobility. These conditions create mobility opportunity. The demands can be met on the supply side by properly motivated recruits to and graduates from the educational process among the native-born, or through immigration — that is, through the importation of the necessary skills and qualifications from outside.

Upgrading of the labour force has been taking place throughout the present century; at the beginning less than one-quarter (24 per cent) were in white-collar and service occupations. By 1931 the proportion had risen to one-third (34 per cent) and by 1961, as we have noted, to over one-half. Over the same period the secondary manufacturing, manual or blue-collar occupations made up 28 per cent of the labour force in 1901 and 27 per cent in 1961 (Ostry, 1968: Table 2). Thus, through all these transitional six decades the proportion in manufacturing remained relatively constant at a little over one-quarter. The great shifts were from the bottom, the agriculture and primary occupations. This would seem to be an unusual form of transition for industrial societies. According to Colin Clark's classic model of economic development (Clark, 1951) there is an expansion out of primary occupations into secondary and later into tertiary occupations. The inter-generational mobility counterpart of this economic transition would be the sons of primary workers moving into secondary occupations and those of secondary into tertiary. The increasing occupational demand at the higher levels would draw up mobile sons and daughters of workers from below. However, the secondary level of occupations in Canada never expanded in the present century, creating an unusual pattern of occupational transition.

The relative stability of the secondary sector might reflect the peculiar hinterland conditions of the Canadian economy, which as host to large-scale foreign investment, particularly in resource industries, has had an "entrepôt" component of management and commercial links with external investors (Clement, 1975). This condition might have led to the unusually large service sector. In fact, Canada has a larger proportion of its labour force in service occupations than the United States, which is certainly considered to be the more advanced of the two societies. There is no doubt, as we will examine later, that immigration played an important role in meeting the tertiary-level occupational demands. It will be one of the tasks of this study to analyse the relative contributions of native-born workers and immigrants to this mobility process.

EDUCATION AND OCCUPATIONAL UPGRADING

Upgrading of the labour force to meet the demands of changes in the occupational structure has two aspects. One is the greater number of jobs requiring high levels of training, and the second is that many jobs over a period of time require more education and training to perform them well. Perhaps in this second case there is some inflating of educational requirements, but clearly not always. Professionals such as engineers and physicians probably require more training to perform their jobs well in the 1970s than they did in the 1920s, and at lower levels of the occupational structure complex machinery no doubt increasingly requires more training than formerly.

The occupational upgrading with respect to education can be illustrated for Canada for the decade 1951 to 1961, during which the proportion of the Canadian labour force with 13 or more years of schooling rose from 10 to 16 per cent and those with 9 to 12 years of schooling from 39 to 43 per cent. Within specific occupational groups, the managerial for example, the proportion with 13 or more years of schooling rose from 18 to 27 per cent, for the professional, from 59 to 66 per cent, and for the commercial and financial from 12 to 17 per cent. Manual occupations in manufacturing had minor increases in their educational levels with 4 per cent with 13 or more years of schooling in 1951 and 6 per cent in 1961. For these occupations the proportions with 9 to 12 years of schooling rose from 38 per cent to 41 per cent. For primary occupations, most of them in farming in 1961, no more than 3 per cent had 13 or more years of schooling, and as late as that time only 28 per cent had as much as 9 to 12 years of schooling — clear evidence of the educational handicap of rural workers when they move to cities and some explanation of the fact that, as earlier studies have shown, they end up, in the main, in unskilled occupations (Canada, Dominion Bureau of Statistics, 1953: Table 11: 1963a, Table 17).

Although in terms of education the quality of the labour force improved during the 1950s, the improvement was to begin from a depressed level. At the beginning of the period of economic growth that followed the Second World War more than half (53 per cent) of the male labour force had no more than eight years of schooling. The proportion with such little schooling dropped to 44 per cent by 1961 and 32 per cent by 1971 (Dominion Bureau of Statistics: 1958; 1963a; Statistics Canada, 1977).

Generally speaking, Canadian educational institutions were slow to adapt to the increased demands placed on them by the changing occupational structure. In 1951 only 46 per cent of the secondary school age population, 14-17 years, were in school. The proportion rose to 66 per cent in 1961 and to well over 80 per cent by 1970. Compared to the United States, Canada lagged behind in the production of an educated labour force. The United States had 76 per cent of the secondary school age population in school in 1951 and well over 90 per cent by 1970. (Illing and Zsigmond, 1967: Table 3.2).

At the university level there was also an expansion from a relatively low starting point after the Second World War. In 1951 only 4 per cent of the college age population, 18 to 24 years, were in universities in Canada. The proportion rose to 7 per cent in the early 1960s and 12 per cent in 1971. Thus the higher retention rates in secondary education were followed through by the late 1960s by increased enrolments at the university level. But Canada still had some distance to go to catch up with the United States in higher education. In 1965 only 9.4 per cent of the Canadian population 17 years of age and over had either some university education or had graduated from university. The proportion of the United States population was 19 per cent (Porter, 1966: Table 9.4; Zsigmond and Wenaas, 1970).

The expansion of the educational system and the upgrading of the labour force through formal education meant that younger workers would be better educated than older ones. For example, in Canada in 1970 of males 20-24 years old, 52 per cent had completed secondary school. For those 25-44 years the proportion was 37 per cent, for those 45-64, 27 per cent and those over 65, 15 per cent. The proportions of males of the same age groups with some university education or a university degree were 27, 18, 10 and 7 per cent respectively (Macredie, 1971).

If educational attainment is an important factor in occupational attainment, as our theory holds, we might conclude that the relatively low levels of attainment during the early phase of postwar economic growth would be an impediment to upward movement and lead to "mobility deprivation." On the other hand, workers might be moved up even though they were "underqualified." Yet another possibility was to import qualified workers from abroad to make up for the deficiencies in the stock of "human capital." We will see in an examination of immigration and the Canadian labour force that this in fact took place.

POPULATION, MIGRATION, AND THE LABOUR FORCE

Although the growth of the Canadian population noted earlier came more from natural increase — the excess of births over deaths — than from net migration — the excess of immigrants over emigrants — the latter has always been a significant component of population growth in the country. Migration has been dynamically linked to periods of economic expansion and contraction. For example, in the depression decade of the 1930s more people left the country than came into it. The economic boom after the Second World War brought high levels of migration. Between 1951 and 1961, 1.5 million immigrants arrived while at the same time almost half a million people left. High net migration continued through the next decade, with 1.4 million arrivals and .7 million emigrants. Economic growth tends to take place in different countries at the same time. Hence the favourable conditions which gave rise to immigration into Canada also prompted emigration from Canada as people sought to take advantage of opportunities which they believed to exist elsewhere, particularly in the United States. In the generation between 1941 and 1971 the Canadian population almost doubled from 11.5 million to 21.6 million. The larger part came from natural increase, 7.7 million, but the share of net migration, 2 million, was considerable (Statistics Canada, 1974: Table 1.2).

In 1971, 15 per cent of the Canadian population was born outside of Canada. However, this included children, and women who, for whatever reason, were not working for pay and were hence not in the labour force or concerned with occupational attainment. Of Canadian workers, more than one in five were immigrants at that time (Kalbach, 1974: Table 2.6). Immigrants have come from various countries with varying degrees of similarity to the conditions which they found in Canada. Great Britain has traditionally been the most important source. In the 1950s and 1960s about one-quarter of all immigrants came from there, with the proportion falling off to less than one-fifth in the late 1960s and early 1970s (Canada, Department of Citizenship and Immigration, 1962: Table 13). Italy was the next largest source in the two decades after the Second World War, but by the 1970s immigration was falling off from there also. Germany and the Netherlands were also important until the 1960s, before they too fell off as a source. By the 1970s immigrant sources were shifting. The United States was sending more, about 15 per cent, and Britain was sending less than formerly. The proportion coming from Asia and the West Indies between them (18 per cent) was as great as those coming from Great Britain, the traditional source (Statistics Canada, 1974: Tables 13, 15).

Not only were immigrants varied with respect to their countries of origin, they were also different with respect to the educational levels and work experience with which they came, and often the amount of occupational competence they brought was associated with their country of origin. In general immigrants from Great Britain and the United States were much better qualified than those from Italy or Portugal, and those from Asia had higher educational qualifications than those from Greece. In part, the reason for these differences were the immigration regulations which were changed during the 1960s to a point system which placed great emphasis on skills. However, the system of sponsorship by which people from abroad could join close relatives remained. So unskilled workers from Italy, Portugal, and Greece could join their relatives who had come earlier, while those from Asia, from where immigration had been previously low, required skills to make up the necessary points.

Thus immigrants were a very heterogeneous group with respect to their preparedness for occupational attainment once they got to Canada. They were polarized around the well educated and the poorly educated. A Labour Force Survey of 1965 indicated that 34 per cent of postwar male immigrant workers had completed high school or attended university, but on the other hand 42 per cent had completed only elementary school or less. Despite this polarization, the immigrant labour force was overall better educated than the native-born, only 24 per cent of whom had completed high school or attended university. Nine per cent of immigrants had graduated from university compared to 5 per cent of the native-born (Lagacé, 1968). Thus some groups of immigrants were better prepared than others and also than native-born workers to advance in the work world.

The relationship between the occupational levels of postwar immigrants and the countries from which they came was demonstrated in a study based on the 1961 census. It showed, for example, that in Ontario, to whose highly industrialized centres more than half of postwar immigrants had come, 14 per cent of those from the United Kingdom and 28 per cent of those from the United States were working in the top two of six class levels based on the socioeconomic scale devised by Bernard Blishen, but less than one-half of 1 per cent of those from Italy were working at that level and about 4 per cent of all other Europeans (Blishen, 1970). About half of all United Kingdom workers were in the bottom two classes, which contained 57 per cent of native-born Canadian workers, but 97 per cent of postwar Italian immigrants and 81 per cent of other European immigrants. These differences in occupational levels for immigrants from different places were equally striking in the other provinces. Similar findings were reported by Goldlust and Richmond who examined the experience of immigrants in Toronto, the city which has received such large numbers. British and American immigrants were found in middle and upper middle class positions, while those from other countries were more often in blue-collar occupations (Goldlust and Richmond, 1974: 203).

The two characteristics of the immigrant labour force just reviewed — the polarized educational levels and the disproportionately large proportion of the better educated and occupationally prepared coming from the United States and United Kingdom — continued through to the 1970s. Moreover, professional workers were increasing as a proportion of all immigrant workers. Between 1968 and 1971, 30 per cent gave professional occupations as their intended occupations, compared to 23 per cent between 1962 and 1967 and 9 per cent between 1946 and 1961 (Canada, Department of Manpower and Immigration, 1972).

There is little doubt that the upgrading of the Canadian labour force that we noted as accompanying the industrial growth of the postwar period was achieved in large measure through immigration. In part, this dependence on external recruitment can be attributed to the slowness of Canadian educational institutions to adapt to the manpower needs of a highly industrialized society. At the time of the 1971 census, for example, over 30 per cent of all architects, one-quarter of physical scientists, over one-quarter of all physicians and surgeons working in Canada had immigrated within the previous twenty years (Statistics Canada, 1975).

Because it creates more high-level occupations than were available previously, industrial expansion is a major source of mobility opportunity. The high levels of skill of some immigrants put them in a better position to exploit emerging opportunities than many of the native-born. It is an important task of this study to determine if they were in fact better able to convert their superior educational resources into greater mobility than were the native-born. Since not all immigrant groups had superior education, we would anticipate considerable differentials in occupational attainment between immigrants from different countries.

Whatever picture we eventually establish of the differences between native-born Canadians and immigrants in occupational attainment, or the role of migration in the mobility process, there will be an important missing segment, that is the occupational experience of emigrants from Canada who would not appear in a sample of the Canadian labour force and who have, so to speak, dropped from sight. As we have seen, for all periods when immigration is high, out-migration has equalled a sizable proportion of immigration. No doubt native-born Canadian emigrants, or immigrants leap-frogging elsewhere or returning home, particularly if they are well educated, all move with some perception of opportunity.

Anthony Richmond, a student of migration in Canada, refers to the migration of the better educated as a multi-way movement between urban and metropolitan centres, in which the net gains and losses by country or large city are a small proportion of the total movement (Richmond, 1974). In this "exchange" of competences between Canada and other post-industrial societies we will never know how well both native- and foreign-born emigrants from Canada have done, because they are not among our sample of the Canadian labour force of 1973.

By the late 1960s immigration regulations were becoming more restrictive in advanced industrial societies, no doubt reducing somewhat this "exchange of competences." For most of the age groups at work in 1973, however, the migration option was a real one, so we will never be able to fill in the missing piece to see how those who chose to leave Canada, either native-born or returning immigrants, have fared. If we consider mobility opportunities at a particular time as a set of vacancies, emigrants made room for those who stayed.

As well as immigration into and out of the country, Canada has seen high levels of internal migration. The off-farm, cityward migration, some of which has been inter-provincial, we have already noted. Some of the inter-provincial moves have been exchanges between cities much as with international migration. From the Second World War to 1961, Ontario experienced a net gain of a quarter-million native-born Canadians from the other provinces. British Columbia also gained large numbers through this native-born movement as did Alberta, as the process of internal shifts continued into the 1970s. The Atlantic provinces, relative to their size, were substantial losers of population (Porter, 1966: Table C4).

Whether migration is cityward, inter-provincial or international it is, for adults, almost always associated with occupational changes. The movement of people has been attributed to the "push" factors of poor economic conditions in places and the "pull" factors of bright economic conditions in other places. Actual or perceived opportunities to do better prompt people to move great distances as well as short ones. In one Toronto study 56 per cent of all immigrant householders, but three-quarters of Greek, Portugese, and Italian respondents, said that their main reason for moving was economic, to improve their standard of living. Another reason frequently given was "to be near relatives and close friends" (Goldlust and Richmond, 1974).

City-to-city "exchange" migration, whether international or internal to Canada, is likely to be associated with job opportunities and hence to have positive effects on occupational attainment. On the other hand, off-farm migration poses problems in the analysis of mobility. There has always been a tendency to regard movement out of farming into urban occupations — the rural-urban transition — as upward mobility. Yet we know from many other studies that from the point of view of social classes in transition the off-farm movement has seen the attrition of a class of independent proprietors whose sons most often become unskilled or semi-skilled wage labourers. The rural worker has few if any skills to offer in the urban labour market. Thus it is difficult to know whether the movement should be interpreted as upward or downward mobility. The matter is further confused by the fact that farming is not a homogeneous occupation because farms vary greatly in their size, scale of operations, and value of products sold. Much of the off-farm migration has been created by technological changes in agriculture reducing the demand for labour, and by the large size of rural families. It is unlikely that high achievement values have been dominant in the off-farm movement, governed as much of it is by necessity. City-to-city migration, on the other hand, is more likely to involve people with skills in search of opportunity where, providing economic conditions are favourable, they can improve their occupational standing.

THE SALIENCY OF ETHNIC PLURALISM

Canada as a "new nation" has been a society of immigrants throughout its history. It has become an ethnically plural society in which membership of a cultural or descent group is of some social consequence. The division which runs deepest, because it is based on language and historical animosity, is that between French- and English-speaking Canadians. Because this division is ineluctably a part of the Canadian past and present, it has provided a rationale for the persistence of ethnic identities for those groups which have migrated to Canada since the late nineteenth century. Unlike the United States, where there has long been the normative pressures of the "melting pot" for immigrant groups to become American, the Canadian outlook has been one of encouraging immigrant groups to retain their identities of origin and some sense of community after arrival in Canada. It scarcely could have been otherwise with almost two hundred years of French resistance to assimilation.

Although the French tend to regard all their non-French fellow citizens as "the English," the fact is that, by and large, the non-French do not see it so. Rather they see themselves as fragmented into a multiplicity of groups. Almost as salient as the French have been the three British ethnicities, English, Scottish and Irish, who were so important in the early history of the country. When European immigrants began to arrive the conditions were favourable for them to identify closely with others from their homelands. This condition was helped by the rural community patterns of settlement when European immigration grew apace up until the First World War, just as it was to be fostered by the urban ghetto pattern of settlement of the heavy European immigration after the Second World War.

Unlike the United States, there has always been an official recognition of ethnicity in that all Canadians are required by the decennial census to state their ethnic origin or their European or other cultural descent group on the male side (see Porter, 1975). Although this definition of ethnicity has a sociological absurdity about it, in that mothers "do not count," it has persisted from census to census, and the more self-conscious members of groups have always welcomed this statistical visibility.

These ethnic communities characteristic of the "English-speaking" part of Canada were strong enough in the early 1960s, when the federal government was establishing the Royal Commission on Bilingualism and Biculturalism, which had as its main aim an examination of the relative positions of the English and the French, to insist that the terms of reference of the commission include an examination of the contribution of the other ethnic groups to Canadian development. In time the commission was to devote a separate volume of its report to the other ethnic groups (Canada, Royal Commission on Bilingualism and Biculturalism, Vol. IV, 1973). On the basis of that volume the federal government was in 1971 to introduce a policy of multiculturalism "within a bilingual framework," and some provincial governments did the same. Thus, a further official stamp was put on ethnic or cultural pluralism.

Although statistics of ethnic groups in Canada are based on responses to the dubious question about the first male ancestor to North America, they are the only ones that are available. Table 2:1 shows the major ethnic groups of the Canadian population during the present century. Several trends might be noted. The first is the declining proportion of those who are of British origin from 57 per cent in 1901 to 45 per cent in

1971. The second is the relatively constant strength of the French from
31 per cent in 1901 to 29 per cent in 1971. The third is the increasing
proportion of non-British, non-French from 12 per cent to 27 per cent
over the seventy years. The largest of these groups in 1971 were the
Germans and the Italians. It is also clear that the third ethnic element is
extremely fragmented.

Table 2:1 shows only those groups who make up at least 1 per cent of
the population. The "Other" category contains perhaps another twenty
groups which individually make up minute parts of the population —
for example, Icelandic, Lithuanian, Roumanian, and Japanese each with
about two-tenths of 1 per cent.

Although statistics are eagerly sought by the leaders of ethnic groups
to demonstrate their viability and vitality, the reality is somewhat
different. Both individuals and groups vary in the degree to which they
want to detach themselves from their countries of origin and become
Canadian. One measure of the tendency to assimilate is language loss. In
1971 while 27 per cent of the population had non-French, non-English
origins, only 13 per cent had a mother tongue other than English or
French. That this assimilation takes place in the direction of English is
indicated by the fact that although the English (British) make up only 45
per cent in terms of ethnic origin, 60 per cent have English as their
mother tongue. A further step towards assimilation through language
for the "other" groups is speaking either English or French in the home.

TABLE 2:1 — Ethnic Origin of the Canadian Population, 1901-1971*

	1901	*1921*	*1941*	*1961*	*1971*
British	57.0	55.4	49.7	43.8	44.6
French	30.7	27.9	30.3	30.4	28.7
German	5.8	3.4	4.0	5.8	6.1
Italian	0.2	0.8	1.0	2.5	3.4
Dutch	0.6	1.3	1.9	2.4	1.9
Polish	0.1	0.6	1.5	1.8	1.4
Scandinavian	0.6	1.9	2.1	2.1	1.8
Ukrainian	0.1	1.2	2.7	2.6	2.2
Indian and Eskimo	2.4	1.3	1.1	1.2	1.3
Other	2.5	6.2	5.7	7.4	8.6
Total	100	100	100	100	100

SOURCE: *Report of the Royal Commission on Bilingualism and Biculturalism,* Book IV, 248, and
        Census of Canada, 1971.
*Newfoundland was excluded from the Canadian Census until 1951.

In 1971, 68 per cent spoke English in the home, 7 per cent neither English nor French, and 25 per cent French (Statistics Canada, 1973). Two important facts emerge. One is that judged by language use there is a strong assimilative tendency towards English-speaking Canada. The other is that the relatively small number who continue to speak their ethnic group language in the home is probably confined to recent immigrants. In other words, the longer groups or their members are in the country the more likely are they to become like English Canadians. They are likely, too, to move out of the ethnic community.

There is no doubt some association between assimilation and occupational mobility. Strong ethnic ties imply attachments to tradition, kinship, and community, a condition which at times can be inimical to the acquisition of competence or achievement values which are so important to the mobility process. Some groups, on the other hand, such as Jews and some Asian groups, have cultures which place particular emphasis on achievement in learning and work so that over time the whole group becomes upwardly mobile. For many groups, however, the opposite is the case and for them strong community attachments, which can well satisfy important needs in an impersonal and technological society, can reduce the chances of mobility. Two perceptive observers of the ethnic group structure of Canada have stated clearly the conflict which exists for many ethnic group members (Vallee and Shulman, 1969: 95).

> ... the more a minority group turns in upon itself and concentrates on making its position strong, the more it costs its members in terms of their chances to make their way as individuals in the larger system ...
>
> Among ethnic minority groups which strive to maintain language and other distinctions, motivation to aspire to high-ranking social and economic positions in the larger system will be weak, unless of course, it is characteristic of the ethnic groups to put a special stress on educational and vocational achievement.

The question of mobility and strong ethnic group attachments is all the more difficult to resolve because of the relationship which exists in almost all, if not all, ethnically plural societies between ethnic affiliation and social status. In such societies, ethnic groups are invariably ranked as being higher or lower and they work at different levels of occupational status. This association between general social ranking and ethnic affiliation can arise from various factors, but in Canada it is related to the period and conditions of immigration. Canadian immigration policy has throughout its history been concerned with labour force needs, and there has been the inclination to view peoples from certain parts of the world as pools from which suitable recruits could be drawn. Their terms of entry have most often been set by the English as the dominant "charter group" of Canadian society. Examples are not difficult to find. Chinese labour was imported in the West to help complete the railways and to work in mines. Eastern European peasants were brought to settle and develop the vast prairie regions where they were given land inferior to that granted to English settlers. Italian countrymen came in large numbers after the Second World War to work in construction industries and the underground sewerage systems of the growing cities. As a result of this relationship between occupational level and labour force needs it is possible to show how the various groups are arranged in an hierarchical fashion through various occupational levels.

Because the matter has been extensively dealt with elsewhere a few illustrations might suffice. For example, from 1931 to 1961 the British have always been over-represented in the higher-level professional and financial occupational categories of the census — that is, their share of these jobs has exceeded that of the labour force as a whole. On the other hand, all the other ethnicities except the Jewish have been under-represented at this level. At the lower levels of primary and unskilled occupations the British have always been under-represented, while most of the others, particularly Italians, eastern and southern European groups, have been considerably over-represented. The French, Canada's co-charter group, have been under-represented in the higher occupations and over-represented in the lower ones (Porter, 1965: 87).

That the ethnic stratification has persisted through to 1971 is clear from Table 2:2. The socioeconomic categories employed are those designed for this study from the 1971 census (Pineo, Porter, McRoberts, 1977: 91-102) and which were briefly discussed in Chapter 1. The categories are ranked from the high professional and management occupations down to the unskilled labouring occupations. The over-representation of the British at the higher levels of the white-collar occupations is clear. With few exceptions all non-British groups are under-represented. The striking exceptions are the Jewish and Asian groups both of whom have considerable over-representation. The Jewish case is explained on the basis of the norms of achievement and mobility which we have already noted. To some extent so is the Asian, but also important in the latter case have been immigration regulations which in the more recent period have put a premium on education for selection for entry. The differences between the British and the French are notable and indicate that the lower status of the French established for earlier periods has persisted. The French are under-represented in the top four categories and over-represented at the lower levels of the blue-collar workers. The transition of French Canada from farming to

TABLE 2:2 — Ethnic Origins by Socioeconomic Status, Male Labour Force, 1971

Occupational level*	British	French	German	Italian	Jewish	Dutch	Polish	Scand.	Ukrainian	Other European	Asian	Native	Total
Professional	11.2	8.3	8.9	3.9	18.1	9.2	8.7	9.2	8.4	8.7	20.3	3.2	9.9
Management	7.6	5.1	5.2	2.0	12.0	5.4	4.3	5.7	4.9	3.6	3.3	2.9	5.9
Semi-professional	3.1	2.6	2.4	1.5	4.8	2.8	2.6	2.6	2.1	2.8	4.9	2.8	2.8
Skilled white collar	12.8	10.3	10.3	8.6	23.9	14.0	9.0	10.4	9.9	9.9	15.4	4.0	11.7
Skilled blue collar	19.9	21.7	24.8	28.7	9.1	23.4	23.5	23.6	20.7	24.2	12.4	20.9	21.2
Lower white collar	11.2	12.4	8.3	10.3	14.5	8.2	9.5	7.6	13.5	9.1	13.3	7.0	11.1
Semi-skilled blue collar	10.5	12.5	10.7	16.0	5.2	10.1	13.6	10.2	10.8	15.4	13.8	17.8	11.5
Labourer	17.5	21.4	15.1	26.5	11.6	15.3	19.6	15.2	17.0	19.3	14.2	32.2	18.6
Farmers	3.9	3.2	9.5	0.4	0.2	9.0	6.4	11.0	9.3	4.3	0.7	1.7	4.3
Farm labourers	2.9	2.4	5.0	1.7	0.3	6.7	3.0	4.5	3.5	2.8	1.8	7.4	3.0

SOURCE: Census of Canada, 1971.

*See Table 2:4: Professions = Categories 1, 2 & 5; Management = 3 & 6; Semi-professions = 4; Skilled white collar = 7 & 9; Skilled blue collar = 8 & 10; Lower white collar = 12 & 14; Semi-skilled blue collar = 13; Labourers = 15; Farmers = 11; Farm labourers = 16.

industry, which had the consequences, as E.C. Hughes noted long ago (Hughes, 1943) of establishing a stratification order of the two charter groups within the industrial structure, had been completed by 1971. In both farming categories there is a smaller proportion of French than English in agriculture and both groups were under-represented there. Other groups over-represented at the lower levels of the occupational hierarchy are Italians, Other European, Polish, and very substantially the native peoples. Ukrainian, Scandinavian, Polish, Dutch, and German are all over-represented in farming, a retention of the historical pattern.

The relationship between occupational level and ethnic origin which has been briefly reviewed is a combination of past patterns of immigration, which have linked particular origin groups to particular occupations, and a later and continuing pattern which tends to reinforce the earlier ones. Thus native-born Canadians of particular ethnic backgrounds will have an occupational distribution which is followed by more recent arrivals and hence ethnic stratification continues. Since all groups are represented in some proportion at the top levels, there is no doubt some mobility, probably enjoyed more by second generation native-born than by first generation immigrants.

Corresponding to this hierarchical arrangement of ethnic groups through the occupational structure there appears to be a subjective counterpart of status ranking of ethnic groups on the part of the Canadian public. One study sought to have a national sample of adults rank ethnic origins according to their general "social standing" in the community. Generally when English-speaking Canadians did the ranking the British ethnicities were the highest, followed by those of western and northern Europe, and at the bottom of the ranking order were native Indians and Asians. More isolated as they have been in the relative cultural homogeniety of Quebec and thus less in contact with immigrant minorities, the French Canadians have a somewhat different view of the status of ethnic minorities. While broad categories of ethnic groups, those from northern or central Europe, for example, were ranked in much the same order by the French, the rankings were at somewhat lower levels. Moreover, the French ranked themselves as high as the British — a compliment which was not returned, since the British ranked the French Canadians a good deal lower than themselves (Pineo and Porter, 1967).

From both objective and subjective perspectives there exists some form of ethnic stratification in Canada. Although it has existed as a feature of Canadian society for a long period of time, how rigid it is, or how much ethnic group membership itself is an aid or an obstacle to achieving higher occupational status, is a question to which our study might provide an answer. It could well be that members of some ethnic groups who are lower in the occupational structure are the more recent immigrants and those at the higher levels — and there are some for all groups — are early immigrants or second generation Canadian-born. If that speculation were correct, then occupational mobility would be a function of length of residence in Canada — not of the groups so much as of individuals. It is not easy, considering the rather continuous flows, to arrange ethnic groups as such by their length of time in Canada. Most of them can in fact be divided into the more recent arrivals who maintain strong community links, and the earlier arrivals and second generation Canadian-born who have dispersed and become adapted to Canadian society.

Anthony Richmond suggests that it is not ethnicity in itself which stands in the way of getting on, but the lower level of education of some ethnic groups. When education is taken into account, members of the various minority groups do as well as native-born Canadians (Goldlust and Richmond, 1974). Thus it would seem wrong to attribute ethnic differences in occupational attainment either to cultural differences — that is differences in values held by different groups — or to discrimination, despite the status rankings on the part of the host society. Whatever cultural differences there may be between groups, many of their members who are immigrants are highly motivated to achieve and are able to transmit high achievement values to their children. In one study of high school students in Ontario it was found that where both parents were immigrants students had higher educational and occupational aspirations than did students whose parents were both born in Canada (Porter, Porter and Blishen: unpublished).

Another aspect of adaptation and assimilation is competence in one of the two Canadian languages. Along with length of residence, language used at work might explain a good deal of the variation in attainment for Canada's minorities. Membership in an ethnic group alone might explain very little. If such were the case, Canada would be following a rational model, since length of residence (experience in Canada) and the use of English, or French in Quebec, can be considered an aspect of competence.

ENGLISH AND FRENCH: THE MAJOR MINORITIES

In any consideration of ethnicity in Canada special attention must be paid to the relative positions of the English and the French. Whether they are considered as Canada's co-charter or co-founding group, or whether the French are looked at as Canada's largest minority, next to the English who statistically speaking are also a minority, the different experiences of the two groups in exploiting the opportunities that have come from industrialization have been through the 1960s and 1970s the major subject of dispute between them.

Anglophone Canadians are an ethnically fragmented group, as we have seen. The French are also somewhat fragmented into three relatively distinct parts: the homeland French in the heart of Quebec province — that is in rural Quebec and the smaller urban centres with Quebec City as the focal point; the French in the bilingual belt, a long geographical corridor stretching from Sault Ste. Marie through the Ottawa valley to Montreal and on to Moncton in New Brunswick; and the "diaspora" French who live in scattered communities, mainly in western Canada (Joy, 1972). These separate groups of French, with different experiences and outlooks shaped often by their degree of contact with surrounding Anglophone Canada and the United States, are themselves almost separate ethnic groups. The Acadians in New Brunswick and the Franco-Ontarians are two examples of French groups different from the *Québécois*. Often in the demands for autonomy the French in Quebec express little concern for these other French groups.

Unfortunately, because official statistics are produced by provinces, or by geographical units within them, it is difficult to arrange the French into the three broad groups into which they fall, since these groups often cross provincial boundaries. In Quebec in 1971, 79 per cent of the population was of French origin. Viewed in another way, the French living in Quebec constituted 77 per cent of all of French origins in Canada. After Quebec, New Brunswick was the province with the highest proportion French, 37 per cent. With the exception of small Prince Edward Island with 14 per cent, all the other provinces had less than 10 per cent French (Statistics Canada, 1974: Table 13.7).

Outside of Quebec, the French tend to be regionally concentrated within other provinces. For example, in northern and eastern New Brunswick they constituted 60 per cent of the population; in northern Ontario, 41 per cent, and eastern Ontario, 32 per cent; and in southern Saskatchewan, 21 per cent (Vallee and Shulman, 1969). Where the French have been more heavily concentrated in non-Quebec regions they are more likely to have retained their language. The French are the bilinguals in Canada. One-third of them can converse in English and French compared to only one-twentieth of those of British origin (Statistics Canada, 1974: Table 11.9). No doubt this bilingual capacity arises from the fact that in order to get on in the work world the ability to speak English is of some advantage. Language capacity is a much more important element for French occupational attainment than for that of the English.

The inequality between the English and the French in the occupational world we have already noted in our general discussion of ethnic stratification. The Royal Commission on Bilingualism and Biculturalism was particularly concerned with this phenomenon and mined the 1961 census for any evidence that it might provide. They found, for example, that based on an index in which all workers equalled 100, British males had incomes from employment equalling 110 while those of French males amounted to 87.7. Surprisingly within Quebec itself the differences were greater: employing the same index the British had incomes equalling 142 and the French 92. Moreover, within a group of 35 large manufacturing enterprises in Quebec, among salaried personnel, the proportion receiving $15,000 or more annually who were French was only 15 per cent while 85 per cent were English. The higher incomes which the English earned were not only because on the average they were more highly educated. At all levels of educational attainment the differences persisted, suggesting that either cultural differences, or discrimination, or some other non-rational factors, were at work in occupational allocation (Royal Commission on Bilingualism and Biculturalism, 1965). Finally, 1971 census data showed that for families where the ethnicity of the head is British the average 1970 income was $8,500 compared to $7,303 where the ethnicity was French and $7,962 where it was some other ethnic group (Richmond and Kalbach, 1980: Table 11.9).

There is ample evidence, then, that in Canada generally and in Quebec in particular, the French have been lower in socioeconomic status than the English and some of the other ethnic groups. In other words, as a group they have benefited least from the occupational opportunities of Canada's industrial and post-industrial development. There has been a tendency to explain these differences in attainment in terms of "culture," that is to say, that in their history and traditions the French Canadians have been less well served than the English in theirs to exploit the economic opportunities or to take the initiative in economic development.

The French are Catholic and the English are predominantly Protestant, and while Max Weber's celebrated theory that the Protestants in Europe and the Protestant sects in North America had greater aptitude for capitalistic exploitation than Catholics may explain early capitalistic development, there is no reason to conclude that in the more recent period the two religious orientations were that important in

explaining differences in attainment. Whatever may have been the
reasons for the earlier growth of capitalism, it has been around long
enough for Catholics, too, to have the appropriate value orientations,
and so explanations of differences in attainments would have to be
found elsewhere.

One alternative explanation has been the differences in the quality
and quantity of education. There is no doubt that the educational
attainment of the French has been considerably lower than that of the
English. For the better educated French, and notably the older age
groups among them, their education has been of the classical type
placing great emphasis on humanistic subject matter and less on skills
related to industrial and commercial activities. In 1931 in Quebec only
24 per cent of young people 15 to 19 years of age were in school
compared to 39 per cent in Ontario. By 1951 the proportion had risen
modestly to 30 and 44 per cent respectively. These differences have
persisted (Porter, 1966: Table G1). Quebec had 29 per cent of males
aged 17 in school in 1961 compared to 62 per cent in Ontario; in 1966
the differences were still considerable, 47 per cent and 72 per cent
respectively (Statistics Canada, 1974: Table 7.4).

The deficiencies in the Quebec educational system were extensively
examined and severely criticized by the Parent Commission, which made
recommendations for sweeping reforms to bring French education into
the modern world (Parent, 1963). These changes were made during the
1960s with the result that Quebec was to have in theory at least one of the
most advanced educational systems in Canada. It is still too early to make
satisfactory judgments about the results of these changes beyond the fact
that in terms of years of schooling — about the only way we can apply a
quantitative measure to educational attainment — the younger age
groups of *Québécois* and *Québécoise* have done much better than the older.

Another problem for the French in "making it" in the occupational
world is that if they are to combine geographical mobility with
occupational mobility they do it at a sacrifice which is not experienced by
English Canadians. That is, they must move out of their linguistic
communities, work in a language which is not theirs and, until recently
could not, and in some parts of the country still can not, have their
children educated in French without considerable difficulty and cost.
Thus, whatever achievement orientations they might have are most
likely to be fulfilled within the more narrow range of Quebec's economic
development. English Canadians, on the other hand, could move
anywhere in Canada, and the United States for that matter, without the
cultural penalty for mobility that the French had to pay.

Another factor which could have affected the capacity of the French to exploit the opportunity structure that emerged with industrialization was the later transition of Quebec than of the English parts of Canada from the rural to the urban way of life. Moving out of traditional occupations such as farming and wood-cutting, they and their children often have had few skills to fit them for anything but unskilled and semi-skilled jobs in the cities.

INEQUALITY AT THE START

In the process of occupational attainment all do not have the same starting point. Industrial societies are marked by a degree of structured inequality of condition which is advantageous to some and disadvantageous to others. Those with greater family resources can afford to have more education, receive more enrichment from their backgrounds, and as a result can better exploit job opportunities than can those with lesser family resources. This inequality of condition — the structure of social class — can be distinguished in several ways. Individuals and family heads will differ in the amount of income they derive from work, the amount of income from wealth, the amount of education they have, and the amount of power or status and prestige that they enjoy in the community. These resources have some relationship with each other. Those who have more education are likely to have higher incomes, higher-status jobs and more power and influence. Differing family resources can be directly (as with money) or indirectly (as with education) inherited, thus perpetuating the inequality of condition across generations.

It is a major task of mobility studies to determine the extent to which these privileges of origin afford advantages in occupational attainment or the extent to which they are reduced so that some degree of equality of opportunity prevails. A high degree of equality of opportunity would require that the differences in family resources as children are being brought up have very little effect on the amount of education they obtain or the occupational level they achieve. Moreover, the extent to which occupational attainment is independent of these resources of family of origin is an indication of rational allocation of individuals to the occupational structure.

However, the inequalities of condition in Canada are formidable. With respect to family income in 1971, the bottom one-fifth of all families had incomes of less than $4,900 while the top one-fifth had incomes of more than $14,200. The bottom one-fifth of family incomes amounted to only 5.6 per cent of all the income earned, while the top one-fifth of families received 40 per cent of all the income, twice as much as it would have if there was equality of income distribution (Statistics Canada, 1974: Table

7.4). There appears to have been very little change in the distribution of income from 1951 when this statistical information first became available. Differences in incomes make for differences in assets. In 1969, families where the head was 35 to 44 years old and with incomes between $5-7,000, average liquid assets were about $1,000 while those with incomes greater than $15,000 have average liquid assets of $7,500. With respect to all forms of assets — property, investments and the like — the top 1 per cent of family wealth holders owned 11 per cent of all family wealth, the top 5 per cent of families owned 27 per cent, and the top 10 per cent, 39 per cent (Statistics Canada, 1974: Tables 7.17, 7.18). The less wealthy half of all families shared between them only one-tenth of all the wealth. Clearly with such inequality of condition between families there are great differences in resources available for rearing and educating children and preparing them for the occupational world.

Educational level of parents is also an important family resource, in that the more education parents have the more are they likely to transmit positive values about education to their children; therefore such children have initial advantages in acquiring the competences which make for occupational success. We have indicated earlier the lag which existed between industrialization in Canada and the development of its educational system. That there was great inequality of condition with respect to educational attainment of parents is indicated by the fact that in 1961 among men 45 to 54 years old, who could have had mature sons in the labour force of 1973, 53 per cent had achieved only elementary education or less, a further 40 per cent had completed high school, 3 per cent had some university, and 4 per cent had completed university (Dominion Bureau of Statistics, 1963: Table 17). For older men, the inequality in educational attainment was greater; for the younger, slightly less so. It is clear that in as much as parental education is a resource that might be converted into children's educational and occupational attainment, it is a resource very unequally distributed.

While differences in accumulated or inherited wealth are the basis of the most striking inequalities in Canada no less than elsewhere, it is the occupational structure which is the basis of the most generalized inequalities. Occupations are the source of differential rewards or income inequalities and they also require generally different amounts of education. All occupational structures within industrial societies assume either a pyramidal or a beehive shape, with the higher-level occupations at the top constituting but a small proportion of the total. As the occupational structure is descended, say from professional and managerial occupations down through white-collar to blue-collar and finally unskilled occupations, larger proportions of the labour force are

TABLE 2:3 — Occupational Distribution* of the Male Labour Force, Canada, 1971

Socioeconomic Classification		
	%	%
Professional	9.9	
		15 (Higher)
Management	5.2	
Semi-professional	3.2	
Higher white collar	10.7	36 (Middle)
Higher blue collar	22.4	
Lower white collar	10.8	
Semi-skilled blue		42 (Lower)
collar	12.7	
Unskilled labour	18.3	
Farm	7.3	7 (Farm)

*See Table 2:2 and Table 2:4.

included. Table 2:3 distributes the male 1971 labour force through the hierarchical occupational classification which was constructed for this study (Pineo, Porter, McRoberts, 1976). Professional occupations, for example, make up 9.9 per cent of the male labour force; higher blue-collar 22 per cent, unskilled labour 18 per cent. With some regrouping, we can see that professionals and managers brought together as an "upper class" make up 15 per cent of the labour force, the middle class, from semi-professionals to higher blue-collar workers, 36 per cent; lower white-collar workers to unskilled labourers, as a lower class, 42 per cent, and farmers 7 per cent. Thus lower-class jobs are far more numerous than higher-class ones and if we consider in addition the well-established demographic fact of lower-class families being larger than higher-class ones, then in any one generation there are many more children of lower-class origins with inferior starting conditions than is the case with upper-class children.

The inequality of condition which stems from the social class structure of occupations has far-reaching effects on the processes of achievement. It means inequality of resources available to families to prepare their children for the attainment process. These are not only financial resources but also such psychological ones as parental encouragement. One factor which we have noted as being crucial to achievement in education and work is motivation. Yet the class structure affects aspirations for attainment in both. For example, in a study of Ontario high school students in 1971, of a grade 12 sample 63 per cent from the highest of six social classes expressed a desire to go to university after high school, but for the lowest of the six social classes only 28 per cent expressed such educational aspirations. For all six social classes there was a diminishing proportion from the highest to the lowest who wanted to go to university. Similar class-related aspirations were found for Grade 10 and Grade 8 students (Porter, Porter and Blishen, 1979). Their occupational aspirations after leaving school were also related to the social class position of their families.

In all industrial societies it has been the task of public education to bridge these inequalities of condition by some equality of educational opportunity, to provide, that is, careers open to the talents found in all social classes. That it has been far from successful in achieving its objective of reducing the obstacles created by unequal starting conditions, has been established for a number of advanced industrial societies. Public education may also have fallen short of its objectives in Canada.

WOMEN AND THEIR LABOUR FORCE PARTICIPATION

One of the remarkable developments within all industrial societies is the increased participation of women in the labour force. Before the time when statistics were kept on the subject, women indeed worked; in the early industrial period they were employed in mines and factories and domestic service and in the rural society they have always had their share of farm work. The growth of the tertiary sector in the later stages of industrial growth opened up a new range of occupations for women in clerical, sales, and service occupations. Women have always tended to be concentrated in particular occupational classifications, often those with less opportunity for advancement, suggesting a process of occupational allocation which considers sex to be an important criterion. Yet, as the proportion of occupations requiring brute strength decreases, there is no inherent or rational reason why women should be restricted to a limited range of work. To some extent the education of women reflected particular social values about their roles, so that when women entered the labour force it was with a different set of competences than men. In the most recent period, however, the women's movement in most industrial societies, and in Canada no less than in others, has succeeded in bringing into question older notions of what was women's work and what was men's. Moreover, in higher education women were rapidly improving their representation, making their exclusion from the top-level occupations on the grounds of their training no longer defensible. The more women acquire the same competences as men, the more it is irrational to exclude them from any sector of the occupational world.

In the most advanced industrial societies where women have achieved legislative support to participate freely in the labour force, they inevitably become competitors with men for the existing occupational opportunities. Up until the present, mobility studies have been almost exclusively concerned with the occupational attainment of men and, indeed, the methodology is linked closely to analysing the differences in occupational attainment between fathers and sons, different positions men alone have achieved at different stages of their work careers. We have yet to devise a satisfactory methodology to cope with the discontinuous type of career which most women have had, involving withdrawals from the labour force in the early stages of child-rearing or after marriage. The pattern may well change as women increasingly secure rights with respect to maternity leave, as day care facilities improve and perhaps, most important of all, as birth rates fall, signifying some rejection of fertility on the part of contemporary women. To bring women into mobility analysis then represents a departure for something of unknown territory, the difficulties of which we elaborate more fully in chapters 7 and 8. At present we limit ourselves to looking at the broad picture of the changing participation of women in the labour force and educational institutions.

In 1951, 23 per cent of women 14 years of age and over were in the labour force. The proportion increased steadily until it reached 39 per cent in 1973. This increase was because of women continuing to work after marriage. Again in 1951, women aged 25-54 constituted 11 per cent of the total labour force, a proportion that rose to 18 per cent in 1971 when men of the same age group were 42 per cent of the labour force (Statistics Canada, 1974: Charts 6.2 and 6.14).

Table 2:4 shows the distribution of the male and female labour force through the various occupational levels. At the higher levels of professional, semi-professional, and technical occupations women are represented in proportions similar to those of men and in some, such as employed professionals, they are over-represented compared to men. Women are correspondingly under-represented in management occupations. Below the management and professional levels, where four-fifths of all the labour force works, men's and women's categories become more clearly separated. There are relatively few female foremen, but a reasonable proportion, compared to men, of female white-collar supervisors. Women are over-represented in all the white-collar groups of clerical sales and service workers. Just over half of all women (55 per cent) worked at these levels and over one-quarter at

60   JOHN PORTER

TABLE 2:4 — Distribution of Males and Females in 1971 Labour Force by Socioeconomic Category

Socioeconomic Category*		Males Per cent	Females Per cent	Total Per cent
Self-employed professionals	(1)	1.0	0.2	0.7
Employed-professionals	(2)	7.1	8.5	7.6
High-level management	(3)	2.0	0.5	1.5
Semi-professionals	(4)	2.8	6.7	4.1
Technicians	(5)	1.8	1.4	1.6
Middle management	(6)	3.2	1.8	2.7
Supervisors	(7)	6.7	4.2	5.8
Foremen	(8)	5.3	0.3	3.6
Skilled clerical-sales-service	(9)	4.0	17.0	8.3
Skilled crafts & trades	(10)	17.1	1.7	11.9
Semi-skilled clerical-sales-service	(12)	7.9	28.4	14.8
Semi-skilled manual	(13)	12.7	7.4	10.9
Unskilled clerical-sales-service	(14)	2.9	9.4	5.1
Unskilled manual	(15)	18.3	8.7	15.1
Farm labourers	(16)	3.0	3.7	3.2
Farmers	(11)	4.3	0.3	3.0

SOURCE: Statistics Canada, Advance Bulletin of the 1971 Census of Canada, March 1974, Catalogue 94-788.
*Pineo, Porter and McRoberts, 1971.

the semi-skilled level where only 8 per cent of men worked. Men, on the other hand, dominate the blue-collar manual sector with one-half of them (49 per cent) in the skilled crafts, semi-skilled, and unskilled operative occupations.

Viewed from the occupational point of view, women do well relative to men. Sixteen per cent of them work in semi- or unskilled manual work compared to 31 per cent of men. It is probable that, by and large, most women who work do so at physically less arduous tasks in more pleasant surroundings than do most men at work, a fact often forgotten when women's demands are oriented to the higher-level occupations where, by the nature of things, as we have seen, only a very few can work whether they are men or women.

When it comes to incomes, however, the picture is quite different. In 1971, the average earnings of women who worked the full year were: in the managerial group, slightly less than one-half that of men; in the professional and technical, three-fifths; in sales, one-third; and in the manual sector, one-half (Statistics Canada, 1974: Table 5.30). Clearly there are significant pay differentials between men and women for similar work, or, because these occupational categories are broad, men get into the better occupations within them than do women. Also men probably have greater opportunities to be upwardly mobile with respect to salary within their occupational group.

Despite these differences in earnings, women on the whole are better educated than men. For example, in 1961 52 per cent of females 15 years of age and over who had left school had completed secondary schooling, but only 42 per cent of men. Although these differences existed for all age groups, they continued to be marked in the younger age groups. For example, 68 per cent of females 20 to 24 had completed secondary schooling compared to 59 per cent of men. Men overtake women at the post-secondary level with 7.5 per cent of all men having some university or a university degree compared to 4.6 per cent of women (Dominion Bureau of Statistics, 1963b: Table 7.2). When women do get to post-secondary education it is more likely to be in the non-university level of the teachers' college, the community college, and nursing education. In 1961, women represented 71 per cent of the enrolments in non-university post-secondary level, 25 per cent among university undergraduates and even fewer, 15 per cent, among graduate enrolments. Throughout the 1960s they made steady improvements, by 1971 reaching 38 per cent of undergraduate enrolments and 23 per cent of post-graduate (Statistics Canada, 1974: Table 4.14). Whatever their level of schooling, and wherever they participated in the labour force, it is clear that women were far behind men in the returns they were receiving to their education.

CONCLUSION

Opportunities for occupational mobility are affected in all industrial societies by particular characteristics within them. Though all profess a belief in equality of opportunity, the extent to which it exists depends on a variety of factors, such as the degree of inequality within the society, the openness of the educational system, the level of urbanization, and the structure of occupations.

In this chapter we have outlined how Canada fares with respect to these factors. We have shown that inequalities are great in income, assets, and educational attainments. A major task of this study will be to determine the extent to which inequalities of origin inhibit equality of opportunity. Though Canada lagged behind the United States in the provision of educational opportunities, there was a vast expansion of education in the 1960s, and it will be important to discover whether younger age groups who have benefited from this expansion have fared better than older age groups in terms of social mobility. During this century Canada has been transformed from a largely rural to a highly urbanized society characterized by a great deal of internal migration. The effect of this large off-farm migration on mobility chances will be a question to explore, as will the general relation between geographical and occupational mobility. As far as the occupational structure is concerned, we have demonstrated that while the secondary level of manufacturing occupations has remained relatively constant, there has been a great expansion of tertiary level service occupations. This, too, is a characteristic that will affect mobility opportunities and we will want to find out how.

In addition to these factors, which are characteristic of all industrial societies to a greater or lesser degree, there are particular features of Canadian society related to its geography and its history that will make a study of occupational mobility within it unique. One is its dependence on immigration to provide the skills necessary for industrial expansion. This, along with the unassimilable French, has made Canada an ethnically plural society. It will be an important task to determine whether immigrants' skills make them better able to exploit opportunities. A related question is the association between assimilation and mobility. Our study might provide an answer to the question of how much ethnic group membership is an aid or an obstacle to mobility. Also we will want to find out whether the historic inequalities between the French- and English-speaking populations have lessened over time.

Another characteristic of the contemporary world that is not unique to Canada is the growing participation of women in the labour force. Previous mobility studies have confined their attention to men, with fathers' and sons' occupations being used as a measure of social mobility. Adequate attention has yet to be paid to the mobility experiences of Canadian women and to the peculiar nature of women's occupational experience, which is so often interrupted for child bearing and rearing. We hope to address these issues also in the chapters that follow, which will explore these various features of occupational mobility in Canada and will attempt to illuminate the Canadian experience.

References

BELL, DANIEL
1973   *The Coming of the Post-Industrial Society.* New York: Basic Books.

BLISHEN, BERNARD R.
1970   "Social Class and Opportunity in Canada," *Canadian Review of Sociology and Anthropology,* 7 (2): 110-27.

CANADA, DOMINION BUREAU of STATISTICS
1953   *Census of Canada, 1951.* Vol. IV. Ottawa: Queen's Printer.
1958   *Statistical Review of Canadian Education.* Census, 1951. Ottawa: Queen's Printer.
1963a *Census of Canada, 1961.* Vol. III, Part I (Bulletin 3.1, 1-13). Ottawa: Queen's Printer.
1963b *Census of Canada 1961,* Vol. 1.2-10. Ottawa: Queen's Printer.

CANADA, ECONOMIC COUNCIL of CANADA
1971   *Design for Decision Making.* Eighth Annual Review, Ottawa: Information Canada.
1978   *A Time for Reason.* Fifteenth Annual Review. Ottawa: Ministry of Supply and Services.

CANADA, FEDERAL TASK FORCE on AGRICULTURE
1969   *Canadian Agriculture in the Seventies.* Ottawa: Information Canada.

CANADA. ROYAL COMMISSION on BILINGUALISM and BICULTURALISM
1965   *The Report, Book III. The Work World.* Ottawa: Queen's Printer.
1973   *The Report, Book IV. The Cultural Contribution of the other Ethnic Groups.* Ottawa: Information Canada.

CANADA. STATISTICS CANADA
1973   *Census of Canada, 1971, Population, Official Language and Language Most Often Spoken at Home.* Vol. I, Part 3 (Bulletin 1.3-5). Ottawa: Information Canada.
1974   *Perspective Canada: A Compendium of Social Statistics.* Ottawa: Information Canada.
1975   *Census of Canada, 1971, Occupations.* Vol. III, Part 3 (Bulletin 3.3-7). Ottawa: Ministry of Industry, Trade and Commerce.
1977   *Census of Canada, 1971.* Vol. III, Part 7 (Bulletin 3.7, 1-6). Ottawa: Ministry of Industry, Trade, and Commerce.
1978   *The Occupational Composition of Canada's Labour Force.* 1971 Census, Profile Studies. Ottawa: Information Canada.

CLARK, COLIN
1951   *The Conditions of Economic Progress.* London: Macmillan.

CLEMENT, WALLACE
1975   *The Canadian Corporate Elite: An Analysis of Economic Power.* Toronto: Carleton Library No. 89.

GOLDLUST, JOHN and ANTHONY H. RICHMOND
1974   "A Multivariate Model of Immigrant Adaptation." *International Migration Review,* 8: 193-225.

HUGHES, E.C.
1943   *French Canada in Transition.* Chicago: University of Chicago Press.

ILLING, W.M. and Z.E. ZSIGMOND
  1967 *Enrolment in Educational Institutions by Province,* 1951-52 to 1975-76. Economic Council of Canada (Staff Study No. 20). Ottawa: Information Canada.

JOY, RICHARD J.
  1972 *Languages in Conflict.* Toronto: Carleton Library No. 61.

KALBACH, WARREN
  1974 *The Effect of Immigration on Population.* Report of the Canadian Immigration and Population Study. Ottawa: Information Canada.

LAGACÉ, M.D.
  1968 *Educational Attainment in Canada.* Dominion Bureau of Statistics, Special Labour Force Survey No. 7. Ottawa: Information Canada.

MACREDIE, IAN
  1971 "The Educational Attainment of the Canadian Labour Force 1960-1970." *Notes on Labour Statistics,* Statistics Canada. Ottawa: Information Canada.

OSTRY, SYLVIA
  1968 *The Occupational Composition of the Canadian Labour Force.* Dominion Bureau of Statistics. Ottawa: Information Canada.

PARENT, A.M.
  1963 *Report on the Quebec (Province) Commission of Inquiry on Education in the Province of Quebec.* Quebec, Que.

PINEO, PETER C. and JOHN PORTER
  1967 "Occupational Prestige in Canada." *Canadian Review of Sociology and Anthropology,* 4(1): 24-40.

PINEO, PETER, JOHN PORTER and HUGH MCROBERTS
  1977 "The 1971 Census and the Socioeconomic Classification of Occupations. *"Canadian Review of Sociology and Anthropology,"* 14(1): 91-102.

PORTER, JOHN
  1965 *The Vertical Mosaic: An Analysis of Social Class and Power in Canada.* Toronto: University of Toronto Press.

  1966 *Canadian Social Structure: A Statistical Profile.* Toronto: Carleton Library No. 320.

  1975 "Ethnic Pluralism in Canadian Perspective." In Nathan Glazer and Daniel P. Moynihan, eds. *Ethnicity: Theory and Experience.* Cambridge, Mass.: Harvard University Press.

PORTER, MARION, JOHN PORTER and BERNARD BLISHEN
  1979 *Does Money Matter? Prospects for Higher Education in Ontario.* Toronto: Carleton Library No. 110.

PORTER, JOHN, MARION PORTER and BERNARD BLISHEN
  1982 *Stations and Callings: Making It Through the Ontario Schools.* Toronto: Methuen.

RICHMOND, ANTHONY H.
  1974 "Migration, Ethnicity and Race Relations." *Proceedings of a Seminar on Demographic Research in Relation to International Migration, Buenos Aires, Argentina, March 1974.* Paris.

RICHMOND, ANTHONY and WARREN E. KALBACH
   1980   *Factors in the Adjustment of Immigrants and their Descendants.* Statistics Canada, Census Analytical Study. Ottawa: Minister of Supply and Services, Catalogue 99-761 E.

VALLEE, FRANK G. and NORMAN SHULMAN
   1969   "The Viability of French Language Groups Outside of Quebec". In Mason Wade, ed. *Regionalism in the Canadian Community.* Toronto: University of Toronto Press.

ZSIGMOND, Z.E. and C.J. WENAAS
   1970   *Enrolment in Educational Institutions by Province 1951-52 to 1980-81.* Economic Council of Canada, Staff Study No. 25. Ottawa. Information Canada.

CHAPTER 3

Mobility and Attainment in Canada: The Effects of Origin

HUGH A. McROBERTS

It is obvious, in our society, and for that matter virtually every other society, that those who have the fortune to be well born will have a distinct advantage over those who were not so fortunate. Further, it is equally obvious as a consequence of this, that by and large the circumstances of offspring will be little different from those of their parents. However, what is less clear is the extent to which this inheritance of the parental lot occurs, the extent to which different groups in society vary in the degree to which it occurs, and how the transmission of the good or ill fortunes of birth occur. These then are the themes, which will be the focus of the analysis in this chapter and throughout the remainder of the book.

When one looks at the structure of most societies, particularly in an historical context, it is clear that until very recently the "inheritance" of social position has been the norm rather than the exception. Indeed, in many societies there were clear rules which insured, to a greater or lesser extent, that such inheritance occurred often in the most literal sense. The extensive and complex rules of the Hindu caste system probably represent the most extreme historical instance of such inheritance rules, but in some cases the rules and customs governing inheritance of property and position in Europe during the Middle Ages seem only moderately less rigid. However, with the changes which have occurred over the last two to three hundred years much of this is believed to no longer be the case. During that period two major and closely interrelated changes have occurred in western societies which have led to the belief that not only does social mobility occur, but that it ought to occur.

The first of these changes was the Reformation, which brought with it not only religious individualism but secular individualism as well. Fundamental to the notion of religious individualism was the denial of a natural hierarchy of men ranked in ever closer communication with God through which all communication with God and ultimately salvation itself must be mediated. Instead, religious individualism stressed the equality of all men before God and the need for each man to work out his own personal salvation directly. As much of the moral justification for social inequalities had rested upon the notion of inequality before God, it is not at all surprising that as these new ideas began to take hold the legitimacy and indeed the "naturalness" of these social relations began increasingly to be called into question.

The second major change was the Industrial Revolution and the replacement of the productive relationships of feudalism with those of capitalism. The norms and rules governing feudalism were typically inegalitarian, ascriptive, and particularistic, and were in general in harmony with the moral and religious beliefs of the pre-Reformation period. Capitalism on the other hand was more at home with the religious and secular individualism of the reformation. (Weber, of course, is the best-known proponent of the relationship between the two, although he is by no means the only one to take up the topic; see, for example, Tawney, 1926.) Whether one factor is causally linked to the other is however not important in this context as there is little dispute that the two developments did aid and reinforce each other, leading to the emergence of an ideological structure which stressed egalitarianism, achievement, and universalism. One of the key features of this emerging ideological structure was the notion that while inequalities of condition would continue to exist (see Davis and Moore, 1944), the position individuals ended up within the socioeconomic hierarchy would be the just outcome of their own efforts or the lack there of.

By the 1930s these beliefs were well established in both popular and academic thought, not just as ideological goals to be striven for but rather as objectives which had already been achieved. The analysis of social mobility had its origins in the skepticism on the part of some sociologists as to whether industrial societies were really as open or meritocratic as the social theorists had argued. Thus, the initial studies of social mobility emerged not so much from an explicit theoretical position of their own, but rather as an attempt to empirically critique the conventional theoretical wisdom of their time. They were, needless to say, quite successful in this effort.

While data which could be used to examine mobility had been gathered as early as the 1920s (see Sorokin, 1927, for examples of this), the first major study of mobility was begun by Glass and his associates at the London School of Economics in 1949 (Glass, 1954). The pioneering work in the United States was carried out by Rogoff with her study of the mobility of men in the city of Indianapolis (Rogoff, 1953). The results of the two studies were in some respects remarkably similar. Both found, using methodologies which were identical but independently derived, that there was substantial occupational inheritance between fathers and sons. Further, they found, even in the event that sons did not inherit their fathers' occupational level, that the occupation in which the sons did end up was unlikely to be greatly different from that of their fathers. There followed a number of other studies of mobility in industrial societies which, using various techniques, led pretty much to the same conclusions. Indeed, the similarities in findings across studies led Svalastoga to observe, "In terms of the product moment correlation coefficient, actual mobility in modern industrial societies may be characterized as corresponding to a coefficient between .4 and .5." (1965:106) It is interesting to note, despite the large number of studies and methodological advances since his observation, that the statement has yet to be falsified.

There can be little doubt that these early studies served to call into serious question some of the more sanguine versions of the theoretical conventional wisdom of the time. In combination with historical events (the Brown decision of the United States Supreme Court was probably the most important of these), these findings focused substantial sociological attention on the analysis and understanding of the whole question of the quality of equality of opportunity. However, the early studies of mobility suffered from two problems. First, they were methodologically flawed. That is to say, the measures which they employed to assess the nature and extent of occupational inheritance did not have all of the properties which the investigators attributed to them. While this issue is raised in the next section of this chapter, it is only fair to note that the early findings have been found to be remarkably robust in their general thrust, and that the new techniques have only modified them in detail, albeit important detail. Secondly, these studies were basically descriptive in nature. They allowed for very detailed examination of the patterns of occupational inheritance and disinheritance, and for assessments of the degree of inequality of opportunity in a society. However, these descriptions, while pointing to the problem and documenting its extent, did little to explain how it was that parents were able in substantial degree to transmit the advantages or disadvantages of their socioeconomic position to their children. In short, we lacked a theory of status transmission.

The status attainment model (or theory depending upon one's semantic disposition) developed by Blau and Duncan in *The American Occupational Structure* represented the response to the latter problem. By the standards of the physical sciences or even of economics it is a very weak theory. On the other hand, by the standards of sociology it is now one the best articulated and certainly the most tested theoretical structures available.

While the two ways of looking at the inter-generational transmission of social position are very clearly related and, as we shall see, do much to inform each other, at the same time they are sufficiently different that an integrated approach to them does neither justice. For this reason the remainder of this chapter is broken out into two relatively discrete sections. In the first we shall present the results of the traditional occupational mobility/inheritance form of analysis. We shall begin by describing the theoretical and methodological problems which are involved in such an analysis, and then we shall apply a current version of the model to our data in order to see what the data can tell us about occupational inheritance and mobility in Canada. In the second major section we shall turn to an examination of the status attainment model. The theory leading to the model will be discussed, and then the model will be applied to our data to further explore the nature of the Canadian stratification system. Before proceeding to these two sections, however, it is necessary to say a few words about the data employed and more particularly about the subset of the data to be analysed in this chapter.

The Selection of a Sub-population

The process by which individuals move from their origins to their adult locations in the division of labour has often been conceptualized as a race. However, as the terms and outcomes of the race have been subjected to scrutiny, it has become increasingly clear that in Canadian society — as in all others — the race is by no means a fair one. Various groups in our society are asked to run on courses which differ not only in length but in the number of obstacles which must be overcome in the running. In addition, even for those who run the same course, there are inequalities at the start. Those who come from more advantaged backgrounds appear to be given a head start in the race, and the remainder of the contestants are disadvantaged in direct proportion to the meagreness of their background resources. The primary purpose of this chapter is to examine both how and to what extent these inequalities at the start affect the outcome of the race. In order to do so I shall focus on a group who arguably at least run on the same track under more or less the same conditions. In later chapters others will focus attention on those who are also forced to run on other more difficult courses (e.g. women, francophones).

The population to be analysed in this chapter is made up of Canadian-born males who were between the ages of 25 and 64 at the time of the survey (July 1973), and who at that time were part of the civilian labour force of Canada. The bounding of the population on age and labour force status is done for purely methodological reasons, as the questionnaire was not designed to deal effectively with the status of those who were either not yet in the labour force because they had not completed their education, or with those who had left the labour force due to retirement. In order to focus in as much as possible only on the effects of background, the analysis is restricted to Canadian-born males. This is a group for whom the process of status attainment should be relatively homogeneous (that is, to return to the earlier metaphor, a group who have run on the same track). These men, of course, represent the largest single component of the Canadian labour force and as such their experiences may be viewed as typifying the mobility/status attainment regimes in Canadian society. For this reason their experiences will also serve as baseline against which we can compare the experiences of other groups in Canadian society who have been forced to run on other tracks more strewn with obstacles.

Fathers and Sons: Occupational Mobility and Inheritance in Canada

The degree of inequality in a society is usually assessed by considering two dimensions of the distributive system of that society. The first is concerned with the degree to which the scarce and desirable goods of that society are apportioned out to the members in a way which is just. The second dimension is concerned with the degree to which access to the positions on which the apportionment of shares are based shows evidence of inter-generational continuity. The former concern refers to the degree of inequality of condition in the society, and the latter, following Duncan's usage refers to the degree of stratification in the society (1968:680-81). More specifically, the degree to which a society is stratified may be defined as the degree to which the position of the members of one generation in the hierarchy of inequality is predictable at a level greater than chance from a knowledge of the previous generation's location. (See Duncan, 1968:681; and Svalastoga, 1965, for similar usages.) It is interesting to note that while this definition is usually interpreted in the context of an expectation that the predictabil-

ity or association will be positive, Svalastoga points out that it also applies
to the situation in which the association is negative, an unusual but
possible outcome, say, in the case of a revolution.

In this section we shall focus on the description of the degree of
occupational stratification in Canada as it can be viewed in a
cross-tabulation of father's occupation against son's. While this examination will not present an exhaustive picture of the degree to which
Canada is a stratified society, occupation plays such a central role in
determining the location of individuals in the broader hierarchy of
inequality that one can safely assert that the degree of occupational
stratification which is observed is a very good measure of the degree to
which a society is stratified in the broader sense of the term. In making
this assessment we shall begin with an examination of the simple
percentage distribution of son's occupation given father's, and from
there proceed to more precise and complex models of the mobility table.
However, it should be remembered that the central question in each case
remains: how closely is the occupational location of the son associated
with that of his father?

Before we look at the relationship between father's and son's

**TABLE 3:1 — Collapsing of 16-Fold Pineo-Porter-McRoberts Occupational
Classification to 10 Categories**

Category Title	Pineo-Porter-McRoberts Titles
Professional and semi-professional	Self-employed professionals
	Employed professionals
	Semi-professionals
Managers	High-level management
	Middle management
Supervisors	Supervisors
Upper white-collar	Technicians
	Skilled clerical-sales-services
Lower white-collar	Semi-skilled clerical-sales-service
	Unskilled clerical-sales-service
Foremen	Foremen
Upper blue-collar	Skilled crafts and trades
Lower blue-collar	Semi-skilled manual
	Unskilled manual
Farmers	Farmers
Farm labourers	Farm labourers

occupations, the classification of those occupations deserves a brief discussion. In the construction of the data base upon which this analysis rests we originally coded the occupational data into sixteen categories based on the occupational classification developed by Pineo, Porter, and McRoberts (1977). However, even with a data set as large as ours, this classification proved to be too detailed. The basic father-son table contains 256 cells, many of which turned out to contain too few cases for a reliable analysis. In order to avoid this problem it was necessary to collapse the categorization from the original sixteen into a more compact ten categories (see Table 3:1 for details). While this collapsing involves some loss of detail in the analysis, it is less serious than the potential errors which could have been introduced by the small cell counts in the original classification.

In Table 3:2 the tabulation of father's occupation by son's occupation is presented in the form of outflow percentages. In arraying the data in this fashion we are asking the question: given father's occupation, what is the likelihood of the son arriving at a particular occupational destination? The general form of the percentage distributions will seem familiar to those who have examined such tables for other industrialized societies. The largest percentage values tend to be clustered around the main diagonal of the table and the values then tail off the further one moves away from the diagonal. This pattern of course indicates that in Canada as elsewhere there is a strong tendency for the son's occupation to be the same as or at least not greatly different from his father's.

The extent of the clustering around the diagonal is by no means uniform, however, across the rows of the table. When we look more closely some interesting details begin to emerge. Perhaps the most striking feature in the table is the way in which it can be seen that farm occupations exist in a supply relationship to the non-agricultural labour force. Throughout the table it is clear that virtually no one with non-farm origins is likely to end up as either a farmer or a farm labourer. Further, over three-fourths of those of farm origins will end up in the non-agricultural sector of the labour force, primarily as lower level blue-collar workers. This is not surprising when one considers the very dramatic changes which have taken place in the Canadian labour force in the inter-generational period. Our sample covers roughly the time span from 1925 to 1973, during which time farming as an occupation has declined from 29 per cent of the male labour force at the time of the 1931 census to less than 10 per cent in 1971. The effect of this structural change in the composition of the Canadian labour force was of coruse to drive the sons of farmers off of the farm where there was no work for them and into the industrial labour force. This can be

TABLE 3:2 — Outflow Matrix for Fathers Occupation by Son's Present Job (Native-born Males 25-64)

Father's Occupation	Son's Present Occupation										Distribution of Father's Occupation
	1	2	3	4	5	6	7	8	9	10	
1. Professional & semi-pro.	**39.4**	18.3	5.9	8.5	7.6	3.7	7.4	8.1	*	*	4.5
2. Managers	28.0	**21.6**	8.1	8.1	8.7	2.9	10.4	10.7	1.2	*	3.6
3. Supervisors	21.8	14.8	**15.3**	9.7	10.3	7.6	9.4	9.9	1.0	*	5.1
4. Upper white-collar	21.9	14.6	8.4	**15.8**	8.8	6.0	12.3	12.0	*	*	3.7
5. Lower white-collar	16.6	11.4	12.6	8.1	**11.1**	5.7	14.7	18.4	*	*	7.3
6. Foremen	13.6	11.2	8.3	8.6	8.9	**13.8**	17.0	16.8	1.3	*	5.8
7. Upper blue-collar	11.9	7.9	7.7	7.4	9.7	9.2	**22.4**	23.0	*	*	17.7
8. Lower blue-collar	8.7	6.8	7.4	5.8	8.7	7.0	21.1	**32.3**	*	*	24.9
9. Farmers	6.8	4.6	4.8	4.5	5.2	8.6	16.2	25.9	**19.9**	3.6	24.7
10. Farm workers	4.5	4.4	3.3	2.7	8.1	6.8	21.1	31.2	10.0	**8.0**	2.8
Total	12.8	8.7	7.5	6.8	8.2	7.8	17.5	23.5	5.8	1.5	100.0

*Cell less than 1 per cent.

very clearly seen in the data where over one-quarter of the fathers were engaged in farming but less than 10 per cent of the sons.

Within the non-farm occupations, the professional and semi-professional occupations show the highest rate of inheritance (the percentage of sons in this occupational group whose fathers were also in these occupations is 39.4 per cent), followed closely by lower level blue-collar workers with an inheritance rate of 32.3 per cent. In the remainder of the table, while staying in the father's occupational stratum is always a likely outcome, it is more likely that the son will end up in a stratum which is close to but not the same as his father's. Amongst those sons whose fathers were either managers or supervisors it is more likely that they will end up as professionals or semi-professionals. In the case of sons whose fathers were in either of the two levels of the white-collar occupations, upward or downward mobility (over short distances) appear to be almost equally likely outcomes. Finally, those of blue-collar origins, while not always working in occupations at the same skill level as their fathers, are more likely than not to remain as blue-collar workers.

These are the basic patterns of observed occupational mobility and inheritance in Canada. They tend to suggest that there is some degree of inter-generational continuity with respect to the occupational location of fathers and sons, and to justify an initial conclusion that there is occupational stratification in Canadian society. However, what these data do not tell us is how intensive this pattern of stratification is, in the sense that we cannot tell to what extent the observed patterns of inheritance and mobility differ from those which could have occurred by chance alone. For example, we have observed that the sons of farmers are more likely to end up in non-farm occupations than in farming, and this has been attributed to the changing structure of the Canadian labour force. In this sense we would expect that the proportional level of inheritance of farm occupations would be low. But, is it lower or higher than could be expected given that this shift in the labour force composition has occurred? Conversely, we have noted that the proportional level of inheritance in the professional and semi-professional occupations is the highest in the table. But is this really surprising when we also point out that over the time period in question this group of occupations has shown the highest rate of growth in terms of their proportion of the Canadian labour force? In order to answer these questions we need to separate out two different types of mobility which are confounded in the percentage analysis in Table 3.2. These different types or sources of mobility are called structural and circulation mobility.

We have already, in the discussion above, touched on the issue of structural mobility; however, it is an issue of such central import to the analysis of mobility that a brief more formal treatment is necessary. An often observed and much commented upon feature of the occupational structures of industrial societies has been the fact that the nature of these structures has been undergoing a transformation and more particularly a transformation along certain very definite lines. In particular, the transformation has been in the direction of a decline in the proportion of workers engaged in the primary sector of the economy (most notably in agriculture) at a very rapid rate, a modest decline in the proportion engaged in the secondary or goods-producing sector, and a marked increase in the proportion of workers in the tertiary sector of the economy. (See Bell, 1973, for an extended documentation and discussion of this trend, and Porter, Blishen, *et al.*, 1971 for a discussion of the Canadian case.) These changes in the economy and their corresponding impact on the structure of the labour force are sufficient in themselves to cause a certain amount of mobility both in terms of constraining the supply of positions in the primary and secondary sectors (mainly farming and blue-collar) which are available for the son's generation, and in terms of increasing demand for workers in the tertiary sector (mainly white-collar and professional positions). The mobility which can be attributed to these changes is what is referred to a structural mobility, in the sense that its source is viewed as being located in the economy in a more general way and as being exogenous to the processes of status transmission.

The second type of mobility is what is called exchange or circulation mobility. This mobility is viewed as that mobility which occurs independently of the mobility which is induced by structural changes in the prevalence of occupational positions. It is the mobility which occurs as the result of the displacement downward of the less able by the upward movement of the more able. As such the patterns of circulation mobility are viewed as the measure of the degree to which a society is open to opportunity or closed, the degree, in other words, to which it is stratified. Thus, if we wish to determine the degree to which the patterns of mobility or inheritance which we observe in the father-son table reflect a stratified society, we need some way to remove from the observed mobility the mobility due to the changes in the structure.

One set of procedures which attempts to do this is based on a manipulation of the percentage table. The results of this approach as applied to our data are presented in Table 3:3. The measure of minimum structural mobility is simply the standard index of dissimilarity (Shyrock and Siegel, 1973) applied to the marginal distributions of father's and son's occupation. The value for this measure of 21.86 per

TABLE 3:3 — Percentage Decomposition of Father's Occupation to Son's Current Occupation Mobility

		%
1.	Minimum structural mobility	21.86
2.	Observed mobile	77.22
3.	Observed circulation (2-1)	55.34
4.	Expected mobile	87.02
5.	Expected circulation (4-1)	65.16
6.	Mobility index ((3/5)×100)	84.00

cent is conventionally interpreted as telling us that due solely to changes in the occupational structure in the inter-generational period, at least one-fifth of the sons in our sample had to be mobile. This, in combination with the fact that 77.2 per cent of the sons in our sample were observed to be mobile (line 2), implies that no more than 55.34 per cent could have been mobile due to circulation mobility (line 3). If we compare these results with what we would expect to find in the situation where son's occupation was unrelated to (more formally, statistically independent of) father's occupation, we find that 87 per cent of the sample would have been expected to be mobile (line 4), and hence that the maximum expected circulation mobility would be 65.16 per cent (line 5). Finally, if we take the observed circulation mobility as a percentage of the expected circulation mobility, we find that the observed mobility is 85 per cent of that which could be expected under independence. This value could be interpreted to signify that there is some degree of occupational stratification. However, the procedure, while descriptively useful, has associated with it a number of problems. First, the measures are sensitive to the number of occupational categories employed (the more categories the higher the value of the index). Secondly, the expected values generated under the model of independence employed are very much dependent on the relative values of the marginal distributions of the table (Blau and Duncan, 1967; Tyree, 1973) and hence the expected circulation mobility is not a margin-free measure. Finally, the margins themselves are not measures of occupational structures and hence the measure of minimum structural mobility does not measure what is claimed for it (Duncan, 1966). This last problem is in fact the most serious, as it is impossible to measure the concept of structural mobility given the information available in a mobility table. This in turn means that the most we can hope for is to remove the effects of the margins of the table from consideration and view the associations which remain as representing the pattern of circulation mobility.

The set of models of the mobility table developed by Goodman (1969, 1972) and elaborated by Hauser (Featherman and Hauser, 1978) provide a solution to the problem of separating out the effects of the margins of the mobility table and the effects of circulation mobility. These models, called log-linear models, are based on an analysis of variance like decomposition of the counts in the table which are additive in their logarithms. The equation describing the father-son mobility table has the following form:

$$ln\ x_{ij} = u + u_i + u_j + u_{ij}$$

This equation presents a decomposition of the mobility table in which the natural logarithm of the cell count ($ln\ x_{ij}$) is viewed as the linear sum of: u, a term which is a function of the average density of cell counts in the table (average cell frequencies); u_i and u_j, which are deviations from that average density due the relative densities of the ith origin category and the jth destination category respectively; and u_{ij} is a deviation net of u_i and u_j which is due to the interaction or association between the ith origin and the jth destination. The standard model of independence between i and j sets the term u_{ij} to zero for all i and j and yields a set of estimated counts which can be compared with the observed counts using the standard Pearson goodness of fit Chi-square referenced against the appropriate degrees of freedom. However, for the analysis which is being carried out here it is more advantageous to use the maximum likelihood ratio Chi-square (G^2) which has the useful property of being additively decomposable within models and between them, a property which the Pearson Chi-square does not have.

Table 3.4 presents the results of a log-linear analysis applied to the father-son table which was presented in table 3. The first model (model 1) tests the nul-hypothesis of no association in the table. That is to say, the model attempts to fit the data under the constraint that u_{ij} is equal to zero for all father-son combinations (all i, j). The value of G^2 is, as would be expected, very large with respect to its degrees of freedom, and the model mis-classifies 17.3 per cent of the cases. This result simply shows that there are significant associations between father's and son's occupations in the table.

Model two is of rather more substantive interest. This model is a quasi-independence model and has as its null-hypothesis the assertion that, if we remove the cases in the main diagonal of the table (father's occupation same as son's) from consideration, there will be no significant

TABLE 3:4 — Selected Log-Linear Models for Father's Occupation and Son's Current Occupation and Son's Current Occupation

Model	G^2*	df	G^2H/G^2T	$\triangle$	P
All males:					
1. P,S	1281.0	81	100.0	17.3	.000
Mobile only:					
2. P,S	506.9	71	39.57	10.0	.000
Mobile over 2 or more levels					
3. P,S	192.1	53	15.00	5.0	.000
Contrasts:					
4. (1 vs. 2)	774.0	10	60.42	7.3	.000
5. (1 vs. 3)	1088.9	28	85.00	12.3	.000
6. (2 vs. 3)	297.7	18	23.23	5.0	.000

*Adjusted for an estimated sampling efficiency of .57 relative to a simple random sample.

association in the remaining cells of the table. Or, to put it another way, the model asserts that if we remove from consideration the expected associations due to occupational inheritance, we would expect those sons who were mobile to be randomly distributed with respect to their origins. While this model does not fit the data, we can see that there has been a very substantial reduction in the G^2, and that only 10 per cent of the cases are misallocated by the model. If we take the G^2 for model 2 as a percentage of the G^2 for model 1 we can see that there has been a substantial reduction of the G^2 between the two models, with only 40 per cent of the association in the table being due to associations in the off-diagonal cells. Further, as can be seen in model 4 which contrasts models 1 and 2, some 60 per cent of the association in the table can be attributed occupational inheritance alone. This in turn suggests that if a son did not inherit his father's occupation, his destination is relatively weakly tied to his origins.

We may also use quasi-independence models to look at other groups within the table who are of interest. In model 2 we examined the association between fathers and sons for those who had been mobile by at least one occupational level. In model 3 we extend this to look at the associations between father's and son's occupations for those sons who were mobile over two or more occupational levels. Again the null-hypothesis is one of no association between father's occupation and son's occupation for this group, and again the model fails to fit the data. However, only 5 per cent of the cases are misallocated by the model and the G^2 is only fifteen per cent of the original G^2 (model 1), indicating that for those who are mobile over two or more levels the effects of origin are very weak indeed.

Overall this analysis gives a picture of the mobility table in which there is a very strong association between father's occupation and son's in the main diagonal of the table (the inheritance cells), which alone accounts for some three-fifths of the total association in the table. When we look at the cells adjacent to the main diagonal (representing upward or downward mobility in single steps) we again find evidence of strong associations between father's and son's occupations accounting for a further 25 per cent of the total association. The remaining association in the table is accounted for by the associations between father's occupation and son's occupation in those cases where the son has been mobile over two or more levels, but these account for only 15 per cent of the total. These results would reflect a mobility structure in which the inheritance of one's father's occupational level was the most usual outcome, followed by mobility to an adjacent occupational level, and in which mobility to occupations beyond this range was relatively rare. This is, of course, very much the picture of the mobility table which we have come to expect from the literature. However, while this type of analysis can be useful in attempting to capture the broad structure of the mobility table, it can, unless interpreted with caution, be misleading as well. This is particularly so if one attempts to conceive of the associations in the subsets of the table which were analysed as being uniform across the cells in those subsets. For example, while most of the association in the table is to be found in the cells on the main diagonal, this does not mean that the association is equally strong in all of those cells, nor does it mean that the association in any particular cell in the diagonal is necessarily stronger than the association in all non-diagonal cells.

If we wish to look at the structure of mobility and inheritance in greater detail and to attempt to locate more precisely those instances in which origins are of very great importance and those in which they barely matter, then we need a method of measuring the association between origin and destination on a cell-by-cell basis which is comparable across cells. For some time it was believed that the indices of association or Rogoff ratios — developed independently by Glass (1954) and Rogoff (1953) — provided a solution to this problem. However, it has since been shown by Blau and Duncan (1967), and more formally by Tyree (1973), that these measures had neither the properties of marginal independence nor of cross-cell comparability which were claimed for them. Similar claims were also made for the use of the parameters of the saturated log-linear model as mobility indices. These claims have also been found to be incorrect (Featherman and Hauser, 1978: 161-63), although the parameters are an improvement on the Rogoff ratios primarily because in the logged form the influence of outliers is reduced (Featherman and Hauser, 1978:163). None the less, as they show, the use of these terms can be every bit as misleading as the use of Rogoff ratios. However, in a recent paper Hauser (1978) has proposed a modified log-linear model of the mobility table which allows us to generate a set of parameters from which we can construct cell-by-cell measures of association which do have the desired properties. In the final part of this section the Hauser model and the results of fitting that model to our data will be presented.

Fitting Hauser's New Mobility Ratios (R*)

In effect what the Hauser model does is to attempt to partition the mobility table into a set of mutually exclusive and exhaustive sub-tables such that the strength of the associations within the sub-tables is the same across all of the cells in the sub-table. Once this partitioning has been accomplished it is then possible to rewrite the model of the mobility table in the following way:

$$ln \ x_{ijk} = a + b_i + c_j + d_k + e_{ijk}$$

Where a is an overall effect (much like u in the earlier model), and b_i and c_j are parameters which reflect row and column effects respectively. The d_k term reflects the relative strength of the set of interactions in the kth sub-table. The e_{ijk} term represents an error term defined in much the same way as the error term in an ordinary least squares regression:

$$e_{ijk} = ln \ x_{ijk} - ln \ \hat{x}_{ijk}$$

Conceptually, what this model allows us to do is to separate the father-son mobility table into a series of k sub-tables (or levels) within which we hypothesize that the strengths of the interactions (or, in Hauser's terminology, the interaction densities) are homogeneous. For example, let us consider the way in which we would deal with model 2 in Table 3.4 under this formulation. In model 2, it will be recalled that the null-hypothesis was that apart from the interactions in the main diagonal, the mobility process was a random one. Using the revised model we could reformulate one version of model 2 in a more specific way as follows:

$$ln\ x_{ijk} = a + b_i + c_j + d_k + e_{ijk}$$
$$k = 1,\ \text{if}\ i = j$$
$$k = 2,\ \text{if}\ i = j$$

If this model were to fit the data it would tell us that the mobility table was one in which there were strong and uniform associations between father's and son's occupations in the main diagonal, and (assuming $d_1 > d_2$) that the father-son associations for those who were mobile were uniform and of a lower order of strength. The magnitude of the difference between d_1 and d_2 would give the difference in the strength of the associations. It is worth noting that if the hypothesis of random mobility had been true then the value of d would have been zero. Of course, the structure of our mobility table is more complex than this simple example. Indeed, the fact that neither model 2 or model 3 in Table 3.4 fit the data is conclusive evidence of the lack of interaction homogeneity in the mobility cells of the table. As a consequence we must attempt to fit a more complex model which employs a greater number of levels.

Once a model has been fit to the data and the parameters of the equation defining the model have been estimated, it is then possible to use this information to calculate the new mobility ratios using the following formula:

$$R_{ij} = x_{ij}\ /(exp\ a \bullet exp\ b_i \bullet exp\ c_j),$$

where the exponentiation (exp) is on the Naperian base. These indices can be interpreted as measures of the strength of association in the cells of the table — the larger the value the greater the association. In substantive terms the values tell us the degree to which it is likely that a son with particular origins will end up in a given destination net of any effects which can be attributed to the inter-generational changes in the margins of the table. These ratios in fact accomplish what the Rogoff ratios claimed to accomplish. Indeed, as Hauser points out, they are analogous to the Rogoff ratio and in the case of strict independence they become identical to it (Hauser, 1978:15-17).

The actual procedure for fitting such a model to the data is tedious and will not be gone into in detail here. It involves a series of approximations beginning with a fairly crude model of the table structure which is iteratively refined over a series of trials. In the case of our data it was found that an adequate fit could be obtained by dividing the table into seven levels. Table 3.5 shows the level to which each cell in the father-son table was assigned in the final model; a 1 denotes the level

TABLE 3:5 — Level Designation for Father's Occupation by Son's Occupation Model (Native Born, Aged 25-64, in Labour Force, July 1973)

	Son's Current Occupation									
Father's Occupation	*1*	*2*	*3*	*4*	*5*	*6*	*7*	*8*	*9*	*10*
1. Professional & semi-pro	2	2	5	5	5	6	6	6	7	7
2. Manager	3	3	5	5	5	6	6	6	7	7
3. Supervisor	4	4	3	5	5	6	6	6	7	7
4. Upper white-collar	4	4	5	3	5	6	6	6	7	7
5. Lower white-collar	5	5	4	5	5	6	6	6	7	7
6. Foreman	6	6	6	6	6	4	6	6	6	7
7. Upper blue-collar	6	6	6	5	5	4	4	5	6	7
8. Lower blue-collar	7	6	6	6	5	5	4	3	7	6
9. Farm	7	7	7	6	6	5	5	4	1	2
10. Farm labourer	7	7	7	7	6	6	4	4	2	1

of highest interaction density, a 7 denotes the level of lowest interaction density. When the P,S,L model was fit to the data using this configuration of levels we obtained a G^2 of 68.75 with 75 degrees of freedom, which in combination with an index of dissimilarity of 3.97 indicates a highly satisfactory fit with the data.

Table 3.6 presents the estimates of the parameters of the model. Comparing the values in columns 1 and 2 of the table allows us to look at the shifts in occupational prevalence between the father's generation and the son's generation. The upper four occupational levels (professional and semi-professional, managers, supervisors, and upper white-collar workers) all show marked growth in the inter-generational period. There is a very small increase in the prevalence of the lower level white-collar occupations. All of the categories of blue-collar worker show some decline, with the decline in the lower blue-collar category being quite marked. The decline in the farm and farm labour groups is quite sharp. None of this is very surprising in the light of the discussion of general trends in the Canadian labour force presented in Chapter 1. Indeed, these are just the sorts of shifts that one would expect to find in a society that is well into the so-called post-industrial transition.

The parameters which are of greater interest are the d's, or levels parameters. These values give a measure of the average strength of density of the interactions within their particular level of the table. To compare these values to each other it is only necessary to take the exponent of the difference between the d's for the two levels to be compared. For example, the average interaction in level 1 is 3.13

TABLE 3:6 — Estimated Parameters (in additive form), Father's Occupation to Son's Occupation, Native-Born Males 25-64

	Father's Occupation b_i	Son's Occupation c_j	Level d_k
1	−.889	.781	2.5332
2	−.740	.333	1.3917
3	−.348	.262	.6580
4	−.658	.064	.3915
5	.140	.188	.1423
6	.063	.040	−.2459
7	.943	.799	−.6192
8	1.232	.993	
9	1.196	−1.414	
10	−.940	−2.046	

$$a = 3.7612$$
$$\text{Model } \ln x_{ij} = a + b_i + c_j + d_k$$

(exp[2.5332 − 1.3917]) times as strong as the average interaction in level 2, and the average in level 1 is 23.39 times as strong as the average interaction in level 7 (exp[2.5332 + .6129]). This then suggests that there is very substantial variation in the strength of the associations between father's occupation and son's occupation. The consequences of the variation can, however, be more clearly appreciated when we turn to examine the new mobility ratios.

Table 3.7 presents the array of the new mobility ratios calculated from the data in Table 3.6. The interpretation of these values (the R^*'s) is exactly the same as for the Rogoff ratios. That is, values of greater than 1 indicate a positive association between origin and destination (the event occurs more often than would be expected by chance alone), values of precisely 1 indicate that there is no association between a particular origin and destination, and values of less than 1 indicate a negative association between origin and destination (the event occurs less often than would be expected by chance). Bearing this in mind we see that, while the configuration of the table is not unlike that of mobility tables in which other measures of association have been used, certain features do stand out more sharply. First, the degree of inheritance among the sons of farmers and farm labourers is very much stronger than among any other cells in the table ($R^*(9,9)$ = 12.8, and $R^*(10,10)$ = 9.31). Interestingly, the next strongest pair of interactions are also found

TABLE 3:7 — New Mobility Ratios ($R^{*}ij$) for Father's Occupation by Son's Occupation (Native-Born Aged 25-64, in Labour Force, July 1973)

Father's Occupation				Son's Occupation					
	1	2	3	4	5	6	7	8	9	10
1. Profession & semi-pro.	4.24	3.10	1.04	1.80	1.45	.82	.76	.69	.91	.87
2. Manager	2.02	2.44	.97	1.24	1.14	.47	.75	.64	.78	.38
3. Supervisor	1.52	1.63	1.80	1.39	1.31	1.11	.64	.56	.66	.26
4. Upper white-collar	1.50	1.58	.96	2.24	1.12	.87	.83	.67	.18	.35
5. Lower white-collar	1.00	1.08	1.30	1.03	1.23	.92	.89	.92	.41	.63
6. Foreman	.70	.89	.72	.90	.83	1.48	.85	.70	.78	.50
7. Upper blue-collar	.79	.83	.86	1.01	1.18	1.30	1.48	1.25	.32	.35
8. Lower blue-collar	.65	.75	.87	.84	1.11	1.04	1.47	1.88	.47	1.03
9. Farm	.50	.53	.59	.66	.68	1.29	1.14	1.40	12.80	4.34
10. Farm labourer	.30	.47	.37	.40	.98	.96	1.41	1.71	5.92	9.31

within the section of the table which deals with the farm sector ($R^*(9,10)$ = 4.34, $R^*(10,9)$ = 5.92), indicating that the son's of farmers are disproportionately likely to become farm labours (could this be because they are waiting for father to pass on the family farm?), and that the sons of farm labourers are disproportionately likely to become farmers (is this perhaps the other side of the coin, where grandfather had a long life — father was still waiting to take over the farm when the son was 16 — and father had a short one?). Indeed, there is a very clear sense in the table of the farm sector being virtually cut off from the non-farm sector of the economy. Not only is there very strong within-sector inheritance and mobility, but the both the in-flow and out-flow interactions which connect these occupations to the rest of the economy are very weak as well. When we look at the out-flow interactions (those between the sons of farmers and farm labourers and all other occupational destinations) we find weak but positive associations between these origins and blue-collar work, and uniformly negative interactions between farm origins and any level of white-collar work. On the in-flow side the interactions between the sons of non-farm sector workers and either of the possible farm sector destinations are, with one exception, negative. Again these results merely confirm what we would have expected on the basis of our earlier discussions. The high degree of within-farm sector inheritance is not, of course, surprising simply because farming is one of the few occupational spheres where direct inheritance of father's occupation, in the literal sense rather than the figurative, is both possible and normatively acceptable.

We can now turn to look at the area of the table which represents the second highest interaction density zone. This area lies in the upper left-hand corner of the table. Here we find the cells for the relationships between professional or managerial origins and professional or managerial destinations. The association between having a father who was a professional or semi-professional and being a professional or semi-professional one's self is, excluding the farm sector, the strongest in the table. The associations between professional fathers and sons who are managers and manager fathers whose sons are themselves professionals are slightly lower but are very much of the same order of magnitude. This is to be expected given the nature of these occupations. First, access to professional occupations is closely tied, in most instances, to educational credentials, in particular to having achieved a university degree. Indeed, during the time period which are covered by our data a university degree was virtually a sufficient condition for a professional occupation. Given this and the fact that the sons of the highly educated (professionals and managers) are far more likely than others to achieve a university education, it is understandable that the degree of association in this cell is quite high. When one further notes that many of the managerial positions in our society are either professional positions as well or at the very least require as a condition of entry professional qualifications, the explanation of the high interactions amongst these four cells is complete.

While the interaction densities in the upper and lower corners of the table are, because of their striking magnitudes, of great interest, the more general pattern of interactions in the table is not without interest as well. If rather than looking at the specific magnitudes of the interactions we simply consider that values of greater than 1 are positive, that values which are equal to (or very close to) 1 indicate no association, and that values which are less than 1 are negative, then we can further clarify the structure. First, it can be seen, as is so common in mobility tables, that all of the interactions on the main diagonal are positive. That is to say, that it is quite common in Canadian society for sons to end up in the same type of occupation as their fathers. There is of course substantial variation in the degree to which this is so depending on the father's occupation, ranging from the very strong associations which we have already discussed through to the quite weak associations which are found for the sons of lower level white-collar workers ($R^*(5,5) = 1.23$), foremen ($R^*(6,6) = 1.48$), and upper level blue-collar workers ($R^*(7,7) = 1.48$). None the less, regardless of origins, sons consistently end up in occupations at the same level as their fathers to a degree that substantially exceeds that which could be expected by chance.

Secondly, if one divides the table into four broad quadrants along the non-manual–manual axes, a second and very important aspect of the structure of mobility in Canada becomes apparent. If we look first at the set of cells which form the lower left-hand quadrant and which the associations between fathers with manual occupations and sons with non-manual occupations, we can see, with only three exceptions (cells [7,4], [7,5], and [8,5]), that the R^*'s are all less than 1, and even in the exceptional cells the differences are very close to 1. Similarly, when we look at the upper right-hand in which the cells representing the associations between fathers with non-manual occupations and sons with manual occupations are located, we see, with only one exception in this case (cell [3,6], which is again very close to 1), that all of the exceptions are negative. In the case of the remaining two quadrants (manual-manual, and non-manual–non-manual), while not all of the cells are greater than unity, those cells on or near to the diagonals are consistently greater than unity (in many instances very much so). These patterns provide very strong evidence for a conclusion that in Canadian society there is a major barrier to both upward and downward mobility which is located along the division between non-manual and manual occupations. Thus, while Canadians are mobile to a degree beyond that which could be expected by chance alone, their mobility is very much a restricted mobility in which they move to occupational groupings which are close to those of their fathers, and in which changes of collar colour are rare.

In summary, then, our analysis shows that while there is a positive association between father's occupation and son's occupation, this association is by no means uniformly strong. For those who were the sons of men working in the farm sector of the economy, or of men who held either professional or managerial occupation, their father's occupation can be seen to have exercised a substantial influence on where they ended up in the occupational division of labour. For the remainder, the influence of father's occupation, while not negligible, is certainly less decisively specific in its influence. Finally, of course, we have seen that there is a major barrier to mobility which divides Canadians along manual and non-manual lines.

In interpreting these results it must be borne in mind that when we look at the observed amounts of total mobility, as opposed to the patterns of circulation mobility with which we have been concerned, we find that while there is indeed much inheritance (23 per cent of the sons had occupations in the same group as their fathers), there is also a great deal of mobility (77 per cent were mobile by at least one occupational level). What the focus on circulation mobility reveals, when we strip away the mobility which is due solely to changes in the occupational structure in order to lay bare the basis nature of the opportunity structure in society, is that this underlying structure is a relatively rigid one in which the fortunes or misfortunes of one generation are typically also those of the next. Although it has been argued that the distinction between structural and circulation does not matter in the sense that the individual who has retained the high status of his birth or escaped the low status of his origins could care less about the source of his good fortune, the distinction is not a trivial one if we wish to understand the operation of the Canadian opportunity structure and what the future may hold for our society.

The sharp contrast which we find between the patterns of observed mobility and the patterns of circulation mobility tell us that because Canada was fortunate enough to be part of the period of tremendous economic growth which was experienced by the western industrial nations during the last half-century, we have been able through structural mobility to enjoy the illusion of being a relatively open society in which a person's location in the occupational structure was relatively independent of his origins. This illusion based on structural mobility is all well and good as long as it can be maintained, or more to the point as long as economic growth can be counted upon to transform the structure of the labour force in the same way as it has in the past. But what happens when the pace of growth falters and slows? When it stops? When, in other words, the changes in the labour force which are necessary for structural mobility do not occur? At that point the dominant source of mobility increasingly becomes circulation mobility, the patterns of observed mobility are the patterns of circulation, with the consequence that we would then (indeed perhaps we are now) be faced with a society which has become, in very short order, much more rigid.

In this section we have examined the ways in which father's and son's occupations are or are not linked. We have seen that the dominant pattern in Canadian society is one in which the occupations of sons are not usually very different from that of their fathers. Given these findings, the question becomes, What are the links which allow the advantages and disadvantages of origin to be so faithfully reproduced? What, in other words, is the *process* of stratification? To give a partial answer to this question we will turn in the next section to the status attainment model.

The Status Attainment Model

The structure of industrial societies is such that with a few exceptions it is only rarely that a father is able to directly confer his occupational position on his son. The obvious exceptions to this are fathers who are farmers or who own their businesses. Even in the latter case direct inheritance is becoming rarer, because unless the business is wholly owned by the father (which usually means that it is a very small firm) the law gives certain rights to minority shareholders which no longer make the transition from father to son automatic. The vast majority of the work force of an industrial society are either employed by others for wages or salaries, or work as members of the professions. While it is no doubt the case that personal connections can be of some assistance in obtaining employment, it is also the case that such factors are of little avail unless the individual is at least minimally qualified for the position which he seeks. Indeed, it is generally the case that the labour market operates in a relatively impersonal and universalistic fashion, with a primary reliance on certification and past performance as the criteria for hiring. As a consequence it is almost impossible for fathers to directly confer their occupations on their sons, although they may, given that their son is qualified for a position, be able to gain him some preference in competition with other qualified sons. It is most unlikely, however, that associations of the magnitude of those which we observed in the last section would arise if this were the only or even the main way in which fathers assisted their sons. However, if direct inheritance of roles is ruled out in most cases, and if the effects of influence on the hiring and promotion process are likely to be small, how are we to explain the degree of stratification which we observe?

The answer lies in looking backward in the socioeconomic life cycle to the period before the son enters the labour force. This is the period in which the son is receiving the training which will prepare him for his working life and in which the advantages and disadvantages of his origins can directly affect his future.

The socioeconomic life cycle is a concept which is employed to map out the sequence of events through which the typical person will proceed over the course of his life. Once we have mapped out this sequence we can then examine how and to what extent the advantages of origin are likely to affect the outcomes of each stage and the transitions between stages. While the life cycle can be broken down into many levels of detail, in this analysis we are only concerned with three broad components: the period during which an individual receives his education, the translation of that education into an occupational position, and the career trajectory from labour force entry to the present. As we have already suggested, the effects of family background on entry and career are likely to be small. Hence most of the inter-generational transmission of advantage and disadvantage must be due to the influence which family background has on educational attainment. This is indeed exactly what the status attainment model argues and what has been found in previous research which has attempted to assess the model. The status attainment model is simply a more systematic statement of this discussion in the form of three main propositions and some sub-propositions which can be stated in either verbal or mathematical form:

1. The greater the socioeconomic resources of a person's family of origin, the higher their educational attainment will be.

Or

$Re = a + b\ F.Ses,$

where Re represents the person's educational attainment, $F.Ses$ a measure (or measures) of the socioeconomic resources of that person's family of origin, and a and b are respectively the intercept and slope of a linear function relating these factors. It is predicted by the model that b will be greater than zero.

2. The higher a person's educational attainment the higher the status of his occupation at the time of labour force entry net of the effects of his socioeconomic background, and the higher the socioeconomic resources of a person's family of origin, the higher the status of his first job again net of the effects of his education.

Or

$$J = a' + b'F.Ses + c'Re,$$

where J is a measure of the socioeconomic status of the respondent's first job and where b' and c' represent the rates of status return to background resources and educational attainment respectively. The model predicts that c' will be very much greater than b'.

3. The higher the status of the person's first job the higher the status of his current occupation. This will remain the case even when the effects of background and educational attainment are controlled for. Further, both educational attainment and background will also have positive effects on current occupational status.

Or

$$C = a'' + b''F.Ses + c''Re + d''J,$$

where C is a measure of the status of the respondent's current (1973) occupation. The coefficients b'', c'', and d'' again represent rates of status return to their respective variables. The model would predict that c'' and d'' will be substantially larger than b''. Thus, the model, while not addressing itself to the specific content of the processes which relates these factors, does answer the following questions: What are the nature and strength of the relationships between the social background variables and the respondents' educational attainments? Given educational attainment, what effect does this, in combination with background, have on occupational status at the time of labour force entry? What effect do all of these factors have on current occupational status? Before we can answer these questions, it is necessary to first define the variables in these equations in terms of the measures in our data and to re-specify the model in terms of these measures.

Measurement and Re-specification

In the previous section we employed a single variable $F.Ses$ to denote the set of factors related to the respondent's socioeconomic background. Following Blau and Duncan (1967) we shall use the combination of father's occupational status (F) and father's educational attainment (Fe) as our core measures of the respondent's socioeconomic background. Father's occupational status was measured using the same question as was used to measure father's occupation in the earlier part of this chapter; that is, we asked for the respondent's father's occupation at the time the respondent was 16 years of age. However, in this instance the occupations have been assigned scores using the Blishen-McRoberts (1976) scale of socioeconomic scores. These scores provide a scaling of the general goodness or desirability of the occupations. (See Goldthorpe and Hope, 1972 for an extensive discussion of the meaning of various occupational scaling procedures.) Additionally, these scores are closely related to the level of income and lifestyle which is likely to be enjoyed by the incumbent of an occuaption, and as such they serve as a good indicator of the overall quality of the resources which the respondent was likely to have had available to him in his youth. Father's education is included as a second and more specific measure of these resources. To obtain the information the respondent was asked to indicate the highest level of education which his father had attained. This information was then scaled by assigning to each level a number which represents the median number of years required to attain that level.

In addition to these two measures of background resources, we have, following Blau and Duncan (1967), and Duncan, Featherman, and Duncan (1972), added a third variable — number of siblings (S) — to the background set as a control. The argument for this is very simple. We assume that, all other things being equal, as the number of siblings grows so will the competition within any family unit for the fixed resources of that unit, and hence that the net return to any given level of family background will decline as a linear function of the number of siblings with which the respondent must compete.

The remaining variables in the model — respondent's education (Re), respondent's first job (J), and respondent's current job (C) — are all measured using single indicators. Respondent's education was measured and scaled in the same way as father's education. First and current occupation were both scaled using the Blishen-McRoberts socioeconomic scores.

The equations to be estimated for the status attainment model can now be re-specified as follows:

$$Re = a + bF + cFe + dS + e_{Re}$$

$$J = a' + b'F + c'Fe + d'S + g'Re + e_J$$

$$C = a'' + b''F + c''Fe + d''S + g''Re + h''J + e_C$$

If the error terms for these equations are uncorrelated, then the coefficients of this set of equations may be estimated using ordinary least squares regression procedures.

The Canadian Status Attainment Model

The basic results of fitting this model to our data are presented in tables 3.8 and 3.9. Table 3.8 displays the means, standard deviations, and zero order correlations for all of the variables in the model. Table 3.9 gives the metric (or unstandardized) coefficients for the equations in the model, the standardized coefficients, and the total and indirect effects for each of the independent variables (see Cohen and Cohen, 1975; and Alwin and Hauser, 1975). In fitting the model as specified above it was found that the variables father's education and siblings had no significant effect on either first or current occupation. These two variables were then dropped from the equations and the coefficients were re-estimated. The results of this re-estimation appear in the table. It is worth noting that the omission of these variables had virtually no effect on the predictive power or the fit of the equations. The R^2 remained unaffected to three significant digits, and in all but one instance the standard errors of the remaining coefficients went down.

The first equation in the model estimates the effects of our social background variables on the respondent's educational attainment. Jointly the three measures of background which we have used account for just over 28 per cent of the variance in educational attainment.

TABLE 3:8 — Means, Standard Deviations and Correlations for Native-Born Males, Aged 25-64 In the Labour Force July 1973.

	Father's SES (F)	Father's Education (Fe)	Number of Siblings (S)	Education (E)	First Job SES (J)	Current Job SES (C)	Mean	Sd
F	—						35.14	13.18
Fe	.493	—					7.34	3.91
S	−.239	−.299	—				4.62	3.28
E	.395	.456	−.340	—			10.93	3.66
J	.401	.352	−.254	.647	—		39.07	14.28
C	.400	.348	−.232	.619	.673	—	44.50	15.01

TABLE 3:9 — Regression Coefficients for a Status Attainment Model for Native Born Males, Aged 25-64 in the Canadian Labour Force, July 1973

| | Dependent Variable | | | | | | Total, Direct, and Indirect Effects | | | | | | |
| | Metric Coefficients[a] | | | Standardized Coefficients | | | On First Job | | | On Current Job | | | |
Independent Variable	Education	First Job	Current Job	Education	First Job	Current Job	Total	Direct	Via Education	Total	Direct	Via Education	Via First Job
Father's occupation	.055 (.003)	.186 (.010)	.123 (.010)	.200	.172	.108	.288	.172	.116	.242	.108	.058	.076
Father's education	.277 (.010)	*	*	.297	—	—	.172	—	.172	.086	—	.086	—
Siblings	-.227 (.011)	*	*	-.203	—	—	-.118	—	-.118	-.059	—	-.059	—
Education		2.262 (.035)	1.189 (.042)		.579	.289	.579	.579	—	.545	.289	—	.256
First job			.466 (.011)			.443				.443	.443	—	—
Intercept	7.994	7.783	8.986										
R^2	.283	.444	.520										

[a] Standard errors in parenthesis.
*Term omitted from the equation as coefficient not significant at .01 level and standardized coefficient less than .1.

Examining the standardized coefficients we can see that of these variables father's education has the strongest effect. Father's occupational status and the number of siblings have effects which are roughly equal in magnitude but opposite in sign (.200 and −.203 respectively). As was expected the coefficient for number of siblings was negative, reflecting the penalty which the respondent suffers due to the dilution of family resources by brothers and sisters. Turning to the metric coefficients we can see that fairly substantial differences in the independent variables would be required to make much difference in the dependent variable. However, as a glance at the correlation matrix also shows, these variables are by no means independent of each other and a change is generally associated with a change in the others in a way such that the effect is cumulative. That is to say, high status occupations are generally associated with high levels of education and with a propensity to have small families. Thus, we can see from equation one of the status attainment model that the socioeconomic status of the family of origin has a substantial impact on the respondent's educational attainment.

The second equation in the model shows how this educational attainment in combination with background affects the respondent's entry status. As can be seen in Table 3.9 these two factors account for over two-fifths of the variance in first job status ($R^z = .444$). It will be noted that the direct effects of the background variables on first job status are small (indeed, the direct effects of father's education and number of siblings are negligible) and that most of the explained variance in this equation is attributable to the very strong effect of educational attainment on first-job status. While education is by itself the most important determinant of first-job status, we must at the same time recall that in the model it is in part determined by socioeconomic background. The variation in first-job status which can be attributed to the effects of background on educational attainment are called the indirect effects of background on first-job status as mediated by education (Alwin and Hauser, 1975; Land, 1969). These effects have been calculated and are given in column 9 of Table 3.9 along with the direct and total effects (Total effect = Direct effect + Indirect effect) for each variable (columns 8 and 7 respectively). It can be seen, while none are as strong as education, that when the indirect effects of the background variables are included, the effect of these factors on first-job status is far from negligible. Indeed, overall it can be shown that the combined effects of socioeconomic background on first-job status account for roughly one-quarter of the explained variance.

In the third equation we turn to examine how background in

combination with entry status and educational attainment affect the respondent's subsequent career. In total these factors account for just over one-half of the variance in current job status ($r = .520$). As in the previous equation the effects of background are small, and only father's occupation has a significant direct effect on current status. Further, and unlike the previous equation, the indirect effects, while not trivial, are small. The most important direct determinant of current status is entry status followed by educational attainment. However, when the indirect effect of educational attainment on current status as mediated through first-job status is considered as well, we can see (column 10) that educational attainment is the most important overall determinant of current status.

Overall the model confirms the major findings of previous status attainment search both in Canada (Turritin, 1974; Cuneo and Curtis, 1975; McRoberts, 1975) and the United States (Blau and Duncan, 1967, Duncan, Featherman, and Duncan, 1972; Hauser and Featherman, 1978). First, it is clear that the key determinant of both labour force entry status and current status is the respondent's educational attainment. Secondly, it is equally clear that the respondent's socioeconomic background is an important determinant of the amount of education which he will receive. In this context it is important to recall that, although studies of educational attainment have succeeded, through the addition of other factors such as grades in school, motivation, and self-concept, in explaining much more of the variance in educational attainment than this reduced model, in every case these new variables have also been found to be in part determined by socioeconomic background (Porter, Porter and Blishen *et al.*, 1982). In summary, we may conclude that the way in which the advantages and/or disadvantages of socioeconomic background are transmitted inter-generationally is through the way in which background effects educational attainment.

However, the question which still must be answered is: How much difference does background make? To answer this question I will now turn to the equations for our model in metric form, and view them as a set of rules which predict how, on the average, individuals with particular characteristics will fare in their socioeconomic attainments. Viewed in this way we can apply the model to two sons of differing socioeconomic backgrounds and see just how much difference their backgrounds would make in their educational and occupational attainments.

Let us begin by describing two fictional sons, A and B. A is a man not unlike the average member of our sample. His father is a semi-skilled blue-collar worker ($F = 35$) with a grade school education ($Fe = 8$), and he comes from a large family with four brothers and sisters ($S = 4$). B on the other hand is a child of privilege. His father is a professional engineer ($F = 65$), who, of course, has a university education ($Fe = 16$). He comes, as well, from a small family with only 1 sibling ($S = 1$). Panel 1 of Table 3.10 shows the attainments which our model predicts for each of these two men. First, we can see that their educational attainments differ by just over four and one-half years; the difference between an incomplete high school education (11.25 years) for A, and a university degree (15.81) for B. The statuses of their first full-time jobs will differ by nearly sixteen points (15.72) or by just over one standard deviation. A's first job with a score of 40 would most likely be as a skilled blue-collar worker or perhaps as a semi-skilled white-collar worker. B's on the other hand with a score of 56 would be in the upper levels of skilled white-collar work or in the lower levels of management. Over the course of their careers to their current occupations the difference in their statuses will increase slightly (from 15.92 to 16.54) and both will be upwardly mobile by about 6 points. Overall then we can again see how closely son's achievements are tied to their backgrounds. A will do better than his father (current job status of 45 for A versus 35 for his father) but at the same time it is most likely that he will remain a blue-collar worker. B will not fare quite as well as his father (current job status of 62 for B versus 65 for his father) but the difference is slight and his score would indicate a professional or managerial occupation.

How much of this difference between A and B can be attributed to the 4.56 years of difference in their educational attainments? To answer this question we can look at the difference which is predicted by our equations under the assumption that A was able to transcend his origins and achieved the same level of education as B. The results of this exercise are presented in panel B of Table 3.10. The difference in outcomes for A and B drops to 5.57 and 6.31 points for entry and current status respectively. This in turn means that of the gross differences in outcomes of 15.72 and 16.54 attributable to background, 65 per cent (10.33 points) of the first job difference, and 62 per cent (10.23 points) of the current job difference is attributable to the differences in educational attainment which can be attributed solely to background. In panel C of the table the conjecture is taken one step further and the model is re-evaluated on the assumption that A not only manages to achieve the same education as B, but that he is equally efficient in translating that education into an entry status. Here we can see the complete breakdown of the difference in outcomes between A and B. The gross difference in current occupational status of 16.85 points can be decomposed as follows: 61.85 per cent of the difference is due to the effect of background on educational attainment, 15.78 per cent of the difference is due to the effect of background on entry status (2.16 points difference), and 22.37 per cent of the difference is due to the direct effect of background on current status. Clearly these results reinforce our earlier conclusion that the major mechanism of status transmission in Canada, as in most other industrial societies, is via the advantages or disadvantages conferred by background in the attainment of education.

Conclusions

To return to the metaphor of the race upon which we drew earlier in this chapter, we have seen that in Canada there is clearly more than a little "inequality at the start," and that those advantages and disadvantages which are present at the start of the race have considerable bearing on its conclusion. To be sure, there are many who manage to overcome their disadvantage to a greater or lesser extent, and even a few who are unable to exploit an advantageous position on the grid. Nonetheless, the simple fact which emerges from the data whether configured as percentage tables, log-linear models, or status attainment models, is that the finishing order and the starting order are very much alike. Or, in other words, that in most instances the work and status of most Canadians will not be very different from the work and status of their fathers. Thus, it remains very much the case that there are still important barriers to equality of opportunity in Canadian society. As I have shown in this chapter one of the important ways in which the advantages of background are passed on is through the effect of parental status on the son's educational attainment. Indeed, this effect alone accounts for over three-fifths of the contribution of background to current status. In the next chapter Jones will extend this analysis to a detailed examination of the ways in which education translates into a career, and to an analysis of career mobility.

Finally, we would remind the reader that this analysis has focused on the effects of origin for a group in Canadian society that is in itself relatively privileged — native-born males. In subsequent chapters the analysis will be extended to a comparison of this group with other less fortunate groups, such as women, and the non-native-born, and to an analysis of some of the members of the native-born Canadian group which have been historically viewed as disadvantaged, such as ethnic and linguistic minorities.

References

ALWIN, DUANE A. and ROBERT M. HAUSER
1975 "The Decomposition of Effects in Path Analysis." *American Sociological Review*, 40 (Feb.): 37-47.

BELL, DANIEL
1973 *The Coming of Post-Industrial Society.* New York: Basic Books.

BLAU, PETER M. and OTIS DUELLEY DUNCAN
1967 *The American Occupational Structure.* New York: Wiley.

BLISHEN, BERNARD R., and HUGH A. MCROBERTS
1976 "A Revised Socioeconomic Index for Occupations in Canada." *Canadian Review of Sociology and Anthropology*, 13(1): 71-79.

COHEN, JACOB, and PATRICIA COHEN
1975 *Applied Multiple Regression/Correlation Analysis for the Behavioral Sciences.* Hillsdale: Lawrence Earlbaum Associates.

CUNEO, C.J., and J.E. CURTIS
1975 "Social Ascription in the Educational and Occupational Status Attainment of Urban Canadians." *Canadian Review of Sociology and Anthropology*, 12: 6-24.

DAVIS, KINGSLEY and WILBERT E. MOORE
1945 "Some Principles of Stratification." *American Sociological Review*, 10: 242-49.

DUNCAN, OTIS DUDLEY
1966 "Methodological Issues in the Analysis of Social Mobility," pp. 51-97 in Neil J. Smelser and Seymour Martin Lipset, ed. *Social Structure and Mobility in Economic Development.* Chicago: Aldine.
1968 "Social Stratification and Mobility: Problems in the Measurement of Trends." Pp. 675-719 in Eleanor B. Sheldon and Wilbert E. Moore, ed. *Indicators of Social Change.* New York: Russell Sage Foundation.

DUNCAN, OTIS DUDLEY, DAVID L. FEATHERMAN, and BEVERLY DUNCAN
1972 *Socioeconomic Background and Achievement.* New York: Seminar Press.

FEATHERMAN, DAVID L., and ROBERT M. HAUSER
1978 *Opportunity and Change.* New York: Academic Press.

GLASS, D.V., ed.
1954 *Social Mobility in Britain.* London: Routledge and Kegan Paul.

GOLDTHORPE, JOHN H. and KEITH HOPE
1972 "Occupational Grading and Occupational Prestige." Pp. 19-80 in Keith Hope, ed. *The Analysis of Social Mobility Methods and Approaches.* Oxford: Clarendon Press.

GOODMAN, LEO A.
1969 "On the Measurement of Social Mobility: An Index of Status Persistence." *American Sociological Review*, 34 (December): 831-50.
1972 "Some Multiplicative Models for the Analysis of Cross-classified Data." Pp. 649-96 in *Proceedings of the Sixth Berkeley Symposium on Mathematical Statistics and Probability.* Berkeley: University of California Press.

HAUSER, ROBERT M.
1978   "A Structural Model of the Mobility Table." *Social Forces*, 56 (March): 919-53.

LAND, KENNETH C., and SPILERMAN, eds.
1975   *Social Indicator Models*. New York: Russell Sage Foundation.

McROBERTS, HUGH A.
1975   "Social Stratification in Canada: A Preliminary Analysis." Ph.D. Dissertation. Department of Sociology, Carleton University, Ottawa.

PINEO, PETER C., JOHN PORTER, and HUGH A. McROBERTS
1977   "The 1971 Census and the Socioeconomic Classification of Occupations." *Canadian Review of Sociology and Anthropology* 14(1): 91-102.

PORTER, JOHN, BERNARD BLISHEN *et al.*
1971   *Towards 2000*. Toronto: McClelland and Stewart.

PORTER, JOHN, MARION R. PORTER, BERNARD BLISHEN, *et al.*
1982   *Stations and Callings*. Toronto: Methuen Press.

ROGOFF, NATALIE
1953   *Recent Trends in Occupational Mobility*. Glencoe: Free Press.

SHRYOCK, HENRY S., and JACOB S. SIEGEL
1975   *The Materials and Methods of Demography*. Washington: U.S. Government Printing Office.

SOROKIN, P.A.
1927   *Social and Cultural Mobility*. Chicago: Free Press (1964).

SVALASTOGA, KAAVE
1965   *Social Differentiation*. New York: David McKay Co.

TURRITTIN, A.H.
1974   "Social Mobility in Canada: A Comparison of Three Provincial Studies and Some Methodological Questions." *Canadian Review of Sociology and Anthropology*. Special issue: 163-86.

TYREE, ANDREA
1973   "Mobility Ratios and Association in Mobility Tables." *Population Studies*, 27: 577-88.

CHAPTER 4

Educational and Occupational Attainment: Individual Achievement

FRANK E. JONES

The focus of the traditional approach to the analysis of occupational mobility or to occupational attainment is on the tension between the relative influence of ascribed and achieved resources of individuals. Thus, earlier studies (Glass, 1954; Rogoff, 1953) seeking to measure mobility in terms of departures from statistical independence of fathers' and sons' occupations, sought to eliminate or to control the effects of the marginal distributions of fathers' and sons' occupations, that is, what is now referred to as structural mobility. Although more recent analyses (Blau and Duncan, 1967; Duncan, Featherman, and Duncan, 1972; Featherman and Hauser, 1978; Hauser *et al.*, 1975; Tyree, 1973) have identified weaknesses in these earlier procedures, the concern, nonetheless, is to separate the influence of "unearned" resources such as social origins, typically indicated by father's occupation, father's education and family size, from that of "earned" resources such as those skills developed through education, as indicated by attained level of education, or years of education, or some measure of scholastic performance, and those skills developed through employment. The tension between unearned and earned, or ascribed and achieved, resources may be perceived to apply to "society" as the unit of concern. Thus, measures[1] of father-to-son mobility may be interpreted as evidence of the operation of value-orientations, such as ascription or achievement (Parsons, 1951), in such societies as Canada, the United States and Great Britain. Measures of father-to-son mobility may also be seen as indicating the extent to which such societies conform to a model of an "open-class" society (Jones, 1961), that is, whether such societies fit the model of modern industrial society (see for example, Levy, 1966; Parsons, 1951, 1960). At the individual level, which is the main focus of models of status attainment, despite the relevance of such models to societal processes, analysis is also concerned with the tension between ascription and achievement, with the emphasis on the relative influence of these resources on individual attainment. In general, the results do not reflect a condition where each resource type acts against the other but, cast in a form assuming an additive relationship among these resource types, they tend to reveal that ascribed resources bolster, directly or indirectly, achieved resources.

This chapter reflects the traditional concern with the tension between ascribed and achieved resources. Thus, the discussion, begun in Chapter 3 where the emphasis was on the significance of ascribed resources, is continued here, but attention is shifted to the influence of achieved resources on occupational mobility and attainment. Specifically, attention is given to the influence of earlier achievements in a person's life on those occurring at later stages. In broad terms, the discussion concerns the influence exerted by education on occupational attainment on entry into the labour force and on the persistence of that influence on later occupational attainment; the influence exerted by occupational experience on post-labour force entry occupational attainment; and the relative influence of education and occupational experience on occupational location and attainment. The task is twofold: to report and to interpret the main findings about these relationships. In some respects, what is reported in this chapter will be familiar to those conversant with the literature on occupational mobility and attainment but the discussion will depart in some degree from those relating to past analyses, such as those cited above. In those analyses, which typically revealed that achieved resources exert a greater influence than ascribed resources on occupational attainment, the conclusion seemed to be that these results demonstrate the operation of a rational matching of the skills possessed by labour force participants to the job opportunities available to them. The present analysis, although conventional in many respects, differs in investigating the possibility that more than one rationality[2] may operate in modern industrial societies and the possibility that the prevailing rationality can be identified. This aspect of the analysis focuses on the relationship between education and first occupation on entry into the labour force and requires the formulation of two models of rational labour force allocation which are tested in terms of three variants of the labour market. The analysis of occupational attainment subsequent to first occupation will follow convention in its use of familiar status attainment models but will also depart from convention by attempting to go behind the familiar measures used in such models to formulate a more abstract model of the relationship.

The analyses to be reported are based on male respondents who were 25-64 years of age in 1973, and include farmers[3] and farm labourers. As in Chapter 3, the analyses will focus on the main findings in the data in the sense that controls by such variables as ethnicity, nativity, and region of residence are not introduced. In effect, the intention is to deal with the overall facts relating to educational and occupational attainment as these pertain to the majority of the Canadian labour force. In the section to follow, some detailed findings on the relationship between education and first occupation are reported. To interpret these findings, the discussion turns to a consideration of the varying demand for and supply of skills which constitutes the labour market. The models which emerge from this discussion are tested in terms of observed and expected values to allow an assessment of the prevailing rationality of occupational location in Canada.

Education and Occupation: Entry into the Labour Force

Education is, as anticipated, positively associated with the occupational level[4] at which a man enters the labour force. This is apparent from the matrix (Table 4.1) resulting from a cross-tabulation which yields moderate magnitudes for ordinal measures of association (gamma = .47, Somers D = .42) and, if education and occupation are treated as interval measures, a Pearson correlation coefficient equal to $r = .62$[5].

The cross-tabulation of first occupation by educational level reveals no surprises: about two-thirds of those with higher academic degrees began their careers in a professional occupation, while almost three-quarters of those without formal education began employment in blue-collar occupations ranging from skilled craftsmen to labourers. The details provided by the 160 cells of the matrix can be summarized by Indexes of Dissimilarity.[6] Thus, if the occupational distribution for each educational level is compared to the overall occupational distribution (Table 4.2), it can be seen that disparities in occupational distributions of those who have attained a given level of education increase as the levels move away, in either direction, from those who have gained some academic or vocational secondary education (Level 3). A comparison of occupational distributions for all pairs of educational levels (Table 4.3) confirms that differential educational attainment means quite different probabilities of occupational allocation on entry to the labour force. In general,

TABLE 4:1 — First Occupation by Education: Percentage Outflow Distribution*

Level of Education†	Self-Employed Professional	Employed Professional	High Managerial	Semi-Professional	Technical	Middle Managerial	Supervisor	Foreman
0	0.0	0.0	0.0	0.0	0.8	0.0	0.0	0.0
1	0.0	0.0	0.0	0.1	0.1	0.0	0.8	1.3
2	0.0	0.2	0.0	0.6	0.4	0.4	0.7	1.5
3	0.0	0.4	0.0	0.9	1.1	0.5	1.5	1.9
4	0.0	1.8	0.3	3.1	2.3	1.5	2.5	1.8
5	0.0	3.2	0.3	4.7	1.6	0.9	2.3	1.6
6	0.1	10.5	1.0	9.5	7.2	3.7	3.1	2.3
7	0.7	44.0	2.1	16.2	3.9	5.3	2.6	1.9
8	37.6	33.8	1.9	8.0	0.1	2.5	0.8	0.4
9	2.5	65.2	3.2	12.2	4.5	2.2	1.4	1.0

Table 4:1 (Continued)

Level of Education †	Skilled White-Collar	Skilled Craftsmen	Farmer	Semi-Skilled White-Collar	Semi-Skilled Craftsmen	Unskilled White-Collar	Labourer	Farm Labourer
0	0.9	18.4	3.8	2.4	21.6	0.0	34.8	17.4
1	0.8	13.7	7.2	2.7	24.2	2.5	27.0	19.6
2	0.8	16.2	7.1	6.7	19.1	2.6	25.2	18.7
3	2.4	18.1	3.6	13.1	19.8	5.0	23.4	8.3
4	7.6	21.6	1.9	16.5	14.7	6.9	14.1	3.3
5	6.7	30.7	1.5	12.0	14.6	4.6	11.7	3.5
6	11.1	13.6	1.9	13.2	8.0	4.7	7.5	2.3
7	7.2	2.6	0.2	6.2	1.8	2.2	2.1	0.8
8	8.4	0.8	0.0	2.0	1.3	1.8	0.0	0.7
9	3.6	0.3	0.0	1.7	1.0	1.0	0.0	0.3

*Cell entries are based on a weighted N=13945 Males, 25-64 years of age; the unweighted N=13361.

† 0 — No formal education
1 — Some elementary
2 — Completed elementary
3 — Some academic high school or vocational high school
4 — Completed academic high school or vocational high school, some post-secondary, some teacher's college or nursing
5 — Completed post-secondary, completed Teacher's college or Nursing, some community college
6 — Completed community college, some university certificate or diploma
7 — Bachelor's degree
8 — Professional degree
9 — M.A. or Ph.D.

**TABLE 4:2 — Indexes of Dissimilarity Between the Occupational Composi-
tion† of Each Education Level and the Overall Occupational
Distribution of the Male Labour Force, Aged 25-64**

Level of Education*	Indexes of Dissimilarity
0	33.26
1	32.68
2	24.68
3	14.95
4	17.96
5	19.55
6	30.05
7	61.26
8	74.06
9	74.62

* For descriptive labels corresponding to codes, see Table 4:1.
† First occupation.

dissimilarity increases as the distance between educational levels
increases. For example, the Indexes of Dissimilarity in occupational
distribution between those having no education and those with some
elementary education is 13.3 and this value increases to a maximum of
94.9 between those reporting no education and those who have attained
a higher academic degree. Of the few reversals reported in Table 4.3,

**TABLE 4:3 — Indexes of Dissimilarity for First Occupation Composition for
All Pairs of Education Level, Males, 25-64**

Level of Education*	0	1	2	3	4	5	6	7	8
1	13.34								
2	14.47	8.14							
3	22.37	22.86	15.63						
4	42.89	43.89	35.89	21.05					
5	45.73	46.73	38.73	25.52	12.31				
6	62.32	58.38	52.92	40.24	27.76	29.07			
7	88.03	84.32	79.40	75.29	63.47	62.54	43.34		
8	94.14	90.91	89.97	87.69	77.58	76.05	61.57	38.26	
9	94.92	93.05	91.78	88.04	80.78	79.04	61.89	24.57	42.89

* For descriptive labels corresponding to codes, see Table 4:1.

the largest reveals a greater difference in occupational distribution between those with a professional degree and those with higher academic degrees, (Index of Dissimilarity = 42.9), than those with an undergraduate degree and those with higher academic degrees (Index of Dissimilarity = 24.6). Those who achieve an academic degree, whatever the level, find employment in different occupations than those who have earned professional degrees.

While the facts which support the generalization that education and occupation on entry into the labour force are positively associated deserve attention, it is perhaps more useful to consider what the association means. Although there may be several possible explanations for the association, the focus here will be on two alternative explanations. The first is a perspective which may be labelled *technical rationality,* which views occupational allocation as a process of fitting persons possessing a given level of education to occupations whose educational requirements are objectively determined. In this perspective, education represents a set of occupationally relevant skills possessed by labour force entrants who find occupations consistent with those skills. A second alternative, termed *employer rationality,* is the perspective which interprets the association between education and first occupation as the result of employers adjusting educational requirements to fit those of job applicants. Although both these perspectives refer to procedures which are rational, they differ in that the first interprets the fit between education and occupation as the outcome of technically dictated efficiency while the other sees the fit as a result of the orientation, and power, of employers to tailor occupational entry standards to the educational composition of the labour market. As these alternatives have gained some prominence as explanations of the relationship of education to occupation, it is useful to consider them as possible explanations of the results presented here even though the available data may not allow a determination of the more adequate explanation.

To formulate a more general proposition concerning occupational allocation, it is necessary to introduce *skill* as a concept. Briefly stated, it is assumed that occupations represent responsibilities which require for their discharge a set of skills, whether technically or managerially determined. Similarly, but from the vantage point of labour force participants, persons who seek or find employment are assumed to possess skills which in some degree are occupationally relevant. Thus the process concerns, essentially, the fit between acquired[7] and required skills.

From the perspective of technical rationality, the fit should be close, since it is assumed that required skills are technologically determined. In a broader perspective, technical rationality may be associated with the functional tradition in sociology that interprets role allocation and, hence, the relationship between education and occupation, in terms of *ascription* and *achievement*. Thus in the functionalist tradition, it is recognized that there are societies where priority is not given to skill as a principle in allocating persons to positions or roles. That is, where age, sex, kinship or ethnicity or some other more or less institutionalized division of people has priority over skill in relation to role allocation. Thus, Parsons (1960:110-16, 1951:177) describes advanced industrial societies as achievement or performance-oriented in contrast to less-developed societies which are ascriptive.[8] Similarly, Levy (1966:62) asserts that "the structures of all relatively modern societies reflect an increasing emphasis on rationality, universalism, functional specificity, and emotional neutrality or avoidance." While these statements refer to various structures and processes of modern societies, they undoubtedly relate to processes of allocation in the occupational structure. If this perspective[9] is valid, it should mean that the occupational distribution of persons in the labour force should be determined entirely on the basis of skills — those skills possessed by labour force participants and those required by employers in any given time period.[10] Within this tradition, since Canada is a modern industrial society, a high correlation between education and occupational location might be anticipated. However, this interpretation could be challenged by those who assume employer rationality to be the operating principle. This position, which focuses on criticism of various aspects of education in modern industrial societies, does not reject rationality as a principle but rather assumes that it is a form of market rationality in which employers when recruiting labour give priority to those with the highest skills.[11] The criticism is rooted in the view that the educational system, including its costs, is simply functional to capitalistic exploitation.[12] In this perspective, the protagonists do not reject skill as the principle of allocation but rather see the employer, as a consequence of trying to maximize the skill of his labour force, as manipulating the fit between required and acquired skills.

Assuming that both perspectives in this controversy view skill as the basis of labour force allocation, it may be helpful to decompose the concept somewhat so that it becomes possible to determine what is required in terms of data. Thus, by thinking of acquired skills as attributes of persons, it is possible to assume that such skills are both genetic and learned and to suggest possible indicators or measures of skills which reflect these sources. For example, I.Q. scores or vocational aptitude scores may be suitable indicators of genetic skills, while education and occupational experience may serve as measures of learned skills.[13] For occupations, it is useful to think of general and specific skills arising out of a set of responsibilities or tasks identified for the occupation. For example, those allocated responsibilities for teaching and research might be expected to possess verbal and logical skills at a general level and knowledge of an academic or professional discipline or some part of it as specific skills. It is necessary, then, to have measures of general and specific skills to describe occupations. Theorizing continued in this vein generates a model which requires occupational allocation to be a consequence of the effects of genetic and learned skills. Thus, the model might be expressed as:

occupational location = genetic skill +
    extra-occupational learned skill +
    intra-occupational learned skill

and might be tested by:

occupation = I.Q. + attained educational level +
    occupational experience.

Although this theoretical model may be acceptable to both perspectives discussed above, a problem exists at the level of measurement. Essentially, the problem is to identify measures which are unambiguous and which are acceptable to both perspectives.

While objective measures for each variable are conceivable—measures of required skills can be determined for specific occupations by experts such as job analysts and measures of genetically and experientially acquired skills are available in the form of a variety of I.Q., vocational aptitude, and educational level tests, there would be little agreement that the reliability and validity of available measures are sufficient to dispel all doubts. The problem of indicators or measurement is all the more difficult where occupational mobility surveys are concerned. In the present case where the data were collected by a government agency, there was no attempt to gather data on genetic skills, and measures of extra-occupational and intra-occupational learned skills were crude. Thus, indicators of extra-occupational learned skills were limited to respondents' reports of attained level of education and number of years of education, making it impossible to make finer distinctions relating to academic performance or to distinguish between cognitive and affective factors as suggested by Gintis (1971). Similarly, information relating to occupational experience was limited to the respondent's occupation on entering the labour force, and for subsequent occuaptional locations, those in 1963 and in 1973, to participation in apprenticeship training, and to some information relating to years of labour force participation. As the occupational information is expressed in terms of relatively broad occupational categories or is transformed to Blishen values, the contribution of any occupational experience to a person's skills can be determined only if one is prepared to accept broad assumptions. Although indicators of these skills remain crude, making interpretation difficult, they appear to represent the present state of the art (see, for example, Blau and Duncan, 1967:187, 402; Kelley, 1973-482) and are used in the present analysis because they have substantive interest and raise important issues in the analysis of occupational attainment and mobility.

Allowing for these limitations in the data, the reported $r = .62$ for education and occupation on entry into the labour force may now be considered in terms of technical and employer rationality. As interest is on first occupation, no occupational experience is assumed and the formal model may be reduced as follows:

First occupation = genetic skills +
    extra-occupational learned skills

and as the data relate only to extra-occupational learned skills, this proposition must be expressed as

First occupation = education.

However, such a formulation does not distinguish between the perspectives of technical and employer rationality as it does not reflect the difference in the "measurement" of occupations that is at the heart of the controversy. That is, whether occupations represent relatively stable technically-determined skills or fluctuating employer-determined skills. The problem would be less severe (1) if models representing different degrees of rationality could be constructed and (2) if an objective measure of occupational skill could be used in testing the models.[14]

As a response to the first condition, it seems useful to construct models in terms of different conditions of the skill market, that is, when the supply and demand for skills are balanced or unbalanced. Thus, if an exactly balanced skill market is assumed, it may be argued that technical and employer rationality would coincide. In other words, if the appropriate skills required for employment are available, an employer would gain no advantage by inflating or deflating the skill criteria for entry into the occupation. However, when there is an imbalance between supply and demand, it may be expected that employer rationality might displace technical rationality.

In a market in which there are as many applicants with high as with low educational qualifications but in which there are unequal occupational opportunities, and assuming that the better educated would have priority, employers might be expected to upgrade occupational criteria. In a market where there are as many opportunities for employment in high-skill as in low-skill occupations but where there are fewer with high education than with low education, employer rationality would have the effect of downgrading skill criteria. In each situation of imbalance, the match between acquired and required skills, anticipated by technical rationality, would be weakened, although it may be assumed to be operative to some degree.

It is possible to provide models representing the three market conditions described above. To begin, these market conditions will be illustrated by models portrayed in the form of a four-celled matrix achieved by dichotomizing the categories of education and occupation. Thus, a model (See Table 4.4, Model One) may depict a situation where the supply of persons who have at least completed high school is equal to that of non-graduates and the demand for high-skill occupations equals that of low-skill occupations. If technical rationality is the wholly operative principle of allocation, all those with higher education would find employment in the higher-skill occupations and all those with lower education in the lower-skill occupations. The other two models describe the situation where there is an unbalanced skill market where employers may upgrade or downgrade occupations rather than conform to the dictates of technical rationality. While these situations are clearly artificial, they do portray what can happen where persons are rationally allocated to occupations but where demand and supply are in disequilibrium.

As the balanced market model yields an $r = 1.00$, it is assumed that this value also represents complete technical rationality, while values less than unity represent departures from technical rationality.[15]

It is possible to portray a fully rational distribution in a larger matrix following the same procedure used for the simple models: by allocating those with the highest education to the highest-skill occupation until the supply is exhausted and then to those with the next-highest educational level and so on. Table 4.5 shows the results of such a procedure using the observed marginals relating to a cross-tabulation of first occupation by education.[16] The model provides a basis for comparison with the observed bivariate distributions. As a means of evaluating observed correlation coefficients, it may be helpful to consider what the maximum correlation coefficient would be under conditions of technical rationality. Under this principle, initial occupation should be fully determined

TABLE 4:4 — Three Models of the Relationship of Education and Occupational Status

MODEL ONE
Occupational skill level

	High	Low	
Complete high school or higher	50	—	50
Incomplete high school or lower	—	50	50
	50	50	100

EDUCATION (Model One)

MODEL TWO
Occupational skill level

	High	Low	
Complete high school or higher	30	0	30
Incomplete high school or lower	20	50	70
	50	50	100

EDUCATION (Model Two)

MODEL THREE
Occupational skill level

	High	Low	
Complete high school or higher	30	20	50
Incomplete high school or lower	0	50	50
	30	70	100

EDUCATION (Model Three)

by attained education, assuming that extra-occupational learned skills are measured by attained education and that measurement error is negligible. However, a correlation equal to unity could only result where frequencies on the values of each variable are equal so that there can be a perfect match between the measured values of the two variables. It is, therefore, useful to determine the effect of specific marginal distributions on the maximum value of the correlation coefficients, assuming, of course, technical rationality. Using observed margins, the Pearson correlation coefficient, based on this redistribution is .96. This means that the observed marginals, in this instance, account for more than 7.5 per cent of the variance.[17] More important, the model provides evidence that the state of the skill market,[18] described in terms of the marginal distributions for education and occupations, exerts some influence on the relations between the two variables. Thus, there is some reason for suggesting that a given state of the market might favour technical rationality or employer rationality as defined above.

It is also possible to test, using the observed data, models corresponding to the equal supply-demand market and to unequal market conditions. To do so a procedure is used which, while preserving the core relationships between the variables, provides estimates of cell frequencies on the basis of marginal distributions set as required (Deming, 1964:96-127). In short, the procedure takes account of the effect of marginals.

Before discussing the results of this operation, however, it is necessary to assess the occupational data as an objective indicator of skills. Ideally, this condition could be met if our occupational data could be directly related to some measures of skill requirements such as those developed by the U.S. Department of Labour (1956, 1966; Fine, 1968) and also developed, on the basis of similar procedures, for the occupations listed in the Canadian Classification and Dictionary of Occupations (Canada, 1971 and 1973). Although expert judgments of the educational skills required for occupations may not be completely independent of employer hiring practices, these two scales, representing levels of skills acquired through general education (GED) and through special vocational preparation (SVP),[19] are widely accepted as objective measures of the training requirements of occupations (see, for example, Berg, 1971:40-60).

However, as the occupational data used in this analysis were available only as coded in terms of Blishen values or in terms of the project classification, it was necessary to approach the problem somewhat differently. As the project classification was based on four-digit 1971 Census of Canada codes which, in turn, are based on CCDO codes,

TABLE 4:5 — Rational Model

Level of education*		Occupations							
	Self-Employed Professional	Employed Professional	High Managerial	Semi-Professional	Technical	Middle Managerial	Supervisor	Foreman
0								
1								
2								
3								
4								
5								
6		373	60	193	271	182	244	233
7		382		321				
8		173						
9	159							
Total	159	928	60	514	271	182	244	233

TABLE 4:5 — Rational Model (Continued)

Level of education*	Skilled White-Collar	Skilled Craftsmen	Semi-Skilled White-Collar	Semi-Skilled Craftsmen	Unskilled White-Collar	Labourer	Farm Labourer	Total
0							109	109
1						630	1,090	1,720
2					87	1,802		1,889
3			332	2,199	502			3,033
4		1,367	1,100					2,467
5	439	1,004						1,443
6	207							1,330
7								754
8								382
9								332
Total	646	2,371	1,432	2,199	589	2,432	1,199	13,459

*For descriptive labels corresponding to codes, see Table 4:1.
†Excludes Farm Owners
Males, 25-64† years of age

average GED and SVP values were computed for each category.[20] When occupation, ordered by average GED values, was correlated with education, the correlation coefficient increased by .025 over the correlation coefficient for education and occupation, based on the arbitrary order of the project classification. This small difference suggests that the use of the project classification as a scale of required skills conforms satisfactorily to an order assumed to be independent of employer influence[21] and that correlations between education and first occupation, to the extent that they depart from unity, may be interpreted as evidence of the operation of influences other than technical rationality on occupational status on entry to the labour force.

With the objectivity of the occupational classification as an ordered distribution of skills established, it is appropriate to interpret in terms of

TABLE 4:6 — First Occupation by Education: Observed Frequencies Males, 25-64 years

| Level of Education[1] | Occupation* | | | | |
	PMT	WC	BC	F	Total
Elementary	30	356	2,569	1,043	3,998
High School	265	1,589	3,300	505	5,659
Post-Secondary	530	876	1,284	130	2,820
Academic/					
Professional	1,107	269	80	11	1,468
Total	1,932	3,090	7,233	1,689	13,945

Gamma	.682	
Somer's D	.456	signs reversed
Pearson's r	.586*	

[1] Elementary   Levels 0, 1, 2
  High school   Levels 3, 4
  Post-secondary   Levels 5, 6
  Academic/
    professional   Levels 7, 8, 9

[2] PMT (professional, managerial, technical) = self-employed and employed professional, high managerial, semi-professional and technical occupations.
  WC (white-collar) = middle managerial, supervisory, skilled, semi-skilled and unskilled white-collar occupations.
  BC (blue-collar) = foremen, skilled and semi-skilled craftsmen and labourers.
  F (Farm) = farm owners, farm labourers.
* ≤ .001

technical and employer rationality the results of comparing the observed matrix for education and first occupation to those based on adjusted marginals which reflect different states of the skill market. Although the analysis is concerned with the 10 x 15 matrix for education and occupation, the effects of the adjustment may be easier to grasp if illustrated by tabulations based on a simplified classification of education and occupation.

While the observed association between education and occupation is clearly evident (see Table 4.6), the effect of a market, in which employment opportunities are equal for occupations at all skill levels and for which there is an equal supply of applicants from all educational levels, is to improve the fit between education and occupation (Table 4.7). Thus those with elementary schooling are less likely to be employed in higher-level occupations while for those with post-secondary education, employment opportunities increase for white-collar and decrease for blue-collar occupations.

Before reporting the results of the adjustments of the large matrix, some comments on the categories used are in order. The ten levels of education and the fifteen-category occupational classification are used so

TABLE 4:7 — First Occupation by Education: Adjusted to Equal Marginal Frequencies, Males, 25-64 years

Level of Education*	Occupation*				
	PMT	WC	BC	F	Total
Elementary	21	275	1,043	2,025	3,364
High School	167	1,127	1,229	840	3,363
Post-Secondary	687	1,280	985	412	3,364
Academic/ Professional	2,489	681	106	87	3,363
Total	3,364	3,363	3,363	3,364	13,454‡

Gamma .763 ⎫
Somer's D .614 ⎬ signs reversed
Pearson r .697† ⎭

* See Table 4-6 for coding details.
† < .001.
‡ Unweighted N=12745.

Whether significance levels should be reported for adjusted data is debatable. If the results of adjustment are viewed as artificial, it would be inappropriate to report significance levels. However, as the adjusted data are based on information obtained from a sample of "real" respondents, there is an argument for reporting on significance.

that variation in the distributions of these measures could be maximized within the limits of the classification systems developed for the analysis. Given the reduction of thousands of occupations to fifteen classes and of various kinds of educational programs to ten levels, only a loose fit can be expected between these sets of categories. Actually, a comparison of average GED values and average educational levels[22] for each occupational class indicates that they correspond reasonably well. As shown in Table 4.8, the mean GED for self-employed professionals is 5.7, equivalent to over sixteen years of schooling, while the mean *level* of education is 7.9, equivalent to professional education. Similarly, the

TABLE 4:8 — Project Occupational Categories: Mean GED and Mean Level of Education

Occupational Category	GED	Level of Education
Self-employed professional	5.7	7.9
Employed professional	5.4	6.7
High managerial	5.1	5.8
Semi-professional	4.6	5.7
Technician	3.8	4.7
Middle managerial	4.5	4.7
Supervisor	3.7	3.9
Foreman	3.5	3.5
Skilled white-collar	3.8	4.2
Skilled craftsman	3.2	3.1
Semi-skilled white-collar	3.0	3.5
Semi-skilled craftsman	2.6	2.7
Unskilled white-collar	2.7	3.7
Labourer	1.8	2.5

EQUIVALENCE KEY

Years of Education	= GED =	Level of Education
17 and over	6	7, 8, 9
13-16	5	5, 6, 7
11-12	4	4
9-10	3	3
7- 8	2	2
up to 6	1	1
—	—	0

mean GED for labourer is equivalent to less than complete elementary schooling while the mean level of education falls between completed elementary school and some high school. The correspondence for the other occupational categories may be assessed by comparing the two means in relation to the equivalence key shown in Table 4.8.

While the possibilities for adjusting the marignals of the matrix may be infinite, the choice of equal proportions in the categories, although not realistic, did permit portrayal of a market where there were equal numbers of persons of differing educational qualifications to fill equal numbers of jobs differing in terms of required skills. While a model could have been constructed by assuming some distribution of unequal proportions in both sets of categories which conforms to a "realistic" balanced market, assuming equal proportions produced a balanced model and made it unnecessary to decide what distribution was most "realistic." Although a model with equal sets of educational and occupational categories would portray a condition where the number of qualified applicants was equal to the number of jobs that correspond in skill levels, it was judged unsatisfactory to expand the educational categories to fifteen or to reduce the occupational categories to ten. The models based on the four-category classifications of education and occupation, however, portray such conditions.

The adjustment of the large matrix produces a similar effect (See Table 4.9) as that reported for the collapsed matrix. What the comparison reveals may be more easily seen by considering persons with some post-secondary education (levels 5 and 6).[23] As the marginal percentages of these categories are relatively unchanged by the adjustment, any difference between expected and observed percentages may be interpreted as a consequence of the simulated change in occupational opportunity. Thus, it may be seen that in a balanced skill market, fewer persons who have obtained some post-secondary education would be expected to be employed in the lower-skill occupations, while more would be expected to find employment in the higher-skill occupations. As the adjustment results in increased demand for most occupational categories, expected percentages for all educational groups are generally higher in most occupational categories, while decreases are generally observed for employed professionals, skilled and semi-skilled craftsmen, semi-skilled white-collar occupations and labourers. On the whole, a marked expansion in opportunities for higher-skilled employment results in gains for most educational levels. At certain educational levels, such as those representing persons with higher academic degrees (Level 9) or those who did not complete high school (Level 3), a balanced market results in an increase and decrease, respectively, of those shares

TABLE 4:9 — First Occupation by Education: Differences* Between Adjusted and Observed Outflow Percentage Distributions

Level of Education†	Self-Employed Professional	Employed Professional	High Managerial	Semi-Profes-sional	Technical	Middle Managerial	Supervisor	Foreman
0	0.0	0.0	0.0	0.0	8.1	0.0	0.0	0.0
1	0.0	0.0	0.0	0.5	0.4	0.0	7.2	11.2
2	0.0	0.1	1.2	1.6	2.3	4.0	5.2	10.8
3	0.0	0.0	0.6	1.5	4.8	3.8	8.1	9.8
4	0.0	− 0.5	2.8	2.5	5.9	7.2	8.6	6.0
5	0.0	− 0.6	3.6	4.7	4.8	4.8	9.0	6.2
6	0.2	− 5.7	7.4	1.3	9.1	10.0	5.6	4.1
7	0.8	−25.7	13.1	0.2	3.9	11.7	3.8	2.6
8	21.6	−23.7	7.6	−2.2	0.0	3.1	0.6	0.4
9	3.1	−36.6	21.5	0.7	4.9	5.0	2.4	1.4
Total	1.2(1) 6.7(2)	6.9 6.7	0.4 6.7	3.8 6.7	2.0 6.7	1.4 6.7	1.8 6.7	1.7 6.7

Level of Education†	Skilled White-Collar	Skilled Craftsman	Semi-Skilled White-Collar	Semi-Skilled Craftsman	Unskilled White-Collar	Labourer	Farm Labourer	Total
0	3.2	-2.3	2.9	-3.6	0.0	-12.0	3.7	0.8[1] / 10.0[2]
1	2.1	-4.9	1.6	-9.5	7.8	-14.4	-1.9	12.8 / 10.0
2	1.7	-7.3	2.5	-9.2	6.7	-15.2	-4.2	14.0 / 10.0
3	3.2	-10.2	0.8	-11.7	8.6	-16.0	-3.3	22.5 / 10.0
4	4.6	-15.1	-4.5	-10.5	5.9	-11.0	-1.9	18.3 / 10.0
5	5.4	-20.2	-2.3	-9.9	5.0	-8.7	-1.9	10.7 / 10.0
6	0.2	-11.1	-7.2	-6.6	0.8	-6.5	-1.7	9.9 / 10.0
7	-0.7	-2.2	-3.7	-1.5	0.1	-1.8	-0.6	5.6 / 10.0
8	-3.0	-0.7	-1.5	-1.2	-0.5	0.0	-0.7	2.8 / 10.0
9	-0.2	-0.3	-1.0	-0.7	0.8	0.0	-0.2	2.5 / 10.0
Total	4.8 / 6.7	17.6 / 6.7	10.6 / 6.7	16.3 / 6.7	4.4 / 6.7	18.1 / 6.7	8.9 / 6.7	100.0 / 100.0

N = 13,459 Males, 25-64 years of age.
1 — Observed Percentage
2 — Adjusted Percentage

* Cell Entries = Adjusted % − Observed %
† For descriptive labels corresponding to codes, see Table 4-1.

of the occupational opportunities whose skill levels are roughly appropriate rather than in an increased inconsistency between educational level and required skills. As a joint consequence of the higher supply of males with M.A.'s and Ph.D.'s and a higher demand from high-skilled occupations, more persons from this educational level would be expected to find employment in high-skilled occupations. Employed professionals represent an anomaly due, presumably, to the slight lessening of demand. Although the percentage of those who did not complete high school decreases, persons at this level could expect to make modest gains among the higher-skill occupations as a consequence of increased demand. Although the overall change for those who have not completed high school and those who have attained higher degrees is similar, Indexes of Dissimilarity for observed and adjusted distributions are equal to 39.0 and 41.2, respectively, the pattern of differences between expected and observed occupational distributions suggests that the marginal adjustments reflect greater technical rationality than the observed distribution.

A comparison of the observed relationship between education and first occupation and those resulting from the three models is more easily grasped when the results are expressed as standard measures of association. Moreover, according to previous arguments, the values for the observed relationship and the three models, as shown in Table 4.10, may be interpreted, in the degree they depart from unity, as departures from technical rationality. In these terms, the greatest departure from technical rationality is observed for the model representing the equal availability of persons with different levels of education.[24]

Essentially, this model represents the situation where there are fewer

TABLE 4:10 — First Occupation* by Education

Model	Gamma	Somer's D	r
Observed	.500	.443	.640†
Equal supply	.497	.440	.604†
Equal demand	.548	.515	.642†
Equal supply and demand	.594	.560	.711†
Fully rational	1.000	.955	.961†

N = 13,459 Males, 25-64 years of age.
*Excludes farm owners
†Level of significance ⩽ .001

lower-educated persons to fill a larger proportion of lower-skilled occupations and higher proportions of higher-educated but without any increase in the relatively low percentages of higher-skilled occupations. In general, the model allows a considerable opportunity for employer rationality, assumed to be biased towards selection of the better-educated, to operate. The result is underemployment, from a skill perspective, of the better-educated, and overemployment of the less-educated (see Table 4.A2).

By contrast, the model which depicts equal demand for all occupational categories but leaves supply as observed yields a higher correlation which may be interpreted as representing an increased influence of technical rationality. In this model, the percentage of high-skill occupations increases substantially except in the case of employed professionals, and the percentages distributed among the lower-skilled occupations decrease substantially (Table 4.A3). Thus, as there would be little advantage in displacing technical by employer rationality, the smaller percentage of higher-educated persons means that they may more easily find first occupations commensurate with their education. At the same time, those with lower educational attainment move upwards to occupations ordinarily demanding higher skills.

Finally, the model which depicts equality in supply and demand, where educational attainment levels and categories of occupational demand are both equal, yields the highest correlation, and compared to the equal supply model reveals an increase of approximately eleven points. Thus, the market conditions depicted by this model seem more favourable for the operation of technical rationality and less favourable for employer rationality.

The magnitude of the observed correlation between education and occupation is similar to that for the model representing equal demand. Although it may be concluded that the influence of technical rationality is more apparent than in the equal supply model, the observed correlation falls short of the maximum correlation of .96, suggesting that technical rationality is operative only to a moderate extent as a distributive principle in relation to occupation on entry into the labour force. Indeed, the present analysis suggests that technical rationality and employer rationality may operate simultaneously to influence occupational distribution although each is differentially influenced by skill market conditions. Furthermore, the analysis suggests that a distribution fully determined by technical rationality alone requires conditions unlikely to be realized in contemporary society: a balance between the supply and demand for skills *and* the disappearance of particularistic and ascriptive criteria in relation to occupational allocation.

Current Occupation: The Influence of Education and Experience

In the analysis of the occupational distribution of labour force entrants, it is reasonable to assume that the appropriate skills relating to the available occupational opportunities are acquired mainly through formal education. Such an assumption would be unrealistic, however, in analyses of occupational attainment at later career stages. This means that the analysis of post-labour force entry occupational attainment must, at some point, abandon bivariate models in favour of multivariate models.

The basis of the analysis of first occupation distribution was the concept of skill. Thus, occupations were observed as sets of required skills and labour force entrants as possessors of occupationally relevant skills, and it was assumed that the distribution of persons into occupational categories was to be explained by a systematic relationship between required and acquired skills. This formulation, allowing for two interpretations of the relationship, was evaluated in terms of self-reported data on education and occupation which were classified in terms of categorical schemes developed in the research. When the analysis shifts to later career stages, in this instance current occupation (1973), it is still possible to base the analysis on the concept of skill but it is necessary to formulate a more complex model. Before introducing such a model, however, some results of the zero-order relationship between current occupation and education are reported.

The Relationship Between Education and Current Occupation

Although education is likely to have its strongest effect when a person enters the labour force for the first time, it may also have a persistent effect on occupational allocation. Moreover, the balance of education and experience is likely to vary for occupations. Thus, for certain professional occupations, no amount of experience can replace a professional degree as a means of entry to the occupation. At other levels, it is realistic to expect that experience can overcome formal educational deficiencies. Given the possibility that education can have a persistent influence on an occupational career, it may be useful to know something about the gross or zero-order association between education and current occupational status before the net effects of education are reported.

On the whole, the relationship between current occupation and education is much the same as its relationship to first occupation. Thus, education appears to have as much influence, as evaluated by Pearson correlation coefficients, on current occupation as it has on first occupation and is almost as influential as first occupation on current occupation. However, the relationship between education and current occupation diminishes when first occupation is controlled, the partial correlation being 0.39. But it is still sufficiently large, in comparison to the partial of .33 between first occupation and current occupation, to support the expectation that education is a persistent influence on occupational allocation. Together, education and first occupation account for 40 per cent of the variance in current occupational status.[25]

As the zero-order relationship between education and current occupation is not substantially different from that between education and first occupation, there is little point in reporting further detailed results. Nonetheless, some findings arising from analysis of the full matrix and from the labour market models are worth reporting.

Among the details revealed by the full matrix (Table 4.A4), it is worth noting that sizable percentages of those reporting no formal education are located in skilled and semi-skilled crafts, even though the heaviest concentration, as might be anticipated, is in the lower occupational categories. Although 70 per cent of those reporting some high school are currently employed as skilled craftsmen or below, about 30 per cent found employment in occupations normally demanding higher levels of education (if the category of foreman is removed, the percentage is about equal to 21 per cent). Similarly, although a considerable majority of those reporting higher education, such as having completed university, are currently employed in higher occupations, some of the higher educated are employed in lower skill occupations.

As the interpretation of the relationship between education and first occupation under varying market conditions also applies to the relationship between education and current occupation, only a few comments on the summary measures reported in Table 4.11 are necessary. Although the results for the two relationships are similar, it may be observed that for current occupation, the Pearson correlation for the condition of equal supply is higher than that for equal demand. It might be expected that technical rationality would be, as in the case of first occupation, least operative where there are equal proportions of persons available at all educational levels but unequal opportunities for occupational levels. However, the relationship between education and occupation under the condition of equal supply is likely modified as a consequence of the attenuated relationship of education to current occupation.

TABLE 4:11 — Current Occupation* by Education

Model	Gamma	Somer's D	r
Observed	.502	.453	.623†
Equal supply	.539	.487	.649†
Equal demand	.520	.488	.615†
Equal supply and demand	.589	.555	.707†
Fully rational	1.000	.960	.975†

N = 12,793 Males, 25-64 years of age; unweighted N = 11,862
*Excludes Farm Owners.
†Level of significance ≤ .001

The summary measures presented in tables 4.10 and 4.11 nevertheless are very similar, indicating that technical rationality is more influential on current occupational location, as it is on first occupation, when opportunities and skill levels are jointly equalized.

The Relationship between Current Occupation and First Occupation

In the model to be presented below, occupational experience is emphasized as an important source of skills relevant to current occupational status. As first occupational status occupies such a prominent place in the model, it seems justifiable, to report some findings resulting from a bivariate analysis of the relationship between first and current occupations.

If technical rationality is assumed to be the major influence on current occupational allocation and if first occupation is assumed to allow the acquisition of new skills or the improvement of existing skills, a positive relationship between first and current occupation may be expected. It is therefore no surprise to find a correlation of .54 (Table 4.12) between these two measures, nor to find that intra-generational transition is marked by a higher degree of stability[26] than inter-generational transition. Even so, almost two-thirds of males aged 25-64 years moved to an occupational category which differs from that at the time of initial entry into the labour force. Of this total mobility, about one-third was accounted for by differences in the marginal distributions for first and current occupational status.

Although a majority of respondents did, in fact, change occupational categories, there was considerable variation among first occupation

TABLE 4:12 — Full and Reduced Models of Occupational Attainment: Path Coefficients*

Dependent	1963 Occupation	First Occupation	Respondent's Education	No. of Siblings	Father's Occupation	Father's Education	R^2
First Occupation	—	—	.522²	-.001	.099²	.003	.314²
First Occupation	—	—	.523	—	.100	—	.314²
1963 Occupation	—	.420²	.274¹	-.016	.085¹	.009	.429²
1963 Occupation	—	.432²	.302²	—	—	—	.422²
Respondent's Current Occupation	.561²	.077²	.207²	.001	.020¹	.022¹	.582²
Respondent's Current Occupation	.565²	.079²	.220²	—	—	—	.581²
Respondent's Current Occupation	.598²	—	.246²	—	—	—	.577²
Respondent's Current Occupation	—	.313²	.360²	-.008	.068²	.027 ·	.402²
Respondent's Current Occupation	—	.323²	.391²	—	—	—	.396²
$\bar{X}$ 7.654	7.149	5.795	10.579	4.579	6.325	7.282	
s.d. 3.973	3.933	3.940	3.734	3.230	3.203	3.975	

TABLE 4:12 (Continued)

ZERO-ORDER COEFFICIENTS

	1963 Occupation	First Occupation	Respondents Education	No. of Siblings	Father's Occupation	Father's Education	R^2
Respondent's Current Occupation	.731	.539	.569	-.198	.264	.327	
1963 Occupation		.599	.540	-.194	.277	.307	
First Occupation			.552	-.183	.253	.299	
Respondent's Education				-.324	.292	.491	
No. of Siblings					-.122	-.280	
Father's Occupation						.395	

N = 7,890 Males, aged 25-64 years; unweighted N = 7,598
*Estimates excluding 1973 occupation are reported in Table 4:A8 and those based on Blishen values for occupational data in Table 4:A9.
[1] $\leqslant$ .01
[2] $\leqslant$ .001

origins and the percentage found in the modal current occupation destinations. Thus, supervisor, the most frequent current status destination for those entering the labour force in unskilled white-collar occupations, claims 15 per cent of their outflow (Table 4.A5), while over 90 per cent of those beginning as self-employed professionals were currently employed in that occupational category. In contrast to inter-generational transition, the stability destination was the modal destination for all origins except unskilled white-collar and farm labourer origins. However, the percentages in these modal destination categories range from 20.6 per cent (semi-skilled white-collar origins) to 90.2 per cent (self-employed professional origins). A majority of males beginning employment as self-employed professionals, employed professionals, high-level managers, and semi-professionals are currently employed in the same category, while between 33 per cent and 49 per cent of those beginning as technicians, mid-level managers, supervisors, foremen, skilled craftsmen, farmers and labourers are currently employed in the same occupational category. Although those who began employment in semi-skilled white-collar occupations had the smallest percentage continuing, over 20 per cent were currently employed in that category. In short, a man entering the labour force at a particular occupational level was most likely to be currently employed at that same level than at any other specific occupational level. However, the chance that such a man would be currently employed at a level other than his entry level varied with the level of his entry occupation. Although a majority of men moved from one level to another, the movement was widely dispersed among destinations. Thus, only 21 of the 240 current destinations, other than the stability destinations, accounted for 10 per cent or more of those employed in a given first occupation.

As the rank order of the percentage of sons found in stability destinations closely resembles the rank order of the occupational categories,[27] stability in the transition from first to current occupation location is seen to be closely related to the income, education, and prestige levels of first occupations. For those who did change from first to current occupations, employed professionals, skilled craftsmen, and supervisors were prominent among the higher ranking[28] destination categories: employed professionals for those beginning as high-level managers, semi-professionals, technicians and skilled white-collar workers; supervisors for those beginning as skilled, semi-skilled or unskilled white-collar workers; and skilled craftsmen for those beginning as foreman, semi-skilled craftsmen, labourers and farm labourers. Finally, 10 per cent or more of those beginning employment as farmers, semi-skilled craftsmen, unskilled white-collar workers and farm labourers are currently employed as labourers.

The transition from initial to current status is marked, on the basis of the 10 per cent criterion, by the impermeability of the white-collar/blue-collar boundary as well as by a strong tendency for those whose initial employment was in farming occupations to move to blue-collar occupations.

A Multivariate Model of Occupational Allocation

Although bivariate analyses of the relationship of education and of initial occupational experience to current occupational status contribute to an understanding of these relationships, it is necessary to pursue the analysis in a form which brings both these influences as well as other known major influences into the model. As a beginning the conventional status attainment model, as presented in the previous chapter, is utilized but this model will be modified as necessary in relation to theoretical considerations.

Stated in relation to skill, the model can be described in these terms:

Required skill = formally acquired skill +
occupationally acquired skill
+ social origins

and could be tested, for example, by

Current occupation = 1963 occupation +
first occupation + education +
father's occupation +
father's education +
number of siblings.

While it may be observed that this model, as it concerns available measures of formally and occupationally required skills, is subject to the ambiguity in interpretation discussed earlier — namely, the relative influence of technical and employer rationality — the previous analysis should allow the conclusion that both these principles are operative. Consequently, the present analysis turns from that problem of interpretation to consider the relevant effects of formally and occupationally acquired skills in the context of issues which concern the reliability of the available indicators for the concepts of the model as expressed above.

The analysis begins, in terms of the conventional status attainment model, by estimating the effects of selected variables on first occupation, with the emphasis on education as an indicator of formally acquired skills. As the analysis proceeds, the effects of education and occupational experience, with first and subsequent occupational status as indicators of

occupationally acquired skills, on occupational status attainment subsequent to labour force entry will be estimated. Finally, the possibility of
analysis using multiple indicators for all variables in the model will be
considered.

Although there is a strong association between education and first and
subsequent occupational statuses, it has been shown in Chapter 3 that
social origin[29] has a substantial direct effect on educational attainment[30]
and also exerts an effect, although mostly indirectly, on occupational
attainment. Thus, in the status attainment model for this sample, social
origin accounts for about 30 per cent of the variance in educational
attainment. However, where first occupation is concerned, the direct
effects of social origin are greatly reduced and education becomes the
dominant influence exerting a direct effect and mediating origin effects.
Thus, for the present analysis, which is mainly concerned with the 1963
occupation and current occupation, social origin variables may be safely
ignored.[31] Consequently, a simpler model than the basic model may be
used to identify direct influences on 1963 occupation. Thus, estimates
with several models, as reported in Table 4.12, indicate that

1963 occupation = education + first occupation

accounts for only a slightly smaller amount of variance[32] than the full
model.[33] The model reveals, moreover, that first occupation exerts a
greater direct effect than education on a person's intermediate
occupational status. Thus, the pattern as revealed so far indicates that a
person's educational attainment is the most important influence on entry
into the labour force but that the point of entry into the labour force, as
expressed in terms of occupational status, exerts the greater direct
influence on post-entry, non-current occupational status. Even so, it is
apparent that education continues to exert a relatively strong effect at
this intermediate career stage,[34] as well as a substantial effect (Table
4.13) which is mediated by first occupation. As education and 1963
occupation, among all the variables included in the model, account for
most of the variance in current occupational attainment, education can
be interpreted as exerting a persistent influence throughout occupational careers.

The concentional occupational attainment model (Duncan, Featherman and Duncan, 1972), enriched by 1963 occupation, used to identify
influences operating on current (1973) occupation, accounts for 58 per
cent of the variance in current occupational attainment (Table 4.12),[35] an
improvement of 18 per cent over the conventional model. If the
convention of dropping variables whose coefficient is less than .10 is
followed, an extremely truncated model survives: respondents' educa-

TABLE 4:13 — Decomposition[1] of Path Coefficients

		Indirect Effects via Respondent's			
Dependent First Occupation Independent Variables	Total Effect	Education	First Occupation	1963 Occupation	Direct
Father's Occupation	.158	.059			.099
No. of Siblings	−.105	−.104			−.001
Father's Education	.206	.203			.003
Respondent's Education	.522				.522
Dependent *1963 Occupation* Father's					
Occupation	.182	.055	.042		.085
No. of Siblings	−.115	−.099	.000		−.016
Father's Education	.203	.192	.002		.009
Respondent's Education	.493		.219		.274
First Occupation	.420				.420
Dependent *Respondent's Current* *Occupation* Father's					
Occupation	.158	.059	.031	.048	.020
No. of Siblings	−.113	−.105	.000	−.009	.001
Father's Education	.232	.204	.001	.005	.022
Respondent's Education	.524		.164	.153	.207
First Occupation	.313			.236	.077
1963 Occupation	.561				.561

N = 7,890 Males, aged 25-64 years.
[1]See Alwin and Hauser (1975).

tion and 1963 occupation with estimated path coefficients of .25 and .60, respectively. Nonetheless, as the full model accounts for only an additional 0.5 per cent of the variance, there is evidence that a person's education and 1963 occupation have, in comparison to other variables thought to be important, a very substantial direct influence in determining 1973 occupation. Similarly, education and first occupation account for 40 per cent of the variance when social origin variables are dropped from the conventional model. As well as having a persistent effect on current occupational status, education's relative contribution is substantial, amounting to 40 per cent of that of experience as reflected by 1963 occupational location.[36] It is noteworthy that education exerts a direct effect slightly less than three times that of first occupation. If occupation is regarded as an indicator of occupationally acquired skills, then it would appear that these are skills accumulated throughout a career but which exert their influence on current occupational status most strongly at later career stages. Thus, as may be seen from Table 4.13, the direct effect of 1963 occupation is much stronger than any of the other variables in the model and it mediates 75 per cent of the effect of first occupation,[37] and 29 per cent of the effect of education.

A Two-Indicator Model of Occupational Attainment

Although the presentation of a multivariate model of occupational allocation has taken the form of conventional occupational status attainment models, these models are seen as expressions of a more abstract theoretical model focused on the concept of skill. Given the abstract nature of this model, it may be unfair to test it on the basis of single indicators of its concepts.[38] Instead the use of multiple indicators to capture the complex reality of status attainment might provide a more appropriate test of the model.[39] In the present instance, this conclusion was reinforced by evidence of the indirect effects of first occupation, noted above, as well as by concern over the weaknesses in the available indicators.

Ideally, construction of a multiple indicator model should be completed before decisions concerning the required data are made. However, in the present instance, the conceptual perspective discussed above was not formulated when decisions concerning the required data were taken. Nevertheless, it seemed useful, if only for heuristic purposes, to attempt to construct a two-indicator model. Two indicators can be identified for each unmeasured variable in the model. As shown in the diagram, required skills, formally acquired skills, and occupationally acquired skills designate the unmeasured variables; the occupational classification categories for first and 1963 occupations designate the measures for occupationally acquired skills; level of education, a ten-category classification, and years of education designate the measures for formally acquired skills; and 1973 occupation, coded in occupational classification categories and by Blishen values, designate the measures for required skills.

| Concepts | required skills | formally acquired skills | occupationally acquired skills |

Indicators	current occupation (project categories)	current occupation (Blishen)	level of education	years of education	first occupation	1963 occupation

To test the model, it is necessary to show that the observed variables are indeed indicators of the unobserved variables. To do so requires estimates of the correlations between the unobserved variables and their empirical indicators. These estimates can be obtained from the correlations of the empirical indicators (see Blalock, 1969; Costner, 1969; Duncan, 1972; Hauser and Goldberger, 1971; and Mayer and Younger, 1974).[40] The test is whether or not there is a single common source of variation for the first set of empirical indicators (for example, the required skills set) and another distinct single common source of variation for the second set (for example, the acquired skills set). In Costner's term (1969:251), the test determines if rX_iY_j is free from "differential bias," where X_i and Y_j are indicators, respectively, of unobserved variables X' and Y'. If differential bias is present, the observed variables are deemed to be inadequate indicators of the unobserved variables. On the basis of a procedure proposed by Mayer and Younger (1974:200-202) as an improvement over other available procedures, differential bias was found to be absent for the relationships between indicators of formally acquired skills and indicators of required skills but not for the relationships of indicators of formally acquired skills and occupationally acquired skills or for the relationships of indicators of occupationally acquired skills and required skills.[41] As the indicators for the unobserved variables were not specified prior to data gathering, it is not surprising that the estimates of the relationship between unobserved variables and their indicators only partly meet the test of adequacy. However, as the estimates were shown to be adequate, using Costner's (1969) admittedly weaker test,[42] it seemed worthwhile to use them to estimate the relationship between the unobserved variables since the main objective of the analysis is to demonstrate its usefulness in developing an improved explanation of occupational status attainment.

The estimated correlations were used to estimate path coefficients for the two-indicator model. The result (Table 4.14) suggests that a two-indicator model could improve prediction of current occupation.[43] In the present instance, the two-indicator model accounts for 13.8 per cent more of the variance[44] than the comparable one-indicator model (Table 4.12, line 5), using project classification categories as measures of occupationally acquired skill. Moreover, the two-indicator model may

TABLE 4:14 — Two-Indicator Reduced Models of Occupational Attainment

Dependent	Occupationally acquired skills	Formally acquired skills	R^2
Required skills	.746	.126	.719

All coefficients significant at .001 level or beyond.
N = 8,599 Males, 25-64 years of age.

ZERO-ORDER COEFFICIENTS*

	Occupationally acquired skills	Required skills
Formally acquired skills	.776	.705
Occupationally acquired skills		.844

TWO-INDICATOR REDUCED MODELS

Excluding respondents whose 1963 occupation = 1973 occupation

Dependent	Occupationally acquired skills	Formally acquired skills	R^2
Required skills	.243	.461	.429

All coefficients significant at .001 level or beyond.
N = 3,458 Males, 25-64 years of age.

provide a better estimate of the relative influence of the two skill types on current occupational location. A comparison of the one-indicator and two-indicator models, in the present instance, reveals that the influence of occupationally acquired skill increases from less than three to almost six times the influence of formally acquired skill.

As the number of years a person has participated in the labour force can be reasonably conceived to be a measure of experience, the model might be tested using first occupation and years in the labour force as indicators of occupationally acquired skill. However, as the estimated correlation between the occupational indicators and occupationally acquired skill ranged from .63 to .98 compared to .18 and .28 for years in the labour force and occupationally acquired skill, years in the labour force, with this combination of indicators, appears to be an unsuitable measure of experience.[45]

These methodological explorations move the analysis away from the conventional models for occupational attainment. Rather than describe the effects of education and prior occupational status on, say, current occupational status, the multiple-indicator model evaluates the relation of formally and occupationally acquired skills to required skills, that is, the fit between the supply and demand for occupational skills. The gain from this conceptualization may be a more accurate estimate of the relative weight of education and occupation in determining current occupational status. Moreover, a multiple-indicator model, by accounting for more variance than the single-indicator model, may enhance the credibility of this perspective as an explanation of the process of status attainment. Perhaps the most important consequence of these methodological explorations is the identification of education and occupation as indicators of explanatory concepts rather than as explanations in themselves.

Summary

In this chapter attention has been given to the effects of achievement, in contrast to those of ascription, on occupational status attainment. The task was twofold: to report the main empirical findings for a body of national data; and to interpret these findings as a contribution to the explanation of occupational status attainment. Although the discussion has moved back and forth between findings and interpretation, the focus, nonetheless, has been on the significance of variations in skill, as offered by labour force participants and demanded by employers, for location in the occupational structure. Whether dealing with the relationship between education and occupation on entry into the labour force, or the persistent influence of education at later career stages, or the influence of labour force experience, the underlying emphasis on the concept of skill has been constant.

The empirical findings resulted from conventional bivariate and multivariate analyses of data relating to the education and the occupational careers of male respondents whose ages were between 25 and 64 years when the data were collected in 1973. Thus, bivariate analysis revealed education to be strongly related to occupational rank on first entry into the labour force and both bivariate and multivariate analyses revealed education to be a persistent influence at all stages of the occupational career for which data were available. However, multivariate analysis revealed that the importance of education as a direct influence on occupational status attainment, subsequent to entry occupation, reduced in comparison to the influence of the immediately prior occupational status. Although social origin clearly exerts a direct influence on *educational* attainment, this analysis reveals that education, first occupation and 1963 occupation outweigh by far the direct influence of social origins on current occupational status. Indeed, the effects of education and first or later occupational status on current occupational status so strongly outweigh the effects of social origins as to suggest that the latter deserve very little further consideration in the analysis of *occupational* attainment. If understanding of occupational allocation is to increase, a more detailed knowledge about the relationship of educational attainment and of prior occupational status to current occupational status is evidently necessary. Moreover, educational policies and practices and labour market conditions operative while persons are of school age and of labour force age clearly require investigation.

After analysis of the data had provided factual answers to questions concerning the relative influence of education and occupational experience on current occupational attainment, it seemed desirable to consider, at a theoretical level, what these results, familiar to students of the literature of occupational mobility and status attainment, might mean. In short, it seemed justifiable to engage in a little theorizing to attach meaning to the empirical findings. Where the relationship of education and occupational attainment was concerned, theorizing took the form of distinguishing between alternative principles for the allocation of labour force participants to occupations. Interpretation took the form of relating these alternatives to the magnitude of correlations between observed indicators. Thus, observed correlations could be used to assess the relevant influence of technical and employer rationality, as the alternatives were labelled. From a different perspective, the relative influence of technical and employer rationality, and, by implication, the magnitude of observed correlations, could be seen to result from the balance or imbalance of the labour market.

A combination of theory and methodological procedure was also used to make sense of the empirical results of multivariate analysis. For this task, the familiar "achievement" variables of the basic status attainment model were further specified in terms of skill. Thus, skills were seen to be possessed by persons, with education, an achievement variable, seen as an indicator of formally acquired skills, and occupation, treated as a source of experience, as an indicator of occupationally acquired skills. These abstract or unobservable variables, then, were related to current occupational attainment which was seen as an indicator of required skills from an employment perspective. Although this mode of conceptualization and a subsequent utilization of procedures improved estimates of the strength of the relationships between unobservable variables and resulted in a gain in the "explained" variance of current occupational attainment, any value attributable to this frankly speculative exercise should not rest on those empirical results. Rather its value should be determined by the extent that it serves as a stimulus to develop explanations of occupational attainment as well as to obtain better data for their testing.

Notes

1. Expressed as departures from independence, summary measures of association, or as the relative importance of measures of such resources when estimated by regression equations.
2. That is, the argument legitimating a decision or set of decisions relating to the selection of personnel.
3. In some instances, which will be indicated in the text, farmers are excluded from the analysis. In all tables, N refers to the sample weighted as described in Chapter 2. The unweighted N is reported occasionally so that the reader may have some indication of the actual case base used in the analysis.
4. Information on education results from questions which asked the respondent to indicate the "highest level of education that you have completed" and from another which asked for a report on "the number of years altogether you were in school" (Appendix 1:1). Information on occupations was obtained from answers to a series of questions which were coded to the 1971 census 4-digit occupational code but made available to the principal investigators in the form of Blishen scale values (Blishen and McRoberts, 1976) and in the form of a categorical classification devised for the project (Pineo, Porter and McRoberts, 1977). As the sixteen categories of the classification, identified hereinafter as the project classification, as ordered by the authors, closely resemble orders based on Pineo-Porter prestige scores, on Blishen values, and on GED and SVP values (see p. 113 above), the categories, treated here, are ordered from self-employed professionals to farm labourers.
5. As indicated in notes 4 and 20, the categories of the occupational classification may be treated as ordered. Therefore, gamma may be used to express the relationship between the occupational classification and the ordered educational categories. As the educational and occupational classifications consist of ten and sixteen categories, respectively, it may be assumed that a Pearson correlation based on such data will not greatly over-

or under-estimate the "true" correlation, i.e., when based on interval measures. For example, Henry (1982) has shown that a correlation based on an interval measure and a fifteen-category ordinal variable will differ, on the average, from the "true" correlation by .077 points. In the present case, the Pearson correlation based on interval measures for education and occupation, years of education and Blishen scale values, is .66, a difference of .04 from the correlation of the two ordinal measures.

6. In the present instance, the Index of Dissimilarity (U.S. Bureau of the Census, 1971:232-33) may be interpreted as reflecting similarity or difference in the significance of education in locating individuals in initial occupational categories. The higher the Index of Dissimilarity between two categories the greater the difference in education between persons employed in them.

7. Acquired skills refer to those skills possessed by a labour force participant whether acquired genetically or through learning.

8. It is evident that this perspective is also related to the functional theory of stratification which holds that occupational roles are valued in relation to the combined influences of demand for valued skills required to meet hierarchized functional requirements and the supply of those skills as influenced by the training period required.

9. For a critique of the model of the achieving society, see Offe (1976).

10. It is assumed that there are limits set by a society's functional requirements which prevent complete abandonment of the principle of technical rationality. Perhaps it is the strength of commitment to technical rationality which distinguishes societies in which work is revered from those in which work is treated as simply necessary.

11. In this perspective, sometimes referred to as "credentialism" (see, for example, Berg, 1971; Featherman and Hauser, 1976:481), education is the indicator of skill, a matter to be discussed below. Employers are seen to be rational in that they may believe that productivity is a function of education, as evidenced by the extent that income is a positive function of education (see, for example, Berg, 1971; Wilkinson, 1965), or that conformity and other traits deemed desirable by employers result from education (see Gintis, 1971).

12. Presumably state capitalism is not exempt from this criticism, although it tends to focus on western moden industrial societies.

13. It is apparent that such indicators, so conceived, are subject to error. Thus, some component of I.Q. and vocational aptitude scores may measure learned rather than genetic skills while some component of the measures of education and occupational experience may reflect genetically acquired skills. Although the issues raised by the controversy surrounding this issue of measurement (see, for example, Jencks, 1973) are important, the formulation of the present argument need not wait on their resolution.

14. For the present analysis, no improvements on the present measures of education are possible.

15. As gamma equals unity if there is a zero cell in a fourfold table, r is a more convenient measure of association for the models and for the actual matrices. Values for ordinal measures are, nevertheless, reported.

16. As the fit between the skills acquired through education is assumed to be looser than for other occupations, farm owners are excluded from these

models of different market conditions. Actually, the summary statistics when farmers are included (Table 4.6) differ only slightly from those reported in the text. Although there is also an argument for excluding welf-employed professionals from these models since, like farm owners, clients rather than employers participate in the market, this category has been retained since entry into the occupation is closely linked to educational level.

17. Although the relationship is monotonic, it is evident From Table 4.5 that it is not strictly linear. Thus, of the variance accounted for by the marginals, about half $(eta^2 - r^2 = .037)$ is due to non-linearity. Although the number of categories for each variable can affect the magnitude of measures of association, as shown by a 4×4 categorization of education by occupation which yielded a Pearson $r = .92$, a 75×25 categorization of these same variables yielded a Pearson $r = .97$, a value closely approximating that reported for the 10×15 table reported in the text.

18. Obviously, the heterogeneity of our sample with respect to age and other characteristics means that the model describes an artificial skill market but one which may be helpful as a device for analysis.

19. The procedure used to determine the educational and training require- ments of each occupation and details of the two scales are given in Canada, Department of Manpower and Immigration (1971, 1973) and U.S. Department of Labour (1956, 1968).

20. The correlation between the order of categories in the project classification and the GED order for those categories, unweighted for labour force distribution, was 0.82 and for SVP, 0.79. These results, as well as further analysis, suggest that the ordered categories of the project classification may be treated as a skill order. It should be noted that because GED and SVP values were not available, farmers and farm labourers were omitted from this analysis. For further details, see Frank E. Jones (1980).

21. It would be unrealistic to assume that GED and SVP estimates are completely free of bias attributable to hiring practices, but in the absence of reliable estimates of bias their objectivity depends largely on the procedures used to determine the estimates. As noted above, there is wide acceptance of these estimates which, presumably, reflects faith in the procedures used.

22. Equivalents of years of education are available for GED values (Canada, 1973).

23. Educational level 5 includes persons who have completed business or trade training or who have completed nursing school or teacher's college or who have attended community college. Educational level 6 includes those who have completed community college or attended university, including those who have obtained a university certificate or diploma.

24. Although the adjustment procedure does not provide a non-zero estimate for an observed zero cell, this constraint was accepted in preference to collapsing categories or adding a constant to zero cells. The observed data and the three models, tabulated as 10×4 matrices to eliminate zero cells, revealed a pattern of Pearson Coefficients comparable to those reported in Table 4.10, except that the observed correlation was the lowest.

25. Statistics for similar analyses reported in this chapter may vary slightly as a consequence of varying sample sizes, mainly as a result of listwise deletion of cases. The partial correlations and the R^2 reported here are based on the zero-order coefficients reported in Table 4.12.

26. Stability refers to those whose origin and destination occupations are the same.
27. For the project classification rank order, the Spearman coefficient = .84; and for the order based on average Blishen values, .71.
28. In terms of destination categories accounting for 10 per cent or more of each first occupation.
29. As measured by father's education, father's occupation, and number of siblings.
30. Although these measures of social origin and family environment account for almost one-third of the variance in attained education, there are other influences which, if measures had been available, might have altered the relative influence of origin variables. Among these, intelligence must be assumed to be prominent. For example, if the correlation coefficients used by Duncan, Featherman and Duncan (1972:89-94) for the relation of I.Q. to the other variables in their model are used with the observed correlations for the present data, the direct effect of intelligence on attained level or years of education appears to be substantial. Even though it is reasonable to expect intelligence to have a strong effect on educational attainment, estimates of this effect cannot be regarded as other than very tentative since the correlations between I.Q. and other variables in the model were not based on data obtained for the Canadian Mobility Study. The results mentioned above simply underline the necessary simplicity of the models presented here.
31. As these variables are included in the model, estimates of path coefficients are reported in Table 4.12, but not discussed.
32. Although I conform to the convention which places emphasis on the causal paths or relationships of the variables included in an explanatory model, there are reasons for retaining an interest in R^2, i.e., variance accounted for by the variables comprising the model. One such reason concerns the relation of variables (and other components of the residual) excluded from the model to the included antecedent variables. In the present instance, since 1963 occupational status is known to be correlated with the antecedent variables included in the conventional model, it seems worth knowing if its effect on current occupational status is independent or redundant. For this purpose, it seems more economical to summarize its effect by reference to R^2 than to refer to individual changes in the estimates of the paths between the variables of the conventional model. Moreover, recognition of the force of the argument (Blau and Duncan, 1967:174-75) that the magnitude of the residual is an ambiguous base for judging a model's explanatory value does not require that one should ignore the possible sterility of analyses which trace relationships between variables which together account for little variation in the dependent variables. This reason for interest in R^2 is particularly pertinent in those instances, common in sociology, where the variance in the dependent variable is not the arbitrary creation of the analyst but an externally determined and interpretable property of the system under study. While R^2 may be more easily ignored where models represent a high degree of theoretical closure, inspection of R^2 may induce a proper constraint on explanatory claims based on models where theory is tentative or are based on empirical generalizations whose theoretical underpinnings need to be worked out.
33. As 1963 occupation is used as an indicator of occupationally required skills

in the two-indicator models discussed below, it was also used in the one-indicator models to facilitate comparison of the relative efficiency of one- and two-indicator models.

As only respondents with continuous participation in the labour force and those who were employed in 1963 could report on occupation for that year, the addition of 1963 occupation to the model reduces the weighted N by almost 3,000. Although there is some variation in the magnitude of path coefficients when the same models are estimated for both samples, the relative importance of the variables in the model are unchanged. Readers may compare results for both samples by comparing Table 4.12 and Table 4.A8.

34. In terms of the conventional criterion which assesses a path coefficient $\geq$ 0.10 as non-negligible.

35. In this analysis, the project occupational classification categories are used as measures of occupational location since we focus on skill as a dimension of occupation. When the Blishen scale is used as a measure of occupation, the enriched model accounts for 69 per cent (Table 4.A9), of the variance compared to 50 per cent for the conventional model.

36. It is easier to convey the absolute consequence of education in terms of Blishen points: each additional level or year of education results in a net increase for current occupation of between three-fifths and four-fifths of a Blishen point, depending on whether the full or reduced model is estimated.

37. Although the correlation between first and 1963 occupations is .60, it is not much greater than that between first and current occupation, $r = .54$. The model, with current occupation dependent, estimated on the basis of those respondents whose first and 1963 occupations were different, revealed very similar results, with increases or decreases of .02 or less for path coefficients for first and 1963 occupations and for education. The result of this analysis also shows 1963 occupation as exerting the strongest direct effect on current occupation.

38. In the distinction made here, a theoretical model states the relationships between unobservable or unmeasured variables while an empirical model states the relationships between indicators or measured variables.

39. Costner (1969:262) has argued that single-indicator models "are strictly untestable unless one assumes very slight measurement error."

40. The estimates are obtained by following the logic or rules of path analysis (Blalock, 1969; Blau and Duncan, 1967:172-73; Costner, 1969) or the logic of factor analysis (e.g., Hauser and Goldberger, 1971). To follow this discussion, a reader may find it helpful to recall that in the logic of factor analysis, it is assumed that empirical variables are correlated with an unobservable dimension or factor.

41. In this procedure, the test statistic, t_2, for the present sample must be equal to or less than 6.6 to reject the presence of "differential bias." The t_2 values were as follows:

Formally acquired skills — required skills = 0.77
Formally acquired skills — occupationally acquired skills = 13.85
Occupationally acquired skills — required skills = 54.85.

42. By Costner's test (1969:251) differential bias was not evident. That is, Costner's equation 7, $(rx_1y_1)(rx_2y) = (rx_1y_2)(rx_2y_1)$, held within these limits:

Formally acquired skills $\rightarrow$ occupationally acquired skills = .012

Formally acquired skills → required skills = .002
Occupationally acquired skills → required skills = .027

43. The two estimates, obtained by Costner's procedure for each relationship among observed variables, were averaged as a basis for computing the estimates for the two-indicator model. Although procedures to obtain single estimates have been recommended (Hauser and Goldberger, 1971), Costner's procedure was judged to be adequate for present purposes.

44. As in the previous assessment of the effects of adding variables to the conventional model, it seems reasonable to assess any gains of the multiple indicator model by comparing its path estimates or residuals with those obtained from single indicator models. The result is less impressive where the Blishen scale is used as the single indicator of occupation with only 3.3 per cent improvement in explained variance. However, comparison is difficult since Blishen values enter into the computations of the improved model only as a measure of current occupation, whereas it is a single indicator for all occupations in the conventional model. The results also differ if the sample includes only those respondents whose 1963 and 1973 occupations were different: for the improved model, explained variance drops to 43 per cent, and for the single-indicator models, using project classification categories or Blishen values, to 28 per cent and 45 per cent, respectively. Moreover, the relative importance of occupationally and formally acquired skills changes under these restrictions. While these differences deserve investigation, the main issue is whether 1963 occupation should be regarded as an indicator of occupationally acquired skills whether or not it differs from 1973 occupation. In this analysis, it is assumed that experience gained in the 1963 occupation can influence location in that same occupation in 1973.

45. In view of the possibility that some foreign-born respondents reported years in the labour force since arrival in Canada rather than their total years of employment, estimates for these correlations were also obtained for the native-born only. Differences between the two estimates and those for all males, age 25-64, were insignificant.

References

ALWIN, DUANE F. and ROBERT M. HAUSER
    1975   "The Decomposition of Effects in Path Analysis." *American Sociological Review*, 40: 37-47.
BERG, IVAR
    1970   *Education and Jobs: The Great Training Robbery.* New York: Praegar.
BLALOCK, H. M., JR.
    1969   "Multiple Indicators and the Causal Approach to Measurement Error." *American Journal of Sociology*, 75: 264-72.
BLAU, PETER M. and O. D. DUNCAN
    1967   *The American Occupational Structure.* New York: John Wiley.
BLISHEN, BERNARD R., and HUGH MCROBERTS
    1976   "A Revised Socioeconomic Index for Occupations in Canada." *Canadian Review of Sociology and Anthropology,* 13: 71-79.

144   *FRANK E. JONES*

CANADA, DEPARTMENT OF MANPOWER and IMMIGRATION
1971, 1973 *Canadian Classification and Dictionary of Occupations.* Vol. 1: *Classifications and Definitions;* Vol. 2: *Occupational Qualification Requirements.*

COSTNER, HERBERT L.
1969 "Theory, Deduction and Rules of Correspondence." *American Journal of Sociology,* 75: 245-63.

DEMING, W.
1964 *Statistical Adjustment of Data.* New York: John Wiley.

DUNCAN, OTIS D., DAVID FEATHERMAN and BEVERLEY DUNCAN
1972 *Socioeconomic Background and Achievement.* New York: Seminar Press.

FEATHERMAN, DAVID and ROBERT HAUSER
1976 "Sexual Inequalities and Socioeconomic Achievement in the U.S., 1962-1973." *American Sociological Review,* 41: 462-83.
1978 *Opportunity and Change.* New York: Academic Press.

FINE, SIDNEY A.
1968 "The Use of the Dictionary of Occupational Titles as a Source of Estimates of Educational and Training Requirements." *Journal of Human Resources,* 3: 364-75.

GINTIS, HERBERT
1971 "Education, Technology and the Characteristics of Worker Productivity." *American Economic Review.* Papers and Proceedings of the 81st Annual Meeting of AEA: 266-79.

GLASS, DAVID V., (ed.)
1954 *Social Mobility in Britain.* London: Routledge and Kegan Paul.

HAUSER, ROBERT, J. N. KOFFEL, H. P. TRAVIS and P. K. DICKINSON
1975 "Temporal Change in Occupational Mobility: Underlying Conceptualization and Empirical Tests." *American Sociological Review,* 40: 279-97.

HAUSER, ROBERT M. and ARTHUR S. GOLDBERGER
1971 "The Treatment of Unobservable Variables in Path Analysis," in H.L. Costner, ed. *Sociological Methodology.* San Francisco: Joosey-Bass.

HENRY, FRANK
1982 "Multivariate Analysis and Ordinal Data." *American Sociological Review,* 47: 299-304.

JENCKS, C. *et al.*
1972 *Inequality: a Reassessment of the Effect of Schooling in America.* New York: Basic Books.

JONES, FRANK E.
1961 *Introduction to Sociology.* Toronto: Canadian Broadcasting Corporation.
1980 "Skill as a Dimension of Occupational Classification." *Canadian Review of Sociology and Anthropology,* 17: 176-83.

KELLEY, J.
1973 "Causal Chain Models for the Socioeconomic Career." *American Sociological Review,* 38: 481-93.

LEVY, Jr. MARION J.
1966 *Modernization and the Structure of Societies.* 2 vols. Princeton: Princeton University Press.

MAYER, LAWRENCE R. and MARY S. YOUNGER
  1974 "Multiple Indicators and the Relationship Between Abstract Variables," in David R. Heise, ed. *Sociological Methodology*. San Francisco: Joosey-Bass.

OFFE, CLAUS
  1976 *Industry and Inequality*. London: Edward Arnold.

PARSONS, TALCOTT
  1960 *Structure and Process in Modern Societies*. Glencoe: The Free Press.
  1951 *The Social System*. Glencoe: The Free Press.

PINEO, PETER C., JOHN PORTER and HUGH A. MCROBERTS
  1977 "The 1977 Census and the Socioeconomic Classification of Occupations." *Canadian Review of Sociology and Anthropology*, 14(1): 91-102.

ROGOFF, NATALIE
  1953 *Recent Trends in Occupational Mobility*. Glencoe: The Free Press.

TYREE, ANDREA
  1973 "Mobility Ratios and Association in Mobility Tables." *Population Studies*, 27: 577-88.

U.S. BUREAU of the CENSUS
  1971 *The Methods and Materials of Demography*. By Henry S. Shryock, Jacob S. Siegel and Associates. Washington D.C.: U.S. Government Printing Office.

U.S. DEPARTMENT of LABOUR, BUREAU of EMPLOYMENT SECURITY
  1956 "Estimates of Worker Trait Requirements for 4,000 Jobs as Defined in the Dictionary of Occupational Titles." Washington, D.C.: U.S. Government Printing Office.
  1966 "Selected Characteristics of Occupations (Physical Demands, Working Conditions, Training Time)." *A Supplement to the Dictionary of Occupational Titles*, 3rd ed. Washington, D.C.: U.S. Government Printing Office.

WILKINSON, BRUCE
  1965 *Studies in the Economics of Education*. Ottawa: Queen's Printer.

TABLE 4:A1 — First Occupation by Education: Outflow Percentages Both Marginals Adjusted to Equal Proportions in Levels and Categories

Level of Education*	Self-Employed Professional	Employed Professional	High Managerial	Semi-Professional	Technical	Middle Managerial	Supervisor	Foreman
0	0.0	0.0	0.0	0.0	9.0	0.0	0.0	0.0
1	0.0	0.0	0.0	0.7	0.4	0.0	8.0	12.6
2	0.0	0.2	1.2	2.3	2.7	4.4	5.9	12.4
3	0.0	0.4	0.6	2.4	6.0	4.3	9.7	11.7
4	0.0	1.4	3.1	5.6	8.2	8.7	11.2	7.9
5	0.0	2.7	3.9	9.5	6.5	5.7	11.4	7.9
6	0.4	5.1	8.5	11.0	16.5	13.9	8.7	6.5
7	1.5	18.4	15.2	16.5	7.9	17.1	6.5	4.5
8	59.3	10.1	9.4	5.7	0.0	5.4	1.4	0.9
9	5.5	28.5	24.8	13.1	9.4	7.1	3.9	2.3
Total	6.7	6.7	6.7	6.7	6.7	6.7	6.7	6.7

TABLE 4:A1 (Continued)

Level of Education*	Skilled White-Collar	Skilled Craftsman	Semi-Skilled White-Collar	Semi-Skilled Craftsman	Unskilled White-Collar	Labourer	Farm Labourer	Total
0	4.1	17.0	5.6	18.4	0.0	23.8	22.05	100.00
1	3.0	9.8	4.6	16.5	10.5	14.7	19.2	100.00
2	2.5	10.1	9.6	11.3	9.5	11.9	15.9	100.00
3	5.7	8.5	14.3	8.9	13.8	8.3	5.4	100.00
4	12.4	6.9	12.3	4.5	13.0	3.4	1.4	100.00
5	12.2	10.9	9.9	4.9	9.7	3.1	1.7	100.00
6	11.5	2.8	6.3	1.6	5.6	1.2	0.6	100.00
7	6.5	0.5	2.6	0.3	2.4	0.3	0.2	100.00
8	5.4	0.1	0.6	0.2	1.4	0.0	0.1	100.00
9	3.4	0.1	0.8	0.2	1.0	0.0	0.1	100.00
Total	6.7	6.7	6.7	6.7	6.7	6.7	6.7	100.00

N = 13,459 Males, 25-64 years of age.
* For descriptive labels corresponding to codes, see Table 4:1.

148 FRANK E. JONES

TABLE 4:2A — First Occupation by Education: Differences* Between Adjusted† and Observed Outflow Percentage Distributions

Level of Education‡	Self-Employed Professional	Employed Professional	High Managerial	Semi-Profes-sional	Technical	Middle Managerial	Supervisor	Foreman
0	0.0	0.0	0.0	0.0	-0.6	0.0	0.0	0.0
1	0.0	0.0	0.0	-0.1	0.0	0.0	-0.4	-0.5
2	0.0	-0.1	-0.1	-0.6	-0.3	-0.3	-0.4	-0.6
3	0.0	-0.4	0.0	-0.7	-0.8	-0.4	-0.7	-0.6
4	0.0	-1.7	-0.2	-2.4	-1.4	-1.1	-1.1	-0.5
5	0.0	-2.9	-0.2	-3.7	-1.0	-0.6	-1.0	-0.4
6	-0.1	-9.1	-0.9	-6.7	-3.3	-2.3	-0.6	0.0
7	-0.6	-30.4	-1.3	-5.8	0.6	-0.8	1.8	2.0
8	-26.7	-15.5	-0.6	1.0	0.0	1.1	1.5	1.4
9	-1.7	-30.3	-1.2	1.3	4.4	1.0	2.8	2.4
Total	1.2	6.9	0.4	3.8	2.0	1.4	1.8	1.7

TABLE 4:2A (Continued)

Level of Education ‡	Skilled White-Collar	Skilled Craftsman	Semi-Skilled White-Collar	Semi-Skilled Craftsman	Unskilled White-Collar	Labourer	Farm Labourer	Total
0	-0.6	0.1	-0.5	0.3	0.0	1.9	-0.5	0.8(1) / 10.0(2)
1	-0.6	0.3	-0.5	0.7	-0.6	2.0	-0.2	12.8 / 10.0
2	-0.5	0.7	-1.1	1.0	-0.6	2.5	0.2	14.0 / 10.0
3	-1.5	1.7	-1.5	2.0	-0.9	3.4	0.5	22.5 / 10.0
4	-4.5	4.9	0.0	3.5	-0.5	4.1	0.6	18.3 / 10.0
5	-4.0	6.8	-0.1	3.4	-0.4	3.3	0.7	10.7 / 10.0
6	-4.8	9.1	4.8	5.5	1.3	5.6	1.4	9.9 / 10.0
7	1.4	6.4	11.2	4.6	3.6	5.5	1.9	5.6 / 10.0
8	9.0	3.9	8.1	6.6	6.5	0.0	3.8	2.8 / 10.0
9	3.8	1.5	6.9	4.5	3.2	0.0	1.4	2.5 / 10.0
Total	4.8	17.6	10.6	16.3	4.4	18.1	8.9	100.0 / 100.0

N = 13,459 Males, 25-64 years of age.
* Cell Entries = Adjusted % − Observed %

† Equal proportions for Levels of Education
‡ For descriptive labels corresponding to codes, see Table 4:1.

TABLE 4:A3 — First Occupation by Education: Differences* Between Adjusted† and Observed Outflow Percentage Distributions

Level of Education‡	Self-Employed Professional	Employed Professional	High Managerial	Semi-Professional	Technical	Middle Managerial	Supervisor	Foreman
0	0.0	0.0	0.0	0.0	11.6	0.0	0.0	0.0
1	0.0	0.0	0.0	1.2	0.6	0.0	6.9	9.3
2	0.0	1.0	4.2	3.5	3.4	6.1	4.5	8.2
3	0.0	1.8	2.0	3.6	7.3	5.9	7.2	7.4
4	0.0	4.2	8.7	5.8	7.4	9.4	5.9	3.4
5	0.0	7.6	10.2	9.1	5.4	5.7	5.6	3.2
6	11.6	3.7	14.9	1.6	5.3	7.4	1.1	0.4
7	25.6	-14.2	14.1	-6.7	-0.5	2.5	-0.8	-0.8
8	59.1	-32.3	-0.9	-7.6	0.0	-2.1	-0.8	-0.5
9	49.9	-40.9	10.6	-8.4	-2.4	-0.4	-0.9	-0.6
Total	1.2(1)	6.9	0.4	3.8	2.0	1.4	1.8	1.7
	6.7(2)	6.7	6.7	6.7	6.7	6.7	6.7	6.7

TABLE 4:A3 (Continued)

Level of Education‡	Skilled White-Collar	Skilled Craftsman	Semi-Skilled White-Collar	Semi-Skilled Craftsman	Unskilled White-Collar	Labourer	Farm Labourer	Total
0	3.8	-3.2	1.7	-5.2	0.0	-12.1	3.5	0.8
1	2.8	-4.6	1.0	-9.5	5.7	-13.1	-0.3	12.8
2	2.0	-7.8	0.5	-10.2	4.2	-15.2	-4.3	14.0
3	4.1	-10.6	-2.2	-12.4	5.0	-15.9	-3.3	22.5
4	4.3	-16.4	-8.6	-11.5	1.0	-11.5	-2.1	18.3
5	4.1	-23.0	-6.0	-11.3	0.8	-9.4	-2.2	10.7
6	-4.0	-12.4	-10.8	-7.4	-2.5	-7.0	-2.0	9.9
7	-4.8	-2.5	-5.6	-1.8	-1.7	-2.0	-0.7	5.6
8	-8.2	-0.8	-2.1	-1.3	-1.8	0.0	-0.8	2.8
9	-3.0	-0.3	-1.7	-0.9	-0.8	0.0	-0.3	2.5
Total	4.8	17.6	10.6	16.3	4.4	18.1	8.9	100.00
	6.7	6.7	6.7	6.7	6.7	6.7	6.7	100.00

N = 13,459 Males, 25-64 years of age.

[1] Observed percentage.

[2] Adjusted percentage.

* Cell entries = Adjusted % − Observed %.

† Equal proportions for occupational categories.

‡ For descriptive labels corresponding to codes, see Table 4:1.

TABLE 4:A4 — Current Occupation by Education: Outflow Percentages

Level of Education*	Self-Employed Professional	Employed Professional	High Managerial	Semi-Professional	Technical	Middle Managerial	Supervisor	Foreman
0	0.0	0.0	0.0	0.0	0.0	0.0	3.8	6.0
1	0.0	0.0	0.0	0.5	0.2	0.7	3.3	6.0
2	0.0	0.2	0.4	0.2	0.9	2.0	5.3	7.9
3	0.1	1.1	1.4	1.3	1.4	3.7	8.1	9.4
4	0.0	4.3	3.7	3.6	2.4	5.8	11.3	8.1
5	0.0	3.8	3.2	6.3	2.1	7.3	7.6	10.4
6	0.4	15.4	7.0	11.3	5.5	8.7	11.0	7.7
7	0.6	43.2	11.5	17.3	2.2	8.6	3.1	2.3
8	39.6	33.9	7.4	6.0	0.3	6.7	1.6	0.8
9	2.4	56.9	16.5	12.0	2.5	4.3	2.9	0.0
Total	1.3	7.6	3.3	4.2	1.9	4.6	7.3	7.6

TABLE 4:A4 (Continued)

Level of Education*	Skilled White-Collar	Skilled Craftsmen	Farmer	Semi-Skilled White-Collar	Semi-Skilled Craftsmen	Unskilled White-Collar	Labourer	Farm Labourer	Total
0	2.7	24.3	4.3	0.3	21.3	0.0	31.9	5.4	0.7
1	1.5	22.7	8.1	3.1	18.7	1.0	30.7	3.3	12.8
2	1.9	22.0	8.7	6.6	15.8	1.4	23.4	3.2	14.5
3	4.0	21.1	6.2	8.6	13.8	2.4	16.1	1.3	22.8
4	8.6	18.8	2.9	7.9	9.6	3.6	8.8	0.7	18.2
5	5.6	26.6	1.8	7.8	7.4	2.0	7.1	1.0	10.7
6	8.5	8.0	2.7	5.3	3.3	1.6	3.0	0.6	9.7
7	4.1	1.7	0.9	1.6	0.5	0.7	1.5	0.3	5.5
8	1.7	0.4	0.0	0.6	1.0	0.0	0.0	0.0	2.9
9	0.0	0.3	0.2	0.5	0.4	0.6	0.5	0.0	2.4
Total	4.7	18.2	4.8	6.2	10.9	2.0	14.0	1.5	100.0

N = 13,432 Males, 25-64 years of age.
*For descriptive labels corresponding to codes, see Table 4-1.

TABLE 4-A5 — Outflow Percentage First Occupation to Current Occupation

First Occupation	Current Occupation							
	Self-Employed Professional	Employed Professional	High Managerial	Semi-Profes-sional	Technical	Middle Managerial	Supervisor	Foreman
Self-employed professionals	90.2	5.5	0.0	0.8	0.0	0.6	2.3	0.0
Employed professionals	0.8	63.5	9.6	7.4	1.3	5.4	2.1	2.4
High managerial	0.0	11.3	57.2	3.4	0.0	10.0	3.2	0.8
Semi-professional	2.8	12.3	8.5	51.8	0.8	5.0	3.1	1.9
Technical	0.0	11.9	5.7	3.4	36.3	5.3	4.7	6.8
Middle managerial	0.0	5.8	11.8	0.9	0.7	49.1	7.0	2.7
Supervisor	0.0	7.7	3.5	3.4	0.5	5.5	43.3	2.9
Foreman	0.7	3.9	3.4	1.6	1.6	3.4	6.0	42.7
Skilled white-collar	0.0	12.8	8.7	6.8	0.9	8.3	14.0	5.0
Skilled craftsmen	0.0	2.2	1.2	2.1	1.3	2.4	4.5	12.8
Farmer	0.0	0.8	0.1	0.1	0.8	2.0	3.3	4.5
Semi-skilled white-collar	0.1	5.3	5.2	2.8	1.4	7.5	16.3	5.1
Semi-skilled craftsmen	0.0	1.8	0.9	1.7	1.5	4.1	4.9	7.0
Unskilled white-collar	0.0	5.1	4.7	4.6	1.1	7.3	15.1	4.6
Labourer	0.0	1.4	1.2	1.1	0.9	2.8	5.4	8.5
Farm labourer	0.1	0.8	0.5	0.2	0.8	1.9	5.2	6.9

TABLE 4-A5 (Continued)

First Occupation	Skilled White-Collar	Skilled Craftsmen	Farmer	Semi-Skilled White-Collar	Semi-Skilled Craftsmen	Unskilled White-Collar	Labourer	Farm Labourer
Self-employed professionals	0.0	0.6	0.0	0.0	0.0	0.0	0.0	0.0
Employed professionals	1.9	1.3	0.8	1.2	0.5	0.4	1.3	0.0
High managerial	7.4	1.4	0.0	4.4	1.0	0.0	0.0	0.0
Semi-professional	2.5	3.5	0.7	2.4	2.5	0.5	1.2	0.6
Technical	6.0	6.3	0.3	2.3	3.1	1.7	5.7	0.6
Middle managerial	8.1	3.2	1.9	2.8	1.5	1.8	2.9	0.0
Supervisor	4.6	4.9	2.3	8.7	5.2	0.4	6.0	1.1
Foreman	5.4	10.1	2.7	5.5	5.1	1.3	6.2	0.2
Skilled white-collar	23.1	5.4	0.3	5.2	3.3	1.7	4.1	0.4
Skilled craftsmen	2.8	47.5	1.6	2.6	8.6	1.7	8.0	0.5
Farmer	2.0	9.7	49.7	2.5	9.2	1.1	11.3	3.0
Semi-skilled white-collar	7.8	8.5	1.0	20.6	6.0	4.0	8.1	0.2
Semi-skilled craftsmen	2.5	18.7	2.4	6.1	29.2	1.6	16.6	1.0
Unskilled white-collar	9.8	8.6	0.8	7.9	8.2	9.7	11.5	0.9
Labourer	3.4	18.9	2.0	6.7	11.4	1.6	33.3	1.4
Farm labourer	2.3	15.6	18.7	3.6	12.7	1.1	20.3	9.1

N = 13,168 Males, 25-64 years of age

TABLE 4:A6 — First Occupation by Education

	Gamma	Somers D	r
Observed	.474	.424	.621
Adjusted to equal supply	.469	.418	.579
Adjusted to equal demand	.537	.506	.635
Adjusted to equal supply and demand	.583	.551	.704
Fully rational 10 × 16	1.000	.955	.965

N = 13,945 Males, 25-64 years of age, including farm owners.

TABLE 4:A7 — Current Occupation by Education

	Gamma	Somer's D	r
Observed	.487	.443	.606
Adjusted to equal supply	.518	.471	.625
Adjusted to equal demand	.510	.480	.607
Adjusted to equal supply and demand	.571	.540	.691
Fully rational 10 × 16	1.000	.968	.980

N = 13,432 Males, 25-64 years of age, including farm owners.

TABLE 4:A8 — Full and Reduced Models of Occupational Attainment: Path Coefficients

Dependent	First Occupation	Respondent's Education	No. of Siblings	Father's Occupation	Father's Education	R^2
First Occupation	—	.561[3]	-.005	.092[3]	.007	.352[3]
First Occupation	—	.560[3]	—	.090[3]	—	.352[3]
Respondent's Current Occupation	.374[3]	.339[3]	-.001	.062[3]	-.011	.439[3]
Respondent's Current Occupation	.382[3]	.359[3]	—	—	—	.435[3]
$\bar{X}$ 7.750	6.119	10.947	4.464	6.404	7.491	
s.d. 4.132	4.184	3.808	3.205	3.262	4.036	

TABLE 4:A8 (Continued)

	First Occupation	Respondent's Education	No. of Siblings	Father's Occupation	Father's Education	RR
			ZERO-ORDER COEFFICIENTS			
Respondent's Current Occupation	.593	.583	-.197	.269	.320	
First Occupation		.587	-.198	.262	.309	
Respondents' Education			-.328	.307	.491	
No. of Siblings				-.126	-.290	
Father's Occupation					.421	

N = 10,820 Males, 25-64 years of age; unweighted N = 10,286.
[3]Level of Significance .001

TABLE 4:A9 — Full and Reduced Models of Occupational Attainment: Path Coefficients

Dependent	1963 Occupation*	First Occupation*	Respondent's Education	No. of Siblings	Father's Occupation	Father's Education	R^2
First Occupation*			.535[4]	-.025[3]	.196[4]	-.001	.421[3]
First Occupation*			.542[4]		.199[4]		.421[3]
1963 Occupation*		.489[4]	.231[4]	-.017[1]	.129[4]	-.007	.531[3]
1963 Occupation*		.490[4]	.233[4]		.128[4]		.531[3]
Respondent's Current Occupation*	.623[4]	.100[4]	.150[4]	.001	.042[4]	.025[2]	.685[3]
Respondent's Current Occupation*	.633[4]	.108[4]	.167[4]				.683[3]
Respondent's Current Occupation*	.686[4]	.203[4]					.677[3]
Respondent's Current Occupation*		.405[4]	.294[4]	-.009	.122[4]	.020[1]	.503[3]
Respondent's Current Occupation*		.405[4]	.303[4]		.131[4]		.503[3]
Respondent's Current Occupation							
X̄ 43.708	41.940	37.780	10.579	4.579	34.724	7.282	
s.d. 14.942	14.530	13.791	3.734	3.230	13.310	3.975	

TABLE 4:A9 (Continued)

ZERO-ORDER COEFFICIENTS

	1963 Occupation*	First Occupation*	Respondent's Education	No. of Siblings	Father's Occupation	Father's Education	R^2
Respondent's Current Occupation	.806	.649	.609	−.237	.424	.377	
1963 Occupation		.689	.591	−.239	.429	.355	
First Occupation			.623	−.243	.420	.369	
Respondent's Education				−.324	.408	.491	
No. of Siblings					−.231	−.280	
Father's Occupation						.499	

N = 7,890 Males, 25-64 years of age.

*Blishen values are used as measures of occupational prestige.

1 ≤ .04
2 ≤ .002
3 ≤ .006
4 ≤ .001

TABLE 4:A10 — Full and Reduced Models of Occupational Attainment: Path Coefficients

Dependent	First* Occupation	Respondent's Education	No. of Siblings	Father's Occupation	Father's Education	R^2
First Occupation		.575[1]	-.025[1]	.178[1]	-.013	.449[1]
First Occupation		.578[1]	—	.175[1]	—	.448[1]
Current Occupation	.448[1]	.285[1]	-.005	.105[1]	.003	.528[1]
Current Occupation	.448[1]	.288[1]	—	.107[1]	—	.528[1]
Current Occupation						
X̄ 44.277	39.142	10.947	4.464	35.293	7.491	
s.d. 15.166	14.550	3.808	3.205	13.544	4.036	

ZERO-ORDER COEFFICIENTS

	First* Occupation	Respondent's Education	No. of Siblings	Father's Occupation	Father's Education	
Current Occupation	.680	.623	-.236	.412	.365	
First Occupation		.650	-.251	.415	.369	
Respondent's Education			-.328	.414	.491	
No. of Siblings				-.231	-.290	
Father's Occupation					.518	

N = 10,820 Males, 25-64 years of age.
*Blishen values are used as measures of occupational prestige.
[1]Level of Significance ≤ .001.

CHAPTER 5

Comparisons over Time

JOHN C. GOYDER

The preceding chapters have reported data on the overall mobility, and forms of status attainment, experienced by a sample of adult Canadians. This aggregated mobility biography mixes all the historical contingencies that might have been important for Canadians of different ages. Someone entering the labour market during the depressed conditions of the early 1930s perhaps encountered a market-wide pressure toward downward inter-generational mobility. One commencing a career in the 1950s may have benefited from a labour market pressure towards upward mobility. Such historical effects are now to be addressed.

A good deal of ingenuity has been expended over the years in advancing hypotheses about the direction that temporal changes in mobility rates should be expected to take. Behind most of these is an approach specifying some features of industrialization (Davis, 1962; Kerr, *et al.*, 1964; Lenski, 1966; Treiman, 1970) that should stimulate mobility in any modern society. In any industrial society, it is thought, there is a trend towards expansion of the upper white-collar labour force (e.g., Blau and Duncan, 1967:429). This results in part from the use of increasingly technical methods of production. Also, the wealth industrialization brings allows the luxury of a large civil service, well-developed university system, and other concerns involving prestigious occupations. Such expansions allow upward "structural"[1] mobility, as workers from lower positions (or family background) move up to fill the new vacancies. In a more fundamental sense, independently of this simple upgrading, the transformation of the labour force is thought to mean (Treiman, 1970:218) that it becomes increasingly difficult for fathers to directly bequeath jobs to sons. This is partly because entrepreneurship typically declines in favour of corporate organization

163

(Mills, 1956). And the increased division of labour (Durkheim, 1964) reflected by an expanding number of job titles means that in a statistical sense the inheritance of father's occupation by a son or daughter becomes less probable. As well, industrial society usually seems to be associated with bureaucractic forms of organization. Bureaucracies are supposed to be impartial in their dealings with the public and meritocratic in their hiring and promotion (Weber, 1958a:33-34). These principles do not always hold (e.g., Blau, 1955) but bureaucracies probably are meritocratic compared to other forms of organization. Another institutional change set in motion by industrialization is said to be a decline in the importance of the family; the basic source of immobility in human societies (Kerr, *et al.*, 1964:18; Weinberg, 1969:8).

The unique aspects of modern industrial society can be represented in terms of changes in values. Blau and Duncan (1967:429) wrote of these changes: "The basic assumption underlying these conjectures is that a fundamental trend towards expanding universalism characterizes industrial society." This is a long-term trend reflected in such sociological abstractions as particularism-universalism, *gemeinschaft-gesellschaft*, mechanical versus organic solidarity, and primary versus secondary relations. It is difficult to satisfactorily measure this drift towards objective rational conduct, and sociologists often seem to shed their scientific standards of evidence when they describe historical societies. But there is enough informal evidence, in the form for instance of literary accounts of life in different times, to make the proposition credible. Whether these changes in values come prior to, or following, the structural consequences of industrialization embodied in phenomena such as the labour force transformation is, of course, a question of longstanding interest to students of social change (e.g., Weber, 1958b).

Features of industrial society such as these have given rise to a "convergence theory" of social mobility, part of a more general point of view arguing that, according to a whole set of social characteristics, societies become more alike over time. The theory has had a controversial intellectual history, both within the context of social mobility studies, and in its wider sense. Some writers have felt that a general trend towards convergence in social characteristics is a fundamental trend brought about by forces associated with industrialization (e.g., Kerr, *et al.*, 1964; Levy, 1966; Moore, 1965, 1966; Bell, 1973). Others have argued that, at the least, convergence theorists have underemphasized differences that remain between societies sharing similar levels of industrialization (e.g., Goldthorpe, 1964; Garnsey, 1975; Payne, 1977).

As applied to social mobility rates, the theory of convergence has usually been formulated with international trends in mind, to provide a rationale for the Lipset-Zetterberg (1956a, 1956b) thesis that considerable mobility is seen in most industrial societies. The theory implies also that each society should progress over time towards higher rates of mobility, eventually converging on some standard "post-industrial" rate (Hazelrigg, 1974). Support for this view has been found in some cross-national research contrasting mobility rates among countries of differing stages of economic development. Several re-analyses of data sets dating (mostly) from the 1950s have found indices of industrialization to correlate substantially with national mobility rates (e.g., Fox and Miller, 1965; Cutright, 1968; Hazelrigg, 1974; Hazelrigg and Garnier, 1976).

Using regression equations developed from this work, quite accurate estimates of a country's overall rate of mobility can be made so long as the requisite data on industrial development are available. Hazelrigg's work, the most recent in the series, allows the calculation of a predicted mobility correlation (Somer's D) using national energy consumption figures as an index of industrialization. This means that even if no Canadian mobility data existed, an estimate could be generated using the formula. Hazelrigg now has two versions in the literature. Applying Canadian energy data to the earlier one (Hazelrigg, 1974) gives a predicted Somer's D of .34 between father's occupation and son's current occupation. A second version of this formula (Hazelrigg and Garnier, 1976) sets the predicted Canadian figure at .37.[2] The actual correlation (.31), computed using the appropriate coding from the Canadian Mobility Study, is not far from the predicted values and reveals that the predictions slightly underestimate the Canadian mobility rate. Canada, that is, has slightly more overall mobility than other societies would at the same level of development. Hazelrigg presents another formula, this time for predicting a measure of net (or circulation) mobility. This is the overall percentage mobile, in a table in which son's occupation has been adjusted to take the same distribution as father's. In the Canadian case, it is found this time that the formula proves extremely accurate when the predicted figure (37 per cent, in the 1976 version)[3] is compared to the actual one (38 per cent) computed from the mobility survey.

The above computations are a way of suggesting that the theory linking industrial development with mobility possesses empirical credibility and can provide plausible predictions about likely trends in occupational mobility in Canada. The country has industrialized rapidly during the twentieth century, and increased social mobility might be expected to have accompanied this. There are, however, at least three qualifications that one might suggest concerning this manner of viewing mobility trends. First, it seems important to ask whether the trends generated by industrialization have occurred rapidly enough to be detectable in the kind of historical analysis that sociologists typically pursue. In our own case, it will be seen that the analysis can span only some forty years. Changes in real mobility patterns may simply be too minor to be noticeable over such a short interval. In the United States, where considerable attention has been given by students of mobility to the question of trends over time, the finding of most observers has been that no clear trends have taken place during the twentieth century (Blau and Duncan, 1967; Duncan, 1968; Hauser, Koffel, *et al.*, 1975). Only among special sub-groups has clear evidence of changes appeared, and it has been suggested that these are something of a "zero sum" enterprise; that is, the trends among sub-groups have been partially offset by small countertrends in the larger society (Featherman and Hauser, 1976).

A second qualification is that we should inquire as to which aspects of "mobility" should exhibit changes. The term would seem, from current usage, to imply several empirical phenomena. Sociologists studying mobility often compare the mean status of different groups or generations within a society. Mean scores reveal nothing about which origins are conducive to mobility, or over what status distances. What they do show, however, is possible patterns of overall structural mobility between generations. In this sense, the comparison of the mean scores for different generations or age cohorts can be considered a study in group mobility. Another empirical pattern implied by "changes in mobility" is an interaction effect whereby the statistical association between father's and son's occupational status is found to alter over time. The strength of the interaction can be assessed under varying degrees of statistical control for the structural component. We shall discuss the implications for theory of the different controls later. The theory linking mobility to pace of industrialization implies a further pattern of findings; that the relative importance of the variables in a regression model of status attainment will shift. This is a still more complicated interaction effect for here it is expected that, over time, the importance of "ascribed" variables (such as family background) will decline in favour of "achieved" variables (such as education, net of background factors) (Goldthorpe, 1964:101; Treiman, 1970). In the analysis described below, these various empirical representations of aspects of mobility are examined separately.

The final reservation to be noted about a simple convergence theory of mobility is that the trends (or some of those described above) may in fact be in reverse to the expected direction. This could occur if Canadian society was undergoing a counter-trend to a long-term master trend of increasing mobility. One such counter-trend might be a very recent one drawing attention to the contemporary economic situation. The rapid pace at which surveys become dated (our data after all were collected in 1973) prevents an absolutely up-to-the-minute assessment of such developments, but some recent Canadian stratification literature has argued in favour of declining mobility rates over quite short periods. Edward Harvey (1974:159-77) examined the first jobs and fathers' occupations of graduates from four Ontario universities and found decreased mobility between 1960 and 1968. Wallace Clement's (1975:182-94) re-examination of elites in Canadian society suggests that recruitment into the corporate elite among sons of working-class fathers has declined between 1951 and 1972. Both studies refer to specialized groups, of course, and do not purport to describe societal trends. A trend of diminishing mobility over much longer intervals has been suggested too and one sees this view particularly, it seems, among the prewar generation of American sociologists. Here, the feeling has been that rates of mobility over the past century in the United States are more likely to have decreased than increased. Part of this conception seems to come from the Turner hypothesis (Turner, 1920) that the frontier is essential for understanding American history. The argument in the United States has been, then, that as the nineteenth century ended and the frontier lands were filled up, the great age of opportunity depicted in Horatio Alger's novels ended (Hertzler, 1952; Chinoy, 1955; Hollingshead, 1952). Canada's frontier was settled somewhat later than the American (Morison and Commager, 1962: 133-64; Morton, 1961:89) and is still the less populated, when one understands the north to constitute the last Canadian frontier. The frontier analysis of mobility trends would thus seem less germane to Canada than to the United States. Another aspect of the thesis of declining mobility in the United States is that the ending of mass immigration after World War One produced a further evaporation of opportunities (e.g., Warner and Srole, 1945).[4] Canada, of course, is still in the midst of heavy immigration and on this count, too, the thesis of a long-term decline in mobility seems less tenable here than in the United States.

Data and Procedures

In the next section data from an internal "cohort" analysis of the Canadian Mobility Study are examined in order to address the matters posed above. There are limitations to the scope of a longitudinal analysis using data collected only at one year and some of these are reviewed below. The question of trends seems important, however, (see, for example, Featherman and Hauser, 1975:245) and a strength of the present survey is that the case base is sufficiently large that the data can support breakdowns by age groups. Such analysis has not been practical in earlier mobility surveys in this country.

One shortcoming of cohort analysis is the likelihood of confusing historical effects with career effects. If one compares, say, father's occupation with son's present occupation there are independent career effects to be contended with. For older respondents, a long time will have elapsed between their fathers' jobs (when respondents were 16) and their own reports of current occupation. The interval will be much shorter among younger respondents. This alone could cause a weaker father-son occupation correlation among older than among younger respondents but such evidence could obviously not be taken to mean that there was more mobility early in the century than now.

The confusion of career and historical effects is so severe when working with current occupation reports that here we rely almost entirely upon comparisons of respondents' first occupations with their fathers' occupations. This ensures that the interval between reports of father's occupation and son's occupation is more or less constant. There are, of course, some limitations to the effectiveness of first occupation reports as indicators of sons' occupational achievements. First occupations may not be representative of what people spend most of their occupational lives doing. This is seen by the imperfect ($r = .54$, from Table 4:12) correlation between first occupation and current occupation. The questionnaire asked people to "describe your first full-time job (for pay or profit) after completing your education." There is some evidence that these instructions were not always obeyed by respondents. Unlikely combinations of education and the year in which the first job was entered were disturbingly frequent.[5]

The same problem has been encountered in other mobility studies (e.g., Blau and Duncan, 1967:166-68) and our question was intended to improve upon the Blau and Duncan version ("Please think about the first full-time job you had after you left school") by insisting upon a first job that was paid work and by using the more generic term "education" in place of "school." It may be conjectured that ego enhancement enters to some degree into reports of first job so that those with ambiguous biographies surrounding the sequence between completing education and entering the labour force select the most flattering of several occupations which conceivably might be considered first jobs. On the other hand, those disposed to exaggerate their career accomplishments may elect the most modest of alternative career origins. These possible selective effects would intrude upon the analysis of mobility trends only if the direction of the bias correlated with age.

The population used in this chapter is restricted to male Canadian-born respondents.[6] A dilemma encountered throughout the analysis was whether respondents aged under 25 or over 65 should be included. Other studies of longitudinal trends (e.g., Blau and Duncan, 1967) have restricted comparisons to those aged 25 to 64 years and we have indications from our own data that this is a wise policy. In particular, the occupation distribution of sons aged under 25 has a serious blue-collar skew because those bound for higher-status occupations were often still in university postgraduate programs and so not in the labour force as yet. On the other hand, comparisons of mobility over only the four decades represented by the 25 to 64 portion of the sample severely restricts the historical depth of the analysis. The decision in the end was that the findings for those aged 18 to 24 were likely to be misleading and should not be reported. Those for people over 64 are reported because the bias does not seem so severe and because this group enhanced the historical depth of the comparison by many years. Nevertheless, one must emphasize that results for this group are more likely to be untrustworthy than those for cohorts in the 25 to 64 range.

Trends in the Mean Socioeconomic Status of First Job

In the Canadian census of 1901, 8 per cent of the male labour force was engaged in managerial or professional occupations. By 1971 this figure had risen threefold to include 25 per cent of the work force (Kubat and Thornton, 1974:153-54). Such occupations dominate the upper range of occupational status scales and it is no surprise to discover that the mean status of first job among succeeding generations of Canadian males has increased. The average status of the first occupation of respondents in different age cohorts (in five-year intervals) is shown in Table 5.1. The table also records the mean scores, by cohort, of father's occupation and respondent's current occupation. The figures include the farming population, with the exception of the right-hand column, which shows the mean first job status of non-farmers. Over the four decades spanned by those aged between 25 and 64 years, mean first occupational status rose by some seven Blishen points. If the over 65 group is included this difference stretches to 8.7 points. It can be seen that the gain in status made between first and current occupation by the respondents now

TABLE 5:1 — Mean Blishen Scores on Father's Occupation and Respondent's First and Current Occupations, by Cohorts

Age in 1973	Date when 16	N*	Mean First Occupation	Mean Father's Occupation	Difference	Mean Current Occupation	Mean First Occupation, Excluding Farmers
25-29	1960-64	2006	41.30	36.90	4.40	44.89	41.43
30-34	1955-59	1638	41.25	36.21	5.04	45.43	41.59
35-39	1950-54	1304	39.53	34.53	5.00	44.91	40.08
40-44	1945-49	1451	37.44	34.65	2.79	44.46	37.93
45-49	1940-44	1257	36.16	33.17	2.99	41.68	36.72
50-54	1935-39	1253	35.41	32.75	2.66	42.08	36.21
55-59	1930-34	1176	34.61	32.62	1.99	41.71	35.41
60-64	1925-29	835	34.15	31.66	2.49	39.32	35.05
65+	1924 or earlier	1303	32.56	29.86	2.70	37.02	33.91

*Computations in Chapter 5 are based on the male, native-born, aged 25 and over sub-sample of the Canadian Mobility Study. Raw N for the sub-sample = 17,594. Case bases reported in tables in the chapter incorporate the standard weight variable (see chapter 1), divided by the factor 300.55, to reproduce the raw N for the study. N's herein vary across tables, on account of changing combinations of missing data.

engaged in the final half-decade of their working lives (60 to 64) is only 5.2 Blishen points — slightly less than the increment in first occupation status registered over roughly the same interval by succeeding generations. In other words, the average upward mobility over a full working career does not quite keep pace with the progressively higher starting point at which each new generation enters the work force (given the usual assumption of an occupational SES scale stable over time). The result is that the current occupation status of those aged 60 to 64 is two points lower than the first occupation status of those (aged 25 to 29) recently entering the labour force.

The increase in first occupation status for those aged 25 to 29, the most recent group in the series, is a minute .05 Blishen points over the immediately prior cohort. Excluding farmers, it can be seen that this cohort actually shows a slight decline in mean status compared to the 30 to 34 age group. The slowdown for the 25-29's is probably at least partially attributable to the tendency for those preparing for high-status jobs to be still in university. Indeed, this factor makes it hard to draw firm interpretations of the results for the cohort. The largest increase over any two adjacent five-year cohorts (2.1 Blishen points) is seen between those entering the labour force in the late 1940s (currently aged 40 to 44) and those beginning careers in the early 1950s (aged 35 to 39). The latter would seem to have benefited from postwar economic conditions. It is to be expected that those entering the labour force during the early 1930s would exhibit diminished mean status over earlier cohorts. In fact, the scores seem to indicate only a diminished augmentation in status for the depression cohort, rather than an actual loss in status compared to earlier cohorts; the mean for the "depression cohort" aged 55 to 59 in 1973 was up one-half Blishen point over the preceding cohort. The costs of the 1930s depression can be detected more distinctly when comparing the difference in mean occupation status between father's and son's occupation for each cohort (column 6, Table 5.1). This mean upward mobility was, at two Blishen points, smaller for those aged 55 to 59 than for any other cohort. Indeed, if an adjustment is made (using a Multiple Classification Analysis; figures not included in Table 5.1) to give first occupation scores with father's occupation controlled we do find a slight downturn in mean status for the cohort entering the labour force during the early 1930s. Although the depression can thus be seen to have impeded the first job status of those entering the labour force during the 1930s, it can also be observed from the current occupation scores in Table 5.1 that the penalty was not permanent. Mean current occupation status for those aged 55 to 59 is more than two Blishen points higher than for the preceding cohort. The data on the socioeconomic costs borne during the 1930s understate matters, of course, because only those who succeeded in finding jobs are included; the loss or deferment of employment during the 1930s is not captured in the results reported in Table 5.1.[7]

It is sometimes difficult to evaluate the importance of occupational status findings because socioeconomic scales such as the Blishen scores are abstracted measures lacking the same face value interpretability that categories such as "white-collar" and "blue-collar" possess. Thus, we may inquire whether an upward movement in mean first job status of some seven points is "important." In the relative scale of determinants of first occupational status, historical period is by no means trivial. The Pearsonian correlation between birthdate and the occupational socioeconomic status of first job is .25. Father's occupational status is a more important determinant of first job, but ethnic status is markedly weaker. City size (at age 16), another variable known to predict occupational status, is of roughly equivalent importance with birthdate. These comparisons refer to zero-order effects. The mechanism whereby birthdate translates into occupational opportunities at the time of first job involves a network of other variables. Birthdate has consequences for the family SES of respondents, it predicts the type of community they are likely to grow up in, and also has implications for the level of respondent's education to be expected. A decomposition of how this process works is shown in Table 5.2. The table was formed by successively introducing additional predictors into the equation regressing first job SES on birthdate and then examining the amount by which each new predictor reduced the regression slope for birthdate. The results are presented in two ways: with farmers included and excluded (in both generations).

It can be seen that the zero-order effect, the simple regression of first job SES on birthdate, is stronger when farmers are included. This reminds us that much of the change in Canadian occupational structure

TABLE 5:2 — Regression of First Job SES on Birthdate, Decomposed into Indirect and Net Effects (Unstandardized Coefficients)

	Gross Effect	Family* Effects	Resp. Educ.	Age of Entry	Net Effect	N
Farmers included	.245	.113	.144	−.025	.013	8032
Farmers excluded	.188	.081	.139	−.023	−.009	5769

*Combined effect of father's occupation, father's education, number of siblings, and community size at age 16.

during this century has constituted a migration off the farms. In both sets of results, most of the historical effect is accounted for by the control variables introduced into the analysis. "Family effects" — a cluster of variables representing father's occupation and education, city size at age 16, and number of siblings — account (in the results incorporating farmers) for some .11 Blishen points of the overall regression coefficient of .25 linking birthdate with first job.[8] When education is added into the equation the regression of first job SES on birthdate decreases by a further .14 Blishen points. The third control variable included in Table 5.2, age at which first job began, was introduced as a correction for the fact that age of entry into the labour force has risen over time. Since age of entry correlates positively with first job SES, it was supposed that part of the overall association between birthdate and first job status included this late entry effect. In fact, controlling for age of entry causes a slight enhancement in the size of the historical effect represented by birthdate. Apparently the slightly later average age of entry among younger cohorts is an epiphenomenon of historical increases in respondent's education and suppresses a small net tendency for age of entry actually to be lower among the more recent cohorts.

Finally, the table shows the remaining "net effect" of birthdate on first job to be tiny; with farmers included each extra year of birth adds an average of .01 Blishen points to respondent's first occupation. In the non-farm version, the net effect takes a minute negative value. We would not interpret either result to mean that there is no historical effect at work. On the contrary, it is historical period which has much to do with the education level of respondents, their parental SES, and the other intervening variables in a model of occupational attainment. What the figures in Table 5.2 provide is a piece of social accounting showing that industrialization sets into play the intervening factors which are associated with first job status; and the small net effect suggests that the important intervening variables have indeed been incorporated into the analysis.

Trends in the Flow From Father's Occupation to First Occupation

Transition tables describing the individual level mobility from father's occupation to respondent's first occupation, for age cohorts, appear in Table 5.3. In order to maintain a reasonably compact and interpretable presentation, occupation was grouped into five broad categories and birthdate was coded into ten-year intervals.[9] A further restriction in the population was instituted in these calculations; cases of very implausible

TABLE 5:3 — Outflow Percentages, Father's Occupation to Respondent's First Occupation, for Age Cohorts

| First Occupation | Father's Occupation | | | | |
	Upper White-Collar	Lower White-Collar	Upper Blue-Collar	Lower Blue-Collar	Farmers
Upper White-Collar					
25-34	39	27	14	10	9
35-44	41	17	9	8	8
45-54	34	12	7	4	5
55-64	30	6	5	4	5
65+	18	7	3	1	2
Lower White-Collar					
25-34	34	33	23	20	17
35-44	31	38	20	19	9
45-54	28	32	17	16	10
55-64	25	39	21	15	7
65+	32	44	15	15	9
Upper Blue-Collar					
25-34	14	23	39	34	33
35-44	17	25	41	33	31
45-54	19	28	49	35	29
55-64	15	26	47	29	26
65+	26	25	50	30	20
Lower Blue-Collar					
25-34	13	17	24	35	35
35-44	11	19	30	40	40
45-54	16	28	26	44	41
55-64	28	28	27	48	44
65+	22	23	31	47	44
Farmers					
25-34	0	0	0	1	6
35-44	0	1	0	1	12
45-54	3	0	1	2	16
55-64	2	1	1	5	18
65+	3	1	2	7	25

combinations of years of education versus age of entering first job were eliminated. It was noted earlier that the first occupation question in the mobility survey was vulnerable to misinterpretations by respondents. The question asked about the first full-time job upon completing education, but some people appear to have reported first jobs that preceded their last year of education. A few respondents reported entering the labour force while in their early teens or even sooner. We expected that some of the older respondents would report early entry and were prepared to accept this as likely to reflect historical reality. Sons of farmers, for instance, no doubt did frequently commence their own farming careers at an early age during the days before the modern minimum school leaving age was established. Reports of youthful entry into the labour force were, however, by no means confined to the eldest cohorts. Claims to have begun work before the age of ten, reports that can hardly be accepted as plausible for any cohort, were in fact most common among the group aged between 35 and 49. In correcting for these implausible reports the principle adopted was that the correction should err in the direction of tampering too little with the original data, rather than too much. Cases were eliminated only if two conditions were met: years of education (question 5 in the questionnaire) plus a constant of five years exceeded the age at which the respondents reported entry into first job; and level of education (question 4) coded into the equivalent years of education completed by those at each level, plus 5, exceeded the age of entry. The reason for these two conditions was that the simple report of years of education (plus the constant to account for preschool years) could sometimes validly exceed age of entry (as when the respondent had repeated years in school). Also, we had some reason to believe that the years of education question tended to be error prone. One eternal student, for example, reported sixty-seven years of education! The correction eliminated in the order of 6 per cent of the first job reports. All the tabulations reported from this point on include the correction.

The first panel of Table 5.3 shows for each ten-year cohort the percentage of respondents moving from one of the five categories of father's occupation into the upper white-collar group. It can be seen that all these percentages are largest for the youngest two cohorts, those aged 25 to 34 and 35 to 44 (the table is arranged so that trends are detected by reading down the columns in each panel). For example, only 1 per cent of sons of lower blue-collar fathers, in the over 65 cohort, entered upper white-collar first jobs. This percentage rose to 4 per cent in both the 55 to 64 and 45 to 54 groups, to 8 per cent in the 35 to 44 cohort, and finally to 10 per cent in the youngest age group. Mobility flows such as these partly reflect the expansion of highly skilled white-collar work in recent decades (later the results are shown with a statistical control for structural changes).

What the percentages in Table 5.3 reveal is that the upward mobility into the highest group, generated by upgrading in the labour force, has had consequences for those of every origin status. Thus, just as more sons of upper white-collar fathers have been able in recent times to maintain a position in that category, so too long-distance upward mobility from farming or blue-collar parental origins into the upper white-collar group has increased markedly over time. Trends involving sons in the lower white-collar category (second panel, Table 5.3) are less distinct and the explanation is probably that the group has not expanded as quickly as the upper white-collar occupations. The most distinct trend in panel 2 is an increasing movement into the lower white-collar level by sons of lower blue-collar workers. This outflow has increased in frequency from 15 per cent of lower blue-collar sons in the over 65 cohort to 20 per cent in the 25 to 34 year old group. Stability within the lower white-collar level is seen to have been greatest in the over 65 cohort (44 per cent) but the decline in percentage over successive cohorts is too erratic to form a pattern. The "inheritance" of an occupation within the same group as the father's does decline quite regularly by cohort in the upper blue-collar group (panel 3). Fifty per cent of sons, aged over 65, of upper blue-collar fathers took first jobs within the same category; the proportion was only 39 per cent in the youngest cohort. Another pattern in panel 3 is the increasing proportion of sons of farmers who have entered first jobs in the upper blue-collar categories.

Among workers in the lower blue-collar occupations (panel 4) are found trends that seem to reflect another particularly strong structural component. The outflow from father's group into first occupations in the lower blue-collar category tends to be greatest among the older cohorts. Downward mobility into this category by sons of white-collar fathers (both upper and lower), for instance, has generally become less common over time although the trend is irregular. Finally, the outflows for sons of farmers (panel 5) follow an expected pattern. The incidence of farm inheritance has, unsurprisingly, declined steadily over time. Mobility into farming by those of non-farming parentage is unusual in all cohorts, especially among the younger ones.

In terms of the simple overall flow between father's occupation and respondent's first occupation, then, an interpretation of increasing upward and decreasing downward mobility over time seems supported. These flows are probably more germane to consideration of the social consequences of mobility than to theories of temporal changes in social structure. If mobility has increased mainly due to structural pressures this does not make it less real for those who have moved to positions of greater status and life chances than their fathers'. The outflows provide, however, the least conservative test of the theory of increasing mobility as a society industrializes. Indeed, if a definition of an industrializing society is that it is one where the farm sector decreases in favour of the industrial sector, and where there is an expanded need for highly educated white-collar labour (Kerr, *et al.*, 1964:14), the interpretation that mobility outflow from father's occupation increases with industrialization becomes tautological.

Most students of mobility trends have felt that a more stringent test of mobility convergence theory is achieved when the effect of labour force transformation is removed by statistical control. In recent work, the popular approach has been to test for trends in net mobility by using log-linear modelling (see Chapter 3 for explanation of the technique). In applying this method to the data in Table 5.3, we shall follow procedures reported by Hauser, Koffel, *et al.* (1975). They examined how closely a model that explicitly did not assume an interaction effect between cohort, father's occupation, and son's occupation, fitted actual trend data. The test handled structural effects by including in the model the marginal distributions of father's occupation and son's first occupation. In other words, estimates of observed cell values for a table cross-tabulating father's occupation by son's occupation by cohort were generated using the simple marginal distributions of the three variables, together with the "two-way interaction" between each pair (if C = cohort, F = father's occupation, and S = son's occupation, the model would be expressed as *FS, FC, SC*). From a cohort analysis of the Blau and Duncan OCGI data, Hauser, Koffel, *et al.* discovered that this model provided a close fit (predicted cell values did not differ significantly from the observed) with the actual data. With collapsed coding of occupation, and the eldest cohort deleted, McRoberts and Selbee (1981) have recently found the same data set to pass the significance test for interaction by cohort in the mobility from father's to son's occupation. For the CMS data (with the youngest cohort deleted, in an attempt to match the U.S. data from 1962) the interaction failed to achieve significance in their analysis. The question of significance hinges in part upon decisions about how "design effect" (the effect for significance testing of departures from random sampling) should be handled. A log-linear analysis of the Canadian data as arranged in Table 5.3 results in an interaction significant at better than the .001 level, but significance is lost if the Chi-square from the log-linear test is deflated by the 0.57 factor employed by McRoberts and Selbee (1981:411). The accuracy of design effect estimates for mobility statistics appears to be controversial (Hauser,· Koffel, *et al.,* 1975:283). And measurement error, which usually has the opposite effect to design effect on significance tests, cannot be corrected for in the CMS data. In a cohort analysis, measurement error may have particularly serious consequences, since the error is likely to correlate inversely with birthdate (see note 12). All things considered, the accurate conclusion may be that father-son mobility interacts with cohort to a borderline level of significance.

The structure-free mobility tables can be presented, by means of the Deming (1943) adjustment, in a form allowing direct comparisons with the percentages in Table 5.3. The father's and son's occupational distributions were adjusted, for each cohort, to match the distributions in the overall table (age 25 and over). That is, the fact that the overall first occupation distribution differs from that for respondents' fathers was allowed to stand but the adjustment did ensure that these changes in distribution were identical within each age cohort of respondents. In short, the strategy was to treat structural effects in intergenerational mobility as a constant.

The adjusted percentages are presented in Table 5.4. A tendency within the non-farm sector, distinct though not entirely smooth, for the proportion of sons taking first jobs within the same category as their father's occupation to decline over cohorts is discernable. The clearest example of this trend is seen in panel 3 of the table. Some 49 per cent of sons of upper blue-collar fathers in the over 65 cohort entered first occupations within the upper blue-collar category. This proportion dropped to 46 per cent in the 55 to 64 cohort, 45 per cent in the 45 to 54 cohort, 42 per cent in the 34 to 44 cohort, and finally to 41 per cent among those aged 25 to 34. In the farming sector the trend runs in the opposite direction; the proportion of sons of farmers taking first jobs as farmers increases very slightly from older to younger cohorts. The actual stability within farming, it was seen (Table 5.3), has decreased over time. What the adjusted percentages (Table 5.4) reveal is that the actual trend can be attributed to the overall decline in farming in Canada. The net trend of a very slight increase over cohorts in the inheritance of farms is offset, in the adjusted table, by a compensating trend of decreasing mobility from farm origins into non-farm categories. Thus, the actual percentages (Table 5.3) show 9 per cent of sons of farmers having entered upper white-collar first jobs, in the youngest cohort, compared to only 2 per cent taking the same route among respondents aged 65 or over. Yet, allowing for the contraction of farming (Table 5.4), the competitive disadvantage suffered by off-farm migrants has increased slightly over time; 8 per cent of farmers' sons in the over 65 cohort entered upper white-collar jobs versus only 5 per cent in the 25 to 35 cohort.

Summarizing, the trend in circulation mobility is probably of

TABLE 5:4 — Adjusted Outflow Percentages

| First Occupation | Father's Occupation | | | | |
	Upper White-Collar	Lower White-Collar	Upper Blue-Collar	Lower Blue-Collar	Farmers
Upper White-Collar					
25-34	30	20	10	6	5
35-44	40	16	8	7	7
45-54	40	16	10	5	6
55-64	43	10	9	7	9
65+	38	17	8	4	8
Lower White-Collar					
25-34	34	31	20	16	13
35-44	32	38	20	19	8
45-54	28	35	19	18	12
55-64	22	40	22	16	8
65+	27	43	17	18	11
Upper Blue-Collar					
25-34	17	26	41	34	30
35-44	18	25	42	34	30
45-54	15	24	45	32	27
55-64	13	25	46	29	27
65+	19	22	49	32	23
Lower Blue-Collar					
25-34	18	23	29	40	37
35-44	11	19	30	40	39
45-54	14	25	25	43	40
55-64	21	24	23	43	41
65+	15	17	26	43	44
Farmers					
25-34	0	0	0	4	15
35-44	0	1	0	1	16
45-54	3	0	1	1	15
55-64	2	1	0	4	14
65+	1	0	1	4	14

borderline statistical significance. The chief feature of the adjusted outflow tables is a tendency for congruency between father's occupation and son's first occupation to decline over time (in all but the farming category). This pattern can be represented in simple statistical fashion using a modification of the log-linear model. If the main diagonal, where fathers and sons fall into the same broad grouping, is blocked (Goodman, 1969), the three-way interaction between the two occupations and cohort now is well short of significance. The temporal trend principally concerns, it might be concluded, the incidence of mobility versus immobility rather than varieties of mobility.

Trends in the Statistical Association Between Father's Occupation and Respondent's First Occupation

We shall now see how different summary statistics represent trends in the overall association between father's and son's occupation. Such statistics are of interest because they identify somewhat different features about a mobility transition table than does a cell-by-cell inspection of simple outflow percentages or adjusted percentages. In a sense, measures of association are supposed to reflect net effects in mobility. The Pearsonian correlation, for example, standardizes variables so that a simple upgrading in occupation status over generations should not affect the correlation between the statuses. This property makes the correlation a useful summary measure of mobility (see for example, Duncan and Hodge, 1963:629-34). In a simpler way, the Chi-square also is at least partially independent of simple structural upgrading or downgrading. In another sense, however, most of the measures may still be affected by an aspect of structural mobility. Most indices of correlation are not independent of the marginal distributions of the variables (Blalock, 1961:116; 1967; 1976; Smith, 1976). The Pearsonian correlation can only reach maximum value when distributions "match" (Cohen and Cohen, 1975:59). To compute measures of statistical association between occupation variables is, then, to capture a hybrid form of mobility, neither purely "gross" nor "net" in the usual understanding of the terms. In our view, mobility so computed allows the most realistic test of the hypothesis linking trends in mobility to industrialization. Table 5.5 (upper portion) shows how several statistics, requiring different levels of measurement and/or assumptions, portray the longitudinal trend in mobility. The first statistic is Cramer's V. Derived directly from the basic Chi-square, it is based on the assumption of unordered categories. It does not, in other words, distinguish mobility over different distances. The statistic simply reacts to any cell entries that

TABLE 5:5 — Measures of Association, Father's Occupation by Son's First Occupation, by Cohort

Cohort	N	Cramer's V	Somer's D	Gamma	Canonical Correlation
A. Actual Trends					
25-34	3152	.185	.252	.335	.322 (.170)*
35-44	2349	.231	.283	.380	.372 (.243)
45-54	2148	.228	.274	.376	.352 (.243)
55-64	1733	.246	.302	.409	.388 (.238)
65+	1141	.261	.377	.507	.432 (.261)
B. Hypothetical Trends: Those attributable solely to structural effects.					
25-34		.205	.273	.362	.338 (.201)
35-44	as	.219	.285	.383	.359 (.222)
45-54	above	.226	.292	.400	.374 (.224)
55-64		.236	.316	.430	.398 (.226)
65+		.241	.355	.481	.423 (.204)
C. Actual Trends less Hypothetical Ones					
25-34		−.020	−.021	−.027	−.016 (−.031)
35-44	as	.012	−.002	−.003	.013 (.021)
45-54	above	.002	−.018	−.024	−.022 (.019)
55-64		.010	−.014	−.021	−.010 (.012)
65+		.020	.022	.026	.009 (.057)

*Second canonical correlation.

vary from those expected from the alignment of the marginal frequencies of the variables being tabulated. The overall trend in mobility, computed thus, is a decline in association between father's occupation and respondent's first occupation, indicating evidence of increased overall mobility in recent times. Next in Table 5.5 is the trend given by Somer's D, a rank order statistic that assumes categories are hierarchial. The trend is again one of declining association slightly broken between the 35 to 44 and 45 to 54 year old cohorts. Gamma (column 5) suggests much the same pattern.

The use of canonical methods in analysing mobility tables has been suggested by some British researchers (Hope, 1972; Duncan-Jones, 1972). The procedure is to treat each category of father's and son's occupation as a dummy variable. All prior assumptions about the ordering of the categories are suspended and the canonical analysis rearranges (and scores) the categories so as to maximize the correlation between the independent and the dependent variables. This feature seems particularly desirable when the farm category is included in a mobility table, because it is difficult to place farming in a rank ordering of occupational status. A further strength of the canonical correlation would seem to be that (like the Chi-square) it relaxes assumptions of linearity. The canonical correlation between father's occupation and respondent's first occupation (column 6, Table 5.5) is .11 points lower in the youngest (25 to 34) cohort than in the eldest (65+). The slight reversal of the trend within the 35 to 54 age groups is again present.

There appears to be controversy within the methods literature over which measures of association are totally margin free (and thus indexes of circulation mobility). Gamma has been said to be such a statistic (Mueller, Schuessler, and Costner, 1970:286), but Blalock (1976) has argued that only the unstandardized regression coefficient is so endowed. Also, it has been thought that on this criterion the canonical correlation is superior to most measures (Duncan-Jones, 1972:204). An effective approach to assessing these claims, within the context of mobility correlations, is provided by work by Hauser, Dickinson, *et al.* (1975) and in the middle portion of Table 5.5 we have adapted their technique to our problem. Hauser performed hypothetical calculations in which a single American father-to-son mobility matrix was successively manipulated, using a Deming adjustment, to take the occupation margins for different decades. Since the intrinsic association within the table had been set as a constant, a margin-free statistic could be expected to remain unchanged even as the margins were deliberately altered. Hauser and his colleagues could then assess the behaviour of different mobility indices by examining which of them did remain invariant. This procedure has been followed, in Table 5.5, taking the father's occupation to first occupation matrix for the entire Canadian sample aged 25 and over (and native-born) as the standard. The matrix was successively weighted by the occupation margins characterizing each age cohort and the measures of association were recalculated to give the "hypothetical trends" presented in panel B of Table 5.5 None of the statistics employed in the analysis described earlier behave in the manner expected of a margin-free measure. All record a gradual but unbroken decline in association, a decline attributable solely to changes in occupational distribution, but changes more complex than a simple upward transformation over generations.

Next, this hypothetical association was subtracted from each of the corresponding actual results seen in the upper portion of Table 5.5. The differences between the actual and expected results appear in the lower part of the table. These we take as an indication of the trends in statistical association resulting from changes in circulation mobility. Computed thus, the test becomes roughly equivalent to the mobility outflow table following Deming adjustment (Table 5.4) or to the log-linear test for three-way interaction. The structure-free test in Table 5.5, however, emphasizes the direction of the overall trend in terms of familiar measures of association, and so allows easy assessment of substantive importance.

Corrected as described above, all four statistics have some features in common. Each yields a trace — but no more — of a trend in the association between father's and son's occupation. The overall spread between the youngest and eldest cohorts is in the order of .03 to .04 correlation points for each of the statistics.

What one makes of the three types of trend presented in Table 5.5, the uncorrected trend, the trend attributable to margin effects, and the net trend, seems largely a matter of sociological judgment. Each addresses different queries and it is a question of which of these concerns is regarded as the most important. The hypothetical trends, for instance, possess importance in their own right. They suggest that the association between occupations over generations varies in strength in different parts of the inter-generational mobility table. As the occupation distribution of fathers and sons in a sample alters over time, different parts of the table are accentuated or diminished and so the overall contingency between generations is seen to change. If this is structural mobility, it is a second order variety, distinct from the simple form where sons take a step in unison up the ladder from their fathers' positions.

An alternative assessment of trends over time in the association, free of structure, between father's occupation and son's first occupation is presented in Table 5.6. The same approach was followed as above, but the Blishen scale was substituted for the five ordinal groups. Farmers were excluded in most of the calculations here because it seems doubtful that farming can be adequately represented by a single.SES score. The socioeconomic scale of occupation is of interest because, being an interval ordering, it allows the use of regression analysis. It is the unstandardized regression coefficient which is generally thought to be the appropriate statistic to compute when making comparisons between sub-groups. Respondents were scored using the first digit of the scale so as to permit the control for structural effects instituted in Table 5.5. The Deming adjustments would have become unmanageable if the full two digits of the scale had been employed.

The first column of results in Table 5.6 shows the Pearsonian correlation (as usual, between father's occupation and son's first occupation). The trend here is akin to those seen in Table 5.5; the

TABLE 5:6 — **Alternative Presentation: Father's Occupation by Son's First Occupation (Coded in Blishen Scores), by Cohort**

Cohort	r	B	Excluding Farm Canonical Correlation	Incl. Farm Canonical Correlation	Standard Deviations† Father's Occupation	First Occupation
A. *Actual Trends*						
25-34	.363	.425	.428 (.320)*	.416 (.340)*	1.29	1.51
35-44	.322	.349	.435 (.292)	.396 (.335)	1.31	1.43
45-54	.353	.353	.585 (.320)	.544 (.389)	1.32	1.32
55-64	.365	.329	.660 (.336)	.636 (.376)	1.36	1.24
65+	.466	.438	.709 (.379)	.667 (.456)	1.35	1.27
B. *Hypothetical Trends:* those attributable to structural effects.						
25-34	.352	.413	.507 (.327)	.478 (.369)		
35-44	.354	.384	.517 (.324)	.501 (.380)		
45-54	.354	.353	.549 (.306)	.517 (.380)	as above	
55-64	.362	.329	.593 (.311)	.551 (.395)		
54+	.396	.372	.674 (.303)	.616 (.383)		
C. *Actual Trends less Hypothetical ones*						
25-34	.011	.012	−.079 (−.007)	−.062 (−.029)		
35-44	−.032	−.035	−.082 (−.032)	−.105 (−.045)		
45-54	−.001	.000	.036 (.014)	.027 (.009)	as above	
55-64	.003	.000	.067 (.025)	.085 (−.019)		
65+	.070	.066	.035 (.076)	.051 (.073)		

*Second canonical correlation.
†Excluding farm.

statistical association between occupations in the two generations has slowly declined over time although in Table 5.6 the 25 to 34 cohort breaks the pattern. The hypothetical correlations, seen in the middle panel of Table 5.6, reveal that margin effects alone would predict such a trend. Subtracting the hypothetical correlations from the observed allows the detection of a trend net of structure. The difference between cohorts, computed this way, becomes very small. Indeed, apart from the over 65 cohort, which stands out as having a markedly stronger correlation than one would expect from the hypothetical result, no trend remains.

The unstandardized regression coefficient appears in column 3 of Table 5.6. This statistic describes a new pattern. Contrary to the Pearsonian correlation, it tends, if anything, to increase over time. The slope for the over 65 cohort (B = .438) is an exception to this pattern as it is slightly greater than that for the youngest cohort (B = .425). The surprising aspect of the regression trend is not that it runs in the opposite direction to the trends seen using other statistics. Slopes and correlations are known to capture different aspects of the association between variables. What is instructive is that the values of the regression coefficients in this analysis are predicatable from the corresponding hypothetical coefficients, seen in the middle portion of Table 5.6. This fact convinces us that the trend observed for the Pearsonian correlation is more than an uninteresting "restriction of range" phenomenon (Cohen and Cohen, 1975:64-65) resulting from the sampling of the cohort sub-groups within the total sample. The shape of the distribution of son's occupation has in fact increasingly over time departed from that for father's. Both distributions are skewed to the right (large proportions in the low status range), but son's occupation in recent cohorts has moved toward a symmetrical distribution. As the distributions have moved out of synchronization, son's occupational SES has necessarily (Cohen and Cohen, 1975:60) become less predictable from father's (hence the declining correlation in Table 5.6, middle) and the slope of son's occupation on father's has (as also observed in Table 5.6) necessarily increased over cohorts. The more steeply sloped regression line expresses the fact that increases in upward mobility correspond to the shifts in distribution. This mobility — a form of heterocedasticity in the relationship between father's and son's SES — occurs in the data for earlier cohorts, but has increased in relative frequency over time. Because the trend toward a symmetrical distribution for occupation is a key consequence of industrialization, we attribute importance to the trend, and to its implications for mobility.

The next results in Table 5.6 (columns 4 and 5) describe the trend when the canonical correlation is employed. These correlations supply stronger evidence of structure-free alterations over time in the association between father's occupation and respondent's first occupation. The decline over cohorts occurs both in the actual and in the hypothetical correlations, but the net trend is in the order of .11 correlation points between the youngest and eldest cohorts. The pattern is essentially the same when farmers are included in the analysis (column 5, Table 5.6).

The net trends (actual correlations less hypothetical ones) have taken a somewhat different form in the alternative presentation than in Table 5.5. In Table 5.5, using five occupation groups, the magnitude of the net trend did not seem to differ greatly according to which statistic was used. In Table 5.6, where the Blishen scale was adopted, the trend is much more marked under non-linear assumptions (canonical correlations) than under linear ones (correlations or slopes). Indeed, conclusions about whether net trends exist depend in Table 5.6 upon whether or not linear assumptions are retained. The structure-free trends in Table 5.5 are smoother over cohorts than those (in linear form) in Table 5.6 where the trend is largely attributable to the over 65 cohort. Finally, in Table 5.5 it was the 35 to 44 year olds that constituted the principal departure from the overall trend while in Table 5.6 it is the 25 to 34 cohort which is the main exception. The detail on trends in the statistical association between father's and son's occupation has admittedly threatened to become overwhelming. A general interpretation is attempted at the conclusion of the chapter but, in part, our point is that caution is in order when concluding that trends in father-son circulation mobility do or do not exist.

Trends in the Relative Importance of Ascribed Versus Achieved Predictors of First Occupation

The final temporal trend to be examined concerns the relative importance of different kinds of predictors in a multivariate model of first occupation attainment. Theory predicts that as a society industrializes, the importance of achieved determinants of SES increases at the expense of ascribed factors.

A test of this theory is shown in Table 5.7. The population is again restricted to non-farmers although the tabulations were also performed with farmers included (not shown). Five family background characteristics — father's occupation and education, respondent's ethnic standing, respondent's family size when he was growing up, and community size at age 16 — are entered under the heading "ascribed statuses."[10]

The joint explanatory importance of the ascribed statuses is represented first by a coefficient of determination (percentage variance explained) and then by the standard error of estimate. The trend, Table 5.7 reveals, has been the expected decrease in the ascriptive importance of the family background characteristics. The variance in first occupation attributable to the five background variables has declined from 31 per cent in the over 65 cohort to 19 per cent in the 25 to 34 cohort. The standard error of estimate, which estimates the standard deviation of the residuals from the regression linking first job with the background variables, is seen to increase over time, showing in another way that our ability to accurately predict first job SES, knowing only father's status, respondent's ethnic status, family size, and community size, has declined.

The regression coefficients describing the trend in the strength of

TABLE 5:7 — Regression Analysis Showing Trends in the Relative Importance of Ascribed Versus Achieved Predictors of First Occupation SES (Unstandardized Coefficients, Nonfarm Population)

Cohort	N	Ascribed Status*			Achieved Status†			Total	
		Variance Explained	B	Standard Error of Estimate	B	Increment in Variance Explained		Total Variance Explained	Standard Error of Estimate
25-34	2120	19.0%		13.46	2.97	28.3%		47.3%	10.86
35-44	1429	18.7%		12.89	2.50	29.9%		48.6%	10.25
45-54	1191	20.7%		11.88	1.86	20.2%		40.9%	10.24
55-64	884	21.5%		10.84	1.55	14.7%		36.2%	9.77
65+	512	31.2%		10.43	1.52	14.7%		45.9%	9.25
Total	6136	21.5%		12.55	2.19	23.4%		44.9%	10.52

*Father's occupation and education, respondent's ethnic standing, respondent's family size when he was growing up, community size at age 16.

†Respondent's education, net of ascribed status.

education as a predictor of first job, seen in the right hand portion of
Table 5.7, are net of the five ascribed statuses. The coefficient can be
considered an indicator of the importance of achieved status since it
estimates the contribution of education in accounting for occupation,
independently of the background family characteristics (all of which
have consequences for education). As in other chapters, education is
scored according to level of schooling attained.

As Chapter 3 showed, over the total population education far
outweighs ascribed status in importance. And, from Table 5.7, the trend
is an ever-increasing importance in education.[11] Among those aged over
65, who would probably have entered the labour force before the
mid-1920s, each year of education added an average 1.5 Blishen points
to first job status. By the youngest cohort, who were starting to enter the
job market by the late 1950s, the increment had risen to an average of
three Blishen points. The results have been presented in ten-year
cohorts, again to maintain a readable table. The trend is smooth when
broken down into five-year cohorts (not shown in Table 5.7) with the
exception of the 55 to 59 year old group. Here, as in the simple mean
first job scores shown earlier, there is a downturn indicative of a
dislocation in the demand and supply for labour skills during the early
1930s.

The coefficient of determination and standard error of estimate are,
like the Pearsonian correlation or standardized regression coefficient,
partially dependent on the distribution of the variables entered in the
analysis. This means that the trend for ascribed variables to diminish
over time in importance is probably partially due to the increasing
normality in the distribution of son's SES. What seems important about
the trend involving education, however, is that the share in the variance
explained due to education, versus the ascribed factors, has increased
markedly over cohorts (column 6, Table 5.7. Further, the variance in
education (not included in Table 5.7) has decreased in each cohort.
When the exercise (described earlier) of fitting varying margins to a
constant table, this time education by first job, is repeated, the predicted
(bivariate) trend that would occur solely because of margin effects is that
education *decreases* in importance over time. In short, the trend observed
in Table 5.7 concerning the relationship between education and first job
SES constitutes, so far as we can tell, a genuine specification according to
historical period.

Canadian and American Patterns Compared

The trends found for Canada are more pronounced than those that

American sociologists seem to find in their country. In the Blau and Duncan study, for example, no tendency for education to assume an increasingly important relationship with first job was discovered (Blau and Duncan, 1967:178, 181). Mobility with all aspects of structure removed may be near to temporally stable in both societies but the Canadian trends concerning both the importance of education and changes in father-to-son mobility under partial control for structure suggest a more than trivial Canadian-American difference.

To make sense of the differences between Canadian and American trend results we shall refer back to the theory linking mobility with industrialization. Although historically the less-developed country, Canada has been industrializing over the past several decades at a faster rate than the United States has. During the past forty years, indices such as the percentage urban and the proportion receiving university education have been catching up to the American rates (Stone, 1967:16; Kubat and Thornton, 1974:121; United States Department of Commerce, 1960:221; 1974:133). It is the more rapid change in the level of industrialization within Canada, we would argue, that accounts for the international differences in rates of change in mobility patterns.

A quantitative representation of this argument can be presented by using the formulas, described earlier, developed by Hazelrigg (1974; Hazelrigg and Garnier, 1976). Hazelrigg's argument was that for any country the overall rate of circulation mobility and the rank order correlation between father's and son's occupation could be predicted knowing only the average rate of energy consumption for that society. It was seen earlier that the substitution of Canadian energy figures into Hazelrigg's formulas produces quite an accurate estimation of both the true rank order correlation between father's occupation and son's current occupation, and the circulation mobility rate. Now, the formula shall be used to generate time series estimates. The 1976 version of the formula was employed, and the results appear in Table 5.8. Average rates of Canadian energy consumption for different decades from the 1920s to the 1970s are entered in the second column of the table. The third column enters the equivalent data for the United States. Ten-year intervals are used in order to emphasize changes over the same interval as in presenting most of the cohort trend results. The energy consumption figures reflect the convergence that has taken place between the two economies over the past six decades. Canadian consumption was only 53 per cent of that in the United States in the 1920s, but by 1975 had reached 90 per cent of the American rate.

The next two columns (4 and 5) in Table 5.8 show the rank order correlation resulting when the energy consumption figures are entered

TABLE 5:8 — Mobility Rates, Predicted from Energy Consumption, for Canada and the United States

Decade	Energy Consumption*		Somer's D†		Circulation‡	
	Can.	U.S.	Can.	U.S.	Can.	U.S.
1920s	3258	6196	.409	.376	.341	.367
1930s	3192	5286	.410	.384	.341	.361
1940s	unknown		—	—	—	—
1950s	5715	8174	.380	.361	.364	.378
1960s	7615	9646	.365	.353	.375	.384
1970s	10,459	11,596	.349	.343	.388	.392
Differences						
1920s-1970s	7201	5400	.060	.033	.047	.025

*Kilograms per capita (coal equivalents). *Source:* Joel Darmstadter, *Energy in the World Economy* (Baltimore: John Hopkins Press), p. 653; United Nations, *Statistical Yearbook* (New York: Publishing Service, United Nations), 1975 and other years. The Darmstadter data run from 1925 to 1965. The 1925 figure is used as an estimate of the 1920s average. UN data are converted, by a linking adjustment, to be equivalent with Darmstadter's.
†Computed from a formula presented in Hazelrigg and Garnier (1976:506).
‡Computed from a formula presented in Hazelrigg and Garnier (1976:504).

into the appropriate Hazelrigg formula. These could be considered rough estimates of the correlations between father's occupation and son's current occupation that might result if a series of mobility samples had been collected each decade in the United States and Canada (the 1920s energy data predict the correlation that would have occurred in 1930, and so on for each decade). The estimates cannot be expected to be exact because, for one thing, we have not used the formula quite properly. The formula was built using energy consumption averaged over the twenty-five years preceding the collection of each study. Using the ten-year averages, a necessary compromise in order to generate a full predicted time series, causes a slight overestimation of the mobility in each decade. Also, of course, the formula is designed to be used with international data. What the exercise of forcing historical energy consumption figures for Canada and the United States into the formula shows is that the predicted decline in the Canadian correlations exceeds that expected in the United States by a twofold margin. The formula takes the logarithm of energy consumption, meaning that the experience from the international comparison of societies at differing levels of industrialization is that there are diminishing returns to mobility resulting from increases in industrialization. Part of the convergence in predicted mobility rates for Canada and the United States is due to this effect; the United States falls on the flatter portion of the curve, where changes in industrialization translate into only small changes in the father-son occupation correlation. Over the years under consideration, Canada fell on a more steeply sloped portion of the curve, and the predicted changes in mobility are accordingly larger. Canada by the mid-1970s lay close to the energy consumption rate prevailing in the United States and in both countries we would not expect, according to the curve, that future changes in the father-son correlation would be very marked.

The final two columns in Table 5.8 show the predicted trend data for the "person-rate circulation" (percent mobile in an adjusted table) in Canada and the United States. Again, the best-fitting curve describing the relationship between energy consumption and the circulation rate takes a log transformation of per capita energy consumption. This curve too suggests that as energy consumption rises the rate of increase in mobility may be expected to slow down. It can be seen that, as before, the predicted change in the Canadian mobility rate exceeds that expected for the United States.

The reliance upon formulas based on international mobility data to generate predicted logitudinal trends can be criticized because of the crudeness of coding in occupation that has, to date, been used in such work. As we noted earlier, the Hazelrigg and Garnier formulas are based on mobility data coded into the familiar white-collar, blue-collar, and farm groups. One must remember too that energy consumption is merely an indicator of industrialization and not a causal variable in itself. If, in the future, energy consumption were to decline due to more efficient usage, while the level of industrial activity stayed level, mobility rates would, we presume, remain unchanged despite the fact that the formulas would predict a decline in circulation together with an increase in the correlation of father's with son's occupation.

Finally, in constructing formulas to express the relationship between mobility and industrialization the issue of net versus structural trends reappears. Hazelrigg and Garnier (1976) have addressed this matter. The rank order correlation, Somer's D, is known to be influenced by the occupation margins. Simple structural upgrading is discounted but not more complex structural effects. The main contribution that Table 5.8 makes is to show that the changes in industrialization (and hence the occupational transformations) have occurred more rapidly in Canada than in the United States, and to express quantitatively the effect this might have on the inter-generational mobility correlation.

The situation surrounding the circulation rates is more complicated.

Up to a point, the Hazelrigg formula linking industrialization with circulation does refer to mobility free of structure. Each father-to-son matrix is adjusted so that the son's occupation distribution matches the father's. Hazelrigg and Garnier also experimented with a formula using a different adjustment, one that set both distributions to equal proportions. They imagined, in other words, that in each country represented in their samples one-third of fathers and sons were farmers, one-third were manual, and the other one-third were white-collar. These rates were found not to correlate with energy consumption. The endeavour to account for differences among nations in rates of mobility would appear to reach end point when such stringent statistical controls are in effect.

Conclusion

It was suggested earlier that over time indices of various aspects of occupational mobility might be expected to change due to the increasing industrial activity that has, to date, characterized most modern societies. In a cohort analysis of national Canadian data, it has been seen that some mobility patterns exhibit more distinct change than others. The simple upgrading in mean status over cohorts is marked and is not surprising; it follows industrialization virtually by definition. And, the importance of education in determining first occupation was seen to have increased over time. This appears to be one of the more robust findings from the analysis and does not disappear even after statistical adjustments for structural effects.

When mobility data are presented as a flow table describing the interchange between father's occupation and son's first occupation, a trend toward increasing mobility is pronounced. When the consequences of changes in occupational distribution over time are statistically removed, the temporal trend is greatly reduced and questions of statistical significance become dependent upon procedural details.

In our judgment, the evidence on balance is that there *has* been a trend toward greater circulation mobility in Canada, but the effect is tiny. Probably it is unrealistic to expect more than a small trend over relatively short historical periods, barring a massive social revolution. Inter-generational mobility is a basic bivariate relationship in social stratification, in which shifts in mediating processes (such as the linkage between family background, education, and occupation) may balance each other out. And a total control for structure trivializes the question of whether industrialization stimulates mobility, in our view. Just as there is a danger of testing convergence theory in a tautological manner which takes as the mobility indicator a characteristic virtually part of the definition of industrialization, so there is danger in exerting statistical controls so powerful that industrialization itself is controlled out of the analysis. For this reason, we view McRoberts and Selbee's (1981:406) conclusion that "there is no trend in mobility. . ." as premature. If industrialization proliferates the occupational roles in a society, so that the variance in son's occupational distribution increases over time, the resulting increase in mobility is more than simply a forced upward step in rank from a generation of fathers to a generation of sons. If mobility data should be conceived as heteroscedastic, with pockets of high and low ascriptive linkage, there is nothing trivial about an industrial transformation which moves a society from the ascriptive into the more achievement-type pockets. The evidence, perhaps seen most unambiguously in the "hypothetical" (but also in the "actual") trends in tables 5.5 and 5.6 is that during the twentieth century in Canada such varieties of second-order structural mobility have increased. This, we conclude, is the most sociologically interesting aspect of the inter-generational mobility results, and offers the most logical test of a convergence theory of mobility.

Convergence theories of mobility rates are, of course, not the only way of approaching questions about mobility trends. Alternative theoretical positions might result in empirical results similar to those shown here but the interpretations and emphasis might well differ. It is true that several of the trends exhibit exceptions which a more historically sensitive interpretation (e.g., Bertaux, 1976) might succeed in making sense of. The approach followed here has been to be cautious about attributing substantive meaning to irregularities in the trend data. Our impression has been that many of the bumps are artifacts of the characteristics of different statistical measures, scales, and procedures. A minute scrutiny of the historical meaning behind each data pattern might lead only to over-interpretation. As well, the method that has been used in assessing mobility trends — the cohort analysis — seems a blunt instrument. The historical period that can be surveyed using the technique is brief, and there are undoubtedly errors in measurement, some of which may very likely correlate with historical period (age of respondent).[12]

Another matter in which alternative interpretations are to be expected is the assessments of the ethical meaning of trends. It seems to be implicitly understood in the convergence approach to mobility trends that the expected patterns, decreasing conjunction between the status of fathers and sons, and the like, are ideologically pleasing. Functional analysis has, of course, always been wary of entering into ethical debates.

194   *JOHN C. GOYDER*

Assessments of the ideological implications of social stratification data often turn out to be exceedingly complicated. Some writers have offered alternative views on the ethical implications of commonly encountered empirical mobility patterns. On face value, for instance, a finding that education net of family background has become an increasingly strong correlate of later occupational success would seem to indicate increasing egalitarianism. Some have argued, contrary to this view, that the finding simply reflects a growing credentialism (e.g., Berg, 1970). The view here would be that employers are linking employment unnecessarily closely to formal educational qualifications.

Even a statistic as rudimentary as the zero order regression of son's occupation on father's occupation admits to alternative ideological implications. Conventional interpretations would argue that a steep slope is ethically displeasing because the achievements of sons are seen merely to be tied to those of their fathers. A more horizontal slope may, however, be no more satisfactory. A group with very low range in current occupation would exhibit a small regression slope, yet this might reflect high ascription, as has been found to be the case for blacks of a decade ago in the United States (Featherman and Hauser, 1976) and to some extent for women. The seeming paradox, then, is that mobility is only possible in a stratified society — one in which there is a distribution of ranks. An unstratified society, exhibiting zero mobility, might be considered satisfactory but only if the homogeneity in status held across the whole society. To find that "ceiling" or "floor" effects induce homogeneity among pockets, such as ethnic groups, within a society is simply to discover another ascriptive criterion governing mobility. And even if the homogeneity is society-wide, it can still be viewed as an ascriptive pocket within the context of international socioeconomic stratification. It is at this point, where one begins to debate the relative merits of an undifferentiated society (where mobility cannot occur) versus one with stratification together with mobility, that personal preference becomes paramount and even a partially objective assessment of the ethical implications of mobility data becomes impossible.

Notes

1. The meaning of the structural versus net mobility distinction is elaborated in Chapter 3.
2. The limitations of the occupation codes in his cross-national data obliged Hazelrigg to rely on a simple non-manual, manual, farm ordering. Hazelrigg averaged energy data over the twenty-five years preceding the collection of the mobility survey for each country. The same source of

energy consumption statistics was used in the present calculations as was used by Hazelrigg (Darmstadter, 1971). We would like to acknowledge our appreciation to Joel Darmstadter, who supplied us with additional year-by-year energy statistics which facilitated the historical comparisons. The earlier version (Hazelrigg, 1974) was based upon data from ten countries, the second version (Hazelrigg and Garnier, 1976) retained five of these and added twelve new studies to the analysis. Two of these were from third world countries. Some of the additions were later studies from countries represented in the earlier formula.

3. There appear to be computational errors in the 1974 version of this formula.

4. Other arguments have also been suggested in favour of decreasing mobility. Several American writers (Sibley, 1942; Hertzler, 1952; Chinoy, 1955; Blau and Duncan, 1967:426) have noted that middle-class fertility rose following the Second World War and that this should have closed up occupational vacancies in upper white-collar jobs. Attention has been called as well to the rise of corporations during the twentieth century, and the damaging consequences of this for entrepreneurship (Mills, 1956; Hertzler, 1952). Along with corporate organization, the growth of unions has been held to be detrimental to individual mobility because unionism places priority on group income gains rather than on individual promotion (Hertzler, 1952).

5. See Chapter 11 for details.

6. Concentration is on males because it was felt that longitudinal tends among females would stretch beyond the scope of this chapter (see Chapter 7 for some data for females classified by age cohort). Foreign-born respondents were omitted because it is difficult to know what historical forces this group is subject to. Their biographies would often include a mixture of experiences, some in the mother country, others in Canada. This mixture is, to be sure, germane to the accurate *description* of mobility in Canada (see, for instance, Chapter 8) but not, without elaborate controls, to the present concern.

7. The proportion of respondents losing their jobs sometime between the ages of 16 and 25 was highest among those currently aged 60 to 64 (6.5 per cent). The proportion descends, with each group, reaching a minimum among the 45 to 49 cohort (2.6 per cent). The rate then rises with each cohort, reaching 5.2 per cent in the youngest group.

8. These factors have been grouped together because it is difficult to order them in sequence of events. The logic of the analysis presented in this section is based upon such an ordering for it employs a set of recursive regression equations.

9. The upper white-collar category is composed of professionals, high-level managers, and semi-professionals. Technicians, middle-level managers, white-collar supervisors, and skilled and semi-skilled clerical and sales workers were coded as lower white-collar. Upper blue-collar consists of foremen, skilled, and semi-skilled crafts and trades workers. Unskilled workers and farm labourers were coded as lower blue collar, and farm owners and managers were coded as farmers.

10. Ethnic status was shown in Chapter 10 to involve important historical trends. It is scored using a scale of ethnic prestige, developed by Pineo (1977).

11. A more detailed analysis of trends in the importance of education, with attention to the university educated, appears in Goyder (1980).

12. A crude indicator of the reliability of occupation reports by different aged respondents is the non-response rate. Non-response on father's occupation rises from 13 per cent among respondents aged 25 to 34 to 17 per cent among those aged 55 to 64. Non-response on first occupation rises more sharply with age: from 9 per cent of those aged 25 to 34 to 17 per cent of those aged 55 to 64. Non-response on education is low for all cohorts: 2 per cent among those 25 to 34, 3 per cent among those 55 to 64 years of age. Some additional signs of the roughness of cohort analysis are suggested by findings emerging from the 1973 replication of the Blau and Duncan study from 1962. Featherman and Hauser (1976) have recently published data comparing relationships between status variables for the eleven-year interval spanned by the two studies. Education has been seen to have increased over the decade in importance as a predictor of occupation, yet an internal analysis of the 1962 data suggested no hint of such a trend across cohorts. And the importance of father's occupation in predicting son's current occupation has decreased by an amount that, amplified over the forty-years covered in a cohort analysis, would represent a marked trend. The fact that only son's first occupation can be compared with background variables (see text, page 168) prevents an investigation of trends in career mobility. It is sometimes suggested that career mobility offsets changes in inter-generational mobility.

References

BELL, DANIEL
  1973   *The Coming of Post-Industrial Society*. New York: Basic Books.
BERG, IVAR
  1970   *Education and Jobs: The Great Training Robbery*. New York: Praeger.
BERTAUX, D.
  1976   "An Assessment of Garnier and Hazelrigg's Paper on Intergenerational Mobility in France." *American Journal of Sociology*, 82 (Sept.):388-98.
BLALOCK, HUBERT H.
  1961   *Causal Inferences in Nonexperimental Research*. Chapel Hill: University of North Carolina Press.
  1967   "Causal Inferences, Closed Populations, and Measures of Association." *American Political Science Review*, 61 (March):130-36.
  1976   "Can we find a genuine ordinal slope analogue?" In David Heise, ed. *Sociological Methodology*. San Francisco: Jossey-Bass.
BLAU, PETER
  1955   *The Dynamics of Bureaucracy*. Chicago: University of Chicago Press.
BLAU, PETER M. and O.D. DUNCAN
  1967   *The American Occupational Structure*. New York: John Wiley.
CHINOY, ELY
  1955   "Social Mobility Trends in the United States." *American Sociological Review*, 20:180-86.

CLEMENT, WALLACE
1975   *The Canadian Corporate Elite: An Analysis of Economic Power.* Toronto: Carleton Library, No. 89.

COHEN, JACOB and PATRICIA COHEN
1975   *Applied Multiple Regression/Correlation Analysis for the Behavioral Sciences.* New York: Lawrence Erlbaum.

CUTRIGHT, PHILLIPS
1968   "Occupational Inheritance: A Cross-National Analysis." *American Journal of Sociology,* 73 (3):400-16.

DARMSTADTER, JOEL
1971   *Energy in the World Economy.* Baltimore: John Hopkin's Press.

DAVIS, K.
1962   "The Role of Class Mobility in Economic Development." *Population Review,* 6 (July):67-73.

DEMING, W. EDWARDS
1943   *Statistical Adjustment of Data.* New York: John Wiley.

DUNCAN, O.D.
1968   "Social Stratification and Mobility: Problems in the Measurement of Trends." In Eleanor Bernert Sheldon and Wilbert E. Moore, eds., *Indicators of Social Change.* New York: Russell Sage Foundation.

DUNCAN, O.D., and R.W. HODGE
1963   "Education and Occupational Mobility: A Regression Analysis." *American Journal of Sociology,* 68:629-44.

DUNCAN-JONES, P.
1972   "Social Mobility, Canonical Scoring and Occupational Classification." In Keith Hope, ed. *The Analysis of Social Mobility.* Oxford: Clarendon Press.

DURKHEIM, EMILE
1964   *The Division of Labour in Society.* New York: Free Press.

FEATHERMAN, D.L., and R.M. HAUSER
1975   "Design for a Replicate Study of Social Mobility in the United States." Pp. 219-51 in Kenneth C. Land and S. Spilerman, eds. *Social Indicator Models.* New York: Russell Sage.

1976   "Sexual Inequalities and Socioeconomic Achievement in the U.S., 1962-1973." *American Sociological Review,* 41 (June): 462-83.

FOX, T.G., and S.M. MILLER
1965   "Economic, Political and Social Determinants of Mobility." *Acta Sociologica,* 9:76-93.

GARNSEY, E.
1975   "Occupational Structure in Industrialized Societies." *Sociology,* 3 (Sept.):439-40.

GOLDTHORPE, J.M.
1964   "Social Stratification in Industrial Society." In P. Halmos, ed. *The Development of Industrial Societies.* Keele: University of Keele.

GOODMAN, L.
1969   "How to Ransack Social Mobility Tables and Other Kinds of Cross-classification Tables." *American Journal of Sociology,* 75 (July):1-40.

GOYDER, JOHN C.
1980   "Trends in the Socioeconomic Achievement of the University Educated: A Status Attainment Model Interpretation." *Canadian Journal of
Higher Education*, 10(2):21-38.

HARVEY, EDWARD
1974   *Educational Systems and the Labour Market*. Don Mills: Longman Canada.

HAUSER, R., P. DICKINSON, H. TRAVIS, and J. KOFFEL
1975   "Structural Changes in Occupational Mobility Among Men in the
United States." *American Sociological Reivew*, 40 (Oct.):585-98.

HAUSER, R, J. KOFFEL, H. TRAVIS, and P. DICKINSON
1975   "Temporal Change in Occupational Mobility: Evidence for Men in the
United States." *American Sociological Review*, 40 (June):279-97.

HAZELRIGG, L.E.
1974   "Cross-National Comparisons of Father-to-Son Occupational Mobility." Pp. 469-93 in J. Lopreato and L.S. Lewis, eds. *Social Stratification: A
Reader*. New York: Harper and Row.

HAZELRIGG, L.E., and M.A. GARNIER
1976   "Occupational Mobility in Industrial Societies: A Comparative Analysis
of Differential Access to Occupational Ranks in Seventeen Countries."
American Sociological Review, 41 (June):498-511.

HERTZLER, J.O.
1952   "Some Tendencies Toward A Closed Class System in the United
States." *Social Forces*, 30 (March):313-23.

HOLLINGSHEAD, AUGUST B.
1952   "Trends in Social Stratification: A Case Study." *American Sociological
Review*, 17 (Dec.):679-86.

HOPE, K.
1972   "Quantifying Constraints on Social Mobility: The Latent Hierarchies of
a Contingency Table." In Keith Hope ed. *The Analysis of Social Mobility*.
Oxford: Clarendon Press.

KERR, L.C., J. DUNLOP, F. HARBISON, and C. MYERS
1964   *Industrialism and Industrial Man*. New York: Oxford University Press.

KUBAT, DANIEL and DAVID THORNTON
1974   *A Statistical Profile of Canadian Society*. Toronto: McGraw-Hill.

LENSKI, GERHARD
1966   *Power and Privilege*. New York: McGraw-Hill.

LEVY, MARION
1966   *Modernization and the Structure of Societies*. Princeton: Princeton University Press.

LIPSET, S.M., and H.L. ZETTERBERG
1956a   "A Theory of Social Mobility." *Transactions of the Third World Congress
of Sociology*, 3:155-77.
1956b   "Discussion on Social Mobility and Class Structure." *Transactions of the
Third World Congress of Sociology*, 3:74-75.

MCROBERTS, H., and K. SELBEE
1981   "Trends in Occupational Mobility: Canada and the U.S." *American
Sociological Review*, 46 (Aug.):406-21.

MILLS, C. WRIGHT
1956 *White Collar.* New York: Oxford University Press.

MOORE, W.
1965 *The Impact of Industry.* Englewood Cliffs: Prentice-Hall.
1966 "Changes in Occupational Structure." In N.J. Smelser and S.M. Lipset, eds. *Social Structure and Mobility in Economic Development.* Chicago: Aldine.

MORISON, SAMUEL ELIOT, and HENRY STEELE COMMAGER
1962 *The Growth of the American Republic.* New York: Oxford University Press.

MORTON, W.L.
1961 *The Canadian Identity.* Toronto: University of Toronto Press.

MUELLER, J.H., K.F. SCHUESSLER, and H.L. COSTNER
1970 *Statistical Reasoning in Sociology.* Boston: Houghton Mifflin.

PAYNE, G.
1977 "Occupational Transition in Advanced Industrial Societies." *Sociological Review,* 25 (Feb.):5-39.

PINEO, P.C.
1977 "The Social Standings of Ethnic and Racial Groupings." *Canadian Review of Sociology and Anthropology,* 14 (May):147-57.

SIBLEY, E.
1942 "Some Demographic Clues to Stratification." *American Sociological Review,* 7 (June):322-30.

SMITH, KENT W.
1976 "Marginal Standardization and Table Shrinking." *Social Forces,* 54 (March):669-93.

STONE, L.O.
1967 *Urban Development in Canada.* Ottawa: Queen's Printer.

TREIMAN, DONALD J.
1970 "Industrialization and Social Stratification." In Edward O. Laumann, ed. *Social Stratification: Research and Theory for the 1970s.* Indianapolis: Bobbs-Merrill.

TURNER, FREDERICK JACKSON
1920 *The Frontier in American History.* New York: H. Holt & Co.

UNITED STATES DEPARTMENT of COMMERCE
1960 *Historical Statistics of the United States. Colonial Times to 1957.* Washington, D.C.: U.S. Government Printing Office.
1974 *Statistical Abstract of the United States.* Washington, D.C.: U.S. Government Printing Office.

WARNER, W. LLOYD and LEO SROLE
1945 *The Social System of American Ethnic Groups.* New Haven: Yale University Press.

WEBER, MAX
1958a *From Max Weber.* H.H. Gerth and C. Wright Mills, eds. New York: Oxford University Press.
1958b *The Protestant Ethic and the Spirit of Capitalism.* New York: Scribner's.

WEINBERG, I.
1969 "The Problem of the Convergence of Industrial Societies: A Critical Look at the State of a Theory." *Comparative Studies in Society and History.* 2 (1):1-15.

CHAPTER 6

Family Size and Status Attainment

PETER C. PINEO

Ascribed characteristics, such as ethnicity or race, are assigned to individuals at birth, and it is most frequently the family into which one is born which determines them. In this sense, the family is the source of ascribed statuses, and insofar as the study of status attainment has at its root the investigation of the differential effects of ascription and achievement, much of the whole endeavour can be said to deal with "family factors." In this section, however, we use the term in a much more restricted sense, to refer to the actual structural characteristics of the family. That is, we are asking not whether the family passively bestows upon individuals characteristics which influence subsequent attainment, but rather whether certain characteristics of the family are active agents themselves in influencing achievement.

Family characteristics, in this limited sense, fall into three natural categories. The first category is the structure of the family of orientation. That is, the characteristics of the family into which one is born — its size, whether it is intact or broken, etc. — could have impact upon attainment. Secondly, the marriage and its characteristics are a distinguishable set of factors. That is, when one marries, who one marries or whether one marries may have consequences. Finally, the family of procreation may also be studied. How many children does one have? How long do they remain dependent? This final category is more likely to be influenced by attainment rather than to influence it, although one of the oldest hypotheses in sociology concerns the idea that men who are careful not to have too many children may rise highest in the stratification order (Dumont, cited in Tepperman, 1975).

Given these three facets of the family, and that for each several

201

different measures are possible, the potential number of hypotheses linking family structure to attainment is very large. But among all these possibilities, one finding stands out in the research done so far: coming from a large family reduces educational attainment. This finding, no more expected on theoretical grounds than many others, recurs in many recent studies of educational attainment; the relationship is of a comparatively large magnitude; and it is found to be of about the same magnitude in studies from varying sources. Discovered serendipitously and still not fully interpreted, it remains the single variable to turn up which now merits routine inclusion in the status attainment model along with the basic variables of the Blau-Duncan model. If for no other reason the relationship is of importance because it links an unusually well-documented demographic phenomenon, the fertility patterns of a society, with a problem of continuing social and sociological significance, educational attainment.

Family Size and Educational Achievement

The family size variable is frequently called, in the literature, "number of siblings" or "sib-size" to emphasize the fact that it is not the number of children the respondent has had which is under consideration but rather the size of the family in which she or he was raised — the family of orientation. It has been found consistently since the time of the original Blau-Duncan study (1967) that the larger the family of orientation the lower the level of schooling an individual will attain. The evidence from the study was first presented by Beverly Duncan (1967) and extended in the Duncan-Featherman-Duncan volume (1972). The zero-order correlation between family size and educational attainment fluctuates from around −.27 up to as high as −.35 depending upon what particular population is examined. It is reduced if controls are introduced. Thus the high reading of −.35 for the male spouse-present experienced civilian labour force, 1962, is reduced to −.23 when controls for father's occupation and farm origin are introduced (Featherman and Hauser, 1976:469).

Featherman and Hauser have presented a re-analysis of the 1962 data to make them comparable to their own 1973 data (1976). Concentrating upon the experienced civilian labour force and upon males and females with spouse present, they found a weaker relationship for females (−.27) than males (−.35). They also found a striking stability of the relationships between 1962 and 1973. While mean number of sibs fell from 4.18 to 3.78 (male reports, with S.D.'s of 2.76 and 2.68, respectively) or from 3.96 to 3.64 (female reports, with S.D.'s of 2.70 and 2.61, respectively), the correlations changed very little. For men, the 1973 correlation was −.36; women, the correlation in 1962 was −.27 and in 1973 it was −.29.

Another recent U.S. study generally confirms these results. McClendon (1976) analysed the NORC General Social Survey, and found for men a zero-order relationship of −.30 and for women −.36. While the gross effect appears somewhat larger for women and thus different from the Featherman-Hauser results, McClendon notes that the direct effects are larger for men than women. He writes: "The direct effects of siblings on years of schooling completed is twice as great for males as for females" (59). The unstandardized coefficients are −.334 and −.150, respectively.

Re-analysis of two data sets, the Douglas data and the Crowther data, by Kerckhoff (1974, 1975) shows that a similar relationship may be found, for males at least, in the United Kingdom. Zero-order relationships ranging from −.26 to −.27, depending upon which measure of educational attainment is used, were found in the Douglas data (1974: 793) and a relationship of −.24 from the Crowther data. Kerckhoff notes, ". . . the correlations involving family size were consistently lower in the English studies than in Duncan's analysis" (794). While smaller, they were still very much in the same general range of strength as the U.S. correlations, however.

Early results for Canada may be found in work done by Curtis and Cuneo (1975). Using a sample of young, urban French- and English-speaking Canadians, they found that results for the English were close to those from the United States or Britain. The zero-order correlations were −.32 for both men and women. For the French, somewhat surprisingly considering the possibility of higher variance in family size for this group, the relationships were weaker: −.20 for men and −.15 for women.

In all, then, some fluctuation in the magnitude of the correlation is found from study to study. Some of the fluctuation may be owing to sampling variability, and some to differences in the precise population being studied. What is impressive is that from various time periods in the United States and from three different countries, correlations are found which not only are always in the same direction but which also adopt quite similar magnitudes — rarely below −.20 or above −.30. No prior theoretical expectations existed to predict that the relationship would be so substantial, and even now quite diverse interpretations are offered. Kerckhoff refers to family size as "another index of the social status of the family of orientation" (1974:791). Others refer to the costs of education and the spreading thin of parental resources in larger families (see Duncan and also Cuneo-Curtis). Interpretations of the effect as being partially brought about by reduced I.Q. levels in children from large families are also suggested (See Duncan Featherman and Duncan, 1972: 88-105).

Another quite extensive body of literature exists which is relevant to the question of the effects of family size upon education. These are what one could call the "high school studies," since they are most typically based on questionnaires completed by high school or other students. Probably the best known of them all is Sewell's longitudinal study of Wisconsin students and the path model used by most of these researchers has become known as the Wisconsin model. Many, but not all, of these studies include measures of family size and concern themselves in passing at least with the relationship between family size and education, usually with education measured as educational *expectations* rather than educational *attainments*. Family size was included as a variable in the three main Canadian studies: Breton's national student survey (1972), Porter, Porter and Blishen's Ontario study (1979) and Anisef's Ontario study (no date, but see MacKinnon and Anisef, 1979). It was not originally included in Sewell's study but was picked up as a measurement in the most recent re-interviewing of his respondents (Sewell, Hauser and Wolf, 1980). Other U.S. studies including the measure are Rehburg and Westby (1967), Hout and Morgan (1975) and Rosen and Aneshenel (1978).

While some of these studies have rather small samples and most of them are only regional in scope, it is reassuring that they all find a negative relationship between family size and educational expectations or attainments. While negative, however, the relationship found in these studies seems consistently to be smaller than that found in the national surveys of adults. The magnitude of the relationship fluctuates between and within samples, but hovers around a value in the low teens — perhaps $-.14$ or $-.16$. Age cannot vary much in a high school sample and this would explain at least some of the difference. But age is similarly restricted in variance in the British studies noted earlier and the correlations from them are not this low. Also, McClendon's analysis of the national NORC data for the United States includes age as a variable (1976: 57) and computations from those data suggest that controlling for age would reduce the relationship only moderately. A second probable cause is that expectations rather than attainments are used as the measure of education. A recent report from the Sewell study (1980) uses attainments rather than expectations and finds a somewhat larger relationship ($-.17$ for males and $-.20$ for females). But there must be some further factor, not evident at the moment, producing lower correlations in samples of high school students.

To some degree, the high school studies would seem a better data source than our national survey to pursue the theoretical question of why family size influences education as it does. These studies contain a wide assortment of social psychological and attitudinal questions that could not be included in a brief questionnaire administered under Statistics Canada sponsorship. But they also have limitations. Age, period, and cohort effects and, quite frequently, community or region, are held constant and confounded in any single study. While comparisons between studies could compensate for this limitation, the job would never be easy and many such studies would be needed to do it. Within these limitations, however, those analysing the high school studies are making some progress. Most of the studies undertake the job of identifying the intervening mechanisms between family size and education, and it seems the relationship can be "explained away" with relative ease. No two studies proceed in the same way, but it appears some mix of variables involving mental ability, grade point average and the amount of outside encouragement given the respondent by others is sufficient to reduce the relationship below the level of significance if not virtually to zero. In particular, "parental encouragement," or more properly the student's perception of the degree of parental encouragement, seems the most potent intervening variable. From these studies the information provided concerning the relative importance of mental ability proves useful, as we show below. On the other hand, explaining the relationship by recourse to parental encouragement seems to be only the beginning of a theoretically satisfying explanation. It leaves unsettled how a cross-national demographic regularity could be brought about by a mechanism as personal and private as parental encouragement.

In analysing family size effects in our national survey data we cannot, as noted, directly pursue the attitudinal and social psychological issues raised in the surveys of high school students. But what the national cross-section permits is an investigation of the demographics of the phenomenon. We are able to see how closely Canada resembles the United States both in the zero-order relationship and at more complex levels of analysis. We can investigate differences within Canada, comparing men with women and the French with the English. Through cohort analysis we observe any changes in the nature of the relationship over time, which is a matter necessarily obscured in the studies of single cohorts of students. Analysis of the national survey cannot solve the theoretical conundrum but can provide guidance in sorting out sampling fluctuations and other extraneous information in the small and/or regional studies. It can also contribute to the solution of the theoretical puzzle because, at the least, it provides broad constraints within which any theory ultimately proposed must exist.

Family Size Effects: English Canada

The Cuneo-Curtis study and the Canadian studies of high school students indicate that the negative relationship between family size and education exists in Canada as elsewhere. The large national cross-section of the mobility study permits a precise test of how closely Canada resembles the United States in the strength of the relationship. To begin, English Canada is first analysed.

English Canada was defined, at this point, as all those giving a language other than French as the one in which they are most comfortable. Some 12,000 males fell into this group.[1] The relationship between family size and educational attainment for them was −.30, quite close to that reported for English males by Cuneo and Curtis, and somewhat less than that reported for males in the United States. The mean family size was 5.03; phrased as "number of siblings" this would be 4.03, midway between the figures from 1962 and 1973 in the U.S. The standard deviation was 2.86, fractionally larger than that from the United States. The Canadian and the U.S. family size questions were virtually identical. The U.S. study did ask the respondent to include adopted siblings; the Canadian study evaded this issue.[2]

As well as providing the zero-order relationships, the earlier analyses of the United States provide estimates of the relationship with controls in place, and so Canada may be compared with the United States at this level of analysis as well. Beverly Duncan identified four variables as important controls. Citing work done earlier by Martin David and others, Duncan used controls for occupation and education of family head[3] and for "family type." By family type she meant whether the respondent was raised in an intact or a broken family. This is a matter of some importance in the United States because of a high incidence of broken families in the black community. The question used in the U.S. study to establish whether the family was intact was, "Were you living with both your parents most of the time up to age 16?" Around 17 per cent answered no to this question (Blau and Duncan, 1967: 332).

The occupation and education of the family head are readily available as controls in the Canadian study, but family type was differently measured. The question referred not to "most of the time up to age 16" but specifically "when you were 16 years old." The two versions of the question produce apparently similar results with 18.5 per cent of the Canadian males and 19.0 per cent of the females saying no. But the similarity to the United States is a coincidence. Among the 17 per cent living with only one parent in the U.S. study, 77.4 per cent reported it was the mother. In Canada, only 57 per cent reported it was the mother. The broken families in the United States were likely then to have been brought about more frequently by divorce or separation, which typically result in the mother having custody. In the Canadian data, the more balanced sex ratio suggests early departures from home by the child or the death of one or another parent are the reasons for the "broken family." These factors would be more common in the Canadian study since the age referred to is 16, rather than "most of the time up to age 16."

Controlling for father's education and father's occupation by including them with family size in a multiple regression does reduce the apparent impact of family size upon educational attainment. The standardized beta is $-.17$, considerably less than the original zero-order correlation of $-.30$. Controlling for family type, as measured in the Canadian study, had no further effect.[4] In fact, family type is a substantial variable in the original Duncan study only for the blacks and for the very oldest cohorts of whites, so the ineffectiveness of the variable in Canada could be owing to something more than just the wording of the question.

The strength of the association between family size and education after these controls is again somewhat lower than the equivalent measure from the U.S. data (Duncan, 1967: 366). But the difference is slight and the best conclusion to draw is that the effects of family size upon educational attainment are remarkably similar for English Canadian and U.S. males.

Equivalent tabulations were made for English-speaking women. In this case all women may be used, not just those working, since the occupational status of the respondent is not involved in the equations. It may first be noted that the mean family size reported by the women, 5.08, is reassuringly similar to that reported by men, 5.03. So also the standard deviations are virtually identical, 2.93 for the women and 2.86 for the men. The equivalence of the means and the standard deviation is reassuring since with the exception of sibling groups which are all of one sex, and for a slight distortion owing to differential mortality by sex, it is a single parameter which is being estimated in both cases.

There is no theoretical reason to expect the correlation between family size and educational attainment to be equivalent for men and women. Popularly held beliefs that education, at the higher levels at least, is more important for boys than girls would, if acted upon, cause the relationship to be higher for women. Data collected so far in the U.S. tend to show, with one exception, a somewhat lower correlation for women. In

Canada, the one prior study, that of Cuneo and Curtis, finds the relationship to be identical for English-Canadian men and women. Simply extrapolating from those results leads to an expectation that the relationships will be identical and this turns out to be the case. Before controls the relationship for women is −.30, exactly the same as that for men. After controls for father's occupation and education, it falls to −.17, again exactly as for men. The final control, for family type, again made no further reduction.

The English-speaking men and women in this sample do not differ to any significant degree in their mean educational attainments. For the men, the mean attainment was 10.85, for women, 10.80. (The number is a somewhat arbitrary code, not quite equivalent to actual years of attainment, as we showed elsewhere.) But the two sexes do differ in the standard deviations. For men, it was 3.70; for women it was 3.23. This difference reflects a pattern which has held through much of Canada's recent history: more men than women have dropped out of school early; more men than women went on to the highest degrees. Thus, in the sample the men show more variation in educational attainment than do the women. As a result of this difference in variability, while the standardized coefficients showed no difference between the sexes, the unstandardized coefficients do differ a little. For men the unstandardized regression coefficient between family size and educational attainment is −.39; for women it is −.32. With controls for father's education and occupation, it was −.22 for men and −.18 for women. Measured this way, family size seems to have slightly larger effects upon the educational attainments of men than of women. From this one should perhaps conclude that family size has operated as part of the causal process resulting in men showing more variation in educational attainment than women. The reverse finding, that the unstandardized are equivalent and the standardized coefficients different, would lead to the conclusion that the factors that increased the variation in male education were wholly exogenous to family size.

Family Size Effects: French Canada

Since the family in French Canada has traditionally been substantially larger than that in English Canada, it seems likely that a different relationship between family size and educational attainment would be found among the French. On purely statistical grounds one might expect a higher relationship. That is because not only would the mean family size be higher among the French, but also the skew in the distribution would result in a higher standard deviation as well. Higher standard deviations are, all other things equal, likely to produce higher correlations.

While this seems most likely from a mathematical point of view, again a simple extrapolation from the results of Cuneo and Curtis would suggest otherwise. They found, despite this likely tendency, that the relationship is lower in French Canada. Their sample was of young urbanites, however, and for this group the old pattern of large families would have eroded. The national sample contains all age groups and so would contain many French who had been raised in the traditional, large family.

The mean family size and the standard deviation are indeed larger for the French. For the males, defined as those "most comfortable" in French, regardless of which province they live in, the mean family size was 7.31, with a standard deviation of 3.44. French women gave a similar report: the mean was 7.30 and the standard deviation 3.46. The standard deviation for the English was, as noted earlier, lower, at around 2.90. But the expected effects of the larger standard deviation upon the zero-order correlation between family size and educational attainment are not found. The correlation was −.30 for the English; for the French it was −.26 for both the men and the women. The Cuneo-Curtis finding is confirmed, rather than the mathematically based expectation. The magnitude of the French-English difference is much less than that found by Cuneo-Curtis, however. Also, the national data show no sex difference in French Canada, while Cuneo-Curtis did find such a difference.

Controls for father's education and occupation and family type reduce the associations among the French down to −.13 for men and −.14 for women, still lower than for the English.[5] The various control variables appear to perform identically for the French and English. The father's education is the most important in all cases and the family type variable of essentially no importance.

The unstandardized coefficients contain no surprises. Since the French males have a higher variation in educational attainment than do the females, the unstandardized regression coefficient between family size and educational level is larger for the males (−.31) than for the females (−.26) but both are lower than the equivalent measures from English Canada. After controls, the unstandardized coefficients are −.15 for the French men and −.14 for the women.

With the exception that the relationship is unexpectedly weaker in French Canada, the statistical results from the two groups are extremely similar. But there is a practical consideration involved in all of this which should not be ignored. Traditionally the French family was larger than the English; the French in our sample reported around two more siblings than the English. Since family size has depressing effects upon educational attainment in both societies, this difference should have real consequences upon the relative levels of educational attainment in the two. The French are, on average, less educated than the English. While the English averaged to around 10.80 on our education scale, the French men averaged 9.42 and the French women 9.40. This difference, which can loosely be thought of as about 1.40 years of schooling, may be partly owing to the size of the family.

Estimates may be made, using the results of the regression analysis, of how much of this difference may be owing to family size. With controls, and using the equations derived from the French cases, the estimate is that about one-third of a year of education appears to be a function of family size. Without controls, the estimate is greater, of course: .71 for men and .57 for women. The difference is owing to the effects of father's education and occupation operating upon achievement through family size. Some, but far from all, of the French-English difference in educational attainment would seem to be a function of differences in family size.

The extent to which differences in family size appear to explain differences in educational attainment would be even greater if the association between family size and education were not smaller in French Canada. Thus, if the coefficients from the English-based equations are applied to the French men, for example, the effects of family size are: gross effect, .89 years; net effect, .50 years. For women the figures are .73 and .41, respectively. Thus, in some auto-corrective way, the structure of French-Canadian society has operated to minimize the effects of the large families.

Reconciling the Differences between the United States, English and French Canada

How may the diverse results from the United States, English and French Canada be reconciled? First, it must be noted that the results are quite similar. The correlation between family size and educational attainment is always negative, and it ranges in size only from −.25 to about −.35, in the adult samples. This is, by the standards of quantitative sociology, a remarkable regularity.

If the difference is to be interpreted, however, one difficulty must be immediately recognized. The two variables involved are inversely related temporally and spatially as well as at the individual level. Thus, recent trends in most western societies have been a movement to lower birth rates simultaneously with a move to higher levels of educational attainment. So also, in the data being considered, the United States, English Canada and French Canada form a gradient from high to low in levels of educational attainment and the perfect reverse gradient, from low to high, in family size. The same kind of pattern can be found across the cohorts in each of the three societies. Thus, differences between societies or cohorts that appear to be a function of family size may equally be a function of differing educational levels.

With this in mind, let us consider the differences with differing family size under view. In the chart below, the slope of educational attainment on family size is plotted against the mean family size. The point of the chart is to suggest that the basic tendency to be found in the data is that as the size of the family falls, the effect of family size upon educational attainment increases. The data from 1962 and the 1972 data for U.S. women do not fit the chart well, so it is an extreme oversimplification. But it does provide a glimpse of order in the comparison which makes the nature of the relationships more comprehensible.

The line in the chart is entered to suggest how this difference could occur. If the relationship between family size and educational level within each society were somewhat curved, rather than a straight line, the differences between the societies could also be found within them; that is, the curve could be of such a character that at the point it passes

CHART A: Mean family size by slope of educational attainment upon family size, males, USA, 1973, English Canada, French Canada

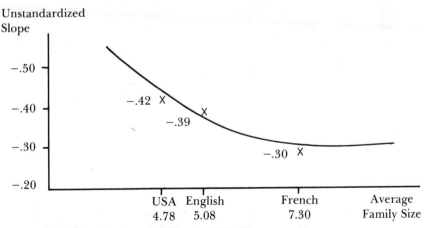

Source for USA: Featherman and Hauser, 1976:467

4.78 in family size, its slope is about −.42, as it passes 5.08 the slope is −.39, and as it passed 7.30, the slope is −.30. Were this true within each society, the shift from one pattern to another could occur automatically as the family size falls and no quantum jump would be needed to create the differences between societies. So also, the cohorts within a society could be expected to conform to the pattern.

Again, this is an idealized version of what the findings might be; it is already known from B. Duncan's work that no neat pattern of change across cohorts is to be found in the United States. But it does again provide a way of describing the general pattern to the results.

If the idea of the relationship being curved can be considered a prediction, based on inspection of the inter-society differences only, as in

CHART B: Educational Attainment (mean) by family size, English and French Canadians, males (N = 20,409, omitting 180 cases giving no language preference. Unweighted N = 20,265)

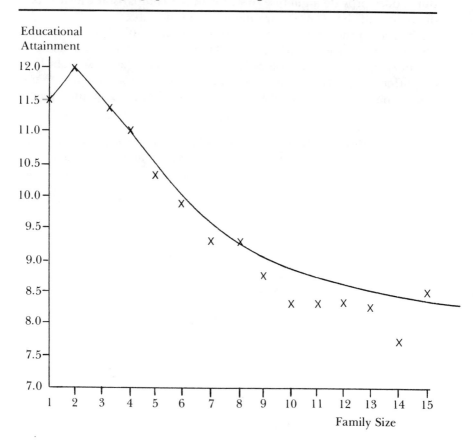

fact it was, actually inspecting the curve can be considered a test of the idea. In Chart B, below, the actual curve of mean educational attainment upon family size for males in the Canadian sample is given. In the main, the idea of a curved rather than a linear relationship seems to have merit. It is not a graceful curve. In the first place, the slightly reduced attainments of the only children work against the explanation offered since, as the mean family size falls, presumably the proportion who are only children would increase and contribute to reducing the relationship. Also, at the other end it does not look so much as if the curve has gradually reducing slope but rather that it becomes flat. Thus, from family size of eight through to fifteen almost no relationship seems to exist between size and educational attainment. Rather, the mean for each family size is found around 8.4 years, reminding one that minimum school-leaving ages do exist and may influence what can happen statistically.

This pattern, if a little messier than might be hoped, does afford a model which helps understand the relationship. Thus, French Canada had a substantial number of families of eight or more children and as this seems to be a zone of no relationship, their number acts to deflate the overall relationship between family size and education. As a society moves from having a substantial proportion of that type down to having very few, the dampening effect disappears and the relationship strengthens. The United States represents this pattern more.

Thus, there seems a built-in tendency within the nature of the relationship for the effect of family size upon educational attainment to increase as family size falls. As noted, the confounding of the two variables means that the tendency could be phrased in terms of "as educational levels increase." But in any case, this tendency is interesting statistically because it seems of sufficient strength to overwhelm the impact of declining variances as family size decreases. It is also theoretically unexpected that as economic development proceeds an ascribed characteristic such as family size should increase rather than decrease in importance.

Table 6.1 repeats the kind of information used to form Chart B, for English and French males separately. It will be noted that the tendency for the curve to become flat is found for both groups. In all, the two curves seem quite parallel, with both groups showing relatively lower attainments among only children as compared to those from somewhat larger families, and with the attainments of the French being some one-half a year behind that of the English for each level of family size.

Both groups also show some slight tendency for the attainment levels in the very largest families (fifteen or more) to be higher than some more

TABLE 6:1 — Mean Educational Attainment by Family Size, French and English Males Separately

Family size	English	N (unweighted)	French	N (unweighted)
1	11.8	757 (690)	10.4	132 (92)
2	12.1	2089 (1905)	11.6	264 (194)
3	11.6	2481 (2296)	10.5	405 (296)
4	10.9	2275 (2265)	10.6	503 (371)
5	10.5	1904 (1972)	9.8	558 (434)
6	9.8	1495 (1645)	9.9	509 (412)
7	9.5	1127 (1266)	9.0	516 (434)
8	9.5	946 (1096)	8.8	431 (399)
9	9.1	691 (854)	8.3	444 (402)
10	8.6	531 (659)	8.2	425 (387)
11	8.6	377 (489)	8.2	372 (346)
12	8.7	257 (347)	8.2	268 (267)
13	9.0	124 (185)	7.8	184 (177)
14	7.7	72 (98)	7.4	119 (117)
15 or more	9.0	48 (70)	8.3	105 (100)
Total		15175 (15837)		5234 (4428)

moderately sized families. Since step- and half-siblings were to be included, what may have happened is that combined families, brought about by remarriage, become particularly numerous in this highest category and this distorts the results. It is also true, of course, that the sample size is small for this largest category (unweighted N is 70 for the English and 100 for the French), making the estimates unreliable.

Family Size and Occupational Attainment

Family size is found, in the United States, to influence occupational attainment principally in an indirect manner, through education. With controls for family background only, which in this case includes father's occupation and farm background, Featherman and Hauser report comparatively large relationships between family size and occupational level, represented by standardized regression coefficients of −.142 for 1962 and −.152 for 1973, for men 20 to 64 years of age. Further controls for educational level reduce this to a mere −.031 in 1962 and −.032 in 1973. Given the sample size, these relationships are statistically significant but are felt to be "substantively trivial" (Featherman and Hauser, 1976:471-73).

A roughly equivalent tabulation of English-Canadian males produces essentially the same results. Using the same population as in the earlier part of this section, less some 1364 cases who failed to report present job, the standardized coefficient, with controls for background and educational level, between family size and occupational attainment is −.032, see Table 6.2.[7] Again the relationship is statistically significant and presumably substantively trivial. The variables used to control for family background were, in this case, father's occupation and education and the measure of whether the family was intact. Farm origin was not used.

In the balance of Table 6.2 the equivalent estimates for French males

TABLE 6:2 — Net Effects* of Family Size upon Occupational Attainment

		Males			Females	
	N	Unstandardized Coefficient	Standardized	N	Unstandardized Coefficient	Standardized
English	10709	−.168	−.032	6953	−.259	−.057
	(10758)	(.043)		(6748)	(.046)	
French	3553	.034	.008	2049	−.242	−.058
	(2938)	(.058)		(1581)	(.077)	

*Net of father's occupation and education, respondent's education, and family type, i.e. whether family intact at age 16.
(Unweighted N and standard errors of the estimates in parentheses).

and for French and English females are given, in standardized and unstandardized form. In all instances the effects are minute. They are statistically significant for all but the French males. The degree of substantive importance can be assessed by considering the contribution to the total variance in occupational status. Even the relatively stronger relationships for the women are so small as to suggest that the direct effects of family size account for some three-tenths of 1 per cent of the variance in occupational status.

With the exception again of the French males, the relationships are, as in the United States, all negative. The negative sign means that those from large families show slightly reduced occupational attainments. The positive association for French males could well be just a sampling fluctuation.

When farmers and those of farm origin are removed from the analysis, all the effects shift to a slightly stronger negative direction. For French males the coefficient moves to become negative, from .008 to −.001. For English males it changes from −.032 to −.045. For English females it changes to −.065 and for French females to −.061.

The tendency for the net effects of family size upon occupational attainment to be somewhat stronger for women than men was found in both the 1962 and 1973 U.S. studies as well as in both English and French Canada. With four relatively independent tests producing the same result, one can probably safely conclude that this is not just sampling fluctuation. It seems to be part of a more general pattern of differences in the effects of family background upon women and men noted by Featherman and Hauser (1976:474). In the Canadian data, for example, net of father's and son's education, family size and family type, the father's occupation relates to the son's .18 in English Canada and .17 in French Canada. The same tabulation for daughters produces standardized betas of only .09 for English women and .02 for the French. These differences are much stronger statistically than the differences in the effects of family size, and it seems likely the family size differences are a by-product of them.

In all, whether farmers are included in the analysis or not, and whether one refers to the data from the males or the females, the conclusion to draw from Table 6.2 is that, as in the United States, the effects of family size upon status attainment are almost wholly indirect, through educational attainment. It is upon the educational system, and the family itself, that attention must be focused in endeavouring to learn why it is that family size has the impact it does upon status attainment.

Family Size and the Intelligence Quotient

In analysing the relationship between family size and educational attainment, Duncan devoted considerable attention to the role played by the intelligence quotient (IQ). Estimates were made suggesting that part, but not all, of the effect of family size occurs indirectly through the IQ (1968:6; also Duncan, Featherman and Duncan, 1972: 88-105).

At the time of this work, it was known that people raised in large families did less well when given an IQ test, but the exact magnitude of the relationship between family size and IQ was not known. Rather the literature, as summarized by Anastasi (1956), contained a large number of varying estimates of the relationship.[8] With careful qualification, Duncan, Featherman and Duncan chose −.30 as the most likely (1972: 94). The result of the choice was that they found that the effect of family size upon educational attainment, which was −.20 with father's occupation and education and the family type held constant, fell neatly into two components. The indirect effect, through IQ, could be represented by a standardized beta of −.10, as could the direct effect. Assuming a different value for the basic correlation would change the results of course. Thus, as Duncan et al. introduced a distinction between IQ at age 12 and IQ at maturity, the results changed, increasing the apparent direct effect of family size upon education from −.10 to −.15, and reducing the indirect effect through IQ accordingly.

Since that work was completed, more recent estimates of the relationship between family size and the IQ have become available from the various studies of high school students described earlier, and they suggest that, if anything, the −.25 relationship assumed between IQ at age 12 and family size was too large. Only the small Rosen and Aneshenel sample produces estimates approaching that size: −.19 for males and −.22 for females (1978: 175). The larger sample from the Sewell panel produces lower estimates: −.14 for males and −.15 for females (1980: 581). Another recent U.S. study of students, although not dealing with educational attainment, also provides recent estimates based on a large sample and these confirm the Sewell et al. results. The correlations, for whites only, are −.13 for males and −.15 for females (Bahr and Leigh, 1978: 334).

While these lower estimates would appear to disconfirm the validity of the Duncan et al. analysis, it must be remembered that their source, the high school studies, also consistently yields lower estimates of the basic relationship between family size and education. The two differences tend to cancel out. Thus, in the analysis given by Sewell *et al.*, path coefficients of −.070 for males and −.095 for females are found between family size and educational attainment after controls for socioeconomic status, maternal employment, rural background and whether the family was intact. Adding IQ to the set of determinants reduces the path coefficients to −.045 and −.074 respectively, a reduction of about the same magnitude as suggested in the Duncan analysis (1980: 571, 573). Mixing the various data sources by substituting the correlation of −.15 into the set of estimates used by Duncan produces a reduction in the path coefficient which is somewhat smaller: from −.20 to −.16.[9] In any case, the role of IQ as a mediator between family size and educational attainment appears relatively modest — the indirect effect is somewhere between 20 and 35 per cent of the total effect.

Can one assume that the Canadian situation is roughly equivalent? Again the crucial information is the strength of the relationship between family size and IQ. The estimates from the Porter, Porter, Blishen data are considerably lower than from the United States: −.06 for males and −.10 for females (1979: 181). Breton does not provide an estimate of the correlation as such but does provide a cross tabulation for males and females separately of family size and IQ (1972:473). The two variables are presented in trichotomies which would attentuate the relationship and even so correlations computed from these data are considerably larger than those from Porter *et al.*: −.15 for males and −.16 for females. With fluctuations this great between studies, certainly no subtle difference between Canada and the United States could be established. If anything, one would tend to conclude that the relationship may be marginally weaker in Canada, just as the basic relationship between family size and education is marginally weaker in Canada. It would follow then that partitioning the Canadian relationship into direct and indirect effects would produce about the same relative split as is found using the U.S. data.

It is difficult to decide what substantive interpretation should be drawn from the observation that around one-quarter of the strength of the relationship between family size and educational attainment is owing to IQ. Since IQ is involved one tends to think of genetic causal effects, but it seems improbable that genetics is involved in any major way. For the basic relationship between family size and IQ to be owing to genetic inheritance there would have to be a negative relationship of some magnitude between the size of the family and the IQ of the parents, and this relationship does not appear to exist. Lacking any evidence of such a relationship, it seems best to conclude that IQ, like grade-point average, is simply an early indication of the growth of superior cognitive skills that ultimately become superior educational attainment. Insofar as this is true, identifying part of the family size–education relationship as being mediated by IQ adds no real theoretical understanding to the sources of the relationship.

Cohort Differences in the Relationship

Since this century has been one of gradually increasing affluence, with periodic setbacks in times of depression, the simplest hypothesis that might be predicted about the relationship of family size and educational attainment would be that economic conditions would create a general trend for family size to disappear as a factor. With prosperity, the hard decisions about which child could get the expensive education would not have to be made. The same line of argument would predict that family size would be a weaker factor in the United States than Canada and stronger in French than English Canada. We have already shown that this pattern does not hold, and have instead suggested that the impact of family size upon educational attainment appears to increase as the society becomes more industrialized. The simple expectation seems, then, to have little likelihood of proving true. It would predict that each successive cohort within Canada would show weaker relationships between family size and educational attainment, with some fall-back into stronger relationships for the depression years.

A possibly more realistic expectation may be formed based on U.S. research. A thorough search for differences in the strength of the relationship of family size to educational attainment across different age cohorts has been made by Beverly Duncan (1967) and more recently replicated by Hauser and Featherman (1975). In both instances the relationship is found to be stable. Not only is there an absence of any trend toward stronger or weaker relationships but also there seems to be an absence of any appreciable variability. In the Duncan analysis of the 1962 OCG data one may perhaps detect a slight tendency for the relationship to be weaker in the very oldest cohort; the Hauser and Featherman replication with the 1973 data did not find even this degree of variation. Duncan's finding that the relationship had "essentially constant magnitude . . . in the thirty-year span following World War I" led her to rule out "changes in economic conditions" or "the timing of innovative social legislation" as factors influencing it (370). These negative results would appear to cast doubt on the idea that institutional or economic factors may underlie the relationship between family size and educational attainment.

While it appears indisputable that the relationship in the United States has been stable since World War I, it does not necessarily follow that this must be the case in Canada. Goyder has shown elsewhere in this volume that the pace of industrialization has been more rapid in recent years in Canada and this can create trends in Canada which have ceased in the United States. As well, the course of development of the educational system in Canada has not parallelled that in the United States. The Canadian system has developed more slowly, and also, because of factors such as the strong provincial control of education, somewhat differently, as some provinces have established secondary and post-secondary facilities much earlier than others.

In Table 6.3 data are presented to test whether the stability across cohorts found in the United States is also to be found in Canada. In it the unstandardized coefficients measuring the effect of family size upon educational attainment, net of father's occupation, education and whether the family was intact at age 16, are presented, for English males and females and French males and females.

The safest interpretation to be drawn from the table is that the coefficients appear to vary more in Canada, particularly French Canada, than they do in the United States. For English Canada the main variation in Table 6.3 takes the form of a peaking of the relationship in the cohort aged 45 to 54 at the time of the survey. This is the cohort which would have been of high school age at the time of the depression of the 1930s. While it is only speculation, we interpret this as a "depression effect." Among the English one may note as well a falling off of the strength of the relationship in the oldest cohort, a pattern that may also be seen in the Duncan analysis as noted earlier.

For French Canada, there is also some evidence of the depression effect for the males as again the coefficient is larger than others for the cohort aged 45 to 54. This is not so for the French females. Rather the coefficients for them come closest to describing an orderly trend toward convergence with the English-Canadian results. The variation in the coefficients for the French males is much too irregular to be called a trend, yet in the youngest cohort there is again a tendency for convergence toward the English pattern. The oldest cohorts in French Canada show virtually no relationship between family size and education.

In all, it appears impossible to conclude from Table 6.3 that a trend either towards increasing or decreasing significance of family size has occurred. All one may conclude with safety is that the stability across cohorts found in the United States is not found in Canada. It may follow from this that two or more counteracting processes are operating in such

TABLE 6:3 — Net effects* of Family Size upon Educational Attainment, by Cohorts, for English Males and Females, French Males and Females

| | *Unstandardized coefficient of family size upon educational attainment (standardized error of the coefficient in parentheses)* | | | |
| | *English* | | *French* | |
Cohort	*Male*	*Female*	*Male*	*Female*
25-34	−.19	−.16	−.13	−.13
	(.019)	(.016)	(.030)	(.025)
35-44	−.19	−.16	−.04	−.10
	(.024)	(.019)	(.034)	(.033)
45-54	−.25	−.20	−.17	−.10
	(.023)	(.020)	(.039)	(.032)
55-64	−.17	−.15	−.07	−.03
	(.027)	(.025)	(.044)	(.045)
65 or older	−.11	−.13	−.03	−.05
	(.031)	(.028)	(.049)	(.042)

Sample size (unweighted in parentheses)

Cohort				
25-34	2873	3030	1033	1092
	(2830)	(3124)	(825)	(861)
35-44	2332	2311	781	781
	(2341)	(2389)	(626)	(634)
45-54	2183	2164	729	772
	(2212)	(2227)	(635)	(678)
55-64	1575	1569	554	551
	(1704)	(1704)	(506)	(490)
65 or older	1357	1593	418	506
	(1698)	(1751)	(415)	(440)

*Net of father's education and occupation and whether the family was intact at age 16.

a way as to cancel out and produce stability in recent U.S. history and fluctuations in Canada. One of these processes may be owing to economic conditions and be shown particularly clearly as a depression effect in Canada, which we next discuss.

The Depression Effect

Prior to her study of the effects of family background upon educational attainment, Beverly Duncan had shown, using 1960 U.S. census data,

TABLE 6:4 — Percentages with Secondary Schooling, by Cohorts, Canada, All Males, 1961

Cohort (age in 1961)	Year aged 16	Percentage with some secondary schooling	Gain ove previous cohort
20-24	1952-56	64.7	+2.6
25-29	1947-51	62.1	+3.7
30-34	1942-46	58.4	+1.9
35-39	1937-41	56.5	+1.6
40-44	1932-36	54.9	+4.9
45-49	1927-31	50.0	+5.6
50-54	1922-26	44.4	+8.0
55-59	1917-21	36.4	+2.7
60-64	1912-16	33.7	+2.7
65-69	1907-11	31.0	+4.9
70+	1902-06	26.1	

Source: *1961 Census of Canada*, Table 102.

that the depression in particular and any periods of high unemployment in general had effects upon the school attainment of males (1965). When jobs are scarce the males stay in school longer. In Table 6.4 we show, using data from Canada's 1961 census, that the same pattern may be found for Canadian males. Each cohort has a higher percentage attending high school than the preceding, and so the gain over the previous cohort shown in the final column of the table is in all cases positive. What is striking is that with the exception of the immediately prior cohort the gains in rates of school attendance were greatest for those of high school age in the depression, the cohorts 45 to 49 and 40 to 44 in 1961. The depression was not a time of major governmental initiatives in providing better access to secondary school; the Provincial School Consolidation Acts, which were the acts which signified a serious attempt by the province to provide universal secondary schooling, were passed either in the 1920s or, more typically, after World War II (Johnson, 1968). The gains in school attendance of the 1930s then occurred as individuals sought out opportunities in what was a rudimentary and stable opportunity structure in Canada.

While these changes in school attendance rates could be demonstrated in the U.S. census, Duncan did not find in her subsequent work that they were of sufficient importance to influence the relationship of family size, or of any of the family background factors, upon school attainment.

TABLE 6:5 — Percentages Getting to High School (sample data), Native-Born French and English Males and Females by Cohorts

Cohorts	English		French	
	Males	*Females*	*Males*	*Females*
25-34	90.1	91.3	77.7	77.6
35-44	76.4	83.6	58.1	51.0
45-54	67.4	74.5	38.8	41.3
55-64	58.7	66.9	34.9	36.2
65 or older	39.0	53.0	22.6	33.0
N	9175	9758	4230	4654
(unweighted)	(10607)	(11257)	(3648)	(3903)

NOTE: See note 10 concerning comparability with census estimates.

What Table 6.3 appears to suggest is that the effects in Canada were of sufficient strength to modify the relationship between family size and educational attainment. For both French and English males the relationship became intensified during the depression. Unlike the United States, in Canada whether the males stayed on in school or not was influenced by the number of children in the family. Those from smaller families did stay in school, those from larger families were more prone to drop out. Either the rudimentary character of the secondary school system in Canada at the time or the greater sharpness of the depression itself may have produced this U.S.-Canadian difference.

While the tendency for males to stay in school during the depression can be seen in the census data, it does not show up clearly in the sample statistics. Sampling fluctuations, the need to work with broader cohorts because of sample size, coupled with differences in the measurement and coding of education[10] appear to blur the results. Tabulations from the sample hint, however, that the pattern of Table 6.4 may largely be confined to the English and that the depression had different consequences for the French. These matters could more efficiently be pursued through more refined analysis of the census results rather than using the sample.

Conclusions

We have noted that the variable of family size has earned a place as part of the basic model of status attainment among U.S. researchers. Its importance is such that its omission from earlier waves of the Sewell longitudinal study of educational attainment was rectified by including it in the recent 1975 follow-up of the panel. It has become, as it were, an establishment variable. Its explanatory power is never large, and so its inclusion is not opportunistic. Rather it seems to have been granted a status as a thoroughly well-established causal factor, the exclusion of which would create small but needless bias in other estimates.

Canada provides an excellent setting in which to test the universality of findings from the American case. Since Canada so closely resembles the United States, any failure of an established finding from the United States to replicate in Canada would lead to serious questioning of it. The possibility that family size has been prematurely included in the basic model is enhanced by noting that in the studies of high school students much of its effect appears to be a by-product of potentially changeful and mutable variables such as the degree of parental encouragement.

Despite this possibility, we find that the Canadian case strengthens the argument for including the variable in the basic model. The estimates of the effects of family size, both at the zero-order level and with controls in place, closely resemble those for the United States both for men and women. Despite quite marked differences in the rates of development of the educational systems, and the traditionally large family in French Canada, both English and French Canada provide estimates quite like those from the United States. The small differences adopt a form which is consistent with the idea that the basic relationship is somewhat curved rather than linear, with the curve having the effect of strengthening the relationship as the mean family size falls.

It is possible that the word "curve" is inappropriate and the real departures from linearity are owing to discontinuities in the continuation rates across the divisions that have been created in the school system between the primary, secondary, and post-secondary levels. Further analysis of these data could pursue this issue.

Canada is also found to closely resemble the United States in the degree and manner in which family size relates to occupational attainment.

Not only does Canada resemble the United States in these basic relationships but also we note that the available estimates of the relationship between IQ and family size also suggest that there is no major difference between the two nations in this respect. The extent to which IQ can "explain away" the relationship between family size and educational attainment appears similar, and of moderate magnitude, in both countries.

The similarities between Canada and the United States both in the strength of the zero-order relationships and in the manner in which they react to the introduction of controls are sufficiently great that the one exception to the resemblance, the tendency for the relationship to fluctuate across cohorts in Canada but not in the United States, is worth special comment. It suggests that the stability across cohorts may be a special feature of U.S. society and not a firm demographic regularity. The relationship may be more time bound than the stability in the United States implies.

Insofar as family size is a significant depressor of educational attainment it is of importance to know exactly how it operates both in order to more fully understand it and to suggest means that can be used to overcome its effects. The search for a theoretical explanation is being pursued in two parallel courses: the large national surveys of adults, and the studies of high school students. The two approaches appear to meet at the point of assessing the role of the IQ as a variable in the relationship, and both reach similar conclusions. The two approaches cannot be expected always to yield immediately congruent results. We detect in the Canadian survey some impact of the depression of the 1930s upon the strength of the relationship, and other fluctuations across age cohorts. Findings of this kind are necessarily slighted in a study of a single cohort of students. In general, the student surveys probably systematically under-estimate the effects of economic conditions and other historical factors. On the other hand, certain findings from the surveys of students remain to be reconciled with the national surveys. It remains puzzling how mediating variables such as parental encouragement could produce major cross-national regularities in the relationship between family size and education. Possibly these are only first approximations to results that may more easily be reconciled, or it may ultimately be observed that variables such as parental encouragement are firmly rooted in enduring features of the social system in ways not currently evident.

Notes

1. The estimate came as part of a regression analysis reported immediately below, and after listwise deletion of missing cases the actual case base was 12,073 (unweighted N equalled 12,468). For subsequent estimates the case bases were: English females, 12,525 (unweighted, 13,163); French males, 4,196 (3,544); French females, 4,415 (3,690).
2. The average family size of 5.03 seems high, but several factors must be remembered. First, this is not the contemporary family which is described, but the family of origin of the respondents. The estimate, then, refers to an earlier point in history. Also, because foreign-born are included it does not

refer only to Canada. Two other factors are more mathematical. Since larger families contribute more sons who potentially can fall into the sample, larger families are over-represented. With this taken into account, by down-weighting the responses of those from larger families, the estimate falls to 3.71, or 4.02 with the French included. Further, since average family sizes are ordinarily computed with the childless included, another correction is required. Imagining that about 15 per cent of all couples may have been childless, including them in the calculation would further reduce the estimate to 3.42, again with the French included. This is close to the estimates of completed family size for the early 1900s given by Légaré and Henripin (1974:69).

3. The term education and occupation of family head is technically correct since on occasion the head is the mother or some third person. Throughout this report we have, somewhat loosely, used "father's education" and "father's occupation" instead.

4. By which is meant it does not alter the estimate of the effect of family size upon educational attainment. There is a very small but significant direct effect, as those from broken families, defined in this way, have slightly lower levels of educational attainment.

5. The difference between French and English Canadians in the strength of the family size–education relationship widens rather than narrows if those of farm origin are excluded from the analysis or if only native-born English Canadians are considered.

6. The departure from linearity is statistically significant for both English and French but not of great magnitude. Eta coefficients expressing the relationship between family size and education are only fractionally higher than the Pearsonian correlations. Statistical significance is possible because of the large sample size. Slight increases in the variance explained of education is achieved if the square of family size is included with family size as explanatory variables.

7. It is tempting to note that the Canadian result is identical to the U.S. 1973 estimate which in turn is essentially identical to the U.S. 1962 one. The exact equivalence is, however, an accident, not only because the control variables and definition of the populations by age are different, but also these are data based on samples. If the Canadian parameter were indeed .032 with a sample of this size (N = 10,709), at the .05 level of confidence, results running from .016 to .049 should be expected.

8. That the relationship was negative has been known for some time and it was once the basis of a major intellectual and social movement, the Eugenicists. Heer provides a brief history of the movement (1975: 63-68). The Eugenicists feared that the excessive fertility of low IQ families would ultimately lower the IQ level of the whole population. Their worries were apparently unfounded as IQ has tended to increase rather than decrease through this century. It is because the issue was a popular social problem, however, that so many measures of relationship between family size and IQ can be found, some based on enormous samples.

9. Logically one should also re-estimate the relationship of IQ to social background variables. One could use the Canadian estimates, which seem low, or the more recent U.S. estimates, which seem high. We continue to use the Duncan estimates for them, and also for the relationship of IQ to educational attainment.

10. The Canadian sample does not immediately agree with the census in estimating school attainment. The sample shows higher levels of attainment, particularly for younger cohorts, than the census. Part of this maybe an upward SES bias, as is characteristic of samples with low completion rates. The balance is probably owing to question differences. The sample question appears to encourage respondents to report more vocational training and other non-formal education than does the census, which rules out courses of short duration or falling into certain subject-matter categories.

References

ANISEF, PAUL
No date   *The Critical Juncture: Educational and Vocational Intentions of Grade 12 Students in Ontario.* Ontario: Ministry of Colleges and Universities.

ANASTASI, ANNE
1956   "Intelligence and Family Size." *Psychological Bulletin*, 53: 187-209.

BAHR, STEPHEN J. and GEOFFREY K. LEIGH
1978   "Family Size, Intelligence and Expected Education." *Journal of Marriage and the Family*, 40(2): 331-35.

BLAU, P.M. and O.D. DUNCAN
1967   *The American Occupational Structure.* New York: John Wiley.

BRETON, RAYMOND
1972   *Social and Academic Factors in the Career Decisions of Canadian Youth.* Ottawa: Manpower and Immigration.

CUNEO, CARL J. and JAMES E. CURTIS
1975   "Social Ascription in the Educational and Occupational Status Attainment of Urban Canadians." *Canadian Review of Sociology and Anthropology*, 12(1): 6-24.

DUNCAN, BEVERLY
1965   "Dropouts and the Unemployed." *Journal of Political Economy*, 73: 121-34.

1967   "Education and Social Background." *American Journal of Sociology*, 72(4): 363-72.

DUNCAN, OTIS DUDLEY
1968   "Ability and Achievement." *Eugenics Quarterly*, 15: 1-11.

DUNCAN, O.D., DAVID L. FEATHERMAN and BEVERLY DUNCAN
1972   *Socioeconomic Background and Achievement.* New York: Seminar Press.

FEATHERMAN, DAVID L. and ROBERT M. HAUSER
1976   "Sexual Inequalities and Socioeconomic Achievement in the U.S., 1962-1973." *American Sociological Review*, 41(3): 462-83.

HAUSER, ROBERT M. and DAVID L. FEATHERMAN
1975   "Equality of Access to Schooling: Trends and Prospects." Working Paper 75-17, Center for Demography and Ecology. Madison: University of Wisconsin.

HEER, DAVID
1975   *Society and Population.* 2nd ed. Englewood Cliffs, New Jersey: Prentice Hall.

HENRIPIN, J. and J. LÉGARÉ
   1974   "Recent Trends in Canadian Fertility." *Canadian Review of Sociology and Anthropology*, Special Issue, "Aspects of Canadian Society" 61-73.
HOUT, MICHAEL and WILLIAM R. MORGAN
   1975   "Race and Sex Variations in the Causes of Expected Attainments of High School Seniors." *American Journal of Sociology*, 81(2): 364-94.
JOHNSON, F. HENRY
   1968   *A Brief History of Education in Canada.* Toronto: McGraw-Hill.
KERCKHOFF, ALAN C.
   1974   "Stratification Processes and Outcomes in England and the U.S." *American Sociological Review*, 39: 789-801.
   1975   "Patterns of Educational Attainment in Great Britain." *American Journal of Sociology*, 80(6): 1,428-37.
MACKINNON, N. and P. ANISEF
   1979   "Self Assessment in the Early Educational Attainment Process." *Canadian Review of Sociology and Anthropology*, 16(3): 305-19.
MCCLENDON, MCKEE J.
   1976   "The Occupational Status Attainment Processes of Males and Females." *American Sociological Review*, 41(1): 52-64.
PORTER, MARION R., JOHN PORTER and BERNARD R. BLISHEN
   1979   *Does Money Matter? Prospects for Higher Education in Ontario.* Toronto: The Carleton Library, No. 110.
REHBURG, RICHARD A. and DAVID L. WESTBY
   1967   "Parental Encouragement, Occupation, Education and Family Size: Artifactual or Independent Determinants of Adolescent Educational Expectations." *Social Forces*, 45(3): 362-74.
ROSEN, BERNARD C. and CAROL S. ANESHENSEL
   1978   "Sex Differences in the Educational-Occupational Expectation Process." *Social Forces*, 57(1): 164-86.
SEWELL, WILLIAM H., ROBERT M. HAUSER and WENDY C. WOLF
   1980   "Sex, Schooling and Occupational Status." *American Journal of Sociology*, 86(3): 551-83.
STATISTICS CANADA
   1963   *Census of Canada: 1961.* Vol. 1, Part 3, Table 102. "Population 10 years of age and over not attending school by highest grade attended." Ottawa: Information Canada.
TEPPERMAN, LORNE
   1975   *Social Mobility in Canada.* Toronto: McGraw-Hill Ryerson.

CHAPTER 7

Educational and Occupational Attainments of Native-Born Canadian Men and Women

MONICA BOYD

"Although social inequality is the subject matter of social stratification studies, little of this work on the position of women has been done by sociologists in the field of social stratification. Indeed, sex has rarely been analyzed as a factor in stratification processes and structures, although it is probably one of the most obvious criteria of social differentiation and one of the most obvious bases of economic, political and social inequalities" (Acker, 1973:340).

This statement emerges from the more general neglect of women in North American sociology (Millman and Kanter, 1977). Summarizing the growing frustration with the sociological relegation of women to the area of marriage and the family, Acker extended the earlier writings of Watson and Barth (1964) by challenging the assumption that women were irrelevant in the area of stratification aside from their family roles and their marital status.

Acker's challenge was timely in two respects. First, the general societal expectation that a woman's place was in the home (see Cook and Mitchinson, 1976) was increasingly divergent from the pattern of growth in the female labour force during the twentieth century. In 1901 only 16 per cent of the adult Canadian female population was actually in the labour force; by 1973 this figure had risen to approximately 40 per cent. This increased labour force participation, much of it occurring in the 1960s and mainly among married women (Labour Canada: Women's Bureau, 1974), rendered questionable the societal and sociological practices of focusing only upon the occupational experiences of males

229

and assigning females the social status of their husbands.

A second reason for the timeliness of Acker's critique was that the increased female labour force participation of the 1960s and early 1970s occurred in the era of renewed attention to equal opportunity. Like many Western nations fashioned from the British and European political and social philosophies of the 1700s and 1800s, Canada adheres ideologically to the principle of equal opportunity which states that access to positions or rewards should not be denied, or granted, to persons on the basis of their ascriptive characteristics, such as sex, race, birthplace, and ethnicity. Rather, individuals should have equal opportunities to compete for social positions and rewards. To use the metaphor of Chapter 3, each individual should have the same opportunity as another to run in a race, and to run a fair race, although clearly not all participants will be winners.

Equal opportunity is a normative principle — one which stipulates how positions and rewards in a society *should* be allocated among its members. In practice, considerable inequality of opportunity with respect to access to positions and rewards exists. In North America, the discrepancy between principle and practice was of particular concern in the 1960s and 1970s, especially with reference to blacks in the United States, the French ethnic-linguistic population in Canada, and women in both countries. All of these groups historically had occupied very different social positions than those held by white, anglo ethnic-linguistic and/or male populations. The social changes of the 1960s and 1970s, including the formation of social movements, challenged the status quo acceptance of these differences, and pointed out that contrary to the principle of equal opportunity, some segments of the population because of their racial, linguistic, or sexual characteristics, did not obtain the same opportunities for achievement as did other members of society.

As a result of the growing labour force participation of women and the increasing saliency of equality of opportunity with respect to gender, sociologists increasingly are comparing the achievements of men and women. For researchers in the status attainment tradition, this comparison means extending life-cycle models of educational and occupational attainments to women. As discussed in Chapter 1, these models were developed in order to better understand the association between father's status and son's status, which is observed in much of the stratification and mobility research. The development of these models of educational and occupational attainment (Carlsson, 1958; Blau and Duncan, 1967; Duncan and Hodge, 1963) greatly refined North American research on the influence exerted by social origins with respect to male educational and occupational achievements. The life-cycle approach revealed that much of the association between social origins and education or occupation was mediated by intervening variables. Social origins were shown to be associated with occupational achievement of men largely because they affect educational outcomes, which in turn influence first job and subsequent occupational attainments.

The use of these models in comparing the statuses of men and women raises at least three questions, which are addressed in this chapter.[1] First, since the models were developed largely in response to studies of male mobility, do the models include those variables which affect the attainments of women? Secondly, for any given model, does the process of educational or occupational attainment differ for men or women? Thirdly, do such sex differences in the attainment process operate to the advantage of men or women?

The Model for Men: Bringing Women In

The first question focuses attention on the independent variables which are conceptualized to affect educational and occupational status outcomes of men and women. Status attainment research has isolated a set of familial characteristics which are known to facilitate the educational and occupational attainments of children. With respect to educational attainment, among the most important of these are the levels of education achieved by the parents, parental income or occupational levels, and the number of children in the family. Parental education is usually positively associated with the education of the offspring — that is, parents with low levels of education tend to have less well-educated offspring, whereas highly educated parents tend to have offspring with high educational attainments. Two possible reasons for this association exist. First, as key agents of socialization, parents transmit to their children what they consider to be appropriate attitudes and expectations about the educational process and the social and practical skills necessary to realize these expectations. Parents reproduce themselves culturally and socially as well as biologically. Secondly, because of its association with socioeconomic status, parental education is also likely a surrogate measure for the economic resources which families provide children in achieving educational goals. Because of the importance of such resources, familial socioeconomic status also is measured directly, either as family or father's income and/or as paternal occupational status. A final factor which affects educational attainment is the number of siblings. In general, the larger the number of siblings, the lower per capita resources available to any one child and the lower is that child's expected educational achievement.

For the most part, these familial characteristics (parental education, family socioeconomic status, and number of siblings) affect subsequent occupational statuses largely because they influence the educational achievements of offspring. However, status attainment studies which include father's socioeconomic status as a family of origin variable show that it also influences first job and current occupational statuses of offspring, above and beyond the effect it exerts via educational attainment. This direct influence of father's occupational status on respondent's occupational status would appear to capture not only the financial resources which father's socioeconomic status represents but also the non-monetary ways in which father's or heads of households' influence the occupational statuses of offspring. For example, offspring can inherit farms, businesses, and even occupations, as when the offspring of a lawyer becomes a lawyer. But the socioeconomic status of the father can affect the status of the offspring in other ways. Fathers may be known to employers, thereby influencing employers' decisions concerning hiring and promotions, or they may assist in the job searches and occupational career planning of offspring because of their own familiarity with a given set of occupations or a given labour market.

With respect to the occupational achievement of sons and daughters, their education also is considered to be an important variable for two reasons. First, it mediates most of the influence of social origins, thereby illuminating the mechanism by which occupational status is tied to social origins. Secondly, it also represents the acquisition of occupationally relevant skills and the attainment of credentials which are used to allocate individuals to occupational positions. Thus it affects not only the first job status but also subsequent occupational statuses. In turn, the status of a first job is related to the status of current occupation, in part because certain occupations have career trajectories associated with them (e.g., factory worker to foreman) and in part because the requirements of certain occupations (e.g., physician) make unlikely recruitment from other occupations (e.g., sociologist).

This set of variables represented by father's education and socioeconomic status, number of siblings, respondent's education, and first job socioeconomic status was the basis for the original model of status attainment, developed by Blau and Duncan (1967) and elaborated by Duncan, Featherman and Duncan (1972). This model is used in several of the initial studies comparing the educational and occupational attainments of American men and women (Featherman and Hauser, 1976b; Treas and Tyree, 1979; Wang, 1973). However, the increased attention to the status attainments of women has either reinforced or prompted the introduction of two additional sets of variables to the early models of educational and occupational attainment: those pertaining to the socioeconomic characteristics of the mother as part of the family of origin characteristics; and those pertaining to additional roles of wife and mother assumed by women.

Recent studies now include maternal labour force involvement in models of occupational attainment for two reasons (Cuneo and Curtis, 1975; Marini, 1980; McClendon, 1976; Sewell, Hauser and Wolf, 1980; Treiman and Terrill, 1975). First, maternal characteristics provide additional information on the family of origin. If a mother worked, one consequence may be an augmentation of financial resources available to the offspring which affects subsequent educational and occupational statuses. Secondly, mothers who work in the paid labour force may influence daughter's subsequent labour force involvement and occupational experiences by simultaneously filling the roles of wife, mother, and employee. They also may impart knowledge about the expectations and demands of the work in the labour force. And they may communicate very specific information about occupational decisions, career planning, and employment markets. This specific information may reinforce the allocative mechanisms of a sex-segregated labour market, in which women are concentrated in occupations labelled as "women's work." Studies of inter-generational mobility of women have observed that because of occupational segregation by sex, occupations held by women are more similar to maternal occupations than to paternal occupations (Rosenfeld, 1978; Stevens and Boyd, 1980; Tyree and Treas, 1974).

In addition to the inclusion of maternal characteristics, the domestic division of labour with respect to breadwinner, homemaker, child-bearer, and child-rearer roles also suggests a second elaboration of the usual occupational attainment model. Both the marital role and the child-rearing role may shape the occupational experiences of women more so than for men. Because of the strong social expectation that men should be the primary providers for the family, marriage and the presence of children serves to reinforce the involvement of men in the labour force. But in the past, this expectation for men has been parallelled by the expectation that women should assume primary responsibility for home maintenance and childcare. Hudis (1976) notes several consequences of the demands incurred by the multiplicity of social roles (wife, mother, and job holder) assumed when marriage is combined with labour force involvement. One consequence may be the rejection of employment altogether; another may be the periodical absence from the labour force which serves to reduce occupational seniority; and a third consequence may be part-time rather than full-time employment. Still another consequence is that within the work world, married women will be allocated to certain jobs and/or occupations. Such allocative mechanisms can result from either labour market practices or individual decisions. Employer perception of familial responsibilities of married women may lead to hiring, job placement, promotion related practices (such as job training) which under-utilize female education and previous job experiences and which depress their mobility (see Boyd, 1982b). Some women also may attempt to reconcile conflict between familial and employment roles by entering occupations and selecting jobs which are compatible with the demands of a family in terms of hours worked, flexibility of the work routine, and commuting distance. Such work, however, might be characterized by lower opportunities for advancement or it may be lower in status or earning than warranted by the workers' education or previous occupational histories (Hudis, 1976; Rosenthal, 1978).

Reflecting these considerations, investigations of female occupational attainments now frequently include measures of labour force involvement and discontinuity and such career contingency variables as marital status and number of children as variables affecting occupational status and wages of women (Featherman and Hauser, 1976b; Goyder, 1981; Hudis, 1976; Marini, 1980; McClendon, 1976; Sewell, Hauser and Wolf, 1980; Suter and Miller, 1973; Waite, 1976; Wolf, 1976).

MALE-FEMALE DIFFERENCES IN ATTAINMENTS AND THEIR CONSEQUENCES

Overall, the inclusion of women in models of status attainment points to the need to include maternal characteristics, and respondent characteristics which reflect the additional female roles of wife and mother. But the inclusion of women and the elaboration of the basic model raises the second and third questions concerning similarities and differences between men and women: Does the process of attainment differ for men and women and how, and do such sex differences operate to the advantage of men or women?

Role-modelling theory and the existence of a sex-segregated occupational structure provide strong rationales for expecting sex differences in the educational and occupational attainment processes of men and women. With respect to educational attainment, "like-sex effects" may exist in which the characteristics of the mothers influence the education of the daughters to a much greater extent than do the characteristics of the fathers and in which the reverse pattern is observed for sons (Boyd,

1982a; McClendon, 1976; Sewell, Hauser and Wolf, 1980; Treiman and Terrill, 1975). This argument concerning like-sex effects is particularly well developed in regard to the influence exerted by parental education where role-modelling theory suggests that offspring model themselves after parents of the same sex. As a result of such modelling, the educational attainment of women should be influenced more by the level of the mother's education whereas the educational attainment of sons should be influenced more by father's educational achievements.

While research generally reveals additional differences between men and women in the effect of other social origin variables on the educational attainment process, there is some ambiguity over the extent and direction of these differences. Studies of high school students indicate that social origins generally have a greater influence on the educational aspirations and attainment for girls than for boys (Alexander and Eckland, 1974; Porter, Porter and Blishen, 1973; Sewell and Shah, 1967; Turrittin, Anisef and Mackinnon, 1982; for more mixed results, see Sewell, Hauser and Wolf, 1980). At least one reason for the stronger association of social background with educational aspirations and attainment of females compared to males may be a preference of parents to give priority to financing and education of sons when money is scarce (Porter, Blishen and Porter, 1973: 134). These findings suggest that the educational attainment of women should be more strongly influenced by such measures of family resources such as paternal socioeconomic status or mother working and more negatively affected by additional siblings which dilute the per capita value of such resources. Some evidence of this for adult men and women is provided by Treiman and Terrill (1975) and by Cuneo and Curtis (1975). However, an analysis of the 1975 follow-up study of a cohort of male and female Wisconsin high school graduates shows that the total effect of father's occupational status and maternal employment on educational attainment is lower for women than men (Sewell, Hauser and Wolf, 1980: tables 8 and 9). In their analysis of married men and their wives in the American 1973 Occupational Changes in a Generation survey, Featherman and Hauser (1976b) also observe the educational achievement of women seems to be less influenced by father's socioeconomic status and by number of siblings than is the case for men.

In addition to their influence on educational attainments, social origins also are expected to differentially affect the first and current occupational attainment processes of men and women. In particular, maternal characteristics are expected to exert a greater influence on the statuses of daughters than on sons while, conversely, father's characteristics are expected to have a greater effect on the occupational attainments of sons than on those of daughters. This expectation derives both from the like-sex effects argument and from the existence of a sex-segregated occupational structure. As discussed above, the like-sex effects argument stipulates that children model themselves more closely after the same-sex parent than after the opposite-sex parent. When extended to occupational status, this argument implies that paternal socioeconomic status will have less influence on the occupational statuses of daughters than on that of sons, and that maternal work characteristics will be more important in determining the occupational status for daughters than for sons. Marini (1980) generalizes the argument further and suggests that like-sex effects will also exist in regard to the effects of maternal and paternal education on the acquisition of occupational status.

The existence of a sex-segregated occupational structure also acts to reinforce the expectation that father's occupational status influences the occupational statuses of sons more so than for daughters and vice versa for mother's characteristics. Sex segregation implies that the occupational attainments of offspring are more similar to those of the same-sex parent (Marini, 1980: 313; also see Rosenfeld, 1978; Stevens and Boyd, 1980; Tyree and Treas, 1974). This association between father-son and mother-daughter occupational attainments not only reflects hiring and job assignment practices in the marketplace, but also the way in which sex segregation constrains parental influence on the subsequent occupational achievements of their offspring. This constraint appears to be very important in understanding the lower influence which father's occupational status has on the occupational status of daughters compared to sons. All of the ways in which fathers influence the occupational attainments of offspring will be curtailed for women to the extent that the occupational structure is sex-segregated. Specific occupational inheritance becomes more difficult for daughters when the occupation to be inherited is firmly entrenched in an all male world (e.g., construction contractor, bricklayer, mechanical engineer) and may well be impossible if sons are available for recruitment. Assistance in the form of pinpointing likely sources of employment or involving offspring in a job-related social network also is less likely, since fathers will tend to know little about the features of female occupations or because daughters are not considered to be legitimate participants in male occupations. For similar but converse reasons, sons may not be as influenced as daughters by having a mother who worked or by her occupational status.

Research in fact confirms the lower influence of father's occupational attainment on daughter's occupational attainments (Cuneo and Curtis,

1975; Featherman and Hauser, 1976b; Marini, 1980; Treas and Tyree, 1979; Treiman and Terrill, 1975) but the evidence is more mixed in regard to the relative influence of maternal work experience on the occupational attainments of sons and daughters. Marini (1980) finds that mother's occupational status exerts a greater influence on the first job statuses of daughters compared to sons but she finds that mother's occupational status has no effect on the current occupational statuses of either sons or daughters. When mother's labour force participation is used as a dichotomous variable, Sewell, Hauser and Wolf (1980: tables 8-9, lines 6 and 12) find that it positively influences the first and current occupational statuses of men but that it has no effect on the first or current occupational statuses of women. Their results are the reverse of what would be expected under the like-sex effect argument, and they can be attributed to the composite nature of the measure. Earlier, we noted that mother's working may be a measure of family resources in addition to serving as a measure of role modelling. If it represents family resources, and if families allocate more resources to sons, then having a mother who worked would enhance the status of sons rather than that of daughters.

Although father's socioeconomic status is expected to be less important for the occupational attainment of women, their own education is expected to play a greater role. This greater influence of education on the first and subsequent statuses of women compared to men is consistent with the relationship between the educational system and the sex segregated occupational structure. Gaskell (1982) notes that training for traditional female occupations, particularly clerical occupations, is more likely to be part of the formal educational curriculum of high schools in Canada and more likely to be recognized as legitimate training by employers. But the link between schooling and male-dominated occupations is weaker. The industrial courses, which would appear to be equivalent high school courses for males, do not provide credentials or skills which are tested or expected on entry to jobs (Gaskell, 1982: 6, 12). Rather, trades training occurs after high school, and for male blue-collar occupations, getting into the labour force and receiving on-the-job training may be more important than high school courses. These sex differences in the relations of formal schooling to sex-labelled occupations of clerical work and trades imply that formal education should be more strongly related to the occupational statuses of women than is the case for men.[2] Education also may be more important in the current occupational attainment process for women because the greater discontinuity in labour force participation forces them to rely on educational attainment instead of work experience as criteria for employment and occupational placement (see Sewell, Hauser and Wolf, 1980: 576).

That first job should have a greater influence on the current occupational attainments of women also is consistent with the patterns of sex segregation in the Canadian labour force. Jobs in which women concentrate are characterized by lower mobility opportunities (Wolf and Rosenfeld, 1978). If this is the case and if the occupational structure is highly sex-segregated, women will experience less career mobility than men, and their occupational status upon entry into the labour force will have more impact on subsequent occupational statuses, including current occupational status (see Marini, 1980: 315).

The above discussion presents the various rationales for expecting sex differences in a model of attainment which includes maternal characteristics, number of siblings, paternal education and occupational status, and — in the case of first and current occupational status — respondent's education and first job attainments. Among women, marriage and motherhood roles also are expected to have additional consequences for their occupational attainments. Specifying what are the consequences of the wife and mother role for the occupational attainments of women is open to two different interpretations. Based on perceptions of the competing demands of family responsibilities, married women may accept or be assigned to occupations which are lower in status, earnings or promotional possibilities than are warranted by their education or previous work experience (Hudis, 1976). If wives and/or mothers hold occupations which offer lower promotional opportunities, first job status will be more tightly associated with the current occupational attainments of these women compared to single women. And, if married women are in occupations which are not commensurate with their educational credentials, education also will have less influence on current occupational attainments of married women. However, a second interpretation concerning the role played by education in the occupational attainment process is offered by Sewell, Hauser and Wolf (1980:576). They argue that education may actually be more influential in determining the current occupational status of women who, because of discontinuous work experience, rely on educational attainment rather than previous work experience as a basis of subsequent occupational placement. Since married women, particularly with small children, are the most likely candidates for labour force exists (see Boyd, 1977; Boyd, Eichler and Hofley, 1975), this argument implies that the influence of education on current occupational attainments should be greater for married women than for single (never married) women. Analytically this implies that education will have a greater effect on the current occupational attainments of married/discontinuous female workers compared to continuous and/or single female workers.

Much of the discussion concerning the status attainment process of married versus unmarried women stresses the consequences of work and family demands for women. The argument that the actual existence or perception of family constraints shape the subsequent occupational attainment process for married women also is used to anticipate the influence of child-bearing on attainment. In addition to the responsibilities associated with the wife role, women with children are faced with reconciling child-rearing responsibilities with occupational demands. Limiting the size of their families is one way in which women may reconcile child-rearing and labour force activities. Alternatively, the presence of children may allocate women to occupations which are lower in status than their skills warrant but which also may have job characteristics which are considered amenable to the meeting of familial demands (see Rosenthal, 1978). The second possibility implies that children depress the occupational attainments of women.

Although the literature stresses the negative consequences of the wife and mother roles on female occupational achievements, it is not clear from the preceding discussion as to whether the sex differences in the attainment process in their entirety will operate to the disadvantage of women compared to men. The third and last question posed in this chapter address this issue of whether or not sex differences in the process of attainment cumulate to the advantage of disadvantage of women or men. This is a useful question for two reasons. First, although sex differences are expected in regard to the influence exerted by the specified indpeendent variables on occupational attainment, the differences may represent a mixture of relative advantages and disadvantages. Depending on the magnitude of these differences and the importance of the independent variables themselves, these differences could cumulate to a strong disadvantage for women compared to men, to an actual advantage, or they could simply cancel each other, with the implication that although the status attainment process differs between men and women, it produces little discernable difference in occupational status outcomes. A second rationale for examining the overall consequences of sex differences in the occupational attainment process arises from the need to distinguish between processual and compositional determinants of occupational status when comparing men and women. The discussion so far focuses intensively on the processual differences between male and female attainment, stressing differences expected with respect to the influence exerted by social origins, education and first job on the acquisition of current occupational status. But this need not be the only cause of occupational status differences between men and women. If men and women differ in their social origins, or in their levels of education and first job status, such sex differences in the stock or composition of these occupationally relevant variables also will enhance or depress the status of one group versus another.[3] In actual fact, these compositional differences are sure to exist for the currently employed population since the female labour force is not randomly drawn from the larger female population (see Gunderson, 1976). Given these differences in composition, our interest in the consequences of sex differences in the occupational attainment process requires two interrelated analyses: first, assessing the overall consequence of processual differences in attainment, and secondly, ascertaining the relative importance of processual differences versus compositional differences in producing the observed differences in occupational status between men and women.

In conclusion, three questions shape our subsequent analyses of the educational and occupational attainments of men and women in Canada. The first question asks if the initial models of male occupational achievement includes those variables which might be expected to influence the attainments of women. This question leads to the inclusion of maternal education and work experience in male and female models of attainment and to the elaboration of the analysis to assess the impact of wife and mother roles. Accordingly, in our analysis we begin with a model of educational and occupational attainment which includes maternal education and a measure of maternal labour force participation.[4] Then we augment this model of current occupational attainment by examining how marriage and motherhood affect the acquisition of female occupational status. In these analyses, we also address the second question on whether or not educational and occupational attainment processes exist. Also central to our analysis is the third question: do the sex differences in the attainment processes operate to the advantage of women or men. Here we assess the overall impact of both processual and compositional differences between men and women in the labour force.

Much of the investigation involves technical terminology appropriate to multivariate analytical techniques. Readers less interested in the methodological details of the analysis may wish to concentrate on the conclusion to this chapter. In addition, the concluding paragraphs of each section also discuss the substantive findings.

In addressing our three questions we have restricted the analysis to the native-born population in Canada, age 25 to 64. The age restriction omits young adults, some of whom will not have completed their education and it also omits those of retirement age whose inclusion might confound the analysis, either because of selective longevity (for example, persons who are better educated, or of higher socioeconomic status in any age cohort may live longer) or because of the selectivity of continued labour participation for those past normal retirement age. The analysis is also limited to the native-born population since data in Chapter 11 indicate nativity differences in the educational and occupational attainment process. Rather than confound the comparisons of males and females by the inclusion of the immigrant population, which is about one-quarter of the population age 25 to 64 in 1973, this chapter examines the educational and occupational attainment process of native-born men and women. Additional analyses on the occupational status of immigrant women are presented in Boyd (1982c, 1984) and in Chapter 11.

Male-Female Differences in Educational Attainment

The investigation begins by examining male-female attainments early in the life cycle. Research conducted in the United States and Canada documents differences in educational outcomes of males and females, with females more likely than males to complete high school but less likely to obtain a college education or a post-graduate degree (Alexander and Eckland, 1974; Robb and Spencer, 1976; Sewell and Shah, 1967, 1968). In addition to sex differences with respect to length of schooling, there exist sex differences in educational curricula. Females predominate in secretarial courses and home economics; males are found in math and shop. Such concentration does not end with high school. Nursing and teaching are two occupations viewed as female and not surprisingly many, if not most, of the students in teachers' colleges or nursing programs are women. In university, females are more likely to major in the humanities or social sciences and less likely to be in mathematics, engineering, law, and medicine (Statistics Canada, 1981; Vickers, 1975). These sex differences in length and type of education are attributed to diverse causes, among them, social origins, the socializing influence of the family, the peer group and teachers, self-concept, the internal structure of schools, and the organization of the educational system itself (Alexander and Eckland, 1974; Gaskell, 1982; Porter, Porter and Blishen, 1973, 1982; Robb and Spencer, 1976; Roby, 1972; Rosen and Aneshensel, 1978; Sewell, Hauser and Wolf, 1980; Sewell and Shah, 1967, 1968; Turrittin, Anisef and Mackinnon, 1982).

Despite the apparent richness of facts describing the educational differences between North American men and women, for the most part Canadian investigations focus on selected groups of people such as high school students or young adults. The 1973 Canadian Mobility data permit a broader overview of educational attainment. Unlike studies limited to students currently enroled in school or to young adults, our data shows the educational stock of all adult Canadians, and permit us to assess the impact of family background on such attainments. We begin the analysis by observing educational differences between adult Canadian men and women. We then examine the effect of social origins on male and female educational attainments. Here we assess the empirical evidence for the like-sex effects model in which maternal characteristics are presumed to have a greater influence than the paternal characteristics on the educational attainments of daughters and vice versa for sons.

Table 7.1 shows how adult men and women age 25 to 64 in 1973 differed in the length and type of education received. Although more women receive and complete an academic high school program, fewer women are university educated. The data in Table 7.1 also show that women are less likely to have entered or completed university and they are less likely to hold an M.A., Ph.D., or a professional degree. Instead, women concentrate in post-secondary programs to a much greater extent than men (24 per cent versus 14 per cent of males age 25 to 64). And, of those women who have received post-secondary schooling, most are from nursing schools or teaching institutions. Despite these differences, men and women on the average have the same educational score of 10.6 (Table 7.2), although the standard deviation of these mean scores indicates that the female educational distribution is more concentrated around this mean than is true for the male distribution. As shown in Table 7.2, native-born Canadian men and women on the average also come from similar social backgrounds as represented by number of siblings, parental education, mother's labour force participation, and father's SES. The slight differences between men and women in social origins in part reflect the deviation of the half boys–half girls sex ratio within families, and the differences between the sexes with respect to emigration from Canada and mortality.

A major concern is to identify the process which produces these outcomes and to measure sex-specific differences in this process. More specifically, we are concerned with the degree to which familial resources differentially influence the capacity of men and women to obtain the educational credentials necessary to compete in the labour market.[5]

Data addressing the importance of family background on educational

TABLE 7:1 — Level of Educational Attainment for Native-born Males and Females, Age 25-64, Canada 1973

	Males	Females
Below high school	31.0	27.8
Zero Schooling, Some Elementary	16.0	13.1
Finished Elementary	15.0	14.7
High school	38.3	39.2
Some Academic	20.6	22.8
Finished Academic	9.4	11.3
Some Vocational	4.4	2.1
Finished Vocational	3.9	3.0
Post secondary-general	11.1	14.4
Some	4.2	4.3
Finished	6.9	10.1
Post secondary: programs	4.2	10.1
Nursing, Teaching	.7	7.9
CEGEP	3.5	2.2
University	11.3	7.8
Some University	4.7	3.0
University Diploma	1.7	2.0
University B.A.	4.9	2.8
Post-university	4.1	.8
M.A., Ph.D.	1.6	.4
Professional Degrees	2.5	.4

attainment are presented in panels 2 and 3 of Table 7.2 for native-born males and females, age 25 to 64, using listwise regression.[6] Table 7.2 provides the regression parameter statistics in the form of both metric and standardized beta coefficients.[7] These data answer two related questions concerning the educational attainment process of native-born men and women. First, do sex differences exist with respect to the influence (or the "effect") of social origins on educational attainment? Secondly, do like-sex effects exist? That is, do fathers influence the educational attainments of sons more so than do mothers, and do mothers, correspondingly, have a great influence on the educational attainments of daughters? With respect to the first question, comparisons of the metric coefficients (Table 7.2, line 3, 4) indicate that the educational attainments of men and women are influenced differently by father's occupational status, father's education, and mother's education and labour force participation. Further, the significant

TABLE 7:2 — Means and Regression Coefficients for a Model of Educational Attainment for Native-born Females, Age 25-64, Canada 1973

	Line Number	Mother's Education	Father's Education	Number of Siblings	Mother in Labour Force	Father's SES	Respondent's Education[a]	Constant^2 or R^2
Means and standard deviations								
Males	(1)	7.382	7.090	4.789	.164	34.542	10.616	
		(3.582)	(3.861)	(3.331)	(.371)	(13.004)	(3.734)	
Females	(2)	7.539	7.214	4.817	.186	34.831	10.555	
		(3.602)	(3.853)	(3.354)	(.389)	(13.001)	(3.190)	
Metric coefficients								
Males	(3)	.214	.176	−.201	.241	.055		6.812
		(.013)	(.012)	(.011)	(.089)	(.003)		
Females	(4)	.245*	.134*	−.185	.127*	.024*		7.778*
		(.010)	(.010)	(.009)	(.072)	(.002)		
Standardized coefficients								
Males	(5)	.205	.182	−.179	.024	.191		.325
Females	(6)	.277	.162	−.194	.015	.097		.306

[a] coded to approximate years of schooling completed. See Chapter 1.
*Significantly different from the corresponding male metric coefficient at the .05 level using a two-tailed test.

difference in the intercepts for the regression equations implies that women on the average get one year more schooling after adjusting for sex differences in social origins and their effects.

What support do these data in Table 7.2 give for the like-sex phenomenon, in which a parent has more influence on the subsequent attainments of offspring of the same sex? According to the like-sex model, the educational characteristics of fathers should have a greater effect than that of mothers on the educational attainment of sons and the reverse should hold for the educational attainment of daughters. Determining whether such is the case requires answering two different questions: first, do maternal and paternal education differ in their influence within each sex group; and, secondly, does the magnitude of the effect of each variable on educational attainments differ between the male and female populations? With respect to the first question, the discussion of like-sex effects suggests that father's education should have a larger impact than mother's education for the educational attainment of sons while the reverse should hold for daughters. Statistical tests (McClendon, 1976) for differences in the effect of maternal and paternal education within each male and female group indicate this pattern of effects for women but not for men. For every unit change in mother's education, females experience a .245 increment in their own education compared to a .13 increment due to the influence of father's education (Table 7.2, line 4). For males, however, the influence of mother's education upon son's education is not significantly different from the influence of father's education at the .05 level (F=2.811).

With respect to the second question concerning like-sex effects, comparisons of the coefficient reveal that maternal education has more influence on the educational attainment of daughters than that of sons (.245/.214) and fathers' education influences sons' educational achievements to a greater extent (.176/.134) than it influences that of daughters'. These data on parental educational influences offer considerable evidence in support of the like-sex effect model. Our findings are consistent with American research by Sewell, Hauser and Wolf (1975) and Treiman and Terrill (1975), but the contradict research by McClendon (1976) who found no evidence in support of like-sex parental effects on the educational attainments of men and women.

The same-sex effects argument is derived from role-modelling theory (see Treiman and Terrill, 1975) and as such it is most applicable to the impact of parental education on the educational attainment of the offspring. However, an argument also can be made that same-sex effects may be observed for the effects of maternal and paternal work-related characteristics on educational attainments of men and women. This expectation derives from the possibility that work characteristics of the mother may shape the work aspirations of the daughter, whereas the work characteristics of the father shape the aspirations of the son, and that such aspirations in turn influence educational performance and achievement. At first glance, this possibility is suggested by the data concerning the greater influence of father's occupational status on the educational attainments of sons compared to daughters. However, the converse expectation that mother's work history would have more influence on the educational attainments of daughters compared to sons is not supported by the data. Instead, having a mother who worked full-time for one or more years during the respondent's elementary or secondary school years significantly effects the attainments of sons but not daughters, a finding which is also observed in American research (Sewell, Hauser and Wolf, 1980). It would appear that in the context of educational attainment, maternal work history and father's socioeconomic status are not only capturing like-sex role modelling by offspring but also are measuring familial resources available for supporting educational aspirations and attainments. As indicators of familial resources, their greater influence on the educational attain-ments of sons rather than daughters is consistent with the observations of Porter, Porter and Blishen (1973) who suggest that parents may be more likely to financially further the educational attainments of sons, particularly when economic resources are scarce.

Overall, the way in which families influence the educational outcomes of children varies for male and female offspring in two important ways. First, the education of the mother has a greater impact on the education of the daughter, thereby suggesting the importance of same-sex role models for female educational achievement. Secondly, women are less affected by the economic resources of their families, as measured by father's socioeconomic status and mother's labour force participation. These weaker linkages between measures of family status and the educational achievements of women are indicative of a more homogen-ous educational model for women. Women are more likely to finish high school (Table 7.1) but, having done so, they are less likely to go on and complete university and professional degrees.

Sex and First Job

The influence of family on the educational attainments of men and women is of interest for two reasons. First, education represents the acquisition of skills and credentials relevant for the labour market. As such it constitutes an investment to which occupational and income rewards accrue. But also it is the first step in the process by which social position is transmitted across generations. This section examines the second stage in this process — entry to the labour market and acquisition of a first job. Since education is a key resource which people bring to the job market, we examine the influence of education on first job attainment and we ask if its impact differs for men and women. But following the logic of the life-cycle model, we retain the prior family of origin characteristics in our models to determine whether they influence first job status net of their effects on educational achievement.

The usual model of first job acquisition is one based on men, and it assumes that most individuals enter the labour force at some point in their lives. Is this the case for women, particularly when education, quite aside from providing labour force related skills, also provides a setting within which young singles meet and many marry? The answer appears to be that the majority of women do at some point enter the labour force. Seventy-eight per cent of the native-born women age 25 to 64 replied to one or more of the four questions on full-time jobs covering a time span from first full-time job to current job. This is a conservative estimate of the labour force involvement of women since questions were not asked about part-time work with the exception of current occupation.

On the average, the first full-time jobs held by native-born women in Canada are about four Blishen-McRoberts points higher in socioeconomic status than those held by men (Table 7.3). As with education, the standard deviations indicate that women are slightly more clustered around the mean than are men. The regression equations presented in Table 7.3[8] address two questions which are central to the analysis of the first job status attainments of Canadian men and women: does the attainment process differ by sex, and if so, do such differences operate to the advantage of men or women? With respect to the first question, sex differences in the first job attainment process exist largely in the direction suggested by our earlier analysis of educational attainment. The total causal effect of maternal education on first job status is over 40 per cent greater among women than men (.755/.533); but, conversely, the total causal effect of father's occupational status on the first job status of women is 30 per cent of the effect observed for men (.091/.303). Mother's labour force participation has an insignificant influence on the first job attainments of women but it increases male first job attainments by one Blishen-McRoberts point. In addition, the number of siblings has a larger negative direct impact on the first job attainments of daughters than it does for sons. Discussion of this finding is postponed to the subsequent examination of current occupational

TABLE 7:3 — Regression Coefficients for a Model of First Job Attainment for Native-born Males and Females, Age 25-64, Canada 1983.

Line Number	Mother's Education	Father's Education	Number of Siblings	Mother in Labour Force	Father's SES	Respondent's Education	Respondent's First Job SES	Constant or R^2
Means and standard deviations								
Males (1)	7.461	7.178	4.716	.165	34.854	10.739	38.791	
	(3.575)	(3.865)	(3.303)	(.371)	(13.079)	(3.704)	(14.260)	
Females (2)	7.857	7.554	4.524	.205	35.933	11.066	42.977	
	(3.571)	(3.856)	(3.254)	(.404)	(13.200)	(2.938)	(12.777)	
Metric coefficients								
Males (3)	.533	.354	-.516	1.041	.303			23.972
	(.053)	(.051)	(.045)	(.376)	(.012)			
(4)	.063	-.017	-.090	.429	.189	2.161		9.002
	(.045)	(.044)	(.039)	(.320)	(.010)	(.038)		
Females (5)	.755*	.358	-.610	-.242*	.091*			33.902*
	(.048)	(.048)	(.043)	(.335)	(.012)			
(6)	.208*	.070	-.210*	-.414*	.050*	2.469*		12.742*
	(.042)	(.041)	(.037)	(.282)	(.010)	(.044)		
Standardized coefficients								R^2
(7)	.134	.096	-.120	.027	.278			.288
(8)	.016	-.047	-.021	.011	.173	.561		.442
(9)	.211	.108	-.155	-.008	.094			.174
(10)	.058	.021	-.054	-.013	.051	.568		.413

*Significantly different from the corresponding male metric coefficient at the .05 level using a two-tailed test.

attainments where a similar pattern of sex differences in the effects of siblings is observed.

The pattern of direct and indirect effects of family origin variables offers mixed support for the argument that same-sex parents have more influence on the first job attainments of their offspring. Mother's education influences the first job attainments of daughters more so than for sons, and its influence persists beyond the completion of schooling for women. But mother's labour force participation has no significant impact on the first job status of daughters, whereas it does influence the first job statuses of sons via increasing their educational attainments (Table 7.3, lines 3-5; also see Table 7.2). As suggested earlier in the discussion of educational attainment, such results contradict the same-sex effects argument and they are consistent with the interpretation that mother's labour force participation is measuring economic resources to a greater extent than role-modelling influences. In contrast to mother's labour force participation, the greater influence exerted by father's occupational status on the first job attainments of sons is consistent with the expectation that same-sex parents serve as role models, although this variable also may be capturing the availability of economic resources for the subsequent attainments of offspring.

Two additional sex differences are especially noteworthy in the regression equations for first job status. First, education has a greater impact on the first job attainments of women compared to men (total causal effect is 2.469 versus 2.161). Secondly, the intercept for the female equation is considerably higher than the intercept for the male regression equation (Table 7.3, lines 4 and 6). These differences are understandable within the context of a sex-segregated occupational structure. Earlier in this chapter, we noted that the occupational structure and the educational system are especially interlocked for female-typed occupations. Training programs and certification which provide direct entry to jobs are provided by Canadian schools but largely for clerical occupations as opposed to trades occupations, where apprenticeship and on-the-job training may be more appropriate entry and hiring criteria (Gaskell, 1982). This implies that formal education is more tightly associated with first job status for many female-typed occupations than for many of the male-typed occupations, and that in turn formal education should have greater influence on the first job status of women. Sex segregation also may underlie the higher female intercept observed in the regression equations (Table 7.3). Although women dominate in the selected service and manufacturing occupations such as waitressing and garment sewing, they concentrate in white-collar occupations. Since white-collar occupations tend to be assigned higher socioeconomic scores (Pineo, Porter, McRoberts, 1977: Table III), one implication of a sex-segregated labour force is that the first jobs of women are on the average higher in socioeconomic status than are the first jobs of men.

The general pattern which emerges from the data in Table 7.3 is one in which the acquisition of first job status is more of a step-by-step process for native-born women compared to men. In particular, the first job attainments of women are less influenced by paternal socioeconomic status and mother's labour force participation, and they are more influenced by educational achievements. In addition, once the effects of social origins and education are taken into account, the first job status of women on the average is about four points higher than the status observed for men. As an overall consequence of these sex differences in the first job attainment process, women tend to have higher first job statuses than men.

Current Labour Force Participation of Native-born Men and Women

The previous sections examine the educational and first job attainment processes of native-born Canadian men and women. Since both education and first job are important factors influencing the subsequent occupational experiences of men and women, the next step should be to compare the roles played by family social origins, education and first job in the current occupational attainment of men and women. However, the extension of the previous analysis to current occupation requires us to think carefully about the male-female comparisons which we are making. Most men and women have held a full-time first job. But subsequent rates of labour force attrition differ significantly for men and women. Women are far less likely to be currently in the labour force and, when they work, they differ from men in the type of work which they do.

Support for these claims is given in tables 7.4 and 7.5 which show male-female differences in labour force involvement by age groups and by education. Table 7.4 confirms what is discussed extensively elsewhere (see Gunderson, 1976; Labour Canada, Women's Bureau, 1978): only 39 per cent of the women age 25 to 64 are in the 1973 labour force, compared to 94 per cent of the native-born men. Age is a factor affecting labour force participation of both sexes but at all age levels the female rate is lower than that for males. Education, too, is associated with the propensity of women to be in the labour force. Only one-quarter of women with an elementary schooling or less are in the 1973 labour force

TABLE 7:4 — Per Cent in Labour Force for Native-born Males and Females Age 25-64, by Age Groups, Education and Marital Status, Canada 1973.

| | Per Cent by Sex | | | |
| | Males | | Females | |
Age, Education and Marital Status	In Labour Force	Not in Labour Force	In Labour Force	Not in Labour Force
N, thousands	3,509	222	1,501	3,891
Total, Per cent	94.0	6.0	38.6	61.4
Per cent				
25-34	98.2	1.8	41.8	58.2
35-44	97.4	2.6	39.3	60.7
45-54	94.5	5.5	39.5	60.5
55-64	81.9	18.1	30.9	69.1
Education				
Elementary[a]	88.7	11.3	26.6	73.4
High school	96.4	3.6	38.1	61.9
Post-secondary	96.8	3.2	47.1	52.9
University[b]	97.0	3.0	57.1	42.9
Marital status[c]				
Single	88.3	11.7	72.9	27.1
Married, spouse present	95.2	4.8	33.5	66.5
Separated	85.2	14.8	53.5	46.5
Divorced	89.6	10.4	66.2	33.8
Widowed	80.8	19.2	44.2	55.8

[a]Includes a few persons with no schooling.
[b]Includes education beyond university.
[c]Based on responses to the Canadian Mobility Survey question on marital status.

compared to nearly three-fifths of women with at least some university education. In contrast, the labour force participation rates of males are virtually unaffected by education for those with more than elementary schooling (Table 7.4). Marriage also has a greater impact on the labour force participation of women compared to men. Only one-third of women who are currently married with a husband present are in the 1973 labour force compared to nearly three-quarters of women who are single.

Not only do native-born men and women differ with respect to labour

TABLE 7:5 — Class of Work for Native-born Males and Females, in the Labour Force, Age 25-64, by Age Group, Education, and Marital Status

Age, Education and Marital Status	Male				Female			
	Full-time Paid[a]	Part-time Paid	Full-time Unpaid[b]	Part-time Unpaid[b]	Full-time Paid[a]	Part-time Paid	Full-time Unpaid[b]	Part-time Unpaid[b]
N, in 000s	3,337	65	6	1	1,078	296	37	49
Total, per cent	97.7	2.1	.2	[f]	73.9	20.3	2.5	3.3
Age								
25-34	97.7	2.1	.2	.0	78.1	18.0	1.8	2.1
35-44	98.5	1.4	.2	.0	69.4	23.1	3.2	4.2
45-54	98.8	1.0	.1	.1	72.0	20.6	2.9	4.6
55-64	96.2	3.6	.1	.1	74.5	20.2	2.4	2.6
Education								
Elementary[d]	97.9	1.6	.5	[c]	67.7	21.2	5.4	5.7
High school	98.2	1.6	.1	[c]	72.2	21.6	2.6	3.7
Post-secondary	98.2	1.7	[f]	.0	76.0	20.4	1.4	2.3
University[e]	96.6	3.4	.0	.0	83.2	14.9	.7	1.2
Marital status								
Single	94.7	3.4	1.7	.2	91.5	8.3	.2	.0
Married, spouse present	98.4	1.6	[c]	[c]	67.8	24.0	3.5	4.6
Separated	97.6	2.4	.0	.0	83.1	16.5	.0	.4
Divorced	96.7	6.3	.0	.0	94.4	5.6	.0	.0
Widowed	92.6	7.4	.0	.0	78.5	20.5	.5	.5

[a] Includes wage and self-employed workers.
[b] Unpaid family workers.
[c] Excludes persons who are in the labour force but had never worked and are currently unemployed.
[d] Includes a few persons with no schooling.
[e] Includes education beyond university B.A.
[f] Less than .1 per cent.

force participation, but also they differ with respect to the class of work performed while in the labour force. As shown in Table 7.5, over 95 per cent of all the males in the labour force hold full-time paid (including self-employed) occupations, and again the tendency to perform this type of work does not vary sharply with either age or education. However, less than three-quarters of the native-born women in the 1973 labour force hold full-time paid jobs. Twenty per cent are part-time workers, and the remainder unpaid family workers. The class of work performed varies with age, and again education has a greater effect on the type of work performed by women than on the type of work performed by men. As revealed in Table 7.5, the higher the educational level, the greater the percentage of women in full-time paid work, and conversely, the lower the proportion in part-time paid work or in unpaid family work. Marriage, too, influences the type of work for women, married women with husbands present having the lowest percentage in full-time paid employment.

The data in tables, 7.4 and 7.5 thus require that considerable thought be given to comparing the occupational attainments of men and women who are employed in the 1973 labour force. By definition, such comparisons ignore over 60 per cent of the native-born female population who are not in the labour force. Even when women are in the labour force, they are not as likely as men to be in full-time paid jobs (Table 7.5). Such class of worker differences between native-born men and women poses a special problem for comparisons of occupational attainment between the sexes. If all men in the labour force are compared to all women in the labour force, the possibility arises that male-female differences will in part reflect the different class of worker distributions of men and women. This possibility can be handled statistically in one of two ways: either by controlling for the class of worker distributions, or else by holding class of worker constant — that is, by comparing men and women within each class of worker category. However, given that 95 per cent of the male labour force participants are full-time paid workers, neither approach is very useful. Although comparisons can be made between full-time paid men and women, the small number of men in the remaining class of worker categories precludes any comparisons with female workers in comparable class of worker categories.

At first glance, a reasonable solution would be to compare the occupational attainments of full-time paid men with full-time paid women and with other classes of worker categories for women. Unfortunately this approach is questionable because of the high item non-response on the current occupation question which was found among part-time and unpaid family female workers. Analysis reveals that 44 per cent of those native-born women who were part-time paid workers or unpaid family workers, did not given their current occupation. Further, a ten-category occupational distribution which is available from the Labour Force Survey portion of the Canadian Mobility Survey indicates that compared to women who did respond, the female non-respondents in part-time or unpaid family categories are disproportionately in service or farm occupations. They also have lower social origins and lower education compared to those who responded to the current occupation question, indicating that the high item non-responses of these women to current occupation is not random. Where occupational data are available, they are for a select group of part-time and family workers.

The particular methodological difficulties associated with the selectivity of item non-response suggests that analyses incorporating or based wholly on the part-time or family workers may be misleading. Minimally, the findings limit our comparisons of male and female occupational attainments to those of the full-time paid workers. Only with this specification can we be sure that we are indeed comparing like populations not only with respect to type of work performed but also with respect to data reliability.

However, one consequence of this decision to compare only the current occupational experiences of full-time men and women is that the full-time paid females are superior to their male counterparts and to other women in terms of social background and other job related characteristics. This superiority results from the fact that different types of work evidently are selective of different types of women. As shown in Table 7.6, women who were not in the 1973 labour force were more likely to be married, to have more children of their own, to be lower with respect to social origins (mean parental education and number of siblings), have less education, a lower first job status, and to have worked fewer years. It is also apparent from Table 7.6 that full-time work and part-time work are held by different types of women. Compared to part-time paid workers and unpaid family workers, full-time paid women come from higher social origins, have more education on the average, have a higher first job status, and higher current occupational status (Table 7.6). They also have fewer children and are less likely to be married, factors which are known to influence the labour force participation and occupational experiences of women.

This selectivity of full-time paid work among women has at least one of two consequences for our comparisons of male-female status attainments. One consequence is compositional: because of the selectiv-

TABLE 7:6 — Characteristics of Native-born Males and Females Age 25-64, Full-time Paid[a] Workers, Other Females in the Labour Force and Females Not in the Labour Force, 1973

Characteristics	In Labour Force			
Means and standard deviations	Full time paid[a]		Other Females	Females not in the Labour Force
	Males	Females		
Mother's education	7.401	7.991	7.489	7.148
	(3.581)	(3.632)	(3.616)	(3.587)
Father's education	7.114	7.631	7.171	6.908
	(3.881)	(3.940)	(3.864)	(3.851)
Father's SES	34.663	36.158	33.876	34.213
	(12.899)	(13.431)	(12.785)	(12.584)
Number of siblings	4.779	4.534	4.693	5.110
	(3.308)	(3.236)	(3.296)	(3.397)
Education	10.523	11.330	10.660	9.807
	(3.630)	(2.935)	(2.997)	(3.267)
First job	38.298	44.484	42.001	41.152
	(13.735)	(12.698)	(12.018)	(12.551)
Current job	43.802	46.502	42.865[c]	—
	(14.604)	(12.831)	(11.686)	—
Number of children[b]	2.665	2.346	2.902	3.102
	(1.944)	(1.938)	(1.850)	(2.041)
Mean age	41.629	40.897	41.706	42.905
	(11.024)	(11.345)	(10.952)	(11.513)
Per cents				
Mother in labour force				
Yes	15.04	20.05	16.01	15.38
No	84.96	79.95	83.99	84.62
Marital status				
Single	9.32	19.98	6.44	3.77
Married	87.18	64.87	84.87	88.14
Separated	1.66	4.69	2.98	2.37
Divorced	1.08	4.32	.80	1.10
Widowed	.75	6.14	4.91	4.61

[a]Wage, salary or self-employed. Excludes unpaid family workers.
[b]Ever married population.
[c]High nonresponse rate, see text.

ity of full-time paid work for women from higher social origins, education, and first job status, the achievements of these women are greater than those observed among full-time paid men. As shown in Table 7.6, full-time paid females on the average are better educated, come from higher social origins, and have higher first job and current occupational statuses than do full-time paid men in the labour force. These univariate comparisons accurately depict the relative achievements of full-time men and women, but they are misleading if generalizations are extended to encompass all men and women. Women not in the full-time labour force have social origins and first and current occupational statuses which more closely approximate those observed for full-time men (Table 7.6), thus implying that the relative status of women compared to men would be depressed by including other workers or women not currently in the labour force (see Marini, 1980: 310).

A second related consequence of the selectivity of full-time paid work among women is that the comparisons of male-female attainment processes may not be representative of the experiences of all men and women who have ever entered the labour force. This will occur to the extent that the "censoring problem" arises as the result of selection into the labour force on the basis of variables related to occupational achievement (see Fligstein and Wolf, 1978; Marini, 1980). For example, women may not be in the labour force because they cannot find jobs and wages which are consistent with their education, previous training, previous work experience, or which cover the costs of providing alternative child care (see Cook and Eberts, 1976). This in turn implies that women who are currently in the labour force, and particularly those in full-time employment, are not a random sample of all women, but rather are those women for whom there is some correspondence between their education, occupational status, and/or wages. If this is the case, then the status attainment process of women currently in the labour force will not be generalizable to all women, and the process may show greater similarity to that of males than would be observed if comparisons were made between all men and women ever in the labour force (Fligstein and Wolf, 1978).

Whether or not the censoring problem actually exists is debated but not yet resolved in the literature. On the basis of their research on the American 1967 National Longitudinal Survey of Mature Women, age 30 to 44, Fligstein and Wolf (1978) conclude that the censoring of results due to restricting analyses to men and women currently in the labour force is minimal. However, indirect support for the existence of a censoring problem is provided by researchers who note that educational and occupational models of attainment differ depending on whether the population studied is women in the labour force, women not in the labour force, or all women (see Marini, 1980:311 for a review).

In light of this ongoing debate, we proceed to examine the attainment process of native-born men and women in the current labour force. But we caution that because the population being examined is that of the full-time paid labour force, the results may not describe the experiences of all those men and women who are in part-time work or who were in the labour force prior to 1973. Subsequent analysis indicates considerable support for this caveat with respect to the current occupational attainments of married women.

Origins and Destinations: The Occupational Attainment Processes of Full-time Paid Native-born Men and Women

In this and subsequent sections, the earlier analysis which examined the relation between social origins, education and first job is extended to consider the influence which these variables in turn exert upon the current occupational status of full-time paid men and women in the 1973 Canadian labour force. We begin with a descriptive comparison of the origin and destination statuses of men and women. Then we consider the process of occupational attainment, using the earlier model in which occupational status is conceptualized as a function of family of origin characteristics and educational and first job attainments. In a subsequent section, we consider an elaboration of this basic model by asking how wife and mother roles also influence the attainment process for Canadian women.

We begin our comparison of the occupational attainments of men and women with a cursory review of the data in Table 7.6. We already have noted the selectivity into full-time work of better-educated women from higher social origins. On the average, native-born women in the full-time paid labour force have first and current occupational statuses which are higher than those observed for men. However, the sex-specific comparisons indicate that the initial advantage held by women with respect to their first job status is subsequently lost over their working life. To illustrate, the average first job status of women is 8.3 points higher than the average for their father's occupational status, whereas the mean first job status of sons is only 3.6 points higher than their fathers. But by the time of the current job, the father-offspring gap in occupational status is much smaller although it still favours women (10.3 for females compared to 9.1 for males). These changes reflect the reduced career mobility of women. Between first job and current occupation, average occupational status increases by 2.0 points for women and 5.5 points for men. The Blishen-McRoberts distributions presented in Table 7.7 provide additional information on these differences in intra-career mobility of women and men. The smaller standard deviations for women on both first and current job (Table 7.6) are indicative of their

TABLE 7:7 — Percent Distribution in Blishen Scores, and Porter-Pineo-McRoberts Occupational Groups for Father's Job and Respondents' First and Current Jobs, Native-born Full-time Paid Workers by Sex, Canada, 1973.

Occupational Metric	Father's Occupation		First Job		Current Job	
	Males	Females	Males	Females	Males	Females
Blishen-McRoberts score						
Total[a]	100.0	100.0	100.0	100.0	100.0	100.0
10-19	2.0	1.2	1.2	.1	.6	.1
20-29	45.2	40.9	29.3	15.9	17.6	13.7
30-39	22.0	22.3	31.7	19.6	26.2	16.7
40-49	17.9	18.7	16.6	20.1	22.8	18.5
50-59	6.4	9.1	10.4	33.8	13.0	35.9
60-69	5.1	6.2	7.9	7.9	16.0	12.0
70-75	1.5	1.5	2.8	2.6	3.8	3.0
Pineo-Porter-McRoberts Classification	100.1	100.0	99.9	100.0	100.0	99.9
Self-employed professionals	.8	1.0	1.1	.3	1.3	.2
Employed professionals	2.2	2.8	6.1	8.4	7.1	8.8
High-level management	1.0	1.2	.4	.3	3.4	.9
Semi-professionals	1.4	1.2	3.3	10.9	3.7	11.2
Technicians	.5	.5	2.0	1.8	1.8	1.9
Middle management	2.6	3.1	1.3	.4	5.2	1.8
Supervisors	4.8	5.0	1.7	1.4	7.7	7.0
Foremen	5.6	5.9	1.7	.1	7.9	.5
Skilled clerical-sales-service	3.0	4.5	4.9	21.4	5.0	23.9
Skilled crafts and trade	17.3	17.4	15.6	.9	17.6	1.1
Semi-skilled clerical-sales-service	5.3	5.9	11.2	28.5	6.3	21.7
Semi-skilled crafts and trade	12.6	10.8	16.0	7.4	10.3	7.9
Unskilled clerical-sales-service	1.7	2.7	4.4	10.3	2.1	7.0
Unskilled manual	12.4	13.8	18.7	7.4	13.6	5.7
Farm labourers	3.2	2.9	7.9	.4	1.5	.2
Farmers	25.6	21.4	3.6	.1	5.5	.1

[a]May not add to 100.0 because of rounding.

concentration in the middle three categories (30-59 points) and their underrepresentation in the lowest and the highest categories (10-29 and 60-79 points). Intra-generationally, there is more change in the occupational status distributions of men than of women, as indicated in the index of dissimilarity which is 17.8 for men and 6.6 for women. Between the first and current job there is a shift out of the low end of the status distribution into the middle and higher status categories for men whereas the change is not as dramatic for women. Consequently, although men and women are represented in almost equal proportions at the higher end of the first job status distributions, women are underrepresented relative to men in the upper tail of the current occupational status distribution (e.g., 60-75).

Table 7.7 also presents the male and female occupational distributions using the occupational classification devised by Pineo, Porter and McRoberts (1977). In displaying the sex segregation of occupations, these distributions shed considerable light on the patterns of career mobility for men and women. For both first and current job, nearly half of the women in our sample are in skilled and semi-skilled clerical, sales and service occupations compared to 16 per cent of the males for first job and 11 per cent for current job. The concentration of women in these occupations and their absence from others (farming, skilled crafts and trades, foremen, high- and middle-level management) explain the male-female differences observed earlier in father-offspring mobility and in first and current job statuses. With respect to inter-generational mobility, the analyses in Chapter 8 and elsewhere (Dunton and Featherman, 1979; Tyree and Treas, 1974) show that gross father-daughter mobility patterns are very much a function of the underlying sex segregration of the Canadian occupational structure. Since paternal occupation is used as the benchmark and since many of the fathers are engaged in blue-collar work, women who tend to concentrate in white-collar occupations will appear to experience greater upward inter-generational mobility than do men. As noted previously, the magnitude of this father-daughter mobility is also enhanced when the Blishen-McRoberts index is used since this measure tends to scale white-collar occupations as higher in status than blue-collar ones (Pineo, Porter and McRoberts, 1977: Table 3). Thus it should not be surprising to observe (Table 7.8) that the gap in the mean father-first job statuses is greater for women than for men. However, despite their higher assigned socioeconomic status relative to blue-collar work, female white-collar occupations have a number of characteristics which affect subsequent mobility opportunities. Such occupations tend not to offer on-the-job training but rather require that training occur prior to employment. Also, they have poorly developed career trajectories, and thus they offer little chance for advancement (Wolf and Rosenfeld, 1978). Given these characteristics, once women initially are allocated into these white-collar jobs, their career mobility is depressed relative to the career mobility of men.

Overall, the data in Table 7.6 and 7.7 are suggestive of sex differences in the occupational status attainment process of the native-born full-time paid labour force. Table 7.8 presents the means and the metric and standardized coefficients for a regression analysis which examines the effects of father's socioeconomic status (when the respondent was age 16), mother's labour force participation, parental education, and number of siblings on the educational, first job and current occupational attainments of Canadian men and women.[9] Of special interest in this section is the attainment of current occupational status by native-born men and women. However, data on educational and first job attainments (Table 7.8, lines 3-5, 9-11, 15-17, 21-23) also are presented since the populations being examined are slightly different from those examined previously. We note that many of the earlier observations which were made with respect to the educational and first job attainments of all native-born men and women are also confirmed for full-time men and women currently in the labour force.[10]

What do the data in Table 7.8 indicate about the current occupational attainment process of native-born men and women in Canada? The data in Table 7.8 show that maternal and paternal education, paternal occupational status, mother's labour force participation and number of siblings all have significant total causal effects on the current occupational status of men and women (lines 6 and 12). However, the magnitude of these effects is significantly different for men and women only with respect to the total causal effect of father's occupational status on current occupational attainment. Net of other social origin variables, a unit increment in father's occupational status increases current occupation status by .327 points for sons but only .096 points for daughters (Table 7.8, lines 6 and 12). Not only does the socioeconomic status of the fathers (or head of household) affect the occupational attainments of women to a lesser extent than for men, but also its influence is exerted earlier in the life cycle for women. Forty-six per cent of the effect of father's socioeconomic status is mediated by education for women compared to 37 per cent for men. Father's occupational status does not continue to directly affect occupational status after women obtain their first full-time job but it continues to have a significant direct effect on the current occupational statuses of sons. This suggests that the transmission across generations of paternal status is more of a step-by-step process for women than it is for men.

Although paternal occupational status does not directly influence the current occupational attainments of women, mother's labour force participation does. The reverse is observed for men, whose attainments are directly affected by paternal occupational status. Mother's labour force experience affects male attainments only very early in the life cycle by favourably influencing the amount of education obtained (Table 7.8; also see tables 7.2 and 7.3). However, the two patterns of parental influences are not equivalent in their impact on occupational attainments. Having a mother who worked does not yield the same increment in status for daughters that father's socioeconomic status does for sons. Net of other social origin variables, education and first job, women receive a 1.6 increment in occupational status if their mother worked compared to a .12 increment received by sons for each unit increment in father's occupational status (Table 7.8, lines 8 and 14). Given these figures, men are advantaged relative to women in terms of same-sex parental influence when their fathers' occupational status is 14 Blishen-McRoberts points or more, which is the case for virtually all the men in the full-time paid labour force (see Table 7.7).

The finding that mother's labour force participation directly affects daughter's current occupational attainments is surprising in light of the insignificant effect of mother's labour force participation on female educational and first job attainments (see Table 7.8, lines 9-11; also see Table 7.2 and 7.3). Perhaps what the findings reflect are the composite nature of the mother's labour force participation variable. Earlier discussion noted that mother's labour force experience was a variable which at its crude level of measurement probably captured both the additional financial resources which the mother's work brought to the family, and the role-modelling effects which might be expected from having had a mother who was in the labour force. As a measure of resources, having a mother who was in the labour force may make little difference to the educational and first job attainments of daughters. but, for those women who are in the full-time paid labour force, having a mother who worked may become an important asset for a variety of reasons, ranging from increased knowledge about the work world to strategies for handling a variety of domestic and work-related responsibilities. Clearly, additional research using more refined measures of the resource versus role model components of the mother working variable is needed to illuminate just why mother's work experience has an impact on the occupational attainments of full-time women.

Among the social origin variables, differences also exist between men and women with respect to the influence of siblings on the current occupational attainment process. The number of siblings influences the current occupational attainment of native-born males because it affects

TABLE 7:8 — Means and Metric Coefficients for a Model of Current Occupational Attainment, Native-born Men and Women in the Full-time Paid[a] Labour Force, Age 25-64, Canada 1973

	Line Number	Mother's Education	Father's Education	Number of Siblings	Mother in Labour Force	Father's SES	Respondent's Education	First Job SES	Constant or R^2
Means and Standard Deviation									
Males	(1)	7.639 (3.547)	7.364 (3.896)	4.584 (3.264)	.158 (.365)	35.177 (13.193)	11.009 (3.638)	39.256 (14.303)	44.811 (15.067)
Females	(2)	8.215 (3.593)	7.916 (3.952)	4.281 (3.138)	.209 (.407)	37.043 (13.592)	11.807 (2.775)	45.617 (12.870)	47.390 (12.841)
Metric Coefficients									
Males									
Education	(3)	.211 (.014)	.156 (.013)	-.199 (.012)	.334 (.099)	.053 (.003)			7.241
First job	(4)	.543 (.057)	.323 (.055)	-.499 (.049)	1.272 (.416)	.305 (.013)			24.089
	(5)	.072 (.049)	-.024 (.047)	-.054 (.042)	.525 (.352)	.186 (.011)	2.235 (.041)		7.903
Current occupation	(6)	.453 (.061)	.393 (.058)	-.453 (.052)	1.184 (.442)	.327 (.014)			28.856
	(7)	-.020 (.053)	.043 (.051)	-.007 (.046)	.434 (.381)	.207 (.012)	2.246 (.045)		12.592
	(8)	-.054 (.048)	.055 (.046)	.019 (.041)	.189 (.344)	.120 (.011)	1.203 (.048)	.467 (.011)	8.903
Females									
Education	(9)	.191 (.019)	.095* (.019)	-.106* (.018)	.173 (.134)	-.016* (.005)			9.312*
First job	(10)	.598 (.092)	.260 (.090)	-.522 (.089)	-.223 (.655)	.085* (.022)			37.769*
	(11)	.042 (.075)	-.016 (.073)	-.213 (.072)	-.725 (.527)	.038* (.018)	2.911* (.083)		10.660*

Table 7:8 (Continued)

	Line Number	Mother's Education	Father's Education	Number of Siblings	Mother in Labour Force	Father's SES	Respondent's Education	First Job SES	Constant or R²
Current occupation	(12)	.442 (.092)	.254 (.090)	-.553 (.089)	1.719 (.655)	.096* (.022)			40.235*
	(13)	-.082 (.077)	-.006 (.075)	-.262* (.074)	1.245 (.542)	.051* (.019)	2.743* (.086)		14.688
	(14)	-.104 (.068)	.002 (.065)	-.150* (.064)	1.625* (.468)	.031* (.016)	1.220 (.092)	.523* (.019)	9.111

Standardized Coefficients

	Line Number	Mother's Education	Father's Education	Number of Siblings	Mother in Labour Force	Father's SES	Respondent's Education	First Job SES	R²
Males									
Education	(15)	.206	.167	-.178	.034	.193			.314
First job	(16)	.135	.088	-.114	.032	.281			.225
	(17)	.018	-.007	-.012	.013	.172	.568		.447
Current occupation	(18)	.107	.102	-.098	.029	.286			.211
	(19)	-.048	.011	-.001	.011	.181	.542		.413
	(20)	-.013	.014	.004	.005	.105	.290	.433	.522
Females									
Education	(21)	.247	.134	-.120	.025	.079			.202
First job	(22)	.167	.080	-.127	-.007	.090			.116
	(23)	.012	-.005	-.052	-.023	.041	.628		.430
Current occupation	(24)	.124	.078	-.135	.054	.101			.113
	(25)	-.023	-.002	-.064	.039	.054	.592		.393
	(26)	-.029	—	-.004	.051	.033	.264	.524	.549

[a] Excludes part-time workers and unpaid family workers. Included self-employed workers.

* Significantly different from the corresponding male metric coefficient at the .05 level using a two-tailed test.

educational attainments which in turn is associated with subsequent occupational attainments. But for women, number of siblings influences current occupational status not only through educational attainment but also because it continues throughout the life cycle to influence directly female first job and current occupational attainments. This significant direct effect of siblings on female occupational attainment is difficult to explain. In addition to acting as a measure of family resources, number of siblings may have a stronger and persistent effect over the life cycle on female occupational attainments because it also may be a proxy measure of nuptial and fertility behaviour in the family of origin which subsequently shape female respondents' wife and mother roles. These roles in turn are hypothesized to negatively affect labour force participation and labour market rewards (see Hudis, 1977). The possibility that number of siblings is in part capturing the effects of wife and mother roles on occupational attainment is suggested by subsequent analyses. Data presented later in chapter show that the direct effect of siblings on female current occupational status is insignificant in models for ever-married women. Among single women, unpublished analysis reveals that siblings do not directly affect the current occupational attainments of women age 35 and older.

In addition to sex differences in the effect of social origin variables on current occupational attainments, sex differences also exist with respect to the influence exerted by education and first job statuses. Both education and first job have a significantly greater total causal effect on the current occupational attainments of women compared to men (Table 7.8, lines 7, 8, 13, 14). Further, decomposing the total causal effect of education on current occupational status into direct and indirect effects via first job shows that first job mediates more of the influence of education on current occupational status for women than for men (56 per cent versus 46 per cent for men). In conjunction with the insignificant direct effect of father's occupational status on the current occupational status of daughters, these results indicate that the current occupational attainment process is more of a step-by-step process for women than it is for men. Father's occupational status affects daughters attainments to a much lesser degree and over a shorter period of the daughter's occupational life cycle than is true for men. And, although mother's labour force participation favourably influences the occupational attainments of daughters, it does not compensate for the lesser influence exerted by father's status. Indeed, education and first job have more influence on the current occupational attainments among women than they do among men.

Such findings concerning the impact of social origins, education, and first job attainments on the occupational attainment process of native-born men and women in the full-time labour force can be interpreted in light of our discussion at the beginning of this chapter. In this discussion we suggested that sex differences in the occupational attainment process reflected not only the availability of economic resources and the existence of sex-specific role models in the family of origin but also the organization of the educational system and the sex-segregated occupational structure. In particular, this greater influence of formal education on both the first job and current occupational attainments of women compared to men is consistent with the fact that training for many female occupations such as clerical work or nursing, occurs within the formal school system (Gaskell, 1982). Our findings also are consistent with the sex-segregated structure of the Canadian labour market. Given the use of sex as a criterion for allocating people into jobs and the resulting sex-specific occupational distributions, it is not surprising to find that father's occupational status does not influence daughter's occupational status to the same degree or in the same way as it does for women. Also sex segregation implies that women are more concentrated in white-collar types of jobs (see Table 7.8) which often offer only very short career ladders. For example, a secretarial position is one where internal mobility is not very great and where few mechanisms exist to ensure mobility between secretarial and other positions. As a result, the status of first job will have more influence on current occupational status for women than for men, who are dispersed through the occupational distribution and who have more occupational mobility opportunities.

Assessing the Difference: Male and Female Current Occupational Attainments

The previous section addressed a question which is central to many studies of social stratification, namely, do differences exist between native-born men and women in the processes by which social origins in general, and paternal socioeconomic status in particular, are transmitted from one generation to the next? The data in Table 7.8 provide an affirmative answer. Compared to male occupational attainment, the current occupational attainment of women is less affected by father's occupational status and more strongly affected by their education and first job attainments. This pattern suggests that occupational attainment is more of a step-by-step process for women than it is for men. Given the finding of sex differences in the occupational attainment process, a second question is what are the consequences of such differences. Does the occupational attainment process of women operate to their disadvantage or to their advantage relative to men? This is an important question in light of the concern in recent years over sexual inequality. The question also is an important one because the data on the characteristics of full-time paid labour force create the impression that women in the labour force do very well, at least in terms of having a higher average occupational status than do men. Such data initially would appear to indicate that despite male-female differences in the process of occupational attainment, this is not translated into occupational disadvantage for women.

However, we noted previously that this portrayal of the data is extremely misleading. In addition to sex differences in the attainment process, compositional differences between men and women are factors influencing their relative occupational statuses. Women, on the average, come from higher social origins, and have higher levels of educational and first job attainments than men, all of which contribute to the higher observed current occupational status of women (Table 7.8). In actuality, the higher mean occupational status of native-born full-time paid females, relative to males, is a function of at least two factors: their characteristics; and the way in which these affect the occupational status attainment process. It is possible that women compared to men in the full-time paid labour force are disadvantaged in their status attainment process but that this disadvantage is masked by the higher social origins, education, and first job statuses of these women.

Two related techniques are used to assess this possibility: the substitution of means technique, and the decomposition of differences in means. The substitution of means technique involves substituting the means for the variables of one group (A) into the regression equation of another group (B), and generating a hypothetical occupational status mean. This hypothetical mean represents the occupational status which group A would have if it continued to have its own average characteristics but had the regression equation of group B. An alternative interpretation is that the hypothetical mean would be the mean characterizing group B if group B had the characteristics of group A but kept its group-specific way of utilizing those characteristics as depicted by the regression equation for group B. The decomposition of means technique uses the data generated from the substitution of means technique. It takes a variety of forms and has been discussed and critiqued widely (Althauser and Wigler, 1972; Blinder, 1973; Boulet and Rowley, 1977; Iams and Thornton, 1975; Sobel, 1979; Winsborough and Dickinson, 1971). The technique which is developed by Winsborough and Dickinson (1971) allows the decomposition of male-female differences in occupational status into three components: a component due to compositional differences between men and women with respect to their average characteristics; a component due to sex differences in the process by which these variables affect occupational achievement;[11] and a component representing the joint interaction of sex differences in composition and process.

Table 7.9 addresses the question of why native-born full-time paid women have higher mean first and current occupational statuses than men.[12] The substitution of means and the decomposition of differences in means techniques suggest that women on the average have higher first job status than do men both because they have higher mean levels of socioeconomic origins and education (see Table 7.8) and also because of a more favourable attainment process, largely reflecting the larger intercept and the greater influence of education on female first job status. As revealed in column 3, Table 7.9, if women had the average male social origin and educational characteristics, but kept the occupational attainment process described in Table 7.8, the average mean first job status of women would be 43.16 Blishen-McRoberts points compared to the observed mean first job score of 45.62 points. Conversely, if women kept their own socioeconomic characteristics, but had the male first job attainment model, the female first job score would be 41.48 Blishen-McRoberts points (Table 7.9, column 4), which is still higher than the observed score for males, but which represents a decline from the actual score of 45.62 points observed for the first job for women. Columns 5 through 8 summarize the results using the decomposition of differences in means techniques. In order for the mean first job status of men and women to be identical, mean first job scores would have to decline by 6.36 points for women (Table 7.9, column 5). Of this six-point decline in first job status, over four points (4.14) would be due to the difference in male-female models of attainment whereby men overall are not as advantaged as are women in the process of attaining first job status. An additional 2.46 points would be lost by giving women the same characteristics as men.

These data in Table 7.9 suggest that women have a higher first job status primarily because of differences in the effect which the variables in general, but education in particular, have on first job, and secondly because on the average, native-born women in the full-time paid labour force have higher socioeconomic origins and educational attainments than men. However, the story changes with respect to the acquisition of current occupational status. Although women have a mean current occupational status score of 47.39 Blishen-McRoberts points compared to 44.81 for men (Table 7.9, columns 1 and 2) the difference reflects the

TABLE 7:9 — Actual and Expected Mean Occupational Status by Sex and Decomposition of Sex Differences in Means, Native-born Full-time Paid Labour Force, Age 25-64, Canada 1973

| Occupation | Actual Mean Occupational Status | | Expected Mean Occupational Status | | Difference (1)-(2) | Decomposition of Actual Sex Differences in Occupational Status | | |
	Male (1)	Female (2)	Male Means[b] Female Equation[b] (3)	Female Means[b] Male Equations[a] (4)	(5)	Amount Due to Composition Equation (6)	(7)	Inter Actions (8)
First job	39.256	45.617	43.156	41.480	-6.361	-2.461	-4.137	.237
current job	44.811	47.390	42.953	48.968	-2.579	-4.437	1.583	.207

[a]Excludes part-time workers and unpaid family workers. Included self-employed workers.
[b]Table 7:8, lines 1 and 2.
[c]Ibid., line 14.
[d]Ibid., line 8.

higher mean socioeconomic characteristics of the women. The decomposition of sex differences in current occupational status reveals that if women had the same compositional stock as men, their average occupational status would decline 4.44 points. But, if their social origins, education, and first job had the effect on current occupational attainment which characterizes full-time paid native-born males, women would actually gain 1.58 Blishen-McRoberts points in their current occupational status. That women do not appear disadvantaged in terms of their higher mean occupational status is misleading. Native-born women in the full-time paid labour force have higher average occupational status compared to men largely because of their higher social origins, education, and first job status compensate for sexual inequalities in the current occupational attainment process.

Occupational Attainment, Marital Status and Children

Thus far, attention has been focused upon differences in the occupational attainments of full-time paid native-born Canadian men and women, age 25 to 64. The model of occupational attainment used is a basic one which conceptualizes occupational status as a function of social origins, education, and first job status. This model derives from investigations into male occupational mobility, and it overlooks other events which may affect the occupational status of women in the labour force. This section examines the impact of two important life-cycle events for women: marriage and child-bearing/child-rearing.

As shown in tables 7.4 and 7.5, marital status is strongly associated with female work patterns. Additional tabulations reveal that only 22 per cent of married women (husbands present) in the Canadian Mobility sample are in the 1973 full-time paid labour force, compared to nearly two-thirds (65 per cent) of the single women and over two-fifths (42 per cent) of separated, divorced and widowed women. Since nearly nine out of every ten native-born women are married, these figures mean that married women are less frequently found in the labour force than their numbers dictate.

The multiplicity of social roles assumed by married women (wife, mother, job holders) not only influences the propensity to be in the labour force, but also may exert a depressant effect on the acquisition of occupational status for those currently in the labour force, either because time and energy cannot be directed solely to job performance or because familial demands allocate women to occupations which are viewed as compatible with wife and mother roles but which are lower paying or offer fewer mobility opportunities (see Hudis, 1976; Marini,

1980; Spitze and Waite, 1980). One consequence may be that educational credentials and previous jobs or occupations will have less influence on the current occupational attainments of married women compared to single women. However, Sewell, Hauser and Wolf (1980) suggest that education may actually have more influence in determining the status of married women, since women with interrupted labour force participation rely more extensively on formal education rather than work experience to obtain new employment.

In addition to the effects of marriage, the child-bearing/child-rearing role has consequences for female occupational attainments. Assuming that children require time and energy, and assuming that the ensuing familial childcare responsibilities are assumed by women, children are hypothesized to depress the occupational attainments of women. At least three reasons underlie this negative association between child-bearing/child-rearing and the occupational status of women. First, employer assumptions about the family responsibilities assumed by women may negatively influence job placement, hiring, and promotional practices of women with children. Secondly, child-bearing and child-rearing — at least during the toddler years — is often associated with exits from the labour force or part-time involvement (see Boyd, Eichler and Hofley, 1976) which may negatively affect the occupational status attainment process. Thirdly, Rosenthal (1978) argues that re-entry women often trade the larger downtown work setting for smaller firms closer to home and schools. If job structures, status, and promotional opportunities are positively related to size of firm, then occupational status could be depressed for re-entry women.

In light of our discussion above and in the introduction, two questions are raised in this section. First, does marital status differentially affect the occupational attainments of men and women in the full-time paid labour force? Secondly, what is the impact of child-bearing and the implied child-rearing responsibilities for the occupational attainments of married women? The analysis addresses both questions by combining responses to the Canadian Mobility survey question on marital status into three categories: single (never married), married, spouse present (hereafter referred to as married) and other (composed of separated, divorced and widowed persons). The rationales for these three categories are both conceptual and pragmatic. Conceptually, the different living arrangements and financial status of the separated suggest that they are more logically included with other marital status groups who often live on reduced incomes (see Boyd, 1977). While it might be desirable to keep even these groups distinct in light of the rather different causes of marital dissolution (marital breakup versus death of a spouse), pragmatically the small numbers in each marital status group force the consolidation of the separated, divorced and widowed into one group.

The first question which concerns the impact of marital status on occupational achievement is answered by examining the characteristics of workers by marital status and by comparing the process of occupational attainment across marital status groups holding sex constant. The data in Table 7.10 reveal rather substantial compositional differences within the full-time paid labour force by marital status among women. Married women with a spouse present tend to be lower in educational attainments and in occupational status than are single women and higher than separated, divorced or widowed women. Single women in the full-time paid labour force have the highest occupational status of all, with an average Blishen-McRoberts score of 50 points, which is also in keeping with their higher average first job status, educational attainment and social origins.

This scenario is reversed somewhat among men where single men have the lowest occupational status and educational achievement compared to other men, and where married men with spouse present have the highest current occupational status of all. Evidently in terms of average occupational status, men with wives present are advantaged relative to other men whereas women who never married are advantaged relative to other women.

Of interest is whether these occupational outcomes reflect differences in the actual status attainment process or whether they reflect compositional differences among marital status groups. Table 7.11 presents the metric coefficients for the current occupational attainment process for men and women by marital status. Within each sex group, these metric coefficients were compared among the three marital status groups (e.g., the coefficients of the single were compared with those for married and separated, widowed or divorced persons, and comparisons were also made between the coefficients for the married and other marital status groups). These comparisons reveal considerable similarity in the occupational attainment process among marital status groups, especially among women. Among ever married men, no statistically significant differences are observed in the occupational attainment process between men who are married with a wife present and those who are separated, divorced or widowed. However, differences in the attainment process are observed between ever-married men and single men. Compared to ever-married men (married with wife present, separated, divorced or widowed), education has less direct influence on the occupational attainments of single men while first job has more

TABLE 7:10 — Means and Standard Deviations for a Model of Occupational Attainment by Marital Status, Native-born Men and Women in the Full-time Paid[a] Labour Force, Age 25-64, Canada 1973

Sex and Marital Status	Line Number	Weighted (N)	Age	Father's Education	Mother's Education	Number of Siblings	Mother in Labour Force	Father's SES	Respondent's Education	First Job SES	Current Occupation
Males											
Single	(1)	661	36.763	7.596	7.990	4.324	.179	34.858	11.209	39.704	42.018
			(11.546)	(4.015)	(3.665)	(3.170)	(.384)	(13.319)	(3.971)	(15.131)	(15.731)
Married[b]	(2)	6,447	41.010	7.335	7.608	4.620	.156	35.214	11.012	39.217	45.174
			(10.853)	(3.877)	(3.535)	(3.275)	(.363)	(13.194)	(3.603)	(14.222)	(14.990)
Other[c]	(3)	238	43.876	7.467	7.487	4.218	.169	35.266	10.424	39.101	43.195
			(10.801)	(4.065)	(3.494)	(3.106)	(.376)	(13.042)	(3.627)	(14.101)	(14.468)
Females											
Single	(4)	460	37.690	8.085	8.481	4.507	.191	38.001	12.766	48.756	50.331
			(12.055)	(4.130)	(3.649)	(3.315)	(.394)	(13.934)	(2.842)	(12.938)	(12.941)
Married[b]	(5)	1,451	38.790	7.842	8.127	4.240	.224	36.664	11.621	45.067	47.040
			(10.448)	(3.887)	(3.568)	(3.085)	(.417)	(13.331)	(2.618)	(12.673)	(12.603)
Other[c]	(6)	301	44.934	8.033	8.252	4.148	.167	37.415	11.245	43.448	44.572
			(11.465)	(3.990)	(3.617)	(3.110)	(.373)	(14.293)	(3.060)	(12.957)	(13.050)

[a] Excludes part-time workers and unpaid family workers. Includes self-employed workers.
[b] Spouse present.
[c] Separated, divorced, or widowed.

(Table 7.11, lines 3, 6 and 9). Further analysis of the attainment process of single and married men suggest two reasons for these results. First, on the average single men are four years younger in age than ever married men (Table 7.10). Since more single men have recently begun their careers, it is not surprising to find that first job is more associated with current occupational status than for other marital status groups. Secondly, a larger proportion of single men than married men have first and current occupations in farming, and this again may be a factor underlying the relationship between first and current occupational attainments.

Among women, no statistically significant differences exist between marital status groups with respect to the occupational attainment process, indicating that compositional differences between single, married and other women underlies the observed differences in current occupational status (Table 7.10). We note that variation exists among marital status groups with respect to the influence exerted by family of origin variables on the attainments of women although none of these are found to be statistically significant under the assumptions of linearity and the sample sizes of each marital status group.

Of special interest is the similarity between marital status groups in influence of education and first job status on the current occupational attainments of women. This finding is at variance with the expectation that compared to single women, education would have more impact on the occupational attainment of married women because of their discontinuous labour force experience. However, this discrepancy between the expectation and the data in Table 7.11 may reflect not the inaccuracy of a model concerning the consequences of marriage so much as a failure to adequately test it because of our research design and the sample under investigation. Our examination focuses upon the 1973 current occupational attainments of the full-time paid native-born labour force. Compared to this cross-sectional approach, a more temporally specified data set in which changes in jobs can be linked to the changing nature of family responsibilities may better illuminate the effects of marriage on the attainments of women. Further, the similarity in the occupational attainment process for single, married, and other women may reflect the possible selectivity of the full-time paid labour force for married women who do not find themselves handicapped by discontinuous work histories or by familial obligations. This selectivity also is emphasized by Marini (1980:360) who argues that analyses based only on currently working women underestimates the tradeoffs between work and family roles.

In the earlier section on labour force participation, we noted that the

TABLE 7:11 — Regression Coefficients for a Model of Current Occupational Attainment by Marital Status, Native-born Men and Women in the Full-time Paid[a] Labour Force, Age 25-64, Canada 1973

Line Number	Mother's Education	Father's Education	Number of Siblings	Mother in Labour Force	Father's SES	Respondent's Education	First Job SES	Constant or R^2
Metric Coefficients								
Males								
Single								
(1)	.777	.176	-.025[d]	4.043[d]	.339	–	–	22.029[d]
	(.201)	(.195)	(.189)	(1.499)	(.048)			
(2)	-.084	-.011	.116	2.291	.222	2.304	–	8.302[d]
	(.175)	(.163)	(.158)	(1.258)	(.041)	(.137)		
(3)	-.067	-.035	.020	.219	.093	.887[d]	.622[d]	4.802[d]
	(.144)	(.134)	(.129)	(1.036)	(.034)	(.137)	(.035)	
Married[b]								
(4)	.439	.400	-.509	.955	.325	–	–	29.654
	(.065)	(.062)	(.055)	(.470)	(.015)			
(5)	.011	.038	-.028	.356	.207	2.222	–	13.128
	(.057)	(.055)	(.049)	(.408)	(.013)	(.048)		
(6)	-.026	.061	.013	.226	.122	1.217	.453	9.356
	(.052)	(.050)	(.044)	(.371)	(.012)	(.052)	(.012)	
Other[c]								
(7)	-.211	1.042	-.367	-.207	.255	–	–	29.569
	(.356)	(.332)	(.307)	(2.377)	(.078)			
(8)	-.544	.415	.011	-2.481	.107	2.604	–	13.615
	(.287)	(.272)	(.248)	(1.916)	(.064)	(.229)		
(9)	-.509	.311	-.082	-2.002	.053	1.703	.365	11.480
	(.270)	(.256)	(.234)	(1.803)	(.061)	(.268)	(.065)	

TABLE 7:11 (Continued)

	Line Number	Mother's Education	Father's Education	Number of Siblings	Mother in Labour Force	Father's SES	Respondent's Education	First Job SES	Constant or R^2
Females									
Single	(10)	.484 (.197)	.303 (.192)	-.529 (.194)	1.115 (1.497)	.065 (.050)	—	—	43.486
	(11)	-.178 (.163)	.098 (.155)	-.400 (.156)	.496 (1.204)	.056 (.040)	2.805 (.177)	—	14.830
	(12)	-.127 (.136)	.049 (.129)	-.290 (.130)	1.256 (1.003)	.058 (.034)	1.084 (.191)	.568 (.040)	8.332
Married[b]	(13)	.371 (.113)	.233 (.113)	-.523 (.111)	1.930 (.787)	.093 (.028)	—	—	40.557
	(14)	-.017 (.097)	-.074 (.096)	-.171 (.095)	1.412 (.664)	.043 (.023)	2.756 (.114)	—	14.577
	(15)	-.078 (.085)	-.070 (.084)	-.087 (.083)	2.050 (.580)	.029 (.020)	1.215 (.123)	.513 (.024)	9.834
Other[c]	(16)	.565 (.245)	.391 (.237)	-.945 (.238)	1.709 (1.861)	.097 (.057)	—	—	36.770
	(17)	-.212 (.216)	.172 (.199)	-.525 (.203)	1.457 (1.559)	.074 (.048)	2.490 (.222)	—	16.114
	(18)	-.212 (.184)	.249 (.170)	-.285 (.174)	-.059 (1.335)	-.002 (.041)	1.304 (.219)	.519 (.049)	8.341
Standardized Coefficients									R^2
Males									
Single	(19)	.181	.045	-.005	.099	.287	—	—	.206
	(20)	-.020	-.003	.023	.056	.188	.582	—	.446
	(21)	-.016	-.009	.004	.005	.079	.224	.599	.629

TABLE 7:11 (Continued)

	Line Number	Mother's Education	Father's Education	Number of Siblings	Mother in Labour Force	Father's SES	Respondent's Education	First Job SES	Constant or R^2
Married[b]	(22)	.103	.103	-.111	.023	.286	–	–	.216
	(23)	.002	.010	-.006	.009	.182	.534	–	.410
	(24)	-.006	.016	.003	.005	.107	.292	.430	.514
Other[c]	(25)	-.051	.293	-.079	-.005	.230	–	–	.205
	(26)	-.131	.117	.002	-.064	.097	.653	–	.491
	(27)	-.123	-.087	-.018	-.052	.048	.427	.356	.553
Females									
Single	(28)	.136	.097	-.136	.034	.070	–	–	.114
	(29)	-.050	.031	-.103	.015	.060	.616	–	.429
	(30)	-.036	.016	-.074	.038	.063	.238	.570	.606
Married[b]	(31)	.105	.072	-.128	.064	.099	–	–	.099
	(32)	-.005	-.023	-.042	.047	.045	.572	–	.359
	(33)	-.022	-.022	-.021	.068	.031	.252	.516	.512
Other[c]	(34)	.157	.119	-.225	.049	.106	–	–	.204
	(35)	-.059	.053	-.125	.042	.081	.584	–	.443
	(36)	-.059	.076	-.068	-.002	-.002	.306	.516	.597

[a]Excludes part-time workers and unpaid family workers. Includes self-employed workers.
[b]Spouse present.
[c]Separated, divorced, or widowed.
[d]Significantly different from the correspondent metrics for married men and separated, divorced or widowed men at the .05 level, using a two-tailed t-test.

selectivity of full-time work among women could influence the composition and/or the occupational attainment process observed for women currently in the full-time paid labour force. In this analysis, indirect support for the existence of censoring is provided by comparing the occupational attainment process of married women in the full-time labour force to that observed for either part-timers or married women not in the labour force. Such comparisons cannot be made for current or last occupational status attainments because of the high non-response rate of part-time women and women not in the labour force to the question on current (or last) occupation. However, data in Table 7.12 and 7.13 on first job attainments supports the argument that married women currently in the full-time labour force are a select group and that their occupational experiences may not be representative of all married women who have ever entered the labour force. Among married women with a spouse present, and among other ever-married women (separated, divorced, widowed), full-time paid workers in 1973 have higher first job statuses, complete slightly higher higher levels of education and come from higher social origins than do other labour force participants (part-time and unpaid family workers) and women not currently in the labour force (Table 7.12). In addition to these compositional differences, the first job attainment process also differs among married women depending on their current involvement in the labour force. Among married women with husbands present, education has a significantly greater effect on first job attainments of full-time paid workers currently in the 1973 labour force compared to women who are not in the labour force or who are part-time or unpaid family workers (Table 7.13, lines 1-3). Among separated, divorced, and widowed women, education has a greater influence on the first job attainments of all women in the labour force compared to women not in the 1973 labour force. When compared with results obtained for single women and for married men in the full-time paid labour force (Table 7.13, lines 7 and 8), these data indicate how a focus only on current labour force participants may minimize first job attainment differences by marital status.[13] If extended to current occupational attainments such selectivity also could dampen differences between single and married women and possibly between men and women.[14]

Overall, the assumption of the marital role does not greatly alter the occupational attainment process for women in the full-time labour force, in large measure, we believe, because of the selective full-time labour force involvement of married women with husbands present. However, even if the spouse role does not directly influence the current occupational achievements of native-born women, the mother role still

MONICA BOYD

TABLE 7:12 — Means and Standard Deviations for a Model of First Job Attainments by Current Labour Force Status, Married, Separated, Divorced and Widowed Women, Native-born Population, Age 25-64, 1973

	Line Number	Age	Father's Education	Mother's Education	Number of Siblings	Mother in Labour Force	Father's SES	Respondent's Education	First Job SES	Weighted (N)
Means										
Married Women										
In full-time paid labour force	(1)	39.167 (10.485)	7.742 (3.870)	8.072 (3.577)	4.307 (3.143)	.215 (.411)	36.529 (13.337)	11.517 (2.657)	44.706 (12.692)	1,609
Other labour force	(2)	39.945 (9.792)	7.386 (3.836)	7.768 (3.523)	4.400 (3.224)	.198 (.399)	34.728 (12.953)	11.173 (2.882)	43.138 (11.774)	739
Not in labour force	(3)	40.248 (10.904)	7.514 (3.847)	7.779 (3.550)	4.543 (3.274)	.187 (.390)	35.705 (12.949)	10.786 (2.886)	42.180 (12.619)	3,923
Other Women										
In full-time paid labour force	(4)	44.998 (11.456)	8.023 (4.017)	8.306 (3.558)	4.222 (3.137)	.174 (.380)	37.280 (14.325)	11.247 (3.004)	43.157 (12.845)	333
Other labour force	(5)	46.762 (12.472)	7.919 (4.238)	7.862 (3.654)	4.938 (2.948)	.107 (.312)	34.480 (13.895)	10.664 (3.049)	39.357 (12.032)	77
Not in labour force	(6)	46.809 (12.043)	6.731 (3.816)	6.840 (3.498)	4.994 (3.495)	.206 (.405)	34.985 (13.180)	9.810 (3.377)	38.133 (12.128)	281

TABLE 7:13 — Metric Coefficients for a Model of First Job Attainments by Labour Force Status for Select Sex and Marital Status Groups, Native-born Population, Age 25-64, Canada, 1973

	Line Number	Father's Education	Mother's Education	Number of Siblings	Mother in Labour Force	Father's SES	Respondent's Education	Constant	R^2
Metric Coefficients									
Married Women									
In full-time paid labour force	(1)	.004 (.089)	.161 (.089)	-.204 (.085)	-1.220 (.613)	.027 (.021)	2.890 (.103)	10.226	.417
Other labour force	(2)	.039 (.129)	.231 (.134)	-.160 (.116)	-.010 (.874)	.088 (.030)	2.192[a,c] (.135)	14.213[f]	.392
Not in labour force	(3)	.174 (.058)	.250 (.060)	-.201 (.052)	-0.173 (.415)	.041 (.014)	2.335[a,c] (.064)	13.207[f]	.400
Separated, Divorced, Widowed Women									
In full-time paid labour force	(4)	-.102 (.185)	-.050 (.205)	-.392 (.191)	1.928 (1.481)	.158 (.046)	2.294 (.217)	14.007	.404
Other labour force	(5)	.014 (.411)	.206 (.402)	-.940 (.373)	-5.389 (3.249)	.032 (.101)	2.158 (.390)	18.748	.510
Not in labour force	(6)	-.044 (.266)	.125 (.233)	-.396 (.187)	1.261 (1.541)	.065 (.052)	1.670[b] (.214)	20.648[b]	.309

TABLE 7:13 (Continued)

	Line Number	Father's Education	Mother's Education	Number of Siblings	Mother in labour Force	Father's SES	Respondent's Education	Constant	R^2
Single Women[c]	(7)	.063 (.148)	-.048 (.157)	-.223 (.151)	-1.232 (1.159)	.006 (.039)	2.971 (.164)	12.182	.462
Married Men[d]	(8)	-.059 (.050)	.086 (.052)	-.103 (.044)	.236 (.372)	.190 (.012)	2.197 (.044)	8.559	.440

[a]Significantly different from the corresponding coefficient for married women with husbands present who are in the full-time paid labour force.

[b]Significantly different from the corresponding coefficient for separated, divorced or widowed women who are in the full-time paid labour force.

[c]In the full-time paid labour force.

[d]Spouse present and in the full-time paid labour force.

[e]Significantly different from the corresponding coefficient for single women in the full-time paid labour force at the .05 level using a 2-tailed t-test.

[f]Significantly different from the corresponding coefficient for married men, spouse present in the full-time paid labour force at the .05 level using a 2-tailed t-test.

may. Table 7.14 presents the results of our regression investigation into whether or not children depress the occupational achievements of married women. The population under investigation is married women who are in the full-time paid labour force and whose husbands are present (e.g., not separated). The data presented are presented for two groups, age 25 to 34 and 35 to 44, since our analyses for women age 45 and older revealed that the number of children born had no significant effect on current occupational attainments. The absence of any effect of children for older women is not surprising. Since it is the child care function which is hypothesized to depress female occupational achievements, younger women should be more affected by number of children born. Children may not dampen the current attainments of older women either because the children are older or because they are no longer living at home or because the time elapsed between child-rearing and current occupational status attenuates the relationship.

The data in Table 7.14 support the argument that children result in a dimunition of occupational status for married women under age 45 in the full-time paid labour force. After taking into account social origins, education and first job, married women age 25 to 44 lose between seven and eight-tenths of a Blishen-McRoberts point for each live birth. This effect is similar in magnitude to that observed by Marini (1980) in her analysis of 1973-1974 United States data, and it contrasts with the insignificant net effect which children have on the attainments of married men age 25 to 44 (unpublished tabulations). While small in magnitude, the depressant effect of number of children is not substantively trivial. Two children represent a loss of over one and half Blishen points, which is comparable to the magnitude of mobility between first and current job experience by women under age 45 (Table 7.14, columns 7 and 9).

In conclusion, although the initial comparison of the occupational attainment process among single, married and separated, divorced or widowed women revealed no statistically significant differences in the occupational attainment process, these findings must be understood within the overall association between marital status and labour force participation. In contrast to nearly two-thirds of all single women between the age of 25 and 64 years, less than one-fourth of all married women with husbands present are in the 1973 full-time paid labour force. Analyses of the first job occupational attainment processes for married women by labour force status support the argument that these full-time workers are a select group of married women, and the results suggest (but do not confirm) that such selectivity may minimize differences in the current occupational attainments of single and

TABLE 7:14 — Means and Regression Coefficients for a Model of Occupational Attainment Including Number of Children, Native-born Married Women with Husband Present, and in the Full-time Paid Labour Force, Age 25-44, Canada 1973

Age Group	Father's Education (1)	Mother's Education (2)	Number of Siblings (3)	Mother in Labour Force (4)	Father's SES (5)	Respondent's Education (6)	First Job SES (7)	Number of Children (8)	Current Occupation (9)	Constant R^2 (10)
Means and Standard Deviations										
25-34	8.887 (4.016)	8.928 (3.469)	3.636 (2.712)	.337 (.488)	38.723 (13.238)	12.409 (2.260)	47.638 (12.352)	1.030 (1.179)	49.223 (12.235)	
35-44	7.819 (4.221)	8.134 (3.352)	4.555 (3.320)	.280 (.498)	35.343 (13.235)	11.354 (2.470)	44.486 (12.048)	2.951 (1.772)	45.944 (12.738)	
Metric Coefficients										
25-34	-.026 (.100)	-.117 (.110)	-.059 (.127)	2.886 (.678)	-.032 (.027)	1.141 (.189)	.596 (.033)	-.766 (.283)		9.381
35-44	.067 (.137)	.173 (.165)	.134 (.146)	3.537 (.949)	-.015 (.039)	1.213 (.251)	.507 (.050)	-.801 (.270)		10.165
Standardized Coefficients										
25-34	-.009	-.033	-.013	.115	-.034	.210	.602	-.074		.587
35-44	-.022	.046	.035	.138	-.016	.235	.480	-.120		.511

married women. However, if being a wife does not influence the attainments for these full-time paid women, being a mother does — at least for married women (husbands present) who are less than 45 years of age. Young married women lose slightly under one Blishen-McRoberts point for each child ever born. This depressant influence of children on occupational status of married women with husbands present sets these women apart from single women and from married men. Single women for the most part have no children and hence are not negatively influenced by the child-bearing/child-rearing roles. Neither are married males under the age of 45. Overall, being married is not without consequence for the occupational attainments of women — it influences the labour force participation of women in the labour force, and it is associated with the birth and presence of children, which in turn dampens the achievements of younger women in the full-time paid labour force.

Summary

The preceding analysis which investigates the impact of marital status and child-bearing on occupational status attainments of full-time paid native-born women offers mixed support for the argument that the wife and mother roles influence the occupational statuses of women. Among younger married women with husbands present, children exert a modest depressant influence on occupational achievement — an impact which is not observed for young married men, nor by definition for most young single women in the labour force. But being married, as opposed to having children, has little impact on the occupational attainments of women. That marriage fails to strongly differentiate the occupational experiences of native-born women may be attributed to the exclusion of women not in the labour force and part-time and unpaid family workers from the population under investigation. Data on first job attainments of married women show that full-time paid women are a select group of women. Labour force participation per se and the study of part-time versus full-time work may provide clearer indication of the impact of marriage and family responsibilities on the achievements of women.

The interest in the effect of marriage and motherhood on the occupational statuses of women is motivated by the desire to better understand sex differences in the occupational attainment processes which exist for the full-time paid native-born labour force. The analysis of the full-time paid labour force reveals that women compared to men on the average have higher first and current job statuses. But the higher mean current occupational status of women compared to men in the full-time paid labour force in part reflects their higher social origins, and their higher education and first job statuses.

With respect to both first job and current occupational attainment, women compared to men benefit from their higher origins and higher educational skills, a phenomenon which in part reflects the selectivity of full-time paid employment for these women (see Table 7.6). But in addition, education has a greater effect on first job attainment among women, and this plus other differences in the matric coefficients and regression equations gives them a further advantage in first job attainment. But this advantage does not persist. Compared to men, women on the average are handicapped in the current attainment process, in large measure because they do not benefit directly from the effect of father's occupational status and because their current occupational status is more closely tied to the status of their first job. The substantive impact of such handicaps is reflected in the reduced career mobility of women relative to men. Between first and current occupation, the average occupational status for the full-time paid labour force increases by two points for women and by 5.5 points for men.

The above findings concerning the occupational attainments of native-born men and women underscore Acker's observation that sex is indeed a basis of social differentiation and stratification. The results concerning sex differences in the educational and occupational attainment process in Canada suggest that sex-role socialization and a sex-segregated occupational structure may be two important and reinforcing mechanisms of differentiation and stratification. The educational attainments of offspring are influenced more by the educational attainments of the same sex parent, a finding which theoretically can be linked to same-sex role modelling. At the same time, the stronger impact which father's occupational status and mother's labour force participation has on male educational compared to female attainments is consistent with the observation that families may not give financial support as readily to women for post-secondary schooling, particularly those coming from lower social origins (Porter, Porter and Blishen, 1973).

Over the work life of Canadian men and women, father's occupational status continues to influence the occupational attainments of sons more so than daughters. These findings are consistent with occupational role modelling and with the existence of a sex-segregated work world. Role-modelling theory stipulates that offspring develop occupational aspirations in keeping with parental occupational roles. A sex-segregated occupational structure will further reinforce the tendency of sons to model themselves after fathers and daughters to model themselves after mothers. Specific occupational inheritance from fathers becomes difficult for women when that occupation is defined as suitable only for a male incumbent, and it may not be considered if sons are available for recruitment. Also, a sex-segregated work world minimizes the potential contribution of assistance in the form of job searches and career planning since fathers may not be as familiar with female-typed occupations or because daughters may not seek or be considered to be legitimate participants in male-typed occupations.

The analysis of the status attainment process for first full-time job provides other findings which are consistent with a sex-segregated occupational structure. Sex segregation implies the allocation of women into certain jobs designated as suitable primarily for women and the denial of access into a wider range of jobs socially defined as appropriate for men. The result is that many of the first full-time jobs for women are in the white-collar sector whereas proportionately blue-collar first full-time jobs predominate more for men (see Table 7.7). Education plays a role in producing these sex-segregated outcomes. Our research finds that formal educational attainment has a larger influence on the first job attainments of women compared to men, a finding which may reflect the training provided within some high schools for clerical and service occupations. Formal education has less influence on the first job attainments of men, a finding which in turn is consistent with the tendency to rely on apprenticeship and on-the-job training as entry and hiring criteria for trades occupations (see Gaskell, 1982).

The first job status attainment process operates to the advantage of women compared to men, in part because of the greater influence of formal education and in part because women are more likely to be initially employed in higher status positions. However, once first job is obtained, sex segregation may mean a substantial curtailment of career mobility for women. Women who initially find themselves in first jobs of higher socioeconomic status relative to their male counterparts may soon discover that such positions have fewer internal promotional possibilities. Furthermore, it may prove difficult to move from female-typed jobs into other work. Conversely, because of a long-standing tradition within the work world that supervisory positions are filled by males, men rather than women may find such occupations opening up to them. Certainly this argument is compatible with the greater of career mobility experienced by men vis-à-vis women, with the changes in the occupational distributions between first and current occupation (Table 7.10) and with sex differences in the attainment process. Our findings indicate that once having obtained their first full-time job, women are disadvantaged relative to males in obtaining subsequent increments in occupational status.

Notes

1. There is a fourth question which we consider elsewhere (Boyd and McRoberts, 1982): Should occupational status measures be used in studies of male-female comparisons? In this study, occupational status is measured by the Blishen-McRoberts scale (Blishen and McRoberts, 1976) which is similar to the Duncan (1961) socioeconomic index used in American research. The derivation of these indices raises two concerns over the use of socioeconomic indices in comparisons of male and female occupational attainments. First, socioeconomic indices are generated by regressing the prestige ranking of a limited number of occupations on the education and income of males in each occupational category. Because a male reference population is used to construct the socioeconomic indices, the question arises as to whether this scale provides an appropriate measure of occupational status for women (see Boyd and McRoberts, 1982; Guppy and Siltanen, 1977). Unfortunately, during the course of the data analysis we were not able to address this question since only the Blishen-McRoberts scale derived from male census data was available at the time of the data release. Later, Blishen and Carroll (1978) did construct a socioeconomic scale specific to women. After comparing the two socioeconomic scales specific to employed Canadian men and women, Blishen and Carroll (1978) conclude that on average the socioeconomic scores for men and women are quite similar, and that either the male-derived index or the female-derived index may be used in analyses of male-female status attainments. Similar conclusions are reached by Boyd and McRoberts (1982) who compare male-female occupational attainment models using both the Blishen-McRoberts index and the Blishen-Carroll index. Research by McClendon (1976: 53-54) and Treiman and Terrill (1975: 175-76) provide additional support for this use of the Blishen-McRoberts scores.

   In addition to the reference population used, the sensitivity of such socioeconomic indices for detecting male-female labour force inequalities is also questioned (Boyd and McRoberts, 1982; Sewell, Hauser and Wolf, 1980; Treas and Tyree, 1979). The similarities in occupational status between men and women and in the acquisition of status which is generally observed in studies of male-female occupational attainments (Cuneo and Curtis, 1975; Featherman and Hauser, 1975b; McClendon, 1976; Treas and Tyree, 1979; Treiman and Terrill, 1975; Wang, 1973) contrast sharply with the observed sex segregation of occupations, and differential promotional opportunities. The contrast is not surprising since by their very construction these socioeconomic indices are not intended to capture such aspects of male-female inequalities in the labour force. The hierarchy of occupations scaled by socioeconomic indices closely corresponds to the perceived "goodness" of an occupation — a goodness which is evaluated in terms of the socioeconomic attributes and desirability of the occupation in question (see Featherman and Hauser, 1976a; Featherman, Jones and Hauser, 1976; Goldthorpe and Hope, 1972). By virtue of the occupational metric used, and the theoretical framework employed (Horan, 1978), analyses of male-female occupational status attainments do not, and cannot, directly measure other dimensions of sexual inequality such as access to elite jobs, sex segregation, and reduced mobility opportunities due to participation in a secondary versus a primary labour market. However, as shown in this chapter and elsewhere (Sewell, Hauser and Wolf, 1980), socioeconomic indices are not wholly insensitive to these features of labour force inequality. Occupational status distributions, inter-generational and intra-generational changes in occupational status, and models of attainment show sex differences which are remarkably consistent with these other features of the sexual division of labour.

2. The stronger effect of education on current occupational status among women can be interpreted in another way. Marini (1980: 314, 350) argues that the stronger effect in part reflects the selectivity of labour force participation among all women. She argues that analysis based on currently employed women tend to overestimate the effect of education on current status and that the relationship hypothetically expected is one in which education has less rather than more of an impact on the occupational attainment of women compared to men.

3. This can readily be shown by example. Let us assume that for every year of schooling completed, there is a 1.2 increment in male occupational status and a 2.2 increment in female occupational status. Under an assumption that men and women have identical levels of schooling — Grade 12 completion — this processual differences confers a 1.2 status point advantage on women ($12 \times 1.1 = 1.44$ versus $12 \times 2.2 = 2.64$). But this relative advantage will alter if women have more or less education than do men. Assuming that women have an average of thirteen years of schooling and men an average of ten years, the advantage for women becomes a gain of 1.66 occupational status points (e.g., 10×1.2 versus 13×2.2).

4. Ideally, the same information on work characteristics should be available for mothers and fathers, implying that our model should contain information on the socioeconomic status of the occupations held by both parents. Unfortunately, detailed information on the occupation of mothers suitable for coding in Blishen-McRoberts scores was not collected in the Canadian Mobility Study. In its place a measure of whether or not the mother worked full-time during the respondent's elementary or secondary school years is used. This is an imperfect but not unreasonable proxy for several reasons. First, it captures the role-modelling effects on the females' job performance which might be expected from having had a role model for the simultaneous tasks of wife, mother, and worker. Secondly, it captures part of the additional financial resources which the mother's work brought to the family and which were available for supporting the children's career aspirations (see Marini, 1980; Rosenfeld, 1978; Stevens and Boyd, 1980).

5. This transmission process is clearly mediated by a variety of intervening factors including the organization of the educational system itself (curriculum and streaming practices) and the manner in which parents, peers, and teachers affect the information of student aspirations. The Canadian Mobility data do not permit a consideration of these factors but the interested reader may consult such sources as Gaskell (1982), Porter, Porter and Blishen (1973, 1982) and Turittin, Anisef and Mackinnon (1982) for an extended review and analysis of other Canadian data on this topic.

6. Listwise regression, not pairwise regression, is used in this chapter for several reasons. First, a comparison of listwise and pairwise derived means tests for random patterns of non-response and the use of indicator variables (Cohen and Cohen, 1975: 268-271; Kim and Curry, 1977) also indicated existence of response selectivity for higher socioeconomic individuals. As discussed in Cohen and Cohen (1975) and Kim and Curry (1977), pairwise regression is warranted if and only if the data are randomly missing. If they are not — and they are not for the native-born full-time paid labour force population — results of a pairwise regression must be treated with considerable skepticism (Cohen and Cohen, 1975; Kim and Curry, 1977). Secondly, the need to perform tests for sex interactions requires the use of listwise regression since pairwise regression includes the effects of differential item non-response across populations and does not produce a pooled equation for the entire population which corresponds to the sex specific equations (see Treiman and Terrill, 1975:185).

7. Because betas are influenced by the standard deviations of the variables in any regression model, and because standard deviations vary between populations, the size of the betas of the variables influencing education of males should not be compared with the size of the betas for females (Kim and Mueller, 1976). Similarly, R^2 should not be compared across populations (Hanchuk and Jackson, 1979: 20-22, 78). These statistics are included here and elsewhere in the chapter only for the sake of completeness and for the benefit of those who may wish to use the results for purposes other than the cross-sex comparison. Unlike standardized coefficients, the metric coefficients presented in Table 7.2 can be directly compared for the male and female populations. These statistics indicate the change in the dependent variable which is produced by a unit change in a given independent variable, net of the effects of other independent variables. As a result, metric coefficients indicate the substantive impact (or "effect") which an independent variable has on the dependent variable. Asterisks attached to the female metric coefficients indicate that sex differences in the metric coefficients are statistically significant at the .05 level or less according to a two tail t-test using dummy variable regression. Increment to R^2 tests which are used in chapters 11 and 12 provided the same substantive conclusions (Cohen, 1968; Specht and Warren, 1975).

8. These equations are presented in a format which highlights the total causal effects of social origins and educational attainment on first job status and which indicate the extent to which education mediates the influence of social origin variables in the attainment of first job (Alwin and Hauser, 1975). The first, or reduced form, equation (e.g., line 3 or line 5, Table 7.3) shows the total causal effect of each social origin variable in the model. The coefficients for education in the second equation (lines 4 and 6, Table 7.3) indicate its total causal effect, while the remaining coefficients in the equation indicate the direct effects of social origin variables on first job status. The extent to which education mediates the total causal effect of these social origins variables can be easily calculated from the first and second equations. For example, of the total causal effect of fathers' SES on the SES of the first job of sons, about 62 per cent is direct (.189/.303=.62) with the remainder, about 38 per cent, affecting first job status via its prior influence on educational attainment (1 − .62 = .38).

9. As is the case for Table 7.3, the data indicate the total causal effects of the

independent variables and the mediating role played by intervening variables (Alwin and Hauser, 1975). For each dependent variable, one or more reduced form equations are first estimated (e.g., lines 4, 6, 7) followed by an equation which contains all of the relevant independent variables (e.g., lines 5, 8). As discussed in note 8, for any given independent variable, a comparison of the coefficients within a set of given equations indicates the magnitude of the total causal effect and the extent to which the total causal effect of a variable is mediated by subsequent variables (see Alwin and Hauser, 1975).

10. In terms of their educational attainments, men are more influenced by father's education, father's occupational status and by number of siblings and having a mother who was in the labour force (Table 7.8, lines 3 and 9). Furthermore, paternal occupational status continues to exert a greater influence on the first job attainments of sons compared to daughters and its influence is more direct (61 per cent of the total causal effect versus 47 per cent for women for father's SES). In contrast, daughters are not only less affected by father's status in their first job attainments, but they are more negatively influenced by the persistent influence of number of siblings. For men, virtually all of the total causal effect of siblings on first job attainment is mediated by education (Table 7.8, lines 4 and 5) but for women there remains a significant direct effect of number of siblings on first job status after controlling for education (Table 7.8, line 11). Also, education has a stronger effect on the first job attainments of women compared to men.

11. Because not all of the independent variables used in this analysis have an absolute zero-point, it is not possible to distinguish between the effects of the payoffs for these independent variables and the impact of sex differences in intercept terms (see Althauser and Wigler, 1972:111).

12. In most applications of decomposition techniques, the group which is chosen as the standard for conceptual reasons also have values for the dependent variables in question which are higher than those observed for the remaining group(s) (see Marini, 1980; Winsborough and Dickinson, 1971). In our case, because we are interested in asking how well women do relative to men, men are the standard. However, because of the selectivity of full-time work among women, women have higher occupational status on the average than men. Given the empirical simplicity of comparing a lower status population to a higher status population, we could have reversed our decomposition procedures selecting women as the standard. When this is done, the magnitude of the results changes slightly, but the conclusions are not substantially altered. However, the focus shifts from how women do relative to men to how well men do relative to women. For this reason, we have presented our results with men as the benchmark population.

13. For example, if the first job attainments of single women are compared with those of married women currently in the full-time labour force, no statistically significant differences are observed in the impact exerted by education on the first job attainments of the two groups (Table 7.11, lines 7 and 13). But education has a smaller effect on the first job attainments of married women not engaged in full-time paid work (Table 7.12, lines 2 and 3). Additional research shows that inclusion of these women in the first job attainment models leads to the conclusion that education exerts a lesser influence on the first job attainments of married women with husbands present compared to single women. This latter conclusion differs from the

one of similarity which is reached when comparing only single and married women currently in the full-time labour force.

14. Among married women currently in the full-time paid labour force, education has a greater impact on first job attainments than it does for married men — a finding which parallels the earlier investigation of male-female differences in first job attainments. This finding persists when the first job attainment processes of all currently married men and women (including those not in the labour force) are compared. Intercept differences observed in Table 7.11 between married men and women in the full-time labour force also describe the entire population of currently married men and women with spouses present.

References

ACKER, JOAN
   1973   "Women and Social Stratification: A Case of Intellectual Sexism." *American Journal of Sociology*, 78 (January): 936-45.

ALEXANDER, KARL L. and BRUCE K. ECKLAND
   1974   "Sex Differences in the Educational Attainment Process." *American Sociological Review*, 39 (October): 668-82.

ALTHAUSER, ROBERT P. and MICHAEL WIGLER
   1972   "Standardization and Component Analysis." *Sociological Methods and Research*, 1 (August): 97-135.

ALWIN, DUANE F. and ROBERT M. HAUSER
   1975   "The Decomposition of Effects in Path Analysis." *American Sociological Review*, 40 (February): 37-47.

BLAU, PETER and OTIS DUDLEY DUNCAN
   1967   *The American Occupational Structure*. New York: John Wiley.

BLINDER, ALAN S.
   1973   "Wage Discrimination: Reduced Form and Structural Estimates." *Journal of Human Resources*, 8 (Fall): 436-55.

BLISHEN, BERNARD R. and HUGH A. McROBERTS
   1976   "A Revised Socioeconomic Index for Occupations in Canada." *Canadian Review of Anthropology and Sociology*, 13 (February): 71-79.

BLISHEN, BERNARD R. and WILLIAM K. CARROLL
   1978   "Sex Differences in a Socioeconomic Index for Occupations in Canada." *Canadian Review of Sociology and Anthropology*, 15: 352-71.

BOULET, JAC-ANDRÉ and J.C. ROBIN ROWLEY
   1977   "Measure of Discrimination in the Labour Market: A Comment." *Canadian Journal of Economics*, 10 (February): 149-54.

BOYD, MONICA
   1977   "The Forgotten Minority: The Socioeconomic Status of Divorced and Separated Women." Pp. 46-71 in Pat Marchak, ed. *The Working Sexes*. Vancouver, B.C.: University of British Columbia, Institute of Industrial Relations.

   1982a   "Sex Differences in the Canadian Occupational Attainment Process." *Canadian Review of Sociology and Anthropology*, 19 (February): 1-28.

1982b   "Occupation Segregation." *Proceedings: Conference on Sexual Equality in the Work Place.* Ottawa: Labour Canada, Women's Bureau.

1982c   "Sex and Generational Achievement: Canada." Presented at the International Sociological Association World Congress, Mexico City, Mexico.

1984   "At a Disadvantage: The Occupational Attainments of Foreign Born Women in Canada." *International Migration Review.*

BOYD, MONICA, MARGRIT EICHLER and JOHN R. HOFLEY
1976   "Family: Functions Formation and Fertility." Pp. 13-52 in Gail C.A. Cook, ed. *Opportunity for Choice.* Ottawa: Statistics Canada.

BOYD, MONICA and HUGH A. MCROBERTS
1982   "Women, Men and Socioeconomic Indices: An Assessment." Pp. 129-59 in Mary Powers, ed. *Socioeconomic Status: Concepts and Measurement Issues.* Washington, D.C.: American Association for the Advancement of Science.

CARLSSON, GOSTA
1958   *Social Mobility and Class Structure.* Lund: CWK Gleerup.

COHEN, JACOB
1968   "Multiple Regression as a General Data-Analytic System." *Psychological Bulletin,* 70: 423-26.

COHEN, JACOB and PATRICIA COHEN
1975   *Applied Multiple Regression/Correlation Analysis for the Behavioral Sciences.* Hillsdale: Lawrence Erlbaum Associates.

COOK, GAIL C.A. and MARY EBERTS
1976   "Policies Affecting Work." Pp. 143-202 in Gail C.A. Cook, ed. *Opportunity for Choice.* Ottawa: Statistics Canada.

COOK, RAMSAY and WENDY MITCHENSON, eds.
1976   *The Proper Sphere: Women's Place in Canadian Society.* Toronto: Oxford University Press.

CUNEO, CARL J. and JAMES E. CURTIS
1975   "Social Ascription in the Educational and Occupational Status Attainment of Urban Canadians." *Canadian Review of Sociology and Anthropology,* 12 (February): 6-24.

DUNCAN, OTIS DUDLEY
1961   "A Socioeconomic Index for All Occupations." Pp. 109-38 in Albert J. Reiss Jr. *Occupations and Social Status.* New York: Free Press.

DUNCAN, OTIS DUDLEY and ROBERT W. HODGE
1963   "Education and Occupational Mobility." *American Journal of Sociology,* 68 (May): 629-44.

DUNCAN, OTIS DUDLEY, DAVID L. FEATHERMAN and BEVERLEY DUNCAN
1972   *Socioeconomic Background and Achievement.* New York: Seminar Press.

FEATHERMAN, DAVID L. and ROBERT M. HAUSER
1976a   "Prestige or Socioeconomic Scales in the Study of Occupational Achievement." *Sociological Methods and Research,* 4 (May): 402-22.

1976b   "Sexual Inequalities and Socioeconomic Achievement in the U.S., 1962-1973." *American Sociological Review,* 41 (June): 462-83.

FEATHERMAN, DAVID L., F. LANCASTER JONES and ROBERT M. HAUSER
  1975 "Assumptions of Social Mobility Research in the United States: The Case of Occupational Status." *Social Science Research*, 4 (December): 329-60.

FLIGSTEIN, NEIL and WENDY WOLF
  1978 "Sex Similarities in Occupational Status Attainment: Are the Results due to the Restriction of the Sample to Employed Women?" *Social Science Research*, 7 (June): 197-212.

GASKELL, JANE
  1982 "Education and Job Opportunities for Women: Patterns of Enrolment and Economic Returns." Pp. 257-306 in Naomi Henson and Dorothy E. Smith, eds. *Women and the Canadian Labour Force*. Ottawa: Minister of Supply and Services Canada. Catalogue No. CR22-8/1981E.

GOLDTHORPE, JOHN and KEITH HOPE
  1972 "Occupational Grading and Occupational Prestige." Pp. 19-80 in John Goldthorpe and Keith Hope, eds. *The Analysis of Social Mobility: Methods and Approaches*. Oxford: Clarendon Press.

GOYDER, JOHN
  1981 "Income Differences Between the Sexes: Findings from a National Canadian Survey." *Canadian Review of Sociology and Anthropology*, 18 (August): 321-42.

GUNDERSON, MORLEY
  1976 "Work Patterns." Pp. 93-142 in Gail C.A. Cook, ed. *Opportunity for Choice*. Ottawa: Statistics Canada.

GUPPY, L.N. and JANET SILTANEN
  1977 "A Comparison of the Allocation of Male and Female Occupational Prestige." *Canadian Review of Sociology and Anthropology*, 14(3): 320-30.

HANUSHEK, ERIC A. and JOHN E. JACKSON
  1977 *Statistical Methods for Social Scientists*. New York: Academic Press.

HORAN, PATRICK
  1978 "Is Status Attainment Research Atheoretical?" *American Sociological Review*, 43 (August): 534-41.

HUDIS, PAULA M.
  1976 "Commitment to Work and to Family: Marital Status Differences in Women's Earnings." *Journal of Marriage and the Family*, 38 (May): 267-78.

IAMS, HOWARD M. and ARLAND THORNTON
  1975 "Decomposition of Differences: A Cautionary Note." *Sociological Methods and Research*, 3 (February): 341-52.

KIM, JAE-ON and JAMES CURRY
  1977 "On the Treatment of Missing Data in Multivariate Analysis." *Sociological Methods and Methodology*, 6 (November): 215-40.

KIM JAE-ON and CHARLES MUELLER
  1976 "Standardized and Unstandardized Coefficients in Causal Analysis." *Sociological Methods and Research*, 4 (May): 423-38.

LABOUR CANADA. WOMEN'S BUREAU
  1974 *Women in the Labour Force: Facts and Figures* (1973 Edition). Ottawa: Information Canada.

1978 *Women in the Labour Force: Facts and Figures* (1977 Edition). Part I: *Labour Force Activity.* Ottawa: Minister of Supply and Services. Canada Catalogue No. L38-30/1977-1.

LONG, LARRY H.
1978 "Womens' Labour Force Participation and the Residential Mobility of Family." Pp. 226-38 in Ann H. Stranberg and Shirley Harkess, eds. *Women Working.* Palo Alto, California: The Mayfield Publishing Co.

MARINI, MARGARET
1980 "Sex Differences in the Process of Occupational Attainment: A Closer Look." *Social Science Research,* 9 (December): 307-61.

MCCLENDON, MCKEE J.
1976 "The Occupational Status Attainment Processes of Males and Females." *American Sociological Review,* 41 (February): 52-64.

MILLMAN, MARCIA and ROSABETH MOSS KANTER
1977 *Another Voice.* New York: Anchor Press.

PINEO, PETER C., JOHN PORTER and HUGH MCROBERTS
1977 "The 1971 Census and the Socioeconomic Classification of Occupations." *Canadian Review of Sociology and Anthropology,* 14 (February): 91-102.

PORTER, JOHN, MARION PORTER and BERNARD R. BLISHEN
1982 *Stations and Callings.* Toronto: Methuen Press.

PORTER, MARION R., JOHN A. PORTER and BERNARD R. BLISHEN
1973 *Does Money Matter? Prospects for Higher Education.* Toronto: York University Institute for Behavioural Research.

RICHMOND, ANTHONY H.
1967 *Post War Immigrants in Canada.* Toronto: University of Toronto Press.

ROBB, A. LESLIE and BYRON G. SPENCER
1976 "Education: Enrolment and Attainment." Pp. 53-92 in Gail C.A. Cook, ed. *Opportunity for Choice.* Ottawa: Statistics Canada.

ROBY, PAMELA
1972 "Structural and Internalized Barriers to Women in Higher Education." Pp. 121-40 in Constantina Safilios-Rothschild, ed. *Toward a Sociology of Women.* Lexington, Mass.: Xerox College Publishing.

ROSEN, BERNARD C. and CAROL S. ANESHENSEL
1978 "Sex Differences in the Educational Occupational Expectation Process." *Social Forces,* 57 (September): 164-86.

ROSENFELD, RACHEL ANN
1978 "Women's Intergenerational Occupational Mobility." *American Sociological Review,* 43 (February): 36-46.

ROSENTHAL, EVELYN R.
1978 "Working in Mid-Life." Pp. 239-56 in Ann H. Stromberg and Shirley Harkess, eds. *Women Working.* Palo Alto, California: The Mayfield Publishing Co.

SEWELL, WILLIAM H. and VIMAL P. SHAH
1967 "Socioeconomic Status, Intelligence and the Attainment of Higher Education." *Sociology of Education,* 40 (Winter): 1-23.

1968 "Parents' Education and Children's Educational Aspirations and Achievements." *American Sociological Review,* 33 (April): 191-209.

294 *MONICA BOYD*

SEWELL, WILLIAM H., ROBERT M. HAUSER and WENDY C. WOLF
  1980 "Sex, Schooling and Socioeconomic Status." *American Journal of Sociology,* 86 (November): 551-83.
SPECHT, DAVID A. and ROBERT WARREN
  1975 "Comparing Causal Models." Pp. 46-84 in D.R. Heise, ed. *Sociological Methodology.* San Francisco: Jossey-Bass Publishers.
SPITZE, GLENNA D. and LINDA J. WAITE
  1980 "Labour Force and Work Attitudes." *Sociology of Work and Occupations,* 7 (February): 3-32.
STATISTICS CANADA
  1981 *Education in Canada.* Catalogue 81-229.
STEVENS, GILLIAN and MONICA BOYD
  1980 "The Importance of Mother: Labour Force Participation and Inter-generational Mobility of Women in Canada." *Social Forces.*
SUTER, LARRY and HERMAN MILLER
  1973 "Income Differences Between Men and Career Women." *American Journal of Sociology,* 78 (January): 962-74.
SOBEL, MICHAEL E.
  1979 *Components of Difference Between Two Means: Some Statistical Tests.* Working Paper 79-1. Center for Demography and Ecology. Madison: University of Wisconsin.
TREAS, JUDITH and ANDREA TYREE
  1979 "Prestige Versus Socioeconomic Status in the Attainment Processes of American Men and Women." *Social Science Research,* 8: 201-21.
TREIMAN, DONALD J. and KERMIT TERRELL
  1975 "Sex and the Process of Status Attainment: A Comparison of Working Men and Women." *American Sociological Review,* 49 (April): 174-200.
TRYREE, ANDREA and JUDITH TREAS
  1974 "The Occupational and Marital Mobility of Women." *American Sociological Review,* 39 (June):293-302.
TURRITTIN, ANTON H., PAUL ANISEF and NEIL J. MACKINNON
  1982 "Gender Differences in Educational Achievement: A Study of Social Inequality." Unpublished Paper. Department of Sociology, York University, Toronto.
VICKERS, JILL M.
  1975 "Women in Universities." Pp. 199-240 in Matheson Given, ed. *Women in the Canadian Mosaic.* Toronto: Peter Martin Associates.
WAITE, LINDA
  1976 "Working Wives: 1940-1960." *American Sociological Review,* 41 (February): 65-80.
WANG, LINDA
  1973 "The Female Status Attainment Process and Occupational Mobility." M.A. Thesis. Madison: Department of Sociology, University of Wisconsin.
WATSON, WALTER B. and ERNEST A. BARTH
  1964 "Questionable Assumption in the Theory of Social Stratification." *Pacific Sociological Review,* 7 (Spring): 10-16.

WINSBOROUGH, HALLIMAN and PETER DICKINSON
1971 "Components on Negro-White Income Differences." *Proceedings of the American Statistical Association*, Social Statistics Section: 6-8.

WOLF, WENDY C.
1976 *Occupational Attainments of Married Women: Do Career Contingencies Matter?* Working Paper No. 76-3, Center for Demography and Ecology. Madison: University of Wisconsin.

WOLF, WENDY C. and RACHEL ROSENFELD
1978 "Sex Structure of Occupations and Job Mobility." *Social Forces*, 56 (March): 823-44.

CHAPTER 8

Occupational Mobility among Women

JOHN C. GOYDER

The distinction, noted in Chapter 2, between occupational status attainment and occupational mobility analysis is particularly pertinent to the study of sexual stratification. The preceding chapter compared models of status attainment for the two sexes. Such an approach, it was seen, allows a simultaneous accounting of the relative importance to each sex of a full range of social background variables germane to occupational achievement. The present chapter compares occupational mobility among men and women. A major conceptual distinction between the mobility and attainment approaches concerns the scaling of occupation. Scales of SES, the previous chapter noted, capture only one dimension of the importance to stratification of occupational roles. It is likely, as the stress in that analysis upon sexual segregation of occupations implied, that an occupational SES scale hides part of the inequality between the sexes. Mobility analysis works with occupations coded into broad groupings carrying something loosely approximating a social class meaning. New analytical compromises are required in mobility analysis, however, as the coding of occupations into what are, at best, ordinal categories makes analysis involving many variables cumbersome. Thus, a mobility analysis cannot be expected to include the multivariate complexity of status attainment modelling.

Despite these differences, the two approaches yield several similar substantive conclusions about sexual stratification in Canada. The finding, for example, of a lower linkage in SES scores among fathers and daughters than among fathers and sons reappears in the present chapter in the form of greater occupational inheritance among men than women. In at least one instance, the mobility analysis permits a more

297

thorough exploration of sex differences detected initially in the status attainment analysis. A greater increase in occupational status over the career among men than women was reported in Chapter 7. The mobility analysis allows an explicit test of conjectures advanced previously concerning the importance for this of the sex typing of occupations. Both chapters find the distinction between single and married women to be important, though the manner in which this variable is manipulated in the respective analyses highlights the different conceptual directions emphasized in mobility versus attainment analysis.

Where the previous chapter focused upon native-born men and women working full-time, the population in the present analysis is expanded to all respondents, aged 25 to 64, and part- as well as full-time occupations are included. The rationale was that a chapter on mobility should, above all, perform the descriptive function of tabulating the mobility representative of working women in Canada. Mobility analysis traditionally is sensitive to the consequences of macroeconomic context (as manifested in changes over time in occupational distributions). This context is germane to all workers, and the claims of this principle were judged to outweight the costs of the possible responses biases outlined in Chapter 7.

Intra-Generational Mobility among Women

> At times I'm certain I'm being groomed for something higher up, but as I have only hazy notions of the organizational structure of Seymour Surveys I can't imagine what. . . . I couldn't become one of the men upstairs; I couldn't become a machine person or one of the questionnaire-marking ladies, as that would be a step down. I might conceivably turn into Mrs. Bogue or her assistant [supervisors], but as far as I could see that would take a long time and I wasn't sure I would like it anyway.

The quotation is not from an interview. It is a passage from a Margaret Atwood (1969:19, 20) novel in which the character, Marian McAlpine, describes her job in a market research firm. While fictional, the quotation has a familiar ring of authenticity to it and articulates what must be the fundamental proposition to be tested in an assessment of sexual differences in career mobility; that women do not enjoy the same opportunities that men do. Such a proposition implies a number of possible empirical patterns. The quotation suggests that disproportionately large numbers of women, like our fictional character, can only find employment in dead-end clerical jobs. Women are said to have the probabilities for career mobility set against them from the beginning because they are excluded from occupations with good chances for advancement. Writers who have documented the occupational segregation in the labour force of Canada (Women's Bureau, 1975; Armstrong and Armstrong, 1975; Siltanen, 1976) and other countries (Coser and Rokoff, 1971; Gross, 1972; Ferris, 1971; Martin and Poston, 1972; Silver, 1973; Williams, 1975) have drawn attention to this form of discrimination. Part of the reason that occupational segregation has been considered worthy of careful investigation would seem to be the unequal chances for mobility that the segregation creates.

Even when men and women do begin careers at the same level, it has been said (e.g., Henshel, 1973:56) that it is the men who are favoured for promotions. Thus, a statistical equalization of the female and male first occupation distributions might not be expected to fully eliminate mobility differences between the two groups. This matter, too, has received some attention in the feminist literature and the discrimination is most frequently documented in the case of professional occupations, school and university teaching, for example, where there is a fairly small number of clearly demarked ranks (e.g., Epstein, 1970; Fuchs, 1975; Henshel, 1973:72-94; Hughes, 1973; Reskin, 1976; Smith, 1975). The data for a labour force–wide assessment of this question have not heretofore been available in Canada.

Conventional wisdom about male and female mobility also holds that where men and women are both found to be mobile over their careers men may expect mobility over greater distances up the organizational ladder. This, too, has been examined in case studies of occupations, again usually at the professional level. It has been shown, for instance, that while all academics begin at the lecturer or assistant professor level, men are found to dominate the full professorships and administrative posts while women more often move up only one rank, to the associate professor level (Ferber and Loeb, 1973; Smith, 1975:360-61).

Finally, it has been suggested that women who wish to pursue upwardly mobile careers must bear costs not expected of men. Women in American graduate schools are found to be less likely than men to be married (Feldman, 1973:984). A wider study of American female workers has demonstrated a general tendency for women in higher occupations and income brackets to be less likely to be married than those in lower status employment (Havens, 1973). Meissner *et al.* (1975) have described Canadian data showing another cost borne by working women: husbands with wives in full-time employment render little more assistance with housework than do men whose wives do not work. It may be expected that the group of women most willing to bear costs such as these will exhibit the career mobility patterns most resembling those for males.

There has been some tendency within the feminist literature to analyse' male-female differences in mobility at the level of individual occupations.[1] This approach has value for its ability to circumvent the issue of how to scale occupations in a way that will make ranks on the hierarchy equivalent for male and female incumbents of occupations. A study, say, of people in academic life looks at a single occupational category and can generate data sensitive enough to describe differences in speed of promotion up the ranks of the organization. We have suggested that much of the hypothesizing about female mobility has originated from such investigations. The contribution that a large population-wide sample such as ours would seem to offer is that it allows an assessment of the general applicability of the kind of hypotheses that we have mentioned above. While adding to the picture in this way, some of the richness characterizing single-occupation studies must inevitably be lost.

A scale suitable for ranking the occupational status of a representative sample of men and women is insensitive to rankings within occupations, a dimension that appears to be of considerable importance for comparing males and females. Indeed, the average advantage of men in the labour force, stressed by feminist writers, is all but undetectable in some scales. When current occupations are scaled on an index of socioeconomic standing (Chapter 7), it is seen that the average score for males is actually slightly lower than for females. The problem is that the scale of SES is intended to denote the standing of occupational roles themselves, and is, in fact, usually computed from data for male incumbents. A scale computed from female education and occupation information has been found to correlate highly with the male scale (Blishen and Carroll, 1978) but such a scale assumes that occupational roles bestow the same prestige on every incumbent. Guppy and Siltanen (1977) have shown that publicly evaluated prestige scales ranking male and female incumbents of occupations attribute an average of five extra points to men. It is not known whether the public intends this difference to make allowance for male advantages in rank within occupations or whether the five-point margin estimates some overall augmentation in social standing that accrues to the male role. At present there does not appear to be consensus among sociologists over whether independent prestige scales for sub-groups within societies are advisable (c.f., Haug, 1973; Treiman and Terrell, 1975:175-176). Departing from the logic of an overall assessment of the prestige or ("desirability") (Hope and Goldthorpe, 1974:12) of an occupational role invites the confusing situation of a scale for all the important sub-groups in the labour force.

In this chapter we employ the ordinal scale of occupational groups, introduced in Chapter 2, which categorizes several broad families of occupation. The scale has a face value interpretability lacking in the more abstracted prestige or socioeconomic indexes of occupations and appears to capture the sexual segregation of occupations somewhat more clearly than does the Blishen scale (frequency distributions for each sex, using a collapsed version of the scale, appear in Table 7.11). The ordinal scale allows one to note the white-collar–blue-collar distinction, something not possible in socioeconomic scales. It also distinguishes skill levels, particularly at the lower end of the scale. But the scale cannot do a great deal to handle the intra-occupational variation among the sexes. Because of this, it is well to remember that some risk is run of underestimating the segregation by sex in the labour force, and this seems likely to cause some truncation of differences between the sexes in career mobility.

We have followed in this chapter the rank ordering of the scale suggested by Pineo, Porter, and McRoberts (1977) and seen in Table 3.1.[2] It might be asked if the ordering should be changed for female workers. In trying to answer this question, we have employed ratings from the prestige scale reported by Guppy and Siltanen (1977) for male and female incumbents of occupations. Eighty-seven of the ninety titles used by Guppy and Siltanen could be classified on the ordinal scale and twelve of the fifteen categories contained at least one of these titles. Computing means for titles within each of the categories gives a reading of how the public perceives the status of males and females within each grouping. The ordering of the scale produced by this method correlates .86 and .70, for females and males respectively, with the ordinal scores assigned by Pineo, Porter and McRoberts. By this criterion there would not appear to be serious problems with the rank ordering for either sex. One lesson learned from this comparison is that the manual–non-manual boundary appears to hold greater importance in the female labour force than among males. Within each skill level, the public attributes slightly greater prestige to manual than to non-manual occupations for male incumbents but for females this rule is reversed with non-manual employment receiving considerably higher scores. The prestige scale penalizes males working in traditional female occupations (e.g., telephone operator) and females working in traditionally male pursuits (e.g., sheet metal worker). The fact that many of the traditional female occupations are classified in the non-manual portion of the scale, with male occupations falling frequently into manual categories, appears to account for the sharper manual–non-manual boundary among females.

Female and Male Patterns Compared

The differences in occupational distributions between men and women seem sufficiently large that they are likely to dominate any comparisons of "raw" patterns of mobility among the two groups. That is, if we classify current occupation by first occupation, and compare inflow and outflow percentages for men and women separately, the likelihood is that most of the results will simply rediscover the fact that women are concentrated in lower white-collar occupations and men over-represented at the ends of the occupational scale. There is something of a tradition in mobility research of eliminating marginal differences in a mobility transition table so that the net or inherent patterns may be discovered. This has involved some variation of the strategy of creating cell frequencies, within the table, that are unaffected by the margins of the table. Our approach here is to present initially the unadjusted female mobility table along with matching male cell entries which have been adjusted (Deming) so that the overall male margins are identical for those in the female part of the table. That is, we begin by describing a female table that *is* a combination of net and structural effects, and exert statistical control only on the male table, in order to achieve a more sensitive comparison of mobility between the groups. These results are shown in Table 8.1, with female entries in the upper portion of each cell, and male results in the lower portion. The raw female cell frequencies would seem to possess a descriptive reality lacking in higher order statistical workings of the data. We observe, for instance, that flow into and out of the two divisions of clerical and sales work encompasses the mobility patterns of a very large number of women. Indeed, if there is such thing as a typical pattern of career mobility for Canadian women, it must surely involve movements involving these groups. Flows involving the farm labourer category, which are of some interest and importance in the actual male transition table (discussed in Chapter 3), are numerically too minor to be important for females. The male data shown in Table 8.1 do not possess this descriptive reality. Instead, the male entries provide the comparative reference point of a statistically created society of males in which men are found in each occupation group with the same frequency as women.

Overall, it can be said that females are the less likely to be mobile between their first and their current occupations. Every diagonal cell is greater for females than for males. For example, of 619 females who began their careers in a professional occupation, 434 (70 per cent) were also currently engaged in a professional occupation. In contrast, only 371 (60 per cent) of an identical (adjusted) number of men reporting first jobs in the professional category also said that their occupation in 1973 was a profession. Following the convention of considering the professional occupations as holding, as a group, the highest social status, it could be said that those who reported a professional first occupation and a current occupation in some other group were downwardly mobile.[3] The difference between men and women in the proportion remaining in the same category over the career span measured by the first and current occupation questions is greatest in the foremen category. Here only 5 per cent of the men compared to 58 per cent of women who began careers as foremen were found in the same category in their current occupation. The high-management and middle-management categories show the next largest male-female differences in outflow. In each case women who are currently managers usually began their careers as managers (our categories hide the fact that they may have progressed up the ranks of management over this interval). Most of the male managers, both high and middle, reported that their first jobs were in other categories. The smallest difference in career stability occurs in the semi-skilled clerical and sales group. Fifty per cent of women and 48 per cent of men reported both first and current occupations that were classified within this group. The margin of difference between the sexes in outflow from the unskilled clerical and sales group is also minute (four percentage points). These last two results provide some hint of the consequences of standardizing the male transition table to the female marginals. The standardization increases the males at the traditional female occupation level of low skill white-collar work; we have observed that outflow differences between the sexes are small at this level, and so the adjustment has the effect of reducing the differences in overall stability between the two groups.

Generally, the difference in the male and female outflows is greatest at the upper end of the ordinal scale. The Pearsonian correlation between position on the ordinal scale and the similarity in outflow (assessed by index of dissimilarity scores for differences between males and females along each row of Table 8.1) is $r = .37$ (using as observations scores for each of the fifteen occupation groups and scoring professionals = 15, down to farm labourers = 1). Thus, we may say that the patterns of outflow are most similar between the sexes at the lower end of the occupational hierarchy.[4] Such a finding would suggest that to generalize only from studies of professional or managerial occupations will cause some over-estimation of the magnitude of sexual differences in career mobility. On the other hand, since the greatest sexual differences in career mobility do occur at the upper end of the occupation hierarchy it is appropriate from the point of view of influencing government policy

TABLE 8:1 — Current Occupation by First Occupation, for Females and Males (Male Margins Adjusted to Match Female Margins)

Current	Professionals	High Management	Semi-Professionals	Technicians	Mid-Level Management	Supervisors	Foremen	Skilled Clerical-Sales	Skilled Crafts-Trades	Farmers	Semi-Skilled Clerical-Sales	Semi-Skilled Crafts-Trades	Unskilled Clerical-Sales	Unskilled Labourers	Farm Labourers	N
Professionals	434	4	39	12	1	0	0	41	0	0	51	5	11	3	1	603
	371.3	1.7	59.3	9.1	1.4	0.7	0.7	83.6	2.7	0.1	42.4	6.9	14.7	4.4	0.5	
High Management	13	7	9	0	0	0	0	6	0	0	2	1	6	0	0	45
	9.2	1.7	6.9	0.9	0.6	0.4	0.1	12.0	0.3	0.0	8.6	0.7	2.9	0.8	0.0	
Semi-Professionals	65	5	558	4	6	2	2	47	7	0	53	3	17	6	2	776
	79.3	1.2	470.4	6.0	0.6	0.4	0.0	101.6	5.9	0.0	51.8	15.1	30.6	8.3	0.1	
Technicians	7	0	6	86	0	3	0	6	2	0	13	8	4	5	0	139
	11.4	0.0	6.6	56.2	0.3	0.5	0.0	12.7	3.3	0.2	22.7	11.7	6.2	5.9	0.3	
Mid-Level Management	7	0	5	1	15	0	0	26	0	0	38	6	11	4	0	119
	12.4	0.7	9.7	2.0	5.7	1.5	0.1	26.9	1.4	0.1	29.4	7.7	10.3	4.4	0.9	
Supervisors	8	0	10	7	7	47	2	112	15	0	115	31	47	27	0	464
	15.0	0.6	15.6	4.8	2.1	31.0	1.1	116.3	7.0	0.5	164.8	23.9	55.8	21.9	0.5	
Foremen	1	0	2	0	0	0	11	0	0	0	1	9	4	5	1	32
	1.9	0.0	1.2	0.9	0.1	0.3	1.0	5.4	2.6	0.1	6.7	4.4	2.2	4.5	3.6	
Skilled Clerical-Sales	29	0	45	5	5	13	2	1,000	7	0	371	35	103	25	0	1,634
	48.3	5.5	54.1	25.4	10.5	14.4	4.4	835.4	18.9	1.3	339.7	51.8	157.8	59.8	0.6	
Skilled Crafts-Trades	1	0	0	0	0	1	0	4	47	2	23	18	9	18	1	125
	2.3	0.1	4.9	1.7	0.2	1.0	0.5	12.5	20.2	0.4	23.7	24.9	8.7	20.9	3.0	

First Occupation

TABLE 8:1 — (Continued)

Current	First Occupation															N
	Professionals	High Management	Semi-Professionals	Technicians	Mid-level Management	Supervisors	Foremen	Skilled Clerical-Sales	Skilled Crafts-Trades	Farmers	Semi-Skilled Clerical-Sales	Semi-Skilled Crafts-Trades	Unskilled Clerical-Sales	Unskilled Labourers	Farm Labourers	
Farmers	0 / 1.6	0 / 0.0	1 / 0.4	0 / 0.1	0 / 0.2	0 / 0.5	0 / 0.2	1 / 0.9	1 / 0.9	4 / 2.6	5 / 3.6	1 / 3.9	1 / 2.7	2 / 1.1	8 / 4.4	23
Semi-Skilled Clerical-Sales	35 / 36.5	0 / 4.8	48 / 79.2	3 / 4.4	26 / 32.1	2 / 5.1	2 / 5.1	250 / 217.2	28 / 20.0	0 / 2.0	1,095 / 1,055.0	125 / 149.0	173 / 148.3	110 / 136.4	6 / 12.8	1,914
Semi-Skilled Crafts-Trades	9 / 6.7	0 / 0.7	11 / 25.7	1 / 1.1	5 / 7.4	0 / 1.9	0 / 1.9	15 / 55.0	16 / 27.5	3 / 2.9	98 / 123.8	373 / 290.9	38 / 34.8	76 / 61.4	19 / 18.0	723
Unskilled Clerical-Sales	9 / 14.3	0 / 0.0	19 / 11.4	3 / 2.8	4 / 1.7	3 / 1.4	3 / 1.4	72 / 73.2	8 / 14.7	0 / 0.9	180 / 222.5	49 / 41.8	229 / 195.5	38 / 34.8	6 / 4.0	627
Unskilled Labourers	2 / 8.7	0 / 0.0	4 / 7.6	0 / 1.1	2 / 5.1	2 / 1.4	2 / 1.4	18 / 40.5	10 / 15.1	5 / 2.1	103 / 99.4	60 / 97.4	54 / 51.1	229 / 162.0	17 / 16.9	515
Farm Labourers	2 / 0.0	0 / 0.0	1 / 5.3	0 / 0.0	0 / 1.5	0 / 0.0	0 / 0.0	3 / 6.8	1 / 1.4	11 / 0.8	11 / 3.8	5 / 8.0	7 / 9.2	16 / 16.0	16 / 10.6	54
N	619	17	758	140	106	31	19	1,600	142	14	2,198	738	752	570	83	7,787

*Population: For all tables in Chapter 8, males and females, aged 25 to 64 (females only in Table 8.4). N's are those after weighting by the standard CMS weight variable, downweighted to reproduce actual overall sample size by the factor 1/300.55. Raw N (before nonresponses on occupation questions) equals 16,416, for females, as in Chapter 3, for males.

that the feminist literature has drawn attention to this section of the labour force. We find also that (despite the equalization of the male and female occupation margins) male and female outflows in Table 8.1 are the most alike in occupation groups in which women are over-represented. There is a correlation of −.48 between the proportionate representation of females versus males in each (current) occupation and the dissimilarity in outflow percentages between each sex. Further, this relationship is independent of position on the occupation scale. When occupation rank is partialled out, the correlation of −.48 changes by only .04 points. Such a finding suggests some interesting possibilities for *post hoc* hypothesizing, although the hypotheses would refer mainly to mobility within specific occupations. It could be conjectured, for instance, that in occupations where women form a majority, anti-feminist attitudes are the most effectively combated. In occupations where there are very few women, such as administrative posts in business, sexist values may be well developed, making it particularly difficult for those women who are in the occupation to progress.

Some analyses of mobility transition tables involving comparisons between adjusted and unadjusted cells have made use of a statistic known as the "Freeman-Tukey deviate" (Freeman and Tukey, 1950). Chase (1975:489-90) has used this statistic in mobility analysis and describes some of its properties. It provides a significance test somewhat similar to the conventional Chi-square test, and interpreted in this way we find that only three of fifteen diagonal cells (farm, semi-skilled clerical and sales, farm labourers) fail to show male-female differences at the .05 level of significance. (The Freeman-Tukey deviates are shown in Appendix 8.1; negative signs indicate more females than males in a cell and vice versa.) The chief benefit of calculating this statistic would seem to be that it draws attention to the fact that some of the large percentage differences between male and female entries in Table 8.1 are based on small sample sizes. The point here would not be so much that small sub-samples may give unstable results but that categories with few women do not contribute in any great amount to the mobility patterns which women typically experience. For example, although we have reported the strong percentage difference in male and female outflow from the high level management category, the Freeman-Tukey deviate for this difference (−2.44) places it eleventh of the fifteen groups in importance, comparing along the diagonal cells. Important though the mobility patterns of high-level female managers are from an analytical point of view, they involve only some one-half of 1 per cent of females reporting current occupation in our sample. On the other hand, the statistic draws attention to some relatively modest percentage differences that involve large absolute numbers. It emphasizes, for instance, the higher outflow among males from the skilled clerical category (−5.43), along with similar patterns in the semi-skilled crafts/trades (−4.50) and unskilled labourers (−4.79) groups.

With females exhibiting a stronger tendency to be non-mobile between first and current occupation, it may be expected that males will be over-represented in at least some other career paths. Among the categories of high female employment, the skilled clerical and sales group contributed the greatest number of cells in Table 8.1 in which males outnumber females. It can be seen, for example, that downward mobility from the technicians and middle-management categories into skilled clerical and sales current positions is more characteristic of males than females. Upward mobility from the three lowest groups on the ordinal scale into skilled clerical-sales current occupations also is more typical of males (remembering again, that the male portion of Table 8.1 uses adjusted data). All these male-female differences exhibit a large value for the Freeman-Tukey deviate. Outflow from the skilled clerical-sales category also reveals some distinct patterns among males in the adjusted data shown in Table 8.1. Males are the more likely to move up from this group to professional or semi-professional employment, but they also show the greater downward movement into the semi-skilled crafts/trades and unskilled labourer groups.

It is hard in a cell-by-cell inspection of Table 8.1 to draw conclusions about the question of whether men exhibit the greater "long distance" mobility over several levels or indeed whether upward versus downward mobility is the more characteristic of male respondents. These questions we endeavoured to answer with some summary tabulations and these are presented in Table 8.2. The upper panel of the table records the percentages upwardly mobile, downwardly mobile, and stable. The table shows results for the female and male data in Table 8.1, as well as for the male table before adjustment. Upward and downward mobility was divided into long distance and short distance components. We arbitrarily selected mobility over two categories or less on the ordinal scale as representative of mobility over a short distance. Because of the heterogeneity within categories, some of this mobility may have very little vertical component at all. Long distance mobility is any movement over three or more categories. Table 8.2 reveals that over half of all women in the sample were categorized in the same group when they reported first occupation and occupation in 1973. This proportion is considerably greater than the percentage of males in the unadjusted table (35.1 per cent) who did not change categories. Adjusting the male data in the manner described previously brings this proportion closer into line with the female figure (45.1 per cent) but, as the detailed inspection of Table 8.1 revealed, outflow is still greater among male respondents. The "unadjusted" males exhibit the greatest long distance upward mobility (35.0 per cent). Females rank second on this dimension, however, ahead of the males in the adjusted table. Similarly, on downward mobility women rank behind males in the unadjusted table, but ahead of the males who were adjusted; females are less likely than adjusted males to move downward from first to current job over either a long or short distance. The lower panel of Table 8.2 describes the pattern of upward and downward mobility after setting aside those who were stable over the period surveyed. This allows a more sensitive comparison between the three groups as to which was more likely to achieve mobility over a long distance. The pattern of greater downward mobility among males in the adjusted table might be thought to be an inevitable consequence of the larger diagonal entries among females. On the contrary, it can be seen in the lower panel of Table 8.2 that even when focusing on mobile respondents the female advantage over adjusted males persists. Some 39 per cent of mobile females moved upwards over more than two positions on the scale compared to 17.9 per cent of adjusted males. And long distance downward mobility is still

TABLE 8:2 — Percentages Upwardly and Downwardly Mobile from First to Current Occupation, Females and Males (Adjusted and Actual)

Percentage of Total	Women	Men Adjusted	Actual
Upwardly mobile — long distance	18.3	9.8	35.0
Upwardly mobile — short distance	9.5	21.9	12.4
Stable	53.3	45.1	35.1
Downwardly mobile — short distance	8.0	9.3	8.1
Downwardly mobile — long distance	10.9	13.9	9.4
N	7,787	7,787	13,163
Percentage of Mobiles			
Upwardly mobile — long	39.3	17.9	53.9
Upwardly mobile — short	20.4	39.9	19.1
Downwardly mobile — short	17.0	16.9	12.5
Downwardly mobile — long	23.4	25.3	14.5
N	3,637	4,278	8,549

somewhat more characteristic of these males (25.3 per cent) than of females (23.4 per cent). In both panels of Table 8.2 the greater upward and lesser downward mobility among males in the unadjusted table remains marked.

The findings for adjusted males involve a hypothetical group and such results are difficult to interpret. The results do emphasize again the importance of differences in distributions between the sexes. The obvious interpretation of these results would seem to be that, other things equal, differences in mobility patterns between females and males could be expected to diminish as sexual segregation in the labour force declines. We have seen that the data in Table 8.2 also suggest a more subtle finding: that women enjoy some net advantage over males once account has been taken of the differences in margins. It is here that the hypothetical character of the adjusted male table may cause the results to be prone to misinterpretation. Statistically adjusting a male mobility table to eradicate sexual segregation in occupations cannot be considered equivalent to a social experiment in which such a society is actually created. We have noted already the hint in the mobility tables that males enjoy a relative mobility advantage in occupations in which they are over-represented. The standardization accentuates the importance of occupations in which females are over-represented, and where they may have the advantage over men, because it moves men into these occupations without actually removing occupational segregation in the real society. A social experiment which really equalized the sexual representation of the labour force could be expected to neutralize any relative advantage held by females in female occupations. Figures we might insert in Table 8.2 for men adjusted by means of a real elimination of occupational sex-typing cannot be guaranteed to resemble those reported using statistical standardizations.[5]

To this point, we have examined the entire group of females (and males) aged 25 to 64 who reported codable occupations for the time they entered the labour force and for the time the survey was enumerated in 1973. For descriptive purposes this would seem the correct strategy; such a group captures the experiences of the largest possible proportion of working women in Canada. It is useful also to examine theoretically interesting sub-groups of women, and this shall now be done. It was mentioned earlier that career women may have to bear costs not expected of men. In particular, it seems probable that women who interrupt their careers in order to bear children may suffer a competitive disadvantage over males. Suter's (1973:971) research on income attainment in the United States has suggested this. If so, a corollary might be that the females who come closest to matching male levels of career mobility are those who have had uninterrupted employment from first to current job. Such a group might be said to have paid the cost of foregoing at least part of the possible emotional satisfaction of traditional family life in favour of pursuing career goals. Unmarried continuous career women might be said to have paid even higher costs and could be expected to exhibit the mobility patterns the most similar to those for men.

The CMS questionnaire was designed to capture interrupted versus continuous employment histories. The key question asks: "Since you began your first full-time job, was there a single period of one year or more when you were not working for pay or profit?" The question is awkwardly worded, and gave the alarmingly high no answer rate of 27 per cent among women and only a somewhat more acceptable 12 per cent refusal among men. Because of the importance of career continuity, we endeavoured to salvage the question by classifying as continuous both those women who did answer the question, responding no (reporting no interruptions), or who gave no answer, but skipped the following question which asked about the year that the interruptions began. The inference made here, of course, is that those who did, in fact, have continuous careers would not report a year when an interruption began. Indeed, the instructions in the questionnaire were designed to skip continuous career respondents past this question.

Log-linear models provide a concise way of assessing differences between the male and female mobility transition tables and results using this technique are shown in Table 8.3. The upper panel (A) gives results for all the working men and women aged 25 to 64 years. The second panel (B) analyses only women who were classified as continuously employed from first to 1973 occupation. Single continuous career women only were used for the analysis summarized in the third panel (C). In all the comparisons the full group of males aged 25 to 64 was retained. An alternative approach would have been to truncate the males in each comparison in the same way as for females. We preferred to maintain a fixed reference point against which to compare patterns for different subsets of females.

Three models for predicting mobility from first occupation to current occupation, specifying by sex, are shown in Table 8.3. The first model is a deliberately naive one which enters only the one-way interactions (simple marginal frequencies on first occupation, current occupation, and sex), and it is considered to be a "baseline model." Model 2 makes a more realistic endeavour to predict the actual cell values. It predicts the cells using, in addition to the one-way interactions, the two-way interaction between first and current occupation. In other words, the model recognizes that there is an association, in each sex, between a person's first and current job. However, this model intentionally omits the fact that the occupational margins on first and current occupation are known to differ by sex. Looking at panel A in Table 8.3, it can be seen that this model (number 2) achieves a considerable reduction over the baseline model in the likelihood ratio Chi-square between the observed and fitted cell values. This model could be considered analogous to examining male-female differences in mobility in a transition table in which the original margins for each sex were preserved. Model 3 estimates the importance of the male-female differences under more stringent assumptions. In this model, all the two-way interactions are included, so that the model takes account of the fact that sex is related to first and current occupation. This model is constructed under assumptions equivalent to those incorporated in Table 8.1 (in which male margins were standardized to the female ones). In panel A of Table 8.3, the log-linear analysis essentially provides an alternative presentation of the data already discussed. The models do supply some information not captured in the previous presentation, however. First, they provide an overall significance test of the interaction effect between sex, first, and current occupation. We see in Table 8.3 (panel A) that for the total group of males and females aged 25 to 64 the sexual differences in mobility easily pass the test. Secondly, the models allow one to partition the relative importance of different factors contributing to this interaction. The proportionate reduction in the magnitude of the Chi-square has been described (Goodman, 1972; Hauser, *et al.*, 1975:285) as roughly equivalent to a partitioning of variance in regression analysis. The Chi-square in the baseline model can be loosely treated as an indicator of total unexplained variance.[6] Model 2 reduces this "variance" by a proportion of 74 per cent; model 3 achieves an additional 25 per cent reduction.[7]

The figures for continuous career women (panel B, Table 8.3) reveal a somewhat complicated finding when they are compared to the corresponding values for all women (panel A). We will concentrate here upon the values of the index of dissimilarity. It is the most trustworthy indicator in such comparisons because the simple Chi-square values are influenced by the overall sample size and this diminishes in each panel in Table 8.3. What the index of dissimilarity reveals is that, in a "zero-order sense," it is true that the mobility patterns of women most closely resemble those for men when the comparison is restricted to continuous career women only. In reaching this conclusion we are comparing values of the index for Model 2 in panels A and B and observing that the index of dissimilarity score drops from 24.7 for all women to 19.2 for

TABLE 8:3 — Log-Linear Models of the Mobility from First to Current Occupation, Classified by Gender

A. For all males and females reporting a first and a current occupation:

Model: Description	Notation	LR	DF	p	IOD
1. One-way interactions (baseline model)	(F)(C)(G)	32,690	420	.000	46.4
2. Interactions of first occ. by current occupation	(F,C)	8,568	224	.000	24.7
3. All two-way interactions	(FC)(FG)(CG)	493	196	.000	4.3

B. For all males and females who reported uninterrupted employment from first to current occupation:

Model: Description	Notation	LR	DF	p	IOD
1. One-way interactions (baseline model)	(F)(C)(G)	25,413	420	.000	43.8
2. Interactions of first occ. by current occupation	(FC)	5,607	224	.000	19.2
3. All two-way interactions	(FC)(FG)(CG)	578	196	.000	5.1

C. For all males, and continuous
career females who are single

		LR	DF	p	IOD
1. One-way interactions	(F)(C)(G)	15,130	420	.000	37.0
2. Interactions of first occ. by current occupation	(FC)	1,761	224	.000	7.1
3. All two-way interactions	(FC)(FG)(CG)	167	196	>.5	1.7

Note: LR — Chi-square likelihood ratio
DF — Degrees of freedom
p — Probability of fit
IOD — Index of dissimilarity between expected and observed

Key to Notations: F — First occupation
C — Current occupation
G — Gender

continuous career women. Model 2, however, is the simplified situation in which no allowance is made for the fact that occupational distribution is related to gender. When one looks at results for the more powerful Model 3, it can be seen that the situation changes. Here, the resemblance in mobility patterns for men and women is no longer greater among continuous career women; the index for these women (5.1) is actually slightly greater than that for all women (4.3). This finding allows us to conclude that the greater similarity in mobility between men and continuous women observed in Model 2 is due to the fact that continuous career women have first and current occupational distributions that, compared to those for all women, are relatively similar to the male distribution.

When the female sample is further truncated by selecting only women who are both continuous career and single (including separated and divorced) the sexual differences in career mobility are diminished in all the models. In Model 2 the index of dissimilarity for this group (panel C) sinks to 7.1 from the value of 24.7 for all women. And even with the restrictive assumptions built into Model 3, the differences in mobility between men and women are reduced among single continuous career women. The index of dissimilarity in this model sinks from 4.3 in panel A (all women) to 1.7 in panel C (single continuous women). Even if the occupational distribution of single continuous career women was no different from that for all women we would still expect, from these results, that the single continuous women would exhibit the mobility patterns closest to those for males. Indeed, the Chi-square results for Model 3 in panel C show that there is no statistically significant difference at all between the career mobility achieved by men and by single continuous career women (this is partially due to the truncation in sample size in panel C).

Net Effects in Female Career Mobility

We have heretofore concentrated on comparing patterns of career mobility between females and males. This seems of first priority because the male-female inequality in opportunities is the principal problem to which those in the feminist movement react. It can be seen, however (Table 8.1), that patterns of career mobility in each sex share some basic features. Women, along with men, are observed to share a likelihood of remaining in the same group over their career from first to current occupation. And, the movement that does occur tends in each sex to be over short distances on the scale rather than over very long distances. It is seen in Table 8.1, for instance, that only some one-half of 1 per cent of women commencing work in the unskilled labour category subsequently moved into professional work. Now a closer examination of female mobility from this point of view is made. We noted earlier that the raw figures in Table 8.1 include both net and structural effects; while such figures have descriptive value, they may hide important properties of the social structure. Are there, for instance, natural upward or downward progressions that females typically follow between first and current occupation? It might be expected, for example, that women beginning employment in semi-skilled crafts or trades would frequently upgrade their skills to the skilled craft or trade level. The 2 per cent outflow from semi-skilled to skilled crafts and trades observed in Table 8.1 would not suggest that this is a very promising prediction. However, the test of the hypothesis is prejudiced by the small proportionate size of the skilled crafts/trades group in the female labour force, and by the relatively large number of women with semi-skilled craft or trades occupations. To answer such questions about natural mobility ladders, the marginal effects must be removed. This can be accomplished by examining lambda coefficients for the interaction of first occupation by current occupation.[8] The coefficients are reported in Table 8.4. They denote net effects from a log-linear model of female career mobility in which the effects due to the simple marginal distributions of first and current occupation are controlled. Only the female sample was analysed here. The coefficients may be interpreted by bearing in mind that a positive value indicates some probability (net of margin main effects) for the first and current occupations concerned to occur together; a negative lambda tells one that the two occupations do not occur frequently as a pair. Put another way, the lambdas signify the odds of any respondent being found in each cell, again with the stipulation that margin effects are represented by a separate set of coefficients.

One can see in Table 8.4 that some frequently travelled paths of career mobility do exist for Canadian women. For every first job the greatest probability is that women will be found in the same group when current occupation is measured. But after this the probabilities generally are that mobility will take place within the manual or the non-manual sectors. For instance, it might be supposed that unskilled manual labourers would be more likely to upgrade into semi-skilled blue-collar work than into semi-skilled clerical or sales positions. The supposition is well founded according to the lambda coefficients in Table 8.4; the probability of a female worker having an unskilled labourer first occupation and semi-skilled crafts/trades job ($\lambda = 1.2$) exceeds the probability of such a person moving into semi-skilled clerical-sales work ($\lambda = .7$). Farm labourers exhibit a strong probability ($\lambda = 2.4$) of subsequently

TABLE 8:4 — Lambda Effects for the Interaction of First Occupation and Current Occupation for Females

First Occupation	Professionals	High Management	Semi-Professionals	Technicians	Mid-Level Management	Supervisors	Foremen	Skilled Clerical-Sales	Skilled Crafts-Trades	Farmers	Semi-Skilled Clerical-Sales	Semi-Skilled Crafts-Trades	Unskilled Clerical-Sales	Unskilled Labourers	Farm Labourers
Professionals	3.82	1.48	1.46	0.30	0.39	-0.72	-0.53	0.39	-1.21	-1.56	-0.13	-0.75	-0.77	-1.77	-0.40
High Management	1.62	3.26	1.35	-0.04	0.05	-1.19	0.74	-1.32	0.06	0.81	-2.03	-1.32	-1.34	-1.01	0.36
Semi-Professionals	1.33	1.03	3.51	0.06	-0.01	-0.61	-0.12	0.74	-2.40	-0.56	0.09	-0.65	-0.14	-1.28	-1.00
Technicians	1.31	-0.78	-0.18	3.78	-0.18	0.19	-0.59	-0.25	-1.27	-0.52	0.01	-0.46	0.04	-1.24	0.13
Mid-Level Management	0.10	0.12	1.10	-0.47	3.06	-0.01	0.31	-1.74	-0.36	0.38	-0.51	-0.65	0.18	-1.44	-0.06
Supervisors	-1.64	1.10	-0.49	0.84	-1.01	2.31	-0.32	0.92	-1.00	-0.25	0.88	0.02	-0.20	-0.46	-0.70
Foremen	-0.83	-0.30	-1.29	-0.29	-0.20	-1.44	3.62	0.05	0.92	0.56	-0.66	-1.57	0.36	0.35	0.12
Skilled Clerical-Sales	0.69	-0.04	0.36	-0.63	0.87	1.08	-2.42	3.14	-0.89	-1.25	1.04	-1.04	0.48	-0.55	-0.84
Skilled Crafts-Trades	-2.13	-1.01	0.11	0.01	-1.50	0.69	-0.82	-0.16	3.06	0.35	0.46	0.62	-0.06	0.48	-0.09
Farmers	-0.63	0.49	-1.10	-0.10	-0.01	-1.25	0.68	-1.37	1.62	2.95	-2.08	0.57	-1.40	1.33	0.31
Semi-Skilled Clerical-Sales	0.17	-1.73	-0.26	-0.63	0.51	0.67	-2.05	1.41	0.03	-0.68	1.78	0.08	0.66	0.43	-0.39
Semi-Skilled Crafts-Trades	-1.09	-1.26	-2.01	-0.12	-0.30	0.04	0.77	0.04	0.76	-1.01	0.59	2.38	0.34	1.01	-0.15
Unskilled Clerical-Sales	-0.66	-0.11	-0.71	-1.07	-0.04	0.14	-0.29	0.80	-0.22	-0.81	0.60	0.49	1.57	0.46	-0.15
Unskilled Labourers	-1.33	-2.15	-1.18	-0.35	-0.45	0.12	0.43	-0.08	0.97	-0.80	0.67	1.20	0.30	2.42	0.23
Farm Labourers	-0.72	-0.70	-0.68	-1.29	-1.19	-0.04	0.59	-2.56	-0.08	2.39	-0.71	1.10	-0.02	1.30	2.62

becoming farm owners. Inheritance or purchase of farms by women might be thought to be unusual, but this evidently is relatively more common than other career paths female farm labourers may take. Unskilled clerical-sales workers are, according to the lambda coefficients, more likely to enter skilled or semi-skilled clerical-sales occupations than any other destination (except remaining in unskilled clerical-sales work). Outflow from first occupations in the semi-skilled crafts and trades is, as predicted above, largely into other manual categories. The strongest movement is downward ($\lambda = 1.0$) into unskilled manual work. The probabilities of upward mobility from semi-skilled crafts/trades into the skilled manual or into the foremen group are also strong (both λ's = .8). Transition into white-collar work at the same (semi-) skill level is not so likely ($\lambda = .6$).

A mathematically necessary feature of any mobility transition table is that those in the lowest category cannot be downwardly mobile, nor do those in the highest category have any room to achieve upward movement. The best that those beginning careers in the professional category can do is to remain in the same group, and it can be seen that the probability is ($\lambda = 3.8$) that such women will succeed in this. Those who are downwardly mobile from the upper white-collar categories generally slip by only a few categories. Even here, however, we observe that the long distance downward mobility that does occur is likely to take place within the non-manual sphere. There is some probability, for instance, that women holding professional status first occupations will be downwardly mobile into the skilled clerical-sales group ($\lambda = .4$); it is improbable ($\lambda = -1.2$) that such mobility into the skilled crafts or trades category would occur. Within the upper white-collar occupations certain mobility paths appear to hold for females. In particular, there is a tendency for those starting as technicians to upgrade into the professional level ($\lambda = 1.3$). Oddly, the same progression into semi-professional work does not appear. Another oddity is that supervisors are likely to become high-level managers ($\lambda = 1.1$) but not to move into middle-level management ($\lambda = -1.0$). Some of the lambda coefficients at the upper end of the scale are based upon very small case sizes (see Table 8.1) and the dangers of over-interpreting these are as great as is the vulnerability of percentages computed from a small base.

Inter-Generational Mobility

The difficulty women may face in achieving career mobility has been the first topic discussed here because this seems to us to capture the primary social problems aspect of female occupational mobility.[9] Consciousness among women of discrimination in opportunities for advancement over the working career seems particularly high; higher than consciousness that males may be more upwardly mobile from their father's status than females are. It would seem difficult for women to make their own informal comparisons, as participants in society, between the typical inter-generational mobility achieved by men and women. Such comparisons would require some detailed biographical knowledge of their male work peers. Promotions are an easily visible phenomenon which rate high consciousness among workers, and differences in speed of advancement among females and males may be striking. In addition, informal comparisons of inter-generational mobility rates in each sex would seem difficult to make because of the dissimilarity between the occupations typically held by males and females. From the overall occupational distributions for each sex it can be anticipated that much female movement from family status will involve a transition from a blue-collar father's to a white-collar daughter's occupation. It is often confusing nowadays to sort out the relative status advantages of such moves, particularly where the skill level is constant. To the extent that women do identify inequalities in chances for inter-generational mobility, it seems likely that they formulate the problem in terms of the sexual segregation of occupations that we noted earlier. And, as the following results show, we find that this is indeed the essential aspect of sexual differences in inter-generational mobility.

Summary information about mobility patterns from father's occupation to son's and to daughter's first and current occupations is shown in tables 8.5 and 8.6. The tables record the percentages moving upwards and downwards in each detailed transition table. The transition tables, upon which these tables are derived, are presented in Appendices 8.2 and 8.3, and use the same fifteen category occupation scale employed previously. And, as before, an arbitrary distinction between long and short distance mobility is made by classifying movements over more than two categories as long distance mobility. The tables show figures for the actual or unadjusted male data, and for male transition tables in which the father's and respondent's occupation margins have been standardized to match those for the female sample.

It can be seen, comparing the female and "actual" male percentages in Table 8.5, that the males are by a margin of some ten percentage points more likely to take first occupations within the same occupation grouping as their fathers. Such a finding is in accordance with common sense and has been suggested as a hypothesis in an American study (DeJong, *et al.*, 1971:1,034). It is customary to pass businesses and farms on to the eldest son in a family. And fathers seem to pass on skills or

TABLE 8:5 — Percentages Upwardly and Downwardly Mobile from Father's To First Occupation, Females and Males (Adjusted and Actual)

Percentage of Total	Women	Men Adjusted	Actual
Upwardly mobile — long distance	27.9	28.7	22.9
Upwardly mobile — short distance	17.1	16.2	12.1
Stable	9.2	10.0	19.1
Downwardly mobile — short distance	21.2	21.3	15.2
Downwardly mobile — long distance	24.6	23.7	30.7
N	11,104	11,104	12,648
Percentage of Mobiles			
Upwardly mobile — long	30.7	31.9	28.3
Upwardly mobile — short	18.8	18.0	15.0
Downwardly mobile — short	23.4	23.7	18.8
Downwardly mobile — long	27.1	26.4	38.0
N	10,083	9,991	10,230

informal apprenticeships to sons but not to daughters. Both interpretations might be said to be partially a consequence of the sexual typing of occupations. It may be that fathers frequently perceive their occupation as inappropriate for their daughters, or at least feel that a woman would encounter difficulties in entering the occupation. The figures in Table 8.5 for adjusted males statistically eliminate the sexual differences in first occupation distribution. The adjusted figures reveal that after compensating for these margin effects the proportions of males and females having first occupations within the same group as their fathers are all but identical. The difference between the sexes shrinks from ten percentage points to less than one point. The convergence between male and female percentages seems remarkable considering the crudeness of the standardization. The adjustment is crude in two senses. As noted previously, such a correction for sexual segregation of occupations is only approximate because of the heterogeneity of each group. We would not expect the detailed occupation distribution of males and females within each category on our scale to be identical. Also, there is a crudeness due to the interpretations placed upon diagonal entries in a mobility transition table. To make sense of the diagonals, it seems the

**TABLE 8:6 — Percentages Upwardly and Downwardly Mobile from Father's
To Current Occupation, Females and Males (Adjusted and
Actual)**

Percentage of Total	Women	Men Adjusted	Actual
Upwardly mobile — long distance	34.4	34.0	36.8
Upwardly mobile — short distance	16.3	16.9	14.8
Stable	8.6	9.6	17.6
Downwardly mobile — short distance	19.4	19.3	12.2
Downwardly mobile — long distance	21.2	20.2	18.6
	100%	100%	100%
N	7240	7240	12,201
Percentage of Mobiles			
Upwardly mobile — long	37.7	37.7	44.7
Upwardly mobile — short	17.8	18.7	17.9
Downwardly mobile — short	21.3	21.3	14.8
Downwardly mobile — long	23.2	22.3	22.6
	100%	100%	100%
N	6617	6546	10,052

most sensible to think of the inheritance of specific occupations: either of
businesses being passed on from generation to generation, aspirations
for particular callings being socialized into the new generation, or of
processes such as informal apprenticeships of sons or daughters under
their fathers. It is difficult to hypothesize about the inheritance of
occupation groups. The groups are statistical categories invented by
researchers and, like "objective" social classes, may have little meaning
for those categorized in them. But even though the comparison of
diagonal entries for each sex provides only the most rudimentary tap of
true occupational inheritance in each group the adjustment performed
on males is sufficiently powerful to render the new male patterns
indistinguishable from those for females. Indeed, none of the percentages for females and males in the adjusted table differ by more than one
percentage point. We have already noted that it is difficult to imagine all
the characteristics of a society in which a transformation of the male
labour force into the female one was actually engineered but we have no

grounds from our data for believing that the overall proportions of upward, downward, and stable mobility patterns in such a society would differ by sex.

Along with the relatively high incidence of diagonal entries in the actual male table, we observe in Table 8.5 that males are less likely than females to be upwardly mobile and more likely to be downwardly mobile. In sum, women would appear to enjoy the advantage in mobility from father's occupation to first occupation. It can be seen, for instance, that 27.9 per cent of the women compared to only 22.9 per cent of the men (unadjusted) moved upwards by more than two categories on the occupation scale. Even if one takes account of the higher overall movement out of father's group among women the proportionate higher upward mobility among women remains. This is seen in the lower portion of Table 8.5, where the percentages are recalculated for mobile respondents only. The advantage in favour of women in mobility from father's to first occupation can be seen in another aspect, too. The greater stability within father's group observed among men might offer an offsetting advantage for men, but only if it were the case that men were most likely to inherit at the upper end of the scale and women at the lower end. It would be considered advantageous, for instance, for the son of a doctor to enter medicine. Few would consider it advantageous for the son of a coal miner to take up coal mining. What we find is that here, too, the advantage goes to women. The tendency ($r = -.26$) is for the over-representation of males versus females on the diagonal to be greatest at the lower end of the scale.[10]

To find that women enjoy advantages in inter-generational mobility runs counter to most expectations (DeJong, *et al.*, 1971:1,034). The resolution of the seeming anomaly is found in the career mobility patterns, where it was observed that males enjoy the advantage over females. Males more than catch up by the time of current occupation, and end up enjoying the greater inter-generational upward mobility. Table 8.6 contains the summary of patterns from father's to current occupation. Males, we see, are slightly more likely than females to move upwards from their father's group by more than two positions (36.8 per cent versus 34.4 per cent) and slightly less likely to move upwards over a short distance. Females undergo greater downward mobility than males, both over short and long distances on the scale. When the comparison is restricted to mobiles only (lower portion of Table 8.6) the patterns are accentuated because of a tendency, as in mobility to first job, for males to be the more likely to remain in their father's group (17.6 per cent versus 8.6 per cent). In addition, while we said that the most advantageous occupational inheritance in the transition from father's to first job lay with females, in the mobility from father's to current occupation, the advantage reverses, favouring males. That is, at the upper end of the occupation scale the over-representation of males over females on the diagonal is larger ($r = .24$) than at the lower end. The sexual differences in mobility from father's occupation to current occupation are, like those involving first occupation, erased after the transition table is adjusted so that the occupation margins for male respondents and their fathers match those for females and their fathers. It can be seen in Table 8.6 that the percentages for females and adjusted males are, as in Table 8.5, all but identical.

We have, in this section, relied upon overall summaries of the flows observed in the detailed transition tables from father's to respondent's first and current occupation. In doing this a false impression may have been left, which should not be left uncorrected. It has been said that after adjustment on the occupation marginals the overall upward and downward patterns of mobility involving both first and current occupation are identical for males and females. While this is so, it is also true that an inspection of the female and adjusted male cells in the detailed transition tables (see Appendix 8.2) reveals many divergent patterns between the sexes. These cumulate to a set of sexual differences that are statistically significant. A log-linear model that includes all the two-way interactions between father's occupation, first (or current) occupation, and sex (i.e., that does not assume an interaction by sex in inter-generational mobility) does not fit the actual data ($x^2 = 493$, $DF = 196$, $p = .000$ for first occupation, $x^2 = 352$ for current occupation). The problem is that the differences are uninterpretable in the sense of drawing general conclusions. It seems a case of a statistically significant finding that has no clear meaning.

Summary

When mobility transition tables were simplified to percentage tabulations of the proportions upwardly mobile, downwardly mobile, and non-mobile, it was found that over the career from first to current occupation men were less likely than women to remain in the same group and more likely to move upward on the scale. From father's to first occupation, females were found to hold an advantage over men, achieving greater upward mobility and over longer distances on the occupation scale. From father's to current occupation, however, the consequences of high male career mobility were evident. Men ended up at their current occupations having achieved greater upward mobility from father's occupation and less downward mobility than women.

In the summarized presentation, the differences between the sexes in inter-generational mobility disappeared after adjustment had been made for the different occupation distributions in each gender. The detailed transition tables contained differences between the sexes that, overall, were statistically significant in a log-linear test but these differences did not seem to cumulate into any interpretable pattern. Differences in career mobility were also reduced after adjustment of the male occupation margins. Here, though, interpretable differences in patterns between each sex did remain. Upward mobility over careers was more common among women than among the adjusted group of men, particularly when the movement was over long distances on the scale. There was a marked tendency for females to remain within the same occupation group over the career. This, too, seemed to represent some overall advantage to women because the tendency for women to be less mobile than men was strongest in the higher occupation categories. In examining the sexual differences in career mobility, comparisons were made of how closely the mobility patterns of different sub-groups of women matched those for the total male sample. It was found here that career mobility among unmarried continuous career women gave the closest match with the male patterns.

Our results using large probability samples of men and women seem to support many of the views advanced in more focused research work on women. The findings regarding unmarried continuous career women, for instance, will be no surprise to feminist writers. As well, the sexual segregation of occupations has been an important component of the work by feminist writers and we found that the female occupational distribution was indeed an important aspect of the mobility patterns we examined. In general, the conventional wisdoms about female mobility, which we endeavoured to summarize earlier, seem correct. The chief departure between our results and those from other studies is the advantage in career mobility that women appear to enjoy over adjusted (occupation margins standardized to female distributions) males. The most closely comparable data from other studies might be comparisons of promotion rates which have been made in investigations of single occupations. These have suggested a clear advantage to men. The two types of data, general survey versus individual occupation, are by no means equivalent; our survey data do not address promotion rates at all. Perhaps this is all there is to it. On the other hand, reported at several points in the analysis were instances of a kind of interaction effect whereby sexual differences in mobility or non-mobility were found to vary by occupation group. In some cases these were consistent enough to yield linear correlations describing the trend. In general, we have found the barriers against female upward mobility to be greatest at the upper end of the occupation scale. Since this is where most of the individual occupation studies have been conducted, it is possible that differences in phenomena such as promotion rates would be found to be smaller in, say, lower level white-collar occupations.

If the advantage of survey data is that they allow comparisons of sexual differences in mobility at different levels in the labour force, the disadvantage is the crudeness, mentioned earlier, in the classification of occupations. How would this bias work? Crudeness of coding seems to offer a plausible alternative interpretation to all the findings reported in which male and female differences are said to disappear. The comparison, performed in tables 8.5 and 8.6, for instance, of females with adjusted males undoubtedly oversimplifies the real differences in inter-generational mobility, holding margin effects constant, between men and women. Where we do find differences, however, it seems unlikely that they would disintegrate under a finer coding of occupation. In such cases it might be considered remarkable that sexual differences in mobility can survive the crude coding at all and emerge in a table based on broad occupation groups. Here, if the general rule is that finer coding strengthens relationships, the sexual differences may be understated.

Notes

1. The principal exception to this rule in the Canadian literature is a study reported by Marsden, Harvey and Charner (1975). They compared the mobility of recent male and female college graduates from four Canadian universities.
2. Only a small number of women (N=20 for current occupation) were self-employed professionals and so the two varieties of professionals were combined here.
3. The proportion in a diagonal cell does not by itself denote an advantage or disadvantage of one group over another. The position of the cell would seem crucial for discovering this. To find that a higher proportion of females than males begin careers at the professional level could at face value be taken to indicate an advantage to females. On the other hand, to find a greater proportion of females having both first and current jobs in the unskilled labourer category indicates a disadvantage to females, since they would then be said to be locked into a low-status occupational level. This dimension of sexual differences in socioeconomic status is captured more clearly in the section comparing upward with downward mobility in each sex.
4. We have used the notion of overall dissimilarity in outflow in reporting this finding, but it is also the case, as one might expect, that the margin by which female diagonal entries exceed those for males is greatest at the upper end of the scale. As we noted before, an early entry (and consequent career

stability) into upper-level occupations is not necessarily a disadvantage. Indeed, in terms of lifetime earnings it would doubtless be more advantageous to start a career in a high-ranking occupation than to move up into one from a lower-status first job. On the other hand, there may be psychological rewards from an upwardly mobile career. Another interpretation of these findings, which we would not deny, is that women simply enter into the lower rung of the professional and managerial group of occupations; occupations which can be immediately entered with some educational certification but which do not allow for further upward movement.

5. One odd consequence of the findings discussed above is that if males could combine their (adjusted) probabilities of transition from first to current occupation with the female distribution on first occupation, they would have a considerably improved current occupation distribution over what they actually have. This can be demonstrated by weighting male first occupation to take on the female distribution, multiplying through the male transition table by these weights, and observing the new current occupation distributions. The new distribution increases the proportion professional from 9 per cent to 12.3 per cent. The proportion of high-level managers increases from 3.3 per cent to 5.7 per cent. Groups at the lower end of the scale are diminished. Unskilled labourers, for instance, decrease in frequency from 13.8 per cent to 9 per cent. The weighting evidently accentuates the strongest upwardly mobile patterns in the male table.

6. It seems to be the usual procedure in log-linear analyses of mobility tables to treat, as we have done, the model with one-way interactions as the baseline for the partitioning of variance. It could be argued that an even simpler model, the "equal probability" case where it is assumed that each cell is the same size, should be employed to provide a baseline. The values of the likelihood Chi-square for this model are 55,162.87, 46,586.34, and 41,855.18 for populations A, B and C, respectively, in Table 8.3.

7. Viewed in this way, the differences between the sexes in career mobility patterns seem small. It should be remembered that the variance here is variance in overall congruency between fitted and observed cell values in a contingency table, not variance in individual occupation level. Further, the sexual differences can be made to appear substantial in another working of the data. A Pearsonian correlation may be computed taking as units of observation the number of males and females in each cell in the mobility transition table. This correlation equals .38 for the raw table, and .76 using the adjusted male data described in Table 8.1. Here, we might say that even with assumptions equivalent to those in model 3, we only explain some 58 per cent of the "variance".

8. An alternative way of presenting these results would be to perform a standardization to equalize the row and column marginals in the female table. We would be unhappy with this form of presentation because "zero cells" in the table cannot be properly handled. Zero cells also pose some problems for the lambda coefficients; we follow here the convention of inserting a constant of 0.5 into the zero cells. This solution is not ideal because it still distorts the true data but no better procedure appears to exist. The use of the Deming adjustment in Table 8.1 also involved some zero cells. There were less zero cells in the male table, and this is one reason why we adjusted male rather than female cells.

9. Supporting evidence for this view would appear to be found in the tendency for feminist writers to address primarily career mobility when they write on mobility differences between men and women (e.g., Henshel, 1973; Smith, 1975). The work on movements over generations that has been done would seem to have been more often performed by writers who could be said to be students of stratification and mobility processes per se (e.g., Tyree and Treas, 1974; DeJong, *et al.*, 1971; Treiman and Terrell, 1975; Featherman and Hauser, 1976). This work has often been written from a comparative rather than from a social problems perspective. Chase (1975:483), for instance, has noted of the inter-generational literature in the United States that: "In the last few years, sociologists have been rushing to fill this void in the stratification literature and a number of articles have appeared comparing various forms of men's and women's mobility. The logic behind these comparisons is that in order to discover the distinctive features in one stratification system, it is helpful to compare it with other stratification systems."

10. In computing this correlation we are following similar procedures to those described earlier for the correlations reported on page 303. Again, occupational groups are the unit of analysis, and the rank order of the groups is correlated against the proportionate representation of males versus females. Here, however, the correlation reported is for the actual male percentages, not the adjusted ones. If the adjusted male data are substituted, the pattern of greater male stability in low-status first occupations is greatly diminished ($r = -.07$). The reverse pattern which will be seen for current occupation does persist when the adjusted male data are used ($r = .23$).

References

ARMSTRONG, H., and P. ARMSTRONG
  1975   "Women in the Canadian Labour Force, 1941-71." *Canadian Review of Sociology and Anthropology*, 12 (Nov.):370-84.
ATWOOD, MARGARET
  1969   *The Edible Woman*. Toronto: McClelland and Stewart.
BLISHEN, B.R., and W.K. CARROLL
  1978   "Sex Differences in a Socioeconomic Index for Occupations in Canada." *Canadian Review of Sociology and Anthropology*, 15 (August):352-71.
CHASE, IVAN
  1975   "A Comparison of Men's and Women's Intergenerational Mobility in the United States." *American Sociological Review*, 40 (Aug.):483-505.
COSER, R., and G. ROKOFF
  1971   "Women in the Occupational World: Social Disruption and Conflict." *Social Problems*, 18 (Spring):535-54.
DEJONG, P.Y., M.J. BRAWER, and S.S. ROBIN
  1971   "Patterns of Female Intergenerational Occupational Mobility: A Comparison with Male Patterns of Intergenerational Occupational Mobility." *American Sociological Review*, 36 (Dec.):1,033-42.

EPSTEIN, CYNTHIA F.
1970 "Encountering the Male Establishment: Sex-Status Limits on Women's Careers in the Professions." *American Journal of Sociology*, 75 (May):965-82.

FEATHERMAN, D.L. and R.M. HAUSER
1976 "Sexual Inequalities and Socioeconomic Achievement in the U.S., 1962-1973." *American Sociological Review*, 41 (June):462-53.

FELDMAN, S.D.
1973 "Impediment or Stimulant? Marital Status and Graduate Education." *American Journal of Sociology*, 78 (Jan.):982-94.

FERBER, M., and J. LOEH
1973 "Performance, Rewards and Perceptions of Sex Discrimination Among Male and Female Faculty." *American Journal of Sociology*, 78 (Jan.):995-1,002.

FERRIS, A.L.
1971 *Indicators of Trends in the Status of American Women*. New York: Russell Sage Foundation.

FREEMAN, M.F. and J. TUKEY
1950 "Transformations Related to the Angular and Square Root." *Annals of Mathematical Statistics*, 21:607-11.

FUCHS, V.R.
1975 "A Note on Sex Segregation in Professional Occupations." *Explorations in Economic Research*, 2:105-11.

GOODMAN, L.
1972 "A General Model for the Analysis of Surveys." *American Journal of Sociology*, 77 (May):1,035-86.

GROSS, E.
1972 "Plus ça change? The Sexual Structure of Occupations Over Time." Pp. 339-49 in R. Pavalka, ed. *Sociological Perspectives on Occupations*. Illinois: F.E. Peacock Publishers.

GUPPY, L.N. and J. SILTANEN
1977 "A Comparison of the Allocation of Male and Female Occupational Prestige." *Canadian Review of Sociology and Anthropology*, 14 (Aug.):320-30.

HAUG, M.
1973 "Social Class Measurement and Women's Occupational Roles." *Social Forces*, 52 (Sept.):86-98.

HAUSER, R., J. KOFFEL, M. TRAVIS and P. DICKINSON
1975 "Temporal Change in Occupational Mobility: Evidence for Men in the United States." *American Sociological Review*, 40 (June):279-97.

HAVENS, E.M.
1973 "Women, Work and Wedlock: A Note on Female Marital Patterns in the United States." *American Journal of Sociology*, 78 (Jan.):975-81.

HENSHEL, ANNE-MARIE
1973 *Sex Structure*. Don Mills: Longman Canada.

HOPE, K., and JOHN GOLDTHORPE
1974 *The Social Grading of Occupations*. Oxford: Clarendon Press.

HUGHES, H.M.
1973 "Maid of All Work or Departmental Sister-in-Law? The Faculty Wife Employed on Campus." *American Journal of Sociology*, 78 (Jan.):767-72.

MARSDEN, L.E., E.B. HARVEY and I. CHARNER
1975 "Female Graduates: Their Occupational Mobility and Attainments." *Canadian Review of Sociology and Anthropology*, 12 (Nov.):385-405.

MARTIN, W. and D. POSTON
1972 "The Occupational Composition of White Females: Sexism, Racism and Occupational Differentiation." *Social Forces*, 50 (March):349-55.

MEISSNER, M., E. HUMPHREYS, S. MEIS, and W. SCHEU
1975 "No Exit for Wives: Sexual Division of Labour and the Cumulation of Household Demands." *Canadian Review of Sociology and Anthropology*, 12 (Nov.):421-39.

PINEO, P.C., J. PORTER and H.A. McROBERTS
1977 "The 1971 Census and the Socioeconomic Classification of Occupations." *Canadian Review of Sociology and Anthropology*, 14(1):91-102.

RESKIN, BARBARA
1976 "Sex Differences in Status Attainment in Science: The Case of the Postdoctoral Fellow." *American Sociological Review*, 41 (Aug.):597-612.

SILTANEN, J.L.
1976 "Sex Segregation in the Canadian Occupational Structure." Master's thesis, University of Waterloo.

SILVER, C.B.
1973 "Salon, Foyer, Bureau: Women and the Professions in France." *American Journal of Sociology*, 78 (Jan.):836-51.

SMITH, DOROTHY E.
1975 "Ideological Structures and How Women are Excluded." *Canadian Review of Sociology and Anthropology*, 12 (Nov.):353-69.

SUTER, L., and H. MILLER
1973 "Income Differences between Men and Career Women." *American Journal of Sociology*, 78 (Jan.):962-74.

TREIMAN, D.J., and K. TERRELL
1975 "Sex and the Process of Status Attainment: A Comparison of Working Women and Men." *American Sociological Review*, 40 (April):174-200.

TYREE, A. and J. TREAS
1974 "The Occupational and Marital Mobility of Women." *American Sociological Review*, 39 (June):293-302.

WILLIAMS, G.
1975 "A Research Note on Trends in Occupational Differentiation by Sex." *Social Problems*, 22 (April):543-47.

WOMEN'S BUREAU
1975 *Women in the Labour Force — Facts and Figures*. Ottawa: Information Canada.

APPENDIX 8:1 — Freeman-Tukey Deviates for Table 8-1

First

Current	Professionals	High Management	Semi-Professionals	Technicians	Mid-Level Management	Supervisors	Foremen	Skilled Clerical-Sales	Skilled Crafts-Trades	Farmers	Semi-Skilled Clerical-Sales	Semi-Skilled Crafts-Trades	Unskilled Clerical-Sales	Unskilled Labourers	Farm Labourers
Professionals	-3.11	-1.15	2.94	-0.79	0.46	3.35	1.10	5.50	2.57	0.37	-1.22	0.85	1.09	0.83	-0.33
High Management	-1.07	-2.44	-0.63	1.32	1.00	-1.19	0.36	2.06	0.69	0.00	3.02	-0.06	-1.35	1.21	0.25
Semi-Professionals	1.72	-2.05	-3.86	0.85	-2.93	1.40	1.05	6.47	-0.34	0.00	-0.13	4.30	2.84	0.94	-1.27
Technicians	1.52	0.00	0.33	-3.51	0.65	-1.70	0.82	2.27	0.88	0.56	2.35	1.25	1.04	0.47	1.31
Mid-Level Management	1.80	1.18	1.79	0.90	-2.84	1.82	0.59	0.22	1.76	0.39	-1.43	0.71	-0.14	0.29	0.96
Supervisors	2.14	1.07	1.62	-0.81	0.20	-2.52	1.49	0.43	-2.32	0.93	0.80	-1.31	1.26	-0.98	-0.56
Foremen	0.84	0.00	-0.40	1.29	0.39	0.66	-4.27	3.87	2.52	0.35	3.13	-1.64	-0.84	-0.13	-0.18
Skilled Clerical-Sales	3.15	3.89	1.33	5.59	5.64	0.43	1.41	-5.43	3.42	1.65	-1.65	2.58	4.84	5.48	4.45
Skilled Crafts-Trades	1.12	0.34	3.62	1.95	0.60	1.41	-0.30	3.08	-4.64	-1.18	0.20	1.54	-0.01	0.70	1.47
Farmers	1.85	0.00	-0.48	0.41	0.51	0.95	0.50	0.10	0.07	-0.62	-0.54	1.96	-0.50	1.34	-1.32
Semi-Skilled Clerical-Sales	0.30	3.61	3.96	-0.73	0.81	1.18	1.74	-2.13	-1.58	2.15	-1.21	2.07	-1.93	2.40	2.29
Semi-Skilled Crafts-Trades	-0.71	1.09	3.52	0.98	0.24	1.05	2.09	7.09	2.53	0.08	2.48	-4.50	-1.73	0.24	-0.18
Unskilled Clerical-Sales	1.62	0.00	-1.88	0.44	0.04	-1.21	-0.89	0.17	2.06	1.33	3.02	-1.03	-2.29	-0.49	-0.75
Unskilled Labourers	3.07	0.00	1.55	3.10	1.46	1.73	-0.25	4.26	1.50	-1.37	-0.33	3.14	-0.36	-4.79	0.04
Farm Labourers	-2.00	0.00	2.56	0.37	0.00	1.82	0.00	1.78	0.49	1.21	-2.57	1.26	-0.51	1.23	-1.41

APPENDIX 8:2 — First Occupation by Father's Occupation, for Females and Adjusted Males

Each cell shows the count (first line) and percentage (second line).

First Occ.	Professionals	High Management	Semi-Professionals	Technicians	Mid-Level Management	Supervisors	Foremen	Skilled Clerical-Sales	Skilled Crafts-Trades	Farmers	Semi-Skilled Clerical-Sales	Semi-Skilled Crafts-Trades	Unskilled Clerical-Sales	Unskilled Labourers	Farm Labourers	N
Professionals	98 / 88.1	26 / 29.3	25 / 17.3	4 / 3.4	34 / 34.3	67 / 57.3	40 / 46.7	44 / 49.3	88 / 106.2	202 / 151.1	35 / 33.9	46 / 70.4	20 / 18.7	58 / 75.7	9 / 14.3	796
High Management	0 / 2.0	3 / 2.0	0 / 0.0	1 / 0.0	0 / 1.1	2 / 2.1	2 / 2.4	2 / 0.0	2 / 2.0	11 / 8.3	1 / 2.1	0 / 1.0	0 / 0.5	1 / 0.5	0 / 0.0	25
Semi-Professionals	84 / 62.4	22 / 19.3	35 / 48.7	5 / 1.9	38 / 35.5	81 / 52.2	70 / 59.5	48 / 48.7	126 / 222.2	239 / 184.6	62 / 54.7	89 / 120.4	27 / 22.6	75 / 78.2	21 / 11.0	1,022
Technicians	21 / 9.8	4 / 6.6	3 / 0.0	2 / 4.3	12 / 6.2	17 / 8.7	6 / 6.5	11 / 3.5	15 / 35.0	27 / 38.5	13 / 8.9	16 / 14.2	10 / 3.2	23 / 26.4	1 / 8.1	180
Mid-Level Management	5 / 1.7	0 / 0.0	3 / 0.8	0 / 0.3	2 / 2.4	5 / 2.3	4 / 2.5	2 / 0.8	2 / 5.1	5 / 7.6	5 / 1.3	0 / 1.1	0 / 1.1	2 / 4.1	0 / 1.3	34
Supervisors	4 / 4.1	5 / 1.0	3 / 0.9	0 / 0.6	6 / 5.8	16 / 19.9	7 / 6.0	7 / 6.1	26 / 30.1	26 / 42.6	9 / 8.8	20 / 6.6	1 / 0.7	8 / 0.7	6 / 1.3	146
Foremen	0 / 1.3	0 / 0.3	3 / 0.2	0 / 0.0	4 / 1.0	2 / 1.2	2 / 3.7	0 / 0.2	6 / 5.4	1 / 11.0	2 / 1.2	7 / 3.2	0 / 0.5	3 / 1.5	1 / 1.3	32
Skilled Clerical-Sales	95 / 87.6	40 / 17.2	45 / 33.3	16 / 15.8	84 / 70.6	169 / 177.6	147 / 197.2	136 / 140.4	437 / 327.1	247 / 338.3	141 / 140.9	221 / 241.0	63 / 65.5	237 / 210.9	32 / 47.8	2,111
Skilled Crafts-Trades	3 / 1.9	0 / 0.7	0 / 1.7	0 / 1.0	3 / 2.5	9 / 4.4	16 / 12.0	2 / 4.1	54 / 43.9	29 / 51.9	10 / 8.2	27 / 34.0	7 / 2.9	35 / 26.4	9 / 8.3	204
Farmers	0 / 0.1	0 / 0.0	0 / 0.1	0 / 0.0	0 / 0.1	2 / 0.0	2 / 0.1	0 / 0.1	0 / 0.4	22 / 22.8	0 / 0.1	0 / 0.1	0 / 0.0	0 / 0.5	0 / 1.6	26

Father's Occupation

APPENDIX 8:2 — (Continued)

First Occupation	Professionals	High Management	Semi-Professionals	Technicians	Mid-level Management	Supervisors	Foremen	Skilled Clerical-Sales	Skilled Crafts-Trades	Farmers	Semi-Skilled Clerical-Sales	Semi-Skilled Crafts-Trades	Unskilled Clerical-Sales	Unskilled Labourers	Farm Labourers	N
Semi-Skilled Clerical-Sales	105.0	18	41	14	80	145	203	115	621	552	210	449	91	430	84	3,158
	105.1	42.9	41.7	14.5	111.0	197.5	167.9	113.5	603.9	532.5	225.1	391.8	98.8	430.0	81.8	
Semi-Skilled Crafts-Trades	8	7	3	0	20	43	52	27	208	259	46	192	16	187	59	1,128
	15.1	4.2	4.8	3.4	15.1	16.1	44.3	14.7	150.6	340.4	27.0	252.3	15.9	156.0	68.0	
Unskilled Clerical-Sales	17	5	13	9	32	43	64	34	181	323	61	169	43	168	71	1,232
	51.5	5.6	21.7	6.2	27.2	68.4	71.8	47.7	246.9	143.3	91.7	143.6	55.9	211.7	38.9	
Unskilled Labourers	2	0	1	3	12	25	40	13	142	184	31	158	21	188	36	855
	9.4	2.2	5.3	1.5	15.5	18.5	32.3	10.1	128.7	253.6	22.4	116.6	13.6	182.1	43.0	
Farm Labourers	1	0	1	0	2	1	1	0	4	110	0	5	1	8	18	155
	0.8	0.1	0.5	0.0	0.7	0.8	0.9	0.7	45	111.4	1.0	3.6	1.1	7.3	21.6	
N	441	133	177	53	329	627	654	440	1,913	2,238	627	1,400	301	1,424	347	

APPENDIX 8:3 — Current Occupation by Father's Occupation, for Females and Adjusted Males

Current Occupation		Professionals	High Management	Semi-Professionals	Technicians	Mid-Level Management	Supervisors	Foremen	Skilled Clerical-Sales	Skilled Crafts-Trades	Farmers	Semi-Skilled Clerical-Sales	Semi-Skilled Crafts-Trades	Unskilled Clerical-Sales	Unskilled Labourers	Farm Labourers	N
Professionals		74	26	18	4	19	48	31	41	66	122	25	38	19	38	10	579
		69.2	24.4	15.2	2.0	33.0	52.8	33.0	31.1	80.5	76.9	33.1	55.9	18.3	47.0	6.7	
High Management		3	3	0	0	2	2	2	1	14	7	2	2	1	2	0	41
		3.1	3.4	1.1	0.3	1.8	3.8	3.2	3.5	6.1	4.6	2.3	2.7	1.1	3.5	0.5	
Semi-Professionals		66	19	32	4	29	52	51	34	102	151	46	62	17	64	9	739
		70.8	12.5	38.2	4.2	39.6	36.2	35.4	56.2	135.1	88.3	34.8	79.3	31.4	72.4	4.6	
Technicians		17	0	4	0	5	13	3	8	13	17	14	15	3	20	2	128
		5.7	1.8	1.5	7.0	5.7	3.8	4.7	5.7	26.6	29.3	6.0	13.9	1.3	12.8	2.4	
Mid-Level Management		11	2	4	1	4	8	4	9	12	20	10	10	3	7	3	106
		7.8	2.6	1.6	0.9	6.7	7.5	6.9	3.6	18.8	16.2	6.9	9.9	2.0	13.1	1.6	
Supervisors		13	3	7	0	12	31	24	15	96	69	35	48	6	56	15	431
		14.6	5.3	4.8	1.9	12.5	45.8	24.6	17.6	74.3	75.4	35.1	53.5	13.1	47.3	5.2	
Foremen		2	0	2	11	3	2	0	2	2	8	3	7	0	4	1	35
		0.7	0.2	0.2	0.0	0.3	1.5	3.3	0.8	7.2	9.7	1.3	4.3	0.4	4.2	0.9	
Skilled Clerical-Sales		65	23	27	2	60	99	98	89	280	186	101	163	50	197	25	1,476
		71.6	14.5	25.9	7.7	37.9	112.9	118.3	98.4	278.1	234.7	104.7	141.3	29.0	175.6	25.6	
Skilled Crafts-Trades		0	0	0	9	9	7	8	4	29	16	6	22	2	16	3	124
		2.0	0.5	1.0	0.6	2.5	3.3	6.5	2.5	27.5	31.6	4.4	18.0	2.3	16.1	5.2	
Farmers		0	0	0	10	0	1	1	1	2	17	1	0	0	0	2	25
		0.1	0.1	0.1	0.0	0.2	0.2	0.3	0.1	0.4	21.3	0.1	0.4	0.1	0.4	1.2	

Father's Occupation

APPENDIX 8:3 — (Continued)

| | | Father's Occupation | | | | | | | | | | | | | | | |
Current Occupation		Professionals	High Management	Semi-Professionals	Technicians	Mid-level Management	Supervisors	Foremen	Skilled Clerical-Sales	Skilled Crafts-Trades	Farmers	Semi-Skilled Clerical-Sales	Semi-Skilled Crafts-Trades	Unskilled Clerical-Sales	Unskilled Labourers	Farm Labourers	N
Semi-Skilled Clerical-Sales		47	9	27	0	45	87	102	69	371	285	116	245	47	233	51	1,741
		26.4	18.0	25.1	6.9	48.2	92.3	85.1	60.9	296.2	336.4	122.9	244.4	54.5	260.5	63.2	
Semi-Skilled Crafts-Trades		11	2	1	4	11	29	31	13	99	207	33	112	18	86	30	683
		8.0	0.6	4.0	0.5	9.8	13.2	29.2	9.4	96.0	211.5	23.1	127.4	10.4	101.4	38.4	
Unskilled Clerical-Sales		14	3	7	4	19	19	28	30	98	119	23	77	26	91	19	577
		38.1	5.2	6.4	4.7	17.2	27.2	38.8	22.3	120.3	93.5	47.5	50.8	26.3	60.7	18.0	
Unskilled Labourers		2	0	2	0	6	13	19	8	60	155	20	73	11	87	35	495
		3.8	1.9	3.1	1.4	8.4	11.4	14.7	9.9	77.8	153.7	15.5	68.1	8.5	88.0	28.8	
Farm Labourers		0	0	0	0	1	0	3	0	4	42	0	2	1	5	3	60
		0.3	0.0	0.8	0.0	0.3	0.3	0.8	0.0	3.2	36.0	0.5	5.0	1.1	3.1	8.5	
N		322	91	129	38	224	412	405	322	1,248	1,419	438	875	200	906	211	

CHAPTER 9

Language and Mobility: A Comparison of Three Groups

HUGH A. McROBERTS

In the previous two chapters Boyd and Goyder have examined the differences between men and women with respect to the process of status attainment and occupational mobility. In this chapter we shall focus on the division of Canadian society by language. While, as later chapters will show, there are other important divisions within Canadian society, the division along the lines of language, in particular French and English, is one which is fundamental to our very make-up as a nation. Indeed, as a nation in which two languages are officially recognized, Canada, while not unique, is a rarity amongst nations. Hence, the way in which language bears on the processes of mobility and status attainment is of more than passing interest.

Viewed from an historical perspective the basic structure of the relationship between the French and English in Canada since 1759 has been one of anglophone domination and francophone subordination in both political and economic terms. This has been especially the case within the province of Quebec. One has only to turn to the work of authors such as Hughes (1943), and Jamieson (1935) to be given a very clear picture of the structure of the Quebec labour force with respect to language in the prewar period. The francophones were disproportionately concentrated in farming and the lower levels of the blue-collar labour force. On the other hand, the anglophones were strongly over-represented in the professional and managerial positions and in the upper levels of the blue-collar occupations. In a very general way this description continues to be an accurate one; however, the situation is a changing one.

335

Beginning in the early 1950s Quebec began a period of relatively rapid modernization which was reflected not only in changes in the occupational and industrial structures of the province, but in the political and ideological structures as well. Francophones began to examine and to question the nature of social and economic institutions in Quebec and began to take the steps necessary to ensure a more equal access on their part to these institutions. The result of this increased awareness and activism on the part of francophone Canadians has been the so-called Quiet Revolution in Quebec, which has had as its consequence a series of inquiries (the Parent Commission, and the Royal Commission on Bilingualism and Biculturalism are two important examples), whose recommendations have resulted in both real changes in the structure of Quebec and Canadian societies, and perhaps as importantly in the way in which francophones and anglophones perceive each other. These changes have made each group more aware of their position vis à vis the other with the result that the relative socioeconomic position of francophones and anglophones has taken on considerable political and rhetorical importance in recent years.

When we turn to the available data to examine the impact of these changes on stratification in Quebec, we find that the picture which emerges is less than clear. For example, Porter presents a tabulation of occupation by ethnicity for the province of Quebec based on data from the 1931, 1951, and 1961 censuses. These data show that within this time period there has been relatively little change in the occupational distributions of the French relative to the English in Quebec. There was as expected a substantial shift overall from agricultural to non-agricultural employment which had a greater impact on the French than on the English. On the other hand, the over-representation of the English in the professional and financial occupations increased by two percentage points in the same period (Porter, 1965:94, Table 3). Regrettably, due to the very substantial changes which Statistics Canada made in the nature of its occupational classification scheme for the 1971 census, it is not possible to extend Porter's table.

By way of contrast when we turn to the two studies of occupational mobility within the province of Quebec (deJocas and Rocher, 1957; Dofny and Garon-Audy, 1969) a slightly different picture begins to emerge. Both studies examine the relative mobility of French and English based on a sample of sons who were born and married within Quebec. They are of particular value because the second study was designed explicitly as a replication of the first based on a ten-year separation in the samples. As a consequence, the authors of the second study were able to present some limited evidence on trends. In the decade (1954-1964) which separates the two samples, there is a drop in the degree of occupational differentiation based on ethnicity. It is still the case that the English are at an advantage with respect to the French, but the trend is towards a lessening of that advantage, especially with respect to the professional and managerial occupational category (1969:288, Table 11). In their analysis of mobility differences their data show a trend towards convergence between the amount of mobility experienced by the two ethnic groups. In the 1954 sample 64 per cent of the French were observed to be mobile compared with 70 per cent of the English. By 1964 the data show that the percentage of the French who were mobile had risen to 75, whereas the corresponding value for the English had declined to 66 per cent (1969:300, Table 22). They go on, however, to argue that this convergence is due primarily to the structural mobility in the marginals of the table where the degree of "minimum structural mobility" as measured by the index of dissimilarity between the father-son marginals of the table, increases by a much greater amount over the decade for the French than for the English, and that the consequence of this is that there has been less "pure mobility" for the French than for the English (1969:300-301). Apart from the fact that their analytic procedures (Rogoff ratios and percentages) do not allow for the separation of marginal and exchange effects, their argument is also flawed unless they are prepared to argue that the observed changes in the relative distribution of occupations by language in Quebec are of such an impermanent nature that they do not in themselves amount to a change in the opportunity structure in Quebec.

Finally, there is the paper by Cuneo and Curtis (1975) in which status attainment models are compared for very small samples of francophone and anglophone men and women in Montreal and Toronto respectively. Their analysis is based wholly on the use of standardized coefficients, which makes comparisons across populations with differing variances risky. However, their data seem to indicate that while francophones are more closely tied to their origins than is the case for anglophones, at the same time they appear to derive a higher rate of return from their achievements than is the case for their anglophone counterparts (1975:15-17). It should be noted that the differences are not large and given the small samples upon which they are based it is difficult to place a great reliance upon these findings.

These analyses then represent the state of our knowledge about the place of francophones with respect to anglophones in the Canadian stratification system at the time when we began the analyses of the data reported in this volume. The only point on which the data seem to be in clear agreement is that, in the occupational division of labour francophones continue to be over-represented in the less well-paid and less desirable occupations and that anglophones are over-represented in the better paid and more desirable occupations. As to whether the process of mobility or status attainment is operating to exacerbate or ameliorate these differences, the data, due both to the samples and methodologies employed, are less than clear.

In earlier work on the Canadian Mobility Study data we carried out an extensive analysis of the differences with respect to mobility and status attainment between francophones within the province of Quebec and anglophones throughout Canada (McRoberts, 1975: Chapter 6; McRoberts *et al.*, 1976). When we compared these two groups with respect to their patterns of occupational mobility we found that, when we controlled (using log-linear models) for the differences in the marginal distributions between the two groups, there were no significant differences between them with respect to the overall patterns of father-son association, the degree of exchange mobility, or the degree of inheritance. From this we concluded that the two groups shared a common pattern of exchange mobility, and that the differences which we find between the two when we look at observed mobility are wholly attributable to the differences between them with respect to the marginal distributions of the tables. These distributions reflected, of course, the expected patterns of francophone advantage and anglophone dis-advantage (1975:174-77; 1976:66-67). In addition, the data were broken out into cohorts and the patterns of mobility from father's occupation to son's first occupation were analysed to see if any evidence of trends in the differences between anglophones and francophones could be found. The results of this analysis tended to be consistent with those reported by Dofny and Garon-Audy (1969). That is we found that, while in the oldest cohort there was a substantial difference between the two groups with respect to exchange mobility (with the francophones being more tied to their origins than the anglophones), as we looked at successively younger cohorts the patterns of exchange mobility became more similar and, indeed, for the youngest cohort no significant difference between the two groups could be found (1976:66).

A similar analysis was carried out on these groups employing the status attainment model. The results of these analyses did throw light on some differences between the francophones and the anglophones. In particular, the models showed that francophones derive much greater benefit from their father's educational attainment in terms of their own educational attainment than anglophones, and that their labour force entry status (first job) is a more important determinant of their current status than is the case for anglophones (1976:73). These results are not greatly at variance with those presented by Cuneo and Curtis (1975), with the exception of the finding on the first job to current job relationship where we find a stronger effect for francophones and they find a slightly weaker effect for francophones vis-à-vis anglophones. When separate models were estimated for cohorts, the results were very much consistent with the matrix analysis — there were substantial differences between francophones and anglophones in the oldest cohort, and for the youngest the models were virtually identical (1976:76-77).

Based on these analyses, we concluded that while francophones continued to be at a disadvantage relative to anglophones in terms of their location in the occupational structure, the trend was towards both a lessening of that disadvantage, and towards a situation in which both groups shared similar processes of stratification. In other words, we concluded that while language continues to be a significant factor in understanding stratification in Canadian society, its importance for this purpose is very much on the wane (McRoberts, 1975:218-22; McRoberts et al., 1976:78-79).

Following the publication of these results a number of comments have been made, primarily with reference to the selection of the populations used for the comparison. In our paper we chose to compare francophones in the province of Quebec with anglophones throughout Canada. This was done because it was (and still is) our belief that this is the most appropriate comparison, in the sense that if one must choose a reference group against which to compare the mobility of francophones, then the rest of the Canadian population constitutes the most reasonable group for that purpose. The patterns of mobility and status attainment in this latter group are then viewed as a set of norms or benchmarks against which the degree of disadvantage of francophones could be measured. However, a number of critics have argued that the paper ought to have included a comparison of francophones in Quebec with anglophones in Quebec as a separate population. In a sense these critics are correct. While a comparison of the French and English within Quebec is not appropriate when the concern is with the place of francophone Canadians in the overall Canadian stratification system, the comparison is nonetheless important if we wish to understand how that system is perceived. This is, we think, particularly so if we wish to understand one of the sources of francophone discontent. When the francophone Canadian considers the stratification structure and his place in it vis-à-vis the anglophones, he does not see the English throughout Canada, with whom he is rapidly catching up. Rather he sees those who inhabit his more immediate milieu — the Quebec English.

But, as we shall see, these are a very odd and privileged group not only in Quebec but in the broader society as well, and when the francophone compares his lot and that of his fellow francophones to this group it is not surprising that his sense of relative deprivation is heightened. As Porter has remarked, "Class becomes real as people experience it" (1965:12). For this reason, then, if no other, an analysis which compares the mobility of francophones and anglophones within the context of Quebec is needed.

In this chapter we shall extend our earlier work by focusing on an analysis of occupational mobility in which three populations will be compared: francophones in Quebec, anglophones in Quebec, and to provide a reference for both, anglophones throughout the rest of Canada. The major thrust of the analysis will be on the comparison of the first two, however. Due to the very small number of cases in our sample of the second population, we shall not attempt a trend analysis, and shall focus entirely on comparisons based on the basic father-to-son mobility table.

In making these comparisons, we shall be concerned with several different aspects of mobility. The first is the simple father-son association. This is the measure of gross or experienced mobility and derives from a direct examination of the mobility matrix. However, in comparing two societies with respect to mobility, the gross mobility can be a misleading basis for the comparison. This is especially so when the degree to which each social structure in the comparison is open to opportunity is in question. It then becomes necessary to decompose the gross mobility into two components: structural mobility and exchange mobility.

Structural mobility is conceived of as that component of mobility that arises purely from the transformation of the occupational structure from the father's generation to the son's generation. For example, if the process of industrial development in a society results in a decline from the father's generation to the son's generation of the percentage of persons working in blue-collar occupations and in an increase in the percentage working in white-collar occupations, then a certain proportion of the sons in that society *must* be observed as mobile regardless of any changes in the underlying opportunity structure of the society.

Exchange or circulation mobility is the mobility which is due to the social structure being open to talent. That is to say, it is throught of as the pattern of upward and downward movement, and stability which arises from the process of the inter-generational transmission of advantages and disadvantages from father to son. In the fully open society, exchange mobility would produce a pattern of independence and a perfectly closed society would produce a pattern of perfect association between father's and son's occupations. When we compare two social structures and ask how open they are, it is their exchange mobility which we ought to compare (see Duncan, 1968, for an extended discussion of this).

Thus, in comparing two groups with respect to mobility, we now have the following situation:

Difference in Observed Mobility = Difference in Structural Mobility + Difference in exchange mobility.

However, in looking at exchange mobility across two groups, it is often the case that the degree of inheritance, which is a common feature of all mobility tables, is such that it masks all other differences. For this reason it is useful, in addition to comparing the total exchange mobility, to look separately at the inheritance cells — those in the diagonal where father's and son's occupation are the same — and at the mobility cells — those where father's and son's occupation are different.

Now in our comparison we have the following:

Difference in Observed Mobility = Difference in Structural Mobility + (Difference in exchange mobility, off diagonal + Difference in inheritance)

Two groups will only be said to have the same "mobility regime" when they do not differ with respect to their overall exchange mobility and with respect to the components of exchange mobility.

In comparing these three groups we shall be concerned with all of these aspects of mobility. In particular, though, the concern will be with differences in exchange mobility, as it is our indicator of the degree to which two groups share a common mobility regime and in turn of the extent to which they differ with respect to the degree of equality of opportunity available to their members.

To establish the linguistic groups of the respondents two questions were asked: one concerned mother tongue; the other was, "What is the language in which you feel most comfortable when talking?" The present analysis uses the second question because it is more likely to represent the respondents' current language affiliation. Those who gave a language other than English or French are omitted. These two major populations are further sub-divided according to their place of residence at the time of the survey, into: francophones in the province of Quebec (FQ); anglophones in the province of Quebec (EQ); and anglophones resident in the remainder of Canada (EC).

The occupational variables are based on the respondent's current

(1973) occupation, and on the respondent's father's occupation (or head of household if father was absent) at the time the respondent was 16 years of age. These were coded into the sixteen-category Pineo, Porter and McRoberts (1977) scale based on the 1971 census classification of occupations. However, the use of the scale in this form is impractical here. The basic father-son matrix involves 256 cells, and the EQ group has less than three hundred cases in it. As a result, it was decided to collapse the sixteen-fold classification into four broad groupings.

Table 9.1 shows how this collapsing was done. The first group represents the executive level of management, professional, semi-professional, and technical workers (PMT). What this group tends to have in common is a general requirement for some post-secondary training as a prerequisite for admission to these occupational roles. Indeed, for the age group which we are examining, it goes further; one could almost say that post-secondary training was a sufficient condition for admission to this group of occupations. The second group contains the broad range of white-collar workers from middle managers and supervisors down to the lowest levels of the routine clerical worker (WC). The third contains a similar range of blue-collar occupations (BC). With respect to variables such as income and status, both groups are relatively internally

TABLE 9:1

Groups:

1. Professional, Managerial, Technical (PMT)
     Categories: Self-employed professional
                          Employed professional
                          Senior managers
                          Semi-professionals
                          Technicians
2. White-collar (WC)
     Categories: Middle-managers
                          Supervisors
                          Skilled white-collar
                          Semi-skilled white-collar
                          Unskilled white-collar
3. Blue-collar (BC)
     Categories: Foremen
                          Skilled blue-collar
                          Semi-skilled blue-collar
                          Unskilled blue-collar
4. Farm (F)
     Categories: Farmer
                          Farm labourer

heterogeneous and overlap each other to a considerable degree. Nonetheless, they do typically represent quite distinct occupational worlds, and as such it is useful to keep them analytically distinct. The final group consists of farmers and farm labourers (F).

Francophones in Quebec versus Anglophones in the Rest of Canada

We shall begin with this comparison as it represents both the baseline comparison upon which the remainder of the analysis will be set, and it represents the point of overlap with our previous work. Table 9.2 presents a series of traditional summary measures of the father-son mobility matrix for each of the three populations of interest. Scanning

TABLE 9:2 — Some Summary Measures of Mobility for Three Populations

	Minimum[a] Mobility	Observed[b] Mobility	Circulation[c] Mobility	Expected[d] Mobility
Francophones in Quebec (FQ)	22.36	56.83	34.47	71.42
Anglophones not in Quebec (EC)	21.91	60.07	38.16	73.47
Anglophones in Quebec (EQ)	26.93	55.55	28.62	72.00

	Expected[e] Circulation	Mobility[f] Index	Pct Down	Index of[g] Association	G[h]
Francophones in Quebec (FQ)	49.06	70.27	7.8	1.51	.57
Anglophones not in Quebec (EC)	51.56	74.01	11.0	1.51	.48
Anglophones in Quebec (EQ)	45.07	63.51	12.6	1.59	.30

[a]Index of dissimilarity (Δ) for father's occupation and R's present (1973) occupation.
[b]Percentage of cases observed to be mobile
[c]$(b - a)$
[d]Percentage expected to be mobile under the assumption independence
[e]$(d - a)$
[f]$(c/e) \times 100$
[g]Glass total index of association = $\Sigma \hat{f_{ij}}/\Sigma f_{ij}$ for $i = j$ only
[h]Goodman-Kruskal Gamma

the first two lines of this table it is clear that what differences there are between the francophones in Quebec and anglophones throughout Canada are relatively small. In terms of structural mobility the amount as measured by the index of dissimilarity would appear to be virtually the same for the two groups. The anglophones appear to show slightly more circulation or exchange mobility than the francophones as can be seen in the third column. This in turn is reflected in the higher mobility index for anglophones (74.01 versus 70.27) and the lower value of gamma (.48 versus .57) vis-à-vis the francophone values. While these measures are useful in summarizing the events in single tables, in that they have a very direct relationship to what is going on in the table, their comparison across tables and particularly across tables with different marginal distributions can be misleading. However, using the models developed by Goodman (1972), and elaborated by Hauser *et al.*, (1975) it is possible to make quite exact comparisons between two or more mobility tables.

Table 9.3 presents the results of this comparison for nine models. Model 1 is the baseline and establishes the magnitude of the G^2 due to the mutual dependence or association (G^2_T) between father's occupation (P), respondent's occupation (S), and group (L, in this case FQ and EC). Model 2 introduces a parameter for the variation due to differences by group in origin (father's occupation). The null hypothesis is, of course, that all of the remaining possible parameters which are not included are zero (i.e., SL = PS = PSL = 0). The null is very clearly rejected, and it can be seen that the inclusion of this factor produces a trivial reduction in the G^2_T (99.33 per cent of G_T^2 remains unaccounted for). Model 3 adds in the parameter for the variation of respondent's occupation by group. The reduction in G_T^2 is again trivial, and this model suggests that the variation between the two groups is only in very small measure affected by differences between them in either origin or destination distributions. Model 4 adds in the term for the association between father's occupation and son's occupation, and has as its null hypothesis that this association is constant with respect to group. Statistically this hypothesis must be rejected. However, in substantive terms it is not clear that this is the best course. The model has an index of dissimilarity of 1.86, indicating that less than 2 per cent of the cases would be misallocated by the model, and that model accounts for all but 1.70 per cent of the total G_T^2. In sum, while the variation in the father-son association with respect to group is statistically significant, it is substantively trivial.[1] The acceptance of this model implies the conclusion that the two groups do not differ with respect to their overall pattern of exchange mobility.

The second set of models in Table 9.3 (models 5-8) test the same set of

TABLE 9:3 — Models for Comparison of FQ with EC

Independence Models

Parameters in the Model	G^2	df	p		$X^2{}_H/X^2{}_T$
1. P,S,L	1060.47	24	.000	17.81	100.00
2. S,PL	1595.75	21	.000	17.70	99.33
3. PL,SL	1575.05	18	.000	17.66	98.04
4. PL,SL,PS	27.28	9	.001	1.86	1.70

Main diagonal blocked

5. P,S,L	363.54	16	.000	12.97	100.00
6. S,PL	350.86	13	.000	12.97	96.51
7. PL,SL	333.07	10	.000	12.75	91.62
8. PL,SL,PS	12.75	1	.000	1.89	3.51
9. Constant Inheritance (4-8)	14.53	8	>.050	.03	—

Decomposition of Independence G^2

	G^2	df	p	%	
1. Due to PL	10.72	3	>.010	0.67	⎱ 1.96
2. Due to SL/PL	20.70	3	.000	1.29	⎰
3. Due to PS/SL,PL	1547.77	9	.000	96.35	
4. Due to PSL/PS,SL,PL	27.28	9	.000	1.70	
Total	1606.47	24	.000	100.00	

hypotheses but with the main diagonal blocked out. Here, only the patterns of mobility (i.e., for those not in the inheritance cells) are compared across the two populations. The pattern which we find is very much like that found when the overall pattern of association is examined. In particular, Model 8 suggests that there is no meaningful variation in the pattern of mobility between the two populations once marginal variations are taken into account. Finally, Model 9 asks whether or not there is any variation between the two populations with respect to the patterns of occupational inheritance. The conclusion is that there are none.

The results of these models are in agreement with those which are presented in the earlier paper when we stated, "This means that in terms of the association between father and son there is no significant difference between the French and English matrices when marginal differences reflecting structural changes are controlled for." (McRoberts, *et al.*, 1976). We went on to suggest that what differences there were between the two groups might be attributable to differences in the marginals, that is to structural mobility. However, an examination of the last panel of Table 9.3 does not, on the whole, support this conclusion. Here we look at the contribution which each of the factors in the model makes to accounting for the total variability in the three-way table. The association between father's occupation and language group accounts for less than 1 per cent of the total variation, and when we add in the association between respondent's occupation and language group it accounts for just over 1 per cent of the variation. In total, variation in the marginals by group accounts for less than 2 per cent (1.96 per cent) of the total variation, which implies that the differences are very small. The lion's share of the variation is due to the constant (with respect to group) association between fathers and sons, which picks up just over 96 per cent of all of the variation. Finally, the variation in the father-son association due to group picks up the remaining 1.7 per cent of the variation. In sum, the models fail to pick up any meaningful variability in either structural or exchange mobility between francophones and anglophones in Canada. Indeed, all possible sources of variability by language group account for less than 4 per cent of all of the variability in the table lending further support to the conclusion of no difference.

The conclusion with respect to no significant differences in structural mobility between the two groups is further confirmed when we return to the percentages. It will be recalled that in Table 9.2 a father-son delta of 22.36 was reported for francophones and a value of 21.91 was reported for anglophones. These values are virtually identical. In Table 9.4, the father's and son's occupational distributions are compared across the two groups. For the professional-managerial and technical group, the francophones are slightly under-represented in the fathers' generation and this under-representation increases by less than one percentage point in the son's. In the white-collar group there is virtually no difference or change. In the blue-collar group the francophone over-representation increases from father to son, but the change is again a small one. Finally, the proportion of francophones in farming declines relative to anglophones in farming from the father's generation to the son's. In short, while the distributions show francophones to be under-represented in the PMT group and over-represented in the blue-collar group, these differences are small.

The results of the analysis thus far show that there is very little difference in any aspect of stratification between the francophones in Quebec and the anglophones in the rest of Canada. We shall now turn to a comparison of francophones in Quebec with anglophones in Quebec where the results will be, not surprisingly, somewhat different.

TABLE 9:4 — Francophones in Quebec (FQ) and Anglophones in the Rest of Canada (EC), Occupational Distributions

Father's Occupation	FQ	EC	FQ - EC
PMT	5.7	7.8	− 2.1
WC	21.1	21.9	− 0.8
BC	43.2	39.8	+ 3.4
F	30.0	30.5	− 0.5
$\quad$ = 3.4			
R's Occupation	FQ	EC	FQ - EC
PMT	19.0	22.3	− 3.3
WC	29.4	29.3	+ 0.1
BC	44.0	38.7	+ 5.3
F	7.6	9.8	− 2.2
$\triangle$ = 5.5			

Comparison of Francophones and Anglophones in Quebec

In Table 9.2, we also have the summary measures of mobility for anglophones in Quebec. Comparing these (line 3) with those for francophones (line 1) it can be seen that overall this group of anglophones are rather more mobile than the francophones. This is shown by both the lower mobility index for anglophones (63.51 versus 70.27) and by the values of gamma (.30 for anglophones in Quebec and .57 for francophones). The most likely source of this difference can be found when we look at the minimum structural mobility measures and note that the anglophone measure is higher (26.93) than the francophone value (22.36), while the total amount of observed mobility is very much the same for both groups. Given this, we would expect to find that much of the difference between the two groups will lie in the differences between their origin and destination distributions.

This expectation is further strengthened when we look at tables 9.5 and 9.6. Table 9.5 compares the occupational distributions of fathers and sons by language. Francophones are substantially under-represented in the PMT groups with respect to origins and this under-representation is even more marked in the destination distribution. In the white-collar group the under-representation of francophones is again marked, but it remains constant across generations. In the blue-collar group the degree of francophone over-representation is

TABLE 9:5 — **Francophones in Quebec (FQ) and Anglophones in Quebec (EQ), Occupational Distributions**

Father's Occupation	FQ	EQ	FQ - EQ
PMT	5.7	14.2	− 8.5
WC	21.1	32.0	− 10.9
BC	43.2	41.2	+ 2.0
F	30.0	12.6	+ 17.4
= 19.4			
R's Occupation	*FQ*	*EQ*	*FQ - EQ*
PMT	19.0	32.9	− 13.9
WC	29.4	40.2	− 10.8
BC	44.0	25.1	+ 18.9
F	7.6	1.8	+ 5.8
$\triangle$ = 24.7			

small in father's generation, and grows to a substantial proportion in the son's. In farming the reverse occurs, with the over-representation of francophones declining across the generations. Overall when we look at these distributions two things emerge. First, it can be seen that the mobility process has tended to increase the under-representation of francophones in Quebec in the upper levels of the work force by comparison with anglophones in Quebec. Secondly, one cannot help but be struck by the degree to which the anglophones in Quebec are an elite group in occupational terms. Nearly three-quarters of them hold positions at the white-collar or professional level and almost one-third are in the professional, managerial and technical group. It might also be noted that they are a very well-to-do group with respect to anglophones

TABLE 9:6 — **Occupation by Language for Quebec**

	English	French	Total
PMT	22.5	77.5	100.0
WC	18.7	81.3	100.0
BC	8.7	91.3	100.0
F	3.8	96.2	100.0
Total	14.3	85.7	100.0
N = 1968*			

*N's may fail to balance +1 case due to the way in which the SPSS Xerox Version 7.0 deals with the truncation of the weighted floating point counts to integers. The percentages are correct.

in the rest of Canada, as a comparison of the distributions in Table 9.5 with those in Table 9.4 will bear out.

However, it must also be noted that, while the anglophones in Quebec are a very privileged group, they are also a very small part of the Quebec labour force. Francophones make up over 85 per cent of the work force in Quebec (Table 9.6) and while they are clearly under-represented in the PMT and white-collar occupational groups, at the same time anglophones cannot be said to dominate at any level. Even in the PMT grouping, francophones make up over three-quarters of the membership.

We shall now turn to an examination of the log-linear models of mobility in order to look more closely at the patterns of structural and exchange mobility for these two groups. The models employed are the same as those which we used earlier in the comparison of francophones with anglophones throughout Canada, only in this case, of course, the comparison is restricted to Quebec.

The models are presented in Table 9.7. Model 4 tests whether there is any difference between the two groups with respect to their overall

TABLE 9:7 — Models for Comparison of FQ with EQ

Independence Models Parameters in the model	G^2	df	p		X^2_{II}/X^2_T
1. P,S.L	656.14	24	.000	21.49	100.0
2. S,PL	592.09	21	.000	20.35	90.2
3. PL,SL	527.64	18	.000	18.23	80.4
4. PL,SL,PS	18.51	9	.029	1.74	2.8
Main diagonal blocked					
5. P,S,L	225.62	16	.000	18.14	100.0
6. S,PL	185.94	13	.000	17.02	82.4
7. PL,SL	142.54	10	.000	14.63	63.2
8. PL,SL,PS	2.92	1	.050	1.30	1.3
9. Constant inheritance (4-8)	15.59	8	.05	.44	—

Decomposition of Independence G^2	G^2	df	p	%
1. Due to PL	64.05	3	.000	9.76 ⎱ 19.58
2. Due to SL/PL	64.45	3	.000	9.82 ⎰
3. Due to PS/PL,SL	509.13	9	.000	77.59
4. Due to PSL/PS,PL,SL	18.51	9	.029	2.82
Total	656.14	24	.000	100.00

pattern of exchange mobility or mobility net of marginal differences. The null hypothesis is that there are no such differences and a delta value of 1.74 clearly indicates that there are not. Model 8 asks if there are any differences between the two groups with respect to the patterns lying off of the main diagonal i.e., differences with respect to the patterns of movement for those who did not remain in their occupation of origin. A delta value of 1.30 for the no difference model (Model 8) clearly indicates that there are no important differences between the two groups. Finally, Model 9 tests for no difference with respect to pattern of inheritance (i.e., the degree to which sons end up in their father's occupational category) between the two groups. Again a delta of 0.44 indicates that no differences exist. In short, in every case the model of no difference between the groups with respect to mobility provides an excellent fit with the data. Substantively, these models confirm that when the differences by language in the occupational distributions are controlled for there is *no difference* in the mobility regimes of francophones and anglophones in Quebec. This is perhaps surprising when we recall the substantial differences between the two language groups with respect to such summary measures as the mobility index and gamma. However, when we also consider the differences between the two groups with respect to occupational distributions this may be less so.

The models which we have considered, it must be noted, look at the patterns of mobility *net* of any effects of structural mobility. Hence, the explanation of any differences will be found in this area. When we look at the decomposition of the $G^2{}_T$ into its components the picture is clarified. We can see that, unlike our findings in the earlier comparison, both the association between father's occupation and language, and the association between sons occupation and language, account for almost 10 per cent each of the total variation. The constant association between father's occupation and son's occupation accounts for only 78 per cent of the total variability in the table, by comparison with 96 per cent when we compared anglophones throughout Canada with francophones.

In summary, when we compare francophones and anglophones in Quebec we find:

1. The anglophones are clearly both with respect to origins and current occupation a very privileged group by comparison not only with francophones, but by comparison with anglophones in the rest of Canada as well.
2. The patterns of exchange mobility do not vary by group. That is, net of the effects of marginal differences the patterns of association, mobility, and inheritance are invariant regardless of language. They share a common mobility regime.

3. The differences in actual experienced mobility between the two groups is structural, or is attributable virtually entirely to the differences between them in occupational distributions.

These conclusions accord fairly closely with those reported by Dofny and Garon-Audy (1969: 299-301). However, the findings here are rather stronger in accent. The difference in distribution are sharper, the similarity in mobility regimes is more clearly seen, and finally the effects of the differences in structural mobility are clearer. The close fit between these findings and their's suggests that we are not just dealing with statistical artifacts.

Anglophones in Quebec

Of late the issue of anglophone migration into and out of Quebec has been much in the news, resulting in part from the different statuses assigned to "Quebec anglophones" and "other Canadian anglophones" under Bill 101. Given this, it is useful to look briefly at these two different segments of the anglophone population of Quebec. When broken out in this way the samples are too small to support a detailed mobility analysis. However, we can look at the marginals of their mobility tables and at some of the traditional summary measures of mobility to suggest what we might find were larger samples to become available at some future date.

Table 9.8 presents the father's and son's occupational distributions for

TABLE 9:8 — **Anglophones in Quebec, Born There (EQB) and not Born There (EQNB), Occupational Distributions**

Father's Occupation	EQB	EQNB	EQB - EQNB
PMT	11.4	22.2	− 10.8
WC	35.5	22.1	+ 13.4
BC	42.9	36.5	+ 6.4
F	10.2	19.2	− 9.0
$\triangle$ = 19.8			

R's Occupation	EQB	EQNB	EQB - EQNB
PMT	27.4	48.3	− 20.9
WC	43.7	30.6	− 13.1
BC	26.5	21.1	+ 5.4
F	2.5	0.0	+ 2.5
$\triangle$ = 21.0			

anglophones born in Quebec (EQB) and for those who were born elsewhere in Canada (EQNB). The former group comprises 74 per cent of the Quebec anglophone population and the latter 26 per cent. When we look at the occupational distributions of the two groups we can see that the difference between them is almost as great as the difference between francophones and anglophones in Quebec. The anglophones born outside of Quebec are very highly concentrated in white-collar and professional work. Indeed, most half of these fall into the PMT category (48.3 per cent). A comparison with Table 9.5 shows that this group is responsible for much of the over-representation of anglophones in the PMT category. Nonetheless the anglophones born in Quebec still remain in a distinctly privileged position with respect to francophones.

When we compare the two mobility tables in terms of summary measures (Table 9.9) we can see that they are very different here as well. Those anglophones born in Quebec have a pattern which is much like that of francophones (Table 9.2), with the difference that they continue to show rather more structural mobility. When we look at the anglophones born outside of Quebec we see a very different pattern. This is a very highly mobile group with both strong structural mobility and low inheritance. Indeed, the association between father's and son's occupation is not statistically significant for this group.

It is likely that this group of migrants are not in fact part of the

TABLE 9:9 — Some Summary Measures of Mobility for Anglophones in Quebec

	Minimum[a] Mobility	Observed Mobility	Circulation Mobility	Expected Circulation	
Anglophones in Que. and born there (EQB)	24.17	58.99	34.82	70.00	
Anglophones in Que. and not born there (EQNB)	34.61	68.29	33.68	74.49	
	Expected Circulation	Mobility Index	Pct Down	Index of Association	G
Anglophones in Que. and born there (EQB)	45.83	75.98	12.1	1.37	.38
Anglophones in Que. and not born there	39.88	84.45	13.9	1.24	.15[b]

[a]See notes to Table 9:3 for description of measures.
[b]$p > .1$

Quebec labour force, but belong rather to a broader regional or national labour force which has some of its more skilled members working in Quebec because that is where some of the head offices happen to be located. Properly then, if we were looking at mobility within Quebec we would want to remove this group from consideration. The main effect of this would likely be to reduce the degree to which structural mobility differentiates the mobility experiences of anglophone and francophone Quebeckers. However, if one compares the distributions in Table 9.5 and Table 9.8 one can see that this reduction would be a small one.

Conclusions

In our analysis we have shown that when the mobility of francophones in Quebec is compared with that of anglophones in the rest of Canada there are no significant differences between the two groups. When we look at the occupational distributions of the two groups there are slight differences between them in favour of the anglophones. However, based on our earlier analysis of cohorts there is every reason to believe that these differences will and indeed are eroding (see McRoberts *et al.*, 1976). Thus, to the extent to which occupational mobility can be viewed as a social indicator of the degree to which a society is open, or of the degree of equality of opportunity in a society, these results suggest that the degree of equality of opportunity enjoyed by francophones within the context of Canadian society does not differ in any meaningful way from that enjoyed by their anglophone compatroits throughout the rest of Canada.

However, as we suggested earlier, when the francophone looks around him to assess how well he is doing by comparison with "les anglais" he does not see all of Canada he sees the anglophones in his own province — Quebec. In doing so, a very different picture emerges. While the basic exchange mobility regime for both groups does not differ significantly, everything else does. The anglophones are a highly mobile group due to their greater structural mobility (particularly the growth of the PMT category of occupations). Secondly, and perhaps more importantly, they are highly over-represented in the cleaner, better paying occupations. Hence it is not surprising that the francophone feels a sense of relative deprivation, and a sense then, that if this is the anglophone condition, he and his fellow francophones have been badly done by as a result of Confederation. Were the experiences of anglophones in Quebec typical of those in the remainder of Canada, francophones would indeed have every right to feel aggrieved. It is precisely the point of this analysis to indicate that this is not the case. The occupational structure and mobility experiences of anglophones in Quebec are clearly not like those of anglophones in the rest of Canada. The anglophones in Quebec are a very privileged group with respect to either population.

This is not the only factor. A francophone looking at this anglophone minority in his province might well conclude that the over-representation of this group in the desirable occupations at the upper end of the occupational hierarchy represents a block to the upward mobility of francophones. In a hypothetical way and with the aid of a few assumptions we can test the extent to which this is true.

Let us assume that forty years ago all of the anglophones in Quebec had left. Secondly, let us assume that the combined occupational distribution of francophones' and anglophones' present jobs represent the provincial occupational demand over that period, which is then to be filled by mobility with francophones. If we now hold origins constant and hold the mobility regime constant, it is possible using a procedure developed by Demming (1964: 115-16), to estimate what the francophone mobility table would be.

Table 9.10 presents the outflow matrix for francophones in Quebec both as observed and as adjusted. In essence the adjusted values are those which would have occurred if there had been no anglophones in Quebec and holding origins and exchange mobility constant. The

TABLE 9.10 — Father's Occupation by R's Present (1973) Occupation: French in Quebec before and After Adjustment*

Father	PMT	WC	BC	F	T		
			R				
Professional, managerial and technical (PMT)	61.8	27.9	10.3	—	100.0	Δ	= 2.0
	(64.6)	(29.2)	(8.3)		(100.0)		
White collar (WC)	29.3	45.1	24.5	1.2	100.0	Δ	= 3.1
	(31.5)	(45.9)	(21.7)	(1.8)	(100.0)		
Blue collar (BC)	15.6	30.8	53.2	.5	100.0	Δ	= 4.0
	(17.6)	(32.7)	(49.3)	(.4)	(100.0)		
Farm (F)	8.7	16.6	50.9	23.9	100.0	Δ	= 3.6
	(10.3)	(18.6)	(49.7)	(20.2)	(100.0)		
Total	19.0	29.4	44.0	7.6	100.0		
	(21.0)	(30.9)	(41.3)	(6.8)	(100.0)		= 3.5

*Adjusted percentages in parentheses. N = 1684

differences, as can be seen, are small. Only 3.5 per cent of the francophones would have ended up in a different cell under these conditions. The majority of these would have been upwardly mobile. The group which would have been most affected is those with blue-collar origins, where 7 per cent would have ended up in a higher category. Overall the differences are very small and the inference that the anglophones in Quebec represent a significant block to the mobility of francophones is difficult to sustain.

In conclusion, this analysis supports the assertion made in our earlier paper that the pattern of linguistic stratification which we have had in Canada is breaking down. Further, through the examination of anglophones in Quebec as a separate population we have shown why the francophone in Quebec may well continue to think otherwise.

Note

1. In this paper while I will report the statistical results I will use a substantive criterion based on the index of dissimilarity to make decisions about the adequacy of fit of a model. If the model leaves less than 2 per cent of the cases improperly fit then it will be treated as having adequately fit the data, and the remaining unincluded parameters will be considered to be substantively trivial regardless of their inferential significance. This problem arises due to the small number of degrees of freedom and the relatively large samples involved. The power of G^2 is particularly sensitive to variations in sample size and as a result substantively equivalent models can differ in their statistical significance solely due to sample size. Thus, when we have as in this case, widely differing sample sizes (from under 300 to over 5,000) for our population, inferential criteria become an unreliable basis for substantive comparison. It should be noted that this strategy is the same as that employed in path analysis using larger samples where paths less than .1 are routinely deleted as substantively trivial. (see Land, 1969:34-35; Sewell, Haller and Ohlendorf, 1970:1,020, for a discussion of this in the case of path analysis).

References

BOYD, MONICA, and H.A. MCROBERTS
    1974 "Design of the 1973 Canadian National Mobility Study on Occupational and Educational Change in a Generation". A paper presented to the North Central Sociological Association Meeting, Windsor, Ontario, May 2-4, 1974. (Mimeo)

DEMING, W. EDWARDS
    1964 *Statistical Adjustment of Data*. New York: John Wiley

DOFNY, JACQUES, and M. GARON-AUDY
    1969 "Mobilites professionnelles au Quebec." *Sociologie et Societes*, 1: 277-301.

356 *HUGH A. McROBERTS*

DUNCAN, OTIS DUDLEY
  1968 "Social Stratification and Mobility: Problems in the Measurement of Trends." Pp. 675-719 in Eleanor Bernert Sheldon and Wilbert E. Moore, eds. *Indicators of Social Change.* New York: Russell Sage Foundation.
FEATHERMAN, D.L. and R.M. HAUSER
  1973 "Design for a Replicate Study of Social Mobility in the United States." Pp. 219-51 in Kenneth C. Land and S. Spilerman, eds. *Social Indicator Models.* New York: Russell Sage.
GOODMAN, LEO A.
  1972 "Some Multiplicative Models for the Analysis of Cross-classified Data." Pp. 649-96 in *Proceedings of the Sixth Berkeley Symposium on Mathematical Statistics and Probability.* Berkeley: University of California Press.
HAUSER, R.M., J.N. KOFFEL, H.P. TRAVIS, and P.K. DICKINSON
  1975a "Temporal Change in Occupational Mobility: Evidence for Men in the United States." *American Sociological Review,* 40: 279-97.
  1975b "Structural Changes in Occupational Mobility among Men in the United States." *American Sociological Review,* 40: 585-98.
LAND, K.C.
  1969 "Principles of Path Analysis." In Edgar Borgatta, ed. *Sociological Methodology.* San Francisco: Jossey-Bass.
McROBERTS, HUGH A., M. BOYD, J. PORTER, J. GOYDER, F.E. JONES, and P.C. PINEO
  1976 "Differences dans la mobilite professionnelle des francophones et des anglophones." *Sociologie et Societes,* (Fall).
PINEO, P.C., J. PORTER, H.A. McROBERTS
  1977 "The 1971 Census and Socioeconomic Classification of Occupations." *Canadian Review of Sociology and Anthropology,* 14:91-102.
SEWELL, WILLIAM H., ARCHIBALD HALLER, and GEORGE W. OHLENDORF
  1970 "The Educational and Early Occupational Status Attainment Process: Replication and Revision." *American Sociological Review* 35: 1,014-27.

CHAPTER 10

Ethnic Origin and Occupational Attainment

PETER C. PINEO AND JOHN PORTER

Canada has, throughout its history, been a society with large numbers of immigrants. We have indicated in Chapter 2 the great variety of places from where these immigrants have and continue to come, and in Chapter 11 we show something of the costs and benefits in terms of occupational mobility of being an immigrant in contemporary Canada. Here we explore what costs and benefits to the individual might arise from the ethnic pluralism which has been created by earlier generations of immigrants. As we have indicated in our review of Canadian social structure, Canada is a society in which ethnic origin or descent group membership is thought to be of some consequence for individuals. The social doctrine that ethnic groups should retain their cultural identity has not been limited to immigrants, for whom no doubt the ethnic community can provide support until they become more familiar with Canadian society. The Canadian-born also have been enjoined to retain their ethnic roots and so the celebrated mosaic is to be formed.

Two Ways of Measuring Ethnicity

Very little is known about whether second and earlier generation Canadians not of British or French origin feel deeply about their ethnic identity or whether they consider themselves dehyphenated Canadians. We suggested earlier that the widespread loss of the ethnic language shown by census data might be an indicator of the loosening of ethnic links. The question by which the Canadian census elicits ethnic origin, "To which ethnic or cultural group did you or your ancestor (on the male side) belong on coming to this continent," is, as we have indicated, of dubious sociological usefulness for tracing descent. The question is difficult to answer and it has been argued forcibly, not without justification, that responses to it are invalid (Ryder, 1955). We take the position, however, that from the point of view of the standards of contemporary survey research the census ethnic question has adequate reliability and validity. We base our position on the results of a series of special tabulations from the sample. The percentage distribution by ethnic origin for males in the sample is virtually identical to the 1971 census, suggesting the question is generally reliable. Cross-tabulations of ethnic origin by language and by birthplace or father's birthplace, where these are relevant considerations, suggest that the question has a level of validity roughly equivalent to other questions routinely used in survey research. Our analysis in this chapter is based on the census question.

To better understand how contemporary Canadians feel about their ethnic identity, we included in the questionnaire a second question: "To which ethnic or cultural group do you feel that you now belong?" We were endeavouring to determine to what extent the census question forced people to acknowledge an ethnicity which might, in fact, have little real importance to them. The second question emphasized the idea of belonging at present to the group. Also, and this is the more important element, unlike the census question, it allowed "Canadian" as a response.

To make the test persuasive we made two further changes. We increased the number of ethnicities offered — including Welsh, Danish, Swedish and others — in order to make the list of options other than "Canadian" broader than in the census question. And, secondly, while we asked people to check only one label, in the few cases (some 150 cases) where people did check more than one we examined the response and if it was something like checking both "Italian" and "Canadian" we coded it "Italian." In these two ways we hoped to load the dice against the response "Canadian" being preponderant. Unfortunately, space restrictions made it impossible to include as options all the possible hyphenated forms — such as French-Canadian or Ukrainian-Canadian. This ultimately limits the effectiveness of the test, of course. Since not all hyphenated forms could be included we decided to include none. French-Canadian and English-Canadian were not offered as options. Finally, it was not possible to arrange for an "other: specify" option. "Other" was allowed as an answer, and around 1,400 of the male and female respondents chose it (3.1 per cent). But they were not asked to give more detail since it was known that the results could not be coded.

Presented with this stimulus, then, the respondents were being tested to see if they would report once again the ethnicity given as their "origin" in the census question or whether they would choose the option "Canadian." The overwhelming majority chose "Canadian" — some 86 per cent. That is, insofar as the results of one question can be relied upon, the image of a Canada in which ethnic identity is of sufficient power to override national identity is now thoroughly out of date, if it was ever true.

A substantial number of those reporting a contemporary ethnic identity other than "Canadian" are, of course, the foreign-born. Almost one-half of those reporting ethnic identities other than Canadian were foreign-born, while less than one-fifth of the respondents in the total sample were foreign-born. With many perhaps not citizens — a question we did not ask — and others not yet at home in Canada, it is reasonable to assume that the foreign-born would report other ethnicities. Table 10.1 shows the full pattern. Just as the foreign-born are a major source of those giving other ethnicities as a response, so also the rate of reporting Canadian becomes extremely high among the Canadian-born — almost 90 per cent for the second generation and over 90 per cent for the third and later generation groups.

Even so, it must be noted in Table 10.1 that the response "Canadian" was the majority response even among the foreign-born. Almost 60 per cent of the foreign-born gave this response. Comparing them with those among the foreign-born who have retained their ethnic identity might well be instructive.

In all, the data suggest that for native-born Canadians ethnicity may be a much less salient part of their identity than is conventionally believed. There are other ways, such as membership in ethnic organizations, participation in cultural events and so forth, by which ethnic communal strengths may be measured and about which we can say nothing (see, for example, Reitz: 1974).

TABLE 10:1 — Present Ethnic Identity by Nativity (per cent)

| | | Canadian-born | |
Response	Foreign-born	2nd generation	3rd generation
"Canadian"	57.4	87.7	91.7
Other	42.6	12.3	8.3
N	4510	3231	12509
(unweighted)	(3666)	(3158)	(13269)

Culture, Achievement and Discrimination

In a society in which ethnic identification is salient there are two reasons why there might be a relationship between ethnic origin and occupational level. They might be called cultural effects and discrimination effects. The first would arise where different ethnic cultures placed different emphases on the value of achievement. There is some evidence that they do. In Canada, before the Quiet Revolution in Quebec, it was often suggested that the traditional culture of French Canada did not value education, ambition, and material acquisition very highly (see Porter, 1965: 99). We deal extensively in another chapter with the differences in occupational attainment between French and English native-born Canadians, but the alleged differences between these two cultures leave us with the question of whether, if other cultures have survived in their traditional forms in Canada, they too might put less emphasis on getting on and achieving in the work world. We know that Jewish culture stresses education and achievement. In other cultures this "achievement syndrome" could be less developed, and indeed if cultural differences have any meaning in the modern world these differences are most likely to be revealed in attitudes about careers and occupations. If there were not such differences we could take that as evidence of a drift to cultural assimilation. Of course, differences in achievement values have also been noted for social class levels so that if particular ethnic groups were over-represented, say in the lower classes, it would not be easy to tell if the culture were that of class or ethnicity.

Moreover, if ethnic cultures do dampen mobility aspirations and if such cultural enclaves, fixed in the Canadian mosaic, are primordial links for individuals, then ethnic saliency can have a cost and prevent structural assimilation. Here we can examine only one side of this relationship. If ethnic affiliation has little or no consequence for mobility, and if ethnic minorities are distributed in fair proportions through the occupational structure, we can infer that a degree of structural assimilation, has been achieved (see Vallee, *et al.,* 1957).

Discrimination effects follow from the attitudes and beliefs held by the members of the dominant or charter group or groups in a society where there are many immigrants. The dominant groups determine the conditions of entry of immigrants, the kinds of work which they might do and the conditions of getting on. The last sometimes requires becoming assimilated and being like the dominant groups: in our case, in the main, the English in Canada. If there are such discriminative elements within the system of inter-ethnic relations, they are likely to persist where strong ethnic identity prevails. Thus, continued ethnic saliency might have a cost also in terms of continued discrimination. Ethnic saliency might also be a device by which the dominant group maintains its privileged position and it might prefer that minority groups retain their ethnic identity and the place in the status order which the immigrant generation had. If ethnicity were found to have effects on occupational attainment it would be difficult to tell whether these were because of cultural differences or because of discrimination. On the other hand, if we found that there were no ethnic effects for second and third or earlier generation Canadians then we might conclude that, immigrants apart, ethnicity has fallen away as an ascriptive attribute in Canadian society. We have shown that most respondents, particularly those who are Canadian-born, now identify themselves as Canadian, and argued that this suggests that ethnicity has not the saliency that it has been believed to have.

Some evidence that the historic association between ethnic origin and occupational level may be diminishing for some groups can be seen from the successive censuses. We have presented the 1971 distribution in Table 2.2. Those from previous censuses for a few selected occupational levels can be found in the earlier work of Porter (1965: 87). Unfortunately, the census distributions for ethnic origin do not separate immigrants from Canadian-born, so that a central question which we are addressing here — the effects of ethnic origin on the occupational attainment of the Canadian-born — cannot be answered from the census data available. Across time comparisons are made difficult also by the fact that census occupational coding has changed, as have territorial definitions of ethnicity. However, we are fully aware from historical evidence that many second and third generation Canadians would have had parents and grandparents who came to Canada as unskilled and impoverished immigrants. The extent to which they have moved out of the "entrance status" of their forebears through occupational mobility can be more satisfactorily established from our survey data, at least for the larger groups in the population.

Occupational Status and Ethnic Status: Evidence from the Census

The census data on ethnicity and occupation presented in one form in Table 2:2 is shown in a different way in Table 10.2, where the mean Blishen scores are given for each of the ethnic groups, including the British and the French, identified in the 1971 census of Canada. No distinction is made here between foreign- and Canadian-born.

Since the means in Table 10.2 are not identical, it is clear that the various ethnic groups do not have identical social standing (as measured by occupational status). But the differences must be put into some perspective, answering the question: are they relatively great or small? One must also ask if they are in the "expected direction."

In C. Jencks, *et al., Inequality,* there is an unusually great attention paid to endeavouring to turn raw statistics into something more intuitively meaningful. Following one of the procedures he uses, the means given in Table 10.2 can be expressed in ways which give a more immediate sense of how great the differences between the ethnic groups may be. To make this possible, the standard deviations in Blishen scores for each group are also given in Table 10.2.

We would contend that the differences between the ethnic groups in occupational status are small. The average French Canadian, for example, is only some three Blishen points behind the average British Canadian. The difference separating the French from such groups as the Germans, the Scandinavians or even the Polish, or Ukrainians, is minute. Three Blishen points are equivalent to the difference between such occupations as bus drivers and welders or between a chemical and a

TABLE 10:2 — Mean Occupational Status of Ethnic Groups as Shown by the Census (Male Labour Force, all ages)

Ethnic groups by Category	Mean	Standard Deviation	Percentage of active male labour force
Charter Groups			
British	42.48	15.32	45.06
French	39.44	14.52	25.76
Western-Northern European			
German	39.39	14.60	6.86
Netherlands	38.97	14.60	2.15
Scandinavian	39.48	14.91	2.02
Eastern-Southern European			
Italian	34.85	12.17	3.78
Jewish	49.94	15.55	1.60
Polish	38.96	14.18	1.69
Ukrainian	38.95	14.47	3.01
Other European	38.17	15.80	4.89
Non-Caucasian			
Asian	43.77	17.02	1.48
Native Indian	32.41	11.69	.75
Total	40.74	14.87	(100.00)

Source: Adapted from 1971 Census of Canada.

mechanical engineer. Such differences must be contrasted to the amount of variation within any group, which is represented by the standard deviation. Using the procedure suggested by Jencks *et al.* (1973: 45) to give some feeling of what the differences between the means represent, one can compute that two men of British ethnic origin picked at random should be expected to differ from one another by some 17.3 Blishen points, the difference between an optician and a longshoreman. Similarly, two French Canadians picked at random should differ by some 16.4 points, the difference between a mining engineer and a tool and die maker. The variation within groups greatly exceeds that between them.

Certain groups do show some distinctiveness. The average occupational status of the Jews is high — at 49.9 Blishen points. Even so, there is appreciable variation within the group — two Jews picked at random should differ by 17.6 points. At the other extreme, the Native Indians are clearly low at 32.4 points. Thus the difference, on average, between Native Indians and Jews is some 17.5 points, comparable to the amount of variation within the Jewish ethnic group itself. But these are the exceptions. For the larger ethnic groups the differences between them are small.

As to whether the differences are in the expected direction one must decide what is to be expected. The ethnic groups in Table 10.2 are organized into four categories: the charter groups; those from western and northern Europe; those from southern and eastern Europe; and the others, mainly non-Caucasian groups. Three elements generate the expectations implicit in this categorization. There is the recognition of a special status for the two founding races, the British and the French. This forms the top group. In the middle, the ethnicities from Continental Europe are organized into two groups based on the distinction developed in the United States between "old" and "new" immigrants. And finally, the special position of the highly visible, non-Caucasian groups is recognized in the final category. No very profound theory goes into forming this arrangement other than the temporal sequences of the great migrations which were similar in Canada and the United States.

If this classification of expectations about the rank order of ethnic groups is not grounded in elegant theory it has one source of corroboration. The Canadian general public largely agrees with it. In 1965 a sample of Canadians (for details, see Pineo, 1977) was asked to report the social standing of Canadian ethnic groups and the results, scored in the same manner as occupational prestige, are given in Table 10.3. It can be seen that, with some exceptions, both English- and

TABLE 10:3 — Social Standing of Ethnic Groups, Canada, 1965

| | Rank given to groups by: | | | |
| | English-speaking | | French-speaking | |
Ethnic groups	X	SD	X	SD
Charter Groups				
British	81.2	21.4	66.0	26.1
French	56.1	27.8	77.6	22.0
Western-Northern Europe				
German	48.7	25.2	40.5	30.0
Netherlands	58.4	22.6	49.7	20.2
Scandinavian	55.0	*	42.0	*
Eastern-Southern Europe				
Italian	43.1	25.0	51.3	22.9
Jewish	46.1	28.0	43.0	28.7
Polish	42.0	22.4	38.0	22.4
Ukrainian	44.3	22.6	40.0	20.5
Other European*	43.0	*	38.0	*
Non-Caucasian				
Asian*	34.0	*	25.0	*
Native Indian	28.3	28.3	32.5	28.2
N	300		93	

*Averages of ratings given to more specific titles, SD's not available.

French-speaking Canadians saw the social standing of the ethnic groups in about the same manner as the classification of Table 10.2. English Canadians would not have included the French among the charter ethnicities perhaps, giving them a rank by social standing lower than the Dutch. The French did see the French as very high, higher than the British. In data not shown, the French ranked English Canadian at 77.6, exactly the same level as they ranked themselves. (The number of French in the sample was small, around ninety cases, so the data should not be overly interpreted).

If the differences in mean occupational status given in Table 10.2 are not great, are they nonetheless in the theoretically predicted direction as judged by the public ranking of ethnic groups? With the outstanding exception of the Asian and Jewish groups, the answer would seem to be yes. Again, excepting these two groups, the British are indeed at the top. The French fall into third place, not second, falling slightly behind the Scandinavians. The northwestern Europeans fall fractionally higher than the eastern and southern. The Italians are appreciably lower than others among the eastern and southern Europeans. The Native Indians are clearly at the bottom.

The rank by social standing collected in the 1965 survey permits a more precise measure of how well the Blishen scores for the various groups could have been predicted. Using the rank given by the English Canadians, and again excepting the Jews and Asians, the rank correlation between social standing and occupational status of the remaining ten groups is .84. Thus, the prediction is quite good. If one worries about the exceptions, their effect is major. Including the Jews and Asians reduces the rank correlation to only .56, a more modest success.

The above correlations must, however, be considered exaggerated since they are based on grouped, or aggregated data, and therefore suffer the problems of the "ecological fallacy," as the variation in occupational status within each ethnic group is totally ignored (Robinson, 1950: 351). Using special programs which will compute correlation coefficients from grouped data — which is the form in which census tabulations are published — individual, as opposed to aggregated, correlations between ethnic and occupational status can be computed. These individual level correlations give a better sense of how much impact ethnicity has upon contemporary occupational status. For ten groups (that is, the Ukrainians and Polish included with "other European"), the correlation between the two is a very modest .07, based on 1971 census results. And no rearrangement of the data substantially increases this correlation. Correlations of .10 are produced for any of the following comparisons: all groups excluding the French-Canadians; the French and British only; the British to all others (grouped as one); the British to all non-charter ethnicities (grouped as one). A smaller correlation, only .04, is produced if the comparison is limited to the non-charter groups only, with both the British and French omitted.

Regardless of how one looks at it, whenever the correlation is computed in a way that makes the individual, not the ethnic group, the unit of an analysis, the association between ethnic standing and the contemporary occupational status of ethnic groups is extremely slight. Whatever differences ethnic groups might have in current occupational status is not derived from the evaluations about them in public opinion. Other factors such as recent immigration and education are important, as we can see from Chapter 11.

Occupational Status and Ethnic Status: Evidence from The Mobility Survey

To examine the relationship between ethnic origin and occupational status we examine the mobility survey data in two different ways. The first establishes correlations between ethnic status, as derived from the

1965 public ranking of ethnicities, and occupational status as derived from the Blishen scale. This simple bivariate relationship is of interest since it gives what is probably the highest reading possible of the relationship between ethnic social standing and occupational status, and hence an upper limit on the possible causal relationship between the two. At this point we assume that the ethnic scale has the properties of an interval scale, an assumption which we make throughout with the Blishen scale. We utilize the entire male sample of 18 years and older. At first foreign- and Canadian-born are considered together and then Canadian-born are considered alone. Age cohorts are also analysed to determine what changes in the association between ethnic status and occupational status there might have been over time. We are assuming here unavoidably a temporal stability of ethnic ranking over time. We have no evidence as we do with the temporal stability of occupational rankings, and the assumption is a questionable one. The expectation would be that the ethnic rankings would not be as marked in later periods as in earlier ones. We also provide the correlations when those respondents who are at present farmers are removed.

Our strategy, then, is generally to extract what historical evidence we can from the survey about the earlier relationships between ethnicity and occupational status, and also to pay particular attention to the immigrants — as described in the study either by immigrants themselves or in the information on father's occupation given by those who are the children of immigrant fathers. We would also note that there are statistically inevitable mobility effects implied if it can be demonstrated that ethnicity was formerly related to occupational status and now is no longer. And the effect would be the reverse of what might be expected — a pattern of catching up would imply higher rates of mobility for those of lower ethnic status.

Our second method abandons the concept of ethnic status and considers ethnic groups as nominal categories in order to establish the direct effect that being a member of an ethnic group has on occupational attainment. We take Canadian-born males only and employ a multiple regression model in which the nominal categories of ethnic groups are treated as dummy variables. Other variables used as controls in the model are: urban or rural upbringing (thus treating the farm problem at the point of social origin rather than as a factor which might distort the ethnic groups' present occupational scores), father's education, father's occupation, number of siblings in the respondent's family, and the education of the respondent.

Mean occupational scores and standard deviations, from the survey data, are presented in Table 10.4. In the upper panel ethnic groups

TABLE 10:4 — Mean Occupational Status of Ethnic Groups as Shown by the Survey (Male Sample, All Ages)

	N (unweighted)	Farmers included $\overline{X}$	SD	N (unweighted)	Farmers excluded $\overline{X}$	SD
Census Groups						
British	7,173 (7,603)	44.38	14.77	6,815 (7,054)	45.51	14.28
French	4,159 (3,619)	40.52	13.86	3,981 (3,402)	41.31	13.65
German	1,080 (1,141)	42.06	15.06	972 (976)	44.18	14.40
Netherlands	368 (357)	41.77	15.87	328 (307)	44.11	15.29
Italian	700 (450)	36.98	12.28	697 (447)	37.04	12.28
Jewish	225 (148)	52.87	15.06	223 (145)	53.08	14.91
Polish	273 (241)	40.78	13.61	260 (218)	41.68	13.33
Ukrainian	539 (545)	40.11	14.55	482 (452)	42.15	14.06
Groups Identified in Sample Only						
English	4,331 (4,663)	43.81	14.54	4,138 (4,374)	44.77	14.15
Irish	1,338 (1,395)	44.69	14.85	1,256 (1,269)	46.11	14.21
Norwegian	173 (191)	42.23	15.01	153 (160)	44.67	14.17
Russian	93 (101)	37.21	12.59	86 (91)	38.50	12.40
Scottish	1,504 (1,536)	45.77	15.19	1,421 (1,411)	47.10	14.56
Other	1,545 (1,305)	41.35	14.99	1,476 (1,199)	42.22	14.79
Total	16,328 (15,692)	42.44	14.67	15,473 (14,451)	43.51	14.32

identifiable both in the mobility survey and the census are listed. The results here, particularly in the first two columns, may be compared to Table 10.2 to assess how closely the survey results reflect the census. The survey results appear to overestimate those from the census by approximately two Blishen points for each ethnic group, with the exception of the French, for which the increase is roughly one point. The overall total is some 1.5 points higher in the survey than the census. The survey appears to have some degree of bias toward the higher socioeconomic status, a bias perhaps inevitable in a voluntary, self-administered questionnaire. Generally, Table 10.4 ranks the groups in the same order as Table 10.2 except for the French, who appear relatively lower in the survey than in the census. Also, included in the top panel of the table is the mean occupational score and standard deviation, with farm owners and operators omitted. In the bottom panel the Blishen scores are given for five ethnic groups (and for a residual "other" category) which can be identified in the survey but do not appear in current census publications. Three of these groups (the English, Irish, and Scottish) are subsumed under the category British in the top half of the table.

Generally, it may be noted that the exclusion of farmers increases the mean and reduces the standard deviation for each ethnic group. This is virtually inevitable since farm owners and managers were given a very low occupational score in the Blishen scale. While a homogeneous group in themselves, at least as Blishen has scored them, they contribute to the variability within the labour force so their exclusion reduces the standard deviations. Also, since farmers appear in different proportions in different ethnic groups, excluding them changes the relative position of the ethnic groups. Thus, for example, while Jews are still at the top, the other groups are less far behind. In the main the discrepancies between tables 10.4 and 10.2 are slight. Once again the means are relatively close, and the observations previously made about the variation within each group as shown by the standard deviations are equally pertinent here. Moreover, the correlation between the status of the present occupation and ethnic status, when computed from the sample, is .11 — well in line with the results of the parallel correlations presented earlier based on the census data.

Table 10.5 presents correlations between ethnic and occupational status for six age cohorts separately, as a test of whether the relationship was stronger in earlier time periods. With the usual reservations about the limitations of cohort analysis, we conclude that stronger associations can be seen in the older cohorts and in the father's generation. Up to 4 per cent of the variance in occupational status has, in earlier time periods, apparently been related to ethnic status.

In the first column of Table 10.5 zero-order correlations between ethnic status and occupational status are given for the respondent's first job, his current occupation and for the occupation he reported for his father. In the top panel of the table the whole male labour force is

ETHNIC ORIGIN AND OCCUPATIONAL ATTAINMENT   369

TABLE 10:5 — Association Between Ethnic Standing and Occupational Status, by Age Cohorts (Male Sample, All Ages)

				Ages			
	Total*	18-24	25-34	35-44	45-54	55-64	65+
Including farmers							
First job	.09	.06	.05	.12	.15	.10	.12
	(15,692)	(1,960)	(3,584)	(2,850)	(2,842)	(2,230)	(2,183)
Present job	.11	.05	.05	.12	.18	.17	.19
	(14,387)	(1,804)	(3,506)	(2,775)	(2,723)	(2,037)	(1,500)
Father's job	.18	.20	.19	.21	.18	.18	.14
	(15,434)	(1,994)	(3,452)	(2,746)	(2,815)	(2,210)	(2,171)
Excluding farmers							
First job	.08	.06	.05	.13	.14	.08	.11
	(14,878)	(1,944)	(3,521)	(2,736)	(2,673)	(2,041)	(1,924)
Present job	.11	.05	.05	.13	.18	.17	.21
	(13,252)	(1,764)	(3,374)	(2,589)	(2,476)	(1,798)	(1,212)
Father's job	.14	.17	.18	.15	.12	.14	.03
	(10,996)	(1,716)	(2,796)	(1,995)	(1,867)	(1,369)	(1,224)
(unweighted N)							

*Includes cases with no information on age.

included; in the bottom panel those reporting their occupations (or their father's) as farm owner and operator are excluded. Farm labourers are included in both sections. Occupation is scored in the 1971 Blishen code; ethnicity is scored according to the social rankings given ethnic groups (see Pineo, 1977).

The comparison of the correlation coefficients for the respondent's present occupation and the one that he reported for his father is clear. Whether farmers are included or excluded the relationship between ethnic and occupational status is greater for the fathers than the sons. That is, comparing the current Canadian labour force with that of a generation ago, remembering, of course, the hypothetical character of the earlier "generation," one finds evidence that ethnicity and occupation were more strongly related in the earlier generation. (At this point the earlier generation has a doubly hypothetical character since some members of it were not even in Canada). In the style of path analysis, one would recommend that ethnic status be included in the diagram as a factor influencing the father's occupation but it would be of less importance as a factor influencing directly the son's occupation. All but a small amount of the current relationship between ethnic status and occupational status ($r = .11$ whether farmers are included or excluded) can be discounted as an inevitable product of the association between ethnicity and the father's occupation working indirectly upon the son's. The first order partials of ethnicity and occupational status for the present occupation, holding constant the father's occupational and ethnic status, are only .04 if farmers are included and .06 if they are excluded, and only .01 among the native-born. Thus, a considerable part of the present, slight, relationship between ethnicity and occupational status appears to be a legacy from an earlier period.

Since the respondent's first occupation occurs earlier in history than does his present job, the existence of a stronger relationship in earlier times should also show up as a stronger relationship of ethnicity to first occupation than to present occupation. The first column of Table 10.5 shows that this is not so. Rather the relationship to first occupation is slightly, perhaps trivially, smaller than the relationship to the present occupation. Low reliability in the reports of first occupation could be a sufficient explanation of the anomaly. We attempt, later, a complicated, alternative explanation involving the interplay of historical trends and lifetime mobility patterns.

The balance of the table repeats the same zero-order correlations for six age cohorts separately. For the two youngest cohorts the pattern is simple. Their reports of their fathers' occupations show evidence of a relationship between ethnic and occupational status; their reports of either their own present occupations or their own first occupations show almost none. One might discount the evidence from the 18 to 24-year-old group, since they have just entered the labour force and may not yet be on any real career trajectory, but identical results are obtained from the 25 to 34-year-old cohort which is well launched into the labour force. The relationship of ethnic status and occupational status for those up to 35 years of age is no more, in fact perhaps a little less, than what should be expected through the indirect path of ethnicity influencing the father's occupational status and hence eventually that of the son. The first order partials are minute and tend to be negative.

For this young group also the effects of leaving farmers in or removing them from the analysis is slight. This is consistent, of course, with the observation that the farming component is not a large part of the contemporary labour force.

As older cohorts are investigated the relationship between occupational status and ethnicity is found to increase in a generally monotonic manner for both first occupation and present occupation. Thus, the correlation of ethnicity with present occupation increases without great irregularity up to .19 when farmers are included and to .21 when they are excluded. Again, the responses from those over 65 may be untrustworthy, but even with them excluded it appears that ethnic status is related to the occupational statuses held by the older respondents in this sample at the time of the survey. It should also be noted that it is among those in the older cohorts that the anomalous pattern of lower correlations with first occupation than present occupation is found. That is consistent with the idea that some factor like ethnic discrimination existed at the beginning of their careers and continued to build up or at least to exert continuing effects throughout their careers. Perhaps the especially low correlation for those now 55 to 64 should be given a different interpretation. It may be that the dislocations of the depression, for this is the period at which that cohort entered the labour force, actually operated in the short run to reduce the relationship between ethnicity and occupational status.

When farmers are included, the relationship of father's occupation with ethnicity shows no trend except for a fall-off in the very oldest cohort. In general, the data in the top panel suggest that a correlation of about .18 has apparently been the normal relationship between ethnicity and father's occupational status and that it has fallen off in the last twenty to thirty years so that now it has been virtually eliminated. That is, the relationship might be said to be typical of Canadian society until World War II and now to have ceased. And throughout this period the relationship was not as strong at the point of entry into the labour force as at peak career or at the end of the career. This is, it is as if the ethnic discrimination, if this is what it was, only partially influenced who were chosen for occupations but intervened more strongly in determining subsequent career progress after entry. If this was the pattern, shreds of it may remain and a build-up of the magnitude of the correlation in later years for those now less than 35 years old is conceivable.

If farmers are excluded from the computations the pattern alters and several inferences may be drawn. For the respondents the correlations change very little; there are, of course, relatively few farmers among the respondents, even the older ones. On the other hand, the correlations of ethnicity with the father's occupation change substantially if fathers who were farmers are omitted. One is reminded that in the parental generation there were many farmers.

The direction of change in the correlation is always in one direction — excluding the farming fathers reduces the associaton. This implies that to a considerable degree the tendency for low ethnic status to go along with low occupational status was a function of the larger number of those of low ethnic status in farming.

Not only are the correlations lower but also, as shown in the final row of Table 10.5, when only the non-farm labour force is considered there is some hint of a trend across the cohorts in the magnitude of the correlations, and it is a trend in reverse to that found for the respondent's occupation. The correlation falls from .17 among the fathers of the youngest respondents to .03 among the fathers of the oldest. The .03 may again be unreliable because of differences in mortality in the oldest cohort and so it seems safest to speak of a trend from .17 down to .14. There is then a slight hint that the relationship of ethnicity and occupational status was a phenomenon which peaked in Canada in the early 1900s. Put another way, one could ask whether the correlation of about .18 found between ethnicity and occupational status early in this century would imply that one even larger, say .25 or even .30, would have been found in the latter part of the nineteenth century. The reports from the oldest respondents about their fathers, who would have entered the labour force in the latter half of the nineteenth century, suggests that this is unlikely. Rather, if the farming sector is omitted, the reverse seems plausible. And even with the farmers included the correlations of ethnicity with father's occupation computed from the responses of the oldest respondents are lower rather than higher. In all, the idea that the relationship between ethnicity and occupational status peaked early in this century, with the arrival of immigrants from central and eastern Europe, seems the most plausible.

Phrased again in path analytic terms, it would appear that ethnic status should be entered as a path explaining the father's, but not the son's, occupational status for the younger cohorts and explaining the son's, but not the father's, occupational status for the older cohorts. Some 3 per cent of the variance is at stake in the older cohorts, much less in the younger ones. With statistical controls the explanation of variance would reduce, probably appreciably. Without such control we cannot establish the extent to which ethnicity "caused" occupational status; what we endeavour to establish in this part of the analysis is whether, regardless of its cause, a substantial link between ethnic and occupational status continues to be, or has been, a feature of Canadian society. We conclude that there has been a moderate link, but that it has now attenuated.

The Effects of Birthplace

Table 10.6 repeats exactly Table 10.5, with the exception that the foreign-born are omitted. Comparing the two tables shows that the basic results can be found, in slightly weaker form, among the native-born. For present occupations, the relationship of ethnic to occupational status falls from .14 to .04 as one moves from those aged 65 or more down to those who are 18 to 24. With the foreign-born included, the relationship fell from .19 to .05 points. In all instances the coefficients computed from the native-born group alone are lower than for the whole sample. It is clearly the existence of a foreign-born component and the entrance statuses held thereby which has enhanced the relationship between ethnic and occupational status. While over 3 per cent of the variance in occupational status appears to be owing to ethnicity when the foreign-born are included it is more like 2 per cent when only the native-born are considered. The other difference is that the virtual disappearance of any ethnic effect appeared to occur some ten years earlier for the native-born, affecting the 35 to 44 cohort.

In Table 10.7 yet another component of the Canadian population is excluded from the computations — those whose fathers were foreign-born. The fall in the magnitude of the correlations which occurred as the foreign-born were excluded does not continue except in the parental generation. For the reports of the respondent's own occupations, that is his first and present one, there is a slight tendency in the reverse. For the twenty-eight correlations within the body of the table which pertain to the respondent's occupation, some sixteen are larger in Table 10.7 than 10.6, five are the same and only seven are smaller. Only two or three of the correlations reachieve the level found in Table 10.6 which included the foreign-born. The safest observation to make is that insofar as the relationship between ethnicity and occupational status in the contem-

TABLE 10:6 — Association Between Ethnic Standing and Occupational Status, by Age Cohorts (Native-born Males, All Ages)

				Ages			
	Total*	18-24	25-34	35-44	45-54	55-64	65+
Including farmers							
First job	.06	.04	.03	.06	.13	.09	.11
	(13,086)	(1,830)	(3,131)	(2,399)	(2,333)	(1,880)	(1,477)
Present job	.07	.04	.03	.05	.14	.14	.14
	(12,043)	(1,682)	(3,065)	(2,326)	(2,227)	(1,711)	(995)
Father's job	.15	.16	.16	.16	.15	.17	.09
	(12,961)	(1,861)	(3,030)	(2,330)	(2,326)	(1,876)	(1,498)
Excluding farmers							
First job	.05	.04	.03	.06	.12	.07	.10
	(12,419)	(1,814)	(3,070)	(2,296)	(2,191)	(1,723)	(1,292)
Present job	.06	.04	.02	.05	.14	.14	.16
	(11,101)	(1,642)	(2,935)	(2,155)	(2,012)	(1,511)	(810)
Father's job	.12	.13	.15	.11	.12	.13	.01
	(9,250)	(1,596)	(2,420)	(1,683)	(1,536)	(1,164)	(825)
(unweighted N)							

*Includes cases with no information on age.

I# ##

ETHNIC ORIGIN AND OCCUPATIONAL ATTAINMENT 375

TABLE 10:7 — Association Between Ethnic Standing and Occupational Status, by Age Cohorts (Males, Third Generation or Later, All Ages)

				Ages			
	Total*	18-24	25-34	35-44	45-54	55-64	65+
Including farmers							
First job	.06 (10,345)	.04 (1,647)	.04 (2,688)	.07 (1,752)	.14 (1,667)	.10 (1,331)	.09 (1,229)
Present job	.06 (9,475)	.03 (1,519)	.03 (2,633)	.06 (1,691)	.14 (1,585)	.15 (1,194)	.12 (823)
Father's job	.10 (10,309)	.13 (1,690)	.13 (2,606)	.10 (1,712)	.08 (1,681)	.10 (1,330)	.05 (1,258)
Excluding Farmers							
First job	.06 (9,876)	.04 (1,633)	.04 (2,639)	.08 (1,682)	.14 (1,580)	.09 (1,233)	.08 (1,081)
Present job	.07 (8,845)	.02 (1,485)	.03 (2,532)	.07 (1,595)	.15 (1,449)	.17 (1,073)	.15 (682)
Father's job	.08 (7,554)	.10 (1,459)	.12 (2,104)	.07 (1,281)	.05 (1,136)	.09 (852)	-.04 (700)
(unweighted N)							

*Includes cases with no information on age.

porary generation is concerned, it makes no difference whether one concentrates upon the native-born population or the population which could be called third generation or more.

The sharp difference between tables 10.6 and 10.7 is in the father's occupation. Here the exclusion of foreign-born fathers produces substantial reductions in *all* the correlations. The pattern may be seen more clearly in Table 10.8, which repeats the correlations representing the relationship between ethnic and occupational status of the fathers, first for the whole sample, then for the native-born only, and finally for those with fathers who were also native-born. The magnitude of the relationship systematically reduces for the total and within each age cohort, whether farm owners and operators are included or excluded from the computations. It is clear that immigration, and the ethnic and occupational status of the immigrants, has been a substantial factor in producing the relationship between ethnicity and occupational status. Yet it is not the only factor. Among those with native-born fathers, some degree of relationship is found, especially, and this may be perplexing, among the younger respondents. Again, the data hint that we have isolated not a long-term historical trend but a pattern which peaked sometime earlier in this century. Tables 10.7 and 10.8 each end with one small negative correlation between ethnic status and occupational status among the native-born fathers of the oldest cohort. This one correlation is of doubtful significance in itself, but it does serve as a reminder that all other correlations — some 134 of them — are positive, which is to say in the theoretically expected direction. That is, the perceptions of the relative standing of Canadians of differing ethnicity collected from a national sample of English Canadians in 1965 does successfully predict occupational status, although very weakly, even when differing age cohorts and differing components according to nativity are examined separately.

A second inference may be drawn at this point. Since it has been shown that immigration is a factor in producing the relationship which has been isolated, it follows also that we have not just rediscovered in various indirect ways some special characteristics of French Canada. Were the only reality to the relationship something to do with a depressed status of French Canadians, including or excluding immigrants should have little statistical effect.

We have presented the results of our analysis so far largely using the Pearsonian product moment correlation coefficient and some closely related measures. The correlation coefficient has the advantage that it can be used in a manner which frees one from concern about the small size of some subcomponents of the sample. It also fits well into the

TABLE 10:8 — Association of Ethnic Standing and Father's Occupational Status, by Nativity Groups and Cohorts (Male Sample, All Ages)

				Ages			
	Total*	18-24	25-34	35-44	45-54	55-64	65+
Including farmers							
All cases	.18	.20	.19	.21	.18	.18	.14
Native-born only	.15	.16	.16	.16	.15	.17	.09
3rd generation or earlier	.10	.13	.13	.10	.08	.10	.05
Excluding farmers							
All cases	.14	.17	.18	.15	.12	.14	.03
Native-born only	.12	.13	.15	.11	.12	.13	.01
3rd generation or earlier	.08	.10	.12	.07	.05	.09	-.04

(N's as in Tables 10.5, 6, 7)

*Includes cases with no information on age.

methodological and theoretical traditions of others who have studied occupational mobility. Thus, we are able, when we report that ethnicity never accounts for more than 4 per cent of the variance in occupational status, to put this result in some perspective by noting that education, in contrast, can explain some 36 per cent of occupational status. But the correlation coefficient also has disadvantages. It is a skittish statistic, reacting in a strong manner to a few cases with extreme charactersitics as easily as to slight differences between substantial numbers of cases. One might well ask whether differences in the relative status of only two or three ethnic groups might be the underlying explanation of the results we have noted. In Table 10.9, then, we repeat the results in a simpler format. The mean status, in Blishen scores, for the current occupation is given for twelve ethnic groups further broken down into four age cohorts. Farm owners and operators are omitted, and both foreign- and Canadian-born are included.

The table must be read with great caution. The sample size for the smaller ethnic groups means that the numbers are very fallible estimates of the actual occupational status of the groups. In the whole unweighted male sample there are only 122 with Russian ethnicity, 232 Norwegians, just 173 Jews. The point of the table is really to demonstrate that the correlational analysis has not given a misimpression. That is, the ethnicity effects it has measured are distributed rather broadly through the various groups, not deriving only from the extreme behaviour of one or two groups.

An equivalent to Table 10.9 could be generated, if a special tabulation were made, from census data and it would provide realistic measures of the change in occupational status of the various groups. For the moment, then, the table should be understood more as a methodological exercise legitimizing the use of the correlation coefficient.

The two extreme cohorts — under 25 and over 65 — are omitted. Here the sample sizes are small and the numbers highly erratic.

A general up-grading of the labour force can be seen from the totals at the bottom of the table. While those 55 to 64 hold jobs which average to a Blishen score of 42.2, those 25 to 34 average to 46.2. That is, a general up-grading of some four Blishen points has occurred during the period represented in the table. In fact, this would be an underestimate since those now 25 to 34 will experience lifetime mobility as well and presumably end their careers with an average score in excess of 46.2.

This general pattern, of the young being some four Blishen points ahead of the oldest, varies markedly from one ethnic group to another. The English show little gain, from 43.6 to 46.7 points, with a peak in the 35 to 44-year-old group. Even less gain, only slightly over two points, is

TABLE 10:9 — Mean Occupational Status of Ethnic Groups by Age Cohorts (Males, 25-64 Years Old), Non-farm

	Total		25-34		35-44		45-54		55-64	
English	46.16	(3,323)	46.72	(1,083)	47.50	(792)	46.01	(812)	43.61	(636)
Scottish	48.49	(1,082)	48.63	(316)	48.68	(283)	49.93	(254)	46.30	(229)
Irish	47.22	(983)	48.36	(334)	47.76	(211)	45.13	(271)	47.63	(167)
Dutch	45.84	(245)	46.64	(64)	45.76	(80)	46.52	(63)	43.37	(38)
French	42.42	(2,627)	43.96	(953)	44.30	(655)	39.90	(606)	39.12	(413)
Norwegian	45.71	(117)	45.71	(46)	47.28	(27)	43.48	(23)	46.30	(21)
German	45.43	(773)	48.03	(274)	46.37	(223)	44.89	(168)	37.32	(108)
Jewish	55.86	(113)	61.02	(40)	57.72	(24)	50.16	(23)	50.88	(26)
Ukrainian	43.67	(352)	48.82	(100)	46.07	(95)	40.64	(82)	36.76	(75)
Italian	37.05	(388)	39.10	(100)	36.61	(145)	35.80	(101)	36.68	(42)
Polish	43.98	(166)	47.74	(40)	46.64	(42)	43.68	(58)	34.48	(26)
Russian	40.14	(68)	40.77	(24)	42.05	(12)	40.48	(15)	37.40	(17)
Total	44.86	(10,237)	46.22	(3,374)	45.78	(2,589)	43.79	(2,476)	42.24	(1,798)

(Unweighted N's in parentheses)

shown by the Scots and a gain of less than one point by the Irish. Thus, the three British groups, always higher than the average for the total labour force, show less gain through the years than does the total.

The Dutch show a gain of some three points when those 45 to 54 are compared to those over 54, but other than that there are no real differences between the cohorts. The sample size is small and the results may be unreliable. The older Dutch are ordinarily above the mean for the total labour force, the younger two cohorts about precisely on the mean.

The French show a regular gain, slightly in excess of that for the total labour force. In all four cohorts their mean occupational status is below that for the total — the gain is not sufficient to constitute a catch-up.

The Norwegians show an erratic pattern, fluctuating above and below the mean for the total. Again, this is a small group and the means may be unrealiable.

The Germans are the first of the lower-status groups to show a clear pattern of catching up. From a position well below the mean, at 37.3, there has been a marked gain of almost 11 points so that the youngest age cohort is above, rather than below, the total population. A similar marked gain is shown for the Jews who, even though the oldest cohort is remarkably high, at 50.9 points, have further increased their status so that the youngest group is the highest in the whole table, at 61.0. Similarly, the Ukrainians have moved from 36.8 up to 48.8, again a movement from below the mean for the total to above it. The Italians do not show the catching up pattern, moving from 36.7 up to only 39.1 through the four cohorts. The Poles show the gain, however, moving from 34.5 up to 47.7. Finally, the Russians show no clear pattern. This is the smallest group in the table and the results are undoubtedly heavily influenced by sampling fluctuation.

In summary, the table substantiates the findings of the correlational analysis. While the results for any particular ethnic group may be unreliable the overall pattern seems clear. The higher-status groups, the British, Norwegians and Dutch, have not increased their occupational status as rapidly as have most of the lower-status groups. Gains by the younger members over the status of the older of 11 or more points are found for the Germans, Jews, Ukrainians, and Poles. The result is a reduction in the distance between groups and a reshuffling of the order. Thus, in the older cohort, if the Jews are excluded, the range from the highest mean to the lowest is 13.1 Blishen points (from 47.6 for Irish down to 34.5 for the Poles). In the youngest cohort the range, excluding the Jews, is only 9.7 Blishen points. Note that the catching-up can occur either through the improvement of the occupations of younger members of the group or through immigration of higher status individuals, and also that career mobility can ultimately change the overall pattern.

Effects of Ethnic Origin: An Alternative Approach

We now turn to the second method of examining the relationship between ethnic origin and occupational status. We drop the notion of ethnic status as derived from the public evaluation of ethnicities and instead consider ethnic groups as nominal categories. Moreover, we are concerned with the effects which ethnic origin, in combination with other background characteristics, might have on the occupational attainment of males who are Canadian-born only. The sub-population examined in this section, then, is native-born males aged 25 to 74 who were in the labour force in 1973 or who retired between 1968 and 1973. The reason for taking in the over 65s and adding those who retired five years previous to 1973 is to increase the numbers of some ethnic groups since, as we have indicated, a national sample even the size of ours yields too small numbers for analysis of all ethnic groups because some ethnic groups are very small fractions of the population.

Even with the extension of the age range we were able to make up only nine ethnic categories. English, French, Scottish, Irish, German, and Ukrainian all have reasonable numbers. Dutch, Norwegian, and Polish are marginal (N = c.100 for the last three depending on the variable). All the other many groups have had to be pooled into "other", a category which includes Jews at the high end of the occupational ladder and probably about twenty or so other groups. The fact is that many of these groups have not been long enough in Canada to have sizable second generations so that with them we are not able to address the question asked in this section: that is, how the Canadian-born of various ethnic backgrounds get on.

As it is, the groups we are able to use represent the charter groups in Canada (English, Scottish, Irish, and French); some of the old immigration from northern Europe (Dutch, Norwegian, German); and the new immigration (Polish and Ukrainian) from eastern Europe. Since it is the new immigration which contained groups culturally most unlike the charter groups, we should be able to make some comparison between those most likely and least likely to succeed if cultural similarity to the dominant groups was of consequence. As in the previous part of this chapter, the ethnic variable is determined by responses to the census question in our questionnaire.

The other variables in the analysis are: respondent's present occupation and father's occupation, coded to their appropriate Blishen occupational scores; respondent's education and respondent's father's education scaled in a way that approximates years of schooling; number of siblings, based on the combined questions asking number of brothers (question 27) and number of sisters (question 29); urban and rural upbringing constructed from responses to question 31 asking where they were living when they were 16 years old (if they responded the same as at present the rural-urban codes were taken from the present classification of the labour force survey). In the multivariate analysis the variables father's education, father's occupation, and number of siblings are combined into one variable called "social origins."

A brief and general answer to our question is given by Table 10.10 where the mean occupational scores of the present generation (our respondents) for each ethnic group can be seen, along with the mean occupational scores of their fathers. The ethnic groups are listed in a rank order from high to low current occupational status of the respondents. Again, we see the three Anglo-Celtic charter ethnicities are at the top with the Scottish the highest of those. The French are at the bottom, unless we consider the "don't knows" as a group reflecting an ethnic denial. "Don't know" was a valid response to the question and in the tabulations they have been kept separate from those who gave no answer. Not only is the "don't know" group lowest in status, but it is as homogeneous with respect to occupational status as any other group as judged by the standard deviation. A third point is that if we set aside the French and the Scottish, all the other groups are remarkably similar in their occupational status and given the variances, as we have emphasized in the previous section, there is no way in which it could be said that these groups constitute "layers" in the occupational class structure (see also Table 2.2 in chapter 2). Nor can it be said that the groups who are descendants of the new immigration are disadvantaged relative to the descendants of either the old immigration or the charter groups.

The same could not be said for the parental generation, where Poles and Ukrainians are considerably below the Anglo-Celtic charter groups. Their considerably lower standard deviations also suggest that they were grouped at the low end of the scale, in part because greater proportions were in farming. (We have noted that although the present generation — the respondents — constitutes a sample of Canadian-born males, their fathers would not constitute a sample of the father's generation, and it is best to consider the fathers the origin points for the sons.)

The extent to which the non-charter ethnicities have gained on the French and the English over one generation can be seen from the difference column in Table 10.10. The difference between the means

TABLE 10:10 — Means and Standard Deviations for Selected Variables by Ethnic Groups. Canadian-born Males 25 to 74 in Labour Force or Retired, 1968-73

Ethnic Group	Respondent's Present Occupation		Respondent's Father's Occupation		Difference son-father	Respondent's Education	Father's Education	Number of Siblings	Percent Rural † Background	N‡
	Rank	Mean*	Rank	Mean		Mean				
Scottish	1	47.20 (15.54)	1	38.22 (14.49)	8.98	11.74 (3.40)	8.90 (3.86)	3.6 (2.8)	32	999
Irish	2	45.12 (14.87)	3	36.02 (13.81)	9.10	11.02 (3.37)	8.03 (3.90)	4.4 (3.0)	38	945
English	3	44.44 (14.60)	2	36.40 (13.65)	8.04	10.79 (3.50)	8.04 (3.83)	3.8 (2.9)	34	2763
Polish	4	43.75 (13.14)	8	31.03 (9.42)	12.72	10.54 (3.32)	4.87 (3.47)	4.6 (2.9)	42	119
Norwegian	5	43.46 (15.57)	7	31.45 (10.78)	12.01	10.89 (3.78)	7.94 (3.80)	4.2 (3.0)	52	117
German	6	43.24 (15.66)	5	32.04 (12.27)	11.20	10.66 (3.42)	6.85 (3.78)	4.7 (3.2)	53	594
Ukrainian	7	42.96 (14.95)	9	28.12 (8.23)	14.84	10.31 (3.88)	4.49 (3.49)	4.6 (3.0)	50	331
Netherlands	8	42.91 (16.48)	6	31.86 (12.56)	11.05	11.44 (3.27)	7.77 (3.86)	4.5 (3.5)	51	92
French	9	41.51 (14.08)	4	33.16 (11.90)	8.35	9.47 (3.95)	5.86 (3.45)	6.4 (3.4)	28	3176
Other		44.46 (14.83)		33.85 (11.38)	10.61	10.95 (3.49)	6.81 (4.03)	4.1 (2.9)	32	720
Don't Know		39.34 (13.13)		32.78 (12.16)	6.56	9.25 (3.74)	6.22 (3.60)	5.1 (3.5)	38	425
All Groups		43.51 (14.73)		34.53 (12.91)	8.98	10.40 (3.72)	7.03 (3.90)	4.8 (3.3)	35	10,282

*SDs in brackets

†Communities of less than 1,000

‡For father's occupation, variable with highest missing data.

for fathers and sons for Poles for example, is 12.72 Blishen points, for Ukrainians, 14.84. The difference for the English is 8.04 and the French 8.35. All the non-charter groups listed gained, it might almost be said, dramatically relative to the English and have overtaken the French.

Thus, the way in which the French have been falling behind some other groups, previously noted in earlier work and shown in Table 10.4 from an examination of aggregate census data, is borne out. The situation is not quite as bleak for the French as it might appear, however, in that the comparison between French and English presented in Chapter 9 shows that the younger cohorts of French are beginning to close the gap with English Canadians.

If we look further at Table 10.10 and compare the present and parental generations in educational attainment, we can see once more how the non-charter groups have gained in relation to the Anglo-Celts. In the parental generation, the mean educational attainment scores were 4.87 for Poles, 4.49 for Ukrainians, but 8.90 for the Scottish and 8.04 for the English, but the present generation of Poles added 5.67 points to their education, and the Ukrainians 5.82, compared to 2.84 for the Scottish and 2.75 for the English. The Germans and Norwegians did even better. The French have the lowest educational levels in the present generation compared to their Anglo-Celtic co-charter fellow country-men.

Thus, it can be seen that as far as the limited range of ethnic groups with which we are dealing is concerned, whatever element they might have retained of the culture of their forebears — and we have no way of saying what if any degree of cultural retention is implied in indicating one's ethnic origin through the census question — their mobility has not been impeded, nor has their educational attainment been lower as a consequence — in fact, quite the opposite seems to be the case. Nor could this be said for the heterogeneous residual category of "other," where educational and occupational attainment is very close to that of the English. Since this group contains Jews with high educational and occupational attainment, and Native Indians who are low on these measures, as well as many other groups whose earlier generations were immigrants to Canada, it would be fairly safe to surmise that on the average their mobility chances have not suffered for being members of non-charter groups.

The same could not be said for the category in Table 10.10 of "don't know." In the present generation they have the lowest mean occupa-tional and educational attainments. They have made only modest gains (about half those of the Poles, for example) in occupational means over their fathers. Moreover, they are eight-tenths third generation or more

Canadian as traced through both their mothers and their fathers. Whoever they are, these ethnic nescients are of low status.

Since we are dealing with native-born Canadians, it is interesting to see what proportions of each of the groups had parents who were also born in Canada, that is who are third generation or more Canadians. These data are presented in Table 10.11. The Poles and Ukrainians, who as we have shown have experienced substantial mobility, are the most recent Canadians of the groups we are dealing with. The French, on the other hand, who in terms of parental birthplace are the most Canadian, have experienced less. The English and Dutch and to some extent Germans are somewhat similar in their "Canadianness." Thus, it would seem that a group's historical recency in Canada does not impede its opportunity as far as the second generation is concerned. If they are born and brought up in Canada they do as well as any. The same, ironically and for many sadly, cannot be said for the French. The movement out of "entrance status" for the non-charter ethnicities seems clear enough. As Canada has moved into its highly industrialized phase, what remains of the "vertical mosaic" is a phenomenon of immigration where, as we have seen in Chapter 9, the "newest" immigration is marked by differences in occupational status. We will now undertake a more elaborate analysis of the process by which the Canadian-born of our various ethnic groups have achieved the status they have.

Ethnic groups will differ in some of the characteristics which are features of Canadian social structure and which could be important for

TABLE 10:11 — Canadian-born Males 25 to 74 by Ethnic Origin, Percent Third Generation or More, 1973

Ethnic Group	N	(unweighted)	Father Canadian-born	Mother Canadian-born
Scottish	1,197	(1,343)	72	73
Irish	1,152	(1,271)	82	79
English	3,414	(4,053)	69	72
Polish	140	(136)	28	43
Norwegian	132	(147)	25	43
German	680	(792)	61	63
Ukrainian	368	(420)	23	36
Netherlands	109	(132)	65	71
French	4,120	(3,716)	96	92
Other	847	(807)	35	45
Don't Know	560	(604)	83	83
Total	12,736	(13,421)		

their mobility opportunity. For example, in addition to the occupational and educational level of fathers, which we take as a measure of their social class origins, they may have grown up in different proportions in rural and urban environments and have come from larger or smaller families. These factors could interplay with other cultural factors stemming from their ethnicity to affect their chances of making it. Although as we have seen they do not suffer in their exploitation of opportunity it will be useful to control for the effects of these other characteristics to get closer to true ethnic effects which can be seen as operating in those somewhat contrary directions, achievement motives stemming from culture or discrimination stemming from selectivity on the part of the host society. We say "get closer to" because with the limitations of our methodology we must include the unknown effects of factors not included in our model, and these inevitably are included in with the ethnicity factor and exaggerate its effect.

We employ a dummy variable regression model similar to that in Chapter 11. The dummy variable technique is necessary because we are assuming ethnicity is a nominal variable. The regression coefficients so obtained are transformed through multiple classification analysis into gross and decomposed effects of ethnicity (expressed as deviations from the grand mean) and of the other variables in the model. The model is:

$$y = a + \sum_i^{10} bEth + \sum_i^{2} bUR + bX_1 + bX_2 + bX_3 + bX_4 + e$$

where

y = 1973 occupation

$\sum_i Eth$ = Ethnic Origin (dummy variables); 10 categories

$\sum_i UR$ = Rural — Urban (dummy variable, 0 = Rural, 1 = Urban)

X_1 = Father's occupation at age 16

X_2 = Father's education

X_3 = Number of siblings

X_4 = Respondent's education

In the analysis X_1, X_2 and X_3 are referred to as "Social Origins."

The results can be seen in Table 10.12 with gross effects shown in column 1. These are the deviations from the grand mean of 44.35 (the mean occupational ranking of all individuals in the subpopulation in the ethnic analysis). With a standard deviation of 15.06 for the total sub-population, the range of ethnic origin means is from one-quarter of a standard deviation above the grand mean (Scottish) to one-sixth of a

TABLE 10:12 — Effect of Ethnic Origin on Mean Occupational Status for Canadian-born Males, 25 to 74 in the Labour Force, 1973, or Recently Retired, in Deviations from the Grand Mean

Ethnic Origin	Gross Effects (1)	Due to Urban Origins (2)	Due to Social Origins (3)	Due to Education (4)	Direct (5)	N*
Scottish	3.802	.473	2.426	.619	.284	867
Irish	1.716	−.300	1.317	.202	.497	783
English	1.044	.055	1.587	−.456	−.142	2,272
Norwegian	.470	−1.422	.675	.988	.229	93
Polish	−.347	−1.004	−1.904	2.098	.463	90
German	−.663	−1.619	−.047	.845	.158	500
Netherlands	−.936	−1.918	.549	2.276	−1.843	81
Ukrainian	−1.173	−1.470	−2.782	2.284	.795	275
French	−2.507	.474	−2.168	−.643	−.170	2,649
Other	.569	.062	−.238	.872	−.127	605

Grand Mean =44.3508
    SD = 15.06
    N = 8215

*Note: These N's were calculated from multiplying the "proportions" in each category (ie., as used in MCA program) rather than the N's, from the breakdown procedure.

standard deviation below (French). Thus, there are some gross variations among ethnic origin groups, although in any comparative context they might be considered moderate. (See Duncan, Featherman and Duncan, 1972: 52). When for each group the gross effects are added or subtracted from the grand mean, they approximate the mean occupational ranks for each group shown in Table 10.10, with the small differences being accounted for by the fact that Table 10.12 is based on list wise deletion. There is nothing in column 1 which we have not already seen; again the Scottish are high and the French low.

In the remaining columns, the gross effects are decomposed into shares which can be attributed to: urban-rural differences at age 16 (column 2); social origins which sums the effects of father's occupation, father's education and number of siblings and which can be taken as a composite measure of class origins (column 3); education (column 4); those which are direct ethnic effects (column 5) including those which, as we have warned, are not included in the model.

If any ethnic group experienced undue advantage in a cultural sense or discrimination through differential power these "true ethnic effects" would show up in column 5, since we will have controlled for differences between the groups in education, social origins, and rural or urban upbringing. Now since, as we have already noted, many of the groups are very close in their occupational status, this exercise may appear overly academic, analogous tò the attempt to establish the contribution to explained variance by all the variables in the model when in fact there is little variance to explain. That is not the object; rather we see here something of the processes by which the non-charter ethnicities have moved from the more depressed status of their forebears to near equality with the Anglo-Celtic charter group.

We can take the Polish group as an example. The mean for their occupational status is not appreciably less than the grand mean. They have suffered some disadvantage because of their rural origins, but not as much as Germans, Dutch, Norwegians, and Ukrainians. In addition, they have been disadvantaged more than the first three by their low social origins. The Ukrainians, who make an important comparison group with the Poles since both are "new immigrants," have been more disadvantaged with respect to rural origins and social origins, particularly father's occupations. As can be seen from column 4, both Poles and Ukrainians have gained much from education. In fact, most of what they have gained as ethnic groups has been through educaton. They have also made most gains in status from direct effects, which, as we have already said, we would like to call ethnicity but which also includes unknown factors.

On the other hand, the present high status of the Scottish can be attributed in part to their urban origin, but above all to the high social origins with which they stated. They gain very little because of superior education or from other ethnic characteristics. The English gain from their social origins and experience negative effects through education relative to the others and gain nothing positive from other ethnic characteristics. Conversely, the low status of the French is almost entirely because of their social origins (large families as well as low father's occupation).

A word of caution is appropriate with respect to the small number of cases for three of the groups in the multivariate analysis. (Numbers are all somewhat higher for each of the individual variables.) For other non-charter groups the number of cases is respectably high, even for Ukrainians whose history in Canada is not unlike that of the Poles. We feel fairly confident in concluding that, for the Canadian-born, ethnic origin can scarcely be considered a relevant characteristic in the allocation of occupational roles. (The position of the French, which is a special case, is examined elsewhere.) For those who are Canadian by birth there has been no lack of achievement on the part of Canada's ethnic groups. We might have found some if the "other" category could have been dealt with more fully. Whoever they may be, they follow much the same pattern although not from as dramatically low social origins as others.

To anyone familiar with ethnic groups in Canada, these findings may not be striking. Many will have formed the impression that the second and third generations of non-charter immigrant groups have moved out of their low-status origins, acquired as much education as Anglo-Celts (and more than the French), ceased to speak their ethnic language, and diffused into the occupational structure of developing urban Canada. It would seem that both cultural and structural assimilation has proceeded apace, although admittedly our ability here to examine cultural assimilation is very limited. We can say, however, that neither cultural effects nor discrimination are evident; nor do ascriptive or particularistic elements dominate over achievement and universalistic elements in the allocation of occupational roles, although some ascriptive elements may continue to lurk in the "other" category. It is likely, too, that for generations beyond the second the assimilative trends are more pronounced. Whether or not the revival of ethnicity on a world-wide scale that followed the Second World War, magnified in Canada because of substantial postwar immigration, might check this assimilative trend has been a matter of speculation. Our evidence suggests that for men born in Canada, and with the exception of the French, it does not matter much for his getting on what ethnic origin he is. We are, of course, dealing with the entire occupational structure. There is, on the other hand, evidence that, with respect to institutional elites, the Anglo-Celts continue to dominate along with French collaborators. If these findings are not consistent with the experience of members of some ethnic descent groups, it must be remembered that for most occupations there is considerable variation within the occupational group with respect to hierarchy and status which we would not have measured.

Conclusions

Our first conclusion drawn from this analysis must be considered a confirmation of results already published. Pineo (1976) and Darroch (1979) have shown, as we show again here, that the overall relationship of ethnic status and occupational status is not great. For the whole male sample, a correlation of .11 between ethnic and occupational status can be derived from the present sample, and this estimate is close to the correlation of .07 found in the 1971 census by Pineo (1976: 119). Since new data are used, however, the sample results are more than just a repetition of the earlier work. They may be considered a confirmation.

The flexibility of the sample data, as opposed to the census, allowed us to further analyse this matter, as the estimate could be recomputed with farmers excluded, for the native-born only, for first occupation, for father's occupation, and the like. Our principal finding is that the correlation has varied over the years. It is as low as .03 for native-born males, 25 to 34 years of age, and as high as .19 for all males, 65 or older. Thus the sample happens to straddle an era in which the relationship between ethnicity and occupational status was at one time of at least moderate strength, explaining almost 4 per cent of the variation in occupation status, and has subsequently virtually vanished. We note, then, that while it was never as strong as earlier analysis might have implied, the vertical mosaic did exist; there was a relationship between ethnicity and occupational status, still observable in the oldest cohorts in the sample. The survey has spanned the period which could be called the collapse of the vertical mosaic.

The data suggest two intriguing possibilities which would need further information to pursue further. There are hints that ethnicity is more strongly related to occupational level later in the career, as the relationships with present occupation are found frequently to exceed those of first occupation. On the one hand this serves as a qualification; the phenomenon may have more power than our estimates for the very youngest Canadian adults suggest, as later studies of the same cohort might show stronger relationships. The other possibility implied by the data is that, as shown by looking at the reports concerning the fathers of our older respondents, ethnicity may have been less strongly related to occupation in the late 1800s than in the early 1900s. That is, the vertical mosaic may have been only a period in Canadian history — a sharpening of the effects of ethnicity during the decades of great immigration. Again one survey is insufficient to settle these matters and over-interpretation of these two possibilities is unwise.

In the first half of our analysis we have considered the relationship of ethnicity without any use of statistical controls. This provided a generous test of the existence of the relationship, but it seemed appropriate as the way to answer the question: "Is it correct to view ethnicity and occupational status as strongly inter-connected factors in contemporary Canada?"

In the second half of the analysis we introduced strong statistical controls for social background, including rural origin, family size, father's education and occupation, and for the respondent's own education. Controlling for social background makes obvious sense, since one is asking whether disadvantages in location (i.e., rural origin) or in the status of one's family of origin are, as it were, the real reasons members of some ethnic groups do less well than others. Such effects are found, as rural origin exerts an especially severe penalty for those of German or Netherlands ethnicity, and depressed family backgrounds negatively effect the Poles, Ukrainians, and French in particular. In controlling for education one is asking a different question. One is endeavouring to determine the extent to which it was education which was used as the ladder by which some groups climbed to higher social status. As one would anticipate this turned out to be the case. Educational attainments explain a large part of the move forward for those of Polish and Ukrainian ethnicity, for example, and have operated to keep the Dutch from being quite so handicapped as their rural origins would suggest. The educational system, then, despite all the current criticism of it, has worked effectively to help minority Canadians overcome the disadvantages of their background.

With these strong controls in place the ethnicity effects which remain are minor. What is left would include what we have called cultural effects and actual discrimination in the work world. Discrimination in provision of educational opportunities would be ruled out by the controlling for education. The final results are not strong but they are striking. If the small Netherlands group and the "other" category are omitted from consideration, our final table shows that after controls are in place only two ethnic groups in contemporary Canada show evidence of their ethnicity having directly handicapped their occupational achievements. The two groups are: the French and the English. While the magnitude of the effect is too small for serious consideration its existence reminds one that any lingering privileges of the charter groups are being effectively challenged in contemporary Canada.

Note

This chapter was initially drafted by Pineo and thoroughly revised in 1976 by Porter. The final portion, following the sub-heading "Effects of Ethnic Origin: An Alternative Approach" is largely Porter's work, excepting the conclusions. I have left the material virtually as it was. P.C.P.

References

DARROCH, A. GORDON
1979 "Another Look at Ethnicity, Stratification and Social Mobility in Canada." *Canadian Journal of Sociology*, 4(1): 1-25.

DUNCAN, O.D., D. FEATHERMAN and B. DUNCAN
  1972   *Socioeconomic Background and Achievement.* New York: Seminar Press.
JENCKS, CHRISTOPHER, *et al.*
  1972   *Inequality: An Assessment of the Effect of Family and Schooling in America.* New York, Basic Books.
PINEO, PETER C.
  1976   "Social Mobility in Canada: The Current Picture." *Sociological Focus,* 9(2): 109-23.
  1977   "The Social Standing of Racial and Ethnic Groupings." *Canadian Review of Sociology and Anthropology,* 14(2): 147-57.
PORTER, JOHN
  1965   *The Vertical Mosaic: An Analysis of Social Class and Power in Canada.* Toronto: University of Toronto Press.
REITZ, JEFFREY G.
  1974   "Language and Ethnic Community Survival." *Canadian Review of Sociology and Anthropology,* Special Issue: Aspects of Canadian Society.
ROBINSON, W. S.
  1950   "Ecological Correlations and the Behavior of Individuals." *American Sociological Review,* 15: 351-57.
RYDER, NORMAN B.
  1955   "The Interpretation of Origin Statistics." *Canadian Journal of Economics and Political Science,* 21(4).
VALLEE, FRANK G., MILDRED SCHWARTZ and FRANK DARKNELL
  1957   "Ethnic Assimilation and Differentiation in Canada." *Canadian Journal of Economics and Political Science,* 23: 540-49.

CHAPTER 11

Immigration and Occupational Attainment in Canada

MONICA BOYD

My dear Father: I thank God I am got to the land of liberty and plenty.
I arrived here on the 9th July. I had not a single shilling left when I got
here. But I met with good friends that took me in, and I went to work
at 6s. per day and my board on to this day. And now I am going to
work on my own farm of 50 acres, which I bought at £55, and I have
5 years to pay it in. . . . I am going to build me a house this fall, if I live.
And if I had staid [sic] at Corsley I never should have had nothing. I
like the country very much. . . . If the labouring men did but know the
value of their strength they would never abide contended [sic] in the
old country.

> Letter from W. Clements (day-labourer of Corsley, Wilts.),
> dated Port Talbot, Upper Canada, October, 10, 1830.
> Appearing in Magrath (1910: 15-16).

The imagery which appears in this 1830 letter is one which stresses
immigrant aspirations, hard work, and status improvement. As discussed by Strauss (1971), it is part of a larger body of images which concern
the immigrant, and which evolved concomitantly with the development
of the North American frontier and with nation-building efforts of the
eighteen and early nineteen hundreds. Such imagery ultimately shaped
not only popular perceptions of immigrant adaptation but also North
American research on the immigrant.

Some of the themes in social science research are negative ones which
question the adaptability of immigrants to a new society and which are

393

concerned with the impact of immigration on racial-ethnic derived conflict and on the economic well-being and mobility opportunities of the native-born. But alternatively, many of these images which are discussed at length by Strauss (1971:79-104) are as positive and as optimistic was W. Clements' letter, and they emphasize the concomitant processes of assimilation and success for the newcomers. The focus on immigrant achievement is a familiar one, well depicted by the Horatio Alger story, but in its most idealized image it contains several assumptions which are common to stratification research on status attainment. First, success is acquired on an individual basis through the hard work and abilities of each immigrant. As a result, theoretical conceptualizations of immigrant achievement gives little attention to the mobility experiences of families or other collectivities (Straus, 1971:4). Secondly, because success is associated with individual hard work and effort, there is an implicit assumption that the host society is one in which there is equality of opportunity.

The central question which arises from the imagery of immigrant success and its underlying assumptions is whether or not such optimism is matched by reality. In fact, do immigrants improve their economic status? Does the status attainment derive from individual efforts and abilities? And does status acquisition occur without impediment or, to use the language of Chapter 3, is the race a fair one?

Responses to these three specific questions require first operationalizing how economic success is to be measured and secondly, making appropriate comparisons of such success. The three questions can be answered using commonly accepted measures of economic status such as occupation or income. However, the comparison of such indicators vary by the questions asked. In the first question, the amount of immigrant status improvement can be studied in several ways. Some studies of assimilation answer the question by comparing the statuses of subsequent generations and showing a gradual improvement over time (Featherman and Hauser, 1978:429-44; Goldlust and Richmond, 1973; Richmond and Kalbach, 1980; and Jones, Chapter 12 in this book). Other researchers focus solely on the experiences of the first generation, comparing indicators of their economic status to either those of their fathers or to those of the native-born. Frequently, career mobility of immigrants also is studied in which the occupational status of the foreign-born before and after arrival in the host country is compared (Goldlust and Richmond, 1973; Richmond, 1967; Rockett, 1978). The general conclusions of these diverse approaches to answering the question on status improvement is that over generations there is an improvement, explained to a large extent by the generational upgrading of the labour force skills and language acquisition. However, the answers are more equivocal with respect to status improvement over the lifetime of the immigrant group. Evidence suggests that immigrants to North America frequently experience initial downward mobility upon arrival. Much of this downward mobility is recouped, but with the exception of the British in Canada, the occupational status measured some years later does not differ appreciably from the immigrants' pre-migration status (Goldlust and Richmond, 1973; Canada, 1974; Richmond, 1967; Rockett, 1978).

In addition to the comparisons of occupational status over the work life of immigrants, comparisons can be made between the economic status of the immigrant and native-born labour force. Such comparisons address the second and third questions posed earlier: does status attainment derive from individual efforts and abilities and/or are the foreign-born and native-born advantaged or disadvantaged in the attainment process? Status attainment research answers these questions by comparing status attainment models for the native and foreign-born labour force. Such comparisons reveal the interplay between ascription, measured by family of origin variables and what are typically thought to be achieved statuses such as education, occupation, and income. They also reveal the similarities and dissimilarities between the foreign and native-born with respect to how labour force relevant skills such as education are used in the acquisition of status, and the extent that one group receives a different return for a resource such as education. Dissimilarities between groups with respect to occupational or income returns to such resources generally are indicative of the existence of some kind of impediment in the status attainment process. Such impediment may exist for immigrants relative to the native-born for at least three reasons: group differences in motivations and aspirations; group differences in the extent of prejudice and discrimination which is encountered (Goldlust and Richmond, 1973); and state-derived labour policies which direct immigrant labour into certain sectors of the economy, characterized by lower achievement possibilities.

Much of the literature on the role of the state labour policies in creating inequalities of opportunities is a response to the evolution and use of temporary migrant labour policies in Europe (Castles and Kosack, 1975; Marshall, 1973; Rist, 1978) and to illegal Mexican migration into the United States (Burowoy, 1976; Bustemente, 1976; Portes, 1978). Canada has not yet developed an intensive use of temporary immigrant labour as has Europe, nor does she appear to experience as massive a large-scale entrance of undocumented aliens as does the United States. Thus the relation between state-derived labour policies and immigrant adaptation has yet to be empirically examined in Canada, although general issues are discussed in Cashmore (1978) and in Richmond and Verna (1978). With respect to the other factors which impede the status attainment of immigrants, Li (1978) reviews the literature on aspirations and contends that group differences in achievement motivation do not explain native-born and foreign-born differences in occupation status. Rather the dominant model adopted is one which is adapted from black-white comparisons in the United States (Blau and Duncan, 1967; Siegel, 1965) and from comparisons of immigrant and immigrant origin groups (Duncan and Duncan, 1968; Featherman and Hauser, 1978; Li, 1978). This model suggests that differences between native and foreign-born workers in the utilization of work-related resources reflects impediments which result from attitudinal and behavioural predispositions in the form of prejudice and discrimination.

Much of the North American research which compares immigrants with native-born workers reveals considerable socioeconomic diversity within the foreign-born population by birthplace. Some birthplace groups do as well as the native-born with respect to occupational status or income; others do not (Blishen, 1970; Duncan and Duncan, 1968; Featherman and Hauser, 1978: 444-75; Li, 1978, 1979; Richmond, 1967, 1979; Goldlust and Richmond, 1973; Richmond and Kalbach, 1980). Such diversity reflects differences between countries in the structure of their economies, in their labour needs, and in their investments in the education and work-related training of their populations. But such diversity is enhanced by the development of restrictive immigrant policies in both Canada and the United States during the twentieth century. As discussed in Chapter 2 and elsewhere (Boyd, 1976; Hawkins, 1972, 1974, 1977; Parai, 1975), Canadian immigration regulations today are selective of highly skilled immigrants although less skilled workers still immigrate on the basis of family ties. Because of the association between country of origin and educational and occupational skills and because of an immigration policy which admits workers on the basis of labour force contribution or family ties, there is an immigrant mosaic in Canada.

Students of immigration adaptation and social stratification examine this immigrant mosaic with several objectives. The first task is to document the relative economic standing of immigrant groups vis-à-vis each other and the native-born population. Having documented the socioeconomic diversity, the central task becomes that of investigating the causes of such diversity. Here the question asked and the method of analysis closely parallel those with respect to the comparisons of the foreign and the native-born groups. Does the variability in economic status by birthplace reflect differences among immigrant groups in variables which are known to affect occupational status, and which in turn are associated with country of origin? Or does the variability reflect an advantage or disadvantage which certain birthplace groups have quite apart from the advantages or disadvantages accruing from their stock of human capital. The exact cause of such advantages or disadvantages often cannot be directly tested from status attainment data sets but discussion again points to differences in aspirations, the existence of discrimination, and the differential allocation and distribution of immigrant groups across segmented labour markets (Bach, 1978; Boyd, 1979; Duncan and Duncan, 1967; Duncan, Featherman and Duncan, 1972; Featherman and Hauser, 1978; Goldlust and Richmond, 1973; Li, 1978; Portes and Bach, 1979). Studies which adopt a status attainment perspective and analyse socioeconomic differentials between many ethnic-immigrant groups tend to stress discrimination after adjustments are made for differences in human capital variables and social origins (Duncan and Duncan, 1967; Duncan, Featherman and Duncan, 1972; Featherman and Hauser, 1978; Li, 1978).

The preceding discussion indicates that the economic status of the immigrant population can be examined in several ways. Two approaches concentrate on temporal changes in status. Here, studies compare status between generation groups or examine the career mobility of the foreign-born generation. The third approach is more cross-sectional in nature. Here the experiences of the foreign- and native-born in the labour force at a given point in time are compared. Often the analysis moves beyond such comparison by investigating the socioeconomic status of detailed birthplace groups.

The first approach to the study of immigrant status is found in Chapter 12, which examines the occupational status of four male generational groups, defined according to respondent and parental birthplace.

This chapter utilizes the other two approaches to study the occupational achievements of immigrants in Canada. In keeping with these approaches, the following questions form the basis of our analysis: How well do immigrants in Canada do vis-à-vis the native-born? Are the foreign-born and native-born similar in how their occupationally relevant characteristics affect their attainments, or do the foreign-born appear to be disadvantaged relative to the native born? And what socioeconomic variations exist for birthplace groups and does such variation in occupational status reflect birthplace differences in variables known to affect occupational status? Answers to these three questions are provided by an analysis of the 1973 Canadian Mobility Survey data on males in the labour force. The chapter concludes with a comparison of the male-female occupational experiences by birthplace.

Educational and Occupational Achievements of Native-Born and Foreign-Born Males

Based on sample weighting procedures developed by Statistics Canada (see Chapter 1), the 11,950 native-born and the 2,571 foreign-born males who were age 25 to 64 and in the July 1973 labour force represent approximately 3,510,000 and 1,018,000 men respectively. Thus, a sizable component, nearly one-quarter (22.5 per cent) of the male labour force age 25 to 64 is foreign-born (these figures exclude the 0.7 per cent of the male respondents in the labour force who did not give their place of birth). Given the relatively large numbers of immigrants in the labour force, their socioeconomic status and mobility experiences not only are of theoretical interest to students of stratification and immigrant adaptation, but also of substantive importance, describing as they do the status of a relatively substantial proportion of the male labour force.

Comparisons of occupational distributions of the foreign and native-born groups suggest only slight occupational differences between the foreign and native-born males. Using three different occupational classifications, Table 11.1 shows only hints of the bipolarity in immigrant occupational skills, which are seen as resulting from an immigration policy which admits immigrants on the basis of either their labour force skills or their family ties. The first panel of Table 11.1 shows that foreign-born male workers are slightly more concentrated at the high end of the Blishen-McRoberts scale (65-74) and at the low end (25-29) than are the native-born. Similarly, the second panel shows the relative over-concentration of foreign-born males in professional occupational groupings and in service, mining, production, fabricational, construction, and trade occupations. The importing of craftsmen to meet Canada's industrial needs is shown in the third panel which reveals that foreign-born males age 25 to 64 are more concentrated in professional, skilled or semi-skilled crafts and trades occupations than are the native-born males who are found to a greater extent in management, clerical, unskilled labourer and farm occupations. But despite such patterns of relative over- and unver-concentration, the differences in the occupational distributions are quite modest, as revealed by indices of dissimilarity (U.S. Bureau of the Census, 1971) of 10, 16 and 9 for the occupational distributions in the first, second and third panels of Table 11.1 A comparison of the mean 1973 occupational status measured in Blishen-McRoberts scores also shows a negligible difference between the

TABLE 11:1 — Occupational Characteristics of Males Age 25-64 in the 1973 Canadian Labour Force by Nativity

Occupational Characteristics	*Nativity*	
	Native Born	*Foreign Born*
Blishen-McRoberts (1976) scores		
15-19	.6	.1
20-24	8.5	6.3
25-29	9.4	15.9
30-34	16.6	14.8
35-39	9.8	10.0
40-44	10.8	10.2
45-49	11.8	9.8
50-54	5.9	7.0
55-59	7.0	4.5
60-64	7.1	6.5
65-69	8.8	10.1
70-74	3.0	4.2
75-79	.7	.4
1971 Census Classification		
Managerial and administration	8.3	7.5
Professional and semi-professional	10.6	15.2
Clerical	6.6	4.9
Sales	11.6	8.0
Service	7.8	10.5
Farming, fishing, logging, trapping	9.7	4.6
Mining, quarry	10.0	12.5
Production and fabrication	10.5	13.7
Construction	11.5	14.6
Transportation	13.3	8.5
Pinio-Porter-McRoberts (1976) Classification		
Self-employed professionals	1.2	1.4
Employed professionals	7.0	9.5
High level management	3.4	2.9
Semi-professionals	3.8	5.0
Technicians	1.8	2.0
Middle management	5.0	3.4
Supervisors	7.4	7.2
Foremen	7.6	7.4
Skilled clerical, sales	4.9	3.7
Skilled craftsmen, trade	17.6	20.2
Semi-skilled clerical, sales	6.3	6.0
Semi-skilled craftsmen, trades	10.4	12.9
Unskilled clerical, sales	2.3	1.2
Unskilled labourers	14.3	13.1
Farmers	5.5	2.6
Farm labourers	1.6	1.6

native and foreign-born male labour force. Foreign-born males age 25 to 64 have a mean of 43.49 Blishen-McRoberts points compared to a mean of 43.61 for native-born males.

However, the native-born and foreign-born similarities in occupational status and in occupational distributions are not in themselves conclusive evidence of economic equality between the foreign and native-born populations. As discussed in subsequent sections, the similarity in mean occupational status lessens considerably when comparisons are made between native and foreign-born male workers in large urban areas, and when the occupational statuses of the foreign-born are presented by country or region of birth. In addition, a univariate comparison such as that presented in Table 10.1 merely indicates whether or not two or more populations differ from one another with respect to a given outcome, notably current occupation. It is possible for two groups to have similar occupational statuses, but to differ both in their compositional characteristics and in the effect of these characteristics on occupational status achievements. Such nativity differences in composition and achievement processes are real possibilities. It would be surprising, if not unusual, to find that native and foreign-born males are identical with respect to family of origin and educational characteristics given the differences between countries with respect to educational training systems and funding and with respect to the structure of their economies, and the possible selectivity of international migration for persons with certain characteristics. Further, it would be equally surprising to find that family background and education exert the same effect on the status attainments of the native and foreign-born males.

The greater effect of social background and education on the occupational status attainment process of the foreign-born compared to the native-born could exist for one or more of the following reasons: (1) the selectivity of migration for persons who are predisposed to achieve (Blau and Duncan, 1967: chapters 6 and 7); (2) the association between economic opportunities and labour mobility which also would imply that migrants are a select group; (3) a tendency for employers to give preferential treatment to immigrants in terms of career opportunities; and (4) an economic structure in which immigrants are highly segregated into staffing multinational corporations where pay scales and promotions are more favourable than in the indigenous firms (see Clement, 1975, for an account of the flow of managers and professionals from the United States into Canada; see also Cashmore, 1978; Richmond, 1969). Alternatively, familial characteristics and education may have less of an effect on the occupational attainment of international migrants to Canada when compared to native-born Canadians because of the economic costs of entering an unfamiliar labour market, the possible difficulties of having educational certification recognized, and the social and psychological stresses of changing linguistic, social, and cultural settings. That there is a "cost" involved in being an immigrant in the Canadian labour force is supported by Richmond's (1967) study which found that over half (53 per cent) of the postwar immigrant sample had experienced downward occupational mobility upon arrival in Canada. Twenty-six per cent of the sample had not made a full recovery by the time of the survey conducted in 1961 (Richmond, 1967:119). Similar patterns are observed in a 1969-1970 study of the foreign-born in Toronto (Goldlust and Richmond, 1973).

Because information was not collected on the occupational statuses of immigrants before and after arriving in Canada, it is not possible to duplicate Richmond's study. However, his observations that downward mobility is characteristic of many immigrants is related to the argument that education and family background variables exert less of an effect on the occupational status of immigrants compared to native-born Canadians. If unfamiliarity with other job opportunities or the labour market conditions lead immigrants to obtain occupations for which they are overtrained, then the result will be a situation in which a lower increment in occupational status per unit increment of education characterizes immigrants compared to the native-born. Further, if immigrants have difficulty in obtaining recognition for educational equivalencies, then the market value of this commodity will be lowered and downward mobility may be expected. A later section will present evidence for the argument that education has less of an effort on the occupational attainments of foreign-born males because of their difficulties in having educational skills recognized at full market value.

Data on mean educational attainment and family of origin variables (Table 11.2) reveal compositional differences between the native and foreign-born males in the Canadian labour force, and they suggest that compared to the native-born Canadians, the educational skills and familial resources of immigrants have less effect on their occupational status attainments. Compared to native-born males, foreign-born males on the average come from slightly higher socioeconomic background as measured by father's education and occupation (columns 9 and 10). Foreign-born males also have fewer siblings and a slightly higher mean level of educational attainment than do native-born males. Since it is generally conceded that fewer siblings, higher socioeconomic origins, and educational attainment tend to be perpetuated across generations, the question arises as to why foreign-born males also do not have a

TABLE 11:2 — Means and Regression Coefficients[a] for a Model of Educational and Occupational Attainment, Males Age 25-64 in the 1973 Labour Force by Nativity

| | Standardized Coefficients | | | | Metric Coefficients[b] | | | | Means and Standard Deviations[c] | |
| | Education | | 1973 Occupation | | Education | | 1973 Occupations | | | |
	Native-born (1)	Foreign-born (2)	Native-born (3)	Foreign-born (4)	Native-born (5)	Foreign-born (6)	Native-born (7)	Foreign-born (8)	Native-born (9)	Foreign-born (10)
Father's education	.298	.445	.016	−.034	.279 (.010)	.414 (.022)	.060 (.040)	−.119 (.084)	7.311 (3.913)	8.200 (4.389)
Father's SES	.201	.187	.178	.201	.056 (.003)	.051 (.006)	.203 (.011)	.208 (.023)	35.048 (13.140)	36.240 (14.848)
Number of siblings	−.205	−.125	−.001	−.074	−.229 (.011)	−.185 (.028)	−.004 (.042)	−.412 (.102)	4.649 (3.290)	3.751 (2.750)
Son's education			.539	.534			2.209 (.041)	2.010 (.084)	10.888 (3.664)	11.306 (4.082)
Son's occupation									44.322 (14.986)	44.086 (15.367)
Intercept					7.948	6.750	12.772	16.327		
R^2					.287	.380	.410	.430		

[a]Listwise regression. The weights used are the general weight, divided by 1/300.5 for the native-born and 1/395.5 for the foreign-born.
[b]Standard errors given in parenthesis.
[c]Standard deviations given in parenthesis.

higher mean occupational status compared to native-born males. Are the foreign-born handicapped in the status attainment process? This possibility can be assessed by comparing the status attainment models ofr the native and foreign-born males.

The basic model of occupational attainment has been developed in earlier chapters (see especially chapters 3 to 6). In these chapters, occupational attainment is conceptualized as resulting from both the transmission of social status across generations and the acquisition of occupationally relevant characteristics. The detailed model stressed is one which traces the effect of family of origin variables, defined as paternal education and occupational status, and number of siblings on the son's current occupational status, by examining the process of educational and first job attainments. However, the model of occupational attainment differs slightly from that analysed in earlier chapters in its omission of first job status as a variable which is both achieved and which mediates the effect of education and family or origin variables on current occupational standing. This deletion of the first job occupational status is required because of the measurement error associated with the first job variable for immigrants. Investigation of the relationship between educational attainment, first job, and age at immigration revealed that at least 13 per cent of the immigrants who answered these questions did not give their first job after completion of education, as instructed by the Job Mobility questionnaire. Instead, they apparently gave their first job upon coming to Canada. This minimum estimate of error associated with the first job variable for the foreign-born varies substantially by age, ranging from 3.8 per cent for males age 25 to 34 to 14.4, 16.6 and 16.0 per cent for males age 35 to 44, 45 to 54 and 55 to 64, respectively. Given the magnitude of this conservative estimate of error, the first job variable is excluded from comparisons of foreign-born and native-born occupational attainments.

In addition to the exclusion of first job, the comparison of native and foreign-born educational and occupational attainments differs from earlier analyses with respect to weighting procedures. Because the actual male labour force population which is represented by the Canadian Mobility sample is so large, standard errors of regression coefficients are extremely small. Earlier analysis corrected for this by downweighting the population estimates by a factor of (1/300.55), so that the standard errors generated would be similar to those obtained in a random sample which is the size of the Mobility Survey (Chapter 1). This works well for investigations of native-born males and for comparisons between men and women. However, when this downweighting procedure is applied to the foreign-born male labour force population, we obtain a population which is nearly 35 per cent larger than our sample population of 2,571 males. Again, this means that sampling errors for regression coefficients of foreign-born males will be much smaller than what we would expect given our actual sample size. Accordingly, when analyses are conducted separately for foreign-born males, a factor of 1/395.5 is applied to ensure that standard errors observed would be those found in a random sample which approximates the actual size of the foreign-born male labour force sample (see Featherman and Hauser, 1978: 511). For the same reason, the subsequent analysis based on residents of large urgan areas is downweighted by a factor of 1/450.0.

The unstandardized regression coefficients in Table 11.2 (columns 5 to 8) show the effect of family background factors on educational and occupational status attainments. These metric coefficients, or b's, indicate how much change in the endogenous, or dependent, variable is produced by a one unit change in the antecedent or exogenous variable, controlling for the effects of other variables in the model. The magnitude of these metric coefficients thus shows the substantive impact or "effect" which an independent variable has on the dependent variable. The table also presents the standardized coefficients for the models of educational and occupational attainments (see Land, 1969). For a variety of reasons (Hanskek and Jackson, 1977:76,94; Kim and Muller, 1976), comparisons should not be made of magnitude of these standardized coefficients between the native and foreign-born groups.

The fact that most male immigrants in the Canadian labour force received their education outside of Canada may at least partially explain some of the nativity differences in educational attainment observed in Table 11.2. As revealed by columns 5 and 6 and confirmed by tests for interaction (Cohen, 1968; Specht and Warren, 1976), foreign-born males receive more education compared to native-born males for each unit increment of father's education (.414 versus .279), controlling for parental socioeconomic status and number of siblings. The differences between the two groups with respect to the influence of number of siblings and father's (or household head's) socioeconomic status are substantively small and statistically insignificant.

Overall, in terms of the regression coefficients for educational attainment, native-born and foreign-born males differ only with respect to the effect of father's education. What underlies the difference is difficult to ascertain, given the absence of both data on emigrants and data which compare the educational attainment of the foreign-born with the educational attainment of their fellow countrymen who remained in their countries of origin. The fact that paternal education has a greater effect on the educational attainment of foreign-born males may simply reflect the selectivity of international migration for high achievers. Alternatively, the differences between native and foreign-born with respect to the influence of father's education on educational attainment may reflect fundamental differences between the educational and stratification systems of Canada and other countries.

With respect to the acquisition of occupational status, a comparison of columns 7 and 8 (Table 11.2) and statistical tests for interaction (Cohen, 1969; Specht and Warren, 1976) indicate that native-born and foreign-born males in the 1973 labour force are similar with respect to the effect of father's or head of the household's occupational status on current occupational status, net of education, and other family background variables. But the two groups differ in the substantive effect exerted by siblings on occupational attainment, with the foreign-born losing four-tenths of a point for each additional sibling, a difference which is statistically significant at the .0005 level. The other significant difference between the native and foreign-born males is found in the influence of education on occupational status attainment. Each additional year of education, net of other background factors, adds a 2.21 increase in occupational status for native-born males. In comparison, each year of education means an educational status increment of 2.01 Blishen-McRoberts points for foreign-born males. This difference is not trivial, for the substantive impact of such differentials increases with the level of education attained. Net of other factors, the nativity difference in the metric coefficient for education means that with only some elementary school education, native-born males are .8 point higher than foreign-born in occupational status. But for males with a doctorate, the disparity in occupational status due to nativity differences in the net effect of education on occupational status becomes 3.9 points in favour of the native-born.

The differential effect of education on occupational attainment for foreign-born males compared to native-born males most probably reflects the difficulties of transferring educational skills across national boundaries. Native-born males who have received their education in Canada have an advantage in that the labour market value of their education is generally understood and accepted by their employers. In contrast, over three-fourths of immigrant males in the Canadian labour force arrived in Canada after age 16; much, if not all, of their education would have been received abroad. These immigrants who have been educated in different educational systems may find that the labour market value of their education is less easily assessed, less applicable to the needs of an industrial labour market and/or equivalencies less easily granted. These problems become particularly acute with respect to the educational training required for law and medicine where recertification according to Canadian criteria is mandatory for most persons not educated in these fields in Canada.

These nativity differences which are observed in the effect of education and size of family of origin on occupational status suggest that the similarity in mean occupational status which is observed in Table 11.2 for the native and foreign-born arises because the slightly higher average socioeconomic origins and educational attainment of the foreign-born offsets these lower effects. The decomposition of differences between the two means (see Chapter 7; also Althauser and Wigler, 1972; Winsborough and Dickinson, 1971) shows this to be the case. According to this decomposition, foreign-born males would gain an additional 1.50 Blishen-McRoberts points if their background and educational resources influenced occupational status according to the magnitudes depicted by the regression equation for native-born males (Table 11.2, column 7). But if they had the socioeconomic characteristics of native-born males, the foreign-born would actually lose 1.37 Blishen-McRoberts points. The interplay of this gain and loss means a very small difference in the mean occupational status of the native and foreign-born males age 25 to 64 in the 1973 Canadian labour force.[1]

In conclusion, although the average status of current occupation is similar for native and foreign-born males in Canada, some differences exist with respect to the effect which family of origin characteristics have on educational attainment and which education in turn has on occupational status. In particular, paternal education has a greater influence on the educational attainment of foreign-born males than it does for the native-born. But educational attainment has less of an effect on the occupational attainments of foreign-born males compared to native-born males. As shown by data presented in Table 11.2, the similarity between native-born and foreign-born males with respect to mean occupational status is due to the fact that even though foreign-born males on the average have higher socioeconomic origins and educational attainment, their educational attainment and number of siblings has less effect on subsequent achievement than is the case for native-born males. As discussed in the next section, when size of geographical residence is held constant, these nativity differences in educational and occupational status and in the attainment process substantially increase.

Occupational Inequalities in Large Urban Centres

The previous section showed that the effect of educational attainment on occupational attainment is smaller for foreign-born males than for native-born males. However, the impact of such differences in the status attainment process is masked by compositional differences between the native-born and foreign-born populations, with the result that the occupational statuses of the two groups are very similar.

The magnitude of occupational differences between the native and foreign-born male labour force is also affected by the urban-rural distribution of the two groups. A comparison of foreign and native-born males in the 1973 labour force reveals that nearly three-fourths (72 per cent) of the foreign-born are concentrated in large urban centres (100,000 population or more) compared to less than one-half of the native-born male population (45 per cent). One-fourth of the native-born reside in rural areas compared to one-tenth of the foreign-born males (Table 11.3). The economic opportunities created by a growing industrial economy have drawn most of the immigrants to Canadian cities with the result that foreign-born and native-born males in the 1973 labour force differ greatly by size of place of residence.

Why should these nativity differences in place of residence minimize the occupational differences between the foreign and native-born male labour force? The place of residence distributions indicate that data for the native-born male labour force are affected by the educational and occupational attainment processes of native-born males not living in large urban areas to a much greater degree than are the data for foreign-born males. Because educational and economic opportunities differ by city size and rural-urban location, it is not surprising to find that the educational and occupational attainment processes of persons residing in different size of place areas are quite different. Thus, any

TABLE 11:3 — Per Cent Distribution of Males Age 25-64 in the 1973 Labour Force and Mean Occupational Status, by Nativity

| | % Distribution | | Mean Occupational Status | | |
	Native-born (1)	Foreign-born (2)	Native-born (3)	Foreign-born (4)	Difference (col. 4-3) (5)
Total	100.0	100.0	43.608	43.489	.119
Large urban centre	45.2	72.2	47.863	44.577	−3.286
Minor urban centre	10.9	7.8	45.434	43.118	−2.316
Other city	7.1	4.3	44.656	43.797	− .859
Small urban area	12.1	5.7	41.945	40.975	− .970
Rural	24.7	10.0	34.962	37.405	+2.443

comparisons of the total native-born male labour force with the total foreign-born male labour force are confounded by occupational status attainment differences by place of residence.

Support for this argument is given by comparisons of native and foreign-born mean occupational status, specific to size of places categories. Within each urban size of place category, foreign-born males on the average have lower occupational status compared to native-born males (Tabel 11.3, columns 3 and 4). Only in rural areas is the average occupational status of foreign-born males greater than that of native-born, and this is due primarily to the relative under-concentration of foreign-born males in farming (4.6 per cent compared to 6.1 per cent for native-born) and a concentration in professional and extractive occupations. Within urban Canada, data in Table 11.3 show that the disparity by nativity in mean occupational status generally increases with the size of the urban areas. Thus, in large urban centres where 72 per cent of the male immigrant labour force reside, native-born males on the average have an occupational status score which is 3.3 points higher than the mean observed for foreign-born. By focusing on the total population, the previous section minimizes the differences in actual occupational status which exist between native and foreign-born males, and compares the educational and occupational attainment processes of foreign-born males who are highly homogeneous with respect to place of residence to that of native-born males who are more heterogeneous.

Since nearly three-fourths of the foreign-born male labour force reside in large urban centres, further understanding of nativity differences in educational and occupational attainment is gained by a comparison of these men with native-born males residing in large urban centres (Table 11.4). Data derived from listwise regression parallelled results in Table 11.3. On the average, foreign-born males residing in cities of 100,000 persons or more, have an occupational status score which is nearly four Blishen-McRoberts points lower than the mean occupational status observed for native-born males in these cities. This difference in mean occupational status is substantively a large one, inasmuch as the average intra-generational mobility is 6 Blishen-McRoberts points for the native-born.

In addition to these nativity differences in mean occupational status, differences between the foreign-born and the native-born with respect to the influences exerted by family background and educational attainment on occupational status are more extensive than suggested by the earlier comparison (Table 11.2). Statistical tests for interaction (Cohen, 1968; Specht and Warren, 1976) indicate nativity differences in the effects of number of siblings and educational attainment on

TABLE 11:4 — Means and Regression Coefficients[a] for a Model of Educational and Occupational Attainment Males Residents of Large Urban Centres, Age 25-64 in the 1973 Labour Force by Nativity

| | Standardized Coefficients | | | | Metric Coefficients[b] | | | | Means and Standard Deviations[c] | |
| | Education | | 1973 Occupation | | Education | | 1973 Occupations | | | |
	Native-born (1)	Foreign-born (2)	Native-born (3)	Foreign-born (4)	Native-born (5)	Foreign-born (6)	Native-born (7)	Foreign-born (8)	Native-born (9)	Foreign-born (10)
Father's education	.270	.454	.036	-.039	.234 (.014)	.420 (.025)	.126 (.064)	-.134 (.104)	8.059 (4.074)	8.241 (4.520)
Father's SES	.169	.184	.111	.205	.043 (.004)	.051 (.007)	.115 (.018)	.212 (.029)	38.600 (13.716)	36.848 (15.013)
Number of siblings	-.208	-.132	-.001	-.081	-.239 (.017)	-.201 (.034)	-.042 (.075)	-.456 (.130)	4.066 (3.074)	3.640 (2.751)
Son's education			.570	.549			2.315 (.070)	2.031 (.105)	11.842 (3.519)	11.448 (4.181)
Son's occupation									49.051 (14.283)	45.166 (15.457)
Intercept					9.262	6.832	16.350	16.886		
R^2					.235	.390	.406	.453		

[a]Listwise regression. The weight used is the general weight, divided by 1/450.0.
[b]Standard errors given in parenthesis.
[c]Standard deviations given in parenthesis.

occupational attainment at the .005, .005. and .05 levels of significance, respectively (Table 11.5, columns 7 and 8). The direct effect of paternal socioeconomic status on the immigrants' subsequent occupational attainments is slightly greater than its effect on native-born attainments. Aside from the selective nature of migration, there is no clear explanation for this finding, or for the nativity differences in size of family effects on occupational status, which remain at about the same magnitude as observed in the analysis for the entire male labour force (Table 11.2).

When the analysis is limited to males in large urban areas, the nativity difference in the effect of education on occupational attainment sharpens. For each additional unit increase in education, native-born males receive about three-tenths of a Blishen-McRoberts point more than do foreign-born males in large urban centres. At twelve years of school, which is very close to the observed means of 11.8 and 11.4 for the native and foreign-born, this difference translates into a 3.4 point difference, to the disadvantage of the foreign-born.

As noted earlier, the fact that the educational attainment has less of an effect on the occupational attainment of the foreign-born male residents of large urban centres may reflect both the experience of downward mobility and the difficulty of transferring educational certification and skills and manpower demands. A third possibility, not heretofore discussed, is that persons who are unable, for reasons of personality, type of training, or quality of education to fully utilize their educational skills in the Canadian labour market, predominate in international migration streams to Canada and/or the decision to remain in Canada. But the point system of Canada's immigration regulations (see Boyd, 1976) cast doubt upon this explanation with respect to immigration. Whether emigration from Canada is selective of those persons whose occupational status is highly influenced by their education is unknown, given the absence of comparable data on emigrants.

Overall, do the observed nativity differences in the effects of background and educational variables on the occupational attainment process account for the nearly 4 point difference between the mean occupation status of the native-born (49.051) and the foreign-born (45.166)? Not entirely, for as discussed earlier, the difference in mean occupational standing can be decomposed into two factors: the differences between the two populations in family background and educational characteristics (Table 11.4, columns 9 and 10); and the differences in the way in which these variables affect current occupational status (the regression equations). This decomposition indicates that nativity differences in background and educational characteristics account for 26 per cent of the differences in mean occupational status by nativity. If foreign-born males in large urban centres had the same characteristics on the average as do the native-born (Table 11.4, column 9), their average occupational status would increase by 1.02 Blishen-McRoberts points. If the characteristics of the foreign-born influence occupational attainment in the manner depicted by the regression equation for the native-born (Table 1.1, column 7), the average occupational status of the foreign-born would increase by 2.81 Blishen-McRoberts points.

Several conclusions may be drawn from the data presented in this section. First, it is clear that the earlier observed initial similarity in occupational status between native and foreign-born males age 25 to 64 in the 1973 Canadian labour force is a function of differentials between the two groups with respect to size of place location. When the analysis is limited to residents of large urban areas, the data show that on the average foreign-born males have a lower occupational status than do native-born males. Since nearly three-fourths of the foreign-born male labour force population (age 25 to 64) resides in large urban centres, it becomes apparent that most foreign-born males in Canada operate in a labour market where their average occupational status is lower than observed for their native-born counterparts. Secondly, only a small proportion of the differences by nativity in mean occupational status can be explained by the family of origin or educational characteristics of the foreign and native-born males in large urban centres. Instead, nativity differences in the status attainment process play an important role. In particular, education has less of an effect on the occupational attainment of foreign-born males compared to native-born males, and this generally overrides the greater influence exerted by father's occupational status on the current occupational status of the foreign-born.

Age at Immigration and Occupational Attainment

So far the analysis has revealed differences in the occupational attainment of foreign and native-born males in the 1973 labour force. The differences are sharpened when the analysis is limited to residents of large urban centres of 100,000 persons or more. Here, the data reveal that much of the lower mean occupational status of the foreign-born compared to the native-born residents of large cities primarily reflects differences between the two groups in how family of origin variables (father's socioeconomic status and number of siblings) and education affect occupational status attainment.

Earlier discussions suggested several possible reasons for the finding that effect of education on occupational attainment is less among foreign-born males than among native-born males: the selection of migration for persons not able to attain occupational success; the experience of downward mobility of any postwar immigrants to Canada (Goldlust and Richmond; 1973; Richmond, 1967); and the problem of obtaining recognition for educational training obtained via a non-Canadian education system. These factors may be operating singly or in unison. Indeed, as noted in previous discussions, the problems of transferring educational equivalencies across national boundaries may result in immigrants taking jobs for which they are overtrained, and thus result in downward occupational mobility relative to the occupations held prior to migrating.

Support for the contention that foreign-born males are disadvantaged in the occupational attainment process because of problems in obtaining recognition for educational skills acquired elsewhere is given by a comparison of males who immigrated to Canada before they were age 17 with those who immigrated at or after age 17. This age break distinguishes among immigrants in several ways. First, the occupational status of the head of the household when the respondent was 16 reflects the status in Canada for immigrants who came to Canada before age 17. In contrast, for persons immigrating to Canada at or after age 17, the occupational status of the household head most probably is that held in the country of origin. Secondly, it is likely that the motives for immigration are different for immigrants arriving before age 17 compared to those who migrated after age 16. Given immigration regulations, the former group most likely immigrated as part of a family and to some extent their migration could be viewed as involuntary. In contrast to these epiphenomenal migrants, persons migrating after age 16 are more likely to have migrated for economic reasons, and many would have completed their education abroad. Indeed, cross-tabulations of age at immigration by completed level of schooling suggest that 85 per cent of males immigrating before age 17 completed their schooling in Canada compared to somewhere between 7 and 18 per cent for males arriving during or after age 17. If difficulties exist in transferring educational equivalencies across national boundaries, the effect of education on occupational attainment of the foreign-born who complete their education in Canada should be larger than the effect of education on the occupational attainment of those foreign-born males who by and large completed their education elsewhere.

Using data for the total male labour force population (columns 1-4) and for residents of large urban areas of 100,000 persons or more, Table 11.5 shows the occupational attainment process of foreign-born males, where the latter are divided into those who last immigrated to Canada before age 17 and those who immigrated to Canada at age 17 or thereafter. A comparison of average socioeconomic characteristics reveal rather marked differences in the composition of the two groups of immigrants (columns 1, 2, 5, 6). Compared to those immigrating at age 17 or later, males who immigrated prior to age 17 have higher educational and occupational attainments, and this difference sharpens when the comparisons are limited to those residents of large urban areas. Males who immigrated prior to age 17 also come from families where on the average, paternal educational attainments are higher and size of family is lower than observed for males immigrating later. Such differences between the foreign-born male labour force, divided by age at immigration, in part reflect compositional differences between the two groups with respect to country of birth. Of the foreign-born males entering Canada before age 17, 38 per cent were born in Britain or the United States, with another 17 per cent born in Germany, France and the Netherlands. In comparison, 23 and 13 per cent of the foreign-born entering Canada at or after age 17 were born in the United Kingdom, the United States or in Germany, the Netherlands and France. The relatively higher status of these birthplace groups is observed and analysed in the subsequent section.

The one exception to the higher socioeconomic origins of the migrants entering Canada before age 17 is the lower occupational status of the head of household compared to that observed for immigrants entering Canada at age 17 or thereafter. No apparent reason exists for this anomaly. The proportion of heads of households who declare farming as an occupation is lower for the young arrivers than for those males entering Canada as adults. Since farmers and farm labourers are assigned a low Blishen-McRoberts score (ranging from 23-30), such figures alone suggest that the paternal socioeconomic status should be higher rather than lower for the immigrants entering Canada before age 17 compared to those who enter later. One real possibility is that our data are picking up the downward mobility experience of immigrants which Richmond (1967) and Goldlust and Richmond (1973) have observed to characterize immigrants during the early years of residence. Since 32 per cent of the male immigrants entering Canada before age 17 last entered within five years of turning age 16, the question of paternal occupations could reflect such downward mobility experiences of the fathers of the foreign-born men in our sample.

With respect to occupational status returns to education and to family background variables, the metric coefficients contained in Table 11.2 and 11.5 indicate that males immigrating to Canada prior to age 17 are

TABLE 11:5 — Means and Metric Coefficients for a Model of Occupational Attainment for Foreign-born Males, Age 25-64 in the 1973 Labour Force by Age at Immigration and Place of Current Residence.

	Total Canada[a]				Large Urban Centre of 100,000 or more[b]			
	Means and Standard Deviations		Metric Coefficients		Means and Standard Deviations		Metric Coefficients	
	Immigrated		Immigrated		Immigrated		Immigrated	
Characteristics	Before age 17 (1)	At age 17 plus (2)	Before age 17 (3)	At age 17 plus (4)	Before age 17 (5)	At age 17 plus (6)	Before age 17 (7)	At age 17 plus (8)
Father's education	8.280 (4.240)	8.183 (4.421)	-.224 (.172)	-.021 (.103)	8.610 (4.403)	8.166 (4.519)	-.412 (.231)	.008 (.120)
Father's SES	33.830 (11.974)	36.916 (15.417)	.208 (.058)	.212 (.027)	35.283 (12.246)	37.104 (15.466)	.271 (.079)	.205 (.032)
Number of siblings	3.033 (2.477)	3.923 (2.793)	-.216 (.257)	-.431 (.120)	2.563 (2.218)	3.864 (2.813)	.114 (.389)	-.487 (.143)
Son's education	11.523 (3.583)	11.280 (4.231)	2.316 (.193)	1.904 (.100)	12.258 (3.492)	11.306 (4.332)	2.439 (.264)	1.897 (.118)
Son's occupation	45.572 (15.000)	43.995 (15.547)	—	—	48.739 (14.705)	44.603 (15.607)	—	—
Intercept	—	—	14.361	16.564	—	—	12.535	17.371
R^2	—	—	.365	.456	—	—	.380	.474

[a]The weights used are the general weight divided by 1/360.0 for foreign-born immigrating before age 17 and 1/409.5 for foreign-born immigrating at age 17 or later.

[b]The weight used is the general weight divided by 1/450.0.

more similar to native-born males than are males entering Canada at older ages. The high negative effect of siblings which was observed earlier for foreign-born males (Table 11.2) is sharpest for those males immigrating after age 16. And with respect to the effect of education on occupational status, a comparison of the data contained in tables 11.2, and 11.5 indicate a larger effect among the foreign-born immigrating before age 17 than among the native-born and the foreign-born immigrating later. The largest discrepancy exists between the foreign-born immigrating before and after age 17. Net of other factors, immigrant males who came to Canada prior to age 17 obtain 2.32 Blishen-McRoberts points for each increment in education compared to an increase of 1.90 Blishen-McRoberts points for the foreign-born who enter Canada at age 17 or later. Again, the magnitude of the differences sharpens when only residents of large urban centres are examined. Here the data show the greater influence of education on occupational status among immigrant workers who came to Canada before age 17 and for those who came later (2.44 and 1.90 respectively; Table 11.5, columns 5 and 6). While such differences may seem small at first glance, at a completed high school level (coded 12), these differences imply an occupational status gap of 6.5 Blishen-McRoberts points to the advantage of the immigrant who enters Canada prior to age 17. As discussed earlier, this advantage may well reflect the difficulty of translating educational equivalencies across international boundaries and the comparative advantage which exists for those immigrants whose educational experiences preclude the need to obtain educational equivalencies. Many of the foreign-born males who immigrated to Canada piror to age 17 have received some or all of their education within the Canadian educational system; probably most have received their last year of education in a Canadian school. This educational experience means that the educational skill acquired by the time of entry into the labour market is likely to be expressed in a currency which is easily assessed by Canadian employers. In contrast, the educational training received by persons completing their education outside of Canada appears undervalued in the Canadian labour market relative to its actual worth. As a result, such persons receive a return on educational attainment which is lower than that received by persons educated in, and exiting from, Canadian schools. Since 78 per cent of the foreign-born male labour force between 25 to 64 years of age arrived in Canada at 17 or later, such educational underevaluation has considerable substantive impact on the occupational experiences of the foreign born labour force.

Occupational Attainment by Country of Birth

So far the educational and occupational attainment of the native and foreign-born male labour force has been examined. While such an investigation summarizes the similarities and differences which exist by nativity, it overlooks the cultural diversity which exists within both the native and foreign-born populations. Not only have past immigration and differential emigration and fertility created an ethnically diverse population but also the increasing ease of transportation, coupled with the postwar emergence of many new nations, means that Canada receives immigrants from any different countries. In 1974 alone, the Department of Manpower and Immigration (1975, Table 9) used nearly two hundred separate country of birth categories to depict the birthplace of immigrants entering Canada during that year.

Country of birth is of interest not only as a demographic characteristic but also because it is intimately tied to occupational stratification in Canada. In the past, immigrants from certain countries, such as Great Britain, have been observed to hold occupations of high status, whereas immigrants from other countries have generally concentrated in occupations of lower status (Blishen, 1970). The cause of this ranking is much discussed. Such stratification in part arises from the association between country of origin and labour force skills. But, as discussed at the beginning of this chapter, such ranking also may reflect the existence of discriminatory practices which stratify birthplace groups in terms of social and occupational suitability. Thus, British immigrants may concentrate in high skill occupations because they have the education and the training required for entry into such occupations. At the same time, however, they may be advantaged by the existence of a stereotype which views persons born in Great Britain as occupationally desirable, beyond the value of the skills which they have to offer. Conversely, persons born in another country may not be equipped with labour market skills and/or they may be handicapped by a label which defines them as less acceptable, or else as acceptable only for certain occupations.

Hypothetically, such stereotypes do not operate in an economically efficient job market when skills are purchased by a would-be employer according to a rational criteria. However, the possible impact of sentiment with respect to the occupational stratification of immigrants is not to be underestimated. Vociferous arguments arose during the latter half of the nineteenth century concerning the desirability of recruiting from Great Britain, and it more generally encouraged the immigration of persons considered culturally compatible with Canadian society. Immigrants from Asian and southern and eastern European countries were often depicted as problematic both in terms of under-cutting wage levels established for resident Canadians but also more generally in terms of cultural assimilation (see Palmer, 1975). The debate over the desirability of persons according to country of origin has continued throughout the twentieth century and is reflected in immigration regulations prior to 1962.

Because of the ideological component to immigration policy, and the association between country of birth and occupational skills, a number of questions arise which are pertinent to any study which investigates the occupational attainment of immigrant groups. The first task, of course, is to assess what occupational differences exist by birthplace; the second task is to ask why. Do some groups have a higher occupational status than others because they come from higher socioeconomic origins or because they have higher than average levels of education? Or does there seem to be an advantage which still remains even after background variables and occupational skills are considered? Conversely, are some birthplace groups likely to be characterized by unskilled or semi-skilled occupations because they lack the skills necessary to obtain higher status occupations? Or does there seem to be a persistent occupational disadvantage which is associated with membership in that birthplace group?

These questions are examined for males with respect to the following birthplace groups: Canada, United States, United Kingdom, the Netherlands, Germany, Italy, Portugal and Greece,[2] other western European countries, Poland, other eastern European countries, and other areas of the world. While a more detailed classification of country of birth would have been greatly preferred, such a classification was not feasible given the small number of men in the Job Mobility sample who came from countries other than those cited above. That is, using the detailed classification system of the Canadian Mobility questionnaire causes the analysis to be based on subsamples containing small numbers, with the result that statistical analyses are affected by sampling variability. As a result, a country of birth classificatioin is used which represents the major countries of origin for the foreign-born labour force in Canada in 1973. The classification is based on instructions and categories used in the Canadian Mobility questionnaire.

The resultant country of birth distribution for the Canadian male labour force in 1973 is shown in Table 11.6. For the 1973 foreign-born male labour force, Great Britain and Italy have been the major suppliers of manpower, followed by persons born in eastern European countries. Only about 23 per cent of the latter category were born in Ukraine despite the large-scale migration of this group to Canada during the early 1900s and the late 1920s. The relatively small representation of Ukrainians in our sample and the resulting decision not to analyse them separately reflects the fact that many of these early pioneers are over age 65 in 1973 and are not included in the population analysed here. Ukrainians as an ethnic group, which includes not only first generation migrants but also their descendants, is much larger and the occupational attainment of this group is analysed in Chapter 10.

Students of migration will correctly note that questions pertaining to birthplace and ethnicity are frequently plagued by changes in boundaries, particularly with respect to the Austro-Hungarian Empire and other eastern European areas. Since respondents were instructed to check country of ˙birth according to present-day boundaries, the possibility arises that birthplace categories do not correspond to the national and social context in which those individuals lived. The problem is minimized by the inclusion of Ukrainians in other eastern European groups but persists to some extent for persons born in Poland. Cross-tabulations of birthplace by ethnicity for the foreign-born population reveals that of males in the labour force who were born in Poland, 7 per cent give their ethnicity as Ukrainian and 13 per cent give their ethnicity as German. Because such slippages may reflect problems with the ethnicity question used by the Canadian census (see Ryder, 1955; DeVries, 1974), as well as with the question on birthplace, we have noted, but not corrected for, the inconsistency.

Characteristics of Immigrants by Country of Birth

Despite the fact that the specifications age 25 to 64 and in the labour force reduce much of our foreign-born sample to postwar immigrants, the pattern of immigration by country of birth closely parallels the discussion based on migration flows which is found in Chapter 2. These trends may be seen in Table 11.6 which presents period of immigration data for the prewar period, during the 1950s and then by years which correspond to changes in Canada's immigration policy in 1962 and 1967. Reflecting the historical exchange of people and manpower across contiguous borders, two-fifths of the males who are born in the United States and in the Canadian labour force immigrated prior to the postwar period. Because immigration from Great Britain has been relatively continuous, approximately one-fifth of the males born in the United Kingdom immigrated prior to the postwar period. It would appear that the concentration of eastern European migration during the early part of the twentieth century is still mirrored in the figures observed for persons born in Poland and other eastern European areas.

TABLE 11:6 — Population and Period of Immigrations by Country of Birth, Males Age 25-64 in the 1973 Labour Force

Country of Birth	Population[a] No. (thousands)	%	Total	Period of Immigration ≤1945	1946-50	1951-56	1957-62	1963-67	1968-73
Canada	3,510	77.5	na	na	na	na	na	na	na
United States	57	1.3	100.0	40.4	3.9	4.9	8.3	10.6	31.9
United Kingdom	210	4.6	100.0	21.5	13.7	19.2	14.4	18.3	12.9
Netherlands	65	1.4	100.0	1.6	15.9	55.8	16.1	6.1	4.5
Germany	54	1.2	100.0	3.4	10.7	48.8	24.6	8.2	4.3
Italy	180	4.0	100.0	1.9	5.6	38.9	28.8	18.7	6.0
Portugal, Greece	56	1.2	100.0	—	7.7	5.3	33.9	38.9	21.9
Other Western Europe	77	1.7	100.0	11.3	7.7	33.7	14.7	18.7	13.9
Poland	47	1.0	100.0	23.0	30.6	27.1	7.7	10.4	1.2
Other Eastern Europe	110	2.4	100.0	17.3	24.0	25.9	16.1	8.9	7.7
Other	161	3.6	100.0	2.9	7.6	11.6	11.1	20.5	46.3

[a]Excludes .7 per cent of the labour force who did not respond to the country of birth question.
na. Not applicable.

What is particularly striking about Table 11.6, however, is the relatively recent importation of manpower from nations other than the United States, the United Kingdom and eastern European countries. The majority of males in the 1973 labour force who were born in the Netherlands immigrated in the 1950s, partly in response to the need for agricultural workers as perceived by the Canadian government and the population pressures at home (see Petersen, 1955). German-born males and males born in other western European countries in the labour force also predominated in the postwar migration flows. No doubt reflecting the considerable refugee movements of nationals displaced by World War II as well as the Hungarian Revolution in 1957, immigration of males born in Poland and other eastern European countries was heaviest in the decade following the war and tapered off during the 1960s and 1970s.

Italian immigration is often depicted as a postwar phenomenon despite the large influx of men during the 1880s and 1890s to work on railway and other large construction projects. The data in Table 11.6 show that 98 per cent of the males born in Italy who are now in the 1973 labour force immigrated after World War II, but that nearly two-fifths came during 1951-1956. The proportion of the Italian-born males who came in subsequent years have steadily been declining. In contrast, just as the decline in immigration from Great Britain appears to have been compensated for by the increase in persons born in the United States (also see Boyd, 1976), so too, the decline in the proportion of Italians in the labour force who have immigrated in recent years has been partically offset by an increment in the late 1950s and 1960s of immigrants from Greece and Portugal.

Prior to 1962, entry into Canada was regulated by criteria based on country of origin, with the result that the immigration of persons from Asian countries was sharply curtailed. The 1962 immigration relations, however, removed much of the discrimination against persons of non-European origin and explicitly used occupational skill and family relationships as the main criteria for entry. These changes were reaffirmed and further elaborated in the 1967 immigration regulations, and more recently in the 1976 Immigration Act (see Boyd, 1976). The effect of these changes are clearly shown in the data on the period of arrival for males in the labour force who were born in countries outside of North America and Europe. Two-thirds of these men have entered Canada since 1962 with nearly one-half (46 per cent) arriving after 1967. Reflecting the labour selectivity of immigration policy, many of these immigrants are in high skilled occupations (Parai, 1965, 1974).

Because of variations in period of immigration, birthplace groups differ in the number of years, or duration, spent in Canada. As shown in Table 11.7, which presents data based on the population used in subsequent listwise analyses, variations in mean years spent in Canada parallel the trends observed in Table 11.6. Most recent immigration to Canada, however, has been destined to large metropolitan areas such as Montreal, Toronto, and Vancouver, with the result that the foreign-born population is heterogeneous not only with respect to duration in Canada but with respect to urban-rural residence.

Additional differences exist by birthplace for males in the 1973 Canadian labour force. Differences between sending countries with respect to educational systems and levels of industrialization as well as an immigration policy based on family reunification and manpower recruitment means considerable association exists between country of birth and occupational skills. The variations in mean family background status, education and occupational status of the foreign-born male labour force population by country of birth are presented in Table 11.7. Generally, persons born in the United States or in the United Kingdom come from high social origins (defined as high mean paternal education, father's or head of household socioeconomic status, and few siblings), and have high mean educational and occupational levels of attainment. Conversely, persons born in Italy, Portugal, or Greece have low social origins, and the lowest mean educational and occupational status of all the groups. In between these extremes of social family origin, education and occupational characteristics, persons born in Germany, the Netherlands or other western European countries, on the average come from higher social origins and have higher mean education and occupational status than do persons born in Poland and other eastern European countries.

With the exception of coming from rather large families of origin (mean number of siblings is 4.7), persons born in the remaining areas of the world come from high socioeconomic origins and have high levels of occupational attainment which are equal, if not superior to those of persons born in western Europe (columns 4, 5, 8, 11). The high status observed for this residual category reflects response to the immigration policy of the 1960s which facilitated not only the reunification of families but also the importation of highly trained manpower (Boyd, 1976; Hawkins, 1972; Parai, 1975). In the Canadian Mobility study data, 46 per cent of immigrant males in the labour force who were not born in Europe, the United Kingdom, or the United States, have come to Canada after 1967, and 30 per cent of these are professionals or managers according to the 1971 Statistics Canada classification of occupations. Since immigration of non-western or North American

TABLE 11:7 — Socio-demographic Characteristics Pertaining to the Occupational Attainment of Males Age 25-64, in the 1973 Labour Force by Country or Region of Birth

Country of birth	Canada	USA	UK	Germany	Nether-land	Italy	Portugal, Greece	Other, Western Europe	Poland	Other East-ern Europe	Other
Means and Standard Deviations											
Father's education	7.311	9.775	9.994	9.552	9.345	4.761	4.584	9.720	6.443	7.980	8.952
	(3.913)	(4.606)	(3.331)	(4.246)	(3.719)	(2.988)	(3.563)	(4.353)	(3.956)	(4.155)	(4.760)
Father's SES	35.048	42.153	41.288	36.142	35.533	27.261	27.164	39.482	33.085	33.496	41.200
	(13.140)	(16.424)	(13.547)	(13.007)	(15.923)	(7.410)	(9.340)	(16.620)	(12.702)	(14.728)	(16.455)
Number of siblings	4.649	3.392	2.711	3.114	5.013	4.492	4.289	2.974	3.474	3.248	4.727
	(3.290)	(2.860)	(2.186)	(2.680)	(2.927)	(2.602)	(3.047)	(2.414)	(2.157)	(2.511)	(3.023)
Respondent's education	10.888	13.492	12.651	12.813	11.864	7.904	7.543	11.998	10.766	10.848	12.887
	(3.664)	(4.043)	(3.038)	(2.801)	(3.143)	(3.798)	(3.678)	(3.599)	(4.600)	(4.068)	(3.023)
Respondent's 1973 occupation	44.322	49.290	50.466	46.243	43.984	35.400	31.507	46.336	41.298	41.258	47.865
	(14.986)	(16.929)	(13.929)	(13.894)	(15.963)	(11.586)	(7.894)	(15.570)	(14.944)	(14.617)	(15.743)
Age	41.002	43.070	43.030	39.441	41.800	41.187	40.249	41.731	49.177	46.918	38.317
	(11.139)	(12.168)	(11.140)	(10.059)	(10.008)	(9.651)	(8.074)	(11.417)	(9.339)	(9.944)	(9.867)
Duration		21.433	20.100	18.850	18.891	15.596	9.185	17.684	25.395	22.975	9.650
		(20.571)	(14.610)	(8.878)	(6.993)	(6.875)	(5.009)	(11.849)	(12.123)	(12.678)	(9.652)
(Na)											
Percent Distribution											
Urban-rural residence	100.0	100.0	100.0	100.0	100.0	100.0	100.0	100.0	100.0	100.0	100.0
Large urban centre	45.7	58.2	71.2	59.8	42.1	86.0	82.1	72.7	67.8	66.5	83.3
Other urban	30.3	25.6	19.5	22.3	26.4	11.1	17.3	17.6	23.2	17.1	11.3
Rural areas	24.0	16.2	9.3	17.9	31.5	2.9	.6	9.7	9.0	16.4	5.4

[a]Characteristics pertain to sample used in listwise regression, Table 11:8

[b]Standard deviations given in parentheses.

hemisphere aliens was sharply curtailed before 1962, most of these men would not have had relatives in Canada to sponsor their entry and thus most would have immigrated on the basis of their occupational skills. Although data from the Department of Manpower and Immigration are not readily available, the criteria used to admit persons born in other regions are undoubtedly more variable, reflecting refugee movement, family reunification, and Canadian manpower requirements.

In addition to showing the variations with the foreign-born male labour force with respect to social origins, education and occupational status, data in Table 11.7 also reaffirm the position of various immigrant groups relative to native-born Canadians. As noted by Blishen (1970) who used 1961 census data, persons born in the United States and the United Kingdom have a mean occupational status which exceeds that observed for the native-born male labour force. Persons born in western Europe also have a mean occupational status which approximates or is greater than that of native-born Canadian males. On the other hand, persons born in southern or eastern European countries on the average have a lower occupational status compared to the native born. Similar rankings are observed with 1971 census data on occupational categories (Richmond and Kalbach, 1980). Such patterns once again indicate the biopolar effect which immigration had upon the Canadian occupational structure. Not only is immigration used to recruit highly trained manpower to the Canadian economy; it also operates to fill the lower-status occupations. The result is an occupational structure in which native-born males on the average occupy the middle range of occupations and where the occupational position of immigrants is closely related to country of origin.

Differences in Occupational Attainment by Country of Birth

As discussed above, the occupational stratification by country or region of birth parallels the variations in social origin and educational attainment. Country of birth groups with a high mean occupational status on the average come from high social origins and have high levels of educational attainment relative to other groups, and vice versa.

In keeping with status attainment research, the question arises as to whether the higher and lower occupational statuses of various birthplace groups reflect their stock of resources or whether such differences also reflect advantages or impediments faced by various groups in the labour market. One way to address this question is to use Multiple Classification Analysis (MCA) which is a form of dummy variable analysis in which one or more of the independent variables such as sex or nativity is a categorical or nominal variable (Andrews, Morgan and Sonquist, 1971). The statistical model is additive, which means that the effect of independent variables such as social origins and education on occupational status is assumed to be the same for all place of birth groups. The model does permit compositional differences between groups, and it indicates the contribution in occupational status points which are attributable to the specific socioeconomic characteristics of birthplace groups. This technique also indicates the variation in occupational status which remains for birthplace groups after statistically adjusting for differences in educational attainment. The differences in occupational status rankings which remain between birthplace groups may be interpreted as reflecting the effect per se of membership in these birthplace groups and the relative advantage or disadvantage of such membership. However, because the occupational status scores generated are net of variables included in the analysis, it is possible that the adjusted differences between birthplace groups reflects the influence of variables which are associated with birthplace (such as knowledge of Canada's charter languages) but which are not explicitly included in the analysis.

The MCA analysis results, which are presented in Table 11.8, are expressed as deviations from the grand mean of 44.268 Blishen-McRoberts points observed for the male labour force age 25 to 64. Column 1 presents the deviations from the grand mean which are observed for all country of origin groups before statistical adjustments for differences in composition are made. Within limits of the rounding error, these deviations when added or subtracted to the grand mean of 44.268 will correspond to the mean occupational statuses of Table 11.7, line 5. The analysis is downweighted by a factor of 1/300.5, since using group specific weights violates the MCA requirement that $\Sigma P_1 d_1 = 0$ where P_1 is the proportion of the population in the ith group and d_1 is the deviation from the grand mean.

Column 2 of Table 11.8 presents the deviations from the grand mean which remain after statistical adjustments are made for compositional differences by birthplace groups in age, place of residence distributions and in mean social origins (defined as paternal education, paternal occupation and number of siblings) and education. Column 2 is labelled as "net effects" since it presents the effects of birthplace which operate directly on occupational status controlling for other variables in the model.

Column 3 is calculated as the difference between the first two columns in Table 11.8. It indicates the relative increment or decrement in

TABLE 11:8 — Variations in Occupational Status of Males, Age 25-64, in the 1973 Labour Force by Country or Region of Birth

| | Gross Effects[a] (1) | Net Effects[b] (2) | Total (3) | Indirect Effects | | | Actual Unweighted[e] N (7) |
				Due to Age, Size of Place[c] (4)	Social Origins[d] (5)	Education (6)	
Canada	.054	.558	-.504	-.459	-.141	.096	8,275
United States	5.022	-.187	5.209	.075	3.680	1.455	144
United Kingdom	6.198	.674	5.524	1.334	3.480	.710	406
Netherlands	-.284	-2.090	1.806	-.698	1.231	1.273	149
Germany	1.975	-2.464	4.439	.946	1.698	1.795	110
Italy	-8.868	-2.216	-6.652	2.987	-4.817	-4.822	257
Portugal, Greece	-12.761	-5.311	-7.450	2.947	-4.786	-5.611	86
Other Western Europe	2.068	-1.665	3.733	1.603	2.549	-.419	130
Poland	-2.970	-3.072	.102	-.029	-.580	.711	73
Other Eastern Europe	-3.010	-3.308	.298	.313	.383	-.398	208
Other	3.597	-2.524	6.121	3.066	1.228	1.827	270

[a]Deviations from the grand mean of 44.268.

[b]Deviations from the grand mean controlling for age, size of place of residence, family origin variables and respondents education.

[c]Deviations from the grand mean, controlling for membership in four age cohorts: 25-34; 35-44; 45-54; 55-64 and for size of place of residence. Size of place residence is defined as residence in one of two areas: large urban centres of 100,000 or more population and the remainder of Canada.

[d]Social origin variables are father's education, occupation of household head when the respondent was age 16, and the number of siblings.

[e]Regression analysis was carried out by weighting the sample to be representative, but by downweighting the results by a factor of 1/300.50.

occupational status which birthplace groups receive because of their age, place of residence distributions, and because of their mean social origin and educational attainments. For example, of the actual 6.198 advantage enjoyed by the males born in the United Kingdom relative to the average status of 44.268 Blishen-McRoberts points for the male labour force, 5.524 points are due to their age and place of residence composition and to their generally high social origins and educational attainments. Conversely, of the 8.868 point lower than average occupational status of the Italian-born, 6.652 points are attributed to their sociodemographic characteristics. This overall contribution can be further decomposed into three additional components: occupational status points which are attributable to the differing age and residential distributions of the birthplace groups; the points which are due to the social origin composition of birthplace groups; and the points which reflect the net effect of place of birth on educational attainment.

Column 4, Table 11.8, presents the changes in mean occupational status which are due to age and urban-rural distributions of birthplace groups. Since residence in large urban centres compared to smaller ones and rural areas is associated with higher mean occupational status (see Table 11.3), groups which are highly concentrated in large urban areas are likely to receive a positive increment in occupational status, and vice versa for groups more geographically dispersed.

In a similar fashion, column 5 represents the effect of birthplace operating through social origins, net of age and place of residence, and column 6 in 11.8 represents the effect of birthplace, net of age distribution and social origin factors, which operates via education. A positive value in column 6 indicates that a given group benefits occupationally because its average educational attainment is higher than the average observed for the entire labour force, net of age and social origins. Similarly, a negative value indicates that a given group loses occupational status because of its lower than average educational attainment, relative to the average observed for the total population after controlling for age and social origins. Since the utility of expressing data in this form becomes clearer by example, we now turn to a discussion of the substantive findings.

Of the many themes appearing throughout the sociological and demographic literature on immigrant groups in Canada, the theme stressing the higher status of the British immigrant relative to all others is perhaps the best known (see Blishen, 1970; Richmond, 1967). This theme is reaffirmed by the Canadian Mobility study. The data in tables 11.7 and 11.8 show that with respect to occupational status, persons born in the United Kingdom are advantaged relative to all other groups, including native-born Canadians. Much of this advantage, however, is due to their stock of socioeconomic characteristics which in turn are associated with occupational achievement (Table 11.8, columns 1-3). Of the 5.524 increment in occupational status which males born in the United Kingdom have as a result of their socioeconomic characteristics relative to other groups, their age and place of residence composition account for 1.334 points. Their very high average social origins (see Table 11.7) contribute an additional 3.480 points and net of social origins, their high average educational attainment accounts for an additional .710 Blishen-McRoberts points. Thus, although immigrant males born in the United Kingdom do retain a slight occupational status advantage after adjustments are made for the higher than average characteristics (Table 11.8, column 2), it is clear that the observed higher than average occupational status in large measure reflects their social origins.

It is interesting to compare this pattern with that observed for persons born in the United States and for the native-born Canadian worker. The data in Table 11.8, columns 4 to 6, indicate that males born in the United States and in the United Kingdom both have higher mean occupational status than average in part because of their superior social origins relative to other groups. But, unlike the U.K. birthplace group, the age-residence composition of United States' born immigrants contributes little to their occupational status, and they receive a 1.5 increment in occupational status for their higher than average education. In contrast to the experience of both the United States and the United Kingdom birthplace groups, social origin characteristics do not have as much impact of the occupational status of native-born Canadians as do their age and place of residence composition. Although Canadian-born males in the labour force lose .141 Blishen-McRoberts points in occupational status because of their social origins, they lose a further .459 points because they are more likely than other birthplace groups to reside in smaller size places where mean occupational status is lower than in lage places (see Table 11.3) and because of their age distribution (Table 11.7).

The data contained in Table 11.8 also illustrate the way in which sociodemographic characteristics of immigrants can negatively affect occupational status. Males born in Italy, and Portugal and Greece have occupational statuses which are 8.868 and 12.761 below the average observed for the entire male labour force (Table 11.8, column 1). Of the 6.652 and 7.450 point disadvantage which can be attributed to the demographic and social characteristics of these immigrant groups, the decomposition presented in columns 4 to 6 indicates that the Italian-born lose about 4.8 occupational status points because of their social origins (see Table 11.7) and an additional 4.8 points because of their lower than average educational attainments. However, this does not translate into a net 9.6 disadvantage for the Italian-born because of their higher concentration in large urban centres. Age and residential location increase the occupational status of the foreign-born Italians by 2.9 points, with the result that the combined effect of sociodemographic characteristics accounts for about 6.7 points of the overall 8.9 disadvantage (Table 11.8, columns 3 to 6).

The overall patterns of birthplace differentials in gross occupational status (Table 11.8, column 1) reflect the group differences in composition and the impact of such variables on occupational status. But, as indicated by column 2 in Table 11.8, some of the relative advantages and disadvantages which characterize birthplace groups is offset by the negative effect of membership in such birthplace groups (Table 11.8, columns 2 and 3 sum to column 1). Because differences by birthplace groups in age, social origins, education, and urban residence have been statistically controlled, the data in Table 11.8, column 2, may be interpreted as the effects of membership in the various groups, although, as indicated earlier, it also includes the effects of variables which are associated with birthplace but which are not included in the analysis. If the data are interpreted in this manner then a comparison of columns 1 to 3 indicates the varying experiences of the immigrant male labour force with respect to occupational attainment. Because of their sociodemographic characteristics, males born in the United States or in the United Kingdom have an occupational advantage of over 5 Blishen-McRoberts points relative to the overall mean, and this advantage is only mildly offset by the .674 point advantage and the .187 loss in occupational status which is associated with membership in the United Kingdom and United States birthplace group, net of other factors. Males born in the Netherlands, Germany, Poland, and eastern Europe also have a sociodemographic profile which operates to their advantage (Table 11.8, column 3) but this advantage is offset by larger negative effects associated with membership in these groups. On the the other hand, males born in Italy, and Portugal and Greece are doubly handicapped. Their average sociodemographic characteristics are below those other groups and this partly is responsible for their lower occupational status. At the same time, these groups are also affected by the loss in occupational status associated with being born in southern European countries.

It is important to note that foreign birth is associated with a lower occupational status for many birthplace groups. After controls are made for age, social origins, education, and size of place of residence, only males born in Canada and the United Kingdom have mean occupational statuses higher than the overall mean of 44.268 (Table 11.8, column 2). As discussed earlier, the preponderance of negative deviations fro the grand mean for all non-United Kingdom countries of birth may reflect a variety of factors operating with varying importance for various groups: psychological factors such as achievement striving; linguistic capabilities; familiarity with the labour market; location in segmented labour markets; quality of education; and/or discrimination. Without further specification of the model of occupational attainment, it is impossible to determine the relative importance of any of these possible factors. However, the evidence is clear: if country of birth groups were similar with respect to age, social origins, education, and size of place of residence, foreign-born males, excluding those born in the United Kingdom, would have a lower mean occupational status than native-born males. Further, the relative disadvantage varies greatly by country with the negative effect being the greatest for males born in southern or eastern European countries.

In the migration literature, the lower occupational skills of southern European birthplace and language groups are well documented (see Hawkins, 1972; Li, 1978, 1979; Richmond, 1979; Richmond and Kalbach, 1980). However, what is surprising is the greater disadvantage of males born in Portugal and Greece relative to Italian-born males. This disadvantage in mean occupational status arises because of a 5.3 point loss in occupational status associated with being born in Portugal or Greece, controlling for differences in social origins, education, age, and place of residence. As noted earlier, this loss of mean occupational status which is associated with birthplace reflects the influence of variables associated with country of birth, but not explicitly included in the model. Thus, as is the case for all foreign-born males of non-United Kingdom birth, the loss in occupational status, net of other social origin, education, and size of place of residence (column 2, Table 11.8) undoubtedly reflects a variety of factors, such as familiarity with the Canadian labour market, participation in an ethnically defined labour market, and linguistic ability. In turn, all of these factors are associated with length of time spent in Canada. Generally, the longer a foreign-born person resides in a host country, the more likely is the acquisition of language skills and familiarity with local and national labour markets. As tables 11.6 and 11.7 show, the immigration of most of the male labour force born in Portugal or Greece has occurred very recently. Hence, it is possible that the lower occupational status of these men reflects in part the recency of arrival in Canada.[3]

If the lower mean occupational status observed for Greek and Portuguese males in the Canadian labour force in column 2, Table 11.8, reflects recency of arrival, then statistical adjustments for duration of years spent in Canada should substantially reduce these inequalities. These adjustments are presented in Table 11.9, which presents the mean occupational statuses of foreign-born birthplace groups as deviations from the grand mean of 44.335. Because length of time spent in Canada is a meaningless variable for most native-born Canadians, the latter were excluded from this analysis, and numbers should not be compared directly with those in Table 11.8. However, findings based on Table 11.9 parallel those based on Table 11.8. Table 11.9, column 1, once again reveals that foreign-born males differ greatly in mean occupational status by country or region of birth. Males born in the United States and the United Kingdom have the highest mean occupational status of all foreign-born males in the labour force, whereas males born in Italy, Greece or Portugal have the lowest. Taking into account the differences between groups with respect to social origins, education, age, and place of residence considerably reduces these differentials between birthplace groups (column 2). But the pattern in

TABLE 11:9 — **Variations in the Occupational Status of Foreign-born Males, Age 25-64 in the 1973 Labour Force, Net of Duration in Canada**

| | | Net Effects[b] | |
	Gross Effects[a] (1)	Excluding Duration (2)	Including Duration (3)
United States	5.590	.370	.173
United Kingdom	6.385	2.754	2.627
Netherlands	−.804	−.362	−.428
Germany	2.541	−.015	−.129
Italy	−9.096	−1.437	−1.321
Portugal, Greece	−12.234	−4.060	−3.659
Other Western Europe	2.292	.879	.873
Poland	−3.483	−1.794	−1.977
Other Eastern Europe	−2.734	−1.448	−1.556
Other	3.782	.069	.279

[a]Deviations from the grand mean of 44.335.
[b]Deviation from the grand mean of 44.335, controlling for membership in four ten-year age groups, father's education, occupation of the head of the household when the respondent was age 16, number of siblings, respondent's education, and residence either in a large urban centre of 100,000 population or more or other areas.

which Italian and southern Europeans have lower than average occupational status still remains despite some shifts in relative ranking (Italians move from second-lowest to fourth-lowest, above males born in Poland and other eastern European countries). Additional statistical adjustments for differences between the birthplace groups with respect to number of years spent in Canada changes the overall picture very little. Even after differences in age, social origins, place of residence, education, and duration in Canada are taken into account, persons born in Portugal and Greece still have a mean occupational status which is 3.66 points below the mean observed for all foreign-born males in the labour force. Italians have a mean which is 1.32 points below the overall mean. Further, persons born in Poland and other eastern European countries also remain occupationally disadvantaged, and persons born in the United States, the United Kingdom, and in "other" areas continue to have the highest occupational status of all. In short, there appear to be occupational inequalities between foreign-born males by country of birth which cannot be attributed to differentials in social origins, education, place of residence, or duration spent in Canada. The inequalities may well reflect the influence of social and economic variables not explicitly excluded in the model. However, it is difficult to ignore the pattern of inequalities which clearly show that birthplace in the United States, the United Kingdom, or nothern or western European countries confers an occupational advantage compared to birthplace in southern and eastern European countries. This pattern not only parallels historical sentiment on the cultural desirability of national origin groups; it also suggests the persistence over time of the resultant structure of occupational stratification.

The Double Negative: Occupational Attainment by Sex and Birthplace

The data presented in the previous section indicate that birthplace operates to differentiate and stratify the male Canadian labour force. However, the picture concerning the stratification of immigrants is oversimplified by the exclusion of women from the analysis. In reality, the occupational stratification of the entire immigrant population in Canada depends not only on birthplace but also on sex. The status of immigrant women in the Canadian labour force can be understood as reflecting the combined negative impact of sex and birthplace or the "double negative" effect. As discussed by Almquist and Wehrle-Einhorn (1978), Epstein (1973) and Seidman (1978), individuals are frequently disadvantaged by membership in negatively evaluated status groups which are defined by such ascriptive criteria as race, sex, or nativity. Such disadvantages can be compounded by membership in two or more of these negative status groups. In this context, the double negative concept implies that immigrant women should display occupational characteristics which reflect the double disadvantage of being female and being foreign-born. To the extent being female connotes participation in a sex-segregated occupational structure, immigrant women in the labour force should display occupational characteristics which are more similar to those observed for native-born women than to those observed for native and foreign-born males. However, being foreign-born also may confer a disadvantage. In such a case, immigrant women should occupy lower status occupational positions compared to native-born women. Further, if considerable stratification by birthplace exists within the immigrant labour force, the lower occupatgional status of immigrant women relative to native-born females and to males may be more characteristic of some birthplace groups than of others.

Minimally, the double negative concept suggests that workers in the labour force should be stratified by sex and by native-born/foreign-born status with the lowest positions held by immigrant women. Empirical research is consistent with the double negative concept. Boyd (1975) and Arnopoulos (1979) note that immigrant women appear to bear a double burden with respect to their standing in the labour force. Like that of immigrant males, the labour force characteristics of female immigrants in Canada in part reflects the association between immigration policy, particularly admissions criteria, and country of origin characteristics. But, in addition, as females, foreign-born women are more likely than men to be in the labour force as part-time workers and relative to both men and to native-born women, they are located disproportionately ". . . in the poorly paid labour market sectors where they work as domestics, chambermaids, building cleaners, dishwashers, waitresses, sewing machine operators and plastics workers. Ignored by unions and inadequately protected by labour legislation, they occupy the bottom rung of the 'vertical mosaic' " (Arnopoulos, 1979:3).

However, the double negative concept goes beyond a simple documentation of the relative occupational positions of sex and nativity groups in the labour force. An ensuing question is why the positions of groups in the labour force are influenced by sex and nativity. One possibility is that occupational variations among sex and birthplace groups reflect compositional differences between the groups with respect to variables such as education which are known to affect occupational standing. Thus, occupational differences might be observed between immigrant men and women or between immigrant women and native-born women because of sex or country of origin differences in the educational system and in work training programs. A second possibility is that immigrant women are disadvantaged occupationally because of their membership per se in a given sex or nativity group. At least three reasons can be given for the existence of this double negative effect, net of occupationally related characteristics. First, employer discrimination by sex and birthplace may exist, which operates to the disadvantage of one group over another. Alternatively, and perhaps concurrently, the formation of ethnically and linguistically bounded local economies, which is a feature of immigrant receiving societies, may shape the employment patterns of female immigrants more so than men. Such shaping might arise from non-North American norms concerning the male approval over the place of work for females (see Kosack, 1976, for a description of this with respect to European women) as well as from the tendency of males rather than females to be the first to receive the instruction offered by Canadian language training programs. Finally, several researchers (Kosack, 1976; Petras, 1979; the Working Party on Women Migrants, 1978) suggest that double disadvantages of immigrant women derive from the more general exploitation of workers in a class society and from the relation between core-capitalist economies and those of the dependent economies of the periphery.

With respect to analyses of immigrants in the Canadian labour force, the double negative concept raises two questions. First, do the characteristics of workers in the labour force suggest the existence of the double negative in which foreign-born women are lower in occupational status than native-born females and native and foreign-born males in the labour force? Secondly, do such differentials reflect group differences in work related skills, or is there evidence of sex and/or nativity advantages or disadvantages which suggest that membership in a double negative status group confers a disadvantage per se for immigrant women? In particular, are all immigrant women affected by the double negative phenomenon, or does stratification by birthplace operate to mitigate the disadvantage for some birthplace groups but not for others?

In keeping with the rationale provided in Chapter 6, these two questions are answered with data for the full-time paid (wages, salary and self-employment income) members of the labour force. With respect to the first question, the data presented in Table 11.10 indicate a differentiation of the Canadian labour force by sex and nativity which is consistent with the double negative concept. Foreign-born women age 25 to 64 have on the average the lowest occupational statuses of all four sex-nativity groups. Depending on place of residence (total Canada or

TABLE 11:10 — Occupational Status and Distributions for the Native and Foreign-born Full-time Paid Labour Force by Sex and Place of Residence, 1973.

| | Total Canada | | | | Large Urban Centres[b] | | | |
| | Males | | Females | | Males | | Females | |
	Native-born (1)	Foreign-born (2)	Native-born (3)	Foreign-born (4)	Native-born (5)	Foreign-born (6)	Native-born (7)	Foreign-born (8)
Actual Sample n	11,359	2,467	3,434	858	3,447	1,501	1,313	609
Current Occupation Status								
Mean	43.8	43.5	46.5	42.8	48.0	44.6	48.6	43.1
standard deviation	(14.6)	(15.1)	(12.8)	(14.0)	(14.2)	(15.2)	(12.1)	(14.2)
1971 Census Classification	(100.0)	(100.0)	(100.0)	(100.0)	(100.0)	(100.0)	(100.0)	(100.0)
Managerial and administration	8.5	7.6	4.7	3.7	12.2	8.8	5.7	3.9
Professional and semi-professional	10.7	15.2	23.6	19.9	14.5	16.6	24.1	19.1
Clerical	6.5	4.9	36.7	28.7	8.7	5.6	43.4	29.6
Sales	11.8	8.0	8.0	7.7	14.0	8.8	7.1	7.7
Services	7.5	9.9	14.0	13.6	8.2	11.1	9.5	12.3
Farm, fishing, logging	9.6	4.6	.5	1.0	1.1	1.3	.1	.6
Mining, quarry	10.0	12.7	3.5	3.8	7.9	11.6	2.1	4.3
Production, fabrication, assembly and repairs	10.8	13.9	6.5	18.0	11.1	14.1	5.2	19.3
Construction trades	11.3	14.6	.1	.0	9.0	14.4	.1	.0
Transportation, crafts	13.3	8.6	2.4	3.7	13.3	7.7	2.7	3.2

TABLE 11:10 — (Continued)

	Total Canada				Large Urban Centres			
	Males		Females		Males		Females	
	Native-born (1)	Foreign-born (2)	Native-born (3)	Foreign-born (4)	Native-born (5)	Foreign-born (6)	Native-born (7)	Foreign-born (8)
Pineo-Porter-McRoberts Classification	(100.0)	(99.8)	(99.9)	(99.9)	(99.9)	(100.1)	(100.0)	(100.0)
Professionals	8.4	10.9	9.0	7.0	11.3	12.1	9.1	7.2
Managers, administrators	8.6	6.5	1.7	2.0	11.9	7.0	3.4	2.4
Semi-professional, technicians	5.5	7.2	13.1	10.7	7.0	7.6	13.3	10.3
Supervisors, skilled white-collar	12.7	10.8	30.9	25.3	15.1	12.0	35.8	26.4
Foreman, skilled crafts and trades	25.5	27.7	1.7	2.9	23.1	26.2	1.3	2.9
Farmers and farm labourers	7.0	4.2	.4	.5	.8	1.4	.0	.2
Semi- and unskilled white-collar	8.4	6.8	28.7	23.9	10.5	8.0	27.3	22.5
Semi- and unskilled crafts and trades	23.9	25.7	13.6	27.6	20.2	25.8	9.8	28.1

urban centres of 100,000 or more persons), foreign-born women have average occupational status scores which are between 2 to 5 points lower than those of native-born women. Their lower occupational status in part reflects their occupational distribution. Of all sex and nativity groups, foreign-born women are the most occupationally concentrated in the service and in the production, fabrication, and assembly occupations, the latter reflecting their extensive employment in the garment industry (see Arnolopoulos, 1979).

The relative standing of foreign-born women compared to native-born women and men is refined somewhat by data on various birthplace groups (Table 11.11). As was shown for men in the preceding section, birthplace stratifies the female full-time paid labour force. The average occupational status for women born in the United Kingdom or in the United States is higher than average status observed for native-born women, which in turn is higher than the average occupational status of women born in western Europe, eastern Europe or other regions. Like their male counterparts, women born in the United Kingdom or in the United States come from higher socioeconomic origins and have higher educational achievements than do persons from other birthplaces. The western European birthplace group has the lowest socioeconomic origins, education and occupational statuses of all birthplace groups, a finding which reflects the inclusion of the southern European birthplace groups in this category (see Table 11.8).

In addition to birthplace, sex also stratifies the immigrant full-time paid labour force. Compared to males born in the same region, being female is associated with an occupational status which on the average is nearly equal to (United Kingdom, United States, and eastern European) or lower (western European and "other" birthplace groups). Such sex differentials are consistent with the considerable variation in the socioeconomic and sociodemographic characteristics of the various male and female birthplace groups (Table 11.11). Parallelling the findings observed earlier for the native-born paid labour force (Chapter 6), immigrant women come from slightly higher social origins (defined by father's occupational status, father's education, and number of siblings) than do their male counterparts. Depending on the birthplace group, women have educational attainments as high or slightly higher than the average observed for men. Demographically, their average age is slightly under a year younger than observed for men and they are more likely than males to reside in urban areas of 100,000 persons or more.

The data in Table 11.11 suggest that the similar or lower occupational statuses of female birthplace groups relative to men may reflect group differences in occupationally relevant characteristics rather than the

TABLE 11:11 — Sociodemographic Characteristics Pertaining to the Occupational Attainment of Males and Females in the 1973 full-time Paid Labour Force, Age 25-64, by Country of Birth.

	Males					Females				
	Native Born (1)	United Kingdom U.S.A. (2)	Western Europe (3)	Eastern Europe (4)	Other (5)	Native Born (6)	United Kingdom U.S.A. (7)	Western Europe (8)	Eastern Europe (9)	Other (10)
Father's education	7.337 (3.900)	9.977 (3.685)	6.957 (4.359)	7.555 (4.162)	8.946 (4.795)	3.849 (3.953)	10.329 (3.345)	6.978 (4.096)	9.262 (4.591)	10.203 (4.507)
Father's SES	35.085 (13.112)	41.579 (14.361)	31.914 (13.111)	33.121 (14.086)	41.285 (16.665)	36.796 (13.577)	42.616 (14.111)	32.160 (12.814)	41.389 (16.748)	42.504 (17.235)
Number of siblings	4.637 (3.283)	2.865 (2.377)	4.150 (2.803)	3.303 (2.438)	4.591 (2.903)	4.328 (3.142)	2.808 (2.441)	3.549 (2.490)	2.747 (2.050)	4.743 (3.094)
Respondents education	10.927 (3.622)	12.826 (3.328)	9.851 (4.139)	10.861 (4.230)	12.847 (3.528)	11.711 (2.809)	12.703 (2.838)	9.185 (3.880)	11.751 (3.937)	12.115 (3.849)
Respondent's 1973 occupation	44.464 (14.926)	50.105 (14.690)	39.713 (14.129)	41.486 (14.727)	47.590 (15.703)	47.021 (12.912)	49.338 (11.708)	37.174 (13.274)	41.692 (16.194)	45.031 (14.890)
Age	41.009 (10.992)	42.895 (11.285)	41.052 (9.852)	47.223 (9.750)	38.227 (9.741)	32.851 (11.286)	41.295 (11.672)	39.326 (9.353)	47.213 (9.653)	35.930 (9.278)
Percent Distribution										
Place of Residence										
Large urban centre	45.7	67.8	71.9	68.1	82.9	54.0	75.9	85.8	77.1	84.4
Other urban centre	30.4	21.4	17.5	17.6	11.6	30.8	17.3	10.5	17.5	12.6
Rural area	23.9	10.8	10.6	14.3	5.5	15.2	6.8	3.7	5.4	3.0

[a]Characteristics pertain to sample used in listwise regression, Table 11.12.
[b]Standard deviations given in parenthesis.

TABLE 11:12 — Variations in Occupational Attainment of Males and Females in the 1973 Full-time Paid Labour Force, Age 25-64, by Country or Region of Birth

Sex and Birthplace	Gross Effects[a] (1)	Net Effects[b] (2)	Total (3)	Net Effects, Due to			Actual Unweighted N.[e] (7)
				Age, Size of Place[c] (4)	Social Origins[a] (5)	Education (6)	
Males							
Native-born	−.315	.585	−.900	−.571	−.325	−.004	7,958
United Kingdom, U.S.A.	5.326	.085	5.241	.651	3.345	1.245	529
Western Europe[a]	−5.064	−2.366	−2.698	1.332	−1.658	−2.372	711
Eastern Europe[b]	−3.294	−3.082	−.212	−.037	−.010	−.165	269
Other	2.811	−2.628	5.439	2.501	1.058	1.881	254
Females							
Native-born	2.242	.898	1.344	.138	.266	.940	2,244
United Kingdom, U.S.A.	4.559	−.725	5.284	1.394	3.507	.383	221
Western Europe[a]	−7.605	−3.918	−3.687	2.577	−1.784	−4.480	180
Eastern Europe[b]	−3.086	−6.555	3.469	.731	3.082	−.344	75
Other	.253	−3.616	3.869	2.909	1.774	−.814	106

[a]Deviation from the grand mean of 44.779.

[b]Deviations from the grand mean controlling for age, size of place of residence, family origin variables and respondent's education.

[c]Deviations from the grand mean, controlling for membership in four age cohorts: 25-34; 35-44; 45-54; 55-64; and for size of place of residence. Size of place of residence is defined as residence in one of two areas: large urban centres of 100,000 or more population and the remainder of Canada.

[d]Social origin variablkes are father's education, occupation of household head when the respondent was age 16, and the number of siblings.

[e]Regression analysis was carried out by weighting the sample to be representative, but by downweighting the results by a factor of 1/300.50.

existence of the double negative effect. But the MCA analysis presented in Table 11.12 which adjusts for these sex and birthplace differences in sociodemographic characteristics offers support for the existence of the double negative effect. Net of their age, place of residence, socioeconomic origins, and education, foreign-born birthplace groups have occupational statuses below the average for the full-time paid labour force. However, immigrant women in the full-time paid labour force have net occupational statuses which are not only below those of native-born women but also are lower than those observed for immigrant males in the same birthplace categories (Table 11.12, column 2).

Although these data indicate a double negative effect which operates to the disadvantage of foreign-born women, the MCA analysis also indicates that the effect is much less pronounced for foreign-born women who are born either in the United Kingdom or the United States. Women born in these two countries do have a net occupational status (Table 11.12, column 2) which is nearly one point lower than the average observed for the full-time paid labour force and which is six-tenths of a point lower than that observed for men who are born in the United Kingdom or in the United States. Such data suggest that the double negative of "immigrant and female" is less of a factor in occupational achievements of those immigrant women who are members of traditionally preferred groups (e.g., United Kingdom and the United States) than it is for groups which in the past have been labelled as undesirable (such as the Asians, the eastern European origin groups at the turn of the century). In addition, the pattern of lower status displayed by non-United Kingdom or non-United States female birthplace groups may reflect the influence of a variable such as facility in one of the two charter languages, which may be associated with birthplace but which is not explicitly included in this analysis.

Conclusion

A prominent concern of Canadian commentators, legislators, and social scientists is the adaptation of the immigrant to a new country. This concern has resulted in the past in restrictive immigration policies whose purpose was to exclude those deemed ill suited for the Canadian culture. But in addition to such negative images, the concern has also fanned an image of immigrants as hard-working, striving, and ultimately successful participants in the economic and social structure of the receiving society. This image has motivated many of the questions asked in this chapter, for implicit in such imagery is the assumption of equality between native and foreign-born in the utilization of their talents and abilities. Our analysis of such equality begins with the central question of this book and examines the process of status inheritance from one generation to the next, for both foreign and native-born males in the 1973 labour force, using a model in which occupational status is determined by father's education, occupation, number of siblings, and respondent's education.

The data from the Canadian Mobility study show native and foreign-born males to be similar with respect to average occupational status. But such similarity in outcomes masks differences in the acquisition of occupational status. It appears that the composition of the foreign and native-born population only partly accounts for differences and similarities in educational and occupational outcomes and that education exerts a greater influence on the occupational attainments of native-born males compared to foreign-born males in the 1973 labour force. These differences between foreign and native-born males with respect to the effect of education on occupational attainment increases when urban-rural residence is held constant. Here the analysis reveals that most foreign-born males operate in an urban labour market where their average occupational status in 1973 is 4 points lower than that of native-born males who also reside in large urban centres. Again, this inequality partly reflects differences between the two groups with respect to occupational status returns to family origin variables and education. Approximately one quarter of the 4 point difference is attributable to the fact that both foreign and native-born males differ with respect to social origins (paternal education and occupational status and number of siblings). Subsequent analysis suggests that the problem of obtaining equivalent market value for education received outside of Canada handicaps foreign-born males with respect to occupational attainment.

A subsequent section of this chapter asks if differences in occupational status exist among immigrants according to country of birth. The data show that males born in the United States and the United Kingdom have an average occupational status which greatly exceeds that of native-born Canadians. On the average, males born in Germany and other western European countries (excluding the Netherlands) also have higher occupational statuses, whereas males born in Italy, Greece, Portugal, Poland and other eastern European countries have lower occupational statuses. Much of the higher occupational statuses of birthplace groups, when compared either to Canadians or to the entire labour force, is due to differences between immigrants with respect to social origins (number of siblings, father's education and occupation) education and urban-rural residence in Canada. When these differences are taken into account, only males born in Great Britain continue to have an average occupational status which exceeds that of Canadian-born males. For the most part, foreign birth handicaps males in the attainment of occupational status. Some birthplace groups overcome this disadvantage because of high social origins, education, or a favourable urban-rural distribution. But not all groups are successful. When only the foreign-born male labour force population is analysed by country of birth, the pattern of occupational status conforms closely to historical images concerning the cultural, social, and occupational desirability of origin groups.

In addition to birthplace, sex also acts as an axis of occupation stratification. In keeping with this perspective, immigrant women in the Canadian full-time paid labour force are observed to have occupational statuses which are lower on the average than those of other sex and nativity groups and which appear to reflect not only their level of occupational status related resources, but also their membership in two negative status groups: female and foreign-born. However, with this group of female immigrant workers, considerable stratification exists by birthplace, and the analysis indicates that the double negative of being female and foreign-born is less of a factor for the occupational attainments of women born in the United States and in the United Kingdom.

Overall, then, the analysis conducted in this chapter tempers the imagery of immigrant success and social equality. Handicapped in the process of occupational attainment by the lower effect of educational attainment on occupational attainment, foreign-born males work predominantly in an urban labour market where, on the average, their occupational status is lower than that of native-born males. But while such occupational inequalities characterize the foreign-born males as a group compared to their native-born counterparts, substantial differences exist within the foreign-born population by country of birth. Some groups, notably males born in the United Kingdom and the U.S., have high occupational statuses compared to other groups. These patterns of occupational inequality which exist among the foreign-born population are not wholly accounted for by differences in social origins, education, urban-rural residence, or length of time spent in Canada. It is a pattern which persists among immigrant women, and their relative occupational standing, in turn, further emphasizes the importance of birthplace and sex as factors underlying the Canadian mosaic.

Notes

1. The gain and loss in occupational status will not sum to the actual difference in occupational status means between the foreign and the native-born because the decomposition of means technique includes a third term to represent interaction between compositional differences and equation differences.
2. Immigrants born in Greece and Portugal were combined in order to retain additional information on southern European immigration. Otherwise, given the smallness of the subsamples, they would have had to be combined either with the Italian or other western European birthplace groups.
3. It may well be that language skill rather than duration is a more powerful explanatory variable accounting for the differentials between birthplace groups. However, initial cross tabulations of the language questions did not suggest much discriminatory power associated with them for foreign-born males. Most males checked English or French as the language spoken on the job, most comfortable in speaking and known well enough to carry on a conversation. This issue, however, has not been fully explored.

References

ALMQUIST, ELIZABETH M. and JUANITA L. WEHRLE-EINHORN
   1978   "The Double Disadvantaged: Minority Women in the Labour Force."
         In Ann H. Stromberg and Shirley Harkess, eds., *Women Working*. Palo
         Alto, California: Mayfield Publishing Co.
ALTHAUSER, ROBERT P. and MICHAEL WIGLER
   1972   "Standardization and Component Analysis." *Sociological Methods and
         Research*, 1 (Aug. 1972): 97-135.
ARNOPOULOS, SHEILA
   1979   *Problems of Immigrant Women in the Canadian Labour Force*. Ottawa:
         Report for the Canadian Advisory Council on the Status of Women.
ANDREWS FRANK, JAMES MORGAN and JOHN SONQUIST
   1971   *Multiple Classification Analysis*. Ann Arbor: University of Michigan,
         Institute for Social Research.
BACH, ROBERT L.
   1978   "Mexican Workers in the United States: A Study of Migration and
         Social Change." Ph.D. dissertation. Department of Sociology, Duke
         University, Durham, North Carolina.
BLAU, PETER and OTIS DUDLEY DUNCAN
   1967   *The American Occupational Structure*. New York: John Wiley.
BLISHEN, BERNARD R.
   1970   "Social Class and Opportunity in Canada." *Canadian Review of Sociology
         and Anthropology*, 7, (2):110-27.
BLISHEN, BERNARD R. and HUGH A. MCROBERTS
   1976   "A Revised Socioeconomic Index for Canada." *Canadian Review of
         Sociology and Anthropology*, 13 (Feb.): 71-79.
BOYD, MONICA
   1975   "The Status of Immigrant Women in Canada." *Canadian Review of
         Sociology and Anthropology*, 12 (Nov.): 406-16.

1976 "Immigration Policies and Trends: A Comparison of Canada and the United States." *Demography*, 13: 83-104.

BUROWAY, MICHAEL
1976 "The Functions and Reproduction of Migrant Labour. Comparative Material from Southern Africa and the United States." *American Journal of Sociology*, 81 (March): 1,050-87.

BUSTEMENTE, JORGE
1976 "Structural and Ideological Conditions of Undocumented Mexican Immigration to the United States." Pp. 145-47 in W. Boyd Littrell and Gideon Sjoberg, eds. *Current Issues in Social Policy*. Beverley Hills, California: Saga Publications.

CANADA, DEPARTMENT of MANPOWER and IMMIGRATION
Canada Immigration and Population Study. Three Years in Canada. Results of the Longitudinal Survey. Ottawa: Information Canada.

CASHMORE, ERNEST
1978 "The Social Organization of Canadian Immigration Law." *Canadian Journal of Sociology*, 3: 409-29.

CASTLES, STEVEN and GODULA KOSACK
1973 *Immigrant Workers and Class Structures in Western Europe*. London: Oxford University Press.

CLEMENT, WALLACE
1975 *The Canadian Corporate Elite: An Analysis of Economic Power*. Toronto: Carleton Library No. 89.

COHEN, JACOB
1968 "Multiple Regression as a General Data Analytic System." *Psychological Bulletin*, 70: 426-43.

DUNCAN, BEVERLY and OTIS DUDLEY DUNCAN
1968 "Minorities and the Process of Stratification." *American Sociological Review*, 33 (June) 356-64.

DUNCAN, OTIS DUDLEY, DAVID L. FEATHERMAN and BEVERLY DUNCAN
1972 *Socioeconomic Background and Occupational Achievement*. New York: Seminar Press.

EPSTEIN, CYNTHIA F.
1973 "Positive Effects of the Multiple Negative." *American Journal of Sociology* (Jan.): 912-35.

FEATHERMAN, DAVID L. and ROBERT M. HAUSER
1978 *Opportunity and Change*. New York: Academic Press.

GOLDLUST, JOHN and ANTHONY H. RICHMOND
1973 "A Multivariate Analysis of the Economic Adaptation of Immigrants in Toronto." Paper presented at the annual meeting of the Canadian Sociology and Anthropology Association, Queen's University, Kingston.

HANUSKEK, ERIC A. and JOHN E. JACKSON
1977 *Statistical Methods for Social Scientists*. New York: Academic Press.

HAWKINS, FREDA
1972 *Canada and Immigration: Public Policy and Public Concern*. Montreal: McGill-Queen's University Press.
1974 "Canadian Immigration Policy and Management." *International Migration Review*, 8: 5-22.

1977   "Canadian Immigration: A New Law and a New Approach to Management." *International Migration Review,* 11: 77-94.

KIM, JAE-ON and CHARLES MUELLER
1976   "Standardized and Unstandardized Coefficients in Causal Analysis." *Sociological Methods and Research,* 4 (May): 423-38.

KOSACK, GODULA
1976   "Migrant Women: The Move to Western Europe: A Step Towards Emancipation?" *Race and Class,* 4 (Spring): 364-79.

LAND, K.C.
1969   "Principles of Path Analysis." Pp. 30-37 in E.F. Borgatta, ed. *Sociological Methodology.* San Francisco: Jossey-Bass Publishers.

LI, PETER S.
1978   "The Stratification of Ethnic Immigrants: The Case of Toronto." *Canadian Review of Sociology and Anthropology,* 15 (Feb.): 31-40.
1979   "Ethnic Stratification in Toronto: A Reply to Richmond." *Canadian Review of Sociology and Anthropology,* 16 (May): 231-36.

MAGRATH, C.A.
1910   *Canada's Growth and Some Problems Affecting It.* Ottawa: The Mortimer Press.

MARSHALL, ADRIANA
1973   *The Import of Labour: The Case of the Netherlands.* Rotterdam: Rotterdam University Press.

PARAI, LOUIS
1965   *Immigration and Emigration of Professional and Skilled Manpower During the Postwar Period.* Economic Council of Canada, Special Study No. 1. Ottawa: Queen's Printer.
1974   *The Economic Impact of Immigration.* (Manpower and Immigration: Canadian Population Study.) Ottawa: Information Canada.
1975   "Canada's Immigration Policy 1962-1974." *International Migration Review,* 9: 449-78.

PETERSEN, WILLIAM
1955   *Planned Migrations. The Social Determinants of the Dutch-Canadian Movement.* Berkeley, California: University of California Press.

PINEO, PETER C., JOHN PORTER and HUGH MCROBERTS
1976   "The 1971 Census and the Socioeconomic Classification of Occupations." *Canadian Review of Sociology and Anthropology,* 14 (Feb.): 91-102.

PETRAS, ELIZABETH
1979   "Caribbean Labor Migrations in a Global Labor Market." Paper presented at the annual meeting of the American Sociological Association, Boston, Massachusetts.

PORTES, ALEJANDRO
1978   "Toward a Structural Analysis of Illegal (Undocumented) Immigration." *International Migration Review,* 12 (Winter): 469-84.

PORTES, ALEJANDRO and ROBERT L. BACH
1979   "Dual Labor Markets and Immigration." Paper presented at the meeting of the American Association for the Advancement of Science, Houston, Texas.

RICHMOND, ANTHONY H.
1967   *Postwar Immigrants in Canada.* Toronto: University of Toronto Press.

1969   "Sociology of Migration in Industrial and Postindustrial Societies." Pp.
238-81 in John A. Jackson, ed. *Migration*. New York: Cambridge
University Press.

1979   "Comments: Ethnic Stratification of Immigrants in Toronto." *Canadian
Review of Sociology and Anthropology*, 16 (May): 228-30.

RICHMOND, ANTHONY H. and RAVI P. VERNA

1978   "The Economic Adaptation of Immigrants: A New Theoretical
Perspective." *International Migration Review*, 12 (Spring): 3-38.

RICHMOND, ANTHONY H. and WARREN E. KALBACH

1980   *Factors in the Adjustment of Immigrants and their Descendants*. Statistics
Canada Census Analytical Study. Ottawa: Minister of Supply and
Services, Catalogue 99-761E.

RIST, RAY

1978   *Guest Workers in Germany: The Prospects for Pluralism*. New York: Praeger
Publishers.

ROCKETT, IAN RICHARD HILDRETH

1978   "Immigration, Ethnicity and Occupational Mobility: The Experience of
Recent Male Immigrants to the United States." Ph.D. dissertation.
Department of Sociology, Brown University, Providence, R.I.

RYDER, NORMAN

1955   "The Interpretation of Origin Statistics." *Canadian Journal of Economics
and Political Science*, 21: 466-79.

SEIDMAN, ANN

1978   "The Triple Jeopardy of Black and Other Minority Women." In A.
Seidman, ed. *Working Women: A Study of Women in Paid Jobs*. Colorado:
Westview Press.

SIEGEL, PAUL

1965   "On the Cost of Being a Negro." *Sociological Inquiry*, 35: 41-57.

SPECHT, DAVID A. and ROBERT WARREN

1976   "Comparing Causal Models." Pp. 46-84 in D.R. Heise, ed. *Sociological
Methodology 1975*. San Francisco: Jossey-Bass Publishers.

STRAUSS, ANSELM L.

1971   *The Contexts of Social Mobility: Ideology and Theory*. Chicago: Aldine
Publishing Company.

U.S. BUREAU of the CENSUS

1971   *The Methods and Materials of Demography*. By Henry S. Shryock, Jacob S.
Siegel and Associates. Volume I. Washington, D.C.: U.S. Government
Printing Office.

DEVRIES, JOHN

1974   "Language Maintenance and Shift Among Canadian Ethnic Groups,
1971." Unpublished Manuscript. Department of Sociology and Anthropology, Carleton University, Ottawa.

WINSBOROUGH, HALLIMAN H. and PETER DICKINSON

1971   "Components of Negro-White Income Differences." American Statistical Association. Proceedings of the Social Statistics Section. Pp. 6-8.

WORKING PARTY on WOMEN MIGRANTS (RUTH PADRUN and JEAN GUYOT, eds.)

1978   *Migrant Women Speak*. London, England: Search Press Limited.

CHAPTER 12

Nativity: Further Considerations

FRANK E. JONES

For a society where immigration is assumed to be an important factor in its development, a comparison of the educational and occupational attainment of those who were born in Canada and those who emigrated here provides valuable information. As there is a persistent interest in the adjustment of those who come to Canada, the educational and occupational attainments of native-born Canadians can provide criteria, albeit arbitrary, for such an assessment. As the presence of immigrants in sufficient numbers may also provoke prejudice and discrimination, it is obviously important to compare, on a factual basis, the successes of immigrants and native-born in areas of activity where success is judged to have prime importance in the lives of individuals.

Although the analysis reported in Chapter 11 does not directly address the question of immigrant adjustment, nor prejudice or discrimination, the facts concerning the comparative educational and occupational attainment of the native-born and foreign-born are undeniably pertinent to those broad concerns. These facts indeed are sufficiently important to justify the further analysis reported in this chapter. Here, however, the objective will be to differentiate the native-born in terms of the historical depth of their ties to Canada. In effect, the objective is to assess the generational status of the native-born within the limits allowed by the data. Thus, the attainment of those whose parents were native-born may be compared to the attainment of those whose parents were immigrants. Moreover, the position of the foreign-born may be assessed in relation to the different generational statuses of the native-born.

In Chapter 11 it was shown that differences in educational and occupational attainment were not strikingly different for native-born

447

and foreign-born males, aged 25 to 64, although the processes of educational and occupational attainment, in terms of the direct effects of the main independent variables, were shown to vary markedly in relation to birthplace. This result seems to be consistent with Porter's description, in Chapter 2, of immigrants to Canada as representing an occupational mixture; some find employment in lower-status occupations which do not attract Canadians, while others fill high-status occupations where demand had outrun the supply of native-born. However, if immigration selection procedures were not directed to meeting shortages in the higher-skill, higher-status occupations, it would be reasonable to expect that a native-born Canadian would have had the advantage over the foreign-born, whether a landed immigrant or a naturalized Canadian, in acquiring the appropriate values and attitudes which contribute to successful educational and occupational attainment. Thus, those seeking work will have acquired attitudes appropriate to the work place through their experience in the family and in school, while employers, having greater familiarity with Canadian school systems and with a similar exposure to Canadian values and traditions, would be more likely to judge, in instances where jobs are open to competition among the native-born and foreign-born, the Canadian applicant to be more suitable. In such circumstances native-born Canadians with both parents native-born[1] might be expected to have the highest educational and occupational attainment, having the advantage over the native-born of foreign-born parents and the purely foreign-born, that is, the foreign-born of foreign-born parents. For the foreign-born to achieve comparable success, in terms of average educational and occupational attainment, they must assimilate the appropriate values and attitudes or demonstrate sufficient superiority and technical competence to overcome their cultural disadvantages. This argument suggests that it might be useful to distinguish among the native-born — those whose parents are native-born — from those with one or both parents immigrants, as these latter may exert a downward effect on the average educational and occupational status of the native-born.

The present analysis is restricted to a subsample of male respondents aged 25 to 64. As a means of establishing generational status, respondents were sorted into categories on the basis of the birthplaces of father, mother and the respondent's own birthplace, the cross-tabulation yielding eight categories (see Table 12.1): four birthplace categories for the native-born: those with both parents native-born (NBNBNB); those with only fathers native-born (NBFBNB); those with only mothers native-born (FBNBNB); and those with both parents foreign-born (FBFBNB); and a similar set of birthplace categories for the foreign-born.

TABLE 12:1 — Frequency* Distribution of Males, aged 25-64 years, in Terms of Categories Based on the Birthplaces of Respondent and Respondent's Parents

Father	Mother	Birthplace Son			Total
		Native-born	Foreign-born	Missing	
Native-born	Native-born	8,830	50	0	8,880
Native-born	Foreign-born	566	33	1	600
Foreign-born	Native-born	874	20	4	898
Foreign-born	Foreign-born	1,705	2,382	0	4,087
Missing	Native-born	63	4	0	67
Missing	Foreign-born	25	8	0	33
Native-born	Missing	258	5	5	268
Foreign-born	Missing	121	120	0	241
Missing	Missing	495	86	55	636
		12,937	2,708	65	15,710

*Unweighted frequencies

For the analysis reported here, five birthplace categories were established to order the respondents on a continuum of acculturation, ranging from the purely native-born to the purely foreign-born.[2]

Findings

Contrary to the acculturation hypothesis which would anticipate the highest educational and occupational attainment for the purely native-born and would imply that the small differences between the native-born and foreign-born reported in Chapter 11 result from a downward effect on the mean exerted by the native-born whose parents were immigrants, this analysis which controls for respondents' and parental birthplaces confirms that the purely native-born have the lowest means on education and current occupation and next lowest on first occupation.[3] Indeed, it is the native-born with one immigrant parent (NBFBNB and FBNBNB) who are consistently most successful in educational or occupational attainment, followed by the purely foreign-born, with the native-born of completely immigrant parentage falling in most instances except first occupation in next-to-last place (Table 12.2).[4] Although differences in mean values for the birthplace categories in adjacent ranks are small, the difference between the first and last ranking categories amounts to about one educational level or one year of schooling and is equivalent to the difference between completing and dropping out of high school. Although determination of the point when differences in Blishen values become non-trivial is largely arbitrary, Blishen values are sometimes reduced to a scale based on the first digit and a five-point difference represents half an interval on such a scale. In these terms, the close to four point difference on current occupation between the purely native-born and the native-born with a foreign-born mother should not be dismissed as unsubstantial. At any rate it is apparent that the rank order of these results does not support the acculturation hypothesis in which educational and occupational status are seen as a function of exposure either of the respondent of his parents to Canadian traditions, a conclusion which seems justifiable, even though cultural exposure is only roughly controlled by using birthplace as a measure.[5]

What explanation is best supported by the results shown in Table 12.2 is not immediately apparent. The possibilities include: (1) an explanation which assumes that the native-born with one or both parents immigrants are marginal men responding in different ways to their marginal status; (2) an explanation which emphasizes the influence of parents as facilitating or impeding the formation of their offsprings' values which bear on educational and occupational attainment; and (3) an explanation which assumes marked differences in motivation between different birthplace categories.

Marginal man theory (Stonequist, 1937) holds that much of the behaviour of human beings can be understood as responses to the pressure of conflicting value systems. As applied to immigrants, it is assumed that they are, through socialization, in some degree committed to values learned either in the country of origin or in the country of immigration through the influence of parents and contact with others of the same country of origin.[6] However, immigrants are seen as exposed, in varying degree, to the values of the country of immigration, and as finding themselves, especially in the social context of education and occupation, having to respond to prevailing attitudes and values. Thus, depending on the relative pressure from opposing or contrasting attitudes or values and the cost a person is willing to bear, an immigrant may conform to either the prevailing values or the traditional values or may try to minimize the conflicts by compromise or through withdrawal. Although rather detailed information on social contacts and on attitudes

NATIVITY: FURTHER CONSIDERATIONS 451

TABLE 12:2 — Means* and Standard Deviations for Basic Model Variables, Males, Aged 25-64, by Birthplace Category

Birthplace Category	Level of Education	Years of Education	First Occupation	Current Occupation	Father's Occupation	Father's Education	No. of Siblings	Mother's Education
NBNBNB	10.06 3.85	10.69 3.89	37.68 13.79	42.87 14.62	34.36 12.96	6.87 3.82	5.17 3.42	7.24 3.57
(N)	(8,779)	(8,176)	(7,805)	(7,439)	(7,552)	(7,889)	(8,726)	(7,738)
NBFBNB	11.37 3.39	12.01 3.56	40.66 14.61	46.61 14.87	38.35 14.45	8.27 3.94	3.88 3.03	8.60 3.48
(N)	(626)	(592)	(583)	(569)	(566)	(577)	(612)	(564)
FBNBNB	11.25 3.48	11.80 3.65	39.98 14.11	45.48 14.94	36.38 13.06	7.73 4.09	3.83 2.92	8.23 3.54
(N)	(967)	(921)	(904)	(875)	(878)	(864)	(959)	(857)
FBFBNB	10.57 3.40	10.89 3.37	37.50 13.18	43.90 14.77	32.27 11.28	6.61 3.96	4.35 3.04	6.38 3.62
(N)	(1,886)	(1,747)	(1,720)	(1,680)	(1,616)	(1,606)	(1,867)	(1,584)
FBFBFB	10.87 4.11	10.98 4.41	39.02 14.86	43.22 15.17	35.60 14.64	7.98 4.39	3.83 2.76	7.25 4.00
(N)	(3,378)	(3,105)	(3,068)	(2,994)	(2,881)	(3,036)	(3,294)	(2,986)

*Differences in means were not statistically significant in the following comparisons:
NBNBNB and FBFBNB on First Occupation
NBNBNB and FBFBFB on Current Occupation, Mother's Education
NBFBNB and FBNBNB on Level of Education, Years of Education, First Occupation, Current Occupation, Siblings
NBFBNB and FBFBFB on Father's Education, Siblings
FBNBNB and FBFBFB on First Occupation, Father's Occupation, Father's Education, Siblings
FBFBNB and FBFBFB on Years of Education, Current Occupation
All other comparisons between means were statistically significant at the .001 level or beyond with the exception of NBNBNB and FBFBNB — Years of Education (.025) and NBFBNB and FBNBNB — Mother's Education (.05).

and values is required to test the marginal man theory thoroughly, a simplified version relating to the present data can be tested if the native-born of full or partial immigrant parentage and the purely foreign-born are regarded as marginal men. In terms of marginality, then, the most marginal would be the purely foreign-born, then the FBFBNB category, with the NBFBNB and the FBNBNB categories being similar in marginality. The problem is anticipating the response to marginality. There is evidence which suggests that persons caught in a situation of conflicting pressures are likely to withdraw from the situation. Thus, the cross-pressured voter tends not to vote (Lipset, 1963:211). Simmel, who, as Lipset notes, offered the first general statement on the consequences of cross-pressures (Lipset, 1963:77) states, for example, "that external and internal conflicts arise through the multiplicity of group-affiliation(s), which threaten the individual with psychological tensions or even a schizophrenic break" (Simmel, 1964 [1922]: 141). Further, in discussing group affiliation in the family, he observes, ". . . the overlapping of group affiliation inevitably resulted in this case in rather extensive withdrawal of the individual from all social ties." In a discussion of examples of cross-pressures in the Middle Ages, he comments, "This relationship was so contradictory that later on the vassals either entered the community of townspeople proper or withdrew from it altogether" (ibid.: 145, 148). In the case of marginal men a possible conclusion is that the cross-pressures of two value systems could suppress achievement motivation and that marginals will be less successful in educational and occupational attainment.

In the present case, those in the more marginal categories are, indeed, less successful than those in the less marginal categories. However, the fact that the native-born with one immigrant parent are most successful, when compared to the two groups representing "pure" but conflicting or contrasting values, suggests that a response to marginality may also take the form of a greater effort to achieve in relation to non-marginal groups. Thus, consistent with Simmel (141-42), who observed that the conflicts which may result from "a multiplicity of group affiliations" are not necessarily negative, but may serve to unify "the inner unity" of personality, it is also possible to conclude that marginality can stimulate competitive effort for occupational status attainment. At best, the marginal hypothesis without a specification of the conditions favouring withdrawal or participation provides but a partial explanation of the results.

An an explanation for the results for all five birthplace categories is difficult to formulate, a better strategy may be to attempt an explanation that focuses on the differential success of the native-born of immigrant parentage and of the foreign-born. To that end, interest may be directed to the possible impeding consequences of either being foreign-born or having one or more foreign-born parents in relation to the acquisition of a given set of attitudes and values, and will be formulated here as the *impedance hypothesis*, namely, the greater the magnitude in the difference between the values of the individual and the values of the host culture, the greater the impedance to acculturation. Although the impedance hypothesis has not been identified as such in the literature on migrants, it is perhaps implicit in explanations which emphasize (See for example, Parsons and Bales, 1955: Chapter 2), the relative roles of father and mother in socialization or acculturation. In the present instance, where the concern is the development of a commitment to prevailing Canadian values of individuality, competitiveness and high achievement in relation to educational and occupational attainment, it may be suggested that father and mother, as socialization agents, exert their influence in somewhat different forms. Thus, for sons, the father may be seen as a role model — as a person who is or has been actively engaged in an occupational role and whose occupational attainment represents a comment on the relevance of educational attainment to occupational success. By contrast, the nother, while less likely to be a role model for her son, can reinforce commitment to the prevailing values through her expression in a variety of activities associated with child-rearing. Although there may be variation in the significance of fathers as role models and mothers as value carriers, it is reasonable to hypothesize that commitment to prevailing attitudes and values will be strongest where both parents are native-born, weakest where both are foreign-born, and will vary depending on which parent is foreign-born where there is only one foreign-born parent. Put another way, the presence of two foreign-born parents provides the greatest impedance to value acquisition while low impedance will be associated with native-born parents.[7] Further, in this model, if it is assumed that the father as an occupational role model exerts a stronger effect than the mother as value reinforcer, the anticipated order in educational and occupational attainment for the native-born of immigrant parentage would be NBFBNB, FBNBNB, FBFBNB.

The order of means on education and on first and current occupation conform exactly to the anticipated order (Table 12.2). Although the differences in means are small, the fact that most are statistically significant and that the order holds for all variables provides a measure of support for the impedance hypothesis. Moreover, the difference between NBFBNB and FBFBNB is over a year on the average in education. The NBFBNB and FBFBNB also differ by over three Blishen points on first occupation and almost two and three-quarter points on current occupation. At the same time, it must be observed that the differences between NBFBNB and FBNBNB are smaller, and most could be attributed to sampling error, suggesting that either a foreign-born father does not impede that much more or that the value reinforcement of the native-born mother effectively overcomes father's impedance effect.

In the case of the native-born with foreign-born parents, and of the purely foreign-born, it can be argued that parents who emigrate may impede their son's acquisition of Canadian values and traditions less than those parents who remain in the old country. However, analysis of these two birthplace categories, controlled for immigration status of the father, showed that average educational attainment and current occupational attainment for native-born with father foreign-born but mother native-born and for the native-born with both parents foreign-born is about one level higher, on the average, for those whose fathers emigrated to Canada compared to those whose fathers did not emigrate.[8] It might be further assumed that length of residence in Canada would be positively associated with lower impedance; however, analysis failed to support the hypothesis in this respect as the tendency among those whose fathers *did* emigrate revealed higher educational attainment for those whose fathers emigrated more recently compared to those whose fathers emigrated in an earlier period.[9]

If it can be assumed that respondents, who identified themselves as Canadians in response to a question on ethnic identity, have acquired Canadian values and traditions to a greater degree than those who reported another ethnic identity, it is possible to test the hypothesis that acquisition of such values and traditions facilitates educational and occupational attainment. Again, although skewing in all categories is towards Canadian identity, except the purely foreign-born, among whom, nonetheless, 55 per cent identify as Canadians, analysis provides some support for the hypothesis: for all birthplace categories those identifying as Canadians reported higher levels of education than those claiming other identities, with differences varying from .025 to .071 of a unit on the educational scale; and for all categories except the native-born with father foreign-born, a higher current occupational status than those claiming other ethnic identities, with differences ranging from 0.51 to 1.86 Blishen points.[10]

Although the impedance hypothesis may account for the order of magnitude of mean values on the basic model variables for second generation Canadians, i.e., birthplace categories NBFBNB, FBNBNB and FBFBNB, the values for either the purely native-born or the purely foreign-born are, respectively, lower and higher than anticipated. Although differences in mean values between the purely native-born and purely foreign-born are small, as foreshadowed by the analysis reported in Chapter 11, the *ranks* of both these categories are different than anticipated. In terms of the five birthplace categories under consideration, the purely foreign-born stand third in mean educational and occupational attainment, except for current occupation where they yield to FBFBNB. However, as Canadian immigration policy has moved steadily in the direction of selecting immigrants in relation to the occupational requirements of the Canadian labour force (Lawrence, 1973) and this selection appears to favour the more highly skilled (Blishen, 1970), the high level of educational and occupational attainment of those belonging to this category possibly relates to immigration selection criteria. When period of immigration is controlled, the impedance hypothesis appears to gain support. Table 12.3 reveals that the mean values for levels and years of education, first and current occupation for the foreign-born who immigrated before 1947 to the lower than all values presented in Table 12.2, a result which holds when age[11] is taken into account. Values for educational and current occupational attainment of the foreign-born who immigrated after 1946 continue to be lower than for the native-born with one parent foreign-born. The higher ranking educational and occupational attainment of the post-1946 foreign-born, compared to their pre-1947 counterparts, is evidence of successful application of immigrant selection criteria.

As the impedance hypothesis would anticipate the highest values for the purely native-born, the fact that this category has the lowest educational and current occupational attainment and next to lowest on first occupation, suggests that this hypothesis, at best, is only useful in accounting for the ordering of the other birthplace categories on the selected variables. This unanticipated result calls attention to the risk attached to focusing on birthplace alone as a measure of socialization resources in relation to educational and occupational attainment. Although the birthplace categories under analysis here are similar in terms of several background variables (see Appendix 12.2), such as age and marital status, they clearly differ in terms of ethnicity. Although ethnicity has a relatively weak effect on educational and occupational attainment, it may be that the effect is strong enough to depress the mean for all purely native-born. Indeed, while the analysis in Chapter 11 reveals that ethnicity has little effect on occupational attainment (see also Goldlust and Richmond, 1974), it also shows that there are small differences in mean values in educational and occupational attainment between ethnic groups. Thus, if there are marked differences between English and French in educational and occupational attainment, a

TABLE 12:3 — Means[1] and Standard Deviations for Basic Model Variables, Foreign-born Males, Aged 25-64, by Period of Immigration

Birthplace Category	Level of Education	Years of Education	First Occupation	Current Occupation	Father's Occupation	Father's Education	Mother's Education	No. of Siblings
FBFBFB								
to 1946	9.80 3.58	9.98 3.31	34.22 12.82	41.68 14.57	32.53 12.45	7.44 3.74	7.08 3.66	3.69 2.83
(N)[2]	(361)	(333)	(324)	(311)	(313)	(320)	(318)	(357)
After 1946	11.14 4.16	11.25 4.52	40.05 15.11	43.86 15.32	36.28 14.94	8.10 4.46	7.34 4.03	3.81 2.75
(N)	(2,685)	(2,497)	(2,485)	(2,434)	(2,324)	(2,443)	(2,413)	(2,636)

[1]Differences between means for Mother's Education and Number of Siblings were not statistically significant. All other comparisons between means were statistically significant at or beyond the .004 level except Current Occupation (.02).

[2]Ns for the two immigration periods do not sum to Ns given in Table 12:2 because of missing information on date of immigration.

control for ethnicity may modify findings which show the purely native-born to have the lowest educational and occupational attainment among birthplace groups.

Although analysis of variance reveals that there are significant differences between birthplace categories, between ethnicities, characterized as British, French, and other, and reveals a significant interaction between ethnicity and birthplace, the analysis shows unambiguously that the differences attributed to ethnicity were much greater than those attributed to either birthplace or interaction between the two independent variables. However, inspection of the means of these ethnic categories, within birthplace categories (see Table 12.4, which reports results for educational attainment) do not suggest that the lowest rank for the purely native-born is mainly a consequence of lower attainment by either the French or the other ethnicities in comparison to the purely native-born British. Rather, the analysis reported in Table 12.4 shows that the rankings of the different ethnic categories tend to follow birthplace rankings. Thus, although mean values for the British tend to

TABLE 12:4 — Mean Years of Education, Males, Aged 25-64, by Birthplace and Ethnicity

	Mean	*S.D.*	*N*
NBNBNB			
British	11.55	3.68	3,200
French	9.96	3.95	3,372
Other	11.33	3.74	791
NBFBNB			
British	12.34	3.39	363
French	11.43	4.10	89
Other	11.87	3.46	94
FBNBNB			
British	12.09	3.56	516
French	10.40	4.61	52
Other	11.84	3.61	312
FBFBNB			
British	11.21	3.28	794
French	9.48	3.78	43
Other	10.76	3.41	837
FBFBFB			
British	12.14	3.36	767
French	12.90	4.95	61
Other	10.53	4.68	2,104

be higher than for those of the other ethnicities, including the French, *within* each birthplace category the rank orders of the ethnicities by birthplace tend to be consistent with birthplace order when ethnicity is not controlled. That is, the rank order for British NBNBNB, British NBFBFB and so on is consistent with the rank order for the categories in general. This seems to hold fairly well, with some exceptions, for the variables reported. A finer breakdown of ethnicity, which allows the examination of mean values for English, French, Irish, Scots, and other European and other non-European, reveals essentially the same result, i.e., that the rankings of the birthplace categories in the various ethnicities tend to follow the general rankings of the birthplace categories. It is a necessary conclusion then, that to be purely native-born, whatever the ethnic affiliation, provides no advantage in educational or occupational attainment over the other birthplace categories and that, within the small differences between the mean values for the birthplace categories, the purely native-born have the lowest record of achievement.[12]

While the impedance hypothesis provides an explanation for the order of mean educational and occupational attainment among the native-born with one or both parents foreign-born and the purely foreign-born, it obviously cannot account for the last place position of the native-born.[13] It is possible that achievement motivation is stronger among the other birthplace categories in that those who immigrate might be assumed to be more strongly committed to achievement since they move to a new country to improve status and living conditions and, presumably, are willing to devote the required energy to achieve these objectives. If this is the case, it would seem to apply to our respondents who are immigrants as well as those who are native-born but with foreign-born parents. In contrast, the purely native-born may be either less achievement-oriented or, if as achievement-oriented as those belonging to other birthplace categories, fail to devote the requisite energy to, or be willing to accept the necessary costs of, achievement. However, if motivation and the required action to realize high aspirations were stronger among the foreign-born than the native-born, the pattern of educational or occupational attainment would not be as found here but rather the purely foreign-born would have the highest attainment followed by the native-born with both parents foreign-born and then the native-born with either father or mother foreign-born. Although one might speculate about motivational differences and accept on the basis of the research literature that such differences exist, our results do not actually lend much credence to such speculation. Whatever the motivational differences between birthplace categories and whatever the discrimination practised in relation to the allocation of educational and occupational opportunities, this analysis reveals that differences in average attainment are small,[14] forcing the conclusion that neither a person's birthplace nor his parents' birthplace gives much advantage in educational and occupational attainment.

THE ATTAINMENT PROCESS

Although differences between *average* educational and occupational attainment among birthplace categories are small, there could be differences in the attainment process itself. For example, the association between origin status and educational or occupational attainment may differ for persons who are foreign-born or who are native-born but have foreign-born mothers or fathers from those who are purely native-born. To investigate such possible differences, the five birthplace categories were compared in terms of estimates for the status attainment model. This comparison showed that the pattern of attainment was similar for all birthplace categories but that there were differences in the effects of specific variables in the model.

In terms of the standardized coefficients of the conventional path model (Table 12.5), all categories show the familiar pattern of a strong direct effect for father's education, with lesser effects for father's occupation and family size on education attainment. However, the usual balance between the father's occupation and family size does not appear for the native-born with father foreign-born nor for the purely foreign-born. As expected, respondent's education exerts the strongest direct effect on first occupational attainment, with father's occupation displaying values within the expected range, while father's education and family size exert slight effects. The results for current occupational attainment are also similar to those reported in the research literature, with first occupation, followed by respondent's education exerting the strongest direct effects. While father's occupation continues to exert a direct effect of sufficient magnitude to justify keeping it in the model for the purely native-born and the purely foreign-born, it is somewhat stronger than usual for the other birthplace groups. The strength of the model, as assessed by explained variance, varies in relation to educational attainment, from 38 per cent for the purely foreign-born to 21 per cent for the native-born with both parents foreign-born, but values are very similar for both first and current occupational attainment in all groups.

The similarity of the attainment process is also apparent when educational and occupational attainment are predicted for each group by substituting mean values for a given birthplace group in the equation

TABLE 12:5 — Basic Educational and Occupational Attainment Model: Path Coefficients, Males, Aged 25-64, by Birthplace Category

Birthplace	N	Respondent's First Occupation	Respondent's Level of Education	Father's Occupation	Father's Education	Number of Siblings	R^2
NBNBNB	5,974						
Respondent's level of education				.184	.332	−.189	.299
Respondent's first occupation			.558	.170	(.020)	−.024[1]	.442
Respondent's current occupation		.456	.281	.107	(.014)	(.010)	.533
NBFBNB	478						
Respondent's level of education				.195	.319	−.170	.270
Respondent's first occupation			.620	.188	(−.060)	(−.031)	.483
Respondent's current occupation		.403	.328	.145	(−.025)	(−.020)	.547
FBNBNB	710						
Respondent's level of education				.267	.171	−.201	.228
Respondent's first occupation			.559	.168	(−.020)	(−.040)	.424
Respondent's current occupation		.383	.303	.147	(.023)	(.034)	.484
FBFBNB	1,251						
Respondent's level of education				.208	.223	−.215	.213
Respondent's first occupation			.620	.127	(−.018)	(−.003)	.445
Respondent's current occupation		.425	.306	.064	(.023)	(−.007)	.493
FBFBFB	2,360						
Respondent's level of education				.190	.438	−.129	.378
Respondent's first occupation			.586	.204	−.058	−.037	.464
Respondent's current occupation		.454	.269	.107	(−.010)	−.060	.546

[1]p < .025, all other estimates except those enclosed in parentheses, p < .01 or less.

TABLE 12:6 — Observed and Expected* Mean Values for Educational and Occupational Attainment, Males, Aged 25-64, by Birthplace Category

Birthplace Category	Respondent's Education Observed	Expected	First Occupation Observed	Expected	Current Occupation Observed	Expected
NBNBNB	10.61	10.61	38.55	38.55	43.71	43.71
NBFBNB	11.81	11.52	41.77	42.01	47.88	47.05
FBNBNB	11.86	11.31	41.37	41.76	46.66	46.66
FBFBNB	11.03	10.51	38.45	39.02	44.62	43.76
FBFBFB	11.27	11.24	40.32	40.29	43.97	45.07

*When mean values for basic model variables, by birthplace, are inserted in the equation for the purely native born.

as solved for the purely native-born (Table 12.6). Even so, these findings reveal differences relating to birthplace. Generally, the expected results reflect a balancing of the general superiority in origin and educational achievement of native-born sons with one parent native-born and the purely foreign-born against processual advantages and disadvantages which vary in relation to the specific dependent variable. Thus, the lower expected values for education reflect the higher origins, in terms of average father's occupation, father's education, and family size, of the native-born son with one parent foreign-born and of the purely foreign-born. Similarly, the higher expected values for first occupation suggest that the advantages of the purely native-born outweigh their origin handicaps. The interplay between origins, education, and first occupation attainment and processual advantages is apparent in the results for current occupation.

Given the similarity of the attainment process, revealed by the findings reported in Tables 12.5 and 12.6, is there any point in analysing the native-born and foreign-born separately, or in extending that analysis, as in the present chapter? The answer is clearly in the affirmative, even though differences in metric coefficients, shown in Table 12.7, are for the most part small. This conclusion follows from a series of simultaneous tests of the model for the five birthplace categories.[15] These tests revealed the models to be significantly different, beyond the .001 level, and the individual equations, beyond the .01 level. This result justifies the decision to control for birthplace in the analysis. Further tests[16] provide unambiguous evidence that, for the entire model, both the purely foreign-born and the purely native-born differ significantly from each of the other birthplace categories *except* from the native-born

TABLE 12:7 — Basic Educational and Occupational Attainment Model: Metric Regression Coefficients, Males, Aged 25-64, by Birthplace Category

Birthplace	N	Constant	Respondent's First Occupation	Respondent's Level of Education	Father's Occupation	Father's Education	Number of Siblings	R^2
NBNBNB	5,974							
Respondent's level of education		7.450		2.093	.053	.328	-.212	.299
Respondent's first occupation		9.901			.183	(.074)	-.099[1]	.442
Respondent's current occupation		8.769	.478	1.103	.120	(.053)	(.045)	.533
NBFBNB	478							
Respondent's level of education		8.537		2.789	.044	.269	-.193	.270
Respondent's first occupation		(3.986)			.189	(-.229)	(-.158)	.483
Respondent's current occupation		9.276	.401	1.470	.146	(-.094)	(-.103)	.547
FBNBNB	710							
Respondent's level of education		9.198		2.483	.065	.137	-.237	.228
Respondent's first occupation		6.507			.181	(-.072)	(-.209)	.424
Respondent's current occupation		5.541	.404	1.418	.167	(.088)	(.190)	.484
FBFBNB	1,251							
Respondent's level of education		8.635		2.502	.064	.198	-.249	.213
Respondent's first occupation		6.214			.158	(-.065)	(-.014)	.445
Respondent's current occupation		8.421	.467	1.356	.087	(.089)	(-.036)	.493
FBFBFB	2,360							
Respondent's level of education		6.716		2.183	.053	.412	-.192	.378
Respondent's first occupation		9.850			.210	-.203	-.197[1]	.464
Respondent's current occupation		11.832	.463	1.013	.110	(-.035)	-.351	.546

[1]p < .025, all other estimates except those enclosed in parentheses, p < .01.

sons whose fathers are native-born but whose mothers are foreign-born (Table 12.8). In most instances, the individual equations for the purely foreign-born differ significantly from those of other birthplace categories. Such differences are observed less frequently between the purely native-born and other birthplace categories. In summary, results shown in Table 12.8 reveal a pattern of differences in terms of degree of foreign birth: the purely foreign-born differing most often from all others, the native-born with both parents foreign-born differing next less frequently, and so on. While the second-highest number of significant differences is observed for the purely native-born, the pattern of such differences also reflects degree of foreign birth.

As the evidence of significant differences between models and equations justifies the analysis which controls for respondents and parental birthplaces, it is appropriate to comment on the estimates of coefficients shown in Table 12.7.[17]

Controlling for respondent's and parental birthplace provides additional evidence of the differences which emerge from a comparison of the native-born and the foreign-born. Thus, in relation to respondent's

TABLE 12:8 — Results of Significance Tests: Basic Model and Individual Equations Paired Comparisons of Birthplace Categories

Comparison	Model	Current Occupation	First Occupation	Education
NBNBNB				
NBFBNB	n.s.	n.s.	<.05	n.s.
FBNBNB	<.001*	n.s.	n.s.†	<.001
FBFBNB	<.001	n.s.	<.01	<.001
FBFBFB	<.001	<.001	n.s.†	<.005
NBFBNB				
FBNBNB	n.s.	n.s.	n.s.	n.s.
FBFBNB	n.s.	n.s.	n.s.	n.s.
FBFBFB	n.s.†	n.s.	.025	<.005
FBNBNB				
FBFBNB	n.s.	n.s.	n.s.	n.s.
FBFBFB	<.001	<.005	n.s.	<.001
FBFBNB				
FBFBFB	<.001	.01	<.025	<.001

*As recommended (Specht and Warren, 1975:57), ϵ .001 is the criterion for tests of models, and 0.25 for tests of equations.
†< .05 but > .025

education, differences in the direct effects of father's education between the purely native-born and the purely foreign-born is less pronounced than revealed by the analysis where the native-born were not differentiated in relation to parents' birthplace. Differences between the native-born and the foreign-born appear to be primarily attributable to differences between the purely foreign-born and native-born sons with either one or both parents foreign-born. Thus, differences between estimates for father's education and father's occupation are greater between the purely foreign-born and native-born sons with one or both parents foreign-born than the differences between the purely foreign-born and the purely native-born. It may be noted that all birthplace categories differ significantly from the purely foreign-born for the equation for educational attainment (Table 12.8). While the effects of father's education are higher for native-born sons whose fathers are native-born but mothers foreign-born, than for native-born sons whose fathers are foreign-born, these differences are not statistically significant.

Although significant differences in relation to current occupational attainment were found only between the purely native-born and purely foreign-born, and between the latter and the native-born with foreign-born fathers and native-born mothers, certain differences among all birthplace categories are worth noting. Origin effects tend to be stronger for the native-born with one or both parents foreign-born than for the purely native-born or purely foreign-born: father's occupation is strongest for the native-born with one parent foreign-born; father's education is strongest, negatively, for the native-born whose mothers are foreign-born, and almost as strong, positively, for the native-born whose fathers are foreign-born or where both parents are foreign-born. In terms of fathers' occupation, the purely foreign-born and the purely native-born differ more from the native-born with both parents foreign-born, than they do from each other. While family size operates differently among various birthplace categories ranging from $-.35$ for the purely foreign-born to .05 for the purely native-born, it is difficult to detect a pattern. Family size, however, may contribute to the significant differences between the purely foreign-born and the purely native-born with foreign-born fathers.

When measures of son's performance in relation to current occupational attainment are examined, it would appear that having one or both parents foreign-born is an advantage for sons who are native-born in that the respondent's own education counts for more than for those who are purely native-born or foreign-born: about one-half a Blishen point more on current occupation for each educational level for these sons in comparison to the purely native- and purely foreign-born. However, first occupational attainment has the strongest effect for the purely native-born, even though the average occupational attainment of the purely native-born is less than that of the other four groups.

REFLECTIONS ON THE ANALYSIS OF STATUS ATTAINMENT

The practice of reporting the effects of uninterpreted variables is a shortcoming in the presentation of the basic educational and occupational status attainment model. Usually the effects of father's education, father's occupation, and the other measures are reported without much consideration for their theoretical significance. This practice leaves the reader to speculate on what father's or respondent's education *means*, what father's occupation *means* and so on. And yet, to understand the process of educational and occupational attainment and the very strong effects of the measures included in the basic model, accounting for 40 per cent or more of the variance for occupational attainment, it seems necessary to know what the various measures actually represent.[18] It is possible, of course, to assume that father's occupation represents family social status and reflects certain values and resources that are relevant to the educational and occupational attainment of offspring. Moreover, support for these interpretations of father's occupation can be mustered from the research literature. However, use of occupation alone cannot allow identification of the unobserved variables and it is possible that all three (status, values, and resources), in addition to others unknown, are represented in any association between father's occupation and other observed variables. Similarly, as there is apparently no clearly identifiable connection between a person's education and occupational attainment, either as these are usually measured or in reality, except for a narrow spectrum of occupations, it is impossible to state unequivocally what is represented by information about the number of years or the level of education reported by respondents in these surveys, as it relates to vocational preparation. Thus, some researchers or readers may interpret these measures of education to represent some quantity of technical skills while others may interpret them as evidence of the acquisition of certain modes of response, such as passivity, self-discipline, and so forth.

These shortcomings in research design are to be regretted. With better measures[19] it might be possible to go beyond speculation in interpreting differences in results for various comparison groups. In the present instance, although most differences between birthplace categories are small, it might advance explanation of the process if such differences as exist could be explained and if the explanation could be tested by unambiguous indicators or measures of the concepts. Similarly, it would be advantageous to be able to *explain* the variable return, identified in Chapter 11, for the native-born and the foreign-born, on origin and on the respondent's educational achievement for occupational attainment — that is, to be able to say what the native-born and the foreign-born utilize from their backgrounds and education to attain similar occupational statuses.

In the present instance, if the educational attainment of those with native-born fathers but foreign-born mothers is compared to those with foreign-born fathers and native-born mothers or both parents foreign-born, it would appear that having a native-born father is an advantage: he will, on the average, have more education and it will count for more — about twice as much as for foreign-born males who marry native-born women and have native-born sons and over 35 per cent more than the foreign-born fathers who marry foreign-born women and have native-born sons. Although the native-born fathers of the purely native-born have less education than fathers in the other groups, excepting the native-born with both parents foreign-born, it counts for more than the education of fathers in all other groups except the purely foreign-born.

If a father serves as a role model, and his education and occupation represent values and material resources relevant to a son's educational and occupational attainment, it is plausible that native-born fathers will be more effective role models in that the value component represented by educational and occupational attainment contributes, status for status, more than that of foreign-born fathers. While mothers may not be role models, their educational attainment[20] may also represent values and resources and again the education of the native-born mother should, through its value component especially, contribute, for a given level of attainment, more to a son's educational and occupational attainment than that of a foreign-born mother. Thus, in terms of the impedance hypothesis, it may be anticipated that native-born parents exert less impedance than foreign-born parents. While a mother's education may exert a direct effect on a son's educational attainment, it may also operate by reinforcing the effects of the values and resources represented by father's education and occupation. The addition of mother's education to the basic model for educational attainment yields results which support this argument. Thus, a comparison of metric coefficients (Table 12.9) for the native-born reveals that the effect of parental education is always greater for native-born mothers or fathers over their foreign-born counterparts.[21] Moreover, for the two mixed parent groups (NBFBNB and FBNBNB), it is apparent that the native-born parent's education makes the greater direct contribution. There is no

TABLE 12:9 — Expanded Educational Attainment Model by Birthplace Category, Metric Coefficients, Males, Aged 25-64

Birthplace Category	Mother's Education	Father's Education	Father's Occupation	Number of Siblings	R^2	N
NBNBNB	.252	.101	.055	−.183	.337	6624
NBFBNB	.160	.215	.041	−.201	.312	504
FBNBNB	.242	.066	.056	−.227	.306	764
FBFBNB	.089	.166	.063	−.233	.234	1355
FBFBFB	.236	.262	.051	−.151	.399	2520

Zero-order coefficients: Mother's Education × Father's Education

NBNBNB	.690
NBFBNB	.588
FBNBNB	.550
FBFBNB	.737
FBFBFB	.808

ready explanation for the finding that mother's education has a greater effect than father's for the purely native-born or the purely foreign-born, although the small differences in the effects of mother's or of father's education could be interpreted as a situation where the material resources of the foreign-born compensate in some way for the values and resources available to the purely native-born. Why mother's education, whether foreign-born or native-born, should have the greater effect cannot be explained in terms of the impedance hypothesis. However, if sons have closer or more frequent contact with their mothers than with their fathers, that proximity could permit the mother to exert a greater influence on son's education. Obviously, such an explanation does not hold for the native-born with both parents foreign-born.

As the contributions of parents' education to son's current occupational attainment operate almost entirely through son's education (see Table 12.10), interpretations of the model for current occupational attainment in terms of the impedance hypothesis may focus on either the total effect (Alwin and Hauser, 1975:42) or on the indirect contributions through son's education. The findings are similar to those relating to educational attainment providing support for the impedance hypothesis. Thus, for native-born sons, native-born parents contribute more than foreign-born parents. For those sons characterized by mixed parental birthplace, the contribution of the native-born parent is greater than that of the foreign-born. Results for the purely native-born and the purely foreign-born and the native-born with both parents foreign-born

TABLE 12:10 — Current Occupational Attainment Model by Birthplace Category

Birthplace Category	Total Effect	Direct	Effects of Mother's and Father's Education		R^2*	N
			Indirect Via			
			Respondent's Education	First Occupation		
NBNBNB					.534	5832
Father's education	.124	.016	.099	.009		
Mother's education	.128	.000	.129	−.001		
NBFBNB					.542	461
Father's education	.117	.006	.145	−.034		
Mother's education	.034	−.057	.082	.009		
FBNBNB					.486	698
Father's education	.043	.015	.034	−.006		
Mother's education	.158	.026	.127	.005		
FBFBNB					.495	1222
Father's education	.060	−.003	.086	−.023		
Mother's education	.119	.037	.058	.024		
FBFBFB					.55	2289
Father's education	.093	−.030	.129	−.006		
Mother's education	.152	.045	.131	−.024		

*For complete model

where mother's education exerts a stronger effect than father's education, are again less readily explained.

This attempt to interpret differences and solutions to regression equations which express the basic model may only be regarded as suggestive. Although there may be value in the impedance hypothesis which anticipates that a person's educational and occupational attainments will be influenced by parental values and resources, better measures of these concepts must be constructed and better data made available before the hypothesis can be adequately tested. Indeed, better data may stimulate more precise formulations of the impedance hypothesis so that it would better reflect the complexity of the attainment process.

Summary

As immigration has been an important factor in the development of Canada, comparison of the educational level and the occupational level of attainment of immigrants and native Canadians is more than a matter of passing interest. Indeed, a comparison of the attainment of immigrants to that of native Canadians is a way of assessing the adjustment of immigrants, a matter of considerable importance to the whole society. Moreover, as immigration policies often provoke questions concerning the relative advantages and disadvantages of immigrant and native-born status, of questions concerning favourable and unfavourable prejudice and discrimination, a comparison of educational and occupational attainment in terms of birthplace is surely relevant.

The analysis reported in this chapter contributes to such a comparison by extending the basic comparison of the native-born and foreign-born through differentiating respondents in terms of "generation status." Thus it was anticipated that there would be differences among respondents depending on whether their forebears were early or late immigrants to Canada. The analysis revealed important facts about the consequences of birthplace and generational status even though only a crude measure of the latter concept was possible.

Thus, the analysis shows that differences in educational and occupational attainment between birthplace categories are small, but it also shows that within this narrow range of differences, the native sons with one parent native-born experience greater educational and occupational attainment, on the average, than the other three categories of native-born sons or the purely foreign-born. It is also evident that the purely native-born are clearly in last place.

Although it may be banal to assert that educational and occupational attainment are the result of complex processes, it is surely a correct assertion. Nonetheless, as the analysis reveals that average educational and occupational attainment rank closely parallels rank on measures of origin, it may be concluded that part of the advantages of those ranking higher, especially with respect to educational attainment, results from a more advantageous start. These advantages are modified by differences in process — for example, the higher educational and occupational return on father's education for the purely native-born compared to native-born sons whose fathers are native-born but whose mothers are foreign-born. Moreover, the analysis suggests that the variable contributions mothers and fathers make to attainment are systematically related to birthplace. This finding, most evident for education, can be interpreted in terms of the effects of material and value resources represented by each parent.

In the conflicts which arise as Canadians perceive their social referents along different dimensions, the advantages and disadvantages of native birth have been a central concern. To some, the advantages of many generations of residence in Canada are obvious while to others it is equally obvious that the fruits go to the highly competitive newcomers. This analysis, while inevitably glossing over individual differences and circumstances, nonetheless makes clear that neither birthplace nor generational status confer advantages or disadvantages which relate directly to educational or occupational attainment.

Notes

1. The only available measure of in-depth Canadian heritage.
2. See Appendix 1 for further details concerning the categorization and assignment to the five birthplace categories of cases where information on birthplace was missing.
3. As noted in Chapter 11, information on first occupation may be less reliable for the purely foreign-born than for native-born respondents.
4. Although the standard weight used in the study results in an over-representation of the purely foreign-born, the adjusted weight used in Chapter 11 for this birthplace category is not used in the analysis undertaken for this chapter. Only fractional differences in results were obtained from computations based on the standard and the adjusted weights for the variables used in the analysis.
5. While the birthplace categories provide a rough measure of generational status in the sense that one might assume that those categorized as NBNBNB have had the longest exposure to Canadian traditions and values; the native-born with one or both parents immigrants, the next longest exposure; and the foreign-born as having the least exposure, it is quite possible for a person who is foreign-born whose foreign-born parents immigrated here, say in 1923, to have had fifty years of exposure to Canadian values and attitudes at the time of the survey, while a respondent falling into the FBFBNB category who was born in Canada in 1953, would have only twenty years' exposure. However, as the mean ages for the birthplace categories are very similar, except for the native-born with both parents foreign-born (FBFBNB), it seems justifiable to treat these birthplace categories as representing varying exposure to Canadian traditions and values. The average age of the native-born with both parents foreign-born is 48, about three to five years older, on the average, than those falling into the other categories.
6. See, for example, Breton (1964), who argues that acculturation is impeded to the degree that an ethnic group experiences institutional completeness in the country of immigration.
7. The impedance hypothesis in focusing on the socialization resources of parents and respondents places the emphasis on what the person brings to educational or occupational situations and assumes that processes operating in those situations, such as discrimination in relation to various opportunities, affect the members of the different birthplace groups equally.
8. For first occupation, the pattern held only for the native-born with both parents foreign-born (FBFBNB). Information on mother's immigration status was not obtained.
9. However, the pattern did not hold for the purely foreign-born, possibly

because post-1946 immigrants, who predominate, have relatively high educational and occupational attainment. While those results are relevant, they require cautious interpretation, as the native-born group with one or both parents foreign-born are heavily skewed towards fathers who have immigrated while the purely foreign-born are skewed in the opposite direction.

10. Again, no clear pattern was evident for first occupation.

11. Pearson correlation coefficients for age and education and for age and occupation suggest that older respondents were likely to have less education, $r = -.28$, and less markedly, lower occupational attainment, $r = -0.19$ and -0.12 for first and current occupation, respectively. As the pre-1947 foreign-born were older than those in the native-born categories whose average ages were similar to the post-1946 foreign-born, mean values on education and occupational attainment were computed for those in the four native-born groups whose age ranged between 46 and 62, precisely equivalent to $\bar{X} \pm 1\sigma$ for the pre-1947 foreign-born. Although all values for these categories were lower than those reported in Table 12.2, the pre-1947 foreign-born ranked next to lowest on education and lowest on first and current occupation.

12. It is interesting to note that these data reveal a low negative relationship between length of residence in Canada and educational or occupational attainment for the purely foreign-born. While such a finding might appear to contradict a generalization by Goldlust and Richmond (1974:209) which stresses the importance of length of residence as an important determinant of immigrant adaptation, including economic adaptation, it would appear, given the purely native-born have the lowest record of achievement, that adaptation for immigrants means lower levels of attainment.

13. Although it is plausible that variations in the ethnic composition of birthplace categories account for the order of educational attainment (see Table 12.4), standardization on the basis of equal proportions of British, French, and Other Ethnic results in only fractional changes in the means for all birthplace categories and change in rank for NBNBNB from last to next to last. This result is consistent with the foregoing discussion which reveals that generally any ethnic NBNBNB would rank lower on attainment variable means than that same ethnic group in any other birthplace category.

14. As Blishen values may mask differences in occupational distribution, tabulations in terms of the project occupational classification were obtained. These showed that birthplace categories differ in their occupational distributions but not to any marked degree. Indexes of Dissimilarity range from 7.88 to 17.96, with a mean of 12.5.

15. Following procedures developed by Specht and Warren (1975), the results of Box's tests for differences between variance and covariance matrices indicated that there were significant differences between the birthplace categories. This finding was confirmed by a test for differences, using a procedure which takes into account the estimates provided by all equations included in the model, as well as by a procedure which allows a test for differences between each equation. Reference to tests at the level of the model and level of equation relate, respectively, to these procedures.

16. The results of paired comparisons are given in Table 12.8. Another procedure was to exclude birthplace categories cumulatively in terms of a gradient of assumed cultural difference: a test for all birthplace categories,

except for the purely foreign-born, was undertaken, followed by a test excluding native-born sons whose parents were foreign-born (FBFBNB) *and* the purely foreign-born, and so on.

17. Tests at the level of models or of individual equations established whether there were statistically significant differences between birthplace categories. As marked differences between estimates of coefficients for individual variables could be assumed to account for differences found at the level of model or of equation, it seemed unnecessary to test at the level of individual variables. Moreover, testing at the latter level might give undue emphasis to relatively small differences in estimates.

18. While it may not matter what the measures represent for purposes of prediction, it matters a great deal for purposes of explanation.

19. The imperious demands of comparative research and the urge to replicate can place barriers in the way of the improvement of measurement and of explanation in social research.

20. Occupational data for mothers are not available since 85 per cent of respondents reported their mothers as not employed in either part-time or full-time jobs during the period of respondent's primary and secondary education.

21. Tests of significance for the model and for individual equations yielded results very similar to those for the basic model but significant differences between the purely native-born and purely foreign-born were not observed except for the equation for current occupation.

Appendix 12:1 — Birthplace Categorization

Although cross-tabulation of respondent's and parents' birthplace yields four birthplace categories for the foreign-born, there is only a small number of foreign-born with only one parent foreign-born. These groups are excluded from the analysis.

The small number of foreign-born with native-born parents appeared to be somewhat anomalous in relation to the analysis of educational and occupational attainment in that some of these respondents could have been born abroad but lived from infancy or early childhood in Canada, while others might have indeed lived abroad through their formative years. From the point of view of the acquisition of "Canadian" values and attitudes, those born abroad but who returned to Canada in infancy or early childhood would be very similar to native-born Canadians of native-born parents, while the others might more closely resemble the foreign-born. It seemed reasonable to assign these fifty respondents to the purely native-born if the respondent reported Canada as place of residence to age 16 but to the purely foreign-born if they were resident outside of Canada at that age. In fact, as 76 per cent of this group reported immigration to Canada before the age of 16 and 82 per cent reported Canada as place of residence at age 16, almost all these respondents were assigned to the NBNBNB category.

As the categorization procedure revealed that birthplace information was missing for about 8 per cent of the males, aged 25 to 64 years, it seemed sensible to attempt to assign cases with missing values to the "pure" birthplace categories — i.e., those shown in the upper half of Table 12.1. As is evident from the table, most of the missing information was for parental birthplace.[1]

The remaining 1,245 cases for which information was missing on parental birthplace were assigned to "pure" categories on a probability basis. For example, as respondents identified as XXNBNB could be NBNBNB or FBNBNB, the 63 respondents were assigned to the pure categories in a ratio of 8,830:874 or roughly ten to one. While this procedure increased the number of cases in each birthplace category on all the variables used in the analysis, it did not result in marked changes in values. For example, the mean Blishen value for current occupation for the pure NBNBNB category was 43.1 and 42.9 for the pure and assigned category. In general, the mean values for the pure and assigned cases declined slightly from those when computation was restricted to pure cases but there was no change in the ordering of the resulting values. In brief, assigning missing value cases to the pure categories increased the case base for computation on the various variables but did not produce substantially different results than when the analysis was restricted to pure cases. As it seemed sensible to report results based on the maximum number of cases for which there was information available, results reported here are based on the combination of pure and assigned cases. As in the analysis reported in Chapter 11, farm owners and farm labourers are included in the computations.[2]

NOTES

1. Initial tabulation identified 146 cases where information was missing on respondent's birthplace. Eighty-one of these cases were assigned either to the purely native-born if both parents were native-born or to the purely foreign-born if both parents were foreign-born. This procedure reduced the number of cases where information was missing on respondent's birthplace to 65.
2. Table 12.A1 shows the final frequencies used as a basis for analysis.

Appendix 12.2 — Background Characteristics

As controls for background characteristics were not, for the most part, introduced in the analyses reported in this chapter, a report of similarities and differences between the five birthplace categories may be helpful in evaluating the findings presented here. The purely native-born, the native-born with one immigrant parent and the post-1946 foreign-born are similar in average *age*, while the native-born with both parents foreign-born and the pre-1947 foreign-born are somewhat older. *Marital status* is similar among all categories, with 86 per cent to 89 per cent married. There was greater similarity than difference in relation to *linguistic usage and background:*

- with the exception of the purely native-born, English was the language spoken on the present job for all groups — 89 per cent to 94 per cent;
- except for the purely native-born, and the purely foreign-born, the other categories were alike in reporting English as the most comfortable language used — 91 per cent to 95 per cent;
- with respect to speaking English or French, except for the purely native-born, some 82 per cent to 93 per cent in the birthplace categories reported an ability to speak English only, with bilingualism reported about as often by the native-born with one immigrant parent as by the purely foreign-born, but most often by the purely native-born and least often by the native-born with both parents foreign-born;
- although the majority in all birthplace categories except the purely foreign-born reported English as mother tongue, the categories varied with respect to neither English nor French as mother tongue.

The purely-native-born were slightly less geographically mobile than the other native-born groups:[1]

- 54 per cent of the purely native-born report that they are living in the same town as they were at age 16 compared to 43 per cent to 45 per cent of those in other native-born groups;
- the native-born of foreign-born parents more frequently reported the prairie provinces as provinces of residence at age 16 than the purely native-born.

On *religious affiliation*, the majority of the native-born with one or both parents foreign-born reported themselves as Protestants, while the purely native-born were somewhat more Roman Catholic than Protestant — 48 per cent versus 44 per cent. The purely foreign-born were about equally divided between Protestant and Roman Catholic but 15 per cent reported their religious affiliations as other than these two.

The birthplace categories differ in terms of *ethnicity* (Table 12.A2). More French than British (English, Irish, and Scots are identifiable) are found among the purely native-born — 45.5 per cent versus 43.9 per cent. The British are in the majority among the native-born with one parent foreign-born, but these two groups differ in that the non-British, non-French ethnicities are found twice as frequently among the native-born sons whose fathers are foreign-born than among those whose fathers are native-born. Non-British, non-French ethnicities are most prominent, slightly over 50 per cent, among native-born sons whose mothers and fathers are foreign-born, although the British are also strongly represented (46.9 per cent). As the majority of the purely foreign-born are neither British nor French, this category clearly differs from the others.

NOTE

1. The foreign-born, as might be anticipated, are the most mobile in terms of the available measures of geographic mobility.

References

ALWIN, DUANE F. and ROBERT M. HAUSER
   1975   "The Decomposition of Effects in Path Analysis." *American Sociological Review*, 40:37-47.
BLISHEN, BERNARD R.
   1970   "Social Class and Opportunity in Canada." *Canadian Review of Sociology and Anthropology*, 7:110-27.
BRETON, RAYMOND
   1964   "Institutional Completeness of Ethnic Communities and the Personal Relations of Immigrants." *American Journal of Sociology*, 70:193-205.
GOLDLUST, J. and A.H. RICHMOND
   1974   "A Multivariate Model of Immigrant Adaptation." *International Migration Review*, 8:193-225.
LAWRENCE, BRUCE
   1973   "Canadian Immigration Policy: Some Sociological Implications." M.A. Thesis, McMaster University.
LIPSET, SEYMOUR M.
   1963   *Political Man*. New York: Doubleday (Anchor Books).
PARSONS, TALCOTT and ROBERT F. BALES
   1955   *Family, Socialization and Interaction Process*. Glencoe: The Free Press.
SIMMEL, GEORGE
   1964   *The Web of Group Affiliations*. Trans. Reinhard Bendix. New York: The
   (1922)   Free Press of Glencoe (Collier-MacMillan).
SPECHT, DAVID A. and RICHARD D. WARREN
   1975   "Comparing Causal Models." In David R. Heise, ed. *Sociological Methodology 1976*, San Francisco: Jossey-Bass.
STONEQUIST, EVERETT V.
   1937   *The Marginal Man: A Study in Personality and Culture Conflict*. New York: Scribner.

TABLE 12:A1 — **Final Birthplace Category Frequencies Used in the Analysis**

Birthplace Category	Unweighted	Weighted
NBNBNB	9,594	9,014
NBFBNB	958	982
FBNBNB	605	638
FBFBNB	1,886	1,924
FBFBFB	2,608	3,441
Total	15,710	16,064

TABLE 12:A2 — **Ethnic Affiliation: Per cent Distribution Males, Aged 25-64 Years**

Ethnicity	NBNBNB	NBFBNB	FBNBNB	FBFBNB	FBFBFB
British	43.9	67.0	58.4	46.9	25.0
French	45.5	16.3	5.9	2.7	2.0
Other	10.6	16.6	35.8	50.4	72.9
Total	100.0	99.9	100.1	100.0	99.9
	(7,854)	(578)	(919)	(1,797)	(3,190)

TABLE 12:A3 — Zero-order Correlation Coefficients, Means and Standard Deviations by Birthplace Category, Males, Aged 25-64 years

	First Occupation	Level of Education	Number of Siblings	Father's Occupation	Father's Education
NBNBNB (N = 5974)					
Current Occupation	.684	.621	-.234	.410	.378
First Occupation		.644	-.260	.409	.386
Level of Education			-.339	.400	.487
Number of Siblings				-.242	-.318
Father's Occupation					.512
X̄ : 43.71	38.55	10.61	4.98	35.01	7.19
s.d. 14.94	14.28	3.81	3.39	13.23	3.86
NBFBNB (N = 478)					
Current Occupation	.680	.652	-.227	.432	.338
First Occupation		.676	-.228	.410	.328
Level of Education			-.274	.399	.456
Number of Siblings				-.208	-.200
Father's Occupation					.529
X̄ : 47.88	41.77	11.81	3.74	38.93	8.54
s.d. 14.84	14.90	3.31	2.90	14.76	3.93
FBNBNB (N = 710)					
Current Occupation	.629	.601	-.197	.420	.292
First Occupation		.632	-.250	.392	.265

TABLE 12:A3 (Continued)

	First Occupation	Level of Education	Number of Siblings	Father's Occupation	Father's Education
Level of Education	.654		-.310	.398	.349
Number of Siblings				-.249	-.249
Father's Occupation					.478
Current Occupation					
X̄ : 46.66	41.37	11.86	3.56	37.09	8.08
s.d. 15.17	14.37	3.24	2.74	13.34	4.04
FBFBNB (N = 1251)					
Current Occupation		.616	-.215	.311	.254
First Occupation		.657	-.319	.235	.240
Level of Education			-.313	.328	.346
Number of Siblings				-.210	-.244
Father's Occupation					.337
Current Occupation					
X̄ : 44.62	38.45	11.03	4.16	32.48	6.78
s.d. 15.34	13.96	3.46	2.99	11.19	3.90
FBFBFB (N = 2360)					
Current Occupation	.693	.631	-.257	.449	.408
First Occupation		.659	-.224	.456	.409
Level of Education			-.269	.474	.579
Number of Siblings				-.213	-.226
Father's Occupation					.585
Current Occupation					
X̄ : 43.97	39.62	11.27	3.78	36.08	8.18
s.d. 15.51	15.31	4.11	2.77	14.86	4.37

CHAPTER 13

Internal Migration and Occupational Attainment

PETER C. PINEO

Since economic development is now, and presumably always will be, somewhat uneven across different parts of the country, some flow of internal migration to adjust labour supply to demand seems a permanent requirement of Canada as well as all other industrialized nations. The effects of such migrations upon individuals and ultimately upon the structure of the society pose a series of questions of interest to sociologists; in this chapter we concentrate upon one consequence of migration, asking about the extent to which migration is rewarded by giving increased occupational status to the migrant. If labour mobility benefits the whole society through producing a more efficient fit between labour skills and occupational requirements, it would seem reasonable to expect part of the economic gain to show as increased occupational mobility for the migrants themselves.

The migration data coming from this survey are unusually rich. In most studies of status attainment, the migration questions are limited to a measure of whether the respondent moved between communities after age 16, and the size of the community of origin and destination. This survey included more questions. Return migrants, those who left the original community but returned again to it, can be identified, as well as Multiple migrants, those who have moved repeatedly between communities. In addition, a series of questions were asked dealing with movement between the provinces. These questions allow an identification of:

- those who moved permanently to another province after age 16;
- those who moved, but returned to the original province;

479

- those who moved to a new province before age 16.

We assess the effects of each of these patterns of migration upon occupational attainment, dealing mainly with the native-born male labour force excluding those of farm origin.

Since the sample for this survey was large, special analyses could be made of various sub-groupings of Canadian society. Many possibilities exist, and in this analysis we examine only those men with farm background who enter the urban labour force, the French within the province of Quebec, and working women. The data also permit the investigation of differences in the process of occupational attainment among migrants and non-migrants, through constructing separate causal models for each group, and this possibility is briefly pursued again among the non-farm, native-born males only. Other possibilities, such as an analysis of income differences or an extensive analysis of educational attainment are not pursued at this time but are possible with these data.

As a background to the analysis, the magnitude of provincial and community differences in occupational structure is first established. Overall rates of internal migration in Canada are discussed and briefly compared to those in the United States.

Differences in Occupational Structure

Is geography an important element in the relative distribution of occupations in Canada at this time? How much do the provinces differ in the jobs which are available? How much variation is there between communities of differing size?

Political and popular concern with regional disparities and have-not provinces would lead to an expectation that major differences would be found between the provinces in occupational level. This sample is well designed to test for such differences since it is stratified by province so that the true sample size (unweighted N) for even the smallest province is over two hundred cases. The results are given in Table 13.1 which shows the occupational structure of each province, using the occupational classification developed for this study (Pineo, Porter and McRoberts, 1977). To make the table readable the sixteen categories of the code have been reduced to seven, and farmers have been omitted.

The table shows that the provinces do differ in occupational composition, and the differences are generally in the expected direction with Atlantic Canada showing lower levels than the balance. But what is perhaps more striking is that the differences are only moderate in magnitude. The basic occupational profile in each province is similar.

TABLE 13:1 — Occupational Composition of the Provinces (Male Labour Force, All Ages, Farmers Excluded)

Percent of Labour Force Classified As:	Nfld	PEI	N.S.	N.B.	Que	Ont	Man	Sask	Alta	B.C.	Total
Professional, managerial	9.5	2.9	7.5	8.6	10.4	12.1	11.0	10.5	11.9	9.6	10.9
Semi-professional, technical	4.0	2.6	4.1	4.6	5.9	6.3	7.2	4.3	5.5	4.8	5.8
Middle managers, supervisors	7.3	9.4	10.9	10.5	11.3	12.6	11.7	13.1	14.2	10.7	11.9
Clerical-sales	12.0	13.0	11.9	12.1	15.8	14.5	13.5	16.4	14.8	14.0	14.6
Foremen, skilled crafts, trades	24.1	30.2	29.9	31.9	23.2	27.0	29.4	25.8	25.9	29.7	26.4
Semi-skilled crafts, trades	16.4	18.2	15.5	13.8	13.0	11.4	10.8	8.0	9.7	12.9	12.1
Unskilled farm labour	26.7	23.7	20.2	18.5	20.4	16.1	16.4	21.9	18.0	18.3	18.3
Weighted N	358	70	520	376	4,494	6,456	709	537	1,197	1,912	16,628
(Unweighted N)	(919)	(222)	(1,361)	(889)	(3,183)	(4,305)	(830)	(752)	(1,246)	(1,872)	(15,579)

Each province has some jobs in the highest categories, and it is never more than a minority of the labour force. And each province has its share of semi-skilled and unskilled. While Prince Edward Island stands out, among the other provinces none has less than 7 per cent falling into the professional managerial category and none has more than 12.1 per cent. At the other extreme, each province has at least 16 per cent who are classified as unskilled labour or farm labourers. If the occupational classification is assumed to be an interval level measurement, an eta coefficient can be used to represent the degree of association. The coefficient is only .077.

Alternative arrangements of the data do not change the results a great deal. If the eta coefficient is computed using the full sixteen categories of the occupational classification, including the farmers, it is virtually identical (.078). If the Blishen-McRoberts scores for occupation are used instead of the classification, making the assumption of an interval level of measurement more tenable, the coefficient is slightly larger at .102, and, with farmers included, it increases to .120. Provincial differences in the structure of the female labour force are even smaller. An eta coefficient measuring provincial differences in the Blishen-McRoberts scores for the female labour force, excluding farmers, is only .056. By any test, little more than 1 per cent of the total variation in occupational level appears to be owing to differences in the provincial occupational opportunity structures. Nor would combining the provinces into regions alter the picture because, of course, if the provinces do not differ greatly in occupational structure no combination of them into regions could produce differences.

In all, the differences between the provinces are, at this point in history, sufficiently small to suggest that no major gain should be expected in occupational level simply in exchange for making a move between provinces. And conversely, no great loss in occupational status should be expected to be incurred by those who choose to remain within their province of birth. It has been argued earlier in this volume (see Chapter 2) that provincial boundaries are poor material to use in dividing Canada into economic regions, and the evidence of Table 13.1 supports this viewpoint.

More substantial differences are to be found if community size rather than province is investigated. The categories used to code community size were: over 100,000; 30,000 to 99,999; 15,000 to 29,999; less than 15,000; and rural. Table 13.2 shows the occupational structure for each of these categories. The occupational code is again the sixteen category occupational classification, reduced to seven classifications and with farmers omitted. Again one sees considerable variation within each

TABLE 13:2 — Occupational Composition by Community Size (Male Labour Force, All Ages, Farmers Excluded)

			Community Size			
Percentage of Labour Force Classified As:	*Rural Non-Farm*	*Less than 15,000*	*15,000 to 29,999*	*30,000 to 99,999*	*100,000 or more*	*Total*
Professional, managerial	4.7	7.4	11.5	11.4	13.7	10.9
Semi-professional, technical	3.6	4.9	4.6	6.7	6.7	5.8
Middle managers, supervisors	8.3	12.5	11.2	10.8	13.3	11.9
Clerical-sales	9.0	11.5	14.8	13.8	17.3	14.6
Foremen, skilled crafts, trades	29.9	30.1	27.5	29.8	23.6	26.4
Semi-skilled crafts, trades	16.7	12.8	12.7	11.1	10.4	12.1
Unskilled, farm labour	27.8	20.8	17.7	16.4	15.0	18.3
Weighted N	3,038	1,835	1,109	1,815	8,831	16,628
(Unweighted N)	(4,689)	(2,427)	(1,172)	(1,331)	(5,960)	(15,579)

community-size category as professional or managerials are found even in the rural–non-farm category, and unskilled workers are found in communities of every size. Yet the overall pattern is stronger. The largest cities have 13.7 per cent in the highest occupational category and no province reached this level. The rural–non-farm category shows 27.8 per cent falling into the unskilled labour and farm labour category, which again is a larger percentage than in any single province. Measures of association show the pattern more clearly. While the relationship between province and occupational level in Table 13.1 could be represented by an eta coefficient of only .077, that between community size and occupational level is .194.

Community size differences are considerably larger than provincial differences no matter now the data are arranged. If the Blishen-McRoberts scores are used the eta coefficient between community size and occupation is .221, which is again much larger than that found for province (.102). Including farmers raised the measure even further, to .297, but since farmers are by definition rural, and were given a very low occupational score, this more substantial coefficient is a by-product of the codes which are used. Since the community size categories can be considered to form an interval scale, the correlation coefficient can also be computed. It is typically only fractionally less than the equivalent eta coefficient: the tabulation yielding an eta coefficient of .221, for example, gives a correlation of .216. Finally, the community size differences are also greater than provincial differences for women as well as men. The eta coefficient measuring community size differences in Blishen-McRoberts scores for women is .118; the equivalent coefficient for provincial differences was only .056. For men, while only about 1 per cent of the variation in occupational level is interprovincial, more like 4 per cent of the variation is inter-community. For women both figures are much less, but the ratio is about the same as community effects are about four times as strong as the provincial ones.

Is this pattern of weak provincial differences and stronger community-size differences a recent development? A rough test of this possibility can be performed. If one assumes that the respondent's first job can safely be used as a proxy measure of earlier history — a contentious assumption — tabulating it against province or community of residence at age 16 can provide a rough measure of the strength of the effects some years ago. The comparison with the contemporary measures is imperfect since only the native-born population can be used and in the case of community size the coding categories for community at age 16 are different than for present community. Nonetheless, the basic pattern is similar. Among the non-farm male labour force, the first job, coded in Blishen-McRoberts scores, relates to province of residence at age 16 with an eta coefficient of .107, which is quite close to the coefficient of .102 found between current job and province. And the size of community at age 16 relates to first job with an eta coefficient of .232, again closely resembling the .221 found between current job and community size. Since the comparisons are rough, modest trends could be hidden, but in the main the pattern seems the same.

Judging from these results only, one could reasonably expect that movement between communities of differing size will have stronger effects upon occupational level than would migration across provincial boundaries, and this turns out to be the case, as is shown later. One might also reasonably expect that the amount of migration would be quite modest, since quite small flows of population would be sufficient to erase the modest differences in occupational level which are found. But the actual rates of migration, shown below, seem well in excess of the minimum that would be required merely to fit occupational demand to supply.

Amount and Type of Migration

How many, then, do move? Taking movement between the provinces first, we can show from the 1961 census that some 12.3 per cent of the Canadian population were enumerated in a province other than the one in which they were born (Kalbach and McVey, 1971:89). It is, of course, the native-born population which is relevant, and the figure includes children. The adult native-born males in our sample showed an incidence of some 13.8 per cent having permanently switched provinces between age 16 and the present. If earlier moves are also included, some 17.0 per cent permanently switched provinces between their birth and the time of the study. This would appear to be in excess of what would be needed to adjust population to the opportunities available. But what is more striking is that this is the percentage who shifted provincial boundaries permanently. When we inquired how many had ever had a permanent residence in another province since age 16 some 32.4 per cent reported they had at least one. More lived elsewhere and returned than settled permanently in another province.

Much of the inter-provincial migration may be just a shuffling around among the smaller provinces. The proportions reporting they have lived elsewhere are particularly low for Quebec, of course (20.8 per cent), and for Newfoundland (22.8 per cent). Ontario is also below average, at 29.2 per cent. The highest rates are reported by residents of Alberta and British Columbia (52.0 per cent and 55.3 per cent, respectively). The other provinces show above average rates: for New Brunswick, 36.8 per cent reported having lived elsewhere; for Nova Scotia, 34.1 per cent; for Prince Edward Island, 39.2 per cent; for Manitoba, 37.3 per cent and for Saskatchewan, 38.6 per cent.

Movement between communities also shows high rates. In all, some 49.0 per cent of the native-born male respondents reported a permanent move to some other community, including 18.8 per cent who reported moves between communities of the same size, and 30.2 per cent who moved between communities of differing size. Further, when asked if they ever lived permanently in another community since the age of 16, some 64.4 per cent said they had done so. By subtraction, it would appear that a quite substantial percentage, some 19.5 per cent, move to another community after age 16 and then return to the original community.

In all, the picture which emerges is of a flowing of population between provinces and between communities which is vastly greater than that required by variations in opportunity structures. Shifts of as few as 5 or 10 per cent of the male labour force is all that would be required to cancel out the differences in occupational level between provinces and communities that we have noted; in fact almost one-third report some movement between provinces and almost two-thirds between communities.

Is all this moving about a new phenomenon? Would one find evidence from the questionnaires completed by the older respondents that thirty or more years ago movement between communities or provinces was less frequent? One could expect to find the oldest showing more geographic mobility since the years at risk are necessarily greater. Table 13.3 shows the incidence of migration for differing age cohorts.

TABLE 13:3 — Incidence of Migration by Age Cohorts (Male, Native-Born Labour Force, All Ages)

Percentages Reporting	18-24	25-34	35-44	45-54	55-64	65+	Total
Same city now as at age 16	71.8	49.6	45.2	46.1	47.3	45.4	51.1
Never moved between cities since 16	60.2	31.1	29.0	30.2	30.6	31.7	35.4
Never moved between provinces since 16	80.8	69.9	65.4	61.0	63.5	65.3	67.6
Same province now as at age 16	92.5	87.5	85.4	82.7	84.0	84.2	86.3
Same province now as at birth	88.8	83.5	81.5	80.4	81.3	82.8	83.1

The picture which emerges from Table 13.3 is remarkable. There is no evidence of the years at risk having any appreciable effect. Rather the rates of migration are very similar for all cohorts over 25 years of age. The only distinctive cohort is the 18 to 24-year-old group which shows much less migration than the balance. The picture in the table is of a society in which, as it were, people moved quite frequently during the year in which they were 25 and rarely or never at any other time. It is known that migration is a phenomenon of young adulthood but the table would appear to exaggerate the effect. Probably the high proportion of stayers in the youngest age cohort is exaggerated by the fact that the movers of this age are notoriously difficult to capture in a survey research sample.

If the years at risk must play a role, the table could be taken to imply a trend. The 49.6 per cent reporting they live in the same city among those 25 to 34 years of age may dwindle as they age so that when they become 65 or more it will be appreciably less than the 45.4 per cent reported by those now 65 or more.

These high rates of internal migration are not peculiar to Canada, however, at least in comparison with the United States. From the censuses Canadians appear to migrate more than do Americans, but the Canadian rates are inflated by the larger number of immigrants in Canada. When native-born Canadians are compared to Americans, as in Table 13.4, the Americans show higher rates. In all but the youngest age cohort, the Americans show about a 5 per cent higher incidence of migration, defined here as reporting a different community of residence at the time of the interview than at age 16. If the percentages are compared diagonally, so that the Americans age 25 to 34 are compared to Canadians aged 35 to 44, a partial correction is made for the fact that the studies are ten years apart in time. Even so, the rates are lower in Canada than the United States.

In this comparison, however, as in so many migration statistics, the problem of the equivalence of units makes it difficult to be sure of the

TABLE 13:4 — Percentages of Migrants by Age Cohorts, Canada and the U.S.

	25-34	*35-44*	*45-54*	*55-64*
U.S.A. – 1962 (Blau-Duncan 1967:510)	55.8	60.0	58.3	63.0
Canada – 1973 (native-born males)	50.4	54.8	53.9	52.7

differences. Thus, insofar as community boundaries vary from one nation to the other the meaning of living in the same community may not be identical in the two.

Permanent Intercommunity Migration

The measure of migration used in Table 13.4 is the one used most frequently to date in studies of occupational attainment and it is the one for which comparable U.S. data are available. It is a dichotomy which classifies each respondent according to whether the present community of residence is the same as that at age 16. As this is only one of several measures of migration in the Canadian study it must be given a more specific name. Hereafter we will refer to it as "permanent intercommunity migration." Return migrants, that is, those who left the original community but eventually returned to it, are classified as non-migrants in this measurement and the term "permanent" is included in the name to note this fact.

The effects of migration, measured in this way, upon occupational attainment have been described for the United States (Duncan, Featherman and Duncan, 1972). Evidence of a small positive relationship between migration and occupational attainment was given. Below we show that the Canadian data produce similar results. We later show that the effects of migration vary when different varieties of migration are considered and different categories of the population are examined.

Since it has been established in the United States by Duncan, Featherman and Duncan, and can also easily be demonstrated for Canada with data from this sample, that the effect of migration upon those of farm origin is quite different from those of non-farm background, the analysis first concentrates upon those with non-farm background. The definition of "non-farm" differs somewhat from that used in the United States: we do not exclude those whose fathers were farm labourers; we do exclude those sons who were themselves farmers.

For the non-farm labour force, defined in this way,[1] there is a small positive relationship between permanent migration to another community after age 16 and occupational attainment in Canada as in the United States. The zero-order relationship, in standardized form, is .13 if only those over 24 years of age are tabulated. If the younger men are included, these still in the years of most active migration, the relationship is lower, at .12. In general, since the migration patterns of those under 25 are so different from the others (see Table 13.3) they are excluded in the analysis which follows, as are the foreign-born.

In unstandardized form, which may convey the extent of the

relationship more vividly, the migrants are found to have Blishen-McRoberts scores some 3.87 points higher than non-migrants (see Table 13.5).[2]

The migrants might well have come from superior social backgrounds. Insofar as they had, the apparent impact of migration upon occupational attainment would be partially spurious. In fact, however, in this sample, the social background of the migrants and non-migrants did not differ appreciably. Correlation coefficients measuring the superiority of migrants' social background over those of non-migrants were: for fathers' education, .06; for number of siblings, .00; and for father's occupation, .05. Such small correlations cannot have great effect upon the results. With these variables controlled for in a multiple regression equation the effect of migration falls to 3.22 Blishen-McRoberts points, meaning that some .65 Blishen-McRoberts points in the lead migrants hold over non-migrants is indirect and owing to high social background (again, see Table 13.5).

There is, however, a quite substantial tendency for migrants to come from smaller communities. This may be represented by a zero-order correlation of 0.23, when size of community at age 16 is related to migration. This factor is of some strength and operates to depress the apparent effect of migration upon occupational attainment, by some .94 points. With size of community, as well as social background, controlled, the apparent effect of migration is increased to 4.16 Blishen-McRoberts points. That is, when compared to others raised in the same-sized communities, the migrants show a higher level of occupational attainment than non-migrants.

Finally, of course, the effects of education must be taken into account. Migrants are better educated than non-migrants; the correlation is .13. Of the total advantage of some 4.16 Blishen-McRoberts points that migrants hold over non-migrants, precisely half, 2.08 points, would seem to be owing to their superior education. We investigate later the evidence in the study about the extent to which the interrelationship between migration, educational attainment and occupational achievement appear to come about because migration acts as a process in which educational attainment is matched more successfully with occupational level.

With educational level controlled for as well, then, the apparent effect of migration falls again, to 2.08 Blishen-McRoberts points. This effect is statistically significant, in the sense that it is many times the value of its standard error. Expressing it in unstandardized form may give a false sense of its importance, however; in standardized form the beta is only .07, and would, by the often used criteria that only betas in excess of .10

TABLE 13:5 — Gross, Indirect, and Direct Effects of Inter-community Migration Upon Occupational Attainment (in Blishen-McRoberts Scores)

| Type of Migration | Gross Effect | Indirect Effects Owing to: | | | Net Effects |
		Social background	Size of community of origin	Education	
Permanent inter-community migration N = 6657 (unweighted N = 6404)	3.87	+ .65	− .94	+ 2.08	+ 2.08
Return inter-community migration N = 3124 (unweighted N = 3181)	2.35	+1.01	+ .01	+ 1.09	+ .24

Population: Native born males, 25 years or older, non-farm (i.e. neither respondent nor father a farm owner or operator) should remain in a path diagram, be dismissed as of trivial magnitude. Perhaps it is desirable that this criteria fall by the wayside. It may be too stringent as it becomes more and more apparent that further explanations of occupational attainment will be brought about only through including a large number of variables each with quite small explanatory power. Migration is, in any case, one variable which turns out to have some remaining explanatory power after education is controlled, and this is rarely so.[3]

Return Migration (Intercommunity)

Not all those classified as non-migrants in the preceding section are truly that. When asked if they had ever lived permanently in another community since age 16, some 42.6 per cent of them reported that they had done so. This is a substantial number; it may, in fact, be somewhat inflated since the definition of "community" was left to the discretion of the respondent.

The question may be raised whether these return migrants resemble migrants who end up in a different community. If the competitive advantage held by migrants derives from their willingness to seek out opportunities in several labour markets, then those who ultimately find the best opportunities in the community from which they originated should be found to do as well as those who ultimately find the best opportunity elsewhere.

A multiple regression analysis parallelling that used in the study of permanent intercommunity migrants can address this question. In this analysis, the intercommunity migrants are omitted and the return migrants are compared to those who report they have never lived elsewhere. Since the bench line for the comparison is different in the two analyses, the comparison is not perfect. Permanent migrants are compared to non-migrants and return migrants; return migrants are compared to those who never moved. But as will be seen, the results of the analysis are so different that this imperfection in the comparison is of little importance.

The effects of return migration upon occupational attainment are positive, but in all respects they are much weaker than the effects of permanent intercommunity migration. The gross effects of return migration are only 2.35 Blishen-McRoberts points while for permanent migration they were 3.87 (see Table 13.5). Controlling for social background reduces the apparent effect of migration by 1.01 points, from 2.35 to 1.34. In contrast to the earlier analysis, community size has little effect. Return migrants come from smaller communities, on average, but the effect is minute ($r = .02$). As a result further controls for community size have essentially no influence upon the strength of the migration effect. It falls from 1.34 to 1.33. Finally, almost all of this effect can be laid to the higher educational status of the return migrants ($r = .12$). With education controlled, the final, direct effect of this kind of migration upon occupational attainment can be measured as only .24 points. The effect via education is 1.09. The net effect of return migration, an as yet imperfectly understood phenomenon, is markedly less than the effect of permanent intercommunity migration, and is not statistically significant.

Multiple Migrations

Just as the non-migrants can be divided into those who never migrated and those who returned, so also the permanent intercommunity migrants may be divided according to the total number of intercommunity moves they report. Multiple moves were common. Among the 3,124 male respondents reporting a permanent move to another community, 2,360 of them, or 75.5 per cent, reported more than one move. A substantial number, 513 cases, reported six to ten moves and 190 reported more than ten moves (for unweighted N's see Table 13.6). Some of those classified as return migrants may also have made multiple moves, but this group is excluded from the above figures. So also, the farm population is omitted.

The question measuring multiple migration was phrased in the following way:

> Since you became 16 years of age, how many times have you moved (changed your place of residence) from one city, town, village or municipality to another? (Count moves inside and outside of Canada.)

This is not a question ordinarily asked in studies of occupational attainment and its value is not yet determined. Neither the reliability nor validity of the question have been established. If it is an adequate question it remains to be determined if those who move frequently show greater occupational attainment than those who move only once or twice. Or, alternatively, it has been suggested that diminishing returns may well set in and those who migrate most frequently could show lower levels of attainment than those migrating less often (see, for example, Grant and Vanderkamp, 1976:68).

Tests for a simple linear relationship between the number of moves and occupational attainment may be made using multiple regression. Omitting the non-migrants and return migrants leads to a test of whether those migrating often achieve more than those migrating only a few times. The usual controls, for social background, size of community at age 16 and education, are used. The resulting estimate of the influence of multiple migration is minute; the coefficient, in standardized form, is only .03. The effect is positive, meaning that more moves generally result in greater occupational attainment, but so small as to suggest that the question is not worth the expense of including in an occupational attainment study.

Another way of estimating the importance of multiple migration is to ask the extent to which adding this extra information to the migration variable increases the impact of migration upon occupational attainment. Thus a variable is created in which the non-migrants are coded zero; the return migrants, one; those migrating once only are given the code of two; those migrating twice are coded three; and so forth. The code can be seen in Table 13.6. Such a variable uses the full range of information, including the idea of multiple migration and also return migration. Simply dichotomizing the population into migrants and non-migrants led to an estimate of the effects of migration, under controls, upon occupational attainment of .072 (see page 489). Using this more complicated variable changes the estimate to .077. The gain is minute. Duncan was apparently correct when he suggested in "Mobility in Britain Reconsidered":

TABLE 13:6 — **Effects of Migration upon Occupational Attainment (Males, Native-born, 25 Years of Age or Older) (Non-farm)**

Migrant Status	N	Unweighted	Gross Effect	Net Effect with Covariates*
Non-migrants	1,794	1,865	0.00	0.00
Return migrants	1,330	1,316	2.35	.22
One move	764	713	2.99	1.27
Two moves	542	476	4.58	2.24
Three moves	508	432	6.57	3.15
Four moves	338	308	6.62	2.85
Five moves	269	238	5.79	2.40
Six to ten moves	513	478	7.13	2.61
Eleven or more	190	188	6.88	3.50
Total	6,248	6,014		(beta) 0.09

*Covariates are: Education, size of community at age 16, number of siblings, father's education, and father's occupational status.

It may well be, however, that most of the information inherent in the migration record can be extracted by a simple classification of respondents as migrant or non-migrant . . . (1972:20)

In the above tests linear regression is used and so there is no check of the possibility that diminishing returns operate to depress the attainments of the most frequent migrants. In Table 13.6 the gross and net effects upon occupational attainment of each level of migration are given. MCA analysis is used to check if a non-linear model yields a better fit. The beta equals .09 and may be compared to the .077 estimate of the effect of migration which came from the regression analysis. The estimate is a little higher. Inspection of the net effects shows a slight tendency to peak among those reporting they have migrated three times between communities, and another peak among those reporting eleven or more moves. The MCA estimate reacts to these peaks and also is undisturbed by variations in the magnitude of the intervals and so produces a higher estimate. On balance, however, the difference is so slight that parsimony would lead to accepting the linear model.

Off-Farm Migration

In the previous analysis only the non-farm population was investigated. Both sons who were farm owner and operators and those who reported their fathers had been farm owner, operators were excluded. This farm population is not small. Some 4,730 men in the weighted sample (or 5,261 without weighting) reported that their fathers had been farm owner, operators — which is 25.9 per cent of all those reporting the father's occupation. Many of these are immigrants, of course, but even among the native-born, 25 years of age or older, 3,306 reported the father had been a farm owner, operator. The majority of these left the farm and so "off-farm migration" is a major migrant stream in recent Canadian history. The extent to which migration was a positive factor in the occupational attainment of these individuals is difficult to ascertain because of the special problems in estimating the socioeconomic status of farm owner, operators and also because of problems of classification. We show, in the first line of Table 13.7, that quite spectacular estimates of the positive impact of off-farm migration can be presented. Also, if these farmers' sons are included with the non-farm population, the whole sample shows quite marked effects of migration. But we suspect these effects are an artifact of the code which happens to be assigned to farmers.

If the top line of Table 13.7 is taken at face value, it suggests that migrants with farm origin show a marked gain of 8.59 Blishen-

McRoberts points when compared to non-migrants with farm origin. The controls entered to generate estimates of indirect and net effects need a word of explanation. In the first place, since all those with farm origin were by definition from the same size of community, there is no point in including a variable of community size as a control (as was done in Table 13.5). By the same logic, there is no point to including the father's occupation as a control variable since all the respondents would have the same score. Yet it is true that farmers are not identical in wealth and so a variable has been used as a proxy for the social status of the father's occupation. The variable is based on the question following the one soliciting father's occupation:

If he owned a farm to do this work, how many people did he usually employ?

Of the native-born farmers' sons, 25 years or older, answering this question, 592 (unweighted N, 707) or 19.5 per cent reported the father typically employed one or more labourers on the farm. We assume these were the wealthier farms and this variable, as a dichotomy, is used in the analysis to replace the variable of father's occupation. We note that the variable has some statistical power, correlating around .20 with the father's level of education and at a similar level with the son's education. These are much lower correlations than are found between father's occupation and education in a non-farm sample. As a mode of differentiating farmers according to social status the question seems weak but of some value.

The controls for social background, including the variable of number

TABLE 13:7 — Gross, Indirect, and Direct Effects of Permanent Intercommunity Migration upon the Occupational Attainment of Sons with Farm Origins*

		Indirect effects owing to:		
Estimates when farm owner, operator:	*Gross Effects*	*Social background†*	*Respondent's education*	*Net Effects*
Coded as 23 (Blishen-McRoberts code)	+8.59	.09	1.64	6.86
Coded as 44 (Prestige score)	+2.41	.08	1.42	.91
N = 2363 (Unweighted = 2,753)				

*Father was farm owner or operator
†Social background is measured by number of siblings, father's education, and whether or not the father employed farm hands.

of farm hands, reduce the effect of migration upon the son's occupational attainment scarcely at all. The indirect effect through education is of some magnitude and it leaves a net effect of migration upon occupational attainment of +6.86, much larger than that found in the non-farm population. In standardized form the effect would be .24.

We make it clear in the second line of the table, however, that it is very likely that this strong effect is an artifact of the score which is assigned to farm owner and operator. The code used in the equations producing the first line of the table was 23, the code given to farmers in the 1971 Blishen-McRoberts classification. It is a very low code, reflecting the fact that farmers report little cash income. It would be as reasonable, however, to assign farmer owners and operators the code of 44, the actual prestige score they were given in the Pineo-Porter study of public evaluations of occupations (1967). This is the code used in the second line of Table 13.7, and when it is used, the picture changes completely. The gross effect is only +2.21, the indirect effects are about the same as with the code of 23, the net effects are only +.91.

We are not suggesting that the second line of the table is correct and the first incorrect. Rather, the point to be made is that until there is some consensus on the proper code to assign to farmers, the effects of off-farm migration are indeterminant.

A second problem with the analysis of Table 13.7 is that it over-simplifies the problem by using merely two categories. Actually the sons of farmers do quite a variety of different things, as shown in Table 13.8.

Table 13.8 accounts for the occupational and migration histories of the 3,296 native-born males, 25 years or older, in the weighted sample, who reported their fathers were farm owners and operators. Some 596 did not give complete information. Another 107 became farm labourers; this small group is omitted from the body of the table. In the table itself,

TABLE 13:8 — Occupations and Migrant Status of Sons of Farm Owners and Operators, Native-born Population, 25 or Older

	Farm owner operator		Non-farm occupation	
Same community as at age 16	402	(598)	569	(750)
Different community than at age 16	178	(250)	1,443	(1,422)
			N = 2,593	(3,020)

Unweighted frequencies in parentheses

the activities of 2,593 respondents are given. Of these, 402 apparently stayed on the family farm, or nearby. The other kind of behaviour that one imagines a farmer's son doing, moving to the city and getting an urban job, accounted for 1,443 cases (although many of these may have moved to rural–non-farm areas rather than cities). But the rest of the cases behaved in a way not ordinarily considered in thinking about off-farm migration. Some remained farmers, but moved to another community. There were 178 such cases. And quite a large number left farming but remained in the community. Some 569 respondents — a non-trivial number — reported that they were not farming but had not moved from the community after age 16. Some may be early migrants, of course. But we note that it cannot be a large number, because the great majority of this group, in answer to another question, reported that they were living with both parents at age 16 (only 15.1 per cent reported they were not living with both parents).

In Table 13.7 the comparison was between the populations described in the two rows of Table 13.8. That is, those who shifted from the community, whether they entered urban jobs or farming, were compared with those who remained in the community, again regardless of their occupations. Other comparisons are, of course, possible, and may be of more significance.

In Table 13.9, a different comparison is made. Those who remained in farming are excluded. Those who migrated and entered the urban

TABLE 13:9 — Gross, Indirect, and Direct Effects of Permanent Inter-community Migration upon the Occupational Attainment of Sons with Farm Origins* Who Are Not Farm Owner, Operators

		Indirect effects owing to:		
	Gross Effects	*Social background†*	*Respondent's education*	*Net Effects*
Sons entering urban occupations or farm labouring (N = 1,848) (unweighted = 2,009)	5.19	.50	1.76	2.93
Sons entering urban occupations (N = 1,758) (unweighted = 1,884)	4.55	.56	1.74	2.25

*Father was farm owner or operator
†Social background is measured by number of siblings, father's education, and whether or not the father employed farm hands.

labour force are compared to those who slid into the urban labour force without leaving the origin community. We ask if this form of behaviour has a penalty. Do those who seem unwilling to leave the original community pay some price in degree of occupational attainment. The numbers in the table suggest they do. The first line of the table includes those who became farm labourers. They are omitted in the second line. In either case, those willing to leave the community showed gross gains of 4.55 or 5.19 points. The indirect effects owing to social background and to the respondent's education are not unlike those found for the non-farm population (see Table 13.5). And the net effects, while somewhat larger, are also roughly equivalent to those found for the non-farm group. It appears that there is about as much at stake in the decision to migrate among those of farm origin who must leave farming as there is for the non-farm population. With farm labourer included the net effect, in standardized form, was .10. With labourers excluded it was .07, essentially identical to the estimate of the effects of migration derived from the non-farm population. If the problems of classification and of the coding of farming as an occupation are properly handled it may appear that the off-farm migrants are not markedly different from the non-farm population.

Education, Occupation and Migration

A second way in which migration may influence the process of status attainment is by altering the magnitude of the causal relationships. In Table 13.10 the results of computing separate regression equations for non-migrants, return migrants and permanent inter-community migrants are given. In the top panel of the table, occupation is the dependent variable. In the bottom panel, educational attainment is the dependent. Since the coefficients are metric, which is to say unstandardized, those in one panel cannot be immediately compared to those in the other. Within the panels, however, any difference in the coefficients in each column signifies that a certain independent variable is exerting more or less causal power for some group of migrants.

In the top panel, one difference would seem to lie in the final two columns. The role that education plays in occupational attainment is greater for the migrant groups than for the non-migrants. Each additional unit of education (which is roughly one year) brings an addition of 1.92 Blishen-McRoberts points for the non-migrants, 2.20 for the permanent intercommunity migrants. Thus, migration functions to increase the rate of return upon years of education, presumably through achieving a better adjustment between skill supply and demand.

TABLE 13:10 — Determinants of Occupational Attainment (and Education Attainment) of Non-Migrants, Return Migrants, and Permanent Inter-community Migrants (Native-born, 25 or Older, Non-farm Males)

A. Determinants of occupational attainment, metric coefficients

Population	Father's Occupation	Father's Education	Number of Sibs	Community Size at Age 16	Respondent's Education
Non-migrants (N = 1,794) (Unweighted = 1,865)	.16 (.02)	.09 (.08)	-.16 (.09)	2.12 (.37)	1.92 (.09)
Return migrants (N = 1,330) (Unweighted = 1,316)	.13 (.03)	.16 (.10)	.05 (.10)	2.12 (.44)	2.20 (.11)
Permanent inter-community migrants (N = 3,124) (Unweighted = 2,833)	.10 (.02)	.09 (.06)	-.07 (.07)	1.12 (.29)	2.26 (.06)

B. Determinants of educational attainment, metric coefficients

Population	Father's Occupation	Father's Education	Number of Sibs	Community Size at Age 16	Respondent's Education
Non-migrants	.05 (.01)	.28 (.02)	-.18 (.02)	.71 (.10)	
Return migrants	.05 (.01)	.23 (.02)	-.19 (.03)	.45 (.11)	
Permanent inter-community migrants	.05 (.01)	.29 (.02)	-.22 (.02)	.43 (.08)	

(Standard errors of the b's in parentheses)

(In standardized form, the betas for the three groups are .49, .51 and .57.)

The other pattern, found in the first panel, is the diminished importance of the variable "size of community at age 16" upon the migrants. The coefficient is over 2 points for both non-migrants and return migrants, but it is only 1.12 for the permanent migrants. Not unexpectedly the effects of the community of early residence are reduced for those who permanently leave. There is nothing mysterious about what replaces this variable. In an equation not shown, community size at present was entered as well as community size at age 16 for the permanent migrants. In this equation, the effect of the first community falls from 1.12 to .86, but the effect of the size of the present community is 1.68 points. Thus, the new community enters as a factor for the permanent migrants, and the sum of the two coefficients would actually exceed that for community size among the non-migrants. Migration does not free one from the influence of the community but merely replaces the effects of one community by those of another.

In both panels of the table the effects of social background, represented by father's occupation, father's education, and family size, appear to fluctuate in a way that leads to no firm interpretations.

The diminishing significance of the size of the community at age 16 upon educational attainment is shown most clearly in the second panel of the table. While community size exerts an influence represented by an unstandardized b of .71 upon the non-migrants it is only .45 for the return migrants and .43 for the permanent inter-community migrants. This is consistent with the idea that a certain amount of migration is a seeking out of educational opportunities not available in the community of origin.

Long-distance Migration

Respondents were asked which province they lived in at birth, at age 16 and at the time of interview. They were also asked how many times they had moved, that is, changed their place of permanent residence, from one province to another since they were 16 years of age. These questions provide measures of the incidence of inter-provincial migration, which may be conceptualized as long-distance migration.

We have shown that the provinces do not differ substantially one from another in occupational structure. From this point of view, one might hypothesize that long-distance, inter-provincial migration would have less pay-off to individuals than does inter-community migration. On the other hand, however, studies by economists suggest that the greater costs of long-distance moves should mean that they occur only when greater pay-off is possible (see, for example, Ritchey, 1976).

Preliminary results suggest that inter-provincial migration has positive effects upon occupational attainment but while the gross effects are about as great as those of inter-community migration, they are predominantly brought about through higher levels of educational attainment and the higher social background of the migrants. Only a small proportion, some 14 per cent of the native-born, non-farm males over 25 years of age, reported that they lived in a different province at the time of interview than at age 16. This group did show higher occupational attainment than the balance. As shown in Table 13.11, the difference was some 4.22 Blishen-McRoberts points, which is a larger difference than that between permanent intercommunity migrants and non-migrants (3.87). The long-distance migrants show more tendency to come from a superior social background than do the intercommunity migrants and so with social background controlled, the effect of long-distance migration upon occupation attainment falls by some 1.64 points. Controlling for social background made a much smaller change in the impact of inter-community migration upon attainment. Educational attainment is also a factor in long-distance migration. The estimate of the extent to which it is superior educational attainment which leads the migrants to high occupational attainment is 1.48 for long-distance migration (see Table 13.11). It was 2.08 for inter-community migrants

TABLE 13:11 — Effects of Inter-provincial Migration upon Occupational Attainment (in Blishen-McRoberts Scores)

| | | Indirect effects owing to: | | |
| | *Gross* | *Social* | | *Net* |
Type of Migration	*Effects*	*Background*	*Education*	*Effects*
Long distance migration (inter-provincial) N = 6,269 (unweighted = 6,038)	4.22	+1.64	+1.48	1.10
Return long distance migration (inter-provincial) N = 4,902 (unweighted = 4,709)	3.05	+1.22	+1.38	+ .45
Early migration (inter-provincial) N = 6,269 (unweighted = 6,038)	2.68	+2.35	+ .37	− .05

Population: Native-born males, 25 or older, non-farm (i.e., neither respondent nor father farm owner, operator).

(see Table 13.5). As a result, controls for both social background and education reduce the effect of long-distance migration to only 1.10 points, which is considerably less than the direct effect of intercommunity migration (2.08, see Table 13.5).

On balance, then, while long-distance migration appears to play a greater role in occupational attainment than does inter-community migration, it is, to a larger extent, owing to the initially higher social background of the long-distance migrants and with this factor and the educational level of the migrants taken into account the net effects of long-distance migration are substantially less than those of inter-community migration. If, in fact, permanent inter-community migration is added as a variable to the equation which generated the estimate of 1.10 as the net effect of inter-provincial migration, the estimate falls to .48, and is non-significant statistically (N = 6222, unweighted = 5986). Thus, knowing a migrant has happened to cross a provincial boundary adds very little if any information relevant to predicting his occupational attainments.

A further category of long-distance migrants may be identified in the sample. This group, forming another 11 per cent of the native-born, non-farm male labour force 25 years of age or older, shows a pattern of "return inter-provincial migration." While reporting that the province of residence at age 16 is the same as that at the time of the interview, they also report having lived since they were 16 for some period of time in another province.

This group may be compared to those who have lived only in one province. The gross, indirect, and net effects upon occupational attainment of this form of migration are given in Table 13.11, where they may be immediately compared to the effects of permanent long-distance migration. The effects of return inter-provincial migration are of some magnitude, but at each point the effects are less than for permanent long-distance moves. Social background again plays a role; the indirect effects through social background are 1.22 Blishen-McRoberts points. So also education is a factor; some 1.38 points of the apparent effect of return long-distance migration is brought about through higher educational attainment. With social background and education controlled, the apparent effect of this form of migration falls from 3.05 to only .45, which is not significantly different from zero.

It was shown earlier, in discussion of Table 13.5, that there were sharp differences in the effect of permanent and return inter-community migration. Permanent inter-community migrants show a gain of some 2.08 points; return inter-community migrants show essentially no gain. So also, moves which are not permanent between provinces do not produce a positive net effect upon occupational attainment.

A final group of long-distance migrants are those who report a change in province of residence between birth and age 16. Some 9 per cent of the native-born male labour force, again 25 years of age or older, show this pattern. These early migrants may be compared to the balance — those who migrated late or who never migrated. In such a comparison they show higher occupational attainment than do those who stayed in their provinces of birth throughout their childhood. The difference is some 2.68 points. Of this difference, however, 2.35 points can be accounted for by higher social origins. As a result, even without educational attainment entered into the analysis, the apparent effect of early long-distance migration falls to a trivial +.37 points. Controlling for educational attainment reduces the effect further to −.05, far from significant statistically. Thus, this early migration has positive impact upon the occupations of the sons only if the gains are realized in the parental generation. It could have been that such migration was at the cost of the parents and the benefits accrued to the child as he was brought near to better educational facilities or a better job market. But such is not the case.

Early migration has, then, no direct effects upon occupational attainment. Long-distance migration, if it happens after age 16, has positive impact upon occupational attainment, but not so great an impact as permanent inter-community migration. The suspicion, voiced in econometric studies that long-distance migrants may pay some penalty for having entered a distant labour market about which they lack full information seems borne out (see Ritchey, 1976:374, for example).

The failure of inter-provincial migration to show strong direct effects upon occupational attainment may again be evidence that provincial boundaries are not of crucial importance at this time in Canada. Migration across lines demarcating different economic regions might show stronger effects.

Migration of French Males

The rates of migration and the effects of migration upon occupational attainment may be examined for the French separately. The French are defined here, as in Chapter 8, as those living in the province of Quebec and reporting that French is the language in which they "feel most comfortable when talking." Since the analysis of the total sample suggested that it was the more important, it is inter-community rather than inter-provincial migration which is analyzed.

Table 13.12 gives the frequencies and effects of migration for English

TABLE 13:12 — Effects of Inter-community Migration upon the Occupational Attainment of French and English

Migrant Category	Quebec French %	Net Effects	All English %	Net Effects
Non-migrants	30.8	0.00	28.0	0.00
Return migrants	20.3	.67	21.5	– .03
One move	15.7	2.01	11.0	1.17
Two moves	10.7	3.00	7.8	2.25
Three moves	9.0	3.94	7.9	2.83
Four moves	4.6	4.62	5.6	2.11
Five moves	2.9	3.97	4.9	2.01
Six to ten	5.2	4.13	9.3	2.21
Eleven or more	.8	2.87	3.9	3.05
Adjusted beta		.11		.08
N		1613		4448
	(unweighted = 1128)		(unweighted = 4613)	

Population: Male, native-born, 25 or older, non-farm (i.e. neither respondent nor father farm owner, operator).
"English" refers to all non-French
Covariates as in Table 13.6.

and French separately. In columns 1 and 3 percentage breakdowns of the two groups according to the various types of migration are given. These percentages show that the English migrate more than do the French. Some 30.8 per cent of the French report no migration as compared to 28.0 per cent of the English. While the percentage of return migrants is higher among the English, the sharper difference is that for all categories of multiple migration beyond three moves the English are more numerous. Only 13.5 per cent of the French report they have moved more than three times compared to 23.7 per cent of the English. Confining the population to French in Quebec might be thought to produce this finding, since inter-provincial migration is excluded. If all French are tabulated, however, the difference diminishes very little. Including those of French origin who now find themselves most comfortable in English might alter the picture, however.

When they do migrate, however, the French seem to gain more than do the English. The gains in Blishen-McRoberts points for the two groups, given in columns 2 and 4, with the exception of only one category are larger for the French. While the adjusted betas may somewhat exaggerate the strength of relationship, because they respond to non-linear differences, they show that the French at .11 do exceed the English at .08.

Migration of Women

The women in the sample may be compared to men in a manner similar to the comparison of English and French. Only working women may be included, however, since those who do not work were not asked their occupations. The analysis is confined to those 25 years of age and older, native-born and non-farm, because this proved to be the proper group to analyse among the males. More detailed analysis may suggest later that a different population should be selected when women are studied.

The expectation we bring to this analysis is that women will be found to be quite similar to men. The results of analyses of the status attainment process among working women in the United States suggest that with the exception of major differentials in income, the relationships to be found when studying women are quite similar to those found in studying men (Featherman and Hauser, 1976). Specifically, then, we would expect a weak, positive relationship (a standardized beta of around .07) between permanent inter-community migration and the occupational attainment of women, with controls for social background, size of community at age 16, and education. We would also expect return migrants to show little gain over non-migrants. The results of the analysis are presented in Table 13.13 and may be compared to Table 13.5 above where men were analysed in the same way.

The expectation that inter-community migration will have the same consequences to the occupational attainment of women as men is not borne out. As shown in the first line of Table 13.13, the impact of permanent inter-community migration is, at all steps, appreciably less for women than men. The gross effect for women is only 1.48, compared to 3.87 for men. Female migrants come from slightly superior social backgrounds and so some of the gross effect (.35 points) is allocated to this. For men, the effect was somewhat larger, at .65 points. Introducing the size of the community of residence at age 16 into the equation again had more influence for men than women. Migrant men attained approximately one Blishen-McRoberts points more than non-migrant men from the same-sized communities; for women the effect was only .39 points. Underlying this is the observation that community size has less impact upon the female labour force. While a zero-order correlation of about .22 exists between occupational status and community size for men (see page 484 above), the equivalent correlation is only about .11 for women.

TABLE 13:13 — Gross, Indirect, and Direct Effects of Inter-community Migration upon Occupational Attainment of Women (in Blishen-McRoberts Scores)

Type of Migration	Gross Effects	Indirect effects owing to:			Net Effects
		Social background	Size of community of origin	Education	
Permanent inter-community migration (N = 4,285) (unweighted = 3,928)	+1.48	.35	−.39	1.14	.38 (n.s.)
Return inter-community migration (N = 1,948) (unweighted = 1,779)	−.24	.54	−.09	.05	−.74 (n.s.)

Population: Native-born women, 25 or older, non-farm (i.e., neither father nor respondent farm owner, operator).

Finally, whatever small effects migration does have upon the occupational attainments of women seem to come about by education. The indirect effect of migration upon occupational status via educational attainment is 1.14 points. While this is less than the 2.08 points found for men, as a proportion of the total effect it is larger. As a result the net effect of migration for women is found to be only .38 points, which is not significantly different from zero. In standardized form the beta is .01.

The observation that community size effects are less for the female labour force than the male and the observation that inter-community migration has little pay-off for women may be two sides of the same coin. Males achieve gains by moving from communities with poorer opportunities to those with better opportunities. But since what opportunities there are for women are more equally distributed through communities of differing size, movement between communities results in no gain. This being said, it remains a problem which will not be addressed at this time, why the male and female labour forces differ in this respect.

In the second line of Table 13.3, those women who spent some time in another community but eventually returned to the community of origin (return migrants) are compared to the non-migrants. Across the whole line the effects are trivial in magnitude. Such women have somewhat superior social background (indirect effect = .54), but do not differ from the non-migrants in either the size of community (−.09) or in education attainment (.05). The gross effect of such migration upon occupational attainment is negative (−.24) and when this is considered in the light of the superior social origins of the women, the overall estimate of the effects of return migration is also negative (−.74), but not significantly different from zero.

The same results may be seen in Table 13.14, where the net gains for men and women migrants are given. The table repeats the result of Table 13.13, but adds the distinction between various degrees of multiple migrants.

The percentage distributions in Table 13.14 permit a comparison of the frequency with which men and women migrate. Slightly fewer women than men are non-migrants, 24.8 per cent compared to 28.7 per cent. But also fewer women are found in the top two categories. In all the difference between the men and women is not great and it mainly takes the form of somewhat less variation in rates of migration for the women than for the men.

The negative pay-off for the female return migrants is shown in the second line of the table (−.81) and may be compared to the slight

TABLE 13:14 — Comparing the Effects of Migration upon Occupational Attainment of Women and Men (Native-born Labour Force, 25 Years of Age or Older)

	Women		Men	
Migrant Category	*%*	*Net Effects*	*%*	*Net Effects*
Non-migrants	24.8	0.00	28.7	0.00
Return migrants	22.8	− .81	21.3	.22
One move	13.9	.42	12.2	1.27
Two moves	9.8	− .39	8.7	2.24
Three moves	9.5	−1.23	8.1	3.15
Four moves	5.2	.22	5.4	2.85
Five moves	4.7	.37	4.3	2.40
Six to ten	7.2	1.22	8.2	2.61
Eleven or more	2.2	−2.57	3.0	3.50
Adjusted beta		.06		.09
N		4095		6248
	(unweighted = 3760)		(unweighted = 6014)	

Population: Native-born, 25 or older, non-farm (neither respondent nor father farm
    owner, operator).
Covariates as in Table 13.6.

positive return for males (.22). While all categories of migrant males show a positive net gain when compared to the non-migrants, the effects for women are as frequently negative as positive.

The adjusted beta coefficients, produced by MCA analysis, are given at the bottom of the table. Since no linear assumptions are involved, the fluctuations from positive to negative in the results from the analysis of women produce a beta approaching in magnitude that of men (.06 compared to .09). If a linear model is applied, however, using multiple regression analysis, the difference is clear. For men, as noted earlier, the standardized beta was .077; for women, it is only .007, and despite a case base of over four thousand, it is not statistically significant.

Conclusions

Most Canadians are migrants. Among the native-born males in all age cohorts over 24 years old, over 60 per cent report having lived permanently in some other community since they were 16. An additional number must have moved before 16. While this incidence of migration is slightly less than that found in the United States some ten years ago, it is nevertheless much more than would seem to be required by the disjunctures in the distribution of occupational opportunities. Perhaps not surprisingly, then, migration results in only very moderate gains in occupational status. Our best estimate of the direct effect of inter-community migration upon occupational status, with education, size of community of origin, and social background controlled, in standardized beta coefficients, is only .07 or .08 for non-farm males. The effect is probably marginally higher for French males than for English. It is, however, virtually non-existent for working women.

Inter-provincial, or long-distance, migration is much less frequent. Some two-thirds of the male population above age 24 report that they have never lived in another province on a permanent basis since age 16. Differences between the provinces in opportunity structures are less than between communities and so also the positive effects of inter-provincial migration are smaller. In fact, with inter-community migration as a control, the effects of inter-provincial migration drop to zero.

The migration questions included in this study are unusually rich and permit an investigation of return inter-community and provincial migration as well as of multiple migration. It is found that these extra measurements do not add appreciably to the explanatory power of a simple dichotomy distinguishing between those who have remained in their community of origin and those who have not. The observation that return migration has no major positive benefits is of theoretical importance, however. Also, the richer measures of migration may be of importance in studies of either educational or income attainment.

The large sample size of the study permits detailed analysis of the role of migration in occupational attainment of sub-groupings of the society. It was observed that among French Quebeckers the rates of migration were lower than for the English throughout the country, but the returns in occupational attainment were higher. Further analysis of this group is possible with these data. So also an extensive, if not conclusive, analysis of off-farm migrants was possible. It was observed that the problem of coding the occupation of farm owner and operator remains unsolved and is of major importance in endeavouring to draw conclusions about the gains and losses occurring to those of farm origin. The large size of the sample made possible a comparison of two special groups with farm background: those who entered urban occupations but did not migrate; and those who both left the community and entered urban occupations. These two groups differed from one another by about as much as migrants and non-migrants with non-farm backgrounds.

The failure of migration to yield any returns to women is perhaps the major substantive finding of the analysis. It requires more analysis and the data would make further analysis possible. The role of community size, and also of province, in the female opportunity structure appears to differ from that of the males.

The migration effects reported in this unit are typically direct effects, with education held constant. But the indirect effects of migration upon occupational attainment via education are of some magnitude, even in the case of women. If this is considered as migration which is *necessary* to achieve education, the combined effect of migration on occupational attainment exceeds the minimum estimates we have provided.

Finally, we would note the extent to which the size of the community of origin or the size of the present community intrudes upon the study of migration. The low rate of return to women of migration is accompanied by an absence of major community differences in occupational levels for women. Migrants who return to the original community show no gain in occupational status. It is possible that the study of migration, at least in present-day Canada, should be approached as a study of differential effects of community size upon occupational and educational attainment.

Migration, like social mobility itself, is probably a pseudo-variable, with its effects necessarily disappearing when both origins and destinations are controlled. What may be novel, however, is the idea that community size alone is the only important characteristic of either the origin or the destination that need be taken into account.

Notes

1. Here and for the rest of this chapter the bivariate statistics and others given are derived as a by-product of either the regression or MCA analysis presented in the accompanying tables and the case base is therefore reduced through listwise deletion to exclude those cases which are no answer on any of the variables described in the relevant table.
2. The form of presentation of the results in much of this chapter follows generally that suggested by Alwin and Hauser (1975). We have not distinguished between total association and total effects as they recommend, however, as the impact of social background upon the relationship between migration and occupational attainment seems of theoretical interest, bearing as it does upon what Duncan, Featherman and Duncan call the "selectivity hypothesis." Thus, our "gross effects" equal the "total association" of Alwin and Hauser.
3. Since it is clear (see Table 13.3) that most migration occurs in the early twenties, one could argue that the effects of migration would be substantially higher for those 25 to 34. At this point the advantages of having moved would be in immediate effect. Older respondents, kept from migrating by family obligations or the like, might show a deterioration in the effects of migration. A run of these 25 to 34 shows no such effect, however. The net effect for this

group of younger adults was 2.22; it was 2.08 for all non-farm males, 25 years or older. The effect via education was 2.24 for the young group and 2.08 for the whole group. The advantages accruing to the migrants, then, persist through the whole career.

References

ALWIN, DUANE F. and ROBERT M. HAUSER
  1975 "The Decomposition of Effects in Path Analysis." *American Sociological Review*, 40(1): 37-47.
BLAU, PETER and OTIS DUDLEY DUNCAN
  1967 *The American Occupational Structure*. New York: John Wiley.
BLISHEN, B.R. and H.A. MCROBERTS
  1976 "A Revised Socioeconomic Index for Occupations in Canada." *Canadian Review of Sociology and Anthropology*, 13 (Feb.): 71-79.
DUNCAN, OTIS DUDLEY, DAVID FEATHERMAN and BEVERLY DUNCAN
  1972 *Socioeconomic Background and Achievement*. New York: Seminar Press.
DUNCAN, OTIS DUDLEY
  1974 "Re-analysis of the 1949 Survey." In J.M. Ridge, ed. *Mobility in Britain Reconsidered*. (Oxford Studies in Social Mobility Working Papers 2). Oxford: Clarendon Press.
FEATHERMAN, DAVID and ROBERT M. HAUSER
  1976 "Sexual Inequalities and Socioeconomic Achievement in the U.S., 1962-1973." *American Sociological Review*, 41(3): 462-83.
GRANT, F. KENNETH and JOHN VANDERKAMP
  1976 *The Economic Causes and Effects of Migration: Canada, 1965-71*. Ottawa: Economic Council of Canada, Minister of Supply and Services Canada.
KALBACH, WARREN E. and WAYNE W. MCVEY
  1971 *The Demographic Basis of Canadian Society*. Toronto: McGraw-Hill.
PINEO, PETER C. and JOHN PORTER
  1967 "Occupational Prestige in Canada." *Canadian Review of Sociology and Anthropology*, 4(1): 24-40.
PINEO, PETER C., JOHN PORTER and HUGH A. MCROBERTS
  1977 "The 1971 Census and a Socioeconomic Classification of Occupations." *Canadian Review of Sociology and Anthropology*, 14(1): 91-102.
RITCHEY, P. NEAL
  1976 "Explanations of Migration." In A. Inkeles, J. Coleman and N. Smelser, eds. *Annual Review of Sociology*.

CHAPTER 14

Summary and Concluding Comments

MONICA BOYD, JOHN GOYDER, FRANK E. JONES, HUGH
McROBERTS AND PETER C. PINEO

The Canadian Mobility Study in Context

It is now time for the collection and standardized manipulation of status attainment data to be placed in the hands of some bureaucratic counterpart of the Bureau of Labour Statistics (Gintis, 1980:15).

Mobility surveys, the above passage suggests, have become "normal science" (Kuhn, 1962) in sociology. Further evidence that such research is now fully institutionalized is found in the increasing tendency for books on social indicators to include chapters on mobility surveys (e.g., Sheldon and Moore, 1968; Land and Spilerman, 1975). To routinize the collection of mobility surveys is not, as we shall emphasize later, to denigrate their importance to social theory. It is because the amount of mobility and form of status attainment in a society is a fundamental component of social structure that collecting such data is important.

The early mobility studies (e.g., Glass, 1954) inquired whether mobility was in fact so free as to be close to the theoretical upper limit represented by what was termed the "perfect mobility model." The evidence, from many countries, demonstrated that this was decidedly not the case. At the same time the mobility discovered in surveys was considerably in excess of the theoretical minimum where every occupational class was inherited from generation to generation. The theoretical issue at stake was how, in industrial societies, the tension between the competition across sub-sectors in a society and the requirement for industrial efficiency in the overall society is to be balanced (Lenski, 1966:24-42). The family, the social class, the ethnic or religious group, the different sexes each hold a vested interest in gaining and perpetuating advantages in the stratification order. Industrial economies in capitalist societies are also closely geared to the profit motive, however, so that efficiency — fitting the best man or woman to the job — is a powerful imperative (Davis and Moore, 1945). A ruling class that permits a too inefficient allocation of manpower defeats its own objectives.

The initial point estimates of just where the modern industrial societies stand on this continuum of low to high mobility, ascriptive to achieved form of status attainment, now are clearly established by a large weight of evidence. Thus, the initial theory question motivating researchers to conduct mobility surveys has been empirically addressed. Interpretative problems will, to be sure, remain, but it is likely that these will increasingly hinge on positions of basic intellectual orientation, not on lack of evidence (see, for example, Berteaux, 1976; Garnier and Hazelrigg, 1976; and references and discussion in Chapter 1).

Increasingly, for the student of mobility surveys, the interest is in working out important second-order problems within the larger theoretical context suggested above. If, in general, mobility is the norm, do all groups within a society share in this overall feature of the social structure? And, is the structure related to a society's level of economic development (see Chapter 2). As a relatively late entrant into the international club of mobility surveys, the Canadian Mobility Study was designed to address questions such as these. We had little reason to believe that the overall mobility and status attainment picture would be greatly at variance with that in societies at a similar level of industrialization. Canada has such a heterogeneous population, however, that a great variety of propositions about internal patterns could be entertained. The strategy in formulating an interview design for the study rested largely on identifying (using common sense and the existing literature on stratification in Canada) the likely bases for differentiation in mobility and status attainment. This national social context, enunciated in Chapter 2, identified French-English inequality as one Canadian social problem so prominent as to be a self-evident focus for analysis in the mobility survey. As well, few societies have so large a foreign-born population as Canada, so the mobility experiences of this group merited detailed attention. As ethnic stratification is another distinguishing feature of Canada, a chapter was assigned to interpreting ancestry as an ascriptive feature of the society. Family composition, known from American research to bear upon socioeconomic achievement, takes on renewed importance in a Canadian study because the compositional differences offer an intervening variable to aid under-standing of the inequality between language, immigration, and ethnic ancestry groups. Migration, again of established importance from other studies, is for many people in Canada a traditional response to regional disparity. This factor, too, deserved attention. Finally, the labour force participation of women in Canada was greatly increasing by the early 1970s. It was no longer plausible to study only the stratification among males, and the Canadian Mobility Study made a major commitment, reflected in the two chapters on the subject, to the study of mobility and status attainment among women.

A second major theme which we perceive in the present generation of mobility studies is the recognition of change over time as a crucial focus of the data (Duncan, 1968). This has been closely investigated in American studies (e.g., Rogoff, 1953; Duncan, 1968; Featherman and Hauser, 1977, 1978) and, in fact, the consensus there has been that overall levels of mobility and form of status attainment change at a ponderous pace at most. This stability may be most characteristic of societies that, like the United States, are in the late stage of industrialization. Few western societies have experienced so massive a social change as the industrialization of Canada during the past three generations. The principal task of future Canadian mobility studies will likely be monitoring the changes between 1973 and the subsequent oil crisis-dominated industrial climate in which a period of stagnation stretches for the foreseeable distance into the 1980s. The 1973 study was from the outset conceived as a benchmark which could in future be replicated. This was one rationale for our preference for a large sample (to minimize chance fluctuations) and an established research design.

A third characteristic of the normal science context of the Canadian Mobility Study is attention to the complexity of inequality. The attainment model, for example, identifies three sources of explanation for the status achieved by an individual or a group. The model clearly signals the importance of endowments. Groups where family background is enriched and education level high are likely to achieve high average status. Endowments, the model reveals, have different effects on occupational status or income among various groups within societies. The effect is double-edged. A strong ascriptive link between father's occupation and son's occupation means both that those of high-status fathers will reap a bonus in their own status attainment, *and* those from low-status origins will bear a disadvantage. Finally, for variables having a "true" zero point, the attainment model identifies an "intercept" effect. This could be visualized as the floor from which each group enters the status race.[1] Given these fine conceptual distinctions, it is not necessarily a failure in analysis if equivocal conclusions are sometimes tendered.

As the following review of findings from the Canadian Mobility Study shall illustrate, no researchers in the field of mobility entirely lose interest in the first-order question of characterizing a society according to the openness of its social structure. The second-order questions identified above are the more prominent, however, and serve as unifying themes underlying our collective work.

The Principal Findings

The first three chapters to report findings (chapters 3.4 and 5) do so on the basis of analysis with very limited controls — i.e., without singling out linguistic, ethnic, and nativity groups which are the subject of analysis in later chapters and without, in a sense, singling out age and sex as they are singled out in other chapters. In short, these chapters provide a report of overall findings about mobility and status attainment for males, subject to certain limitations on age and nativity. The refinements come later.

In terms of mobility, Chapter 3 yields familiar findings. The chapter reveals that in Canada, as in other highly industrialized societies, there is more mobility than stability between generations,[2] that there is more upward than downward mobility,[3] that such mobility tends to proceed at about one step or level per generation, that there is more circulation or exchange mobility than structural mobility, and the mobility within white-collar and blue-collar occupations is greater than mobility between white-collar and blue-collar occupations. Mobility analysis, in the form of bivariate cross-tabulation of educational level, first and current (1973) occupation continues into Chapter 4. These findings are familiar: occupational status on entry into the labour force is, by conventional standards, closely related to level of education, and current occupational status is closely linked to occupation on entry into the labour force. Moreover, educational level has a persistent association with occupational status at career stages beyond entry into the labour force. However, although cross-tabular analysis reported in Chapter 4 establishes an anticipated fact of a positive association between educational and occupational status, the emphasis is on exploring alternative "rationalities" which may explain the relationship between educational and occupational status.

Status attainment analysis, in these chapters, bears out the mobility analysis but clarifies the relationship between family of origin status and current occupational status. In effect, the model reveals that the direct effects of origin status are limited to educational attainment, while education takes over as the main determinant of occupational status on entry into the labour force. Education gives way in turn, although less markedly, to initial occupational status as a determinant of current occupational status. These findings, too, in their general, although not necessarily in their specific, form are representative of status attainment findings reported for other highly industrialized societies such as the United States, Great Britain, and Australia.

We noted above the importance of an historical perspective for understanding mobility and status attainment. To introduce an historical perspective into a "one-time" survey is not simple. Indeed, we argue that the need for an historical dimension in the analysis justifies a periodic repetition of a survey such as the Canadian Mobility Study. Nonetheless, a temporal element may be introduced into survey analysis if the available information allows respondents to be grouped as age cohorts. Thus, each cohort may be regarded as representing a particular historical period. Undoubtedly, there are dangers in interpreting cohorts this way, but in the absence of longitudinal data or of comparable surveys taken at different historical periods, cohort analysis, despite the distortion it may invite, can give some indication whether the trend is to more or less mobility and to varying influence of the principal determinants of status attainment. Such an attempt is reported in Chapter 5 in which the analysis, like those reported in chapters 3 and 4, does not introduce controls. It is, in short, an attempt to detect general trends over a period of more than fifty years. There is, of course, an improvement in occupational status over time, but this is attributable to the changes in the occupational composition of the labour force. The strength of association between father's and son's occupational statuses is seen to have declined over time, but this too is partially attributable to structural effects. Using a variety of analyses, the trend is found to erode as "structure" is operationalized in a successively more comprehensive sense. Under the most powerful techniques which, it is argued, are not necessarily the most sociologically meaningful, the decline in father-son occupational ascription is small. The evidence that education has become more important in determining occupational status on labour force entry does, however, encourage the unqualified conclusion that status attainment increasingly depends on individual achievement. Stronger evidence is needed before we may finally conclude that Canadian society has become more open, but the indications are of greater change in Canada than in the more settled industrial structure of the United States.

Much research confirms the widely held view that the family is an important source of educational aspirations and attainment. Consistent with this literature, our findings, as already noted, show educational attainment to be positively related to a person's family of origin status. Among the more specialized analyses reported in later chapters, those which include family origin variables confirm that family status influences the education of males and females, of French and English, of native-born and immigrants, and of migrant and non-migrant alike. Chapter 12 adds the finding that native-born parents have a stronger influence than foreign-born parents on educational attainment. Together these findings underline the importance of family in the attainment process. We need, however, to know more about the way the family exerts its influence. Unfortunately, our data limit the contribution we might make to such knowledge. We are unable to say whether, for example, families of higher status transmit values which determine higher educational aspirations, whether it is simply a matter of money, or a combination of values and material advantage. We do, however, have information about the size of our respondents' families of origin, and this information is used in Chapter 6 to contribute to our knowledge of how an important structural feature of the family constrains other influences on educational aspirations and attainment which might be generated within the family. Educational attainment is shown to be constrained by family size: as family size increases, educational attainment decreases. And this finding is true for both English- and French-speaking male and female respondents, although it is found to be less constraining for French-speaking respondents despite the greater variation in family size within French Canada. This unexpected result derives partly from the fact that the relationship between family size and educational attainment is found to be curvilinear. While the curve is extremely slight, its cumulative effect is such as to lead to a tendency for family size influences to increase rather than decrease as industrialization has proceeded.

Our study could not include any measure of intelligence for our respondents yet this matter is of importance since it is known that a negative relationship exists between family size and IQ. Information from other research, when added to the data from this study, leads to the suggestion that the role of IQ may have been over-estimated and to the suggestion that further consideration of the role of educational costs in depressing the educational achievements of those from larger families may be the more promising avenue for further research.

A division of labour by sex is a societal universal, but is inter-societally variable. In Canada, as in other highly industrialized societies, although attitudes and actions have operated in the direction of reducing labour force inequality between the sexes, the overall evidence sustains the conclusion that women, in comparison to men, are disadvantaged in various aspects of employment, such as income and access to the full occupational spectrum. Chapter 7, the first of two chapters to deal with the sexual division of labour, asks how women who are employed full-time compare to men, who are, for the most part characterized by full-time employment. The findings suggest the reverse of what might be expected. Women who are employed full-time have, on the average, higher initial and current occupational statuses than males. However, this advantage stems from the fact that women in full-time employment come, on the average, from higher-status families and, consequently, have more education than males. In other words, women must have disproportionately greater resources than males to achieve higher occupational status. We conclude that if the employment resources of men and women were equal, the average occupational status of women would be lower than the average for men. While the analysis in Chapter 7 confirms, as we observed above, that educational attainment is positively associated with family origin status, it adds the information that mother's education is a more important resource than father's education for daughters, while the reverse is true for sons. Additional sex differences in the occupational attainment process among married men and women occur with child-bearing and child-rearing. Number of children depresses the occupational attainment of married women under age 45 but it has no influence on the attainments of married men.

The comparative analysis of the mobility experiences of males and females is continued in Chapter 8. Here, comparisons include women who report part-time employment as well as those who were employed full-time. Analysis of the mobility tables reveals that women have the advantage over men on entering the labour force but lose this advantage at later career stages. Specifically, women, in comparison to their fathers, experienced greater mobility and more mobility over longer "distances" than men but in the transition from first to current occupation, men were less likely to be occupationally stable and more likely to move upwards than were women. When, however, the analyst controls for the different occupational distribution of the two sexes by equalizing the male and female occupational distributions, most of these differences in mobility are eliminated. In short, the actual differences in the kinds of occupations filled, typically by men and typically by women, have important consequences for the mobility of each sex.

Although ethnicity is regarded as an important basis of social identification dividing Canadians, the main message given in chapters 9 and 10 which deal with this phenomenon is that ethnic stratification in Canada is breaking down. Although we cannot say if ethnicity is an important divider in other respects, we can state that it is steadily becoming unimportant as a source of variation in occupational mobility and status attainment. Thus, although the analysis in Chapter 9, limited to the charter groups, reveals that Quebec-born English males have the advantage in occupational status, deriving from structural change in the labour force, over the French, the two groups do not differ in their patterns of exchange or circulation mobility. It is also shown that the Quebec-born English are a particularly privileged group: not only do they have the advantage in occupational status over the French, they also have the advantage over those English who are not Quebec-born, whether these latter reside in Quebec or elsewhere in Canada. The analysis, reported in Chapter 10, which focuses on all the major ethnic groupings, charter or otherwise, confirms and extends the main message of Chapter 9: ethnic stratification is diminishing in Canada. Again, when the ethnic groupings are ordered according to average occupational status, differences can be observed: the Jews and the British groups have attained higher average occupational status than all others but the differences, for the most part, are not great. Indeed, these differences can be accounted for by differences among the groups in family origin status, in areas of residence, and in education, leaving a very small effect attributable to ethnicity.

In Canada, where immigrants form a substantial proportion of the population, concerns focusing on the relative advantages and disadvantages of the native-born and the foreign-born are never far from the surface of popular interest. To some, the immigrants enjoy success won at the expense of the native-born; to others, the native-born reap rewards which accrue, in part, from the employment of immigrants in occupations that the native-born will not accept. The analyses reported in chapters 11 and 12, which face these concerns directly, reveal only small differences in the average values of educational and occupational attainment and considerable similarity in the patterns of inter-generational transference of occupational status for the different generations. These findings suggest that there is little or no advantage in being a second or third generation Canadian.

However, Chapter 11 does show that the average occupational status of foreign-born women employed full-time in the Canadian labour force is lower than that of their native-born female and native-born and foreign-born male equivalents, partly because of differences in occupational status resources but also because of the double disadvantage of being female *and* foreign-born. There are other differences between nativity groups. For example, there are differences in the "occupational value received" for education or social origin. Foreign-born males are not likely to go as far occupationally as the native-born with the same amount of education. Likewise, the purely native-born do better in this respect than the native-born whose fathers are native-born but whose mothers are foreign-born. Even so, the native-born reveal a consistent pattern of coming last in the competition for status.

In a country made up of cities, towns, villages, and rural localities of varying size and in a country characterized by regions varying in their resources and stages of resource development, the idea of leaving one's place of birth to seek a fortune elsewhere is widespread. Despite this persistent call to migrate, and despite the fact that many Canadians, male and female, answer the call, it appears, as Chapter 13 reports, that compared to those who stayed at home, success in the form of a substantially higher occupational status, eludes the migrants. But migration as analysed conforms to a highly abstracted meaning of the word. For example, a form of "pure migration" is isolated when the influence of the size of both community of origin and destination is removed from consideration through statistical controls. Conceived of in this way, migration is found to have little effect upon occupational attainment, but it is noted that this kind of analysis masks very real differences in attainment brought about by the effects of differing labour markets in communities of differing size and complex inter-relationships between migration and educational attainment. The analysis implies that if conceived of in a less abstract manner, with attention paid to specific migratory streams such as the movement off the farms, migration may be found to have greater impact upon both educational and occupational attainment.

Final Reflections

The findings reported summarily above and in detail in preceding chapters of this book derive from a perspective which identifies social stratification as a fundamental element of social structure and consequently mobility and status attainment as important social processes. Thus, the analysis of various aspects of stratification and its related processes is regarded as basic to understanding human society. The objectives of our research were to discover the facts about occupational mobility in Canada and to identify the determinants of educational and occupational attainment. Thus, we provide findings which can be used to assess how Canada measures up to a model of stratification which emphasizes not only the possibility but the necessity of social mobility;

and how Canada measures up to a model of status attainment (or occupational allocation viewed from a societal perspective) in which a person's own abilities and acquired skills will dominate over inherited or ascribed characteristics, such as those flowing from family and ethnic origin.[4]

Although a clearer understanding of the significance of our findings might be achieved through a rigorous cross-societal comparison, it is possible, either by implicit comparison or by regarding our findings in isolation, to suggest where they contribute to our knowledge of Canadian society. Thus, the fact that most mobility in Canada is independent of occupational demand, that the inter-generational association of occupational status is moderate, and that most mobility to date is upward, suggests that Canada compares well with other industrial societies. Moreover, our findings do provide evidence that occupational mobility and status attainment are largely the product of individual ability and acquired skills — that is, that mobility and status attainment are largely the result of individual effort and motivation rather than a return on privileged status. Nonetheless, the relatively heavy influence of family of origin status on education indicates that the mobility process in Canada does not fully conform to a model which assumes zero effects of ascribed characteristics. Even though the 30 per cent of the variance accounted for by family origin status allows for the contribution of individual abilities and skills, such as intelligence, it also allows for the possible effects of environmental factors which may reinforce or frustrate individual ability and effort. Despite the strong evidence from studies undertaken in the United States, notably by Coleman *et al.* (1966) and Jencks *et al.* (1972) that schools and teachers have little influence, compared to family background and individual ability, on educational attainment, others (see for example, Rutter, 1979; Bourdieu and Passeron, 1979) contend that variations in certain elements of the school and educational systems do make a difference.

Occupational attainment contrasts quite sharply with educational attainment in that with the former, direct origin effects almost vanish and, consistent with an emphasis on technical competence, education is revealed to be the dominating effect on occupational attainment on entry into the labour force. Still, as some 60 to 70 per cent of the variance in first occupational attainment is due to factors not identified in the model, other aspects of competence as well as factors which do not reflect competence are likely to influence where a person begins an occupational career. Although education maintains a persistent direct affect on occupational attainment at later career stages, previous employment experience exerts the dominant effect. In the case of current occupation, where education and the occupation held in 1963 account for almost 60 per cent of the variance, the attribution of effects to unknown factors must be considerably reduced. These results imply that a person ends up occupationally by and large where his or her level of education dictates but through a multi-stage process where the influence of education, strongest at the point of entry into the labour force is replaced by the influence of occupational status and experience. It is certainly consistent with the emphasis of our analytic model on individual achievement that a person's final occupation should be primarily determined by his or her previous occupational success and by educational attainment.

What do these findings imply? Does success go to the deserving, those who through various combinations of ability and hard work qualify themselves for the occupations they desire? The evidence is supportive of an affirmative answer, but to insist that ability and hard work are justly rewarded is to assume that educational success depends solely on the objective appraisal of ability and that occupational careers are similarly determined by objective rationality. We know from this study and others that educational success is associated with family status and we know from other studies that conditions internal to the educational system influence educational outcomes. Still, we can say that those who persisted in the educational system long enough to reach the higher levels did enter the labour force at higher occupational levels and did end up with a higher final occupational status. However the successful managed to do so, it is apparent once again that education is an important key to occupational success. Even so, it is possible that the equalization of educational opportunity alone would not increase mobility even if the opportunities were taken and differences in educational attainment reduced. In the case of an over-supply of qualified applicants for employment, it is possible that non-occupationally related resources, such as origin status, and other ascribed attributes, may assume prominence where selection on the basis of occupationally relevant skills is difficult or impossible (see, for example, Davis, 1978). So although educational attainment is a most important element in occupational success, a levelling of educational attainment may not establish fairer competition for occupational attainment. While the norm of equal opportunity requires that educational opportunity be equalized and that the advantages derived from family of origin status be eliminated, something more is needed. Part of the answer, suggested by our findings, is a continued expansion of demand for the services provided by higher skilled occupations.[5]

Among our findings which relate to specific features of Canadian society, we single out for comment those which reveal a persistence in sex differences in occupational attainment that is not found in terms of ethnicity.[6] Although it would be satisfying to explain why sex differences should be more bounded than ethnic differences, only possibilities can be suggested here. Superficially, it could be maintained that the explanation lies in the strength of male chauvinism — a stubborn resistance to the invasion of male territory by women or to a redefinition of the roles of males and females. But this only begs the question: Why should male chauvinism be stronger than ethnocentrism? Perhaps a strong research attack on these different attitudes might lead us to understanding. Certainly, it is reasonable to assume that male resistance to change in sexual definition relates to the self-image of males and, in some respects, to the self-image of females. Since self-image plays a fundamental part in allowing an individual to come to terms with existence, male chauvinism must be regarded as something more than male pig-headedness or macho irrationality. Perhaps the ethnic component of self-image is less salient and assimilation, therefore, easier because the ethnic division, despite its compelling influence on many aspects of human behaviour, is less fundamental than the sexual division between human beings which has its origins, at the very least, in the process of reproduction. Even so, this should not lead to the conclusion that the division is immutable. The division of labour between the sexes, as is well known from cross-societal evidence, is extremely variable. Perhaps, although the difference must still be explained, the application of universal standards in the areas of education and employment simply proceeds more slowly where it concerns sexual identity than where it concerns ethnic identity. Certainly, the difference raises questions about the effectiveness of social action in precipitating change. Action to improve the status of women in Canada has been very prominent since the mid-sixties, while action to reduce the prejudice and discrimination based on ethnicity or nativity has been far more muted. Although the legislation, passed in all provinces, forbidding discrimination on irrelevant bases as an effort to maintain fair competition applies equally to sex and ethnicity, organized efforts to reduce discrimination on the basis of ethnicity or against immigrants in no way compares to the activity put forth on behalf of women or to the prominence given to the cause of women.

Taken separately, improvement in mobility and status attainment for women requires, as for men, a weakening of the link between education and origin status and continual upgrading of the occupational structure. To reduce differences between men and women seems to require, primarily, a reduction of differences in the occupational segregation of the sexes. Achieving such a change is not merely a matter of reducing the hostility or opposition of male workers nor the discriminatory actions of personnel officers, it involves altering a process that begins in the early socialization of women and which is reinforced by teachers, vocational counsellors, and friends. That process presumably is not as universally experienced by those who differ in terms of ethnicity or country of birth.

Issues concerning social stratification and its related processes have generated a great volume of literature in sociology and in other fields. No single study can address all the issues or provide all the relevant facts. A single study can, however, as in the case of the Canadian Mobility Study, add a modest contribution of empirical findings to those produced by a group of contemporary studies, which taken together, increase our knowledge of human society.

Notes

1. Mobility analysis makes a similar distinction. To adjust margins in a mobility table is to remove an endowment and an intercept effect, so that a slope effect characterized in mobility analysis as net transition may be isolated.
2. We note again that mobility rates are influenced by the number of categories used in the occupational classifications.
3. The ratio of upward to downward mobility may be greater or less in Canada than in other societies but we are not, in this discussion, attempting a close comparison between Canada and elsewhere. It is sufficient to observe that the results of mobility and status analysis are very similar among those societies where studies of national scope have been undertaken. Indeed, mobility studies provide strong evidence supportive of the convergence hypothesis.
4. It is an over-simplification to propose that the effects of the attributes of individuals on status attainment are entirely independent of social structure. We do so, possibly, because the education and occupation variables of the status attainment model can be interpreted as evidence of "individual" attainment in contrast to the effects of family of origin size and status which are interpreted as social structural variables. However, a more developed statement of the model might propose that variable attributes of individuals, such as intelligence and motivation, can be assumed to interact with or be conditioned by social structural variables, whether these relate to social structures in which membership and position are determined by birth or to those in which membership and position are determined by competition. It is perhaps apposite to comment, at this point, on the robustness of the model, created by Blau and Duncan (1967), for the analysis of status attainment. The variables specified in the basic status attainment model consistently account for 50 per cent or more of the variance in occupational status attainment despite many creative efforts to expand the model to include variables which quite reasonably might be expected to account, on their own, for a significant proportion of the variance. So far, one result has prevailed: additional

variables add little or nothing to the explanatory power of the basic model, although they may enhance our understanding of the causal relations.

5. Mobility could, of course, improve in a technologically stable period *if* the birth-rate for the privileged status group sharply declined or the death-rate sharply increased, or if the sons and daughters coming from such origins experience a revolution in status aspirations.

6. The exclusion of women who were employed part-time from some of the analyses understates the differences between the sexes. We also found evidence of weak differences between the native-born and foreign-born.

References

BLAU, PETER M. and ORIS DUDLEY DUNCAN
1967 *The American Occupational Structure*. New York: Wiley.

BERTAUX, D.
1976 "An Assessment of Garnier and Hazelrigg's Paper on Intergenerational Mobility in France," *American Journal of Sociology*, 82: 388-98.

BOURDIEU, PIERRE, and JEAN-CLAUDE PASSERON
1979 *The Inheritors: French Students and their Relation to Culture*. Chicago: University of Chicago Press.

COLEMAN, JAMES *et al.*
1966 *Equality of Educational Opportunity*. Washington, D.C.: U.S. Government Printing Office.

DAVIS, CAM
1978 "Factors Effecting the Admittance of Applicants to a Medical School." Ph.D. thesis, McMaster University.

DAVIS, K., and W.E. MOORE
1945 "Some Principles of Stratification." *American Sociological Review*, 10:242-49.

DUNCAN, O.D.
1968 "Social Stratification and Mobility: Problems in the Measurement of Trends." Pp. 675-719 in E.B. Sheldon and W.E. Moore, eds. *Indicators of Social Change*. New York: Russell Sage Foundation.

FEATHERMAN, D.L. and R.M. HAUSER
1977 *The Process of Stratification: Trends and Analyses*. New York: Academic Press.

FEATHERMAN, D.L. and R.M. HAUSER
1978 *Opportunity and Change*. New York: Academic Press.

GARNIER, M., and L.E. HAZELRIGG
1974 "Father-to-Son Occupational Mobility in France: Evidence from the 1960's." *American Journal of Sociology*, 80:478-502.

GLASS, DAVID
1954 *Social Mobility in Britain*. London: Routledge and Kegan Paul.

GINTIS, H.
1980 "The American Occupational Structure Eleven Years Later." *Contemporary Sociology*, 9:12-16.

JENCKS, C., *et al.*
  1972 *Inequality: An Assessment of the Effects of Family and Schooling in America.* New York: Basic Books.

KUHN, THOMAS
  1962 *The Structure of Scientific Revolutions.* Chicago: University of Chicago Press.

LAND, K., and S. SPILERMAN
  1975 *Social Indicator Models.* New York: Russell Sage Foundation.

LENSKI, G.
  1966 *Power and Privilege.* New York: McGraw-Hill.

ROGOFF, N.
  1953 *Recent Trends in Occupational Mobility.* Glencoe, Ill.: Free Press.

RUTTER, MICHAEL, *et al.*
  1979 *Fifteen Thousand Hours.* London: Open Books.

SHELDON, E.B., and W.E. MOORE, eds.
  1968 *Indicators of Social Change.* New York: Russell Sage Foundation.

Statistics Canada   Statistique Canada

Labour Force Survey Division

JOB MOBILITY SURVEY

Authority – Statistics Act, Chapter 15, Statutes of Canada 1970 -71 -72

Name (surname)	(Given names)	This questionnaire will be picked up by your interviewer on

	1 - 5	6 - 8	9 - 12	13 - 14	15	16 - 17
PSU		Segment	Listing	Line	M F	A

Answers to most of the questions in this survey require only a check mark ☑ in the appropriate box. Answers which require a number should be written in the boxes provided. Please remember to write zero where appropriate. If you should have any difficulties with a question note this in the space on the back of the form, and ask your Statistics Canada interviewer for assistance when she returns.

You will find that a number of questions ask about jobs that you or your father have had during your lifetime. In this survey a "Job" is defined as "Working for pay or profit". As a reminder, this expression has been included in brackets after the word "Job" in some questions.

1. In what year were you born?.....................
18 - 20
[1]
(year)

2. Where were you born? (Check one only, according to present boundaries.)

Newfoundland	00	Portugal	17
Prince Edward Island	01	France	18
Nova Scotia	02	Greece	19
New Brunswick	03	Other Western Europe (e.g. Spain, Belgium, Scandanavia, Finland, Austria, etc.)	20
Quebec	04		
Ontario	05		
Manitoba	06	Poland	21
Saskatchewan	07	Ukraine	22
Alberta	08	Other Eastern Europe (e.g. U.S.S.R., Hungary, Balkan States, etc.)	23
British Columbia	09		
Yukon	10		
North West Terr.	11		
United Kingdom	12	Middle East or Asia Minor (e.g. Lebanon, Turkey, Israel, etc.)	24
United States of America	13	British West Indies	25
Italy	14	China or Japan	26
Germany	15	Other	27
Netherlands	16		

3. If you were not born in Canada, answer the following question; otherwise go to question 4. In what year did you last take up residence in Canada? (Do not consider as a break in residence time spent studying abroad, or short visits outside of Canada, e.g. away 6 months or less.)
23 - 24
[1]
(year)

4. What is the highest level of education that you have completed? (If you were not educated in this country check the category which best describes your educational attainment.)(Check only one in the entire list.)

No formal schooling 00
Go to question 6

Elementary school
Some 01
Completed 02

High school
Academic
Some 03
Completed 04

Vocational or technical
Some 05
Completed 06

After high school but not university
Business or trades training: (e.g. secretarial school, hairdressing school, barbering school, trade school, etc.)
Some 07
Completed 08

Nursing school or Teacher's College
Some 09
Completed 10

Community College, Junior College, CEGEP, Technical Institute
Some 11
Completed 12

University
Some 13

Completed:
Certificate or diploma 14
Bachelor's degree 15
Master's degree 16
Doctorate 17
Professional degree (e.g. M.D., L.L.B., C.A., etc.) 18

5. How many years altogether were you in school? ....
27 - 28
[ ][ ]
(years)

6. Aside from regular school, did you ever complete an apprenticeship, a full-time program in a company training school lasting six weeks or more, or training in the Canadian Armed Forces leading to qualification in a trade? .... Yes 0 No 1

7. If you have ever served in the Canadian Armed Forces, answer the following question; otherwise go to question 8. What was your longest period of continuous service? (Do not count service in the cadet, militia, or reserve units.)

	30 - 31		32 - 33
From	[1] (year)	to	[1] (year)

NOW WE WOULD LIKE TO ASK YOU SOME QUESTIONS ABOUT JOBS WHICH YOU HAVE HAD STARTING WITH YOUR FIRST JOB

8. Describe your first full-time job (for pay or profit) after completing your education as indicated above in question 4. (If you never had a full-time job after completion of your education go to question 20.)

(i) What kind of work were you doing? (Give a full description, e.g. selling shoes, motor vehicle repairing, metal machining, clerical work, secretarial work)

(ii) What were your most important activities or duties?(e.g. fitting shoes, auto body work, operating lathe, posting invoices, taking dictation and typing)

4-1101-167.1: 21-3-73

529

(iii) What was your job title? (e.g. manager of shoe department, auto body repairman, lathe operator, invoice clerk, secretary-stenographer)

_____

(iv) In what kind of business, industry or service was this job? (e.g. retail shoe store, auto body repair shop, machine parts mfg., medical clinic)

_____

For office use only   34 - 37 [ ][ ][ ][ ]

(v) If, in this job, you owned a business or farm, or if you were a manager or supervisor, answer the following question; otherwise go to question 8 (vi). How many personnel did you usually employ or have working under you?

None .... [ ] 0

1 - 5 .... [ ] 1

6 - 10 .... [ ] 2

11 - 20 .... [ ] 3

21 - 74 .... [ ] 4

75 or more .... [ ] 5

(vi) In what year did you begin working at this job? .... 39 - 40 [1][ ]   (year)

9. Did you use English or French on your first full-time job? (Check one only)

English but not French .... [ ] 0

French but not English .... [ ] 1

Both English and French .... [ ] 2

Neither English nor French .... [ ] 3

10. From the beginning of your first full-time job until now, in how many years have you worked full-time for pay or profit? (Count as a full year any in which you worked for a period of seven months or more.) .... 42 - 43 [ ][ ]   (years)

11. Since you began your first full-time job, was there a single period of one year or more when you were not working for pay or profit?

No .... [ ] 0 ⟶ **Go to question 16**

Yes .... [ ] 1 ⟶ **Go to question 12**

12. In what year did this period begin? (First period if more than one.) .... 45 - 46 [ ][ ][ ][ ]   (year)

13. At any time after that, did you return to a full-time job (for pay or profit) for a single period of 7 months or more?

No .... [ ] 0 ⟶ **Go to question 19**

Yes .... [ ] 1 ⟶ **Go to question 14**

14. In what year did you return? (Most recent if more than once.) .... 48 - 49 [1][ ][ ]   (year)

15. In the space provided below describe the job to which you returned. (Most recent if more than one.)

(i) What kind of work were you doing? (Give a full description, e.g. selling shoes, motor vehicle repairing, metal machining, clerical work, secretarial work)

_____

(ii) What were your most important activities or duties? (e.g. fitting shoes, auto body work, operating lathe, posting invoices, taking dictation and typing)

_____

(iii) What was your job title? (e.g. manager of shoe department, auto body repairman, lathe operator, invoice clerk, secretary-stenographer)

_____

(iv) In what kind of business, industry or service was this job? (e.g. retail shoe store, auto body repair shop, machine parts mfg., medical clinic)

_____

For office use only   50 - 53 [ ][ ][ ][ ]

(v) If, in this job, you owned a business or farm, or were a manager or supervisor, answer the following question; otherwise go to question 17. How many personnel did you employ or have working under you?

None .... [ ] 0

1 - 5 .... [ ] 1

6 - 10 .... [ ] 2

11 - 20 .... [ ] 3

21 - 74 .... [ ] 4

75 or more .... [ ] 5

GO TO QUESTION 17

16. In the space provided below describe the job (for pay or profit) which you held ten years ago, i.e., in July 1963. (If you were not working at that time describe the last job which lasted 7 months or more which you had prior to July 1963. If you did not have one go to question 17.)

(i) What kind of work were you doing? (Give a full description, e.g. selling shoes, motor vehicle repairing, metal machining, clerical work, secretarial work)

_____

(ii) What were your most important activities or duties? (e.g. fitting shoes, auto body work, operating lathe, posting invoices, taking dictation and typing)

_____

(iii) What was your job title? (e.g. manager of shoe department, auto body repairman, lathe operator, invoice clerk, secretary-stenographer)

_____

(iv) In what kind of business, industry or service was this job? e.g. retail shoe store, auto body repair shop, machine parts mfg., medical clinic)

_____

For office use only   55 - 58 [ ][ ][ ][ ]

(v) If, in this job, you owned a business or farm, or were a manager or supervisor, answer the following question; otherwise go to question 17. How many personnel did you employ or have working under you?

None .... [ ] 0

1 - 5 .... [ ] 1

6 - 10 .... [ ] 2

11 - 20 .... [ ] 3

21 - 74 .... [ ] 4

75 or more .... [ ] 5

- 3 -

17. Describe your present job (for pay or profit) – main job if more than one. If you are not working now, or if you are retired, answer for your last job which lasted 7 months or more.

(i) What kind of work are (were) you doing? (e.g. selling shoes, motor vehicle repairing, metal machining, clerical work, secretarial work)

(ii) What are (were) your most important activities or duties? (e.g. fitting shoes, auto body work, operating lathe, posting invoices, taking dictation and typing)

(iii) What is (was) your job title? (e.g. manager of shoe department, auto body repairman, lathe operator, invoice clerk, secretary-stenographer)

(iv) In what kind of business, industry or service is (was) this job? (e.g. retail shoe store, auto body repair shop, machine parts mfg., medical clinic)

For office use only   60 - 63

(v) If, in this job, you own (owned) a business or farm, or are (were) a manager or supervisor, answer the following question; otherwise go to question 17 (vii). How many personnel do (did) you employ or have working under you?

None .... ☐ 0

1 - 5 .... ☐ 1

6 - 10 .... ☐ 2

11 - 20 .... ☐ 3

21 - 74 .... ☐ 4

75 or more .... ☐ 5

(vi) In this job are (were) you working: (Check one only)

(a) For others for wages, salary or commission? .... ☐ 0

(b) In your own business, farm or professional practice that is:

(i) incorporated? .... ☐ 1

(ii) unincorporated? .... ☐ 2

(vii) If you are now retired or not working, answer the following question; otherwise go to 17 (viii). In what year did you leave the job described above? ....   66 - 67   1 ☐☐ (year)

(viii) Are (were) you working at this job:

Usually 35 hours or more per week? .... ☐ 0

Usually less than 35 hours per week? .... ☐ 1

18. Do (did) you use English or French on the job indicated in question 17? (Check one only)

English but not French .... ☐ 0

French but not English .... ☐ 1

Both English and French .... ☐ 2

Neither English nor French .... ☐ 3

4-1101-167.1

19. From the beginning of your first full-time job (for pay or profit) to the present, how many periods of more than 3 months were you not working for pay or profit?

None .... ☐ 0

One period .... ☐ 1

Two periods .... ☐ 2

Three periods .... ☐ 3

Four periods .... ☐ 4

Five to ten periods .... ☐ 5

Eleven to twenty periods .... ☐ 6

Twenty-one or more periods .... ☐ 7

NOW WE WOULD LIKE TO ASK YOU SOME FURTHER QUESTIONS ABOUT YOURSELF, YOUR FAMILY AND YOUR PARENTS

20. What is your present marital status?

Single (never married)....................... ☐ 0

Go to question 27

Married .... ☐ 1

Separated .... ☐ 2

Divorced .... ☐ 3

Widowed .... ☐ 4

21. In what year were you married? (If you were married more than once, give the year of your first marriage.) ....   72 - 73   1 ☐☐ (year)

22. How many children have you had (count all live births)?

0 .... ☐ 0

Go to question 27

1 .... ☐ 1

2 .... ☐ 2

3 .... ☐ 3

4 .... ☐ 4

5 .... ☐ 5

6 .... ☐ 6

7 .... ☐ 7

8 or more.................................. ☐ 8

23. How many of these children are now living with you?

0 .... ☐ 0

1 .... ☐ 1

2 .... ☐ 2

3 .... ☐ 3

4 .... ☐ 4

5 .... ☐ 5

6 .... ☐ 6

7 or more .... ☐ 7

MALES GO TO QUESTION 27

24. In what year was your youngest child born? ....   76 - 77   1 ☐☐ (year)

25. After your first child was born, but before your last child (if more than one) began school, did you have a job (for pay or profit) for at least one period of 7 months or more?

Yes, full-time (usually 35 hours or more per week) .... ☐ 0

Yes, part-time (usually less than 35 hours per week) .... ☐ 1

No .... ☐ 2

- 4 -

26. After your youngest child began school, did you have a job (for pay or profit) for at least one period of 7 months or more?

Yes, full-time (usually 35 hours
or more per week) .... ☐ 0

Yes, part-time (usually less
than 35 hours per week) .... ☐ 1

No, I did not have a job .... ☐ 2

No, my children are
not yet of school age .... ☐ 3

27. How many brothers do you have? (Count step and half-brothers and those no longer living.)

    0 .... ☐ 0
    1 .... ☐ 1
    2 .... ☐ 2
    3 .... ☐ 3
    4 .... ☐ 4
    5 .... ☐ 5
    6 .... ☐ 6
    7 or more .... ☐ 7

28. How many of your brothers are older than you? (Count step and half-brothers and those no longer living.)

    0 .... ☐ 0
    1 .... ☐ 1
    2 .... ☐ 2
    3 .... ☐ 3
    4 .... ☐ 4
    5 .... ☐ 5
    6 .... ☐ 6
    7 or more .... ☐ 7

29. How many sisters do you have? (Count step and half-sisters and those no longer living.)

    0 .... ☐ 0
    1 .... ☐ 1
    2 .... ☐ 2
    3 .... ☐ 3
    4 .... ☐ 4
    5 .... ☐ 5
    6 .... ☐ 6
    7 or more .... ☐ 7

30. How many of your sisters are older than you? (Count step and half-sisters and those no longer living.)

    0 .... ☐ 0
    1 .... ☐ 1
    2 .... ☐ 2
    3 .... ☐ 3
    4 .... ☐ 4
    5 .... ☐ 5
    6 .... ☐ 6
    7 or more .... ☐ 7

31. When you were 16 years old where were you living:
(Check one only)

In the same city, town, village
or municipality as you are now? .... ☐ 0

In a different city, town, village or municipality of population:
(check according to the size when you were 16, not present size)

    100,000 or more? .... ☐ 1

    20,000 to 99,999? .... ☐ 2

    5,000 to 19,999? .... ☐ 3

    1,000 to 4,999? .... ☐ 4

    Less than 1,000: On a farm? .... ☐ 5

    Not on a farm? .... ☐ 6

32. Where was that?

Newfoundland .... ☐ 00
Prince Edward Island .... ☐ 01
Nova Scotia .... ☐ 02
New Brunswick .... ☐ 03
Quebec .... ☐ 04
Ontario .... ☐ 05
Manitoba .... ☐ 06
Saskatchewan .... ☐ 07
Alberta .... ☐ 08
British Columbia .... ☐ 09
Yukon or North West Terr. .... ☐ 10
Outside of Canada .... ☐ 11

33. Since you became 16 years of age, how many times have you moved (changed your place of permanent residence) from one city, town, village or municipality to another? (Count moves inside and outside of Canada.)

Never moved .... ☐ 0

                            Go to question 35

One time .... ☐ 1
Two times .... ☐ 2
Three times .... ☐ 3
Four times .... ☐ 4
Five times .... ☐ 5
Six to ten times .... ☐ 6
Eleven to twenty times .... ☐ 7
Twenty-one or more times .... ☐ 8

34. Since you became 16 years of age, how many times have you moved (changed your place of permanent residence) in Canada (present boundaries) from one province to another? (Count moves involving the Yukon or North West Territories as inter-provincial moves.)

None .... ☐ 0
One time .... ☐ 1
Two times .... ☐ 2
Three times .... ☐ 3
Four times .... ☐ 4
Five times .... ☐ 5
Six to ten times .... ☐ 6
Eleven to twenty times .... ☐ 7
Twenty-one or more times .... ☐ 8

35. Where were your parents born?
(Check one for each parent.)

	Father	Mother
Atlantic Provinces (Nfld., N.S., N.B., P.E.I.)	☐ 0	☐ 0
Quebec	☐ 1	☐ 1
Ontario	☐ 2	☐ 2
Prairie Provinces (Man., Sask., Alta., N.W.T.)	☐ 3	☐ 3
British Columbia (and Yukon)	☐ 4	☐ 4
United Kingdom	☐ 5	☐ 5
Western Europe (France, Germany, Neth., Italy, Scandanavia, etc.)	☐ 6	☐ 6
Eastern Europe (Poland, Ukraine, etc.)	☐ 7	☐ 7
Other	☐ 8	☐ 8
Don't know	☐ 9	☐ 9

36. Did your father immigrate to Canada? (If yes, indicate the period in which he immigrated.)

No .... ☐ 0
Yes: Before 1911 .... ☐ 1
      1911 - 1920 .... ☐ 2
      1921 - 1930 .... ☐ 3
      1931 - 1940 .... ☐ 4
      1941 - 1950 .... ☐ 5
      1951 - 1960 .... ☐ 6
      1961 - 1970 .... ☐ 7
      1971 - 1973 .... ☐ 8
      Don't know .... ☐ 9

- 5 -

37. (a) When you were 16 years old were you living with both your parents?

Yes .... ☐ 0 ──→ **Go to question 38**

No .... ☐ 1 ──→ **Go to question 37 (b)**

(b) Who was the head of your family when you were 16 years of age? If you had left home by that age, indicate the person who was head of your family at the time you left. (Check one only)

Father .... ☐ 0

Mother .... ☐ 1

Other male .... ☐ 2

Other female .... ☐ 3

38. Now we would like to find out what kind of work your father did when you were about 16 years old. If your father was not the head of your household at that time answer for the person checked in question 37(b). (If you do not know the answer to a particular question indicate this rather than leave it unanswered.)

(i) What kind of work was he doing? (Give a full description, e.g. selling shoes, motor vehicle repairing, metal machining, clerical work, secretarial work)

_____

(ii) What were his most important activities or duties? (e.g. fitting shoes, auto body work, operating lathe, posting invoices, taking dictation and typing)

_____

(iii) In what kind of business, industry or service was this job? (e.g. retail shoe store, auto body repair shop, machine parts mfg., medical clinic)

_____

	94 - 97
For office use only	☐☐☐☐

(iv) If he owned a farm to do this work, how many people did he usually employ?

Did not own a farm .... ☐ 0

None .... ☐ 1

1 - 10 .... ☐ 2

11 - 20 .... ☐ 3

21 - 74 .... ☐ 4

75 or more .... ☐ 5

Don't know .... ☐ 6

(v) In this job was he working:

(a) For others for wages, salary or commission? .... ☐ 0

(b) In his own business, farm, or professional practice that is:

(i) incorporated? .... ☐ 1

(ii) unincorporated? .... ☐ 2

(c) Don't know .... ☐ 3

39. What was your parents' highest level of education? (If your parents were not educated in Canada check the category which best describes their educational attainment.) (Check one only for each parent.)

	Father	Mother
No formal schooling	☐ 00	☐ 00
Elementary school		
Some	☐ 01	☐ 01
Completed	☐ 02	☐ 02
High school		
Academic		
Some	☐ 03	☐ 03
Completed	☐ 04	☐ 04
Vocational or technical		
Some	☐ 05	☐ 05
Completed	☐ 06	☐ 06
After high school but not university		
Business or trades training: (e.g. secretarial school, hairdressing school, barbering school, trade school, etc.)		
Some	☐ 07	☐ 07
Completed	☐ 08	☐ 08
Nursing school or Teacher's college		
Some	☐ 09	☐ 09
Completed	☐ 10	☐ 10
Junior college, College classique, Technical Institute		
Some	☐ 11	☐ 11
Completed	☐ 12	☐ 12
University		
Some	☐ 13	☐ 13
Completed:		
Certificate or diploma	☐ 14	☐ 14
Bachelor's degree	☐ 15	☐ 15
Master's degree	☐ 16	☐ 16
Doctorate	☐ 17	☐ 17
Professional degree (e.g. M.D., L.L.B., C.A., etc.)	☐ 18	☐ 18

40. Did your mother work at a full-time job (for pay or profit) at any time during your primary and secondary schooling?

No .... ☐ 0

Go to question 42

Yes, she worked less than a year .... ☐ 1

Yes, she worked for 1 - 5 years .... ☐ 2

Yes, she worked for 6 - 10 years .... ☐ 3

Yes, she worked for more than 10 years .... ☐ 4

Don't know .... ☐ 5

41. During your primary and secondary education what type of job (for pay or profit) did your mother mainly have? (Check one only)

Professional, managerial, technical (e.g. teacher, nurse, dietitian, department manager, radiologist) .... ☐ 0

Secretarial or clerical (e.g. stenographer, telephone operator) .... ☐ 1

Sales (e.g. saleslady, model) .... ☐ 2

Service (e.g. waitress, hairdresser, baby sitter, nurses aide) .... ☐ 3

Skilled or semi-skilled industrial worker .... ☐ 4

Working on her own account out of her home (e.g. dressmaker, cleaning lady) .... ☐ 5

Farming .... ☐ 6

Don't know .... ☐ 7

42. To what ethnic or cultural group did you or your ancestor (on the male side) belong on coming to this continent? (Check one only)

English .... ☐ 00
French .... ☐ 01
German .... ☐ 02
Irish .... ☐ 03
Italian .... ☐ 04
Jewish .... ☐ 05
Native Indian or Eskimo .... ☐ 06
Netherlands .... ☐ 07
Norwegian .... ☐ 08
Polish .... ☐ 09
Russian .... ☐ 10
Scottish .... ☐ 11
Ukrainian .... ☐ 12
Other .... ☐ 13
Don't know .... ☐ 14

43. To which ethnic or cultural group do you feel that you now belong? (Check one only)

American .... ☐ 00
Canadian .... ☐ 01
Danish .... ☐ 02
English .... ☐ 03
French .... ☐ 04
German .... ☐ 05
Hungarian .... ☐ 06
Irish .... ☐ 07
Italian .... ☐ 08
Jewish .... ☐ 09
Native Indian or Eskimo .... ☐ 10
Netherlands .... ☐ 11
Norwegian .... ☐ 12
Polish .... ☐ 13
Russian .... ☐ 14
Scottish .... ☐ 15
Swedish .... ☐ 16
Ukrainian .... ☐ 17
Welsh .... ☐ 18
Other .... ☐ 19

44. What is your religion?

Anglican................................... ☐ 0
United Church of Canada.................... ☐ 1
Presbyterian .... ☐ 2
Lutheran .... ☐ 3
Dutch Reform............................... ☐ 3
Roman Catholic .... ☐ 4
Ukrainian Catholic .... ☐ 5
Greek Orthodox .... ☐ 5
Jewish .... ☐ 6
Baptist .... ☐ 7
7th Day Adventist.......................... ☐ 7
Methodist .... ☐ 7
Other Protestant .... ☐ 7
Other...................................... ☐ 8
No religion .... ☐ 9

45. What is the language which you first learned to speak?

English .... ☐ 0
French .... ☐ 1
German .... ☐ 2
Italian .... ☐ 3
Ukrainian .... ☐ 4
Indian or Eskimo .... ☐ 5
Netherlands .... ☐ 6
Polish .... ☐ 7
Other .... ☐ 8

46. What is the language in which you feel most comfortable when talking?

English .... ☐ 0
French .... ☐ 1
German .... ☐ 2
Italian .... ☐ 3
Ukrainian .... ☐ 4
Indian or Eskimo .... ☐ 5
Netherlands .... ☐ 6
Polish .... ☐ 7
Other .... ☐ 8

47. Can you speak English or French well enough to carry on a conversation?

English only .... ☐ 0
French only .... ☐ 1
English and French .... ☐ 2
Neither English nor French .... ☐ 3

48. In how many weeks did you have a job (for pay or profit) during 1972?

None .... ☐ 0

Go to question 51

1 - 13 weeks .... ☐ 1
14 - 26 weeks .... ☐ 2
27 - 39 weeks .... ☐ 3
40 - 48 weeks .... ☐ 4
49 - 52 weeks .... ☐ 5

49. How many hours per week did you usually work during 1972?

35 hours or more .... ☐ 0
20 - 34 hours .... ☐ 1
Less than 20 hours .... ☐ 2

50. What was your income (before taxes) from employment during 1972? (Include wages, salaries, tips, commissions, etc. or if you have your own farm, business or professional practice give your net income after deducting business expenses but before taxes.) (Check one only)

No income .... ☐ 00
Less than $2,000 .... ☐ 01
$ 2,000 -   2,999 .... ☐ 02
$ 3,000 -   3,999 .... ☐ 03
$ 4,000 -   4,999 .... ☐ 04
$ 5,000 -   5,999 .... ☐ 05
$ 6,000 -   6,999 .... ☐ 06
$ 7,000 -   7,999 .... ☐ 07
$ 8,000 -   8,999 .... ☐ 08
$ 9,000 -   9,999 .... ☐ 09
$10,000 - 10,999 .... ☐ 10
$11,000 - 11,999 .... ☐ 11
$12,000 - 12,999 .... ☐ 12
$13,000 - 13,999 .... ☐ 13
$14,000 - 14,999 .... ☐ 14
$15,000 - 15,999 .... ☐ 15
$16,000 - 16,999 .... ☐ 16
$17,000 - 19,999 .... ☐ 17
$20,000 and over .... ☐ 18
Net loss .... ☐ 19

- 7 -

51. During 1972, what was your total personal income (before taxes) from all sources (include interest, dividends, rents received, pensions, youth allowances, welfare, etc.)? If you own a farm or are self-employed, state the amount **after** the deduction of business expenses.

No income	☐ 00
Less than $2,000	☐ 01
$ 2,000 - 2,999	☐ 02
$ 3,000 - 3,999	☐ 03
$ 4,000 - 4,999	☐ 04
$ 5,000 - 5,999	☐ 05
$ 6,000 - 6,999	☐ 06
$ 7,000 - 7,999	☐ 07
$ 8,000 - 8,999	☐ 08
$ 9,000 - 9,999	☐ 09
$10,000 - 10,999	☐ 10
$11,000 - 11,999	☐ 11
$12,000 - 12,999	☐ 12
$13,000 - 13,999	☐ 13
$14,000 - 14,999	☐ 14
$15,000 - 15,999	☐ 15
$16,000 - 16,999	☐ 16
$17,000 - 19,999	☐ 17
$20,000 and over	☐ 18
Net loss	☐ 19

THANK YOU FOR YOUR ASSISTANCE

Comments:

Appendix 1:2

Work Completed Additional to this Book

ADSETT, MARGARET A.
  1981   "Sex Differences in Rates of Return from Human Capital to Earnings for Married Full-Time Workers in the Canadian Labour Force: A Case of Women's Work History?" M.A. Thesis. Department of Sociology and Anthropology, Carleton University, Ottawa.

BOYD, MONICA, HUGH A. MCROBERTS, JOHN PORTER, JOHN GOYDER, FRANK E. JONES and PETER C. PINEO.
  1977   "The Canadian National Mobility Study." *Canadian Studies in Population*, 4: 94-96.

BOYD, MONICA and HUGH A. MCROBERTS
  1978   "Design of the 1973 Canadian National Mobility Study on Occupational and Educational Attainment," Working Paper 78-3. Ottawa: Carleton University, Department of Sociology and Anthropology.

BOYD, MONICA and ELIZABETH HUMPHREYS
  1980   "Sex Differences in Canada: Incomes and Labour Markets," pp. 401-420 in Economic Council of Canada, *Reflections on Canadian Incomes*. Ottawa: Minister of Supply and Services, Catalogue No.: EC 22-78/1980E.

BOYD, MONICA
  1979   "Immigrants, Income Attainments and Labour Markets in Canada." Paper presented at the annual meetings of the Population Association of America.
  1980   "The Double Negative: Female Immigrants in the Canadian Labour Force." Paper presented at the Population Association of America.

BOYD, MONICA, DAVID L. FEATHERMAN, and JUDAH MATRAS
  1980   "Status Attainment of Immigrant Origin Categories in the United States, Canada and Israel," pp. 199-228 in Richard Tomasson, ed. *Comparative Social Research*. Vol. 3, JAI Press.

BOYD, MONICA
  1981   "The American Emigrant in Canada: Trends and Consequences." *International Migration Review*, 15: 650-70.

BOYD, MONICA
  1982   "Sex and Generational Achievement: Canada." Paper presented at the International Sociological Association World Congress, Mexico City.

BOYD, MONICA, JOHN GOYDER, HUGH A. MCROBERTS, FRANK E. JONES, PETER C.

PINEO and JOHN PORTER
  1981   "Status Attainment in Canada: Findings of the Canadian Mobility Study." *Canadian Review of Sociology and Anthropology, 18: 657-73.*
  1982   "Sex Differences in the Canadian Occupational Attainment Process." *Canadian Review of Sociology and Anthropology,* 19: 1-28.
BOYD, MONICA and HUGH A. McROBERTS
  1982   "Women, Men and Socioeconomic Indices," pp. 129-59 in Mary Power, ed. *Socioeconomic Status: Concepts and Measurement Issues.* Washington, D.C.: The American Association for the Advancement of Science.
CALLAN, FERN E.
  1979   "The Role of Language in the Income Attainments of Quebec Women." M.A. thesis. Department of Sociology and Anthropology, Carleton University, Ottawa.
  1979   "Recruitment to the Professions: An examination." Departmental Working Paper 79-9. Ottawa: Carleton University, Department of Sociology and Anthropology.
CHAN, DONNA CAMILLE
  1979   "The Status Attainment of Francophones and Anglophones in Quebec: An Application of the Vacancy Competition Model." M.A. thesis. Department of Sociology and Anthropology. Carleton University, Ottawa.
GOYDER, JOHN C.
  1980   "Trends in the Socioeconomic Achievement of the University Educated: A Status Attainment Model Interpretation." *Canadian Journal of Higher Education,* 10: 21-38.
  1980   "Trends in Occupational Mobility in Canada." Paper read at the annual meetings of the Canadian Sociology and Anthropology Association, Fredericton, N.B.
  1981   "Income Differences between the Sexes: Findings from a National Canadian Survey." *Canadian Review of Sociology and Anthropology,* 18: 321-42.
JONES, FRANK E.
  1981   "Age at Immigration and Educational Attainment." *Canadian Review of Sociology and Anthropology,* 18: 393-405.
  1980   "Skill as a Dimension of Occupational Classification." *Canadian Review of Sociology and Anthropology,* 17: 176-83.
  1984   "Age at Immigration and Educational Attainment: Further Explorations." Paper presented at the International Sociological Association World Congress, Mexico City.
MACDONALD, WAYNE and BONNIE SHIELL
  1979   "The Socioeconomic Advantages Associated with Religious Non-Affilation." Paper presented at the annual meeting of the Society for the Scientific Study of Religion, San Antonio, Texas. Available from the authors, Department of Sociology and Anthropology, Carleton University.

McRoberts, Hugh A., John Porter, Monica Boyd, John Goyder, Frank E. Jones and P. C. Pineo
1976   "Francophone-Anglophone Differences in Mobility." *Sociologie et Société*, 8.

McRoberts, Hugh
1975   "Social Stratification in Canada: A Preliminary Analysis." Ph.D. thesis. Department of Sociology and Anthropolocy, Carleton University, Ottawa.

1980   "An Income Attainment Model for Native-Born Canadian Male Wage Earners," pp. 489-510 in Economic Council of Canada, *Reflections on Canadian Incomes*. Ottawa: Minister of Supply and Services, Catalogue No.: EC 22-78/1980E.

McRoberts, Hugh A. and Kevin Selbee
1981   "Trends in Occupational Mobility: Canada and the U.S." *American Sociological Review*, 46: 406-21.

Pineo, Peter C.
1981   "Prestige and Mobility: The Two National Surveys." *Canadian Review of Sociology and Anthropolocy*, 18: 615-26.

Pineo, Peter C., Marian Carbone, Lawrence MacDonald, Carolyn Veccia, Debbie White and Kathy Wilson
(forthcoming)   "Status attainment in Atlantic Canada" unpublished manuscript, McMaster University.

Pineo, Peter C., John Porter and Hugh A. McRoberts
1977   "The 1971 Census and a Socioeconomic Classification of Occupations." *Canadian Review of Sociology and Anthropology*, 14: 91-102.

Selbee, Kevin
1980   "Class and Mobility in Canada: Analysis." M.A. thesis. Department of Sociology and Anthropology, Carleton University, Ottawa.

Stevens, Gillian
1977   "Women's Intergenerational Occupational Mobility: A New Perspective." M.A. thesis. Department of Sociology and Anthropolocy, Carleton University, Ottawa.

Stevens, Gillian and Monica Boyd
1980   "The Importance of Mother: Labour Force Participation and Intergenerational Mobility of Women." *Social Forces*, 59: 186-99.